ARCHITECT'S
DETAIL LIBRARY

ARCHITECT'S DETAIL LIBRARY

Fred A. Stitt

Architect

Editor/Publisher, *Guidelines*

VNR VAN NOSTRAND REINHOLD
New York

DEDICATION

Dedicated to the memory of Howard Friedman, FAIA, Professor of Architecture, UC, Berkeley.

Howard was one of a kind, one of the great, beloved teachers in our profession.

Howard believed architectural education should deal as much with practice as with theory; with function and comfort as much as abstract symbolism; with the future as well as the past.

Howard even believed that a truly elite, first-class architectural education should include training in working drawings and construction details. Some day, thanks to Howard and others like him, it will all come to pass.

Copyright © 1990 by Van Nostrand Reinhold
Library of Congress Catalog Card Number 89-38856
ISBN 0-442-20529-5

Printed in the United States of America

Van Nostrand Reinhold
115 Fifth Avenue
New York, New York 10003

Van Nostrand Reinhold International Company Limited
11 New Fetter Lane
London EC4P 4EE, England

Van Nostrand Reinhold
480 La Trobe Street
Melbourne, Victoria 3000, Australia

Nelson Canada
1120 Birchmount Road
Scarborough, Ontario M1K 5G4, Canada

16 15 14 13 12 11 10 9 8 7 6 5 4 3 2

Library of Congress Cataloging-in-Publication Data

Stitt, Fred A.
   Architect's detail library / Fred A. Stitt.
      p.   cm.
   ISBN 0-442-20529-5
   1. Architecture — Details — Bibliography — Catalogs. I. Title.
Z5943.D48S75   1989
[NA2840]
720'.28'4 — dc20   89-38856
                                                       CIP

PREFACE

This volume is more like a tool kit than a book, a tool kit that can save you about 80% of the time you would normally spend on construction detail research, design, and drafting.

That's because 80% of most detail drafting is RE-drafting. The research is mostly research that's been done before, and most detail design is mainly redesign.

Our building designs are original; we don't use standards, say many architects. If that were completely true, it would mean they do brand-new original designs and details for every roof drain, floor drain, grab bar, door and window frame, brick wall, suspended ceiling, slab floor, and on and on. They don't, of course, but many of them habitually redraft all manner of ordinary standard construction components as if they were being done for the first time.

In fact, every day of the week, thousands of designers and drafters recreate essentially the same construction details over and over again.

There's a better way; a way that's been used for many years by the nation's most productive design firms. That better way is to create a library of standard details. Here's why:

--**A large part of detail drafting consists of sizing and drawing simple standard detail components** such as wood members, steel shapes, wall construction, etc. It's a tremendous time saver to have those components already completed for easy tracing, photocopying, or CADD scanning.

--**A few hundred standard detail components can give you a library of tens of thousands of possible detail combinations.** For example; just thirty drawings--including ten window sections, ten sill types, and ten different wall types--will give you the raw material for one thousand possible detail drawings.

--**You can "build" buildings as you design them by using reduced size copies of details.** You can photocopy footings, walls, floor, and roof construction at reduced size and assemble them into wall sections. Photo-reduce and photocopy the wall sections another 50% and turn them into building cross-sections. Then use the cross-sections as backgrounds for creating exterior elevations.

--**Your standard detail library can become an "office memory"** and be the central part of your office quality control system. Add new information to your standard detail sheets as you gain experience with them on different projects.

--**Especially interesting: It takes virtually no investment to create a standard detail library.** Anyone can start a library instantly by copying and filing the details being done for any new project. The details will be done anyway, so there's no new special drafting required. Later, some can be reused directly. Some will be instructive as references. Some will be copied, partly redesigned and partly reused. The point is that every detail your office does can be reused in some way or other. So why not do all new details in such a way that if they can be reused, it's convenient to do so?

That's where this tool-kit-in-a-book comes in.

This book is designed to expedite the design of original details and to make it easy for you to create your own customized standard detail library. For example:

--The drawings in this book are at the best sizes, scales, and orientation for direct reuse in virtually all working drawing situations.

--The generic detail drawings and complete Composite Detail samples illustrate the best possible formats, including best positioning of notation and dimension lines. All details are sized and oriented to fit within the most widely-used standard detail drawing sheet module: 6" x 5 - 3/4".

--Detail Data Checklists, Notation Checklists and Sample Notes are included to provide ample guidance for detail design and assembly.

--All the detail drawings are generic and readily adaptable to special construction conditions.

In total, this is a comprehensive detail library, tool kit, tracer-book, and CADD resource. Put it to use and you should be able to save hundreds, possibly thousands, of work hours. Best of all, while you're saving all that time, you'll also see an overall improvement in the quality of your production documents.

ACKNOWLEDGMENTS

Thanks to Chandler Vienneau, my former wife and business partner, for a very special and supportive partnership; architect Terry Schilling for helping design the original master detail taxonomy; architects Carol Hickler and Carol Vinolia for the original detail research and drawings; Berkeley architect Dankers Lauderdale for Macintosh computer input; Edward Gadsden for handling the massive job of final input, formatting, and endless revisions; Beverly Patterson, architect-in-training, for extensive design and project management consultation; and my editors at Van Nostrand Reinhold, Everett Smethurst and Cynthia Zigmund, for their endless support and patience.

Heartfelt thanks to you all. This book could not have been done without you.

TO REACH THE AUTHOR

The author welcomes your comments and suggestions. Please write to Fred Stitt, Guidelines, Box 456, Orinda, CA 94563. (Sorry, we can't respond to all letters personally, but all communications are read carefully and all suggestions are given very serious attention.)

Also, if you're interested in news of CADD versions of standard details, please write to the same address or call Guidelines, (415) 254-9393.

CONTENTS

CONTENTS

CONTENTS

CONTENTS

ARCHITECT'S
DETAIL LIBRARY

CHAPTER 1

Instructions

HOW TO USE THIS BOOK

This book is a detail library which includes:

CHECKLIST: HOW TO SET UP A STANDARD DETAIL LIBRARY.
Every detail you do is potentially reusable as a master detail or a reference detail. Here's how to create, file, and retrieve them most conveniently.

DETAIL DATA CHECKLISTS to guide drafters to the best choices of detail components and to suggest special information to show or note with each detail.

SMALL-SCALE GENERIC DETAILS to provide you with "half-size" guides to the regular scale details. You can trace or copy these reduced-sized details and use them to assemble mockups of final detail sheets. You can further reduce them on reduction copiers and assemble the components in small-scale wall sections and cross-sections.

FULL-SCALE GENERIC DETAILS to furnish you with outline detail drawings at the best recommended scales, sizes, and orientation for tracing, photocopying, or computer digitizing.

NOTATION CHECKLISTS to supply you with lists of items that should be noted and drawn in your finished details.

SAMPLE NOTATION lists to give you actual notation that drafters commonly use in varied details of each type. These are reminders and guides, not to be copied without full understanding of the notes your particular project details require.

COMPOSITE MASTER DETAILS to show you finished details with the most commonly required notes and dimensions. These illustrate how FULL-SCALE GENERIC DETAILS should look when completed; they can be used as standard details in their own right.

The Small-Scale, Full-Scale, and Composite Sample Details are clustered according to the Construction Specifications Institute Masterformat specification division system: Sitework details are 02000; Concrete is 03000; Masonry, 04000; etc. The individual detail file numbers are based on the CSI Masterformat 1978 Edition, MP-2-1.

FOR EXPEDITING THE DESIGN AND DRAFTING OF CONSTRUCTION DETAILS:

1)   Find the detail category you're after in the CONTENTS.

2)   Review the DETAIL DATA CHECKLISTS with each detail section for background information about the construction being detailed.

3)   Trace, photocopy, or digitize the detail drawings you want to use. Add your special notation and dimensions.

4)   Make a master copy of your new detail for your Standard or Reference detail files.

5)   Complete the finished detail as required for the project at hand.

Additional information on detail design is included at the beginning of some detail chapters.

CREATING STANDARD DETAILS AND/OR ADDING DETAILS TO A STANDARD DETAIL LIBRARY:

1)   Follow the instructions in the next chapter on HOW TO SET UP A STANDARD DETAIL SYSTEM.

2)   Follow the instructions for detail design and drafting listed above.

HOW TO SET UP A STANDARD DETAIL LIBRARY

This is a model action checklist for setting up a STANDARD DETAIL LIBRARY.
Modify the checklist as you see fit.

Most users of standard details typically adapt 80% of details for any particular project from their library. That's considerable time and money savings and it's a reasonable expectation for any office no matter how varied or original your work may be.

Remember that ALL details you do have potential multiple uses, either as standards for reuse or as reference details, so don't let them go to waste. And remember that you can start a STANDARD DETAIL LIBRARY with the very next detail drawn in your office. It'll be drawn anyway so you may as well do it in such a way as to gain multiple benefits. It doesn't require any significant investment in time and money to set up a system; it just takes communication and monitoring to make sure it's done right. Use this checklist accordingly.

PLANNING AND SCHEDULING

____ Select from the actions listed in the pages that follow and add others of your choosing.
Assign tasks and establish dates for starts, progress reviews, meetings, and completions.

____ Create a file or binder to store data related to planning and managing a detail system.

____ Decide who will be in charge of the detail system. (This may be a tentative or temporary choice for now.)

____ Meet with office staff members to discuss the action steps in this checklist.
If your office size justifies it, establish a task force to research, plan, and implement the system.

____ Start a list of top priority problems and concerns in detailing.

____ Collect comments and suggestions from supervisors.

____ Review past sets of working drawings to identify the types of details that are most readily reusable.

____ Locate any office detail files used in the past, or files currently being used by individual personnel.

____ List possible sources of existing details that might be usable as standards or as reference details.

____ Consider retaining a qualified general contractor to critique some typical samples of your working drawings with you and to help establish rules for effective detailing.

____ Decide how to integrate details with CADD and/or computer data base management.

____ Decide whether you want details to be notated individually or if detail types or clusters should be keynoted on final drawing sheets.

____ Establish a date for deciding who will ultimately be in charge of the system.

____ Create a calendar time line and delegated assignment list for implementing the major phases of researching, planning, and implementing the new or improved STANDARD DETAIL LIBRARY.

____ Notify staff of three requirements in detailing:
____ All details created for new projects will henceforth be filed for long-term reference or for the STANDARD DETAIL LIBRARY.
____ Since details will be used for long-term reference and possible reuse, they will have to follow consistent formats and drafting standards, as described later in this checklist.
____ Since details used as standards will often go through several generations of photo-reproduction and possibly be enlarged or reduced in size, they must be done in ways that ensure top-quality reproduction at every step. Extra sharp, clear drafting will be a must.

WRITE A MASTER LIST OF ACTION STEPS FOR GETTING THE SYSTEM GOING. HERE'S A SUGGESTED MODEL LIST:

____ Establish office drafting and graphics standards for good readability and reproducibility of details.

____ Establish an office detail sheet format so that all details on file are consistent in appearance.

____ Convey the best rules on the steps for creating original details: drawing sequence, notation, scales, dimensioning, leader lines, and simplification techniques.

____ Review the options of detail files you might use and your choices in filing and retrieval systems.
    ____ Filing of Master Details for reuse.
    ____ Filing of reference or "design" details.
    ____ Filing of original construction details.
    ____ Computer filing and retrieval.
    ____ A detail reference catalog.

____ Create file folders and/or three-ring binders, related materials, and procedures for using the details.

____ Establish a jobsite feedback system for upgrading and improving the details.

____ Select reprographic methods for printing final detail sheets.

ENFORCE CONSISTENT DRAFTING STANDARDS:

____ Small lettering is a problem on any job. All hand notation lettering should be at least 1/8" high. Computer-printing or clear typing is preferable for notes and can be a little smaller than 1/8".

____ Light linework tends to fade away, so lines should be consistently black, more differentiated by line width rather than "darkness" or "lightness."

____ Small symbols tend to clog up, so symbols should be large and open. That includes arrowheads, circles, triangles, etc.

____ Crosshatch patterns tend to run together when reproduced, so line patterns should be spaced at least 1/16" apart.

____ Poche made by using grey tone drawing or graphite dust does not reproduce well, so use dot or Zipatone-type patterns to achieve comparable results.

____ Numbers and lettering should not touch linework or they will tend to flow together in reproduction.

USE A CONSISTENT STANDARD DETAIL SHEET FORMAT:

____ Set a size for the detail "cutout window." (I recommend 6" wide x 5-3/4" high as a size and shape that accommodates the largest number of details of different types, scales, and sizes, and still fits evenly within most standard working drawing sheet sizes.)

____ Set standard margin limits for maximum detail profiles: left and right, top and bottom.

____ Set standard sizes and positions for:
    ____ Notation string or keynote code string.
    ____ Dimensions.
    ____ Detail key.
    ____ Title.
    ____ Scale.
    ____ Detail File Number.

____ Create a form for detail reference information and a Detail History Log to be included on standard detail sheets.

TRAINING STAFF

RECOMMENDATIONS FOR CLEAR AND CONSISTENT DETAIL LAYOUT:

____ Draw in sequence from the most general to the most particular.

____ Draw in "layered" phases so that a detail is substantially visually complete at every stage.

____ Keep the exterior face of construction facing to the left and the interior face to the right. (This is a general rule that works well for consistency and readability most of the time. Abandon the rule whenever it fails to support the objective of maximum clarity and readability.)

____ Keep most notation as a list column on the right-hand side of a detail window. Place other notes as appropriate for clarity and to avoid crowding the information.

RECOMMENDATIONS FOR NOTATION:

____ Most notes should be simple names of materials or parts. If more information is required, add the data as assembly or reference notes after the material or part names.

____ Notes should provide information in a consistent sequence:
    ____ Size of the material or part, where size is relevant and not duplicated by a dimension.
    ____ The name of the material or part--generic, not specific names are usually preferred. Don't use product brand names, workmanship standards, or code and reference standards unless your drawings and specifications are one and the same.
    ____ Noted position or spacing of parts unless they are dimensioned.

____ Provide an office nomenclature and abbreviations list, so all drafters will use the same terminology. Such terminology should be consistent with specifications.

____ Arrow leader lines from notes should follow a consistent office standard. Recommended: a short straight line starting horizontally from the note, breaking at an angle to lead to the designated part.

PROPER SCALES FOR DETAIL DRAWINGS:

____ In general stick to two scales: **1-1/2" = 1'-0"** and **3" = 1'-0"**. The scales used throughout this book are the ones most widely used for these details.

____ Use 3/4" = 1'-0" only for the very simplest light framing, landscaping, and cabinet details.

____ 1-1/2" = 1'-0" is used to show simple construction components in roofs, walls, floors, etc.

____ 3" = 1'-0" is mainly used for doors and windows, wall fixtures and connectors, and more elaborate components of the walls, floors, ceilings, etc. When in doubt, this larger scale is preferable.

____ **Half-** and **full-size** details are only for shop drawings or to show the smallest of construction components. Extra-large details take up space and time out of proportion to their usefulness and are rarely justified.

DIMENSIONING:

____ Avoid fractions in dimensions. The smallest practical fraction in most dimensioning is 1/4".

____ Dimension lines should connect only to lead lines extended from the faces of materials, and should not connect directly to material profile lines themselves.

____ Don't duplicate the same dimension on two sides of a detail. Such redundancy is confusing.

____ Use consistent and simple dimension connection symbols--arrows, slashes, or dots.

THE STANDARD DETAIL FORMAT SHEET

DETAIL FILE NUMBER:

dim. lines   break line   ℄   notation boundary   break line

cut mark

dim. line

dim. line

break line

℄

dim. line/
break line

dim. line

title
space

cut mark

DETAIL INFORMATION
References, jobsite feedback, job history

16

SAMPLE SHEET

Below is the detail drawing space. The recommended module, and the module used for the Guidelines Master Details, is 6" wide x 5 - 3/4" high. If you prefer another module, you can still use this format sheet for detail modules of 6 - 1/2" x 5 - 3/4" high maximum, and 5 - 1/2" x 5 - 1/4" high minimum.

(Space for the detail name, scale and file number.)

DETAIL FILE NUMBER: 03305-51

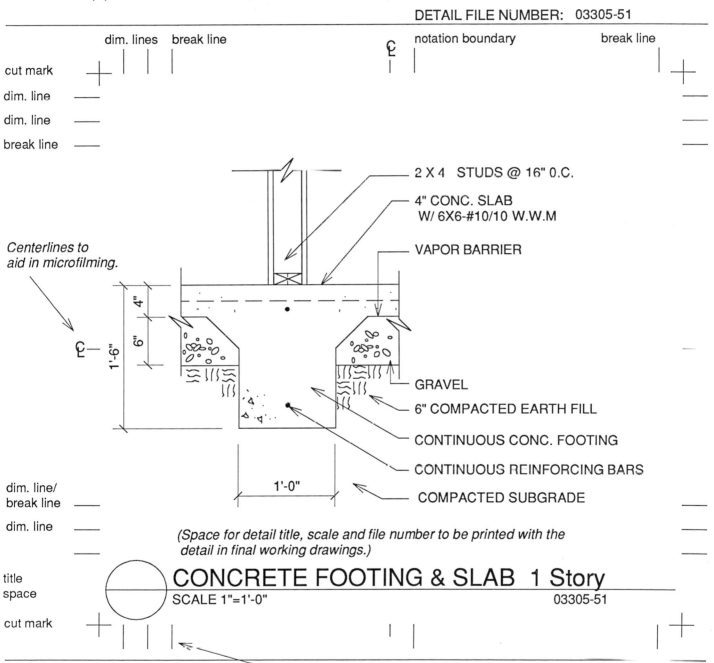

2 X 4 STUDS @ 16" O.C.

4" CONC. SLAB
W/ 6X6-#10/10 W.W.M

VAPOR BARRIER

GRAVEL

6" COMPACTED EARTH FILL

CONTINUOUS CONC. FOOTING

CONTINUOUS REINFORCING BARS

COMPACTED SUBGRADE

Centerlines to aid in microfilming.

(Space for detail title, scale and file number to be printed with the detail in final working drawings.)

CONCRETE FOOTING & SLAB 1 Story

SCALE 1"=1'-0"   03305-51

DETAIL INFORMATION
References, jobsite feedback, job history

Marks show various cut lines, notation, dimension, and face of construction lines. Exterior face of construction is normally at the left, notation blocks normally on the right-hand side. These suggested spacings aid visual consistency throughout your detail system but should be ignored if using them interferes with clarity and ease of detail drawing.

CHAPTER 2

Sitework
02000

DETAIL DATA CHECKLIST

EROSION CONTROL
__Slopes up to 2:1, use stone, broken concrete, or wood grid
__Slopes up to 1:1, use stone or broken concrete set on mortar and with
    mortar between joints
OR
__Use precast unit (concrete with voids for soil)
__Steep slopes, use retaining walls (see later section)

STONE EROSION CONTROL
__Use 4" to 8" diameter round stone
__Hand place on a 3" sand bed

BROKEN CONCRETE EROSION CONTROL
__Each piece should be a minimum of 1' square and 4" thick
__Joints should be tight sand or mortar at least 1" wide
__Set pieces on a 2" sand bed

WOOD GRID EROSION CONTROL
__Lay 2x4s across the slope at 3' spacing; lay 1x4 ties at 8' o.c.
__Fill grid spaces with topsoil and sod or seed, wood chips, gravel, or
    ground cover

PRECAST UNITS EROSION CONTROL
__Set on a 2" sand bed; fill voids with topsoil

SMALL-SCALE GENERIC DETAILS

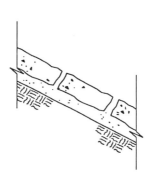

EROSION CONTROL
Concrete
02270-1

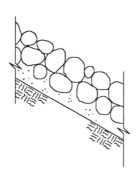

EROSION CONTROL
Stone
02270-11

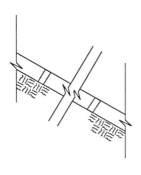

EROSION CONTROL
Wood Grid
02270-21

02270 EROSION CONTROL Concrete, Stone, Wood Grid

FULL-SCALE GENERIC DETAILS

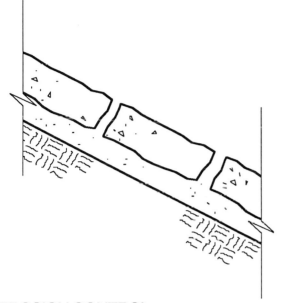

EROSION CONTROL
Concrete
1"=1'-0"   02270-1

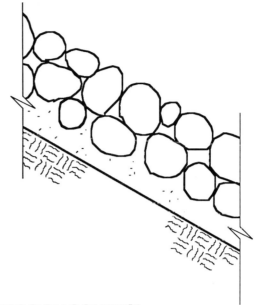

EROSION CONTROL
Stone
1"=1'-0"   02270-11

**NOTATION CHECKLIST,
 SAMPLE NOTATION**

PAVER UNITS
SETTING BED
SLOPE
COMPACTED SUBGRADE

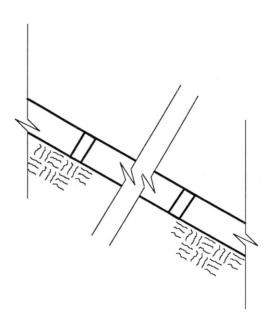

EROSION CONTROL
Wood Grid
1"=1'-0"   02270-21

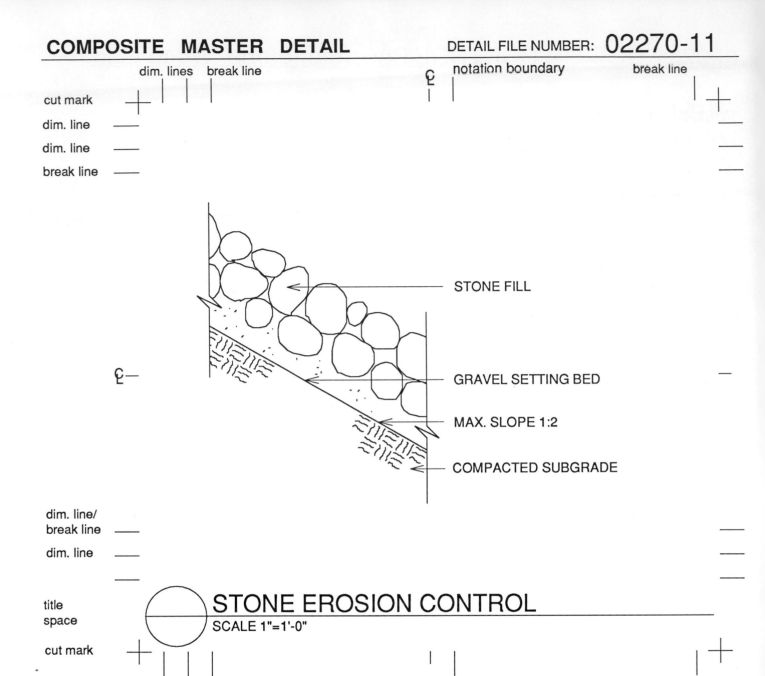

dim. lines   break line

℄   notation boundary   break line

cut mark

dim. line

dim. line

break line

℄—

STONE FILL

GRAVEL SETTING BED

MAX. SLOPE 1:2

COMPACTED SUBGRADE

dim. line/
break line

dim. line

title
space

STONE EROSION CONTROL
SCALE 1"=1'-0"

cut mark

DETAIL INFORMATION
References, jobsite feedback, job history

02401, 02410 FRENCH & TRENCH DRAINS

DETAIL DATA CHECKLIST

DRAINAGE
__Types of pipe for subsurface drains are:
  __Corrugated metal
  __Flexible plastic
  __Concrete
  __Clay tile
  __Asbestos cement
  __Rigid plastic
  __Porous and unperforated
__Install perforated drain with holes facing down
__Drainpipe should be sloped to a sump or outfall
__Grade filter material above and around drainpipe
__Depth and spacing of subdrains depends on soil type (see civil engineering handbook tables)
__Trench drains should slope to a drainpipe

DRAIN INLET COVERS
__Usually precast concrete or cast iron (also ductible iron)
__Frames and grates available for light and heavy loading conditions
  __Shapes available:
    __Round
    __Rectangular
    __Square
    __Linear

GRATES
__In areas of foot or bike traffic, grates must not allow penetration by:
    __Heels
    __Crutches
    __Cane tips
    __Tires
__Must still provide sufficient drainage
__Slotted grating may be used if slots run transverse to traffic direction

SMALL-SCALE GENERIC DETAILS

FRENCH DRAIN
02401-1

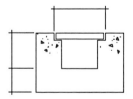

TRENCH DRAIN
02410-1

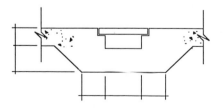

TRENCH DRAIN
02410-2

02401, 02410 FRENCH & TRENCH DRAINS

FULL-SCALE GENERIC DETAILS

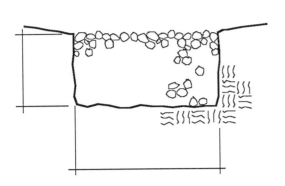

FRENCH DRAIN
3/4"=1'-0"   02401-1

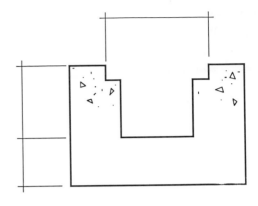

TRENCH DRAIN
3/4"=1'-0"   02410-1

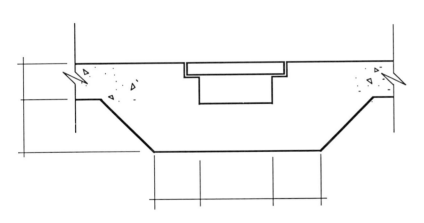

TRENCH DRAIN
3/4"=1'-0"   02410-2

NOTATION CHECKLIST,
SAMPLE NOTATION

FINISH GRADE/PAVING
PAVING BASE
METAL GRATING
METAL GRATING FRAME
CONCRETE BASE
REINFORCING
AGGREGATE
BACKFILL
COMPACTED SUBGRADE

COMPOSITE MASTER DETAIL

DETAIL FILE NUMBER: 02410-1

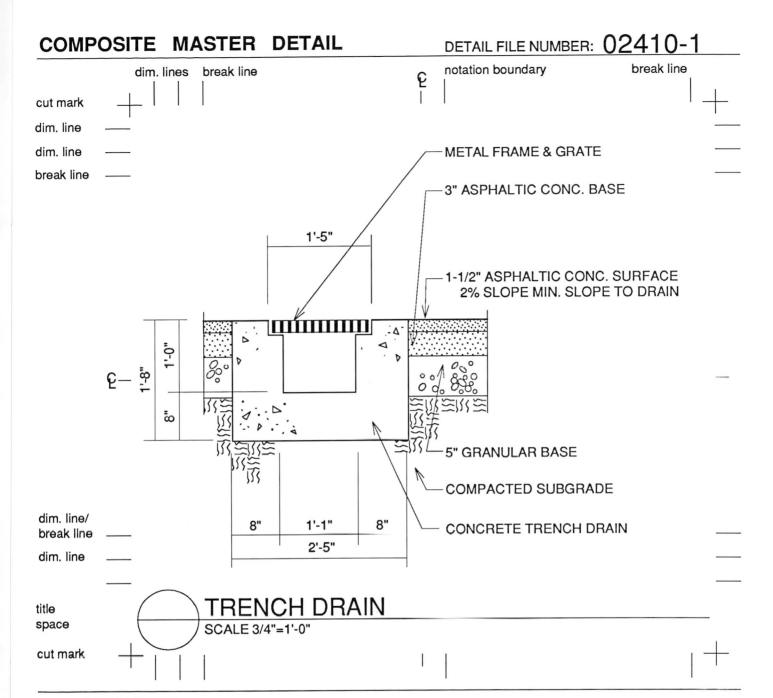

cut mark

dim. line

dim. line

break line

dim. lines   break line

notation boundary   break line

METAL FRAME & GRATE

3" ASPHALTIC CONC. BASE

1-1/2" ASPHALTIC CONC. SURFACE
2% SLOPE MIN. SLOPE TO DRAIN

1'-5"

1'-0"

1'-8"

8"

5" GRANULAR BASE

COMPACTED SUBGRADE

CONCRETE TRENCH DRAIN

dim. line/
break line

dim. line

8"   1'-1"   8"

2'-5"

title
space

TRENCH DRAIN
SCALE 3/4"=1'-0"

cut mark

DETAIL INFORMATION
References, jobsite feedback, job history

02420 (a) DRAINAGE Flumes & Inlets

DETAIL DATA CHECKLIST

CONCRETE FLUMES
__Depth and slope of flume depend on drainage load (see civil engineering handbook tables)
__Exposed edges can be chamfered, tooled, or have a 1/2" to 1" radius
__Reinforcing:
    __Precast concrete curbs may have dowel pins and holes at alternate ends
        __Two #4 bars, one top and one bottom, continuous is common.
    __May have #3 ties or stirrups at 32" to 36" o.c.
    __Two bars at the bottom of the footing may be needed
    __Bars should have 2" cover
__When curb is continuous w/paving, woven wire mesh (WWM) may be turned down into curb
__Compact the subgrade
__Provide ample subgrade drainage
__Expansion Joints
    __Two types needed:
        __Joints in the curb itself
        __Joints between curb and adjacent paving
__Curb joints should occur at approximately 15' intervals, and at all corners
    __Provide 1/4" radius at edge of joints
__ Materials:
    __1/2" preformed expansion joint, held down 1" for sealant on top
    __Heartwood redwood filler strip pour joint, 1/2" flexcell

GRATES
__In areas of foot or bike traffic, grates must not allow penetration by:
    __Heels
    __Crutches
    __Cane tips
    __Tires
__Must still provide sufficient drainage
__Slotted grating may be used if slots run transverse to traffic direction

SMALL-SCALE GENERIC DETAILS

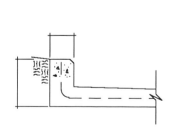

DRAINAGE FLUME/
SPILLWAY
02420-1

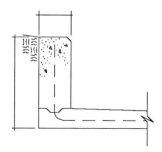

DRAINAGE FLUME/
SPILLWAY
02420-2

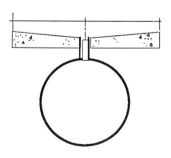

SLOTTED DRAINPIPE
& GRATE
02420-11

02420 (a) DRAINAGE Flumes & Inlets

FULL-SCALE GENERIC DETAILS

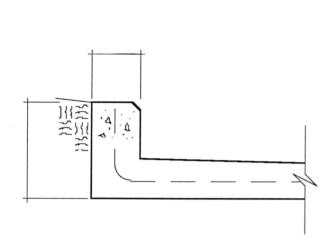

DRAINAGE FLUME/SPILLWAY
1"=1'-0"   02420-1

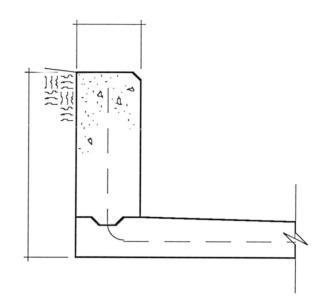

DRAINAGE FLUME/SPILLWAY
1"=1'-0"   02420-2

NOTATION CHECKLIST,
SAMPLE NOTATION

FINISH GRADE/PAVING
PAVING BASE
METAL GRATING
METAL GRATING FRAME
PIPE (TYPE, SIZE, MATERIAL)
CONCRETE BASE
REINFORCING
AGGREGATE
BACKFILL
COMPACTED SUBGRADE

BROOM FINISH CONCRETE
TOOLED EDGE CONCRETE
SLOTTED DRAINPIPE GRATE
6 X 6-10/10 WWM WELD TO GRATE @ 24"O.C.
INI FT FRAME & GRATE
SLOPE FLOOR TO OUTLET

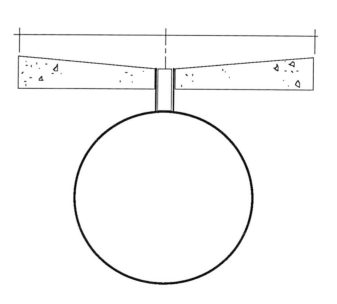

SLOTTED DRAINPIPE & GRATE
1"=1'-0"   02420-11

02420 (b) DRAINAGE Paving Edge

DETAIL DATA CHECKLIST

DRAINAGE
__Types of pipe for subsurface drains are:
    __Corrugated metal
    __Flexible plastic
    __Concrete
    __Clay tile
    __Asbestos cement
    __Rigid plastic
    __Porous and unperforated
__Install perforated drain with holes facing down
__Drainpipe should be sloped to a sump or outfall
__Grade filter material above and around drainpipe
__Depth and spacing of subdrains depends on soil type (see civil engineering handbook tables)
__Trench drains should slope to a drainpipe

SMALL-SCALE GENERIC DETAILS

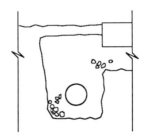

DRAIN @ PAVING EDGE
02420-36

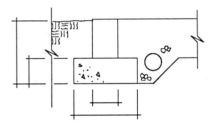

DRAIN @ PAVING EDGE
02420-37

02420 (b) DRAINAGE Paving Edge

FULL-SCALE GENERIC DETAILS

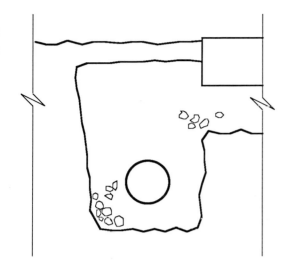

DRAIN @ PAVING EDGE
1-1/2"=1'-0"   02420-36

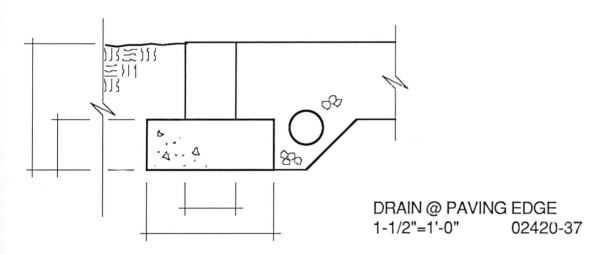

DRAIN @ PAVING EDGE
1-1/2"=1'-0"   02420-37

NOTATION CHECKLIST, SAMPLE NOTES

FINISH GRADE/PAVING
PAVING BASE
METAL GRATING
METAL GRATING FRAME
PIPE (TYPE, SIZE, MATERIAL)
CONCRETE BASE
REINFORCING
AGGREGATE
BACKFILL
COMPACTED SUBGRADE
GRADE
4" PERFORATED PIPE, 1/8" PER FOOT MIN.
 SLOPE TO OUTLET OR DAYLIGHT
PAVEMENT

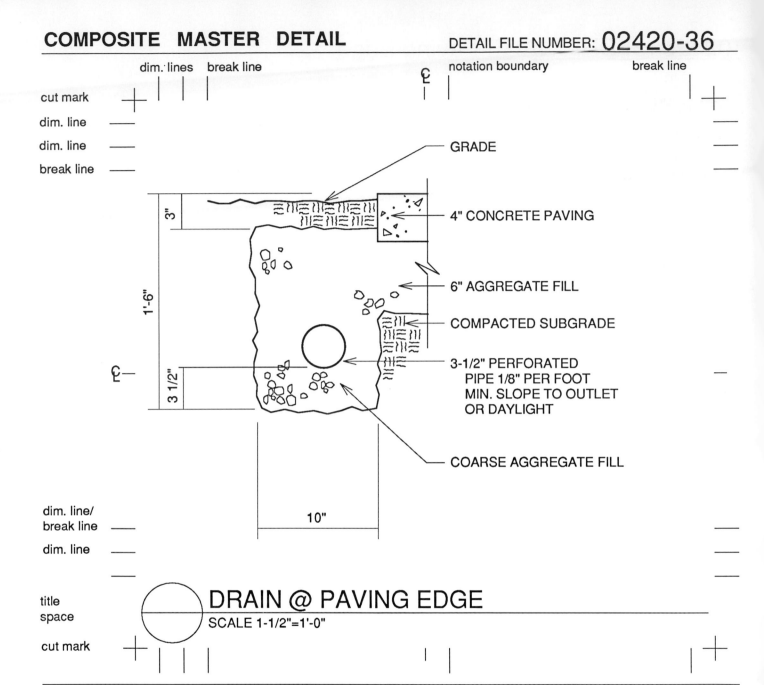

cut mark

dim. lines   break line   notation boundary   break line

dim. line

dim. line

break line

GRADE

3"

1'-6"

4" CONCRETE PAVING

6" AGGREGATE FILL

COMPACTED SUBGRADE

3 1/2"

3-1/2" PERFORATED
PIPE 1/8" PER FOOT
MIN. SLOPE TO OUTLET
OR DAYLIGHT

COARSE AGGREGATE FILL

10"

dim. line/
break line

dim. line

title
space

DRAIN @ PAVING EDGE
SCALE 1-1/2"=1'-0"

cut mark

DETAIL INFORMATION
References, jobsite feedback, job history

32

02420 (c) DRAINAGE Inlets

DETAIL DATA CHECKLIST

MANHOLES
__Spaced 300' to 600' apart for inspection and maintenance
    (Also depends on sewer size and local standards)
__Manhole walls for a combined or sanitary sewer may be:
    __8" brick
    __6" concrete
    __6" solid concrete manhole block or precast concrete units to depth of 12'
__Below 12' depth all brick and block walls shall be 12" thick
__Manholes over 12' deep shall also have a 12' thick base

IINLETS AND CATCH BASINS
__Choice of the unit is subject to local codes and practice
__Spacing depends on the size and type of unit, and the slope of gutter or swale in relation to anticipated
    runoff
__Walls may be:
    __8" brick
    __8" CMU
    __6" poured concrete
    __5" precast concrete

DRAIN INLET COVERS
__Usually precast concrete or cast iron (also ductible iron)
__Frames and grates available for light and heavy loading conditions

GRATES
__In areas of foot or bike traffic, grates must not allow penetration by:
    __Heels
    __Crutches
    __Cane tips
    __Tires
__Must still provide sufficient drainage
__Slotted grating may be used if slots run transverse to traffic direction

SMALL-SCALE GENERIC DETAILS

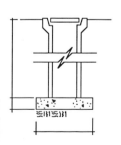
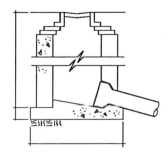
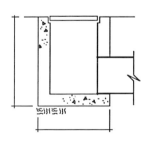
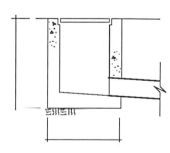

DRAIN INLET
02420-51

DRAIN INLET
02420-52

DRAIN INLET
02420-53

DRAIN INLET
02420-54

02420 (c) DRAINAGE Inlets

FULL-SCALE GENERIC DETAILS

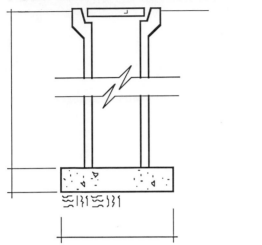

DRAIN INLET
1/2"=1'-0"   02420-51

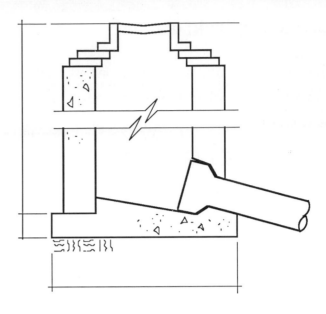

DRAIN INLET
1/2"=1'-0"   02420-52

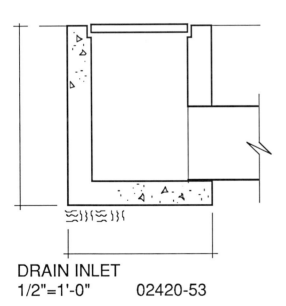

DRAIN INLET
1/2"=1'-0"   02420-53

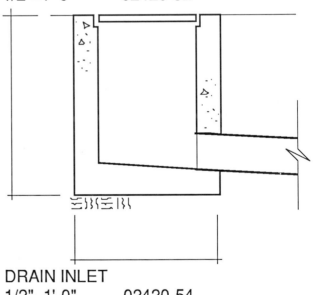

DRAIN INLET
1/2"=1'-0"   02420-54

NOTATION CHECKLIST, SAMPLE NOTES

FINISH GRADE/PAVING
PAVING BASE
METAL GRATING
METAL GRATING FRAME
PIPE (TYPE, SIZE, MATERIAL)
CONCRETE BASE
REINFORCING
AGGREGATE
BACKFILL
COMPACTED SUBGRADE

BROOM FINISH CONCRETE
TOOLED EDGE CONCRETE
GRADE
INLET FRAME & GRATE
PAVEMENT
SLOPE FLOOR TO OUTLET

02431 CATCH BASINS

DETAIL DATA CHECKLIST

MANHOLES
__Spaced 300' to 600' apart for inspection and maintenance
     (Also depends on sewer size and local standards)
__Manhole walls for a combined or sanitary sewer may be:
     __8" brick
     __6" concrete
     __6" solid concrete manhole block or precast concrete units to depth of 12'
__Below 12' depth all brick and block walls shall be 12" thick
__Manholes over 12' deep shall also have a 12' thick base

INLETS AND CATCH BASINS
__Choice of the unit is subject to local codes and practice
__Spacing depends on the size and type of unit, and the slope of gutter or swale in relation to anticipated runoff
__Walls may be:
     __8" brick
     __8" CMU
     __6" poured concrete
     __5" precast concrete

DRAIN INLET COVERS
__Usually precast concrete or cast iron (also ductible iron)
__Frames and grates available for light and heavy loading conditions

GRATES
__In areas of foot or bike traffic, grates must not allow penetration by:
     __Heels
     __Crutches
     __Cane tips
     __Tires
__Must still provide sufficient drainage
__Slotted grating may be used if slots run transverse to traffic direction

SMALL-SCALE GENERIC DETAILS

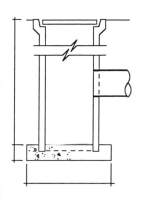

CATCH BASIN
02431-1

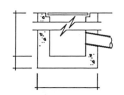

CATCH BASIN
02431-2

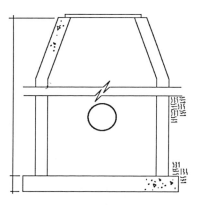

CATCH BASIN 6" Wall
02431-3

02431 CATCH BASINS

SMALL-SCALE GENERIC DETAILS continued

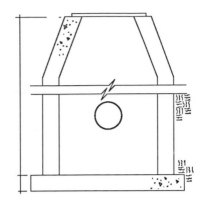

CATCH BASIN 8" Wall
02431-4

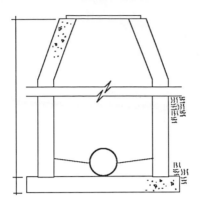

STORM DRAIN & MANHOLE
02431-11

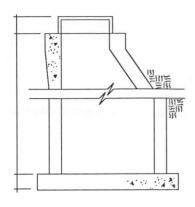

CATCH BASIN
02431-21

FULL-SCALE GENERIC DETAILS

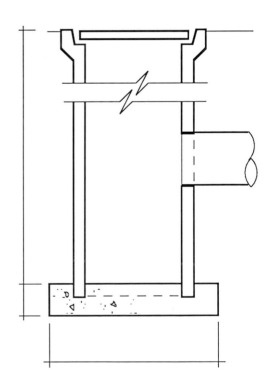

CATCH BASIN
1/2"=1'-0"   02431-1

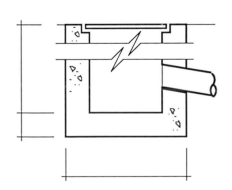

CATCH BASIN
1/2"=1'-0"   02431-2

02431 CATCH BASINS

FULL-SCALE GENERIC DETAILS continued

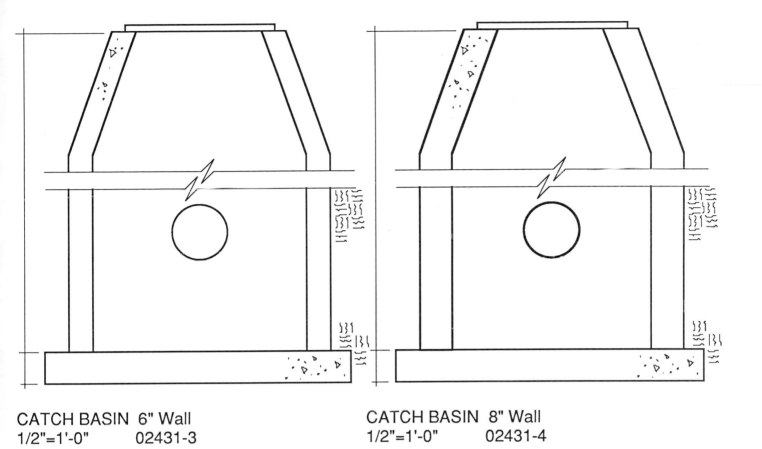

CATCH BASIN 6" Wall
1/2"=1'-0"   02431-3

CATCH BASIN 8" Wall
1/2"=1'-0"   02431-4

02431 CATCH BASINS

FULL-SCALE DETAILS continued

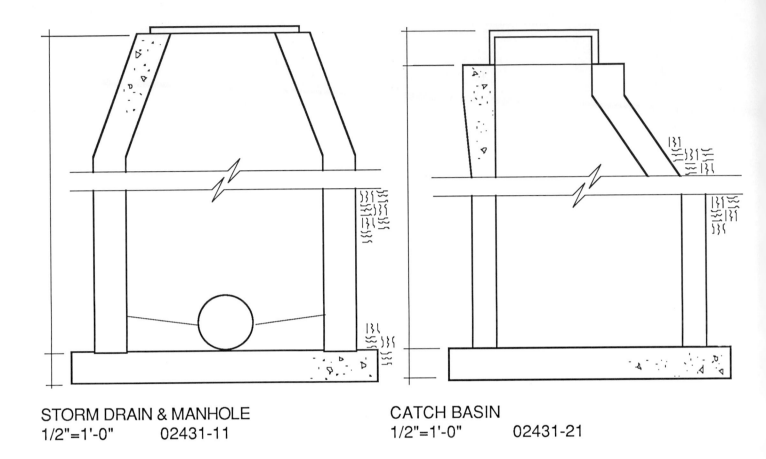

STORM DRAIN & MANHOLE
1/2"=1'-0"   02431-11

CATCH BASIN
1/2"=1'-0"   02431-21

NOTATION CHECKLIST,
SAMPLE NOTES

FINISH GRADE/PAVING
PAVING BASE
METAL GRATING
METAL GRATING FRAME
PIPE (TYPE, SIZE, MATERIAL)
CONCRETE BASE
REINFORCING
AGGREGATE
BACKFILL
COMPACTED SUBGRADE
FLOW (show direction)
#4 BARS @12" O.C. EACH WAY
#3 BARS @10"O.C. EACH WAY

COMPOSITE MASTER DETAIL

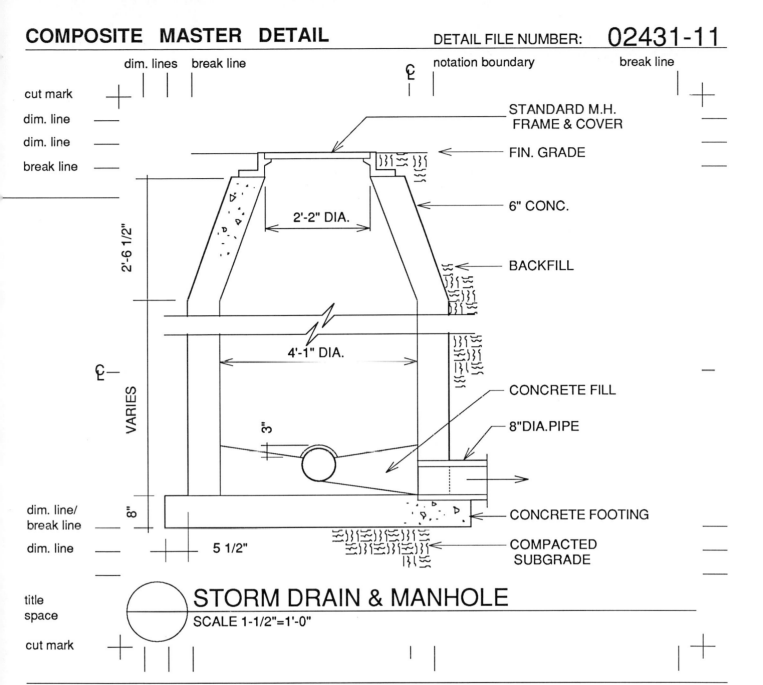

dim. lines   break line   notation boundary   break line

cut mark

dim. line

dim. line

break line

STANDARD M.H. FRAME & COVER

FIN. GRADE

6" CONC.

2'-2" DIA.

2'-6 1/2"

BACKFILL

4'-1" DIA.

CONCRETE FILL

8"DIA.PIPE

VARIES

3"

CONCRETE FOOTING

dim. line/ break line

8"

COMPACTED SUBGRADE

dim. line

5 1/2"

title space

STORM DRAIN & MANHOLE

SCALE 1-1/2"=1'-0"

cut mark

DETAIL INFORMATION
References, jobsite feedback, job history

02435 SPLASH BLOCKS

DETAIL DATA CHECKLIST

SPLASH BLOCKS
__Splash blocks are usually bought as prefabricated units
from landscape supply houses and don't normally require true construction or fabrication detailing.
__Detail drawings are included mainly to show desired sizes and types of blocks and show their
relationship to roof drain downspouts.

SMALL-SCALE GENERIC DETAILS

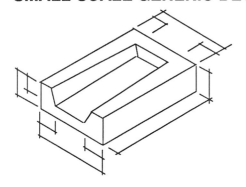

SPLASH BLOCK Isometric
02435-1

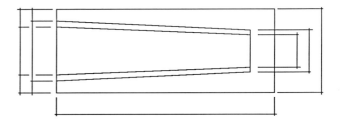

SPLASH BLOCK Top View
02435-6

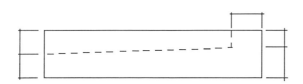

SPLASH BLOCK Side View
02435-7

02435 SPLASH BLOCKS

FULL-SCALE GENERIC DETAILS

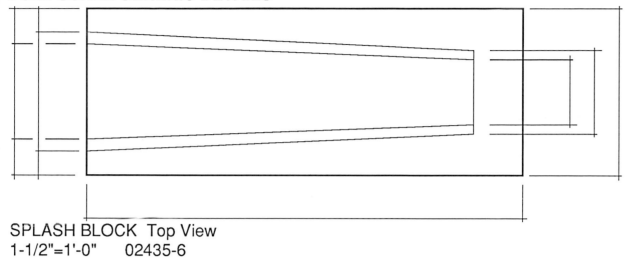

SPLASH BLOCK Top View
1-1/2"=1'-0"   02435-6

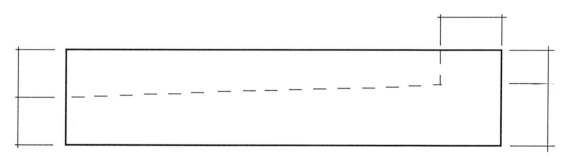

SPLASH BLOCK Side View
1-1/2"=1'-0"   02435-7

NOTATION CHECKLIST, SAMPLE NOTES

PRECAST SPLASH BLOCK
GRAVEL OR PAVEMENT DRAIN
DOWNSPOUT

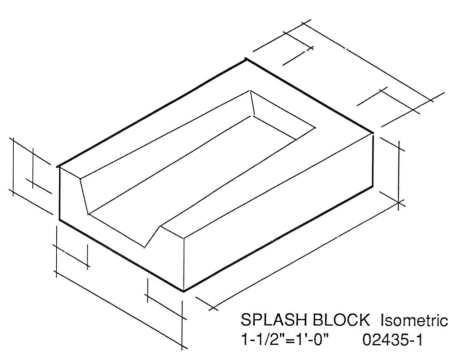

SPLASH BLOCK Isometric
1-1/2"=1'-0"   02435-1

02444 CHAIN LINK FENCE

DETAIL DATA CHECKLIST

CHAIN LINK FENCING
__See manufacturer's data for:
    __Size of pipe
    __Size of mesh
    __Depth of footing
    __Standard spacing of posts
    __Size and spacing of braces

__Special options:
    __Gate size
    __Barbed wire type
    __Barbed wire extension arms
    __Number of wires

SMALL-SCALE GENERIC DETAILS

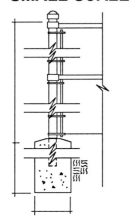

CHAIN LINK FENCE
02444-1

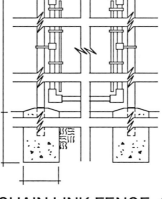

CHAIN LINK FENCE Gate
02444-2

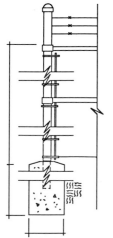

CHAIN LINK FENCE W/Barbed wire
02444-3

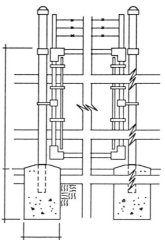

CHAIN LINK FENCE Gate W/Barbed wire
02444-4

02444 CHAIN LINK FENCE

FULL-SCALE GENERIC DETAILS

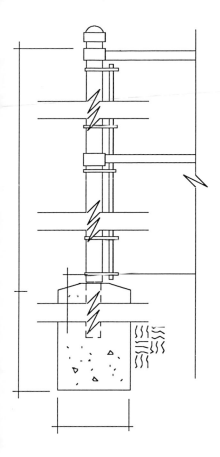

CHAIN LINK FENCE
3/4"=1'-0"   02444-1

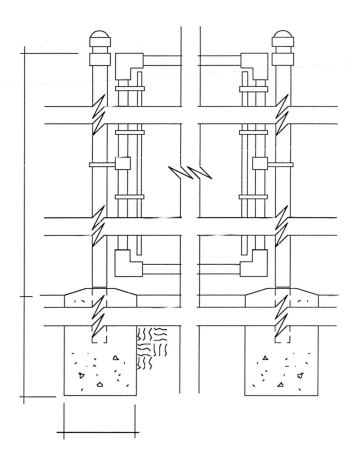

CHAIN LINK FENCE Gate
3/4"=1'-0"   02444-2

02444 CHAIN LINK FENCE

FULL-SCALE GENERIC DETAILS continued

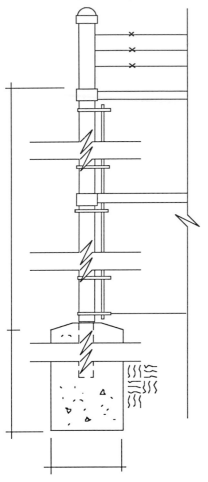

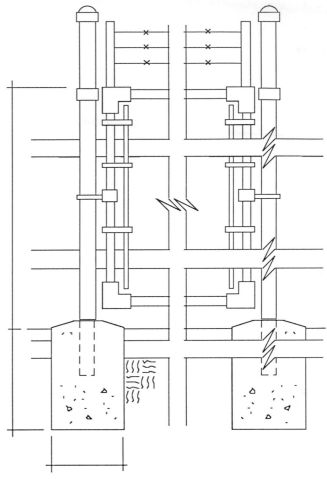

CHAIN LINK FENCE W/Barbed wire
3/4"=1'-0"   02444-3

CHAIN LINK FENCE Gate W/Barbed wire
3/4"=1'-0"   02444-4

NOTATION CHECKLIST,
SAMPLE NOTES

CHAIN LINK FENCE
BARBED WIRE
POST/POST CAP
TENSION WIRE
BRACE RAIL
TIE ROD
FINISH GRADE/PAVING
FOOTING
AGGREGATE BASE

VISE CONNECTORS (connect groundwire
    to fencing/barbed wire)
DOWN CONDUCTOR
COPPER CONDUCTOR CABLE MIN. #6
GROUND ROD MIN. 3/4" O.D.
 BY 8' LONG
BOTTOM SALVAGE WIRE

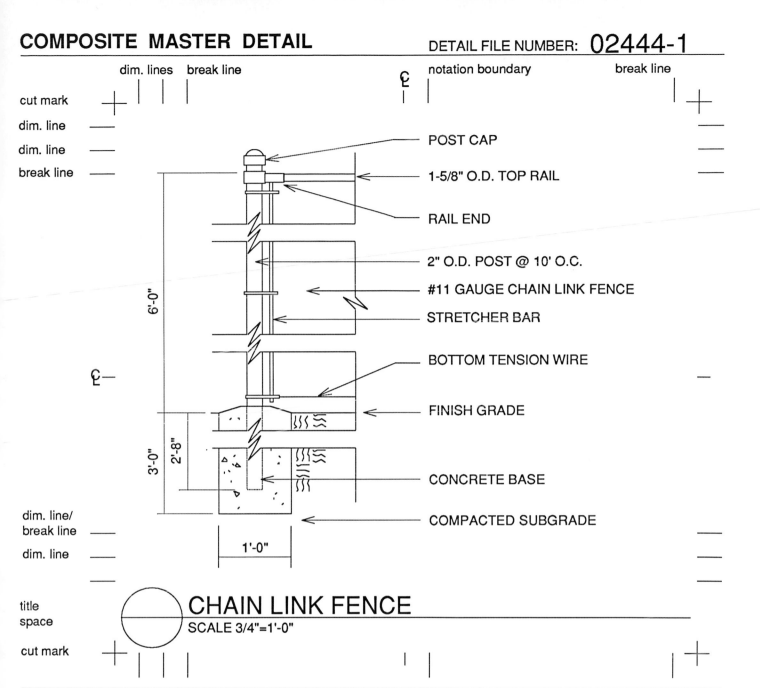

cut mark

dim. lines | break line

notation boundary | break line

dim. line

dim. line

break line

POST CAP

1-5/8" O.D. TOP RAIL

RAIL END

2" O.D. POST @ 10' O.C.

#11 GAUGE CHAIN LINK FENCE

STRETCHER BAR

BOTTOM TENSION WIRE

FINISH GRADE

CONCRETE BASE

COMPACTED SUBGRADE

6'-0"

3'-0"

2'-8"

1'-0"

dim. line/
break line

dim. line

title
space

cut mark

CHAIN LINK FENCE

SCALE 3/4"=1'-0"

DETAIL INFORMATION
References, jobsite feedback, job history

02446 WOOD FENCING

DETAIL DATA CHECKLIST

WOOD FENCING
__Footings for posts should be below frost line
__Below grade, wrap posts with a layer of building paper
    AND
       __Set in a 12" diameter concrete collar on compacted fill
    OR
       __Set on concrete footing or concrete piers with angles or straps to anchor and support posts
    OR
       __Rest the post on gravel (cleats optional)
    AND
       __Fill in the hole with compacted fill
       __Add a stone layer on top of fill if needed for stability
__Common materials sizes:
       __4x4 posts 8' long for 5' to 6' height
       __Supports for 2x4 rails laid flat for clear spans at 4' maximum
       __2x4 rails on edge can span 6' without sagging
__Use dados, lap joints, bolting, and galvanized connectors in detailing
__Avoid butt joints and toenailing
__Use offsets and buttress supports in long lengths subject to wind pressure
__Fence gates are subject to heavy loads and abuse, so use extra-heavy post supports, cross bracing,
    and   heavy-duty hardware
__Slope tops of posts to drain water
__Slope rails or add drain holes to avoid accumulation of water at joints

SMALL-SCALE GENERIC DETAILS

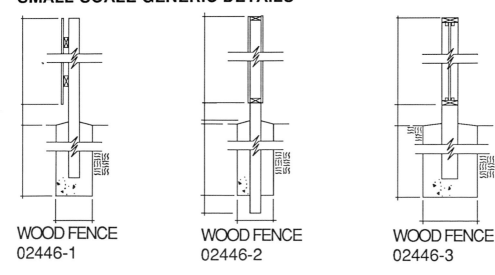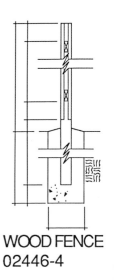

WOOD FENCE
02446-1

WOOD FENCE
02446-2

WOOD FENCE
02446-3

WOOD FENCE
02446-4

02446 WOOD FENCING

FULL-SCALE GENERIC DETAILS

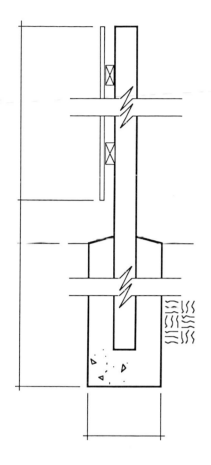

WOOD FENCE
3/4'=1'-0"   02446-1

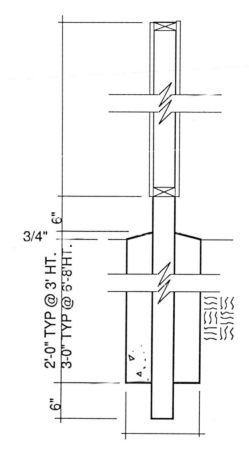

WOOD FENCE
3/4'=1'-0"   02446-2

02447 METAL FENCES

DETAIL DATA CHECKLIST

METAL FENCES
__Metal fences are usually purchased ready-made, or fabricated as variations on
common metal fence types and styles.
__Detail drawings are included mainly to show desired sizes and types and to indicate
anchoring to the ground or pavement.
__See manufacturers' and suppliers' catalogs for design data, details, and specifications.
__See manufacturers' recommendations for anchoring.

SMALL-SCALE GENERIC DETAILS

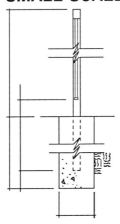

METAL FENCE
02447-11

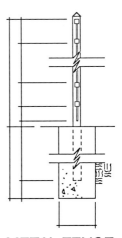

METAL FENCE
02447-12

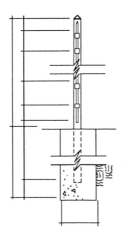

METAL FENCE
02447-13

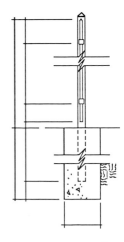

METAL FENCE
02447-14

02447 METAL FENCES

FULL-SCALE GENERIC DETAILS

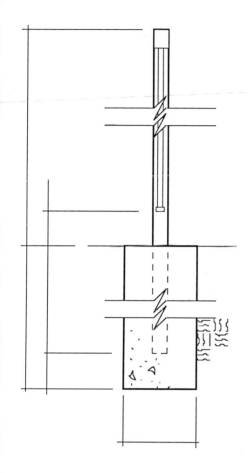

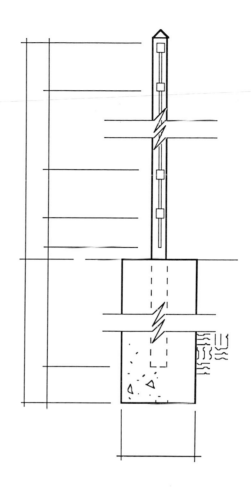

METAL FENCE
1-1/2"=1'-0"   02447-11

METAL FENCE
1-1/2"=1'-0"   02447-12

02447 METAL FENCES

FULL-SCALE GENERIC DETAILS continued

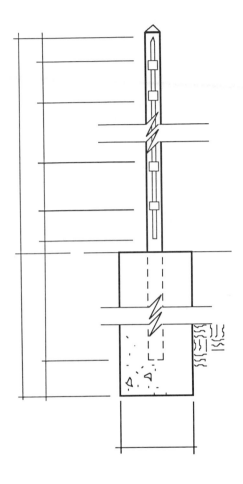

METAL FENCE
1-1/2"=1'-0"   02447-13

METAL FENCE
1-1/2"=1'-0"   02447-14

NOTATION CHECKLIST,
SAMPLE NOTES

INTERMEDIATE RAILS
NEWALS
POST
POSTCAP
PIPE SLEEVE/ANCHOR
FOOTING
BACKFILL
SUBGRADE

12" DIA. CONC. FOOTING
COMPACTED FILL (below footing)
COMPACTED EARTH FILL
METAL POSTS (extend. 6" typ. thru conc. footing,
    max. spacing typ. 6'-7')

02448 FLAGPOLES

DETAIL DATA CHECKLIST

FLAGPOLE BASE
__Footing dimensions are determined by the height of the pole
__See manufacturer's recommendations on footing/height ratio
__Place pole in corrugated tube, and pack with dry sand
__Ground the flagpole for lightning protection
__Pole anchorage as per manufacturer's requirements

SMALL-SCALE GENERIC DETAILS

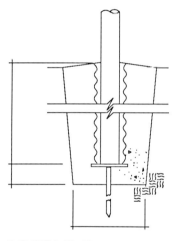

FLAGPOLE Crown
02448-11

FLAGPOLE Crown
02448-12

FLAGPOLE Base
02448-1

FULL-SCALE GENERIC DETAILS

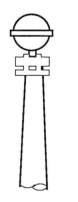

FLAGPOLE Crown
3/4"=1'-0"   02448-11

FLAGPOLE Crown
3/4"=1'-0"   02448-12

02449 (a) MASONRY YARD WALLS

DETAIL DATA CHECKLIST

BRICK YARD WALLS
__Use SW grade brick for weather resistance
__Concrete footings
    __Top of footing below the frost line
    __Minimum footing:
        __10" deep
        __16" wide
        __2-#3 continuous rebars
__Provide cap or coping:
    __Concrete
    __Stone
    __Rowlock brick

__Use Type S mortar for resistance to horizontal forces
__Joints--tooled S or V mortar joints for maximum
    weatherproofing
__Expansion joints--vertical joints at 50' minimum
__Reinforcing--horizontal truss-type wire reinforcing
    every 6th course
__In areas of heavy wind (10 psf or greater):
    __Straight brick walls no higher than 3/4 of the wall
        thickness squared (4' for an 8" wall)
    __Use buttresses, offsets, piers for added support
    __Add vertical reinforcing as per Brick Institute
        handbook

SMALL-SCALE GENERIC DETAILS

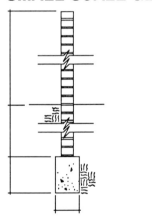

YARD WALL 4" Brick
02449-1

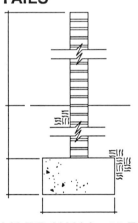

YARD WALL 6" Brick
02449-2

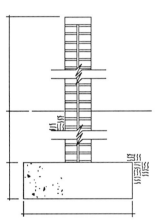

YARD WALL Double 4" Brick
02449-3

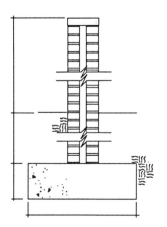

YARD WALL 10" Brick Cavity Wall
02449-4

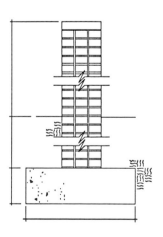

YARD WALL Triple 4" Brick
02449-5

02449 (a) MASONRY YARD WALLS

FULL-SCALE GENERIC DETAILS

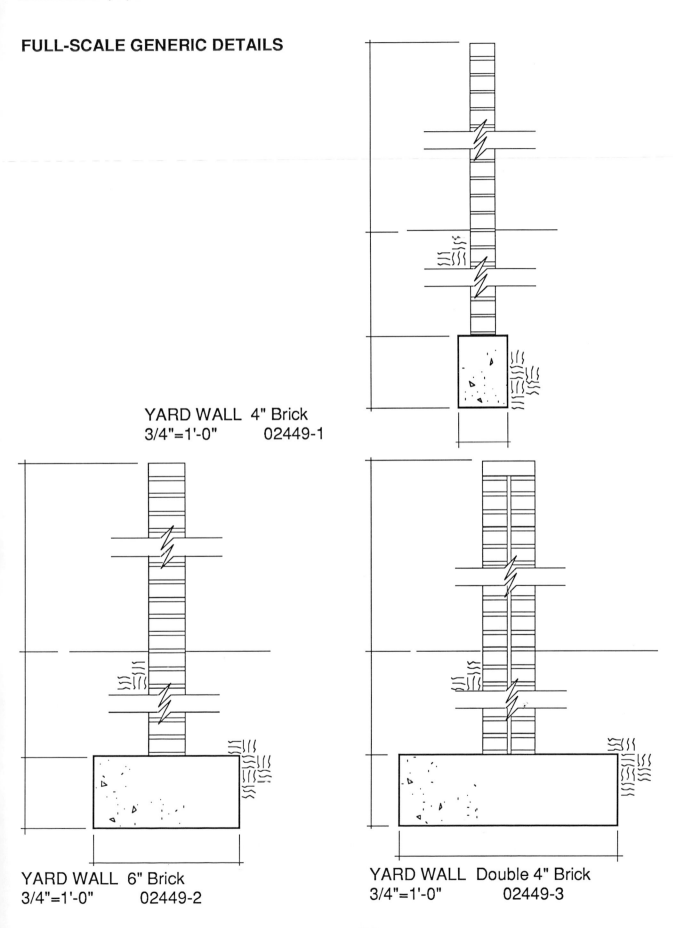

YARD WALL 4" Brick
3/4"=1'-0"   02449-1

YARD WALL 6" Brick
3/4"=1'-0"   02449-2

YARD WALL Double 4" Brick
3/4"=1'-0"   02449-3

02449 (a) MASONRY YARD WALLS

FULL-SCALE GENERIC DETAILS continued

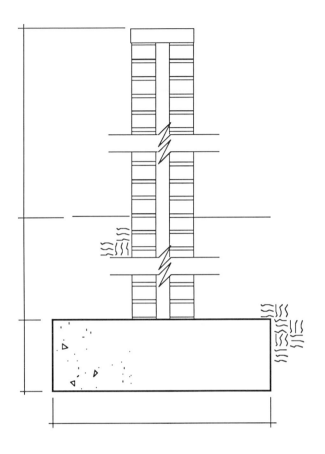

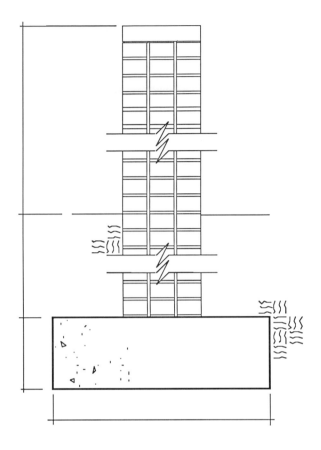

YARD WALL 10" Brick Cavity Wall
3/4"=1'-0"   02449-4

YARD WALL Triple 4" Brick
3/4"=1'-0"   02449-5

NOTATION CHECKLIST,
SAMPLE NOTES

TOP OF WALL ELEVATION
FINISH GRADE/PAVING
WALL CAP (TYPE & SIZE)
MASONRY UNITS (TYPE & SIZE)
REINFORCING
EXPANSION JOINTS (TYPE & SPACING)
FOOTING
AGGREGATE BASE
SUBGRADE
FOOTING DRAIN

HORIZ. CONT. REINF.
FOOTING (reinf.-Typ for a 1' x 3' ftg.-
    3 #3 cont. & #3 bars x 2'-6" @ 12" O.C.)
#4 DOWEL @ 24" O.C. (Typ. tie from block
    wall to ftg.-90° angle 30" vertical & 12"
    horiz. into ftg.)
FILL CELL W/ GROUT @ EACH DOWEL (block
    walls)
WEEP HOLES @ 48" O.C.
EXPANSION JOINTS
CONC. BLK. PILASTER

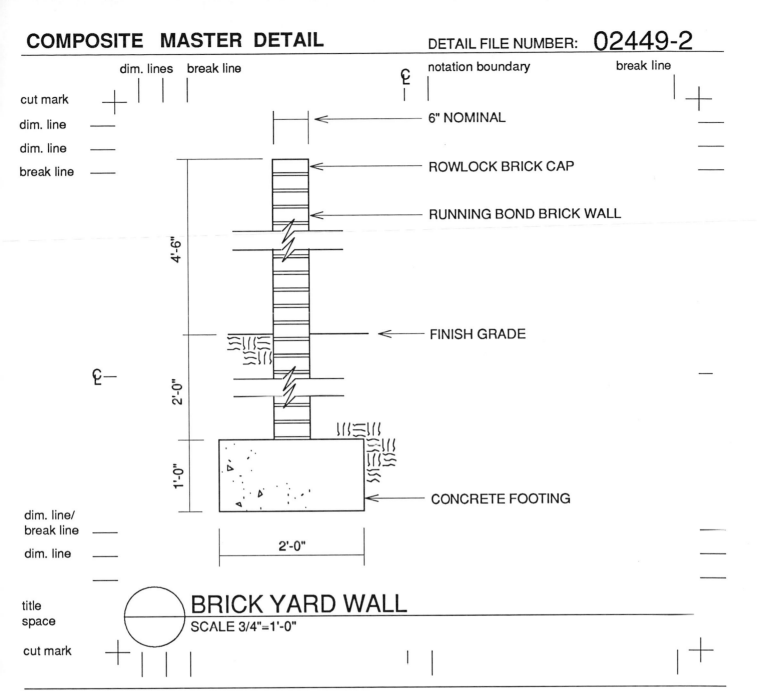

dim. lines   break line   notation boundary   break line

cut mark

dim. line

dim. line

break line

6" NOMINAL

ROWLOCK BRICK CAP

RUNNING BOND BRICK WALL

4'-6"

FINISH GRADE

2'-0"

1'-0"

CONCRETE FOOTING

dim. line/
break line

dim. line

2'-0"

title
space

BRICK YARD WALL

SCALE 3/4"=1'-0"

cut mark

DETAIL INFORMATION
References, jobsite feedback, job history

02449 (b) MASONRY YARD WALLS

DETAIL DATA CHECKLIST

CONCRETE MASONRY UNIT YARD WALLS
__Concrete footings
__Top of footing below the frost line
__Minimum footing:
      __10" deep
      __16" wide
__2-#3 continuous rebars
__Provide cap or coping
__Use Type S mortar for resistance to hor izontal forces
__Joints--tooled S or V mortar joints for maximum weatherproofing
__Expansion joints--vertical joints at 50' minimum
__For an 8" CMU wall, use a 12" CMU pilaster
__Place horizontal reinforcing at 24" o.c., continuous through the pilaster
__Dowel wall to concrete footing with #4 dowels at 24" o.c.
__Fill block cells with grout at each dowel
OR
__Bond beams at top of wall with #5 continuous, at 32" o.c.

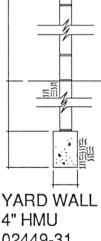

YARD WALL
4" HMU
02449-31

SMALL-SCALE GENERIC DETAILS

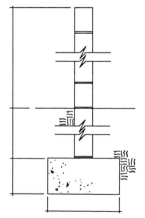

YARD WALL
6" HMU
02449-32

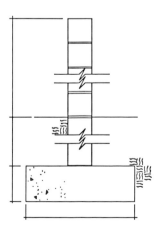

YARD WALL
8" HMU
02449-33

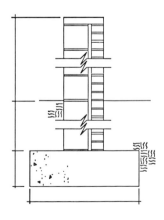

YARD WALL
4" Brick/8" HMU
02449-51

02449 (b) MASONRY YARD WALLS

FULL-SCALE GENERIC DETAILS

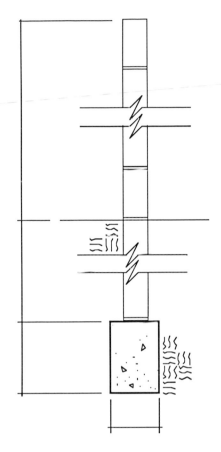

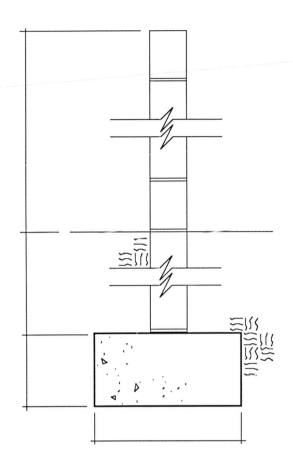

YARD WALL 4" HMU
3/4"=1'-0"   02449-31

YARD WALL 6" HMU
3/4"=1'-0"   02449-32

02449 (b) MASONRY YARD WALLS

FULL-SCALE GENERIC DETAILS continued

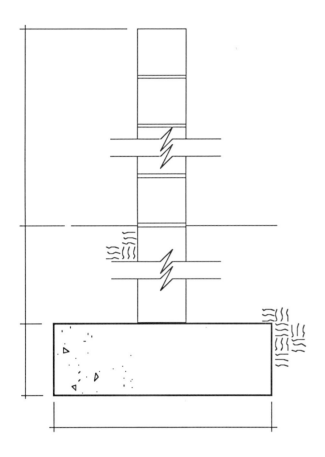

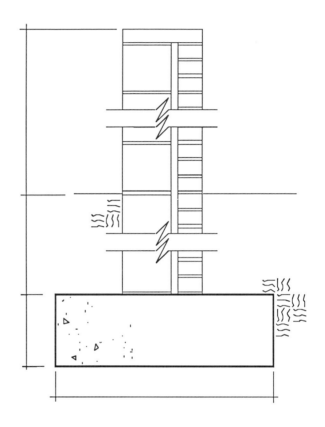

YARD WALL 8" HMU
3/4"=1'-0"   02449-33

YARD WALL 4" Brick/8" HMU
3/4"=1'-0"   02449-51

NOTATION CHECKLIST,
SAMPLE NOTES

TOP OF WALL ELEVATION
FINISH GRADE/PAVING
WALL CAP (TYPE & SIZE)
MASONRY UNITS (TYPE & SIZE)
REINFORCING
EXPANSION JOINTS (TYPE & SPACING)
FOOTING
AGGREGATE BASE
SUBGRADE
FOOTING DRAIN

HORIZ. CONT. REINF.
FOOTING (Reinf.-typ for a 1' x 3' ftg.-
   3 #3 cont. & #3 bars x 2'-6" @ 12" O.C.)
#4 DOWEL @ 24" O.C. (Typ. tie from block
   wall to ftg.-90° angle 30" vertical & 12"
   horiz. into ftg.)
FILL CELL W/ GROUT @ EACH DOWEL (block
   walls)
WEEP HOLES @ 48" O.C.
EXPANSION JOINTS
CONC. BLK. PILASTER

O2451 (a) BOLLARDS Concrete

DETAIL DATA CHECKLIST

BOLLARDS
__Chamfer or round edges
__Add eye bolts or steel rings for chains
__Place rebar in the core of the bollard (vertically) for added strength

SMALL-SCALE GENERIC DETAILS

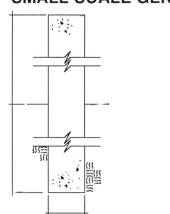

CONCRETE BOLLARD
02451-1

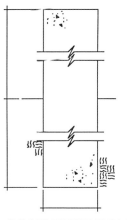

CONCRETE BOLLARD
02451-2

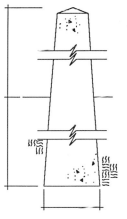

CONCRETE BOLLARD
02451-3

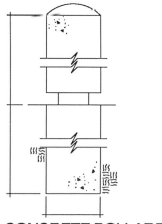

CONCRETE BOLLARD
02451-4

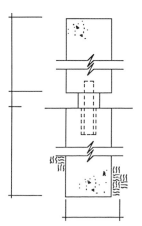

CONCRETE BOLLARD
02451-5

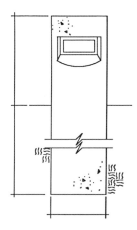

CONCRETE BOLLARD
02451-6

O2451 (a) BOLLARDS Concrete

FULL-SCALE GENERIC DETAILS

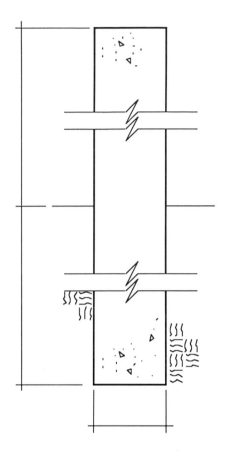

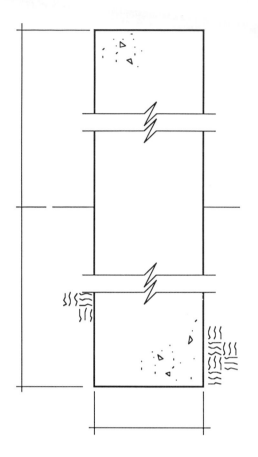

CONCRETE BOLLARD
3/4"=1'-0"   02451-1

CONCRETE BOLLARD
3/4"=1'-0"   02451-2

O2451 (a) BOLLARDS Concrete

FULL-SCALE GENERIC DETAILS continued

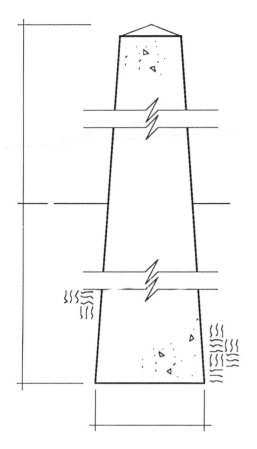

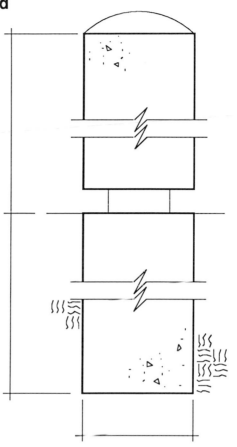

CONCRETE BOLLARD
3/4"=1'-0"   02451-3

CONCRETE BOLLARD
3/4"=1'-0"   02451-4

O2451 (b) BOLLARDS Metal

DETAIL DATA CHECKLIST

GUARD POSTS/BOLLARDS
__Use galvanized metal pipe
__Fill metal pipe with grout or concrete, sloped or
rounded at the top for drainage
__Seal joint between pipe and concrete footing with
a sealant
__Weld eye bolts to pipe or embed in concrete for
chains, etc.

SMALL-SCALE GENERIC DETAILS

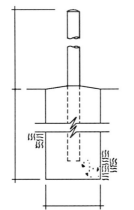

METAL PIPE BOLLARD/GUARDRAIL
02451-31

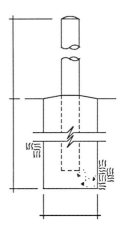

METAL PIPE BOLLARD/GUARDRAIL
02451-32

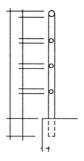

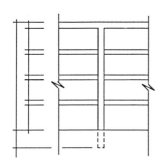

METAL PIPE GUARDRAIL
02451-36

METAL PIPE GUARDRAIL
02451-37

METAL PIPE GUARDRAIL
PIPE SLEEVE 02451-41

O2451 (b) BOLLARDS Metal

FULL-SCALE GENERIC DETAILS

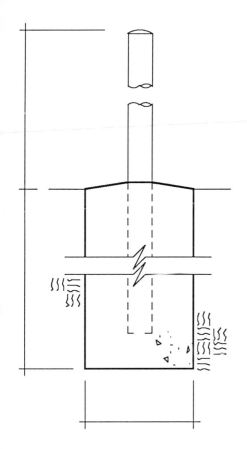

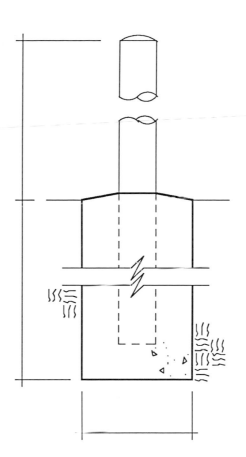

METAL PIPE BOLLARD/GUARDRAIL
3/4"=1'-0"   02451-31

METAL PIPE BOLLARD/GUARDRAIL
3/4"=1'-0"   02451-32

O2451 (b) BOLLARDS Metal

FULL-SCALE GENERIC DETAILS continued

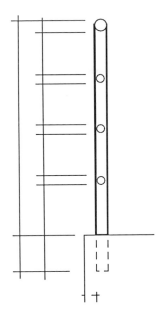

METAL PIPE GUARDRAIL
3/4"=1'-0"   02451-36

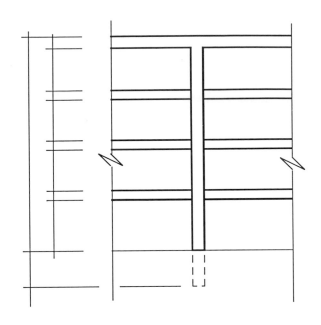

METAL PIPE GUARDRAIL
3/4"=1'-0"   02451-37

NOTATION CHECKLIST,
SAMPLE NOTES

POLE/BOLLARD (SIZE & MATERIAL)
CAP/TOP SLOPE
FINISH GRADE/PAVING
BACKFILL/AGGREGATE/SAND
AGGREGATE BASE
SUBGRADE
TOP RAIL PIPE (MATERIAL & SIZE)
PIPE POST (SIZE & SPACING)
INTERMEDIATE PIPE RAILS (SIZE & SPACING)
PIPE SLEEVE/ANCHOR
PAVING/SLAB/CURB

METAL PIPE GUARDRAIL PIPE SLEEVE
3/4"=1'-0"   02451-41

O2451 (c) BOLLARDS Metal Pipe, Wood

DETAIL DATA CHECKLIST

METAL POSTS/BOLLARDS
__Use galvanized metal pipe
__Fill metal pipe with grout or concrete, sloped or rounded at the top for drainage
__Seal joint between pipe and concrete footing with a sealant
__Weld eye bolts to pipe or embed in concrete for chains, etc.

WOOD BOLLARDS
__Chamfer or round edges
__Add eye bolts or steel rings for chains
__Place rebar in the core of the bollard (vertically) for added strength
__Wood can be treated or untreated
__Treat base of wood bollards with creosote or similar preservative

SMALL-SCALE GENERIC DETAILS

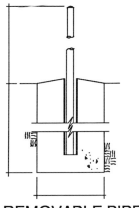

REMOVABLE PIPE
02451-51

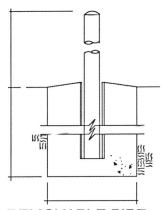

REMOVABLE PIPE
02451-52

WOOD BOLLARD 8" Post
02451-71

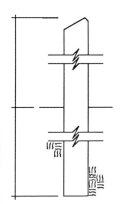

WOOD BOLLARD
6"x8"/8"x8" 02451-72

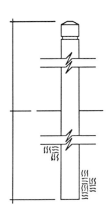

WOOD BOLLARD 6"x6"
02451-73

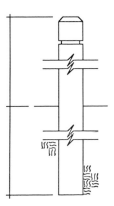

WOOD BOLLARD 8"x8"
02451-74

O2451 (c) BOLLARDS Metal Pipe, Wood

FULL-SCALE GENERIC DETAILS

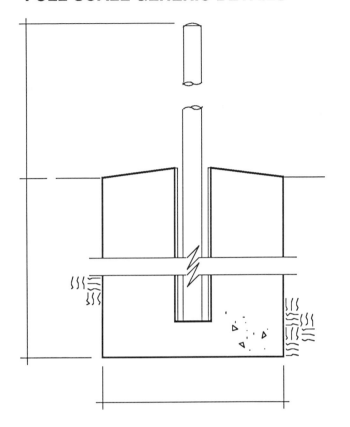

REMOVABLE PIPE BOLLARD/GUARDRAIL
3/4"=1'-0"   02451-51

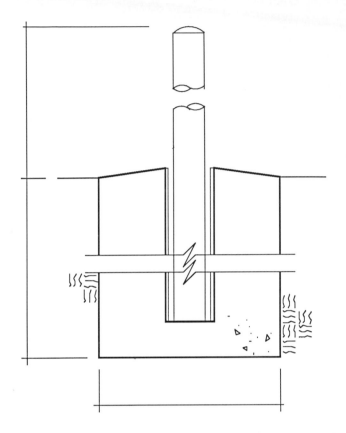

REMOVABLE PIPE BOLLARD/GUARDRAIL
3/4"=1'-0"   02451-52

<u>O2451 (c) BOLLARDS Metal Pipe, Wood</u>

FULL-SCALE GENERIC DETAILS continued

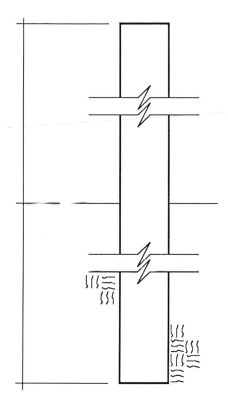

WOOD BOLLARD 8" Post
3/4"=1'-0"   02451-71

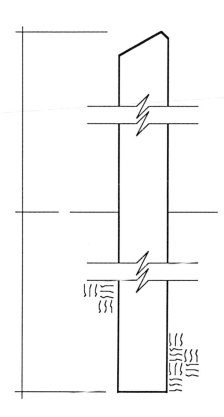

WOOD BOLLARD 6"x8"/8"x8"
3/4"=1'-0"   02451-72

O2451 (c) BOLLARDS Metal Pipe, Wood

FULL-SCALE GENERIC DETAILS continued

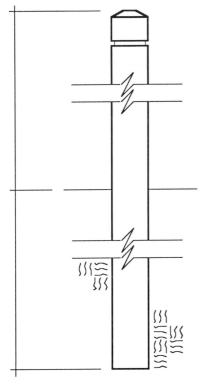

WOOD BOLLARD 6"x6"
3/4"=1'-0"   02451-73

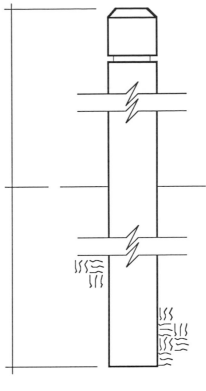

WOOD BOLLARD 8"x8"
3/4"=1'-0"   02451-74

NOTATION CHECKLIST,
SAMPLE NOTES

POLE/BOLLARD (SIZE & MATERIAL)
CAP/TOP SLOPE
FINISH GRADE/PAVING
BACKFILL/AGGREGATE/SAND
AGGREGATE BASE
SUBGRADE
TOP RAIL PIPE (MATERIAL & SIZE)
PIPE POST (SIZE & SPACING)
INTERMEDIATE PIPE RAILS (SIZE & SPACING)
PIPE SLEEVE/ANCHOR
PAVING/SLAB/CURB

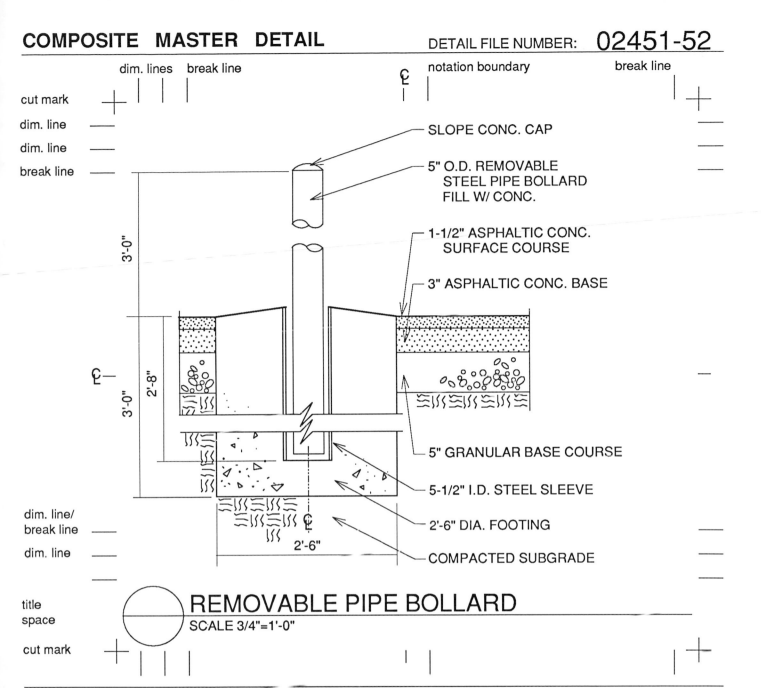

cut mark

dim. lines   break line   notation boundary   break line

dim. line

dim. line

break line

SLOPE CONC. CAP

5" O.D. REMOVABLE
STEEL PIPE BOLLARD
FILL W/ CONC.

1-1/2" ASPHALTIC CONC.
SURFACE COURSE

3" ASPHALTIC CONC. BASE

3'-0"

2'-8"   3'-0"

5" GRANULAR BASE COURSE

5-1/2" I.D. STEEL SLEEVE

dim. line/
break line

2'-6" DIA. FOOTING

2'-6"

dim. line

COMPACTED SUBGRADE

title
space

REMOVABLE PIPE BOLLARD

SCALE 3/4"=1'-0"

cut mark

DETAIL INFORMATION
References, jobsite feedback, job history

02452 SIGNS

DETAIL DATA CHECKLIST

SIGNS
__Street and directional signs are usually purchased ready-made or
   fabricated as variations on common sign types and styles.
   Local highway and street jurisdictions usually provide exact design standards and specifications.
__Detail drawings are included mainly to show desired sizes and types
   and to indicate anchoring to the ground or pavement.
__Besides data provided by governing agencies, see manufacturers' and
   suppliers' catalogs for additional design data, details, and specifications.
__See manufacturers' recommendations for anchoring.

SMALL-SCALE GENERIC DETAILS

SIGN Left Turn
02452-1

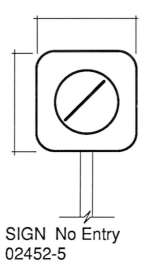

SIGN No Entry
02452-5

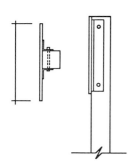

SIGN POST & SIGN CONNECTION
02452-11

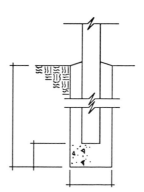

SIGN POST FOOTING
02452-16

02452 SIGNS

**FULL-SCALE
GENERIC DETAILS**

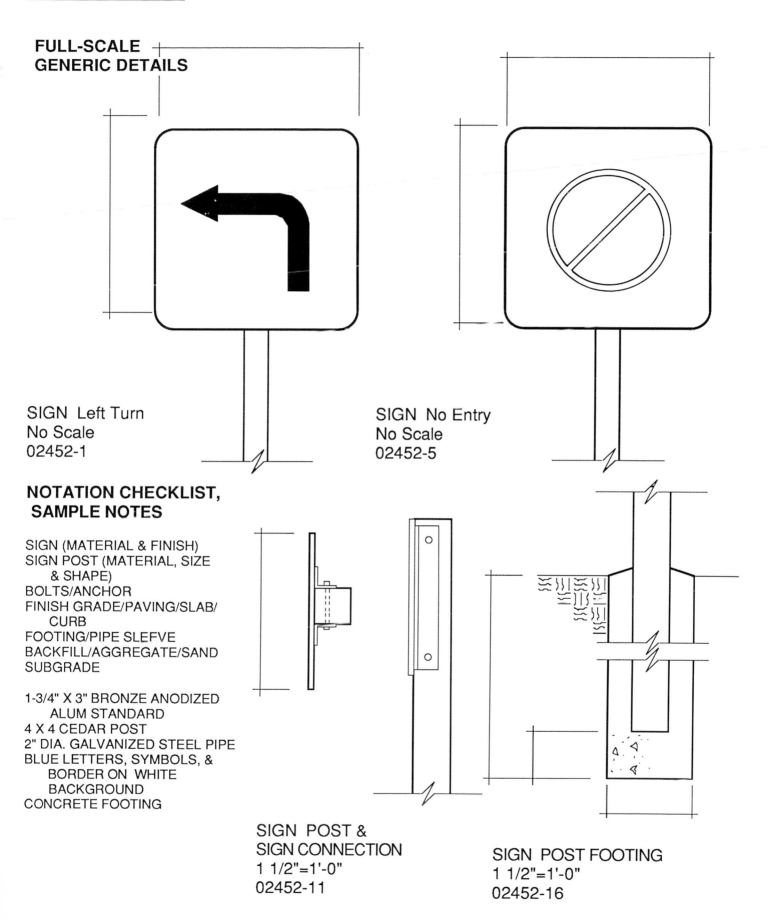

SIGN Left Turn
No Scale
02452-1

SIGN No Entry
No Scale
02452-5

NOTATION CHECKLIST, SAMPLE NOTES

SIGN (MATERIAL & FINISH)
SIGN POST (MATERIAL, SIZE
   & SHAPE)
BOLTS/ANCHOR
FINISH GRADE/PAVING/SLAB/
   CURB
FOOTING/PIPE SLEFVE
BACKFILL/AGGREGATE/SAND
SUBGRADE

1-3/4" X 3" BRONZE ANODIZED
   ALUM STANDARD
4 X 4 CEDAR POST
2" DIA. GALVANIZED STEEL PIPE
BLUE LETTERS, SYMBOLS, &
   BORDER ON WHITE
   BACKGROUND
CONCRETE FOOTING

SIGN POST &
SIGN CONNECTION
1 1/2"=1'-0"
02452-11

SIGN POST FOOTING
1 1/2"=1'-0"
02452-16

dim. lines   break line   notation boundary   break line

cut mark

dim. line ——

dim. line ——

break line ——

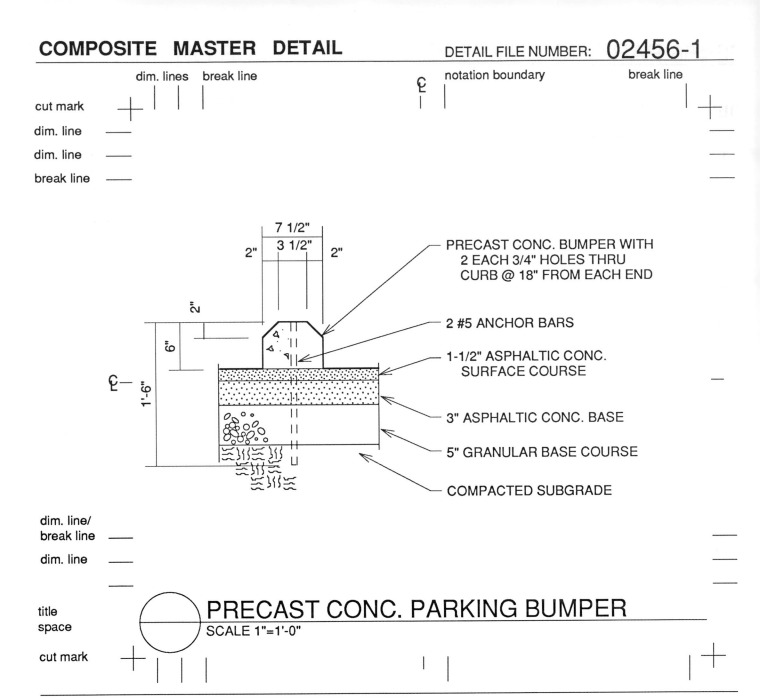

PRECAST CONC. BUMPER WITH
2 EACH 3/4" HOLES THRU
CURB @ 18" FROM EACH END

2 #5 ANCHOR BARS

1-1/2" ASPHALTIC CONC.
SURFACE COURSE

3" ASPHALTIC CONC. BASE

5" GRANULAR BASE COURSE

COMPACTED SUBGRADE

dim. line/
break line ——

dim. line ——

title
space   **PRECAST CONC. PARKING BUMPER**
               SCALE 1"=1'-0"

cut mark

DETAIL INFORMATION
References, jobsite feedback, job history

02457 BICYCLE STANDS

DETAIL DATA CHECKLIST

PRECAST CONCRETE BICYCLE STAND
__Precast concrete
    __3/4" chamfer is typical
    __Available in 4' to 5' lengths
    __Anchor with 3/4" round, 24" long pipe anchor, 2 per bumper
  OR
    __Use 2 #5 bars, 18" long
    __Water drains may also be provided in longer bumpers
       (3-1/2"x 1-1/2" holes at bottom of bumper)

WOOD BOLLARD BICYCLE STAND
__Chamfer or round edges
__Add eye bolts or steel rings for chains
__Place rebar in the core of the bollard (vertically) for added strength
__Wood can be treated or untreated
__Treat base of wood bollards with creosote or similar preservative

BICYCLE RACKS
__Bicycle racks are usually purchased ready-made or fabricated as variations on common types and styles.
__Detail drawings are included mainly to show desired sizes and types and to indicate anchoring to the ground or
    pavement.
__See manufacturers' and suppliers' catalogs for design data, details, and specifications.
__See manufacturers' recommendations for anchoring.

SMALL-SCALE GENERIC DETAILS

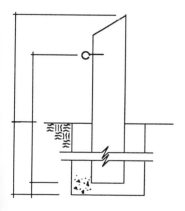

BICYCLE STAND
02457-31

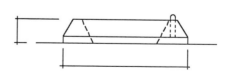

BICYCLE STAND Concrete
02457-1

02457 BICYCLE STANDS

FULL-SCALE GENERIC DETAILS

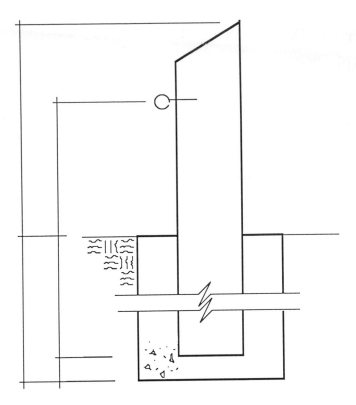

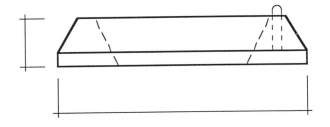

BICYCLE STAND Concrete
1"=1'-0"   02457-1

BICYCLE STAND
1"=1'-0"   02457-31

NOTATION CHECKLIST, SAMPLE NOTES

PRECAST BIKE STAND
U BOLT
GROUT TO PAVEMENT
POLE/BOLLARD (SIZE & MATERIAL)
CAP/TOP SLOPE
FINISH GRADE/PAVING
BACKFILL/AGGREGATE/SAND
AGGREGATE BASE
SUBGRADE
COORDINATE LOCATION W/ ARCHITECT
3'-0" O.C. SPACING TYP.
2" 'U' BOLT (precast conc. product)
BICYCLE RACK RING COLLAR
6" DIA. RINGS,
    BOTH SIDES WHERE REQUIRED

02458 (a) HANDICAP RAMPS

DETAIL DATA CHECKLIST

RAMPS
__See building code and handicap design regulations for slope and
   handrail requirements
__8% slope is typically maximum for wheelchairs for up to 30'
__Provide curbs 4" to 6" high at each side of ramps to prevent side
   runaways or tipping of wheelchairs
__Provide nonslip treatment (abrasive surface or broom finish applied
   across width of ramp)

HANDICAP RAMPS
___Handicap ramps must usually be as per the governing agency's
   design standards and specifications.
___Design standards, specifications and detail drawings are usually provided
   or referenced by the governing agency .

SMALL-SCALE GENERIC DETAILS

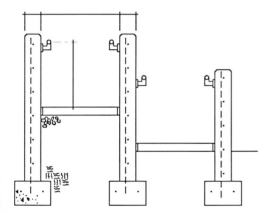

HANDICAP RAMP
O2458-1

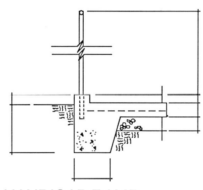

HANDICAP RAMP
O2458-1

02458 (a) HANDICAP RAMPS

FULL-SCALE GENERIC DETAILS

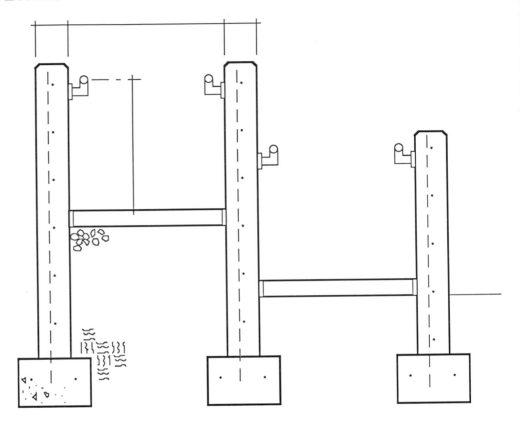

HANDICAP RAMP
1/2"=1'-0"   O2458-1

NOTATION CHECKLIST, SAMPLE NOTES

CONCRETE WALLS/RAMP
REINFORCING
HANDRAILS/BRACKETS
CAMFER
AGGREGATE BASE
COMPACTED SUBGRADE
SEALANT
FOOTINGS

1/4" GROOVES, 3/4" O.C.
STIFF BROOM FINISH ON RAMP SURFACE
TEXTURED CONCRETE
COURSE BROOM FINISH
CONC. GUTTER
CURB TAPER BEYOND
1/2" EXP. JOINT
1/2" JOINT FILLER MATERIAL
TOP OF CURB
REINFORCING
RAMP DOWN

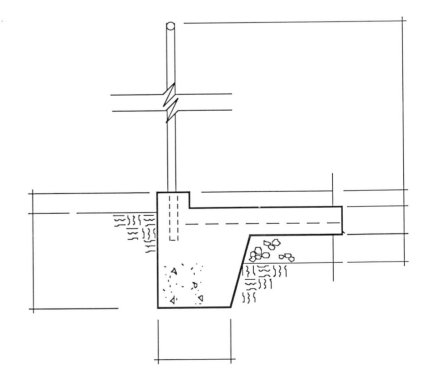

HANDICAP RAMP
1/2"=1'-0"   O2458-1

02458 (b) WHEELCHAIR RAMPS

DETAIL DATA CHECKLIST

RAMPS
__See building code and handicap design regulations for slope and handrail requirements
__8% slope is typically maximum for wheelchairs for up to 30'
__Provide curbs 4" to 6" high at each side of ramps to prevent side runaways or tipping of wheelchairs
__Provide nonslip treatment (abrasive surface or broom finish applied across width of ramp)

SMALL-SCALE GENERIC DETAILS

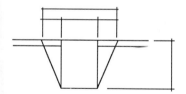

WHEELCHAIR RAMP/CURB CUT
02458-11

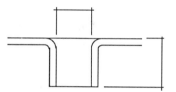

WHEELCHAIR RAMP/CURB CUT
02458-12

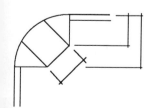

WHEELCHAIR RAMP/CURB CUT Corner
02458-16

02458 (b) WHEELCHAIR RAMPS

FULL-SCALE GENERIC DETAILS

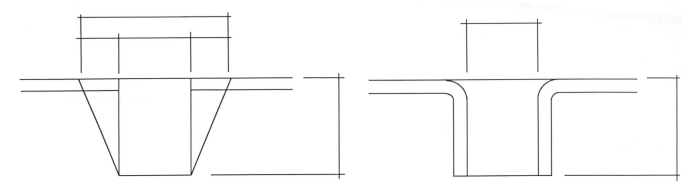

WHEELCHAIR RAMP/CURB CUT
NO SCALE   02458-11

WHEELCHAIR RAMP/CURB CUT
NO SCALE   02458-12

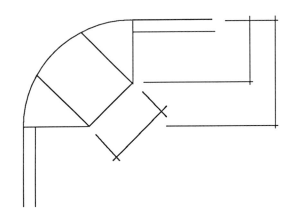

WHEELCHAIR RAMP/CURB CUT Corner
NO SCALE   02458-16

NOTATION CHECKLIST,
SAMPLE NOTES

CURB TYPE
CONCRETE RAMP FINISH
CONCRETE RAMP SLOPE
1/4" GROOVES, 3/4" O.C.
STIFF BROOM FINISH ON
RAMP SURFACE
TEXTURED CONCRETE
COURSE BROOM FINISH
WARP AS REQ'D.

CONC. GUTTER
CURB TAPER BEYOND
1/2" EXP. JOINT
1/2" JOINT FILLER MATERIAL
TOP OF CURB
REINFORCING
SEE   FOR HEIGHT & WIDTH OF CURB CUT
RAMP DOWN

COMPOSITE MASTER DETAIL

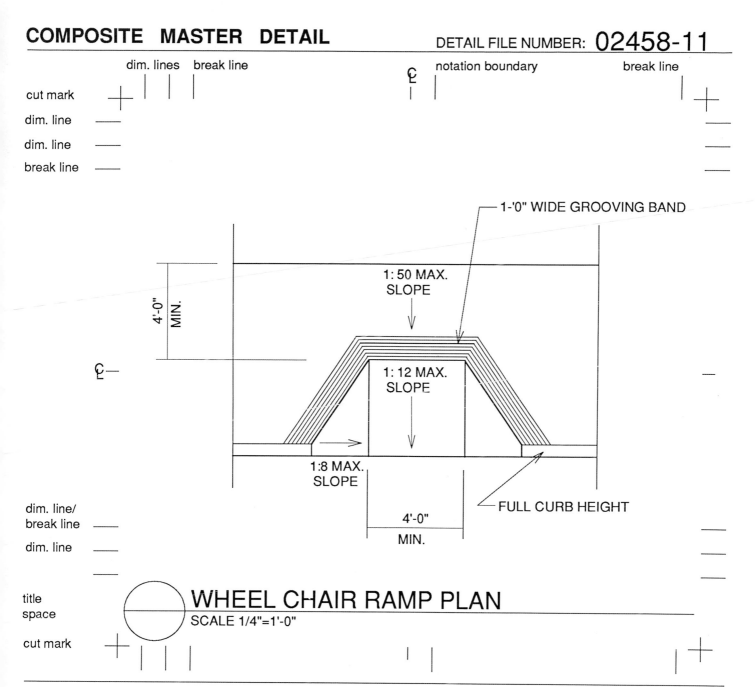

dim. lines   break line   ℄   notation boundary   break line

cut mark

dim. line

dim. line

break line

1-'0" WIDE GROOVING BAND

4'-0" MIN.

℄

1:50 MAX. SLOPE

1:12 MAX. SLOPE

1:8 MAX. SLOPE

FULL CURB HEIGHT

4'-0"

MIN.

dim. line/ break line

dim. line

title space

WHEEL CHAIR RAMP PLAN
SCALE 1/4"=1'-0"

cut mark

DETAIL INFORMATION
References, jobsite feedback, job history

02471 (a) BENCHES

DETAIL DATA CHECKLIST

BENCHES
__Benches are often purchased ready-made, or fabricated as variations on
    common bench types and styles.
__Detail drawings are included mainly to show desired bench sizes and types, and
    to indicate anchoring to the ground or pavement.
__See manufacturers' and suppliers' catalogs for design data, details, and specifications.
__See manufacturers' recommendations for anchoring.

SMALL-SCALE GENERIC DETAILS

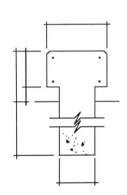

BENCH Concrete
02471-1

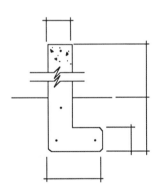

BENCH Concrete
02471-2

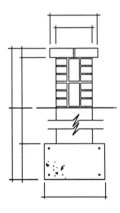

BENCH Masonry
02471-31

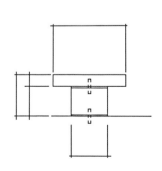

BENCH Marble
02471-51

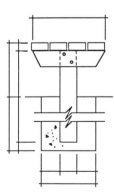

BENCH Wood
02471-71

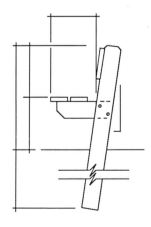

BENCH Wood
02471-72

02471 (a) BENCHES

FULL-SCALE GENERIC DETAILS

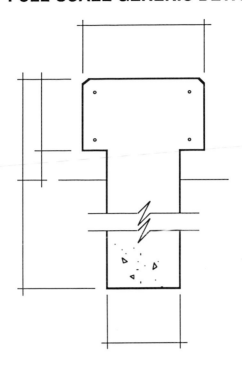

BENCH Concrete
3/4"=1'-0"   02471-1

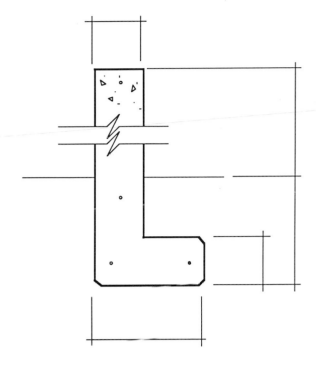

BENCH Concrete
3/4"=1'-0"   02471-2

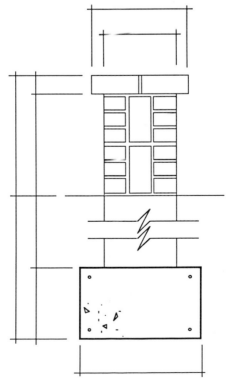

BENCH Masonry
3/4"=1'-0"   02471-31

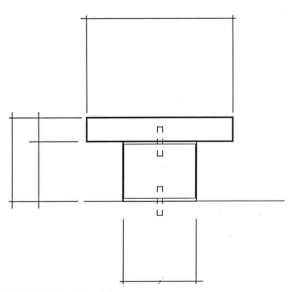

BENCH Marble
3/4"=1'-0"   02471-51

02471 (a) BENCHES

FULL-SCALE GENERIC DETAILS continued

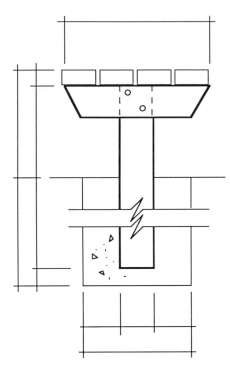

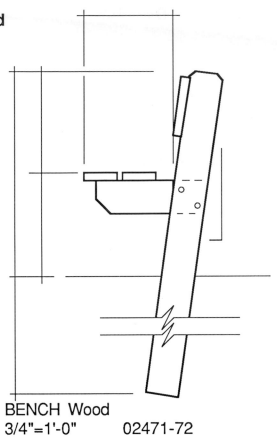

BENCH Wood
3/4"=1'-0"   02471-71

BENCH Wood
3/4"=1'-0"   02471-72

NOTATION CHECKLIST,
SAMPLE NOTES

MATERIAL SURFACE/FINISH
FRAME/SUPPORT
BOLTS/ANCHORS
FINISH GRADE/PAVING
FOOTING
AGGREGATE BASE
SUBGRADE
#4 DOWEL IN 5/8" DIA. HOLE
   (tie CMU bench to supports to slab)
PRECAST CONC. BENCH.
3/4" CAMFER TYP. ALL CORNERS
STEEL INBED PLATES @ 4'-0" O.C. SHIM & WELD
   (to connect precast bench to footing)
SEALANT @ 1/2" FIBER JOINT
#4 BARS CONT. (horiz. approx. 1' O.C.)
#4 BARS VERT @ 3'-0" O.C.
#4 BARS CONT. (@ bottom)
REDWOOD SPACERS, GLUE TO SLAT
   W/WATERPROOF ADHESIVE

REDWOOD SLATS
1/2" X 2" X 3" STL CHANNEL, PAINT 2 COATS FLAT
   ENAMEL
CAP CHANNEL ENDS W/1/8" STEEL, WELD & GRIND
   SMOOTH
NAILER W/ GLUED SPACERS ABOVE
3/4" CONT. CHAMFERED TOP EDGE
3/8" DIA GAL. THREADED STEEL ROD, COUNTER SINK
   NUT & WASHER, PLUG W/1" DIA. X 3/4" HRDWD.
   DOWEL
   SET W/WATERPROOF ADHESIVE
3/8" GAL. LAG BOLT
1/4" DIA X 3" LAG BOLT @ 4 X 4 SUPPORT
1/2" SOLID WD. SPACER @ 4 X 4 SUPPORT
2 X 4 TOE NAILED TO 4 X 4 &
   NAILED TO NEXT 2 X 4 THRU SPACER

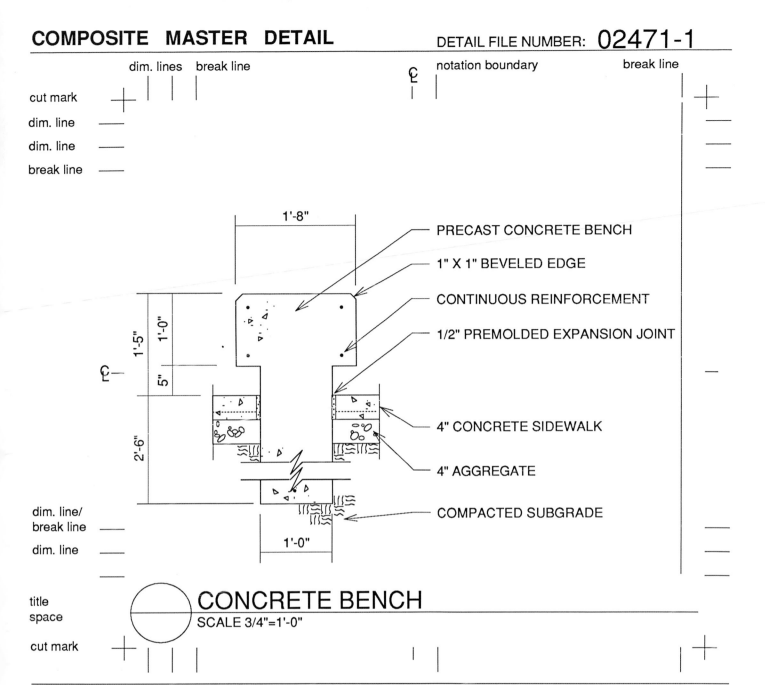

dim. lines break line

notation boundary

break line

cut mark

dim. line

dim. line

break line

PRECAST CONCRETE BENCH

1" X 1" BEVELED EDGE

CONTINUOUS REINFORCEMENT

1/2" PREMOLDED EXPANSION JOINT

4" CONCRETE SIDEWALK

4" AGGREGATE

COMPACTED SUBGRADE

1'-8"

1'-5"

1'-0"

5"

2'-6"

1'-0"

dim. line/
break line

dim. line

title
space

CONCRETE BENCH
SCALE 3/4"=1'-0"

cut mark

DETAIL INFORMATION
References, jobsite feedback, job history

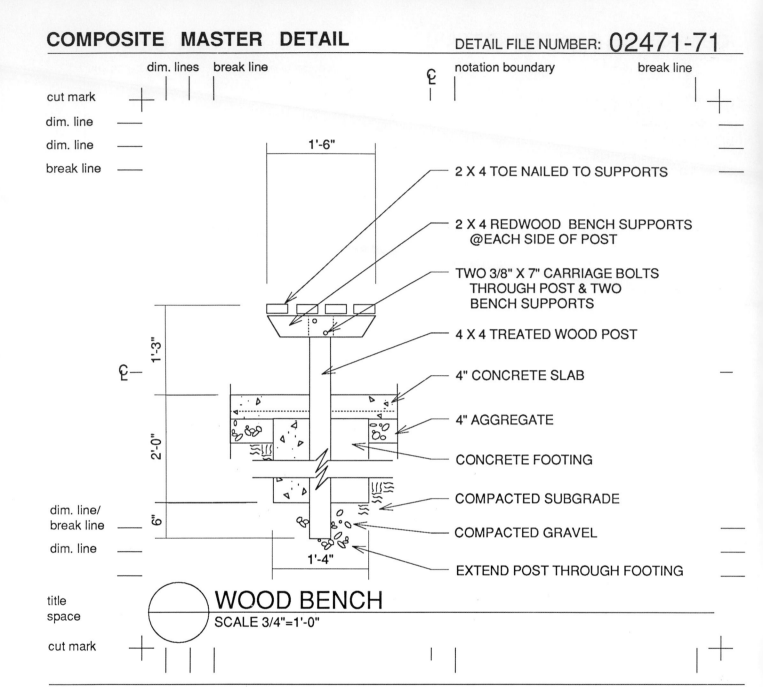

dim. lines   break line

notation boundary   break line

cut mark

dim. line

dim. line

break line

1'-6"

2 X 4 TOE NAILED TO SUPPORTS

2 X 4 REDWOOD BENCH SUPPORTS
@EACH SIDE OF POST

TWO 3/8" X 7" CARRIAGE BOLTS
THROUGH POST & TWO
BENCH SUPPORTS

1'-3"

4 X 4 TREATED WOOD POST

4" CONCRETE SLAB

2'-0"

4" AGGREGATE

CONCRETE FOOTING

COMPACTED SUBGRADE

dim. line/
break line

6"

COMPACTED GRAVEL

dim. line

1'-4"

EXTEND POST THROUGH FOOTING

title
space

WOOD BENCH

SCALE 3/4"=1'-0"

cut mark

DETAIL INFORMATION
References, jobsite feedback, job history

02471 (b) BENCHES

DETAIL DATA CHECKLIST

BENCHES
__Benches are often purchased ready-made, or fabricated as variations
   on common bench types and styles.
__Detail drawings are included mainly to show desired bench sizes and types, and
   to indicate anchoring to the ground or pavement.
__See manufacturers' and suppliers' catalogs for design data, details, and specifications.
__See manufacturers' recommendations for anchoring.

SMALL-SCALE GENERIC DETAILS

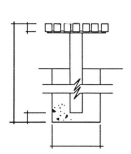

BENCH Wood
W/Metal Frame
02471-81

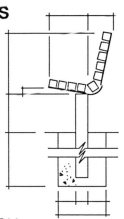

BENCH
Wood W/Metal Frame
02471-82

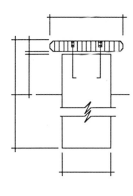

BENCH Wood W/
Concrete/Masonry
Base 02471-91

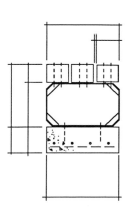

BENCH Wood W/
Metal Frame
02471-83

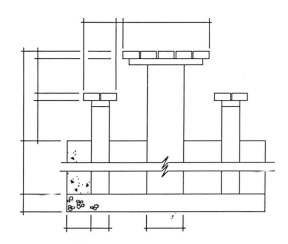

PICNIC TABLE & BENCHES
02471-96

02471 (b) BENCHES

FULL-SCALE GENERIC DETAILS

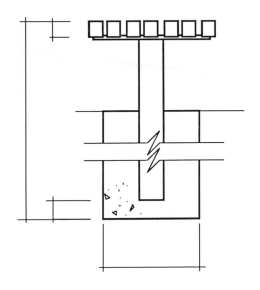

BENCH
Wood W/Metal Frame
3/4"=1'-0"   02471-81

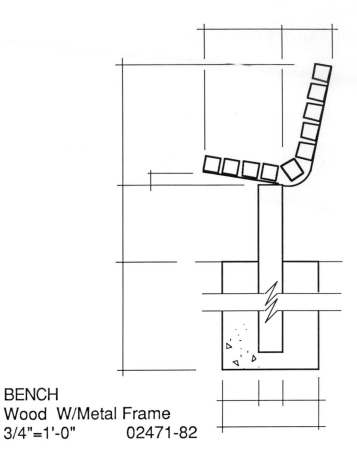

BENCH
Wood W/Metal Frame
3/4"=1'-0"   02471-82

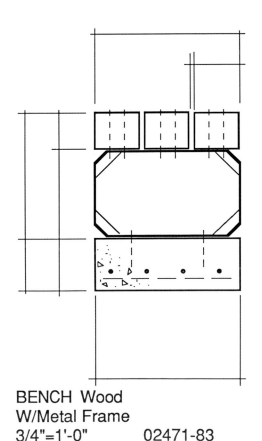

BENCH Wood
W/Metal Frame
3/4"=1'-0"   02471-83

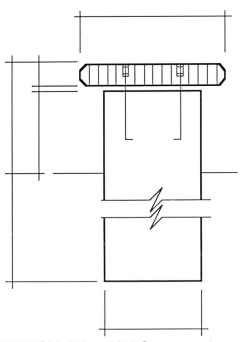

BENCH Wood W/Concrete/
Masonry Base
3/4"=1'-0"   02471-91

02471 (b) BENCHES

FULL-SCALE GENERIC DETAILS continued

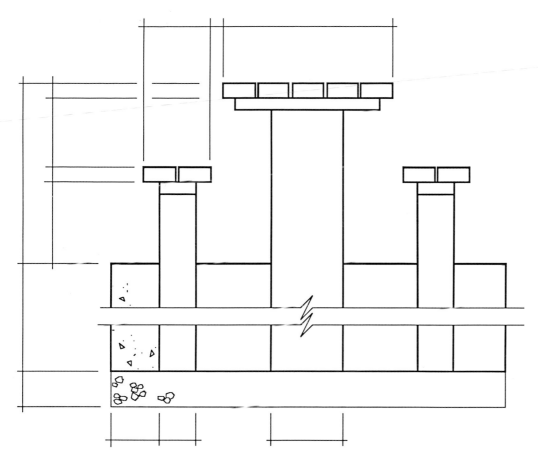

PICNIC TABLE & BENCHES
3/4"=1'-0"   02471-96

02471 (b) BENCHES

NOTATION CHECKLIST, SAMPLE NOTES

MATERIAL SURFACE/FINISH
FRAME/SUPPORT
BOLTS/ANCHORS
FINISH GRADE/PAVING
FOOTING
AGGREGATE BASE
SUBGRADE
#4 DOWEL IN 5/8" DIA. HOLE
   (tie CMU bench to supports to slab)
PRECAST CONC. BENCH.
3/4" CAMFER TYP. ALL CORNERS
STEEL INBED PLATES @ 4'-0" O.C. SHIM & WELD
   (to connect precast bench to footing)
SEALANT @ 1/2" FIBER JOINT
#4 BARS CONT. (horiz. approx. 1' O.C.)
#4 BARS VERT @ 3'-0" O.C.
#4 BARS CONT. (@ bottom)
REDWOOD SPACERS, GLUE TO SLAT
   W/ WATERPROOF ADHESIVE
REDWOOD SLATS
1/2" X 2" X 3" STL CHANNEL, PAINT 2 COATS FLAT ENAMEL
CAP CHANNEL ENDS W/ 1/8" STEEL, WELD & GRIND SMOOTH
NAILER W/ GLUED SPACERS ABOVE
3/4" CONT. CHAMFERED TOP EDGE
3/8" DIA GAL. THREADED STEEL ROD, COUNTER SINK NUT
   & WASHER, PLUG W/ 1" DIA. X 3/4" HRDWD. DOWEL
   SET W/ WATERPROOF ADHESIVE
3/8" GAL. LAG BOLT

1/4" DIA X 3" LAG BOLT @ 4 X 4 SUPPORT
1/2" SOLID WD. SPACER @ 4 X 4 SUPPORT
2 X 4 TOE NAILED TO 4 X 4 &
   NAILED TO NEXT 2 X 4 THRU SPACER
2 X 8
4 X 4
6 X 8 X 16 CMU W/ SOLID GROUT
#4 DOWL (tie CMU bench to supports to slab)
   IN 5/8" DIA. HOLE

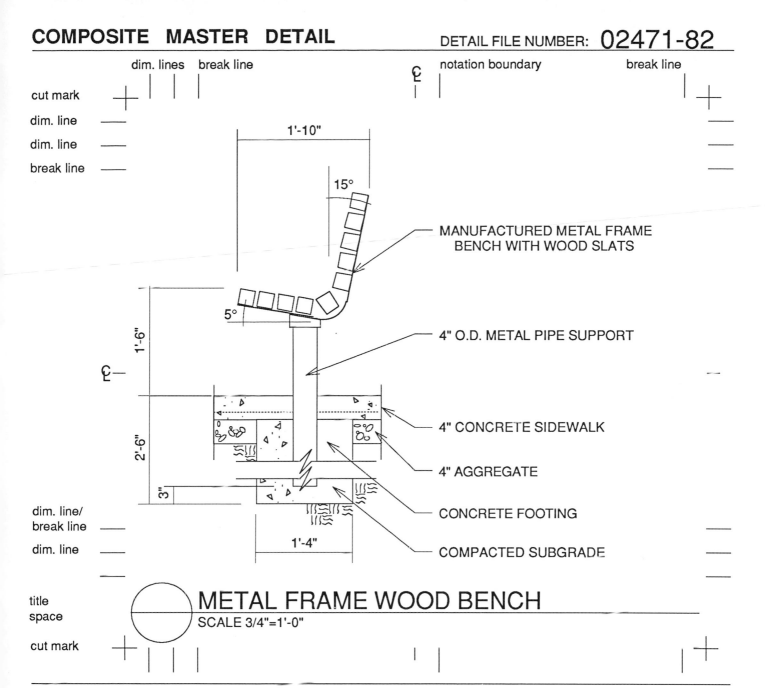

cut mark

dim. lines   break line

notation boundary

break line

dim. line

dim. line

break line

1'-10"

15°

MANUFACTURED METAL FRAME
BENCH WITH WOOD SLATS

5°

4" O.D. METAL PIPE SUPPORT

1'-6"

2'-6"

4" CONCRETE SIDEWALK

4" AGGREGATE

3"

CONCRETE FOOTING

dim. line/
break line

COMPACTED SUBGRADE

dim. line

1'-4"

title
space

METAL FRAME WOOD BENCH

SCALE 3/4"=1'-0"

cut mark

DETAIL INFORMATION
References, jobsite feedback, job history

02478 (a) RETAINING WALLS

DETAIL DATA CHECKLIST

CONCRETE RETAINING WALLS
__Ground slope of 45 degrees or greater requires cribbing or retaining walls
__Walls to 3' high--simple concrete, wood, or planter walls OK
__Walls over 3' --L, T retaining walls or gravity wall
__Place bottom of footing at frost line
__Provide 3" minimum cover for rebar
__Provide 3" diameter weep holes at 4' o.c. (maximum 10' apart)
__Install 1/2" vertical expansion joints every 50'
__Install contraction joints every 25' (1" wide tapered to 1/2" depth)
__Seal expansion and contraction joints with waterstops
__Anchor wall segments to each other at movement joints with:
    __Tapered 2x4 formed vertical key in first pour
   OR
    __1/2" horizontal steel rods, 12" long min. @ 12" spacings with movement sleeves on one side
__Waterproof the earth fill side of wall
__Backfill with gravel, with drainpipe above the footing
__Pipe should drain to storm sewer (may be connected to building footing drains)
__Place filter cloth between gravel and soil backfill

SMALL-SCALE GENERIC DETAILS

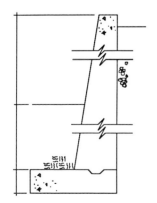

CONCRETE RETAINING WALL L Type
1/202478-11

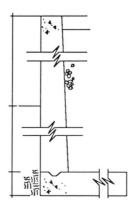

CONCRETE RETAINING WALL L Type
02478-13

02478 (a) RETAINING WALLS

SMALL-SCALE GENERIC DETAILS continued

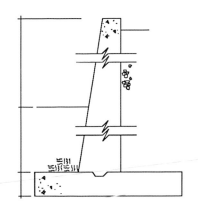

CONCRETE RETAINING WALL T Type
02478-15

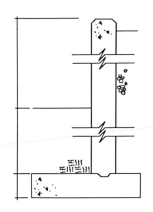

CONCRETE RETAINING WALL T Type
02478-17

FULL-SCALE GENERIC DETAILS

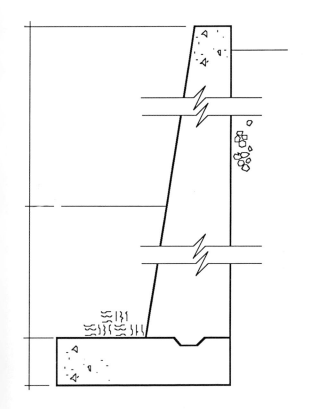

CONCRETE RETAINING WALL L Type
1/2"=1'-0"   02478-11

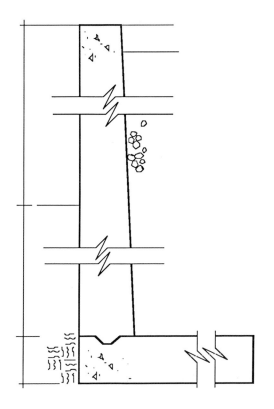

CONCRETE RETAINING WALL L Type
1/2"=1'-0"   02478-13

02478 (a) RETAINING WALLS

FULL-SCALE GENERIC DETAILS continued

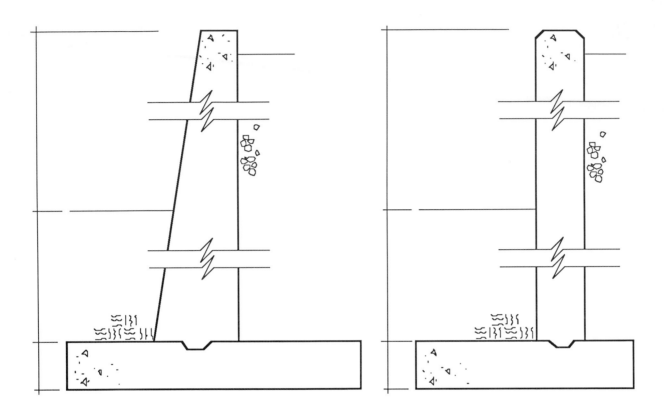

CONCRETE RETAINING WALL T Type
1/2"=1'-0"   02478-15

CONCRETE RETAINING WALL T Type
1/2"=1'-0"   02478-17

NOTATION CHECKLIST, SAMPLE NOTES

TOP OF WALL ELEVATION
FINISH GRADES
ORIGINAL GRADE (DASHED)
EXPANSION JOINTS (TYPE & SPACING)
MASONRY UNIT (TYPE & SIZE)
REINFORCING
WEEP HOLES (SIZE & SPACING)
AGGREGATE DRAIN BED
DRAIN PIPE/DRAIN TILE
COMPACTED SUBGRADE/STRUCTURAL BACKFILL
FOOTING
DAMPPROOFING
POROUS BACKFILL
AGGREGATE BASE

dim. lines   break line

notation boundary   break line

cut mark

dim. line

dim. line

break line

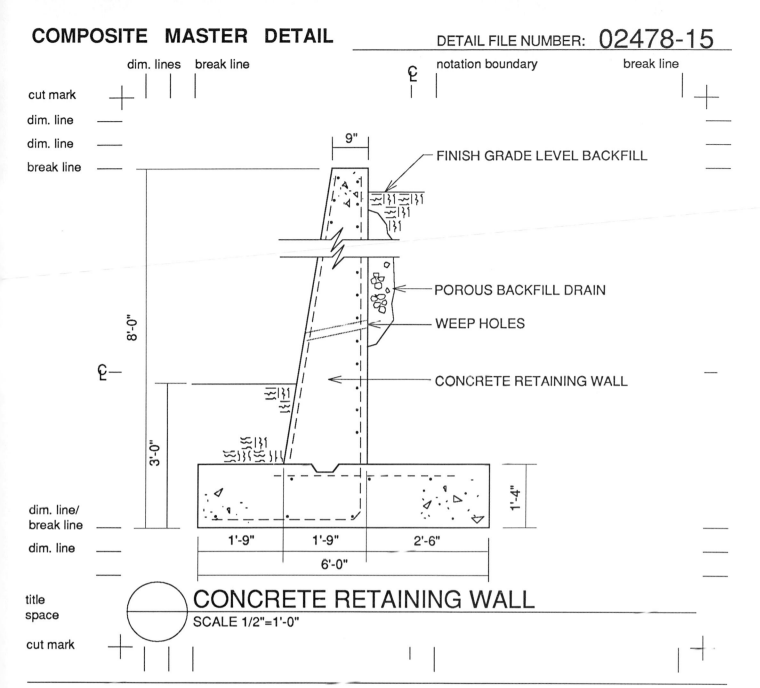

9"

FINISH GRADE LEVEL BACKFILL

POROUS BACKFILL DRAIN

WEEP HOLES

CONCRETE RETAINING WALL

8'-0"

3'-0"

1'-4"

dim. line/
break line

dim. line

1'-9"   1'-9"   2'-6"

6'-0"

title
space

CONCRETE RETAINING WALL
SCALE 1/2"=1'-0"

cut mark

DETAIL INFORMATION
References, jobsite feedback, job history

02478 (b) RETAINING WALLS

DETAIL DATA CHECKLIST

RETAINING WALLS
__Ground slope of 45 degrees or greater requires cribbing or retaining walls
__Walls to 3' high--simple concrete, wood, or planter walls OK
__Walls over 3' --L, T retaining walls or gravity wall
__Waterproof the earth fill side of wall
__Backfill with gravel, with drainpipe above the footing
__Pipe should drain to storm sewer (may be connected to building footing drains)
__Place filter cloth between gravel and soil backfill

BRICK AND BLOCK MASONRY RETAINING WALLS (For walls with minimum horizontal loads only)
__Use SW grade brick for weather resistance
__Top of footing below the frost line
__Provide cap or coping
__Use Type S mortar for resistance to hor izontal forces
__Joints--tooled S or V mortar joints for maximum weatherproofing
__Expansion joints--vertical joints at 50' minimum
__Horizontal and vertical reinforcing as per Brick Institute handbook

DRY STONE GRAVITY RETAINING WALLS
__Tilt stones into the hill
__Batter the wall 2" high
__Base typically 16" wide
__Backfill with gravel, with drainpipe along base of wall at bottom of gravel

SMALL-SCALE GENERIC DETAILS

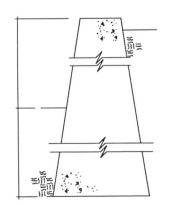 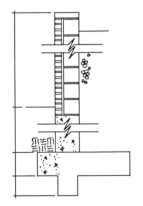 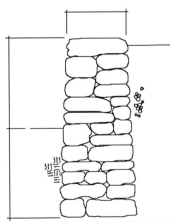

MASONRY RETAINING WALL
Brick & HMU   02478-21

CONCRETE RETAINING WALL
Gravity   02478-19

DRY STONE RETAINING WALL
02478-31

02478 (b) RETAINING WALLS

FULL-SCALE GENERIC DETAILS

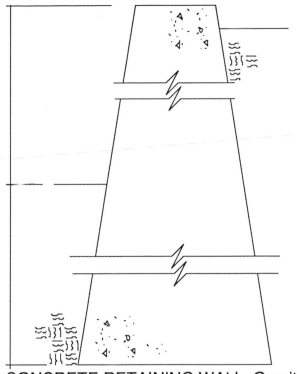

CONCRETE RETAINING WALL Gravity
1/2"=1'-0"   02478-19

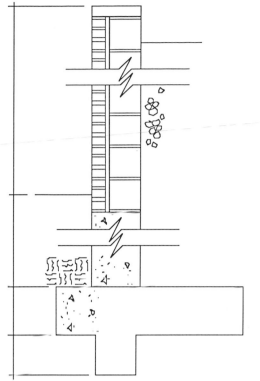

MASONRY RETAINING WALL Brick & HMU
1/2"=1'-0"   02478-21

NOTATION CHECKLIST,
SAMPLE NOTES

TOP OF WALL ELEVATION
FINISH GRADES
ORIGINAL GRADE (DASHED)
EXPANSION JOINTS (TYPE & SPACING)
MASONRY UNIT (TYPE & SIZE)
REINFORCING
WEEP HOLES (SIZE & SPACING)
AGGREGATE DRAIN BED
DRAIN PIPE/DRAIN TILE
COMPACTED SUBGRADE/STRUCTURAL BACKFILL
FOOTING
DAMPPROOFING
POROUS BACKFILL
AGGREGATE BASE

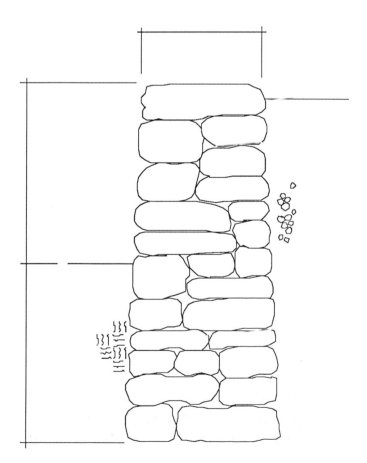

DRY STONE RETAINING WALL
1/2"=1'-0"   02478-31

02479 (a) WOOD PLANTERS/RETAINING WALLS

DETAIL DATA CHECKLIST

POST AND BOARD RETAINING WALLS
__Set posts as deep as the wall is high
__Walls under 2' high don't require weep holes or drains
__For low walls, weep holes drilled into wall may be used instead of drains
__Where drain is needed, run a 6" pipe along back of wall at base
__Walls over 4' high may have their posts tied back to a concrete deadman with a horizontal rods bolted through
   the posts

WOOD RETAINING WALLS
__Stack timbers horizontally
__Support and anchor timbers with:
   __Vertical timbers
   __Concrete piers
   __Vertical steel I-beams
__Tie timbers vertically with min. 2 #4 bars per tie, in 1/2" drilled hole
__Tie back into slope with10' o.c. deadman ties
__Where necessary, use vertical rods at 4' o.c.
__Provide gravel backfill behind filter cloth
__Vertical wood members may be OK for walls up to 4' high, without surcharge, if planted 4' deep

SMALL-SCALE GENERIC DETAILS

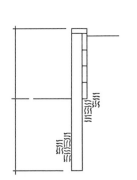

WOOD RETAINING WALL
To 2' High
02479-1

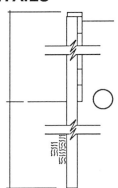

WOOD RETAINING WALL
2' to 4' High
02479-3

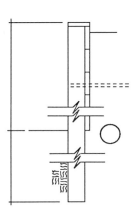

WOOD RETAINING WALL
4' + High
02479-5

02479 (a) WOOD PLANTERS/RETAINING WALLS

SMALL-SCALE GENERIC DETAILS continued

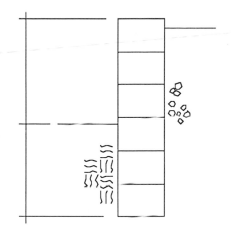

WOOD RETAINING WALL
6x8 Timber/Low
02479-11

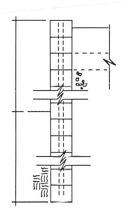

WOOD RETAINING WALL
6x8 Timber/Low
02479-13

FULL-SCALE GENERIC DETAILS

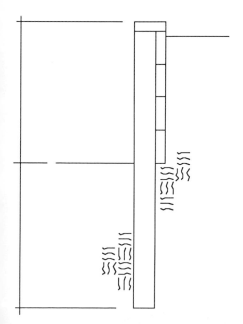

WOOD RETAINING WALL To 2' High
3/4"=1'-0"   02479-1

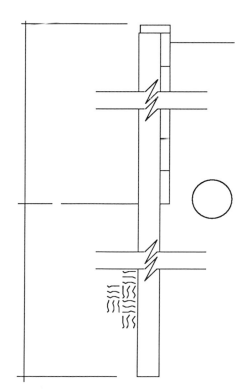

WOOD RETAINING WALL 2' to 4' High
3/4"=1'-0"   02479-3

02479 (a) WOOD PLANTERS/RETAINING WALLS

FULL-SCALE GENERIC DETAILS continued

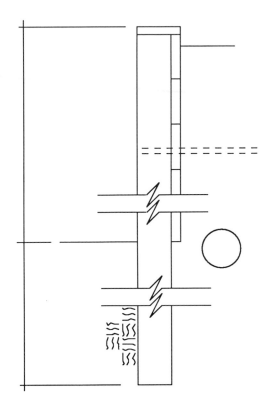

WOOD RETAINING WALL 4' + High
3/4"=1'-0"   02479-5

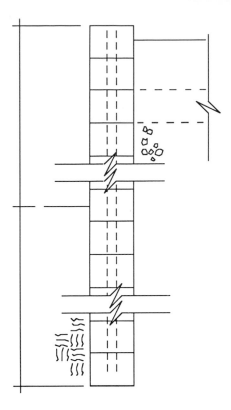

WOOD RETAINING WALL 6x8 Timber/Low
3/4"=1'-0"   02479-13

NOTATION CHECKLIST, SAMPLE NOTES

TOP OF WALL ELEVATION
FINISH GRADES
ORIGINAL GRADE (DASHED)
TIMBER UNITS (TYPE & SIZE)
BOLTS/ANCHORS/ DOWELS
STEEL ROD/WOOD TIE BACKS ('DEADMAN')
AGGREGATE DRAIN BED
DRAIN PIPE/DRAIN TILE
COMPACTED SUBGRADE/STRUCTURAL
BACKFILL
FOOTING
AGGREGATE BASE
POROUS BACKFILL

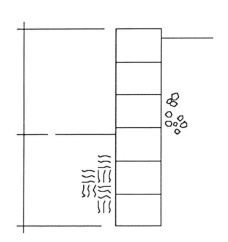

WOOD RETAINING WALL 6x8 Timber/Low
3/4"=1'-0"   02479-11

COMPOSITE MASTER DETAIL

DETAIL FILE NUMBER: 02479-5

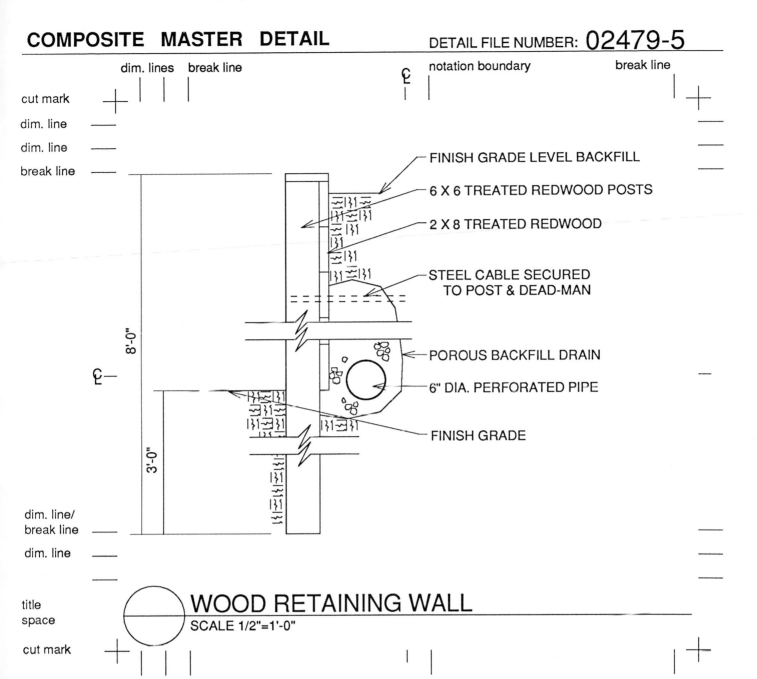

dim. lines   break line   notation boundary   break line

cut mark

dim. line

dim. line

break line

FINISH GRADE LEVEL BACKFILL

6 X 6 TREATED REDWOOD POSTS

2 X 8 TREATED REDWOOD

STEEL CABLE SECURED
TO POST & DEAD-MAN

8'-0"

POROUS BACKFILL DRAIN

6" DIA. PERFORATED PIPE

3'-0"

FINISH GRADE

dim. line/
break line

dim. line

title
space

WOOD RETAINING WALL
SCALE 1/2"=1'-0"

cut mark

DETAIL INFORMATION
References, jobsite feedback, job history

107

02479 (b) WOOD PLANTERS/RETAINING WALL

DETAIL DATA CHECKLIST

WOOD RETAINING WALLS
__Stack timbers horizontally
__Support and anchor timbers with:
    __Vertical timbers
    __Concrete piers
    __Vertical steel I-beams
__Tie timbers vertically with min. 2 #4 bars per tie, in 1/2" drilled hole
__Tie back into slope with10' o.c. deadman ties
__Where necessary, use vertical rods at 4' o.c.
__Provide gravel backfill behind filter cloth
__Vertical wood members may be OK for walls up to 4' high, without surcharge, if planted 4' deep

SMALL-SCALE GENERIC DETAILS

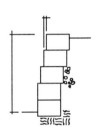

WOOD RETAINING WALL
Battered/Low
02479-15

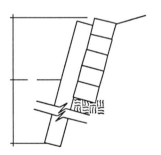

WOOD RETAINING WALL
Sloped/Low
02479-17

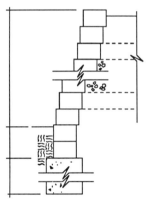

WOOD RETAINING WALL
Battered/High
02479-21

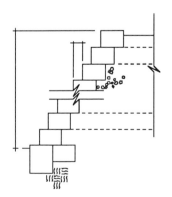

WOOD RETAINING WALL
Battered/High
02479-23

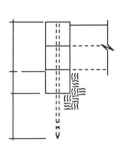

WOOD PLANTER/
RETAINING WALL
02479-25

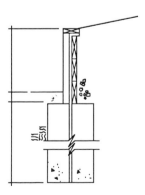

WOOD PLANTER/
RETAINING WALL
02479-31

02479 (b) WOOD PLANTERS/RETAINING WALL

FULL-SCALE GENERIC DETAILS

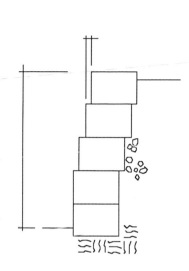

WOOD RETAINING WALL Battered/Low
3/4"=1'-0"   02479-15

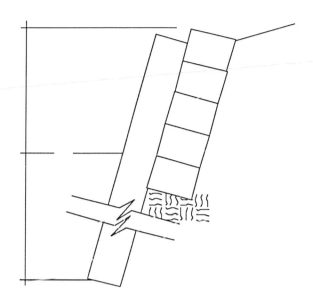

WOOD RETAINING WALL Sloped/Low
3/4"=1'-0"   02479-17

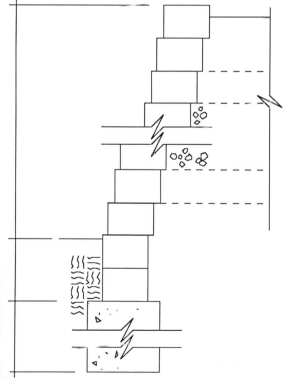

WOOD RETAINING WALL Battered/High
3/4"=1'-0"   02479-21

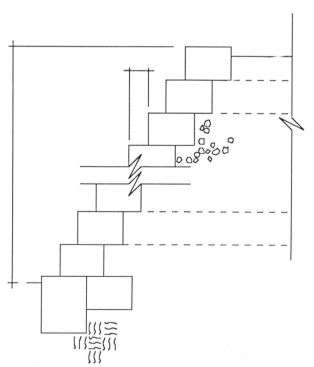

WOOD RETAINING WALL Battered/High
3/4"=1'-0"   02479-23

02479 (b) WOOD PLANTERS/RETAINING WALL

FULL-SCALE GENERIC DETAILS continued

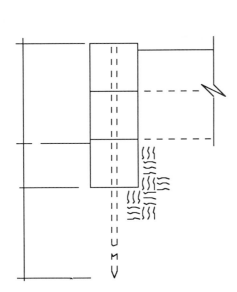

WOOD PLANTER/RETAINING WALL
3/4"=1'-0"   02479-25

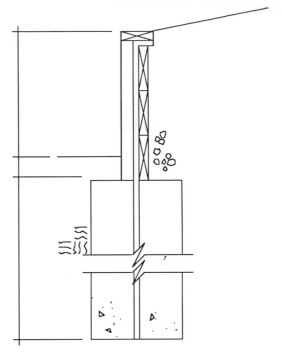

WOOD PLANTER/RETAINING WALL
3/4"=1'-0"   02479-31

NOTATION CHECKLIST,
SAMPLE NOTES

TOP OF WALL ELEVATION
FINISH GRADES
ORIGINAL GRADE (DASHED)
TIMBER UNITS (TYPE & SIZE)
BOLTS/ANCHORS/ DOWELS
STEEL ROD/WOOD TIE BACKS ('DEADMAN')
AGGREGATE DRAIN BED
DRAIN PIPE/DRAIN TILE
COMPACTED SUBGRADE/STRUCTURAL
BACKFILL
FOOTING
AGGREGATE BASE
POROUS BACKFILL

dim. lines   break line

notation boundary   break line

cut mark

dim. line

dim. line

break line

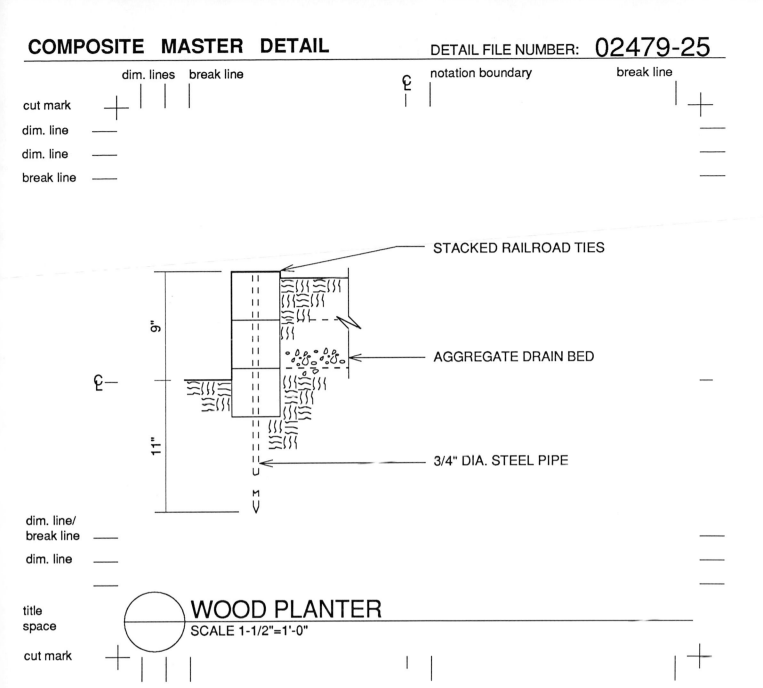

STACKED RAILROAD TIES

9"

AGGREGATE DRAIN BED

11"

3/4" DIA. STEEL PIPE

dim. line/
break line

dim. line

title
space

WOOD PLANTER
SCALE 1-1/2"=1'-0"

cut mark

DETAIL INFORMATION
References, jobsite feedback, job history

02491 (a) TREE PLANTERS

DETAIL DATA CHECKLIST

TREE PLANTING
__Hole should be twice the diameter of the container
__Break subsoil with a pick or otherwise scar the walls of the hole to aid penetration
__Soil ball should rest on firm soil to avoid settling
__Remove burlap from the top of the ball (not necessary to remove from all around root ball)
__Backfill hole with original soil
   OR
      __Use topsoil, peat moss and cow manure in 9" layers, watering each level until settled
      __Do not tamp
__Ground line should be the same as, or slightly lower on the tree, than it was at the nursery
__The water levee around the tree should be 2' to 4' in diameter
__The berm around levee should be 4" high
__Cover levee and berm with 2" of mulch
__Remove any shoots on the trunk within 6" of the soil
__Trunk may be wrapped with tree wrap
__Where tree is planted in a hollow, provide a "land drain" if necessary to dispose of surplus water
      (clean rubble acts as a soakaway)
__Securely stake each tree
__Use 10 ga. twisted wire with a garden hose to wrap around the trunk

SMALL-SCALE GENERIC DETAILS

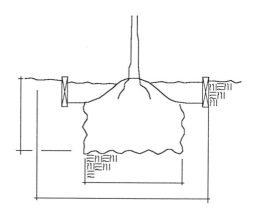

TREE PLANTING
02491-1

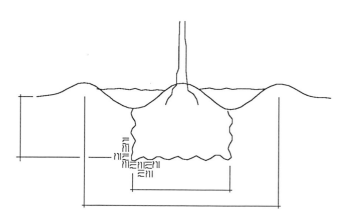

TREE PLANTING
02491-2

02491 (a) TREE PLANTERS

SMALL-SCALE GENERIC DETAILS continued

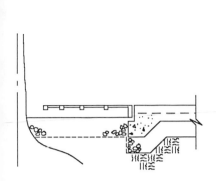

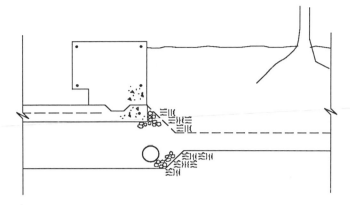

TREE PLANTING GRATE
02491-31

TREE PLANTER BENCH WALL
02491-51

FULL-SCALE GENERIC DETAILS

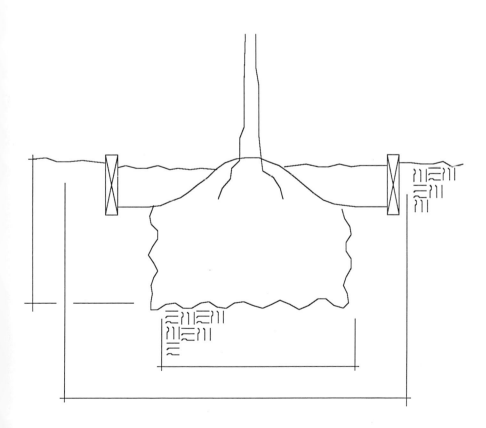

TREE PLANTING
1"=1'-0"   02491-1

02491 (a) TREE PLANTERS

FULL-SCALE DETAILS continued

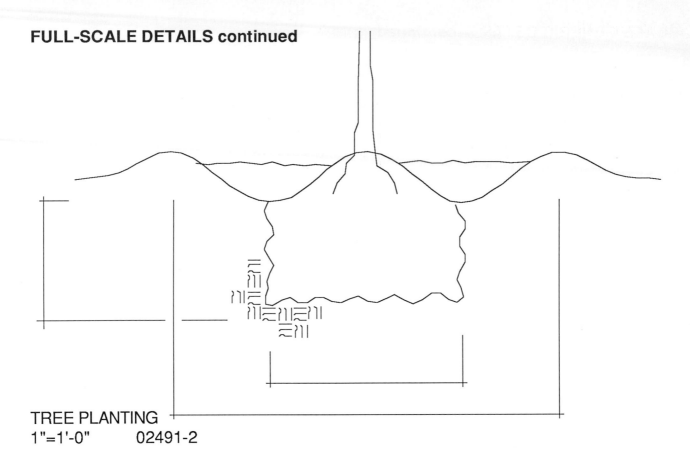

TREE PLANTING
1"=1'-0"   02491-2

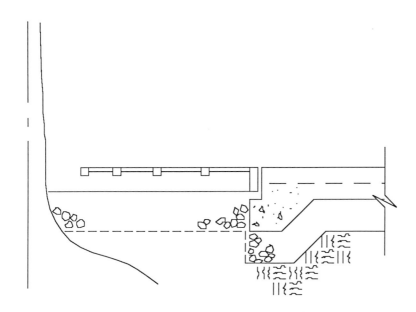

TREE PLANTING GRATE
02491-31

02491 (a) TREE PLANTERS

FULL-SCALE DETAILS continued

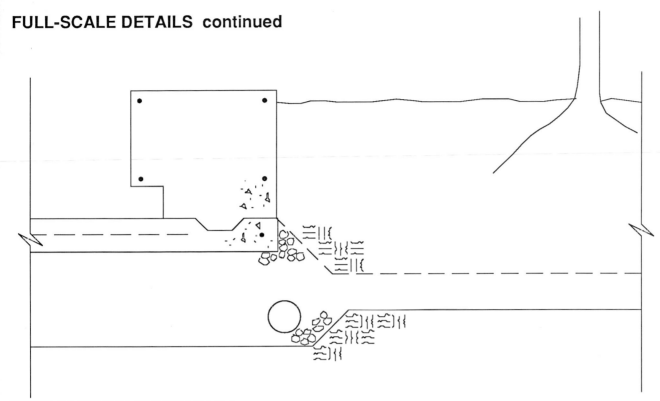

TREE PLANTER BENCH WALL
02491-51

NOTATION CHECKLIST,
SAMPLE NOTATION

TREE/TREEBALL
FINISH GRADE
WATER BASIN
WATER LEVEE
CONTAINER OUTLINE
FIBER MAT
AGGREGATE BASE
BACKFILL
SUBGRADE
TREE GUY/STAKE
REINFORCING
WEEPHOLES (SIZE & SPACING)
AGGREGATE DRAIN BED
DRAIN PIPE/DRAIN TILE
COMPACTED SUBGRADE/
    STRUCTURAL BACKFILL
ORIGINAL GRADE (shown dashed)
POROUS BACKFILL
3" MULCH LAYER (where applicable)
SPECIFIED SOIL MIX

DRIP EMITTER
MICRO TUBING
DRIP LINE
GRAVEL SUMP
PLANT ROOT BALL AT GRADE AS IN NURSERY
REMOVE CONTAINER FROM ROOT BALL
RIGID INSULATION
PLANTER WALL
DRAINAGE LAYER
2 STRANDS #12 GUAGE GALV. WIRE
    FLAG GUY WIRES FOR VISIBILITY W. YELLOW
    PLASTIC RIBBON - 2 PER WIRE
CUT WIRE BELOW SOD
2" X2" X 2' WOOD STAKE, 3 PER TREE, DRIVE
    STAKES FLUSH WITH FINAL GRADE
NEW 3/4" RUBBER GARDEN HOSE AROUND TREE
3" GALV. TURNBUCKLE
WRAP ENTIRE TRUNK W/ APPPROVED MATERIAL
    TO SECOND BRANCH. SECURE @
    2' INTERVALS W/ GRAFTING CORD

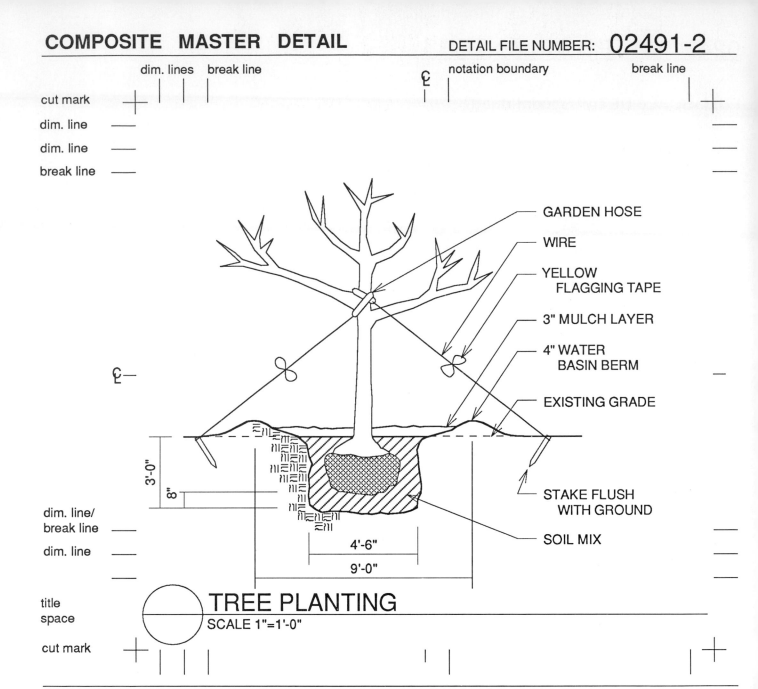

dim. lines break line

notation boundary break line

cut mark

dim. line

dim. line

break line

GARDEN HOSE

WIRE

YELLOW
FLAGGING TAPE

3" MULCH LAYER

4" WATER
BASIN BERM

EXISTING GRADE

STAKE FLUSH
WITH GROUND

SOIL MIX

3'-0"

8"

4'-6"

9'-0"

dim. line/
break line

dim. line

title
space

cut mark

TREE PLANTING
SCALE 1"=1'-0"

DETAIL INFORMATION
References, jobsite feedback, job history

02491 (b) TREE PLANTERS

DETAIL DATA CHECKLIST

TREE PLANTING
__Hole should be twice the diameter of the container
__Break subsoil with a pick or otherwise scar the walls of the hole to aid poor penetration
__Soil ball should rest on firm soil to avoid settling
__Remove burlap from the top of the ball (not necessary to remove from all around root ball)
__Backfill hole with original soil
    OR
    __Use topsoil, peat moss and cow manure in 9" layers, watering each level until settled
    __Do not tamp
__Ground line should be the same as, or slightly lower on the tree, than it was at the nursery
__The water levee around the tree should be 2' to 4' in diameter
__The berm around levee should be 4" high
__Cover levee and berm with 2" of mulch
__Remove any shoots on the trunk within 6" of the soil
__Trunk may be wrapped with tree wrap
__Where tree is planted in a hollow, provide a
    "land drain" if necessary to dispose of surplus water
    (clean rubble acts as a soakaway)
__Securely stake each tree
__Use 10 ga. twisted wire with a garden hose to
    wrap around the trunk

SMALL-SCALE GENERIC DETAILS

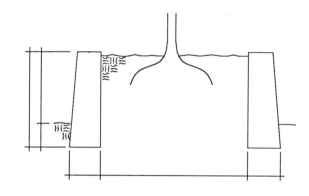

TREE PLANTER ABOVE GRADE
02491-52

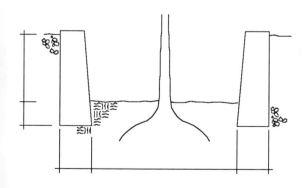

TREE PLANTER BELOW GRADE
02491-53

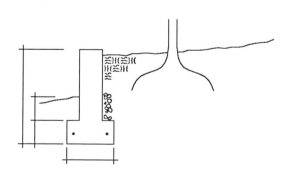

TREE PLANTER ABOVE GRADE
02491-54

02491 (b) TREE PLANTERS

FULL-SCALE GENERIC DETAILS

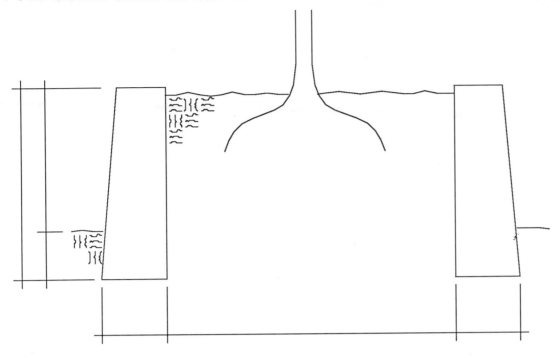

TREE PLANTER ABOVE GRADE
1"=1'-0"   02491-52

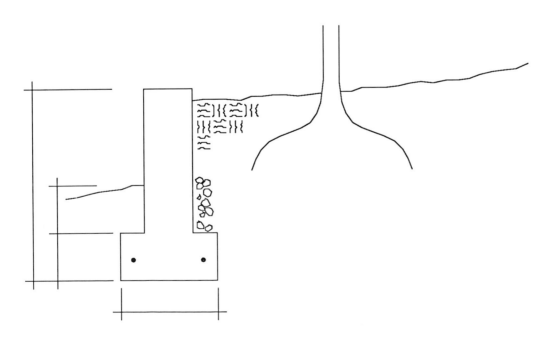

TREE PLANTER ABOVE GRADE
1"=1'-0"   02491-54

02491 (b) TREE PLANTERS

FULL-SCALE GENERIC DETAILS continued

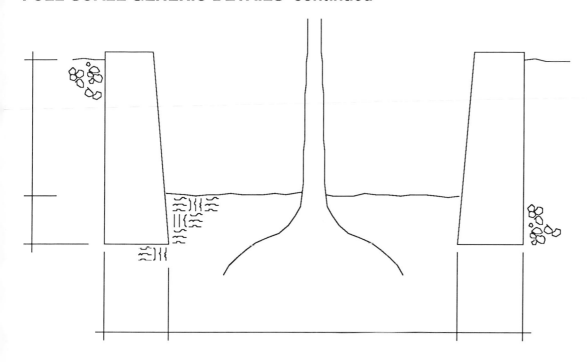

TREE PLANTER BELOW GRADE
1"=1'-0"   02491-53

NOTATION CHECKLIST,
SAMPLE NOTES

TREE/TREEBALL
FINISH GRADE
WATER BASIN
WATER LEVEE
CONTAINER OUTLINE
FIBER MAT
AGGREGATE BASE
BACKFILL
SUBGRADE
TREE GUY/STAKE
REINFORCING
WEEPHOLES (SIZE & SPACING)
AGGREGATE DRAIN BED
DRAIN PIPE/DRAIN TILE
COMPACTED SUBGRADE/STRUCTURAL
BACKFILL
ORIGINAL GRADE (shown dashed)
POROUS BACKFILL
3" MULCH LAYER (where applicable)

SPECIFIED SOIL MIX
DRIP EMITTER
MICRO TUBING
DRIP LINE
GRAVEL SUMP
PLANT ROOT BALL AT GRADE AS IN NURSERY
REMOVE CONTAINER FROM ROOT BALL
RIGID INSULATION
PLANTER WALL
DRAINAGE LAYER
2 STRANDS #12 GAUGE GALV. WIRE
     FLAG GUY WIRES FOR VISIBILITY W. YELLOW
     PLASTIC RIBBON; 2 PER WIRE
CUT WIRE BELOW SOD
2" X2" X 2' WOOD STAKE, 3 PER TREE, DRIVE
     STAKES FLUSH WITH FINAL GRADE
NEW 3/4" RUBBER GARDEN HOSE AROUND TREE
3" GALV. TURNBUCKLE
WRAP ENTIRE TRUNK W/ APPPROVED MATERIAL
     TO SECOND BRANCH. SECURE @
     2' INTERVALS W/ GRAFTING CORD

02507, 02513 PAVING & PAVERS

DETAIL DATA CHECKLIST

WOOD BLOCK OR TIMBER SECTIONS PAVERS
__Preservative treated
__2" minimum depth crosscut, 3" minimum rip cut
__Timber sections 4" to 6" thick are common
__Lay in 4" sand bed

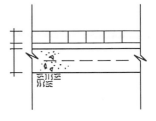

WOOD BLOCK PAVING
On Concrete
02507-1

SMALL-SCALE GENERIC DETAILS

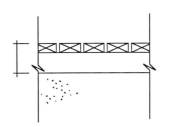

WOOD PLANK
WALKWAY
02507-11

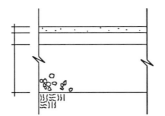

ASPHALTIC CONCRETE
PAVING
02513-1

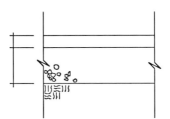

ASPHALT
PAVING
02513-21

FULL-SCALE GENERIC DETAILS

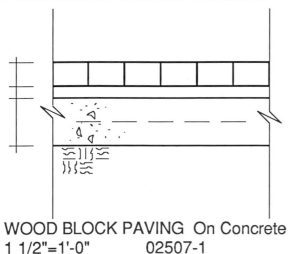

WOOD BLOCK PAVING On Concrete
1 1/2"=1'-0"   02507-1

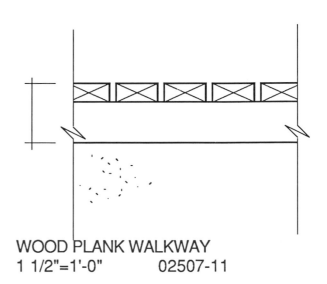

WOOD PLANK WALKWAY
1 1/2"=1'-0"   02507-11

02507, 02513 PAVING & PAVERS

FULL-SCALE GENERIC DETAILS continued

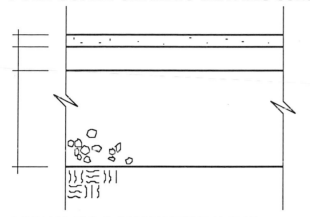

ASPHALTIC CONCRETE PAVING
1 1/2"=1'-0"   02513-1

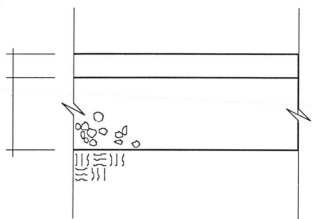

ASPHALT PAVING
1 1/2"=1'-0"   02513-21

NOTATION CHECKLIST, SAMPLE NOTES

PAVER UNITS
SETTING BED
CONCRETE
REINFORCING
SLOPE
CONTROL/EXPANSION JOINTS (TYPE & SPACING)
AGGREGATE BASE
COMPACTED SUBGRADE

ORIGINAL GRADE
FINISH GRADE
PROVIDE CROWN IN CENTER FOR DRAINAGE
SLOPE 1/4" PER FOOT, TYP.
CONCRETE W. 6 X 6 - 10 GAUGE WIRE MESH
CONC. SLAB W. 6 X 6 X #10/#10
CONC. WALK W/ 6 X 6 10/10 W.W.M.
REDWOOD HEARTWOOD JOINT FILLER STRIP
TOOLED JOINTS @ 6'-0" O.C.
1/2" EXPANSION JOINT
JOINT SEALANT & JOINT FILLER ROD
JOINT FILLER BOARD

1"DIA (3/4" to 1" typ.) X 18" DOWEL BARS
   12" O.C. ACROSS SLAB
   (@ exp. jts.) PAINT & OIL ONE END OF DOWEL
EXPANSION JOINT FILLER MATERIAL @ 16" O.C. MAX.
GALV. METAL KEYWAY W/ EDGE EXPOSED
GALV. METAL STAKE PIN
DUMMY JOINTS @ 5'-0" O.C.
PRE-MOLDED EXPANSION JOINT @ 20'-0" O.C. TYP.
PAVING BRICKS IN SETTING BED
SLOPE TO DRAIN AS INDICATED ON PLANS
BRICK ROWLOCK PAVER
SLAB REINF., SEE
VAPOR BARRIER
COMPACTED GRANULAR FILL
4" PEA GRAVEL
SAND CUSHION
COMPACTED EARTH FILL AS REQ'D.
COMPACTED SUBGRADE OR STRUCTURAL BACKFILL
8" CRUSHED AGGRAGATE BASE (@ 6" conc. paving)
6" CRUSHED AGGREGATE BASE (@ 2" asphalt paving)

02514 (a) BRICK PAVING & PAVERS

DETAIL DATA CHECKLIST

BRICK PAVING
__Sizes:
    __4x4, 4x8, 4x12, 6x6, 8x8, 12x12
    __Hexagons: 5-3/4, 8, and 12 inches
__Depth 1-1/8" to 2-1/4"
__Waterproof by placing brick over:
    __15 lb. roofing felt, over 1/2" to 1" stone
      screenings, over 4" gravel
   OR
    __Over 2% neoprene tack coat over 3/4"
    bituminous setting bed, over cutback asphalt
    primer, over a concrete slab
__May be laid with:
    __Mortar joints
      __Require careful tooling to block moisture

    __Sand poured into the joints
    __Nothing in the joints
__Lay over:
    __3" or thicker concrete slab
      __Over 3/4" mortar setting bed
    __4" asphaltic concrete
      __Over 3/4" bituminous setting bed
    __2" to 4" sand base
      __Over firm soil
      __Tamp and level sand
        __Over 15 lb. felt
      __Brush dry sand into joints
      __Add mix of cement with sand for tighter joints
__Provide solid border board support or joints will open
    and pavers will dislodge

SMALL-SCALE GENERIC DETAILS

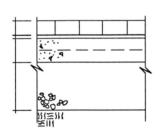

BRICK PAVING
On Concrete
02514-1

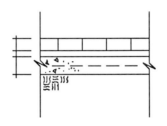

BRICK PAVING
On Sand & Concrete
02514-6

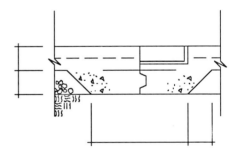

BRICK PAVER
In Concrete
02514-11

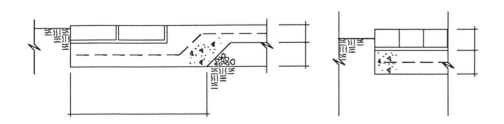

BRICK PAVER EDGE
In Concrete
02514-12

BRICK PAVING EDGE
On Concrete
02514-23

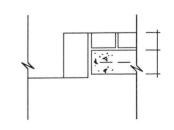

BRICK PAVING EDGE
On Concrete
02514-24

02514 (a) BRICK PAVING & PAVERS

FULL-SCALE GENERIC DETAILS

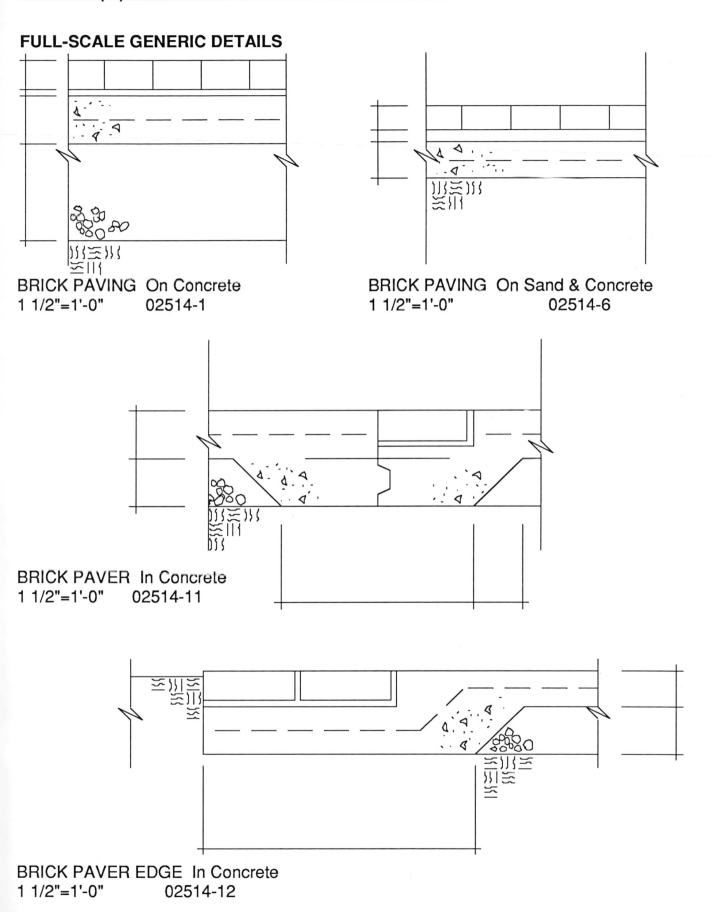

BRICK PAVING On Concrete
1 1/2"=1'-0"   02514-1

BRICK PAVING On Sand & Concrete
1 1/2"=1'-0"   02514-6

BRICK PAVER In Concrete
1 1/2"=1'-0"   02514-11

BRICK PAVER EDGE In Concrete
1 1/2"=1'-0"   02514-12

02514 (a) BRICK PAVING & PAVERS

FULL-SCALE GENERIC DETAILS continued

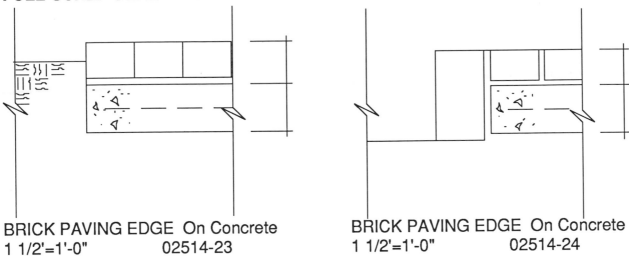

BRICK PAVING EDGE On Concrete
1 1/2'=1'-0"   02514-23

BRICK PAVING EDGE On Concrete
1 1/2'=1'-0"   02514-24

NOTATION CHECKLIST, SAMPLE NOTES

PAVER UNITS
 SETTING BED
 CONCRETE
 REINFORCING
 SLOPE
 CONTROL/EXPANSION JOINTS (TYPE & SPACING)
 AGGREGATE BASE
 COMPACTED SUBGRADE

ORIGINAL GRADE
FINISH GRADE
PROVIDE CROWN IN CENTER FOR DRAINAGE
SLOPE 1/4" PER FOOT, TYP.
CONCRETE W. 6 X 6 - 10 GAUGE WIRE MESH
REDWOOD HEARTWOOD JOINT FILLER STRIP
TOOLED JOINTS @ 6'-0" O.C.
1/2" EXPANSION JOINT
JOINT SEALANT & JOINT FILLER ROD
JOINT FILLER BOARD

1"DIA (3/4" to 1" typ.) X 18" DOWEL BARS
   12" O.C. ACROSS SLAB
   (@ exp. jts.) PAINT & OIL ONE END OF DOWEL
EXPANSION JOINT FILLER MATERIAL @ 16" O.C. MAX.
GALV. METAL KEYWAY W/ EDGE EXPOSED
DUMMY JOINTS @ 5'-0" O.C.
PRE-MOLDED EXPANSION JOINT @ 20'-O" O.C. TYP.
PAVING BRICKS IN SETTING BED
SLOPE TO DRAIN AS INDICATED ON PLANS
SLAB REINF., SEE
VAPOR BARRIER
4" PEA GRAVEL
SAND CUSHION
COMPACTED EARTH FILL AS REQ'D.
COMPACTED SUBGRADE OR STRUCTURAL BACKFILL
8" CRUSHED AGGRAGATE BASE (@ 6" conc. paving)
6" CRUSHED AGGREGATE BASE
   (@ 2" asphalt paving)

02514 (b) PAVING & PAVERS

DETAIL DATA CHECKLIST

BRICK PAVING
__Sizes:
    __4x4, 4x8, 4x12, 6x6, 8x8, 12x12
    __Hexagons: 5-3/4, 8, and 12 inches
__Depth 1-1/8" to 2-1/4"
__Waterproof by placing brick over:
    __15 lb. roofing felt, over 1/2" to 1" stone screenings, over 4" gravel
  OR
    __Over 2% neoprene tack coat over 3/4" bituminous setting bed, over cutback asphalt primer,
        over a concrete slab
__May be laid with:
    __Mortar joints
        __Require careful tooling to block moisture
    __Sand poured into the joints
    __Nothing in the joints
__Lay over:
    __3" or thicker concrete slab
        __Over 3/4" mortar setting bed
    __4" asphaltic concrete
        __Over 3/4" bituminous setting bed
    __2" to 4" sand base
        __Over firm soil
        __Tamp and level sand
            __Over 15 lb. felt
        __Brush dry sand into joints
        __Add mix of cement with sand for tighter joints
__Provide solid border board support or joints will open and pavers will dislodge

SMALL-SCALE GENERIC DETAILS

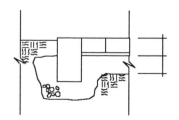

BRICK PAVING EDGE
On Concrete
02514-23

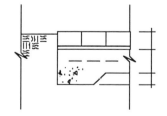

BRICK PAVING EDGE
On Concrete
02514-24

02514 (b) PAVING & PAVERS

SMALL-SCALE GENERIC DETAILS continued

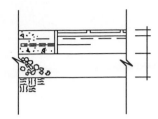

BRICK PAVING
Thin Pavers on Concrete
02514-31

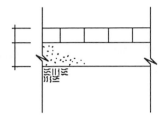

BRICK PAVING
On Sand
02514-34

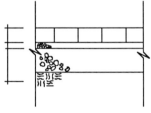

BRICK PAVING
On Aggregate
02514-37

BRICK PAVING
On Asphalt
02514-39

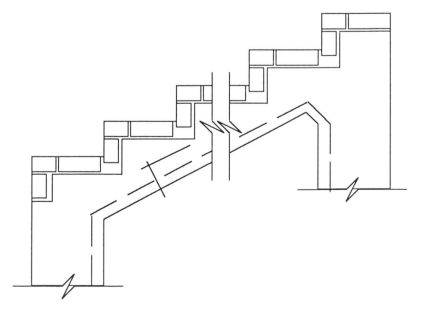

BRICK STEPS
On Concrete
02514-41

02514 (b) PAVING & PAVERS

FULL-SCALE GENERIC DETAILS

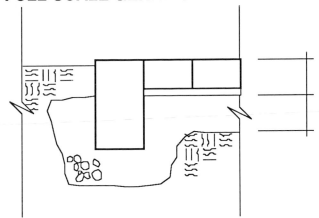

BRICK PAVING EDGE On Concrete
1 1/2'=1'-0"   02514-23

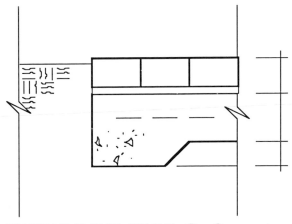

BRICK PAVING EDGE On Concrete
1 1/2'=1'-0"   02514-24

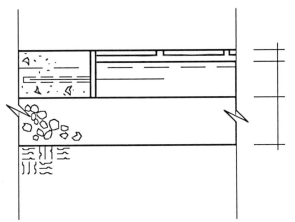

BRICK PAVING Thin Pavers on Concrete
1 1/2"=1'-0"   02514-31

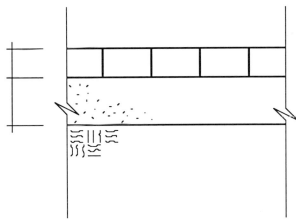

BRICK PAVING On Sand
1 1/2"=1'-0"   02514-34

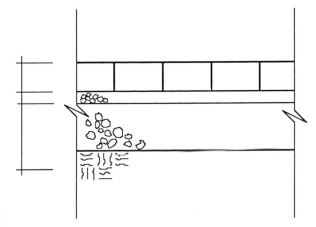

BRICK PAVING On Aggregate
1 1/2"=1'-0"   02514-37

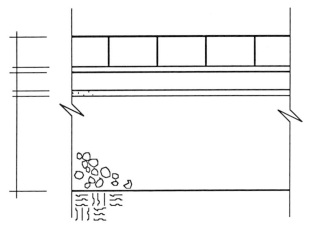

BRICK PAVING On Asphalt
1 1/2"=1'-0"   02514-39

FULL-SCALE GENERIC DETAILS continued

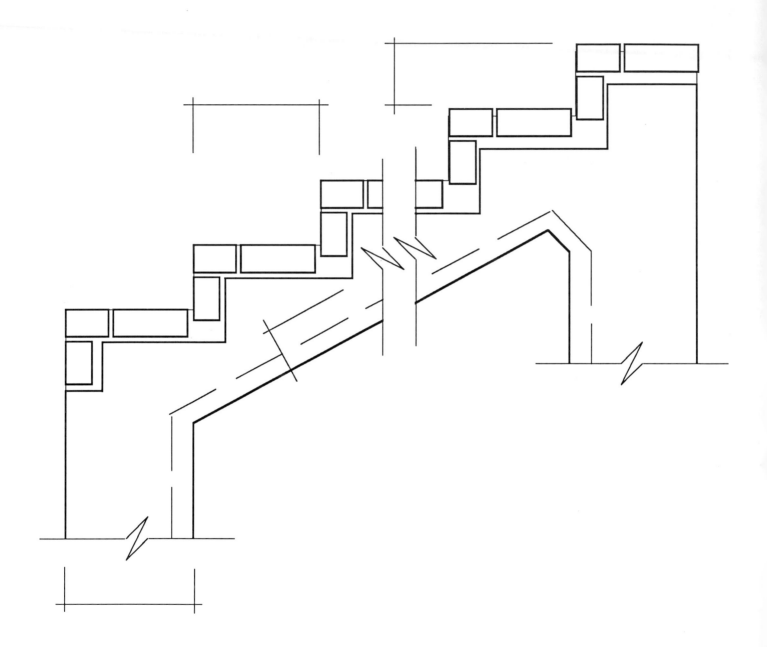

BRICK STEPS On Concrete
Not to Scale 02514-41

02514 (b) PAVING & PAVERS

NOTATION CHECKLIST,
SAMPLE NOTES

PAVER UNITS
SETTING BED
CONCRETE
REINFORCING
SLOPE
CONTROL/EXPANSION JOINTS (TYPE & SPACING)
AGGREGATE BASE
COMPACTED SUBGRADE

ORIGINAL GRADE
FINISH GRADE
PROVIDE CROWN IN CENTER FOR DRAINAGE
SLOPE 1/4" PER FOOT, TYP.
CONCRETE W. 6 X 6 - 10 GAUGE WIRE MESH
CONC. SLAB W. 6 X 6 X #10/#10
CONC. WALK W/ 6 X 6 10/10 W.W.M.
REDWOOD HEARTWOOD JOINT FILLER STRIP
TOOLED JOINTS @ 6'-0" O.C.
1/2" EXPANSION JOINT
JOINT SEALANT & JOINT FILLER ROD
JOINT FILLER BOARD
1"DIA (3/4" to 1" typ.) X 18" DOWEL BARS
    12" O.C. ACROSS SLAB
    (@ exp. jts.) PAINT & OIL ONE END OF DOWEL
EXPANSION JOINT FILLER MATERIAL @ 16" O.C. MAX.
GALV. METAL KEYWAY W/ EDGE EXPOSED
GALV. METAL STAKE PIN
DUMMY JOINTS @ 5'-0" O.C.
PRE-MOLDED EXPANSION JOINT @ 20'-O" O.C. TYP.
PAVING BRICKS IN SETTING BED
SLOPE TO DRAIN AS INDICATED ON PLANS
BRICK ROWLOCK PAVER
SLAB REINF., SEE
VAPOR BARRIER
COMPACTED GRANULAR FILL
4" PEA GRAVEL
SAND CUSHION
COMPACTED EARTH FILL AS REQ'D.
COMPACTED SUBGRADE OR STRUCTURAL BACKFILL
8" CRUSHED AGGRAGATE BASE (@ 6" conc. paving)
6" CRUSHED AGGREGATE BASE (@ 2" asphalt paving)
IRON ORE BASE

02515, 02516 PAVING & PAVERS

SMALL-SCALE GENERIC DETAILS

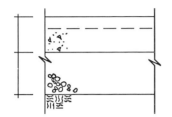

CONCRETE PAVING
6" Driveway
02515-1

ASPHALT BLOCK PAVING
On Sand/Gravel
02515-11

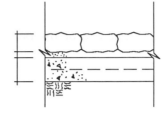

ASPHALT BLOCK PAVING
On Concrete
02516-1

FULL-SCALE GENERIC DETAILS

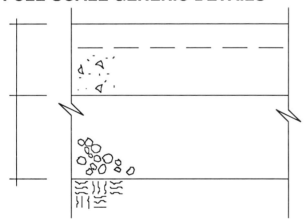

CONCRETE PAVING 6" Driveway
1 1/2"=1'-0"   02515-1

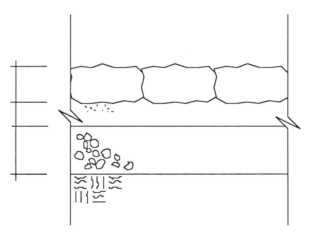

ASPHALT BLOCK PAVING On Sand/Gravel
1 1/2"=1'-0"   02515-11

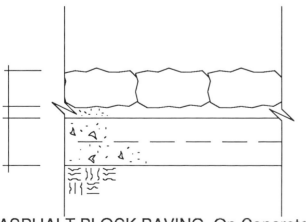

ASPHALT BLOCK PAVING On Concrete
1 1/2"=1'-0"   02516-1

132

02515, 02516 PAVING & PAVERS

NOTATION CHECKLIST, SAMPLE NOTES

PAVER UNITS
SETTING BED
CONCRETE
REINFORCING
SLOPE
CONTROL/EXPANSION JOINTS (TYPE & SPACING)
AGGREGATE BASE
COMPACTED SUBGRADE

ORIGINAL GRADE
FINISH GRADE
PROVIDE CROWN IN CENTER FOR DRAINAGE
SLOPE 1/4" PER FOOT, TYP.
CONCRETE W. 6 X 6 - 10 GAUGE WIRE MESH
CONC. SLAB W. 6 X 6 X #10/#10
CONC. WALK W/ 6 X 6 10/10 W.W.M.
REDWOOD HEARTWOOD JOINT FILLER STRIP
TOOLED JOINTS @ 6'-0" O.C.
1/2" EXPANSION JOINT
JOINT SEALANT & JOINT FILLER ROD
JOINT FILLER BOARD
1"DIA (3/4" to 1" typ.) X 18" DOWEL BARS
    12" O.C. ACROSS SLAB
     (@ exp. jts.) PAINT & OIL ONE END OF DOWEL
EXPANSION JOINT FILLER MATERIAL @ 16" O.C. MAX.
GALV. METAL KEYWAY W/ EDGE EXPOSED
GALV. METAL STAKE PIN
DUMMY JOINTS @ 5'-0" O.C.
PRE-MOLDED EXPANSION JOINT @ 20'-O" O.C. TYP.
PAVING BRICKS IN SETTING BED
SLOPE TO DRAIN AS INDICATED ON PLANS
BRICK ROWLOCK PAVER
SLAB REINF., SEE
VAPOR BARRIER
COMPACTED GRANULAR FILL
4" PEA GRAVEL
SAND CUSHION
COMPACTED EARTH FILL AS REQ'D.
COMPACTED SUBGRADE OR STRUCTURAL BACKFILL
8" CRUSHED AGGRAGATE BASE (@ 6" conc. paving)
6" CRUSHED AGGREGATE BASE (@ 2" asphalt paving)

02517, 02518 PAVING & PAVERS

DETAIL DATA CHECKLIST

STONE PAVING
__Granite paver sizes:
    __4x4, 4x8, 5x8, 8x8, 12x12
__Depths: 2", 3", 4", and 10"
__Install granite on rigid base and mortar for stability and/or if there will be heavy traffic
__Install on flexible base for light traffic
__Slate sizes:
    __4" min. widths x random lengths
__Depths: 3/4" to 2-1/2"
__Install slate on flexible base with no mortar; keep well drained
__Stone thickness in general:
    __3/4" thick if laid on mortar setting bed
    __1-1/2" minimum thickness if laid on sand
__Provide solid border edge support, or joints will open and pavers will dislodge

SMALL-SCALE GENERIC DETAILS

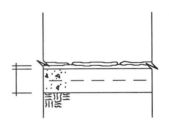

STONE PAVING
On Concrete
02517-1

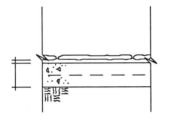

STONE PAVING
On Concrete
02517-2

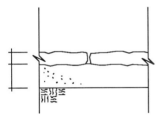

STONE PAVING
On Sand
02517-11

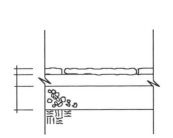

STONE PAVING
On Sand/Gravel
02517-21

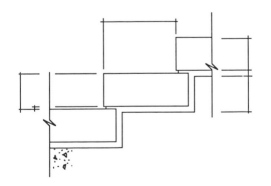

STONE STEPS
On Concrete
02517-31

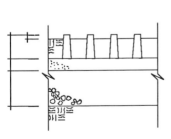

CONCRETE BLOCK
GRID PAVERS
02518-21

02517, 02518 PAVING & PAVERS

FULL-SCALE GENERIC DETAILS

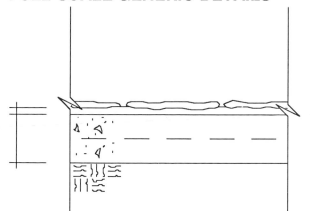

STONE PAVING On Concrete
1 1/2"=1'-0"   02517-1

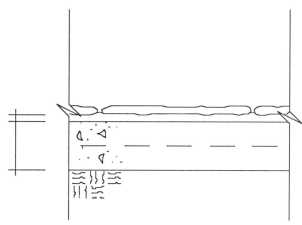

STONE PAVING On Concrete
1 1/2"=1'-0"   02517-2

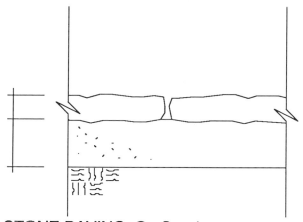

STONE PAVING On Sand
1 1/2"=1'-0"   02517-11

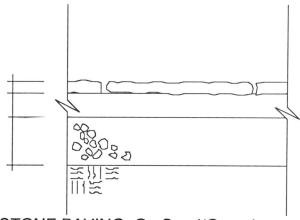

STONE PAVING On Sand/Gravel
1 1/2"=1'-0"   02517-21

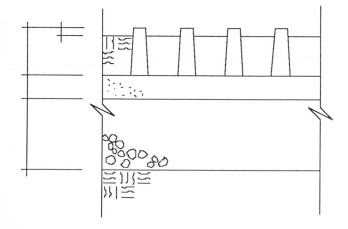

CONCRETE BLOCK GRID PAVERS
1 1/2"=1'-0"   02518-21

02521, 02522 WOOD CURBS & EDGE STRIPS

DETAIL DATA CHECKLIST

WOOD CURBS
__Use redwood, cedar, cypress or treated wood
__Sizes:
    __2x6, 2x8, 6x6, 6x8, and railroad ties
__Hold wood curbs in place with wood stakes, rebar
    or bolts
      __Stakes may be 1x2, 2x2, 2x3, or 2x4, 16" to 24"
        long,
    24" to 48" o.c., and/or at ends of timbers
    __Use 2 20d ga. nails per stake
    __For rebar, use a #4 bar,18" long at each end of
      timber
        __Form a pocket around the bar and fill it with
          concrete

WOOD BORDER BOARDS AND EDGE STRIPS
__Use redwood, cedar, cypress or treated wood
    __Use 2X4s for straight runs
    __Use laminated 1/2" x 4" redwood strips for curves
__Use heavier timber wood curbs to restrain larger
    planter or paver areas and for mowing curbs

02521, 02522 WOOD CURBS & EDGE STRIPS

SMALL-SCALE GENERIC DETAILS

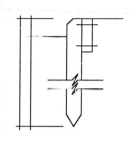

WOOD CURB
02521-11

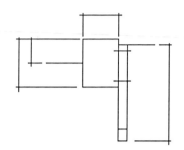

WOOD CURB
02521-12

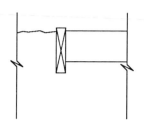

WOOD EDGE STRIP
02522-11

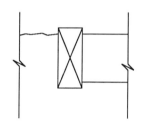

WOOD EDGE STRIP
02522-12

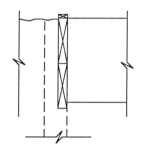

WOOD EDGE STRIP
02522-13

02521, 02522 WOOD CURBS & EDGE STRIPS

FULL-SCALE GENERIC DETAILS

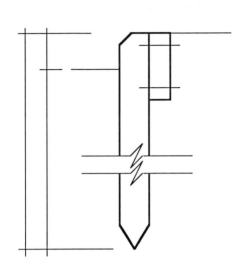
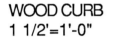

WOOD CURB
1 1/2'=1'-0"   02521-11

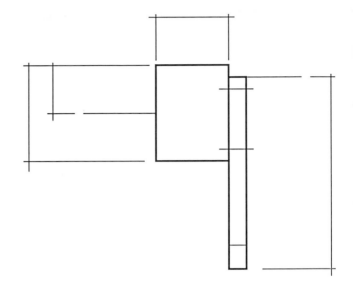

WOOD CURB
1 1/2'=1'-0"   02521-12

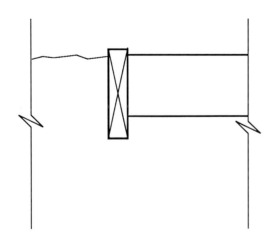

WOOD EDGE STRIP
1 1/2"=1'-0"   02522-11

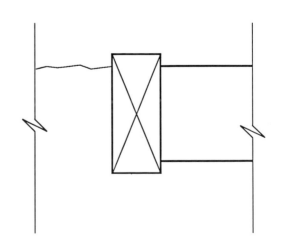

WOOD EDGE STRIP
1 1/2"=1'-0"   02522-12

02521, 02522 WOOD CURBS & EDGE STRIPS

FULL-SCALE GENERIC DETAILS continued

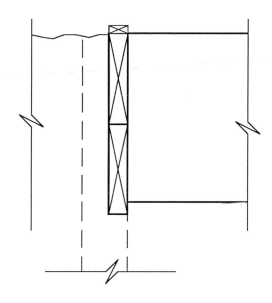

WOOD EDGE STRIP
1 1/2"=1'-0"   02522-13

NOTATION CHECKLIST,
SAMPLE NOTES

FINISH GRADE/PAVING/PLANTING BED
WOOD CURB/PAVING EDGE
PAVING BASE
SUBGRADE
STAKES (MATERIAL, SIZE & SPACING)

FINISH GRADE
ASPHALT-- SEE SITE PLAN FOR THICKNESS & BASE
2 X EDGING, TREATED
2 X CONST. HEART REDWOOD HEADER
2 X 2 X 18" LONG CONST. HEART REDWOOD STAKES
2 X 2 STAKES @ 3'-0" O.C., TREATED
ALL JOINTS TO OCCUR @ STAKES, NAIL HEADER
    TO STAKE W/ 2 - 8 d GALV. NAILS

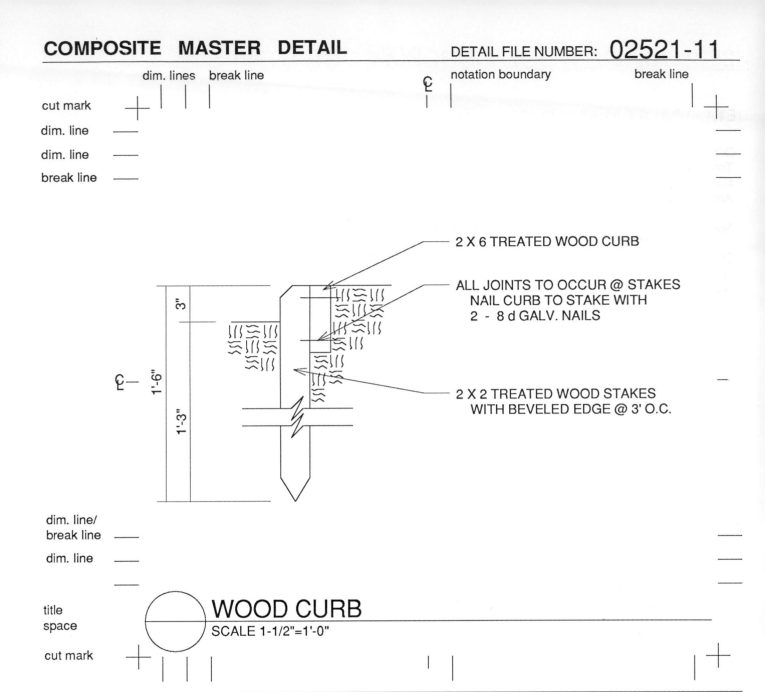

cut mark
dim. lines   break line
     notation boundary   break line
dim. line
dim. line
break line

2 X 6 TREATED WOOD CURB

ALL JOINTS TO OCCUR @ STAKES
NAIL CURB TO STAKE WITH
2 - 8 d GALV. NAILS

2 X 2 TREATED WOOD STAKES
WITH BEVELED EDGE @ 3' O.C.

3"

1'-6"

1'-3"

dim. line/
break line
dim. line

title
space

WOOD CURB
SCALE 1-1/2"=1'-0"

cut mark

DETAIL INFORMATION
References, jobsite feedback, job history

02523 WOOD STEPS (LANDSCAPING)

DETAIL DATA CHECKLIST

WOOD STEPS
__Treated lumber or redwood
__Nail wood treads and risers together with galvanized nails
__Anchor heavy timbers or railroad ties into compacted grade with steel rods
    __3/4" to 1" round, 24" to 36" long steel rods set 12" from each end
__No single riser allowed in any run of walkway or ramp (use 3 minimum risers in any group)

WOOD CURBS
__Use redwood, cedar, cypress or treated wood
__Sizes:
    __2x6, 2x8, 6x6, 6x8, and railroad ties
__Hold wood curbs in place with wood stakes, rebar or bolts
    __Stakes may be 1x2, 2x2, 2x3, or 2x4, 16" to 24" long, 24" to 48" o.c., and/or at ends of timbers
    __Use 2 20d ga. nails per stake
    __For rebar, use a #4 bar, 18" long at each end of timber
    __Form a pocket around the bar and fill it with concrete

SMALL-SCALE GENERIC DETAILS

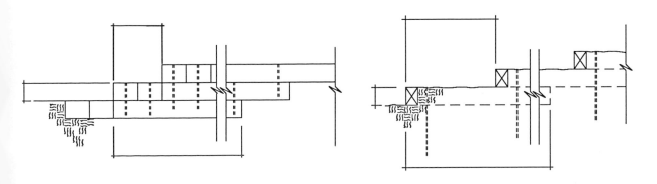

WOOD STEPS
02523-1

WOOD STEPS
02523-2

02523 WOOD STEPS (LANDSCAPING)

**FULL-SCALE
 GENERIC DETAILS**

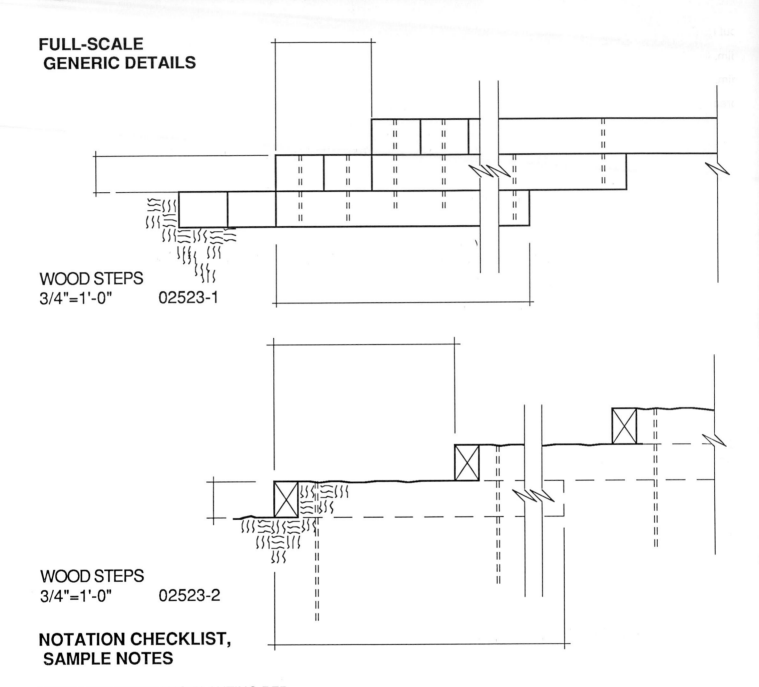

WOOD STEPS

3/4"=1'-0"   02523-1

WOOD STEPS

3/4"=1'-0"   02523-2

**NOTATION CHECKLIST,
 SAMPLE NOTES**

FINISH GRADE/PAVING/PLANTING BED
WOOD CURB/PAVING EDGE
PAVING BASE
SUBGRADE
STAKES (MATERIAL, SIZE & SPACING)

COMPOSITE MASTER DETAIL

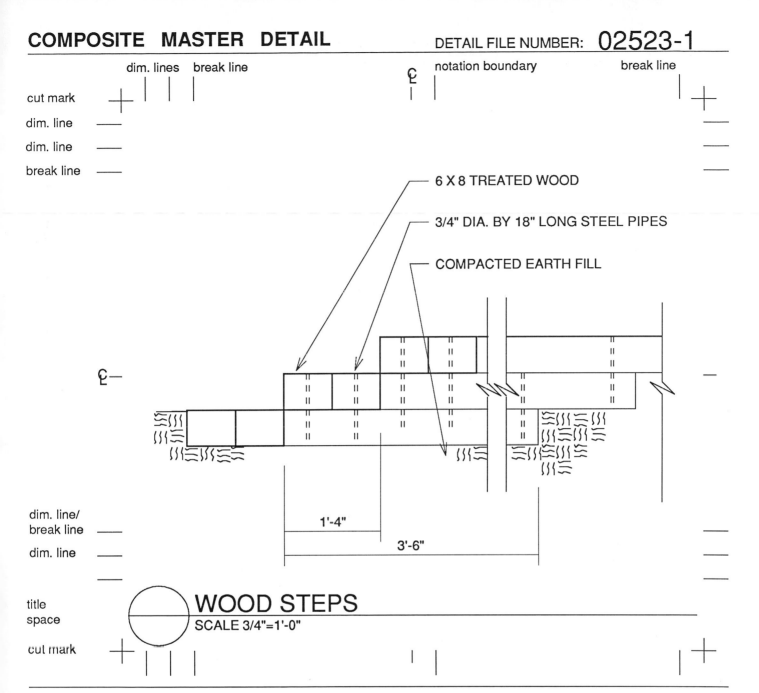

dim. lines   break line

℄

notation boundary   break line

cut mark

dim. line

dim. line

break line

6 X 8 TREATED WOOD

3/4" DIA. BY 18" LONG STEEL PIPES

COMPACTED EARTH FILL

℄

dim. line/
break line

dim. line

1'-4"

3'-6"

title
space

WOOD STEPS
SCALE 3/4"=1'-0"

cut mark

DETAIL INFORMATION
References, jobsite feedback, job history

02524 (a) STONE CURBS, PAVING EDGES

DETAIL DATA CHECKLIST

STONE CURB & GUTTER CURBS
__Stone curb sections come in precut lengths, such as 12' long, straight and curved
__Set stones without mortar in tamped gravel
__Granite is often used in extreme climate areas
__Use expansion joint material such as mastic board at each joint
__Provide backup support such as poured concrete as backing at each joint to help prevent overturning
__Compact the subgrade
__Provide ample subgrade drainage

SMALL-SCALE GENERIC DETAILS

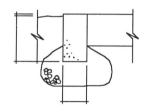

STONE CURB
02524-1

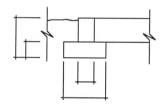

STONE CURB
02524-2

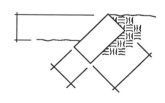

STONE CURB
02524-3

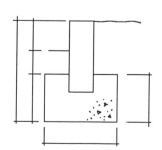

STONE CURB
02524-4

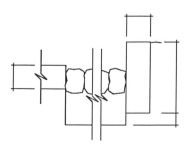

STONE CURB
02524-6

02524 (a) STONE CURBS, PAVING EDGES

FULL-SCALE GENERIC DETAILS

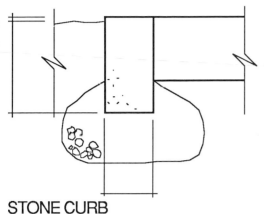

STONE CURB
1"=1'-0"   02524-1

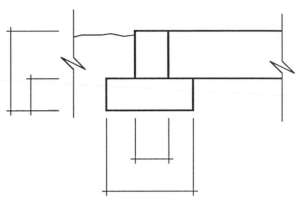

STONE CURB
1"=1'-0"   02524-2

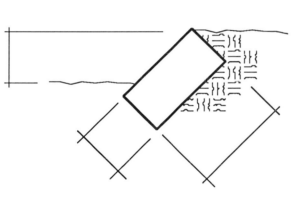

STONE CURB
1"=1'-0"   02524-3

STONE CURB
1"=1'-0"   02524-4

NOTATION CHECKLIST,
SAMPLE NOTES

CURB FINISH (TYPE & MATERIAL)
FINISH GRADE/PAVEMENT
CURB SLOPE/RADII/CAMFER
PAVEMENT SLOPE
AGGREGATE BASE
COMPACTED SUBGRADE
CONTROL/EXPANSION JOINTS (TYPE & SPACING)
SEE SITE PLAN FOR MATERIAL & FINISH GRADE
    @ PAVING
SLOPE GRANITE CURBING 45°
VERTICAL GRANITE CURBING
COMPACTED BANK RUN GRAVEL BASE

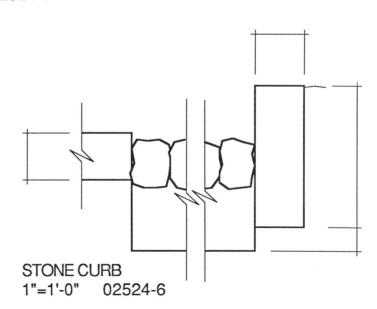

STONE CURB
1"=1'-0"   02524-6

O2524 (b) STONE CURBS, PAVING EDGES

DETAIL DATA CHECKLIST

STONE CURBS & GUTTER CURBS
__Stone curb sections come in precut lengths, such as 12' long, straight and curved
__Set stones without mortar in tamped gravel
__Granite is often used in extreme climate areas
__Use expansion joint material such as mastic board at each joint
__Provide backup support such as poured concrete as backing at each joint to help prevent overturning
__Compact the subgrade
__Provide ample subgrade drainage

SMALL-SCALE GENERIC DETAILS

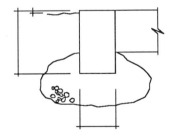

STONE CURB
02524-11

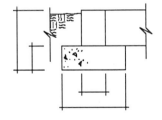

STONE CURB
02524-12

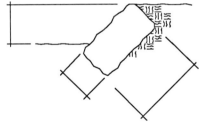

STONE CURB
02524-14

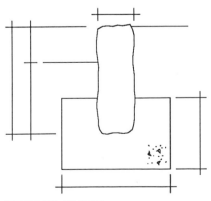

STONE CURB
02524-16

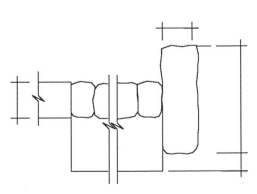

STONE CURB
02524-21

O2524 (b) STONE CURBS, PAVING EDGES

FULL-SCALE GENERIC DETAILS

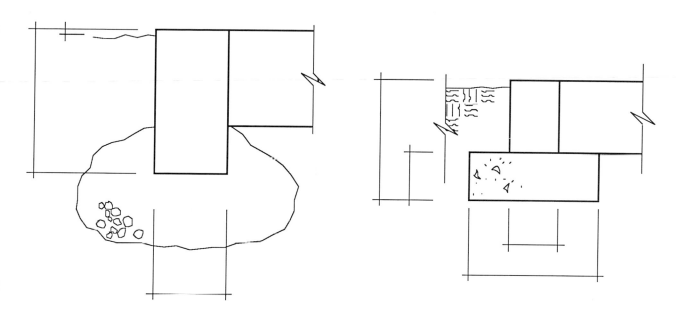

STONE CURB
1 1/2"=1'-0"   02524-11

STONE CURB
1 1/2"=1'-0"   02524-12

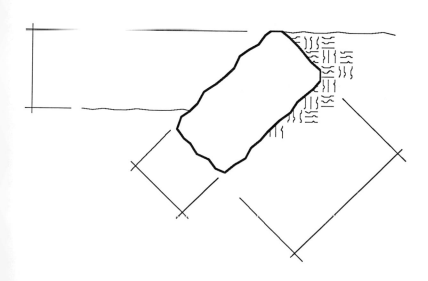

STONE CURB
1 1/2"=1'-0"   02524-14

O2524 (b) STONE CURBS, PAVING EDGES

FULL-SCALE GENERIC DETAILS continued

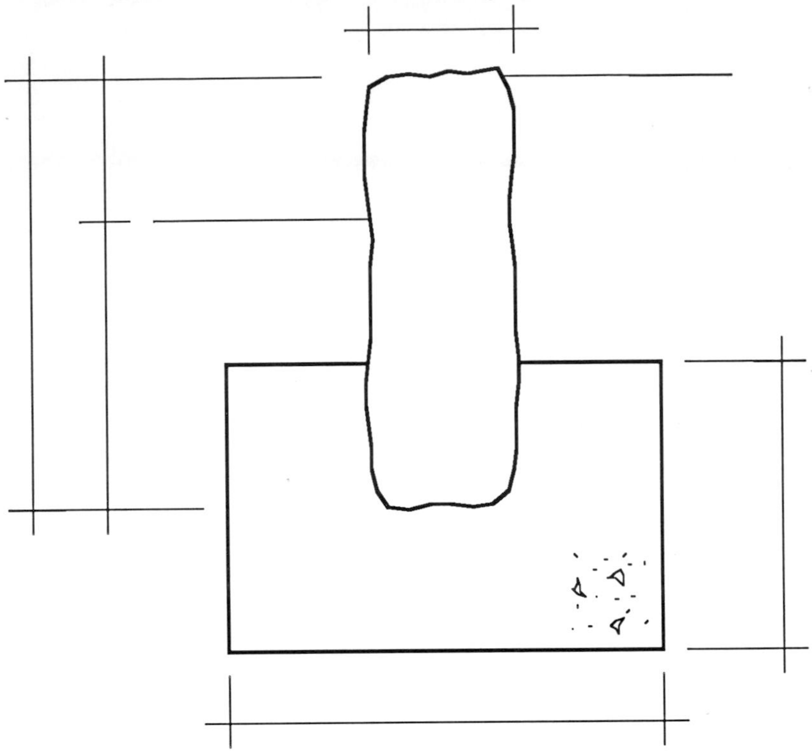

STONE CURB
1 1/2"=1'-0"   02524-16

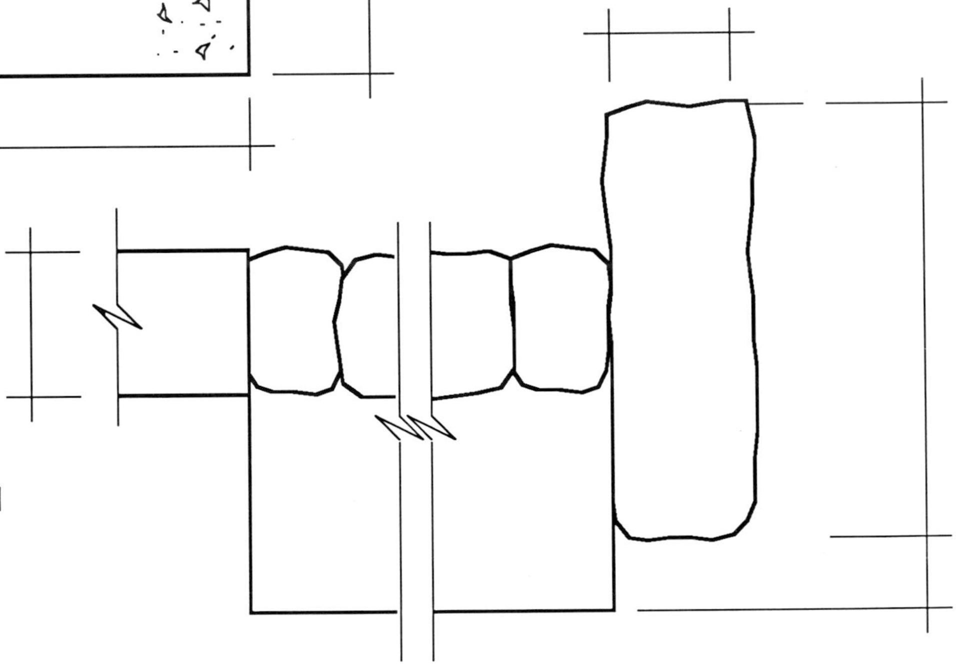

STONE CURB
1 1/2"=1'-0"   02524-21

NOTATION CHECKLIST, SAMPLE NOTES

CURB FINISH (TYPE & MATERIAL)
FINISH GRADE/PAVEMENT
CURB SLOPE/RADII/CAMFER
PAVEMENT SLOPE
AGGREGATE BASE
COMPACTED SUBGRADE
CONTROL/EXPANSION JOINTS (TYPE & SPACING)

SEE SITE PLAN FOR MATERIAL &
    FINISH GRADE @ PAVING
SLOPE GRANITE CURBING 45°
VERTICAL GRANITE CURBING
COMPACTED BANK RUN GRAVEL
BASE

02526 CONCRETE CURBS

DETAIL DATA CHECKLIST

CONCRETE CURBS
__Street curbs must usually follow local road department design standards
__Exposed edges can be chamfered, tooled, or have a 1/2" to 1" radius
__Reinforcing:
    __Precast concrete curbs may have dowel pins and holes at alternate ends
        __2-#4 bars, one top and one bottom (continuous is common)
    __May have #3 ties or stirrups at 32" to 36" o.c.
    __2 bars at the bottom of the footing may be needed
    __Bars should have 2" cover
__When curb is continuous w/walk, woven wire mesh (WWM) may be turned down into curb
__Curb depth below grade varies from 12" to 24"
__Curb width varies from 5" to 7"
__Compact the subgrade
__Provide ample subgrade drainage
__Expansion Joints:
    __Two types needed:
        __Joints in the curb itself
        __Joints between curb and adjacent sidewalk
    __Curb joints should occur at approximately 15' intervals and at all corners
    __Provide 1/4" radius at edge of joints
    __Joint materials:
        __1/2" preformed expansion joint, held down 1" for sealant on top
        __Heartwood redwood filler strip pour joint

SMALL-SCALE GENERIC DETAILS

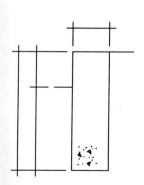
PRECAST CONCRETE CURB
02526-12

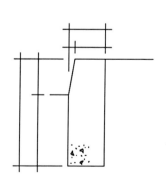
PRECAST CONCRETE CURB
02526-13

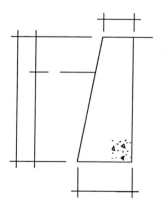
PRECAST CONCRETE CURB
02526-14

02526 CONCRETE CURBS

FULL-SCALE GENERIC DETAILS

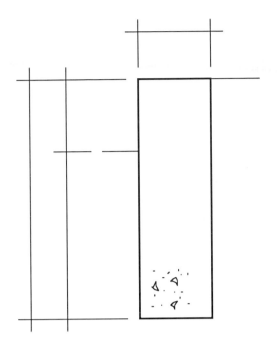

PRECAST CONCRETE CURB
1 1/2"=1'-0"   02526-12

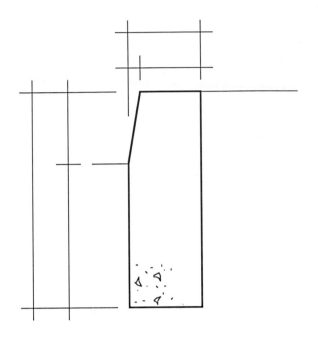

PRECAST CONCRETE CURB
1 1/2"=1'-0"   02526-13

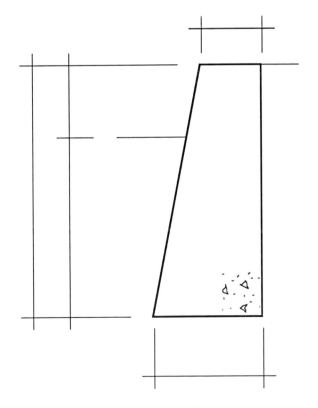

PRECAST CONCRETE CURB
1 1/2"=1'-0"   02526-14

02526 CONCRETE CURBS

NOTATION CHECKLIST,
SAMPLE NOTES

CURB (TYPE & MATERIAL)
REINFORCING
FINISH GRADE/PAVEMENT
CURB SLOPE/RADII/CAMFER
PAVEMENT SLOPE
AGGREGATE BASE
COMPACTED SUBGRADE
CONTROL/EXPANSION JOINTS (TYPE & SPACING)

FINISH GRADE
TOP OF CURB
PAVEMENT
CONCRETE
3/4" RADIUS ON ALL EXPOSED EDGES
1/2" RADIUS EDGE
CONCRETE
REBARS, CONT. TOP & BOTTOM, 2" MIN. COVER
CONC. SIDEWALK
CRUSHED AGGREGATE BASE
6" X 6" - 10 GAUGE WIRE MESH
CAULK
JOINT SEALER
EXPANSION JOINT
1/2" EXPANSION JOINT MATERIAL
BITUMINOUS EXP. JOINT FILLER
RADIUS
3 - #4 BARS CONT.
2 - #5 REBARS CONT.
BITUMINOUS PAVING
COMPACTED GRANULAR BASE COURSE
COMPACTED SUBGRADE OR STRUCTURAL
BACKFILL
2" DIA. DRAIN PIPE THRU CURB

02528 (a) CONCRETE CURBS

DETAIL DATA CHECKLIST

CONCRETE CURBS
__Street curbs must usually follow local road department design standards
__Exposed edges can be chamfered, tooled, or have a 1/2" to 1" radius
__Reinforcing:
    __Precast concrete curbs may have dowel pns and holes at alternate ends
        __2-#4 bars, one top and one bottom (continuous is common)
    __May have #3 ties or stirrups at 32" to 36" o.c.
    __2 bars at the bottom of the footing may be needed
    __Bars should have 2" cover
__When curb is continuous w/walk, woven wire mesh (WWM) may be turned down into curb
__Curb depth below grade varies from 12" to 24"
__Curb width varies from 5" to 7"
__Compact the subgrade
__Provide ample subgrade drainage
__Expansion Joints:
    __Two types needed:
        __Joints in the curb itself
        __Joints between curb and adjacent sidewalk
    __Curb joints should occur at approximately 15' intervals and at all corners
    __Provide 1/4" radius at edge of joints
    __Joint materials:
        __1/2" preformed expansion joint, held down 1" for sealant on top
        __Heartwood redwood filler strip pour joint

SMALL-SCALE GENERIC DETAILS

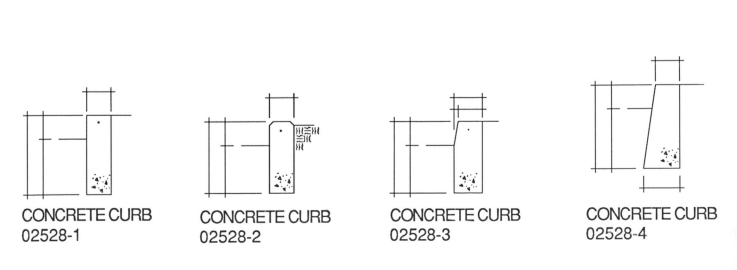

CONCRETE CURB
02528-1

CONCRETE CURB
02528-2

CONCRETE CURB
02528-3

CONCRETE CURB
02528-4

02528 (a) CONCRETE CURBS

SMALL-SCALE GENERIC DETAILS continued

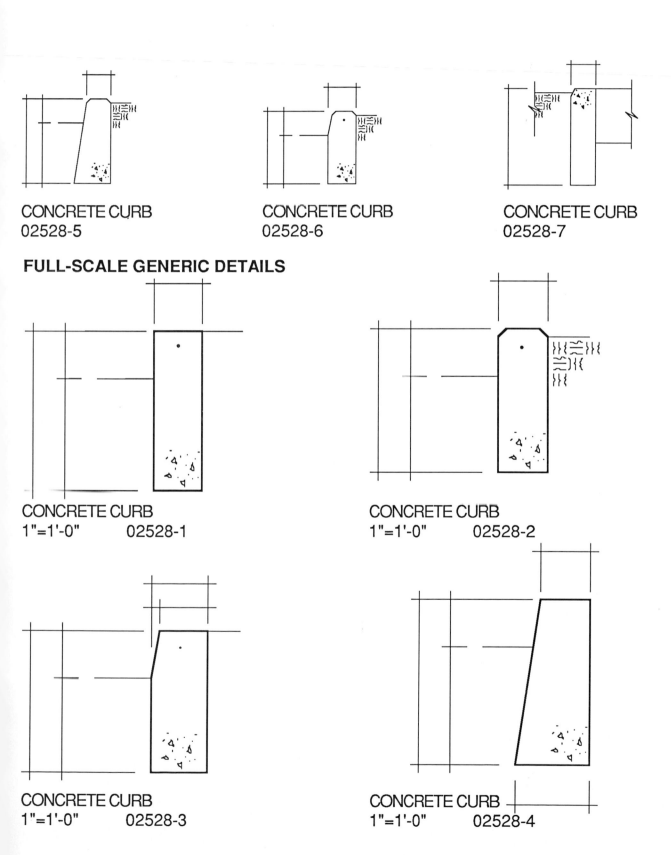

CONCRETE CURB
02528-5

CONCRETE CURB
02528-6

CONCRETE CURB
02528-7

FULL-SCALE GENERIC DETAILS

CONCRETE CURB
1"=1'-0"   02528-1

CONCRETE CURB
1"=1'-0"   02528-2

CONCRETE CURB
1"=1'-0"   02528-3

CONCRETE CURB
1"=1'-0"   02528-4

02528 (a) CONCRETE CURBS

FULL-SCALE GENERIC DETAILS continued

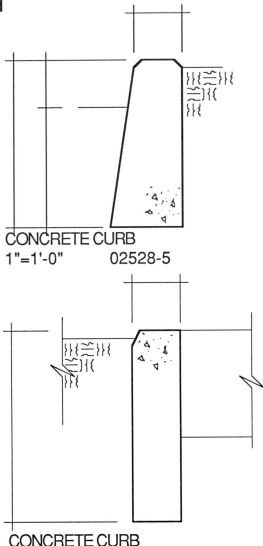

CONCRETE CURB
1"=1'-0"   02528-5

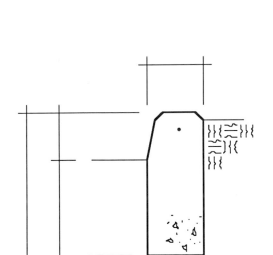

CONCRETE CURB
1"=1'-0"   02528-6

CONCRETE CURB
1"=1'-0"   02528-7

NOTATION CHECKLIST,
  SAMPLE NOTES

CURB (TYPE & MATERIAL)
REINFORCING
FINISH GRADE/PAVEMENT
CURB SLOPE/RADII/CAMFER
PAVEMENT SLOPE
AGGREGATE BASE
COMPACTED SUBGRADE
CONTROL/EXPANSION JOINTS (TYPE & SPACING)
FINISH GRADE
TOP OF CURB
PAVEMENT
CONCRETE
3/4" RADIUS ON ALL EXPOSED EDGES
1/2" RADIUS EDGE
CONCRETE
REBARS, CONT. TOP & BOTTOM; 2" MIN. COVER

CONC. SIDEWALK
CRUSHED AGGREGATE BASE
6" X 6" - 10 GAGE WIRE MESH
CAULK
JOINT SEALER
EXPANSION JOINT
1/2" EXPANSION JOINT MATERIAL
BITUMINOUS EXP. JOINT FILLER
RADIUS
3-#4 BARS CONT.
2-#5 REBARS CONT.
BITUMINOUS PAVING
COMPACTED GRANULAR BASE COURSE
COMPACTED SUBGRADE OR STRUCTURAL
BACKFILL
2" DIA. DRAIN PIPE THRU CURB

dim. lines break line

notation boundary break line

cut mark

dim. line —

dim. line —

break line —

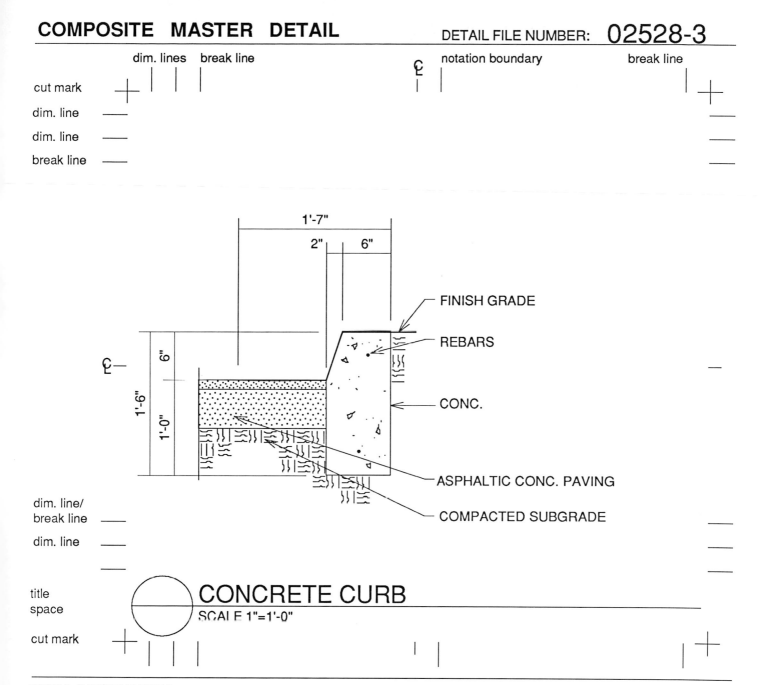

1'-7"

2" 6"

6"

1'-6"

1'-0"

FINISH GRADE

REBARS

CONC.

ASPHALTIC CONC. PAVING

COMPACTED SUBGRADE

dim. line/
break line —

dim. line —

title
space

CONCRETE CURB

SCALE 1"=1'-0"

cut mark

DETAIL INFORMATION
References, jobsite feedback, job history

02528 (b) CONCRETE CURBS

DETAIL DATA CHECKLIST

CONCRETE CURBS
__Street curbs must usually follow local road department design standards
__Exposed edges can be chamfered, tooled, or have a 1/2" to 1" radius
__Reinforcing:
    __Precast concrete curbs may have dowel pins and holes at alternate ends
        __2-#4 bars, one top and one bottom (continuous is common)
    __May have #3 ties or stirrups at 32" to 36" o.c.
    __2 bars at the bottom of the footing may be needed
    __Bars should have 2" cover
    __When curb is continuous w/walk, woven wire mesh (WWM) may be turned down into curb
__Curb depth below grade varies from 12" to 24"
__Curb widths vary: 5" to 7"
__Compact the subgrade
__Provide ample subgrade drainage
__Expansion Joints:
    __Two types needed:
        __Joints in the curb itself
        __Joints between curb and adjacent sidewalk
__Curb joints should occur at approximately 15' intervals and at all corners
__Provide 1/4" radius at edge of joints
__Joint materials:
    __1/2" preformed expansion joint, held down 1" for sealant on top
    __Heartwood redwood filler strip pour joint

CONCRETE CURB & GUTTER
__Minimum gutter slope toward curb is 1-2%
__Radius at curb nose and gutter can be 1" to 3"
__Space curb/gutter expansion joints no more than 30' apart
__An expansion joint or key is also needed where gutter meets paving
__Recommended reinforcing is 2 to 4 bars, #4 or #5
__Compact the subgrade
__Provide ample subgrade drainage

SMALL-SCALE GENERIC DETAILS

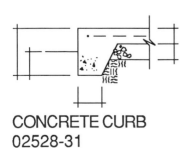

CONCRETE CURB
02528-31

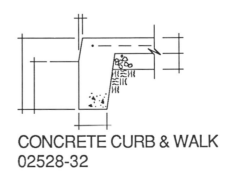

CONCRETE CURB & WALK
02528-32

02528 (b) CONCRETE CURBS

SMALL-SCALE GENERIC DETAILS continued

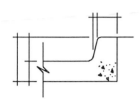

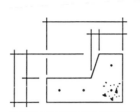

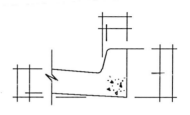

CONCRETE CURB & GUTTER
02528-51

CONCRETE CURB & GUTTER
02528-53

CONCRETE CURB & GUTTER
02528-52

FULL-SCALE GENERIC DETAILS

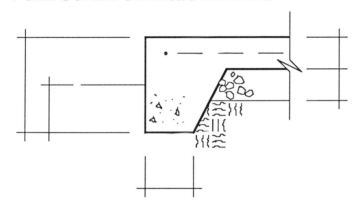

CONCRETE CURB & WALK
1"=1'-0"   02528-31

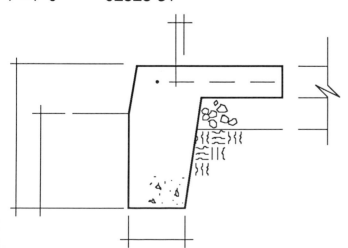

CONCRETE CURB & WALK
1"=1'-0"   02528-32

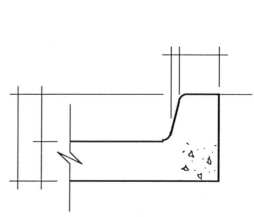

CONCRETE CURB & GUTTER
1"=1'-0"   02528-51

02528 (b) CONCRETE CURBS

FULL-SCALE GENERIC DETAILS continued

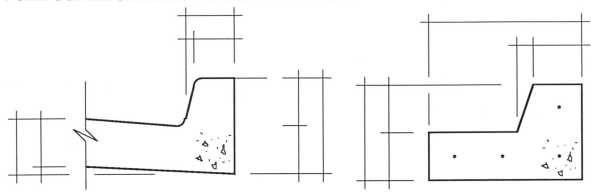

CONCRETE CURB & GUTTER
1"=1'-0"   02528-52

CONCRETE CURB & GUTTER
1"=1'-0"   02528-53

NOTATION CHECKLIST,
SAMPLE NOTES

CURB (TYPE & MATERIAL)
REINFORCING
FINISH GRADE/PAVEMENT
CURB SLOPE/RADII/CAMFER
PAVEMENT SLOPE
AGGREGATE BASE
COMPACTED SUBGRADE
CONTROL/EXPANSION JOINTS (TYPE & SPACING)
FINISH GRADE
TOP OF CURB
PAVEMENT
CONCRETE
3/4" RADIUS ON ALL EXPOSED EDGES
1/2" RADIUS EDGE
CONCRETE
REBARS, CONT. TOP & BOTTOM, 2" MIN. COVER
CONC. SIDEWALK
CRUSHED AGGREGATE BASE
6" X 6" - #10 GAUGE WIRE MESH
CAULK
JOINT SEALER
EXPANSION JOINT
1/2" EXPANSION JOINT MATERIAL
BITUMINOUS EXP. JOINT FILLER
RADIUS
3-#4 BARS CONT.
2-#5 REBARS CONT.
BITUMINOUS PAVING
COMPACTED GRANULAR BASE COURSE
COMPACTED SUBGRADE OR STRUCTURAL BACKFILL

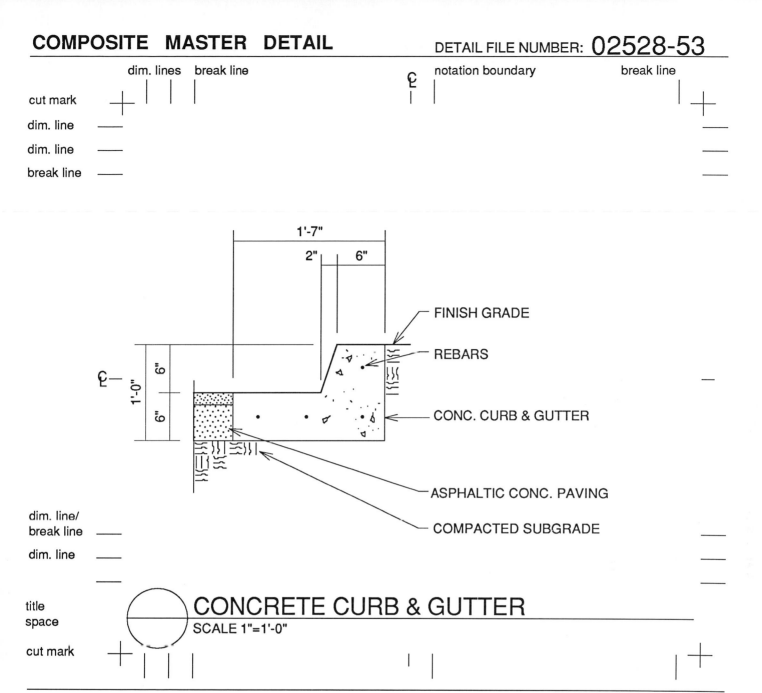

dim. lines   break line   notation boundary   break line

cut mark

dim. line

dim. line

break line

CONCRETE CURB & GUTTER

1'-7"

2"   6"

6"

1'-0"

6"

FINISH GRADE

REBARS

CONC. CURB & GUTTER

ASPHALTIC CONC. PAVING

COMPACTED SUBGRADE

dim. line/
break line

dim. line

title
space

cut mark

CONCRETE CURB & GUTTER

SCALE 1"=1'-0"

DETAIL INFORMATION
References, jobsite feedback, job history

02528 (c) CONCRETE CURBS

DETAIL DATA CHECKLIST

CONCRETE CURBS
__Street curbs must usually follow local road department design standards
__Exposed edges can be chamfered, tooled, or have a 1/2" to 1" radius
__Reinforcing:
    __Precast concrete curbs may have dowel pins and holes at alternate ends
        __Two #4 bars, one top and one bottom (continuous is common)
    __May have #3 ties or stirrups at 32" to 36" o.c.
    __Two bars at the bottom of the footing may be needed
    __Bars should have 2" cover
__When curb is continuous w/walk, woven wire mesh (WWM) may be turned down into curb
__Curb depth below grade varies from 12" to 24"
__Curb width varies from 5" to 7"
__Compact the subgrade
__Provide ample subgrade drainage
__Expansion Joints:
    __Two types needed:
        __Joints in the curb itself
        __Joints between curb and adjacent sidewalk
    __Curb joints should occur at approximately 15' intervals and at all corners
    __Provide 1/4" radius at edge of joints
    __Joint materials:
        __1/2" preformed expansion joint, held down 1" for sealant on top
        __Heartwood redwood filler strip pour joint

CONCRETE CURB & GUTTER
__Minimum gutter slope toward curb is 1-2%
__Radius at curb nose and gutter can be 1" to 3"
__Space curb/gutter expansion joints no more than 30' apart
__An expansion joint or key is also needed where gutter meets paving
__Recommended reinforcing is 2 to 4 bars, #4 or #5
__Compact the subgrade
__Provide ample subgrade drainage

CONCRETE PAVING
__Recommended thicknesses for concrete slabs are:
    __4" for walks, patios, and drives
    __5" to 6" for roads, public sidewalks, and areas with heavy vehicular traffic
__Pour slab over a gravel base 4" to 8" thick, depending on thickness of concrete and nature of soil
__Slope surface of slab 2% or 1/4" per lin. foot minimum
__Surface treatments:
    __To reduce slipperiness:
        __Broom finish
        __Spread abrasive grains on wet concrete
    __To achieve exposed aggregate surface:
        __Sandblast
        __Finish top slab with light water spray before curing and brushing
__Reinforce slab with 4x4x4/4 or 6x6x10/10 woven wire mesh (WWM)
    __Provide 2" cover over the reinforcing

02528 (c) CONCRETE CURBS

DETAIL DATA CHECKLIST continued

CONCRETE PAVING continued
__Expansion Joints:
    __Placement varies with climate
        __Average 30' o.c. in walks
           __15' to 20' squares in larger areas of concrete
    __Dowelling1/2" to 1" diameter dowel in sleeve, graphite coated; 12" to 24" long, 12" to 36" o.c.
    __Gap in slab filled with premolded or poured joint filler
__Control Joints:
    __Can be tooled or saw cut
    __1/8" thick nonferrous strip, or poured joint filler
    __Joint must be 1/4th of the depth of the slab to be effective
    __Edges of slab at joint should have1/8" radius
    __Joints may be dowelled (as above), without sleeve

SMALL-SCALE GENERIC DETAILS

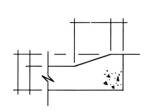

CONCRETE CURB & GUTTER
Iowa Curb
02528-54

CONCRETE CURB & GUTTER
Rolled Curb
02528-55

CONCRETE CURB & GUTTER
W/Swale
02528-56

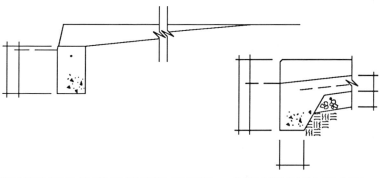

DROPPED CONCRETE CURB
& RAMP
02528-71

CONCRETE CURB
& RAMP
02528-72

STEEL FACED
CONCRETE CURB
02528-76

02528 (c) CONCRETE CURBS

FULL-SCALE GENERIC DETAILS

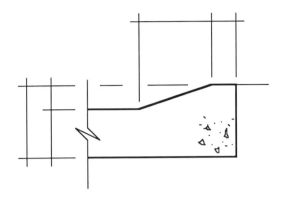

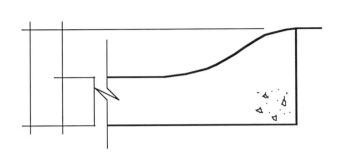

CONCRETE CURB & GUTTER Iowa Curb
1"=1'-0"   02528-54

CONCRETE CURB & GUTTER Rolled Curb
1"=1'-0"   02528-55

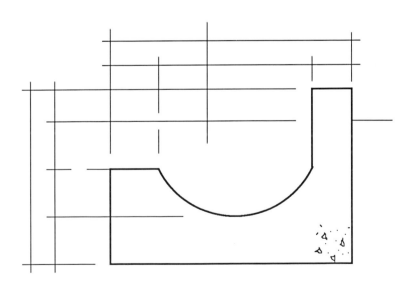

CONCRETE CURB & GUTTER W/Swale
1"=1'-0"   02528-56

02528 (c) CONCRETE CURBS

FULL-SCALE GENERIC DETAILS continued

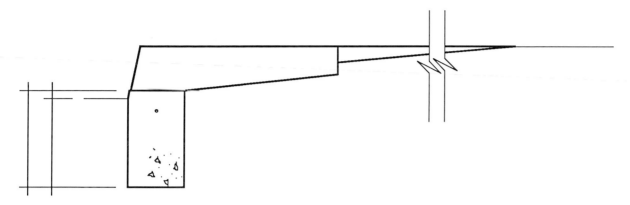

DROPPED CONCRETE CURB & RAMP
1"=1'-0"   02528-71

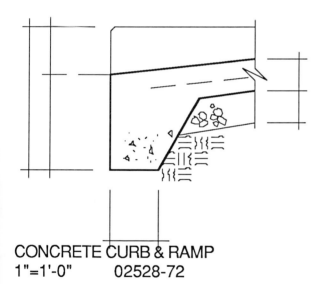

CONCRETE CURB & RAMP
1"=1'-0"   02528-72

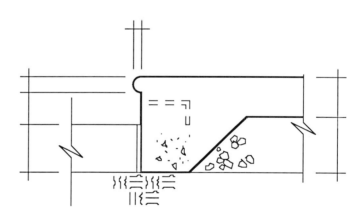

STEEL FACED CONCRETE CURB
1"=1'-0"   02528-76

NOTATION CHECKLIST, SAMPLE NOTES

CURB (TYPE & MATERIAL)
REINFORCING
FINISH GRADE/PAVEMENT
CURB SLOPE/RADII/CAMFER
PAVEMENT SLOPE
AGGREGATE BASE
COMPACTED SUBGRADE
CONTROL/EXPANSION JOINTS (TYPE & SPACING)
FINISH GRADE
TOP OF CURB
PAVEMENT
CONCRETE
3/4" RADIUS ON ALL EXPOSED EDGES
1/2" RADIUS EDGE
CONCRETE

REBARS, CONT. TOP & BOTTOM, @" MIN. COVER
CONC. SIDEWALK
CRUSHED AGGREGATE BASE
6" X 6" - #10 GAUGE WIRE MESH
CAULK
JOINT SEALER
EXPANSION JOINT
1/2" EXPANSION JOINT MATERIAL
BITUMINOUS EXP. JOINT FILLER
RADIUS
3-#4 BARS CONT
2-#5 REBARS CONT.
BITUMINOUS PAVING
COMPACTED GRANULAR BASE COURSE
COMPACTED SUBGRADE OR STRUCTURAL
BACKFILL
2" DIA. DRAIN PIPE THRU CURB

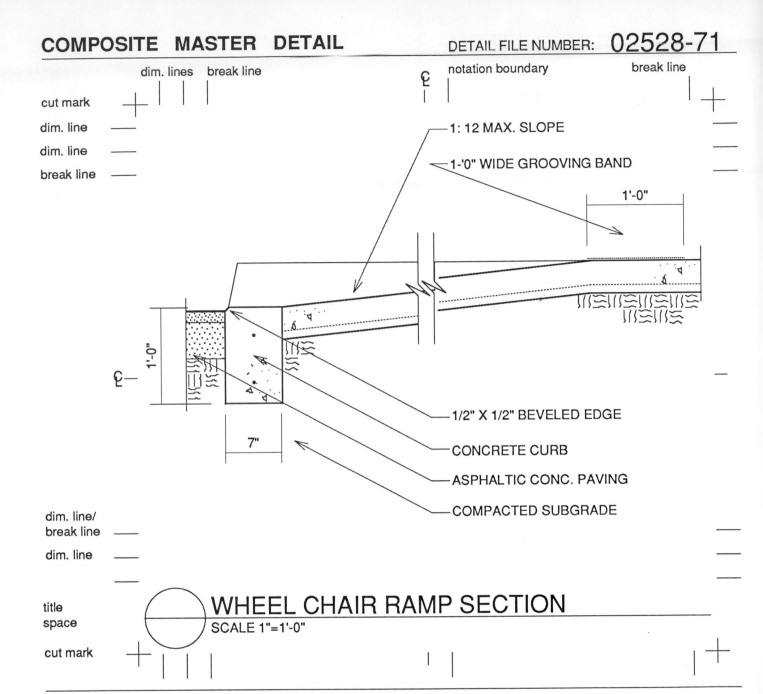

cut mark

dim. lines   break line

notation boundary   break line

dim. line

dim. line

break line

1: 12 MAX. SLOPE

1-'0" WIDE GROOVING BAND

1'-0"

1'-0"

7"

1/2" X 1/2" BEVELED EDGE

CONCRETE CURB

ASPHALTIC CONC. PAVING

COMPACTED SUBGRADE

dim. line/
break line

dim. line

title
space

WHEEL CHAIR RAMP SECTION
SCALE 1"=1'-0"

cut mark

DETAIL INFORMATION
References, jobsite feedback, job history

02529 (a) CONCRETE WALKS & PAVING

DETAIL DATA CHECKLIST

CONCRETE PAVING
__Recommended thicknesses for concrete slabs are:
    __4" for walks, patios, and drives
    __5" to 6" for roads, public sidewalks, and areas with heavy vehicular traffic
__Pour slab over a gravel base 4" to 8" thick, depending on thickness of concrete and nature of soil
__Slope surface of slab 2% or 1/4" per lin. foot minimum
__Surface treatments:
    __To reduce slipperiness:
        __Broom finish
        __Spread abrasive grains on wet concrete
    __To achieve exposed aggregate surface:
        __ Sandblast
        __Finish top slab with light water spray before curing and brushing
__Reinforce slab with 4x4x4/4 or 6x6x10/10 woven wire mesh (WWM)
    __Provide 2" cover over the reinforcing
__Expansion Joints:
    __Placement varies with climate
        __Average 30' o.c. in walks
        __15' to 20' squares in larger areas of concrete
    __Dowelling 1/2" to 1" diameter dowel in sleeve, graphite coated; 12" to 24" long, 12" to 36" o.c..
    __Gap in slab filled with premolded or poured joint filler
__Control Joints:
    __Can be tooled or saw cut
    __1/8" thick nonferrous strip, or poured joint filler
    __Joint must be 1/4 of the depth of the slab to be effective
    __Edges of slab at joint should have1/8" radius
    __Joints may be dowelled (as above), without sleeve

CONCRETE & GUTTERS
__Minimum gutter slope toward curb is 1 to 2%
__Radius at curb nose and gutter can be 1" to 3"
__Space curb/gutter expansion joints no more than 30' apart
__An expansion joint or key is also needed where gutter meets paving
__Recommended reinforcing is 2 to 4 bars; #4 or #5
__Compact the subgrade
__Provide ample subgrade drainage

02529 (a) CONCRETE WALKS & PAVING

SMALL-SCALE GENERIC DETAILS

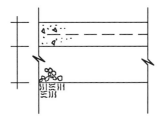

CONCRETE WALK/PAVING
02529-11

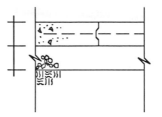

CONCRETE WALK/PAVING
T & G Joint   02529-12

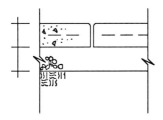

CONCRETE WALK/PAVING
Butt Joint   02529-13

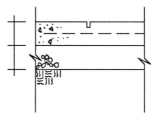

CONCRETE WALK/PAVING
Control Joint   02529-14

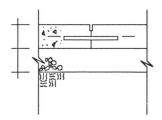

CONCRETE WALK/PAVING
Const. Joint   02529-15

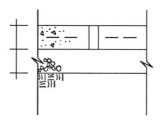

CONCRETE WALK/PAVING
Redwood Divider   02529-16

02529 (a) CONCRETE WALKS & PAVING

FULL-SCALE GENERIC DETAILS

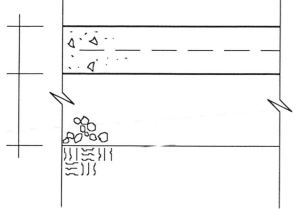

CONCRETE WALK/PAVING
1 1/2"=1'-0"   02529-11

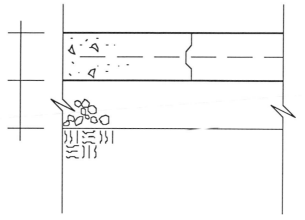

CONCRETE WALK/PAVING T & G Joint
1 1/2"=1'-0"   02529-12

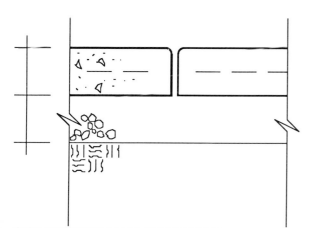

CONCRETE WALK/PAVING
Butt Joint   1 1/2"=1'-0"
02529-13

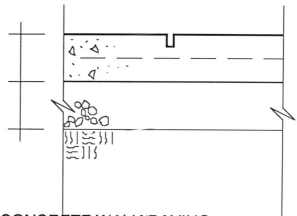

CONCRETE WALK/PAVING
Control Joint   1 1/2"=1'-0"
02529-14

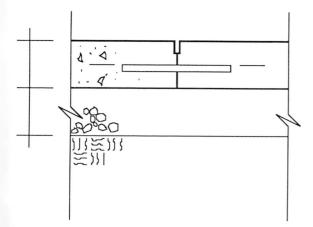

CONCRETE WALK/PAVING
Const. Joint   1 1/2"=1'-0"
02529-15

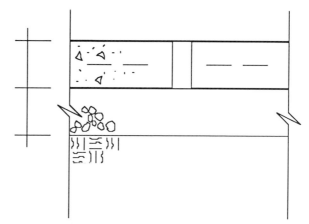

CONCRETE WALK/PAVING
Redwood Divider   1 1/2"=1'-0"
02529-16

02529 (a) CONCRETE WALKS & PAVING

NOTATION CHECKLIST, SAMPLE NOTES

PAVING (TYPE, MATERIAL & FINISH)
SLOPE
REINFORCING
FINISH GRADE
CONTROL/EXPANSION JOINTS (TYPE & SPACING)
AGGREGATE BASE
COMPACTED SUBGRADE
ORIGINAL GRADE
FINISH GRADE
PROVIDE CROWN IN CENTER FOR DRAINAGE
SLOPE 1/4" PER FOOT, TYP.
CONCRETE W. 6 X 6 - 10 GAUGE WIRE MESH
CONC. SLAB W. 6 X 6 X #10/#10
CONC. WALK W/ 6 X 6 10/10 W.W.M.
REDWOOD HEARTWOOD JOINT FILLER STRIP
TOOLED JOINTS @ 6'-0" O.C.
1/2" EXPANSION JOINT
JOINT SEALANT & JOINT FILLER ROD
JOINT FILLER BOARD
1"DIA (3/4" to 1" typ.) X 18" DOWEL BARS
   12" O.C. ACROSS SLAB
   (@ exp. jts.) PAINT & OIL ONE END OF DOWEL

EXPANSION JOINT FILLER MATERIAL @ 16" O.C. MAX.
GALV. METAL KEYWAY W/ EDGE EXPOSED
GALV. METAL STAKE PIN
DUMMY JOINTS @ 5'-0" O.C.
PRE-MOLDED EXPANSION JOINT @ 20'-O" O.C. TYP.
PAVING BRICKS IN SETTING BED
SLOPE TO DRAIN AS INDICATED ON PLANS
BRICK ROWLOCK PAVER
SLAB REINF., SEE
VAPOR BARRIER
COMPACTED GRANULAR FILL
4" PEA GRAVEL
SAND CUSHION
COMPACTED EARTH FILL AS REQ'D.
COMPACTED SUBGRADE OR STRUCTURAL
BACKFILL
8" CRUSHED AGGRAGATE BASE (@ 6" conc. paving)
6" CRUSHED AGGREGATE BASE (@ 2" asphalt
 paving)

02529 (b) CONCRETE WALKS & PAVING

DETAIL DATA CHECKLIST

CONCRETE PAVING
__Recommended thicknesses for concrete slabs are:
    __4" for walks, patios, and drives
    __5" to 6" for roads, public sidewalks, and areas with heavy vehicular traffic
__Pour slab over a gravel base 4" to 8" thick, depending on thickness of concrete and nature of soil
__Slope surface of slab 2% or 1/4" per lin. foot minimum
__Surface treatments:
    __To reduce slipperiness:
        __Broom finish
        __Spread abrasive grains on wet concrete
    __To achieve exposed aggregate surface:
        __Sandblast
        __Finish top slab with light water spray before curing and brushing
__Reinforce slab with 4x4x4/4 or 6x6x10/10 woven wire mesh (WWM)
    __Provide 2" cover over the reinforcing
__Expansion Joints:
    __Placement varies with climate
        __Average 30' o.c. in walks
        __15' to 20' squares in larger areas of concrete
    __Dowelling 1/2" to 1" diameter dowel in sleeve, graphite coated; 12" to 24" long, 12" to 36" o.c..
    __Gap in slab filled with premolded or poured joint filler
__Control Joints:
    __Can be tooled or saw cut
    __1/8" thick nonferrous strip, or poured joint filler
    __Joint must be 1/4 of the depth of the slab to be effective
    __Edges of slab at joint should have1/8" radius
    __Joints may be dowelled (as above), without sleeve

CONCRETE & GUTTERS
__Minimum gutter slope toward curb is 1 to 2%
__Radius at curb nose and gutter can be 1" to 3"
__Space curb/gutter expansion joints no more than 30' apart
__An expansion joint or key is also needed where gutter meets paving
__Recommended reinforcing is 2 to 4 bars; #4 or #5
__Compact the subgrade
__Provide ample subgrade drainage

02529 (b) CONCRETE WALKS & PAVING

SMALL-SCALE GENERIC DETAILS

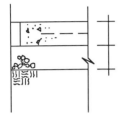

CONCRETE WALK/PAVING
Redwood Joint   02529-17

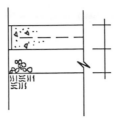

CONCRETE WALK/PAVING
Expansion Joint   02529-18

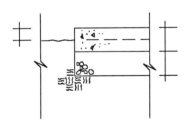

CONCRETE WALK/PAVING @ EDGE
02529-41

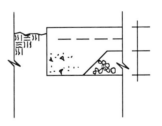

CONCRETE WALK/PAVING @ EDGE
02529-42

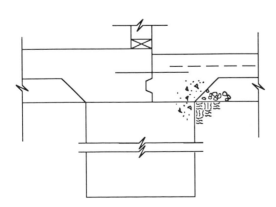

CONCRETE WALK/PAVING @ BLDG FOOTING
02529-61

02529 (b) CONCRETE WALKS & PAVING

FULL-SCALE GENERIC DETAILS

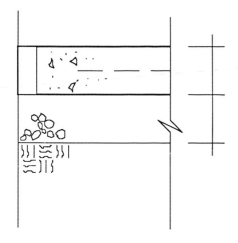

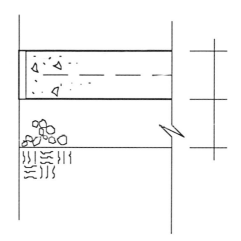

CONCRETE WALK/PAVING
Redwood Joint
1 1/2"=1'-0"   02529-17

CONCRETE WALK/PAVING
Expansion Joint
1 1/2"=1'-0"   02529-18

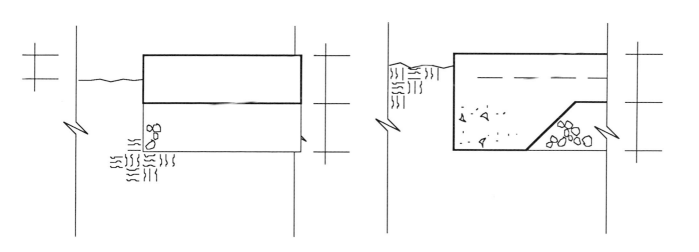

CONCRETE WALK/PAVING @ EDGE
1 1/2"=1'-0"   02529-41

CONCRETE WALK/PAVING @ EDGE
1 1/2"=1'-0"   02529-42

02529 (c) CONCRETE STEPS

FULL-SCALE GENERIC DETAILS

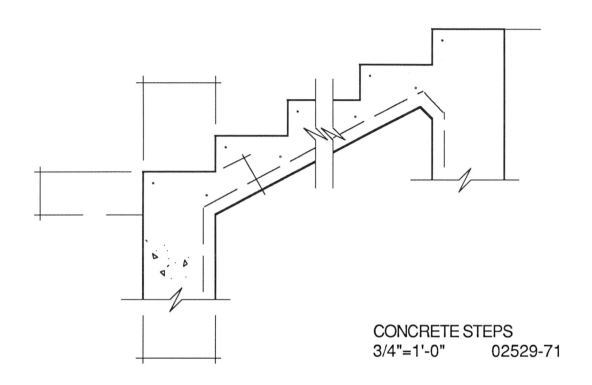

CONCRETE STEPS
3/4"=1'-0"   02529-71

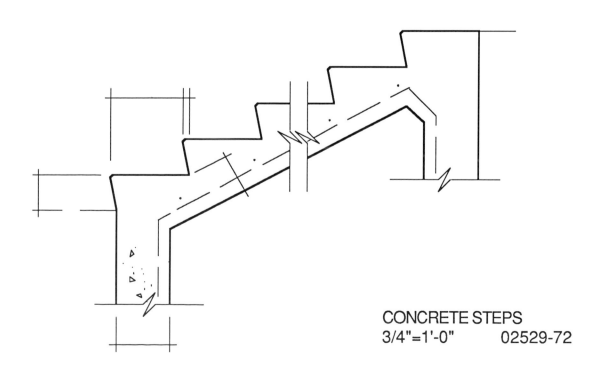

CONCRETE STEPS
3/4"=1'-0"   02529-72

02529 (c) CONCRETE STEPS

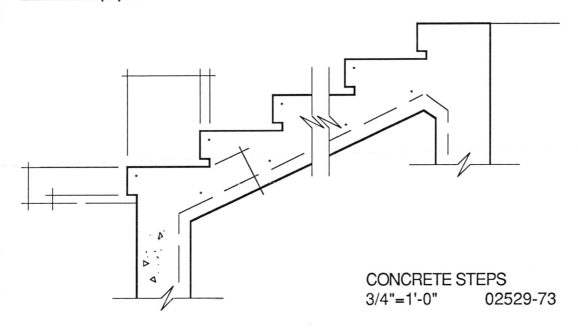

CONCRETE STEPS
3/4"=1'-0"   02529-73

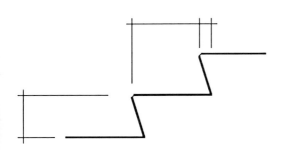

CONCRETE STEPS For Handicapped
3/4"=1'-0"   02529-76

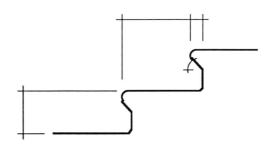

CONCRETE STEPS For Handicapped (ANSI)
3/4"=1'-0"   02529-77

NOTATION CHECKLIST,
SAMPLE NOTES

CONCRETE FINISH
REINFORCING
SLOPE FOR DRAINAGE
METAL NOSING
FINISH GRADES/PAVING
HANDRAIL
HANDRAIL POST PIPE
SLEEVE/ANCHOR
AGGREGATE BASE
COMPACTED SUBGRADE

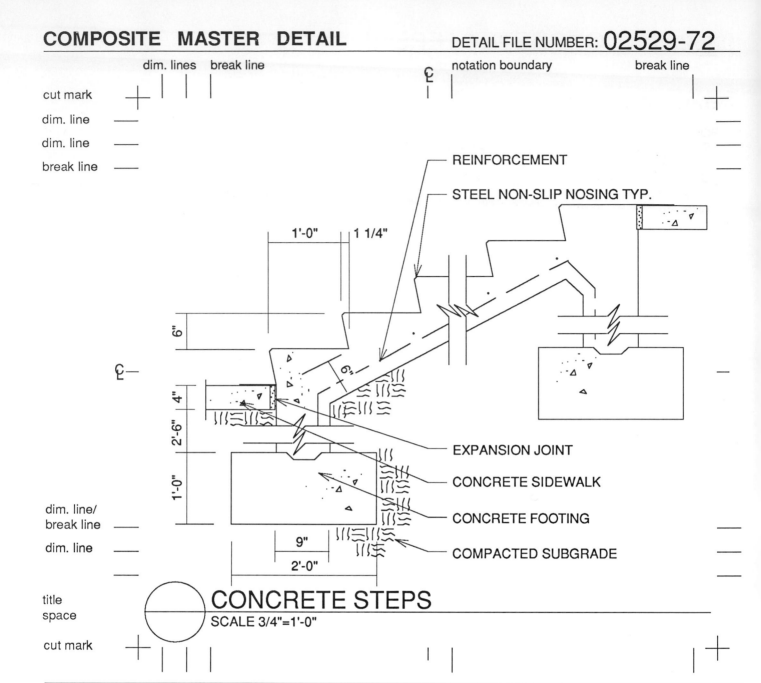

cut mark

dim. lines | break line

dim. line

dim. line

break line

notation boundary | break line

REINFORCEMENT

STEEL NON-SLIP NOSING TYP.

1'-0" | 1 1/4"

6"

6"

4"

2'-6"

1'-0"

EXPANSION JOINT

CONCRETE SIDEWALK

dim. line/
break line

CONCRETE FOOTING

dim. line

9"

2'-0"

COMPACTED SUBGRADE

title
space

CONCRETE STEPS
SCALE 3/4"=1'-0"

cut mark

DETAIL INFORMATION
References, jobsite feedback, job history

02530 SPORTS PAVING

DETAIL DATA CHECKLIST

SPORTS PAVING
__Sports paving must be specified with considerable precision;
   details are mainly to show thicknesses and layering of materials.
__Consult CSI master specifications and athletic facilities handbooks for
   design standards required for specific sports and specific site and weather conditions.
__Also, see manufacturers' and suppliers' catalogs for design data, details, and specifications.

SMALL-SCALE GENERIC DETAILS

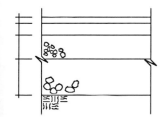

TENNIS COURT PAVING
02530-11

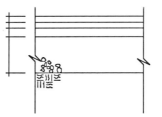

SYNTHETIC TRACK PAVING
02530-12

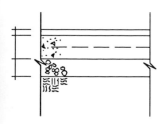

SYNTHETIC SPORTS PAVING
02530-13

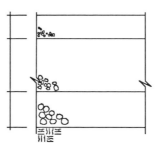

CINDER TRACK
02530-41

02530 SPORTS PAVING

FULL-SCALE GENERIC DETAILS

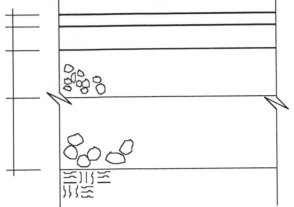

TENNIS COURT PAVING
1 1/2"=1'-0"   02530-11

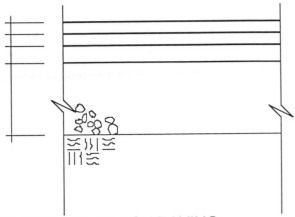

SYNTHETIC TRACK PAVING
1 1/2"=1'-0"   02530-12

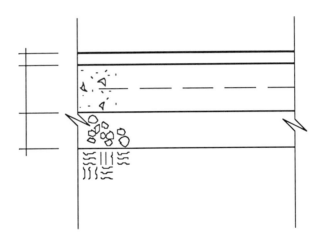

SYNTHETIC SPORTS PAVING
1 1/2"=1'-0"   02530-13

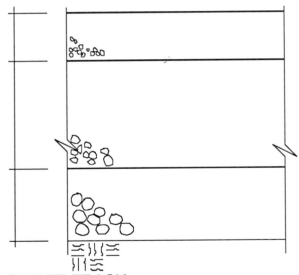

CINDER TRACK
1 1/2"=1'-0"   02530-41

NOTATION CHECKLIST, SAMPLE NOTES

TENNIS COURT:
COLOR COAT
LEVELING COURSE
BINDER
AGGRETATE
GRAVEL
COMPACTED SUBGRADE

CINDER TRACK:
FINE CINDERS
MEDIUM CINDER COURSE
BASE COURSE

SYNTHETIC SPORTS PAVING:
RESILIENT SURFACE
CONCRETE SLAB
REINFORCING
AGGREGRATE BASE
COMPACTED SUBGRADE

SYNTHETIC TRACK:
RESILIENT SURFACE
WEARING COURSE
LEVELING COURSE
BASE COURSE
COMPACTED SUBGRADE

CHAPTER 3

Concrete
03000

DETAIL DATA CHECKLIST FOR FOUNDATION TYPES

For foundation detail types   03305 (a) through (j) & 03306

See each detail type for additional **Detail Data Checklist** data

Note that drain tiles or perforated drain pipe and gravel bed should be added to perimeter wall foundation details as required for drainage.

FOOTINGS & FOUNDATION WALLS

__Footing sizes: Refer to building code for typical sizing for light frame and residential buildings and for
       engineering requirements for larger structures
       __Note soil frost line conditions that effect footing design and depth of footings
__Note elevation points of bottom & top of footings
__Note elevation points and identification of existing grade, finish grade, and compacted grade
__Note reference to foundation plan for footing and grade elevations
__Show cripple wall/floor joist framing
__Redwood or pressure treated wood mudsill: 2x4, 2x6 typical sizes
__Use non-shrink grout a top foundation wall to level the wood mudsill

__Reinforcing bars
       __#4 bars, continuous, centered within 4" of the top and bottom of the footing is typical
       __Minimum clearance from reinforcing bars to outside surface of concrete is 3" but 4" is preferred
       __Higher foundation walls (over 4') often include #4 bars @ 24" o.c. horizontally and vertically
           __Higher walls require engineering computation and detailing

__Dowels
       __#4 deformed rebars typical as anchor dowels
       __#4 plain shape rebar typical for movement joints
       __Use dowels to connect two different pours of concrete

__Treated wood or redwood mudsill connects concrete footing to wood frame
       __2x6 mudsill typical
       __Steel anchor bolts--threaded on top end, bent at end embedded in concrete
           __1/2" x 10" anchor bolt typical for standard residential buildings
           __3/4" x 14" anchor bolt used for larger structures
           __Set anchor bent side down into footing concrete prior to concrete set
           __Attach wood sill to this bolt and secure with nut

__Mudsill and anchor bolts
       __Treated wood or redwood mudsill connects concrete footing to wood frame
           __2x6 mudsill typical
       __Steel anchor bolts--threaded on top end, bent at end embedded in concrete
           __1/2" x 10" anchor bolt typical for standard residential buildings
           __3/4" x 14" anchor bolt used for larger structures
       __Cast-in-place bolts @ 6'-0" o.c., starting 12" from corners typical for residential and other smaller
           frame buildings
       __3/4" x 14" anchor bolts are used for larger structures
       __Space bolts so they don't occur under joists or wall studs
       __Place anchors with bent side down into foundation wall or slab prior to concrete set
       __Attach wood sills, drilled to match bolt holes, and secure with nuts
       __For interior walls, bolt can be shot through wood into concrete with low-power concrete gun
       __Power-driven bolts or anchors are used at closer spacings such as 32" o.c. or 48' o.c.

DETAIL DATA CHECKLIST FOR FOUNDATION TYPES

For foundation detail types   03305 (a) through (j) & 03306

__Girder pockets where a girder bares on a pocket in a foundation wall
    __Allow minimum 4" bearing
    __Provide 1/2" air space at ends and sides of girder
    __Protect bearing ends of girders from moisture with gasket of flashing or building felt

__Redwood or pressure-treated ledgers @ foundation walls
__Post to girder connection
    __Metal post straps, T strap ties, and plywood gussets are typical
__Floor joists, joist hangers, subfloor
    __See local code for span/spacing tables and nailing schedule
__Double floor joists, header joists
    __Usually included at thru-floor openings
    __Under parallel partitions
    __At bathtubs and other concentrated loads

__Flashing
    __Sheet metal, building paper, or combination
    __Design as protective covering to prevent water entry
    __Design to channel rain water that enters back to the outside
    __Use as barrier between dissimilar materials that may corrode each other
    __Building paper flashing--15# typical
    __Metal Flashing--No. 26 gauge galvanized sheet metal typical; affords protection while being
        easy to cut and form on the jobsite

__Thermal Insulation @ perimeter
    __1" rigid insulation board is typical
    __May be thicker in colder climates, as determined by heat loss calculations

__Drainage
    __Perimeter drain tile
        __4" diameter perforated tile pipe is typical
        __Tile pipes separated 1/4" at joints
        __Tile pipe is buried in crushed stone to facilitate drainage
        __Building paper cover to block soil infiltration at tile pipe section ocparations--15# typical
    __Grade site drain away from all sides of the building
    __Provide added soil as necessary to slope and drain directly away from foundation walls
    __Provide side slopes at concrete slab aprons

__Waterproofing
    __Waterproof foundation wall if floor level of interior is lower than exterior grade
        __Use bituminous waterproofing, building felt, or polyethylene film
    __Waterproof concrete floor slabs
        __Provide moisture barrier directly under slab to block ground water
            __6 mil. polyethylene moisture barrier is commonly used but it may deteriorate
                over time
            __Thorough underslab waterproofing requires building roofing felts with tar
                application, like roofing
        __Place slab on 2" to 4" bed of sand or fine, well-compacted gravel

__Termite protection:
    __At contact of wood with concrete
    __Termite-resistant wood treatment
    __Termite shield between wood and concrete
    __Termite-repellent soil treatment under concrete slab
    __Fill hollow masonry unit foundations to block termite entry
    __Keep all wood 12" or more above soil (6" is typical code minimum)

03305 (a) CRAWL SPACE ACCESS & CONC. FOOTINGS

See other DETAIL DATA CHECKLIST for concrete foundations preceding 03305(a)

DETAIL DATA CHECKLIST

CRAWL SPACE
__Crawl space & access
   __24"x18" access is typical with continuous footing below and double joists or header above
   __In wet soil areas, provide vapor barrier with sand cover over soil to block ground water   evaporation
   __In areas infested with rodents, apply a 1" to 2" layer of mesh-reinforced cement on ground
   __Add termite shields and/or other insect barriers as required by local conditions
__Typical crawl space ventilation
   __16" x 8" screen or louver vents between joists
   __Provide 2 sq. ft. of ventilation for each 25 sq. ft. of crawl space area
   __Provide one vent within 3' of each building corner
__Clearances to grade--typical minimum allowable distances:
   __Floor joists--minimum 18" to finish grade.
   __Wood girders--minimum 12" to finish grade.
   __Exterior finish--minimum 8" to finish grade.
   __Greater clearances are recommended to allow for soil build-ups during and after construction
   __Provide greater clearances for special extra-moist conditions, regional insect infestation, etc.

SMALL-SCALE GENERIC DETAILS

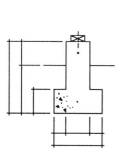

INTERIOR CONCRETE
FOOTING 1-Story
03305-1

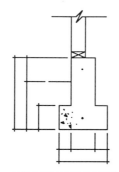

CONCRETE FOOTING
1-Story
03305-2

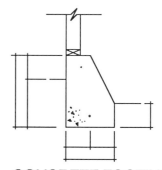

CONCRETE FOOTING
1-Story
03305-3

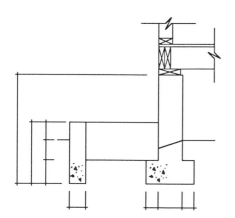

FOUNDATION CRAWL
SPACE ACCESS/AREAWAY 1-St.
03305-81

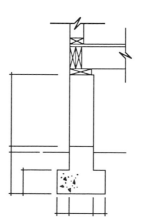

FOUNDATION CRAWL SPACE ACCESS
1 Story
03305-82

03305 (a) CRAWL SPACE ACCESS & CONC. FOOTINGS

FULL-SCALE GENERIC DETAILS

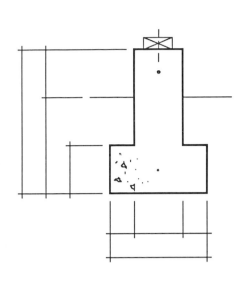

INTERIOR CONCRETE FOOTING 1-Story
1"=1'-0"   03305-1

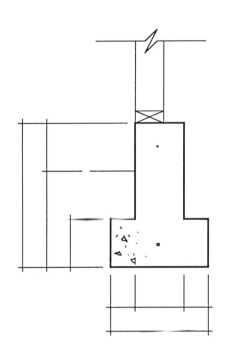

CONCRETE FOOTING 1-Story
1"=1'-0"   03305-2

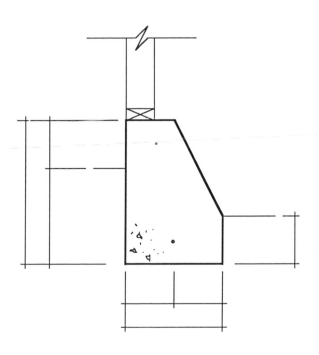

CONCRETE FOOTING 1-Story
1"=1'-0"   03305-3

FULL-SCALE GENERIC DETAILS continued

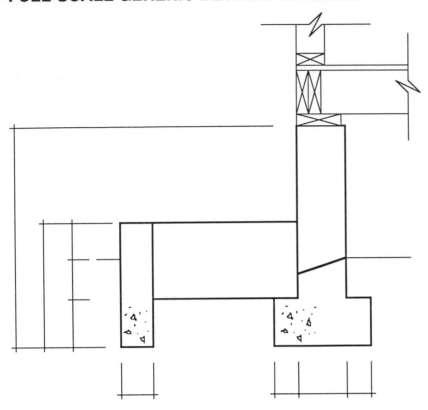

FOUNDATION CRAWL SPACE ACCESS/
AREAWAY 1-St.
1"=1'-0"   03305-81

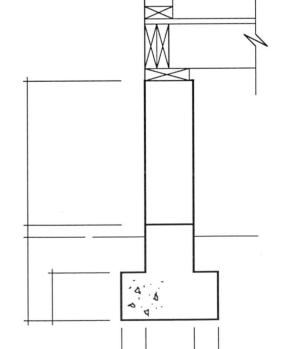

FOUNDATION CRAWL SPACE ACCESS
1 Story
1"=1'-0"   03305-82

03305 (a) CRAWL SPACE ACCESS & CONC. FOOTINGS

NOTATION CHECKLIST,
SAMPLE NOTES

2 X STUDS @ "O.C.
2 X PLATE
SUBFLOOR
2 X SOLID BLOCKING
2 X FLOOR JOISTS @ "O.C.
MUDSILL W/ LEVELING GROUT
ANCHOR BOLTS
REINFORCING BARS
EXTERIOR FINISH GRADE
INTERIOR FINISH GRADE--CRAWL SPACE
INSULATION
TERMITE SHIELD
RODENT BARRIER
VAPOR BARRIER W/ SAND COVER
FOOTING DRAIN TILE
CONCRETE SLAB
WELDED WIRE MESH REINFORCING
WATERPROOF MEMBRANE
CRUSHED ROCK OR TAMPED SAND
STEEL DOWELS
CONCRETE FOOTING
CONCRETE FOOTING REINFORCING BARS
FILLED & TAMPED EARTH

2 X STUDS @ "O.C.
2 X BOTTOM PLATE
SUBFLOOR
DOUBLE 2 X HEADER
2 X FLOOR JOISTS @ "O.C.
MUD SILL @ FOUNDATION WALL
CRAWL SPACE ACCESS OPENING
GRADE
AREAWAY
AREAWAY CONCRETE RETAINING WALL
2" RIGID INSULATION (@ foundation wall or grade
    beam)
DAMPROOFING (@ foundation wall or grade beam)
#15 FELT (over fill surrounding drain tile)
4" DRAIN TILE, SLOPE 1/8" PER 12"
POROUS GRANULAR FILL (minimum: 12" above,
    6" below, & 6" on either side of drain tile)
BACKFILL

03305 (b) CONCRETE FOOTINGS

FULL-SCALE GENERIC DETAILS continued

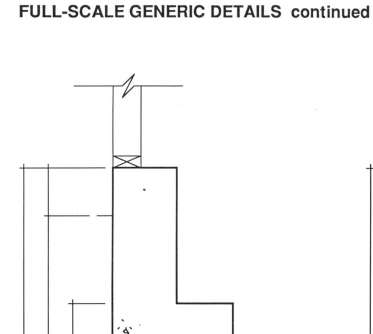

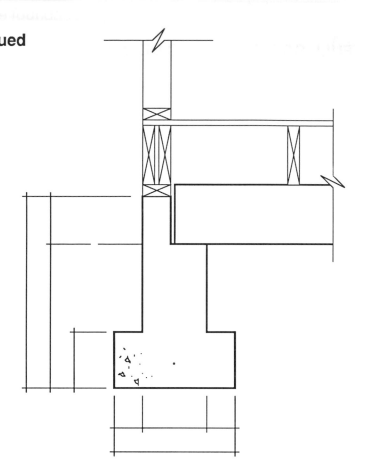

CONCRETE FOOTING
2-Story
1"=1'-0"   03305-9

CONC. FOOTING W/ GIRDER POCKET
1 Story
1"=1'-0"   03305-11

03305 (b) CONCRETE FOOTINGS

NOTATION CHECKLIST, SAMPLE NOTES

2 X   STUDS @   "O.C.
2 X   PLATE
SUBFLOOR
2 X   SOLID BLOCKING
2 X   FLOOR JOISTS @   "O.C.
MUDSILL W/ LEVELING GROUT
ANCHOR BOLTS
REINFORCING BARS
EXTERIOR FINISH GRADE
INTERIOR FINISH GRADE--CRAWL SPACE
INSULATION
TERMITE SHIELD
RODENT BARRIER
VAPOR BARRIER W/ SAND COVER
FOOTING DRAIN TILE
CONCRETE SLAB
WELDED WIRE MESH REINFORCING
WATERPROOF MEMBRANE
CRUSHED ROCK OR TAMPED SAND
STEEL DOWELS
CONCRETE FOOTING
CONCRETE FOOTING REINFORCING BARS
FILLED & TAMPED EARTH

2" RIGID INSUL.(@foundation wall/grade beam)
DAMPROOFING (@foundation wall/grade beam)
#15 FELT (over fill surrounding drain tile)
4" DRAIN TILE, SLOPE1/8" PER 12"
POROUS GRANULAR FILL (typ. min.: 12" above,
    6" below, & 6" on sides of drain tile)
6" COMPACTED EARTH FILL
BACKFILL
FINISH GRADE ELEV.
FINISH FLOOR ELEV.
GRADE BEAM
CONC. FTG. W/#4 REBARS @12"O.C. EA. WAY
1/4" LEVELING PLATE ON
    3/4" NON-SHRINK GROUT
3/4" DIA. ANCHOR BOLTS 14" LONG
1/2" DIA. ANCHOR BOLTS 10" LONG
#3 TIES @ 10" O.C.
2 X 4 KEYWAY
PEDESTAL
BOTTOM OF FOOTING ELEV.
COLUMN CENTER LINE
CONCRETE PIER
4 X 4 POST OR 4 X 8 BEAM ON COL. BASE

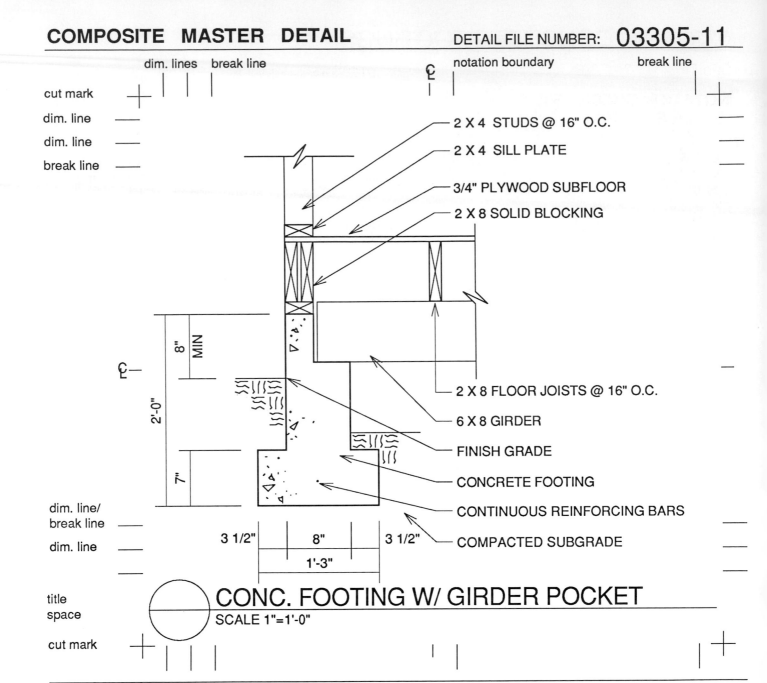

dim. lines   break line

notation boundary   break line

cut mark

dim. line

dim. line

break line

2 X 4 STUDS @ 16" O.C.

2 X 4 SILL PLATE

3/4" PLYWOOD SUBFLOOR

2 X 8 SOLID BLOCKING

8" MIN

2'-0"

7"

2 X 8 FLOOR JOISTS @ 16" O.C.

6 X 8 GIRDER

FINISH GRADE

CONCRETE FOOTING

CONTINUOUS REINFORCING BARS

dim. line/
break line

dim. line

COMPACTED SUBGRADE

3 1/2"   8"   3 1/2"

1'-3"

title
space

CONC. FOOTING W/ GIRDER POCKET

SCALE 1"=1'-0"

cut mark

DETAIL INFORMATION
References, jobsite feedback, job history

03305 (c) CONCRETE FOOTINGS

See DETAIL DATA CHECKLIST for concrete foundations preceding 03305(a)

DETAIL DATA CHECKLIST

FOOTINGS WITH SLAB FLOORS
__T-shaped system
    __Two-pour system with foundation poured first and the slab afterward
    __Place joints at intersections between floor and wall plane
__Interior bearing footings
    __Depth should match exterior footings
    __Avoid unbalanced, concentrated interior/exterior wall loads on soil
__ Interior nonbearing footings
    __Carry only the loads of walls above
    __Minimum thickness as required to accommodate anchor bolt--3" to 4" cover each side

SMALL-SCALE GENERIC DETAILS

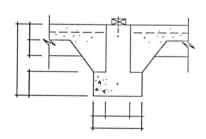

CONCRETE FOOTING
W/ SLAB 1 Story
03305-21

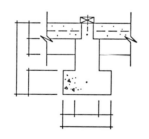

CONCRETE FOOTING
W/ SLAB 1 Story
03305-22

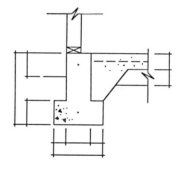

CONCRETE FOOTING
W/ SLAB 1 Story
03305-23

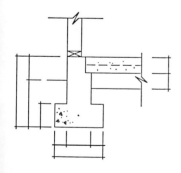

CONCRETE FOOTING
W/ SLAB 1 Story
03305-24

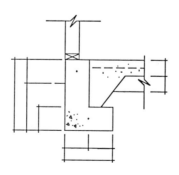

CONCRETE FOOTING
W/ SLAB 1 Story
03305-25

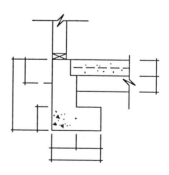

CONCRETE FOOTING
W/ SLAB 1 Story
03305-26

FULL-SCALE GENERIC DETAILS

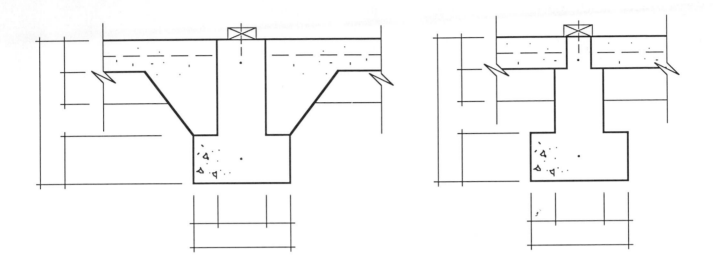

CONCRETE FOOTING W/ SLAB 1 Story
1"=1'-0"   03305-21

CONCRETE FOOTING W/ SLAB 1 Story
1"=1'-0"   03305-22

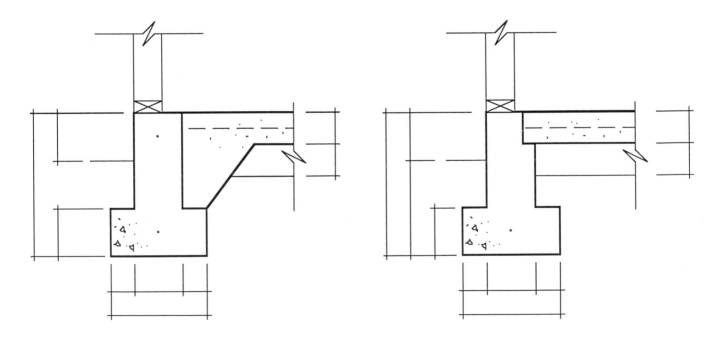

CONCRETE FOOTING W/ SLAB 1 Story
1"=1'-0"   03305-23

CONCRETE FOOTING W/ SLAB 1 Story
1"=1'-0"   03305-24

03305 (c) CONCRETE FOOTINGS

FULL-SCALE GENERIC DETAILS continued

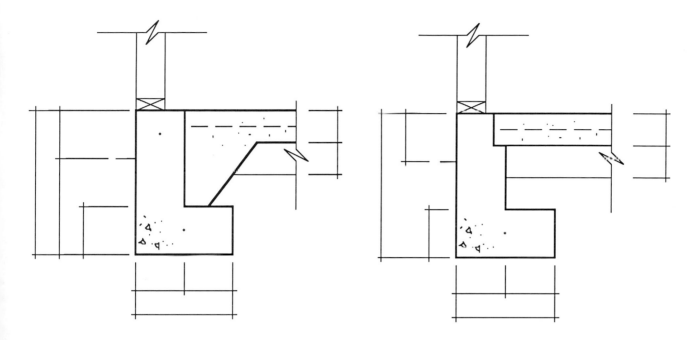

CONCRETE FOOTING W/ SLAB 1 Story
1"=1'-0"   03305-25

CONCRETE FOOTING W/ SLAB 1 Story
1"=1'-0"   03305-26

03305 (c) CONCRETE FOOTINGS

NOTATION CHECKLIST,
SAMPLE NOTES

2 X STUDS @ "0.C.
2 X PLATE
SUBFLOOR
2 X SOLID BLOCKING
2 X FLOOR JOISTS @ "O.C.
MUDSILL W/ LEVELING GROUT
ANCHOR BOLTS
REINFORCING BARS
EXTERIOR FINISH GRADE
INTERIOR FINISH GRADE--CRAWL SPACE
INSULATION
TERMITE SHIELD
RODENT BARRIER
VAPOR BARRIER W/ SAND COVER
FOOTING DRAIN TILE
CONCRETE SLAB
WELDED WIRE MESH REINFORCING
WATERPROOF MEMBRANE
CRUSHED ROCK OR TAMPED SAND
STEEL DOWELS
CONCRETE FOOTING
CONCRETE FOOTING REINFORCING BARS
FILLED & TAMPED EARTH
CONC. SLAB, SEE PLAN FOR REINF.
6" COMPACTED FILL
6" MIN. GRAVEL
REINFORCING BARS
CONT. ANGLES EMBEDDED IN SLAB
    W/ANCHORS
VAPOR BARRIER
NEW COMPACTED FILL
4" CONC. SLAB W/ 6X6-#10/10 W.W.M.
6" CONC. SLAB, SEE FOUNDATION PLAN
    FOR REINF.
#3 @ 12" O.C.
#4 @ 16" O.C. EACH WAY
FORMED METAL KEYED JOINT
1 X 2 SHEAR KEY
DOWELS X @ O.C.
1/8" SAWED JOINT, FILL W/ JOINT FILLER
1/4" X 1/4" SAWED EXP. CONTRACTION JOINT
1/2" ISOLATION JOINT W/ SEALER
1/2" PREFORMED EXP. JOINT FILLER
STOP SLAB REINF. @ JOINT.
FINISH FLOOR
1/2" PREMOLDED FILLER & SEALANT
SEALANT
CONTROL JOINT OR CONSTRUCTION JOINT
2 X 4 SOLE ON 30# FELT

2" RIGID INSUL.(@foundation wall/grade beam)
DAMPROOFING (@foundation wall/grade beam)
#15 FELT (over fill surrounding drain tile)
MIN #12 RAG ROOFING FELT(over fill @drain)
4" PERFERATED PIPE, 1/8" PER FOOT
    MIN. SLOPE TO OUTLET OR DAYLIGHT
4" DRAIN TILE, SLOPE1/8" PER 12"
POUR0US GRANULAR FILL (typ. min.: 12" above,
    6" below, & 6" on sides of drain tile)
6" COMPACTED EARTH FILL
BACKFILL
FINISH GRADE ELEV.
FINISH FLOOR ELEV.
GRADE BEAM
CONC. FTG. W/#4@12"O.C. EA. WAY
1/4" LEVELING PLATE ON
    3/4" NON-SHRINK GROUT
BASE PLATE & LEVELING PLATE, SEE SCHED.
3/4" DIA. ANCHOR BOLTS 14" LONG
#3 TIES @ 10" O.C.
#4 CONT.
2 X 4 KEYWAY
PEDESTAL
BOTTOM OF FOOTING EL.
FOOTING, SEE PLAN FOR MARK / SEE
    SCHED FOR SIZE & REINF.
COLUMN CENTER LINE
CONCRETE PIER
4 X 4 POST OR 4 X 8 BEAM ON COL. BASE

03305 (d) CONCRETE FOOTINGS

See DETAIL DATA CHECKLIST for concrete foundations preceding 03305(a)

DETAIL DATA CHECKLIST

FOOTINGS WITH SLAB FLOORS
__T-shaped system
   __Two-pour system with foundation poured first and the slab afterward
   __Place joints at intersections between floor and wall plane
__Interior bearing footings
   __Depth should match exterior footings
   __Avoid unbalanced, concentrated interior/exterior wall loads on soil
__Interior nonbearing footings
   __Carry only the loads of walls above
   __Minimum thickness as required to accommodate anchor bolt--3" to 4" cover each side

SMALL-SCALE GENERIC DETAILS

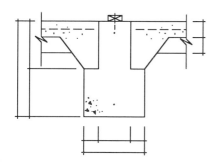

CONCRETE FOOTING
W/ SLAB 2 Story
03305-31

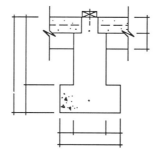

CONCRETE FOOTING
W/ SLAB 2 Story
03305-32

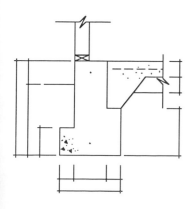

CONCRETE FOOTING
W/ SLAB 2 Story
03305-33

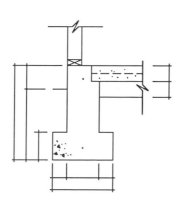

CONCRETE FOOTING
W/ SLAB 2 Story
03305-34

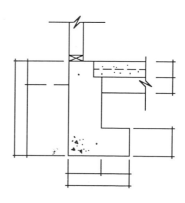

CONCRETE FOOTING
W/ SLAB 2 Story
03305-35

03305 (d) CONCRETE FOOTINGS

FULL-SCALE GENERIC DETAILS

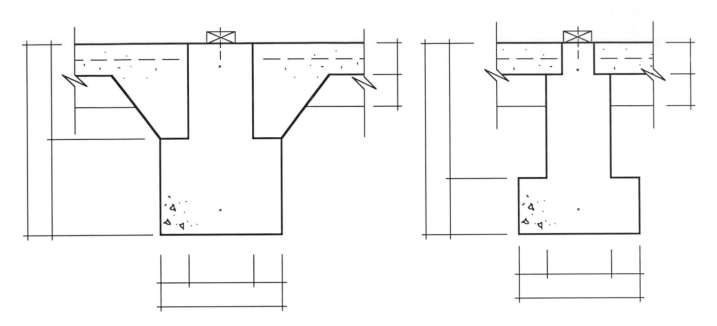

CONCRETE FOOTING W/ SLAB 2 Story
1"=1'-0"   03305-31

CONCRETE FOOTING W/ SLAB 2 Story
1"=1'-0"   03305-32

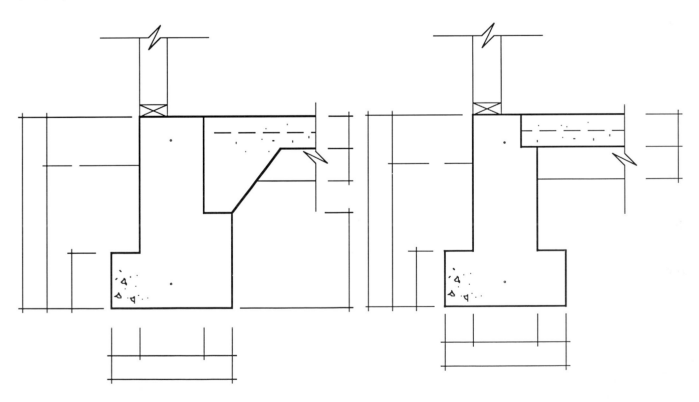

CONCRETE FOOTING W/ SLAB 2 Story
1"=1'-0"   03305-33

CONCRETE FOOTING W/ SLAB 2 Story
1"=1'-0"   03305-34

FULL-SCALE DETAILS continued

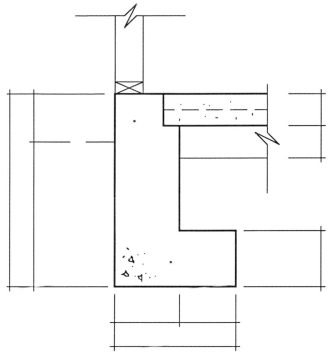

CONCRETE FOOTING W/ SLAB 2 Story
1"=1'-0"   03305-35

NOTATION CHECKLIST

2 X   STUDS @   "O.C.
2 X   PLATE
SUBFLOOR
2 X   SOLID BLOCKING
2 X   FLOOR JOISTS @   "O.C.
MUDSILL W/ LEVELING GROUT
ANCHOR BOLTS
REINFORCING BARS
EXTERIOR FINISH GRADE
INTERIOR FINISH GRADE--CRAWL SPACE
INSULATION
TERMITE SHIELD
RODENT BARRIER
VAPOR BARRIER W/ SAND COVER
FOOTING DRAIN TILE
CONCRETE SLAB
WELDED WIRE MESH REINFORCING
WATERPROOF MEMBRANE
CRUSHED ROCK OR TAMPED SAND
STEEL DOWELS
CONCRETE FOOTING
CONCRETE FOOTING REINFORCING BARS
FILLED & TAMPED EARTH

SEE 03305 (c) FOR SAMPLE NOTATION

03305 (e) CONCRETE FOOTINGS

FULL-SCALE GENERIC DETAILS

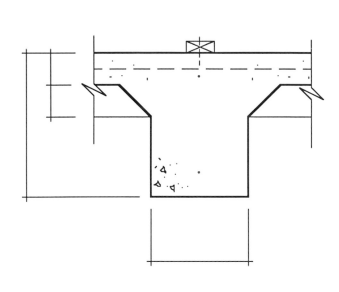

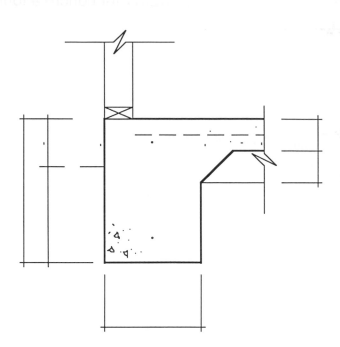

CONCRETE FOOTING & SLAB 1 Story
1"=1'-0"   03305-41

CONCRETE FOOTING & SLAB 1 Story
1"=1'-0"   03305-42

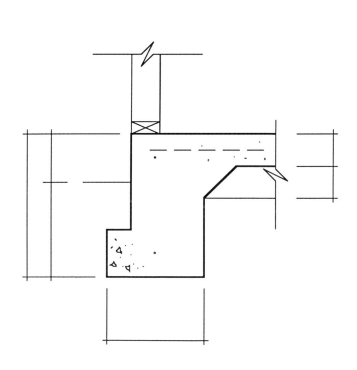

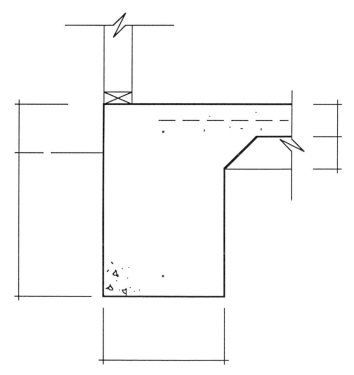

CONCRETE FOOTING & SLAB 1 Story
1"=1'-0"   03305-43

CONCRETE FOOTING & SLAB 2 Story
1"=1'-0"   03305-47

03305 (e) CONCRETE FOOTINGS

FULL-SCALE DETAILS continued

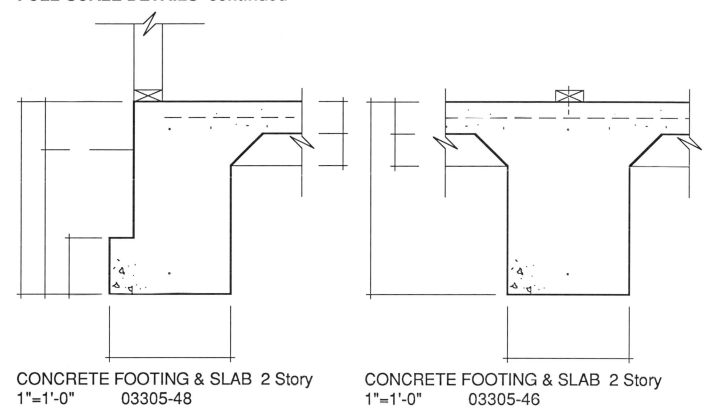

CONCRETE FOOTING & SLAB 2 Story
1"=1'-0"   03305-48

CONCRETE FOOTING & SLAB 2 Story
1"=1'-0"   03305-46

NOTATION CHECKLIST

2 X STUDS @ "O.C.
2 X PLATE
SUBFLOOR
2 X SOLID BLOCKING
2 X FLOOR JOISTS @ "O.C.
MUDSILL W/ LEVELING GROUT
ANCHOR BOLTS
REINFORCING BARS
EXTERIOR FINISH GRADE
INTERIOR FINISH GRADE--CRAWL SPACE
INSULATION
TERMITE SHIELD
RODENT BARRIER
VAPOR BARRIER W/ SAND COVER
FOOTING DRAIN TILE
CONCRETE SLAB
WELDED WIRE MESH REINFORCING
WATERPROOF MEMBRANE
CRUSHED ROCK OR TAMPED SAND
STEEL DOWELS
CONCRETE FOOTING
CONCRETE FOOTING REINFORCING BARS
FILLED & TAMPED EARTH

SEE 03305 (c) FOR SAMPLE NOTES

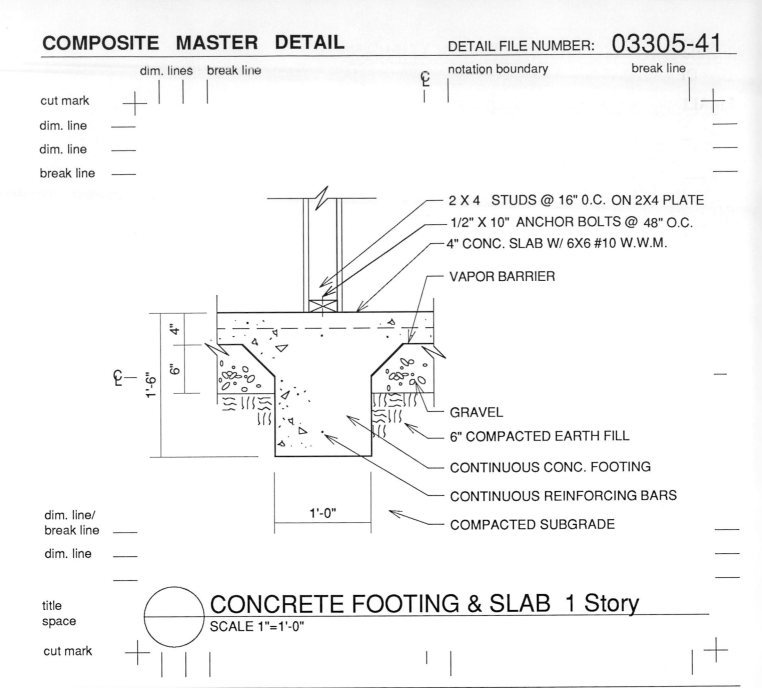

dim. lines   break line

notation boundary   break line

cut mark

dim. line

dim. line

break line

2 X 4 STUDS @ 16" O.C. ON 2X4 PLATE

1/2" X 10" ANCHOR BOLTS @ 48" O.C.

4" CONC. SLAB W/ 6X6 #10 W.W.M.

VAPOR BARRIER

GRAVEL

6" COMPACTED EARTH FILL

CONTINUOUS CONC. FOOTING

CONTINUOUS REINFORCING BARS

COMPACTED SUBGRADE

4"

6"

1'-6"

1'-0"

dim. line/
break line

dim. line

title
space

CONCRETE FOOTING & SLAB 1 Story

SCALE 1"=1'-0"

cut mark

DETAIL INFORMATION
References, jobsite feedback, job history

03305 (f) CONCRETE FOOTINGS

See DETAIL DATA CHECKLIST for concrete foundations preceding 03305(a)

SMALL-SCALE GENERIC DETAILS

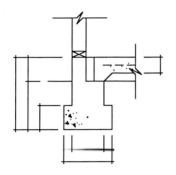

CONCRETE FOOTING
W/ SLAB 1 Story
03305-51

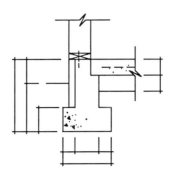

CONCRETE FOOTING
W/ SLAB 1 Story
03305-52

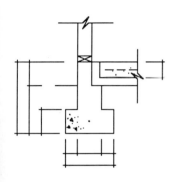

CONCRETE FOOTING
W/ SLAB 1 Story
03305-53

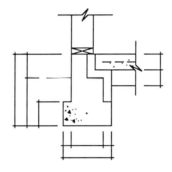

CONCRETE FOOTING
W/ SLAB 1 Story
03305-54

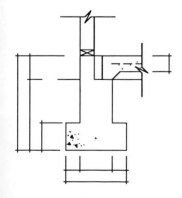

CONCRETE FOOTING
W/ SLAB 2 Story
03305-56

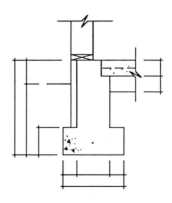

CONCRETE FOOTING
W/ SLAB 2 Story
03305-57

03305 (f) CONCRETE FOOTINGS

FULL-SCALE GENERIC DETAILS

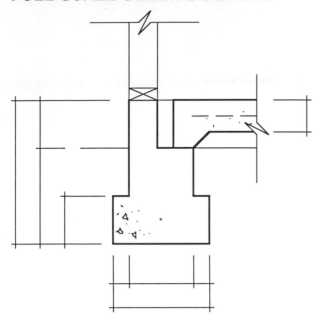

CONCRETE FOOTING
W/ SLAB 1 Story
1"=1'-0" 03305-51

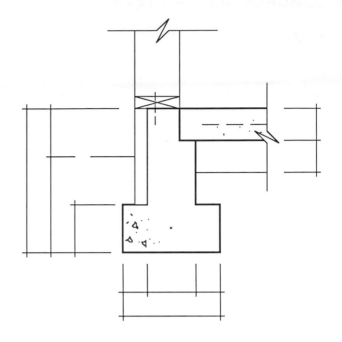

CONCRETE FOOTING
W/ SLAB 1 Story
1"=1'-0" 03305-52

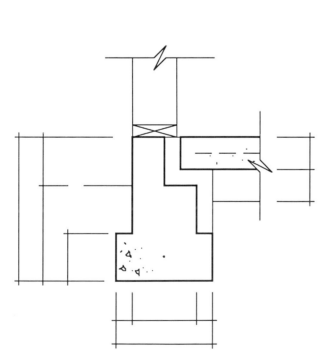

CONCRETE FOOTING
W/ SLAB 1 Story
1"=1'-0"   03305-54

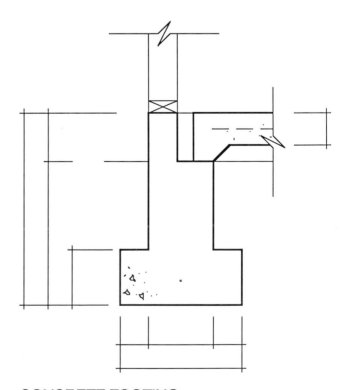

CONCRETE FOOTING
W/ SLAB 2 Story
1"=1'-0"   03305-56

FULL-SCALE GENERIC DETAILS continued

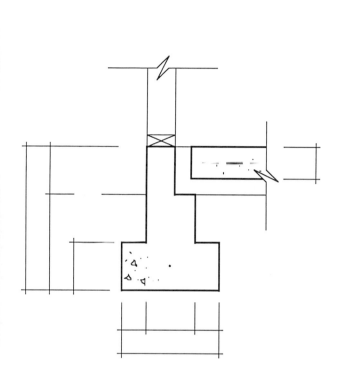

CONCRETE FOOTING
W/ SLAB 1 Story
1"=1'-0"   03305-53

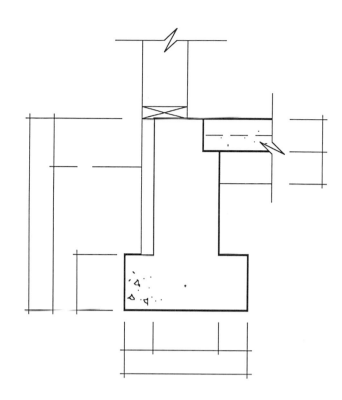

CONCRETE FOOTING
W/ SLAB 2 Story
1"=1'-0"   03305-57

NOTATION CHECKLIST

2 X STUDS @   "O.C.
2 X PLATE
SUBFLOOR
2 X SOLID BLOCKING
2 X FLOOR JOISTS @   "O.C.
MUDSILL W/ LEVELING GROUT
ANCHOR BOLTS
REINFORCING BARS
EXTERIOR FINISH GRADE
INTERIOR FINISH GRADE--CRAWL SPACE
INSULATION
TERMITE SHIELD
RODENT BARRIER

VAPOR BARRIER W/ SAND COVER
FOOTING DRAIN TILE
CONCRETE SLAB
WELDED WIRE MESH REINFORCING
WATERPROOF MEMBRANE
CRUSHED ROCK OR TAMPED SAND
STEEL DOWELS
CONCRETE FOOTING
CONCRETE FOOTING REINFORCING BARS
FILLED & TAMPED EARTH

SEE 03305 (c) FOR SAMPLE NOTES

03305 (g) CONCRETE FOOTINGS

See DETAIL DATA CHECKLIST for concrete foundations preceding 03305(a)

SMALL-SCALE GENERIC DETAILS

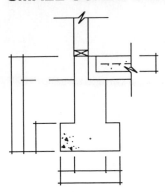

CONCRETE FOOTING
W/ SLAB 2 Story
03305-58

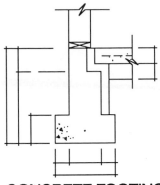

CONCRETE FOOTING
W/ SLAB 2 Story
03305-59

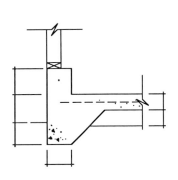

CONC. FOOTING & SLAB
Garage 1 Story
03305-61

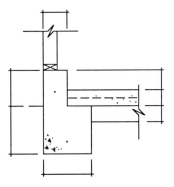

CONC. FOOTING
W/ SLAB Garage 1 Story
03305-63

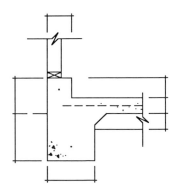

CONC. FOOTING & SLAB
Garage 1 Story
03305-62

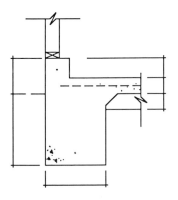

CONC. FOOTING & SLAB
Garage 2 Story
03305-66

03305 (g) CONCRETE FOOTINGS

FULL-SCALE GENERIC DETAILS

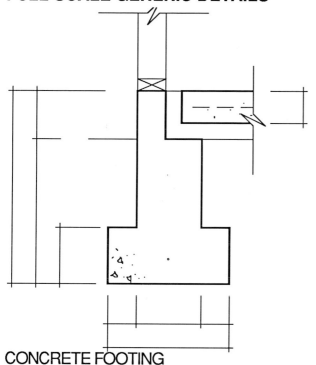

CONCRETE FOOTING
W/ SLAB 2 Story
1"=1'-0" 03305-58

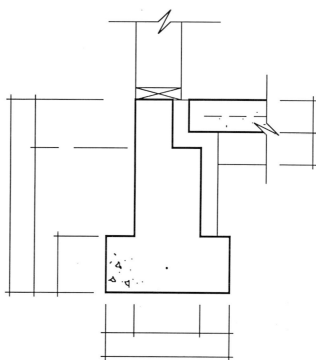

CONCRETE FOOTING
W/ SLAB 2 Story
1"=1'-0" 03305-59

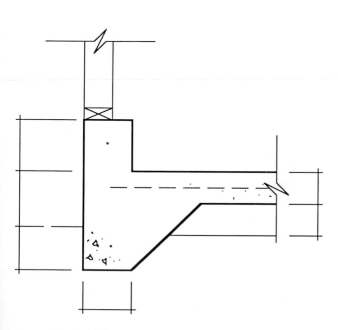

CONC. FOOTING & SLAB
Garage 1 Story
1"=1'-0"   03305-61

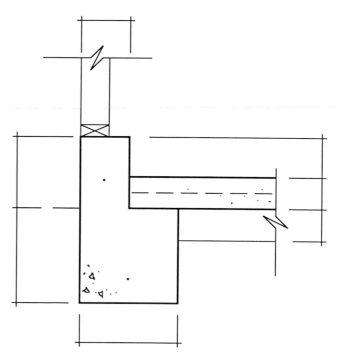

CONC. FOOTING
W/ SLAB Garage 1 Story
1"=1'-0"   03305-63

03305 (g) CONCRETE FOOTINGS

FULL-SCALE GENERIC DETAILS continued

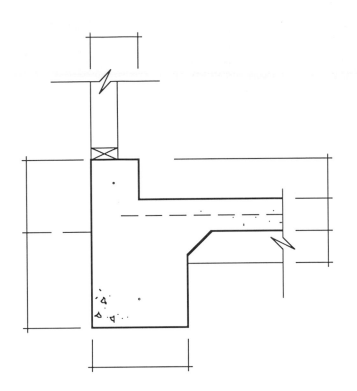

CONC. FOOTING & SLAB
Garage 1 Story
1"=1'-0"   03305-62

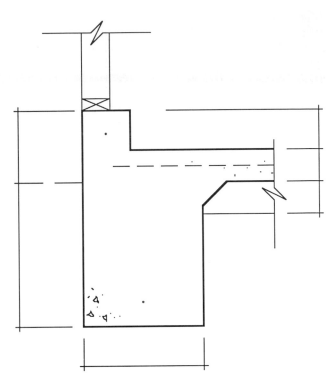

CONC. FOOTING & SLAB
Garage 2 Story
1"=1'-0"   03305-66

NOTATION CHECKLIST

2 X STUDS @   "O.C.
2 X PLATE
SUBFLOOR
2 X SOLID BLOCKING
2 X FLOOR JOISTS @   "O.C.
MUDSILL W/ LEVELING GROUT
ANCHOR BOLTS
REINFORCING BARS
EXTERIOR FINISH GRADE
INTERIOR FINISH GRADE--CRAWL SPACE
INSULATION
TERMITE SHIELD
RODENT BARRIER

VAPOR BARRIER W/ SAND COVER
FOOTING DRAIN TILE
CONCRETE SLAB
WELDED WIRE MESH REINFORCING
WATERPROOF MEMBRANE
CRUSHED ROCK OR TAMPED SAND
STEEL DOWELS
CONCRETE FOOTING
CONCRETE FOOTING REINFORCING BARS
FILLED & TAMPED EARTH

03305 (h) CONCRETE FOOTINGS

See DETAIL DATA CHECKLIST for concrete foundations preceding 03305(a)

DETAIL DATA CHECKLIST

GARAGE SLABS
__5" or 6" thick instead of 4"
__Slope slab to garage door and apron or to floor drain
__Slope apron slab 1" to 3" to driveway
__Separate apron from driveway slab with 1/2" construction joint

SMALL-SCALE GENERIC DETAILS

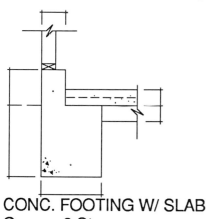

CONC. FOOTING W/ SLAB
Garage 2 Story
03305-67

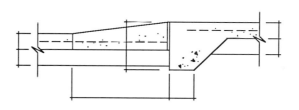

CONC. FOOTING/SLAB
W/ APRON Garage
03305-68

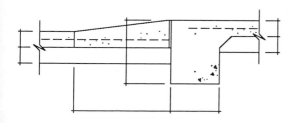

CONC. FOOTING/SLAB
W/ APRON Garage
03305-69

03305 (h) CONCRETE FOOTINGS

FULL-SCALE GENERIC DETAILS

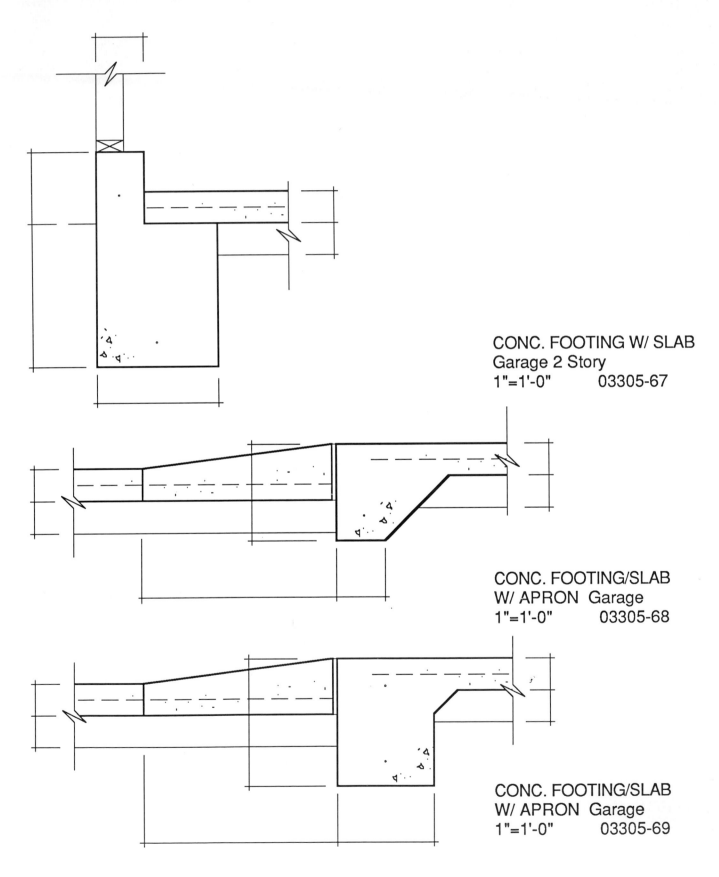

CONC. FOOTING W/ SLAB
Garage 2 Story
1"=1'-0"   03305-67

CONC. FOOTING/SLAB
W/ APRON Garage
1"=1'-0"   03305-68

CONC. FOOTING/SLAB
W/ APRON Garage
1"=1'-0"   03305-69

03305 (h) CONCRETE FOOTINGS

NOTATION CHECKLIST,
SAMPLE NOTES

2 X STUDS @ "O.C.
2 X PLATE
SUBFLOOR
2 X SOLID BLOCKING
2 X FLOOR JOISTS @ "O.C.
MUDSILL W/ LEVELING GROUT
ANCHOR BOLTS
REINFORCING BARS
EXTERIOR FINISH GRADE
INTERIOR FINISH GRADE--CRAWL SPACE
INSULATION
TERMITE SHIELD
RODENT BARRIER
VAPOR BARRIER W/ SAND COVER
FOOTING DRAIN TILE
CONCRETE SLAB
WELDED WIRE MESH REINFORCING
WATERPROOF MEMBRANE
CRUSHED ROCK OR TAMPED SAND
STEEL DOWELS
CONCRETE FOOTING
CONCRETE FOOTING REINFORCING BARS
FILLED & TAMPED EARTH

2" RIGID INSUL.(@foundation wall/grade beam)
DAMPROOFING (@foundation wall/grade beam)
#15 FELT (over fill surrounding drain tile)
4" DRAIN TILE, SLOPE1/8" PER 12"
POROUS GRANULAR FILL (typ. min.: 12" above,
    6" below, & 6" on sides of drain tile)
6" COMPACTED EARTH FILL
BACKFILL
FINISH GRADE ELEV.
FINISH FLOOR ELEV.
GRADE BEAM
CONC. FTG. W/#4 REBARS @12"O.C. EA. WAY
1/4" LEVELING PLATE ON
    3/4" NON-SHRINK GROUT
3/4" DIA. ANCHOR BOLTS 14" LONG
#3 TIES @ 10" O.C.
1/2" DIA. ANCHOR BOLTS 10" LONG
2 X 4 KEYWAY
PEDESTAL
BOTTOM OF FOOTING ELEV.
COLUMN CENTER LINE
CONCRETE PIER
4 X 4 POST OR 4 X 8 BEAM ON COL. BASE
CONC. SLAB, SEE PLAN FOR REINF.
6" COMPACTED FILL
6" MIN. GRAVEL
REINFORCING BARS
CONT. ANGLES EMBEDDED IN SLAB W/ ANCHORS
VAPOR BARRIER
NEW COMPACTED FILL
4" CONC. SLAB W/ 6X6-#10 W.W.M.
6" CONC. SLAB, SEE FOUNDATION PLAN FOR
    REINF.
#3 @ 12" O.C.
#4 @ 16" O.C. EACH WAY
FORMED METAL KEYED JOINT
1 X 2 SHEAR KEY
DOWELS X @   O.C.
1/8" SAWED JOINT, FILL W/ JOINT FILLER
1/4" X 1/4" SAWED EXP. CONTRACTION JOINT.
1/2" ISOLATION JOINT W/ SEALER
1/2" PREFORMED EXP. JOINT FILLER
CONTROL JOINT OR CONSTRUCTION JOINT
STOP SLAB REINF. @ JOINT.
FINISH FLOOR
SEALANT
2 X 4 SOLE ON 30
FELT
SLOPE APRON TO DRAIN AT SIDE

03305 (i) CONCRETE FOOTINGS

See DETAIL DATA CHECKLIST for concrete foundations preceding 03305(a)

DETAIL DATA CHECKLIST

GARAGE SLABS
__5" or 6" thick instead of 4"
__Slope slab to garage door and apron or to floor drain
__Slope apron slab 1" to 3" to driveway
__Separate apron from driveway slab with 1/2" construction joint

SMALL-SCALE GENERIC DETAILS

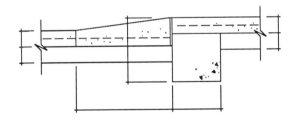

CONC. FOOTING/SLAB
W/ APRON Garage
03305-70

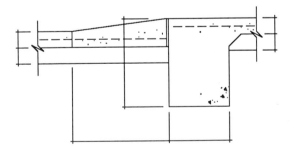

CONC. FOOTING/SLAB
W/ APRON Garage 2 Story
03305-69

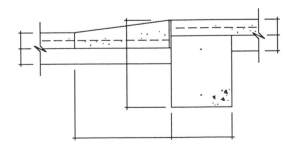

CONC. FOOTING/SLAB
W/ APRON Garage 2 story
03305-72

03305 (i) CONCRETE FOOTINGS

FULL-SCALE GENERIC DETAILS

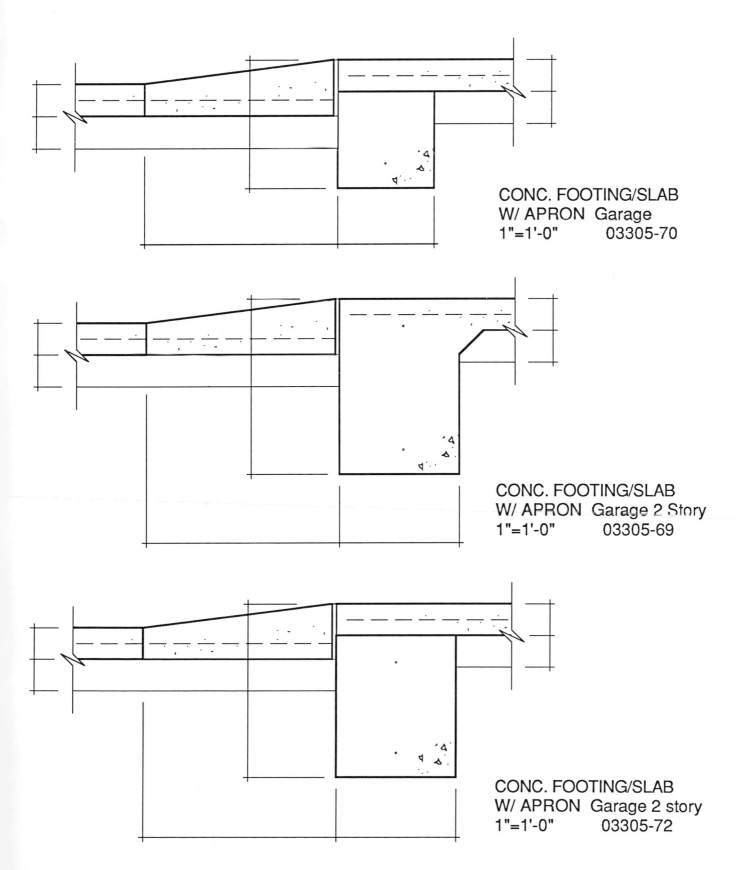

CONC. FOOTING/SLAB
W/ APRON Garage
1"=1'-0"   03305-70

CONC. FOOTING/SLAB
W/ APRON Garage 2 Story
1"=1'-0"   03305-69

CONC. FOOTING/SLAB
W/ APRON Garage 2 story
1"=1'-0"   03305-72

03305 (i) CONCRETE FOOTINGS

NOTATION CHECKLIST, SAMPLE NOTES

2 X   STUDS @   "O.C.
2 X   PLATE
SUBFLOOR
2 X   SOLID BLOCKING
2 X   FLOOR JOISTS @   "O.C.
MUDSILL W/ LEVELING GROUT
ANCHOR BOLTS
REINFORCING BARS
EXTERIOR FINISH GRADE
INTERIOR FINISH GRADE--CRAWL SPACE
INSULATION
TERMITE SHIELD
RODENT BARRIER
VAPOR BARRIER W/ SAND COVER
FOOTING DRAIN TILE
CONCRETE SLAB
WELDED WIRE MESH REINFORCING
WATERPROOF MEMBRANE
CRUSHED ROCK OR TAMPED SAND
STEEL DOWELS
CONCRETE FOOTING
CONCRETE FOOTING REINFORCING BARS
FILLED & TAMPED EARTH

2" RIGID INSUL.(@foundation wall/grade beam)
DAMPROOFING (@foundation wall/grade beam)
#15 FELT (over fill surrounding drain tile)
4" DRAIN TILE, SLOPE1/8" PER 12"
POROUS GRANULAR FILL (typ. min.: 12" above,
     6" below, & 6" on sides of drain tile)
6" COMPACTED EARTH FILL
BACKFILL
FINISH GRADE ELEV.
FINISH FLOOR ELEV.
GRADE BEAM
CONC. FTG. W/#4 REBARS @12"O.C. EA. WAY
1/4" LEVELING PLATE ON
     3/4" NON-SHRINK GROUT
3/4" DIA. ANCHOR BOLTS 14" LONG
1/2" DIA. ANCHOR BOLTS 10" LONG
#3 TIES @ 10" O.C.
2 X 4 KEYWAY
PEDESTAL
BOTTOM OF FOOTING EL.
COLUMN CENTER LINE
CONCRETE PIER
4 X 4 POST OR 4 X 8 BEAM ON COL. BASE
CONC. SLAB, SEE PLAN FOR REINF.
6" COMPACTED FILL
6" MIN. GRAVEL
REINFORCING BARS
CONT. ANGLES EMBEDDED IN SLAB W/ ANCHORS
VAPOR BARRIER
NEW COMPACTED FILL
4" CONC. SLAB W/ 6X6-#10 W.W.M.
6" CONC. SLAB, SEE FOUNDATION PLAN FOR
          REINF.
#3 @ 12" O.C.
#4 @ 16" O.C. EACH WAY
FORMED METAL KEYED JOINT
1 X 2 SHEAR KEY
DOWELS X @   O.C.
1/8" SAWED JOINT, FILL W/ JOINT FILLER
1/4" X 1/4" SAWED EXP. CONTRACTION JOINT.
1/2" ISOLATION JOINT W/ SEALER
CONTROL JOINT OR CONSTRUCTION JOINT
1/2" PREMOLDED FILLER & SEALANT
STOP SLAB REINF. @ JOINT.
FINISH FLOOR
SEALANT
2 X 4 SOLE ON 30# FELT
SLOPE APRON TO DRAIN AT SIDE

03305 (j) CONCRETE FOOTINGS W/ BRICK VENEER

See DETAIL DATA CHECKLIST for concrete foundations preceding 03305(a)

DETAIL DATA CHECKLIST

FOOTINGS WITH MASONRY WALLS
__Considerations for developing a footing for a masonry wall:
    __Weight being supported
    __Soil condition
__Two withe of bricks with solid grout in between rest on footing or on wall
__Use a key, or notched area at top of footing, to secure masonry wall

SMALL-SCALE GENERIC DETAILS

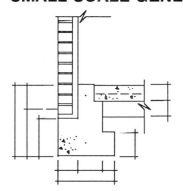

CONC. FOOTING/SLAB
W/BRICK VENEER 1-Story
03305-91

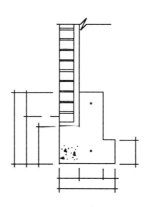

CONC. FOOTING
W/BRICK VENEER 1-Story
03305-92

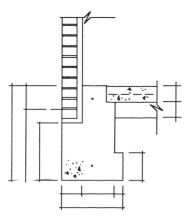

CONC. FOOTING/SLAB
W/BRICK VENEER 2-Story
03305-93

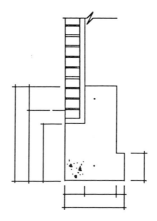

CONC. FOOTING
W/BRICK VENEER 2-Story
03305-94

03306 CONCRETE FOUNDATION WALLS

See DETAIL DATA CHECKLIST for concrete foundations preceding 03305 (a)

SMALL-SCALE GENERIC DETAILS

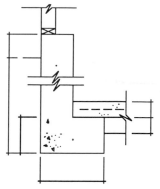

CONC. FOUNDATION WALL
Basement
03306-1

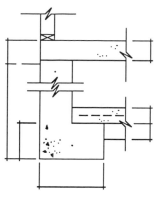

CONC. FOUNDATION WALL
Basement/Slab 1st. Fl.
03306-2

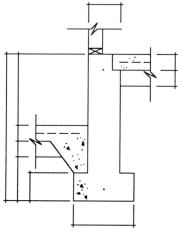

CONC. FOUNDATION WALL
Split Level
03306-11

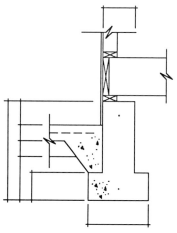

CONC. FOUNDATION WALL
Split Level
03306-12

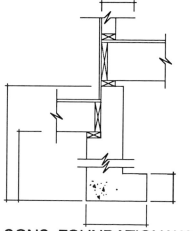

CONC. FOUNDATION WALL
Split Level
03306-13

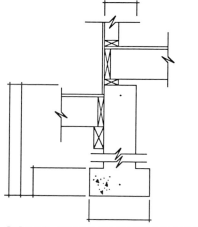

CONC. FOUNDATION WALL
Split Level
03306-14

03306 CONCRETE FOUNDATION WALLS

FULL-SCALE GENERIC DETAILS

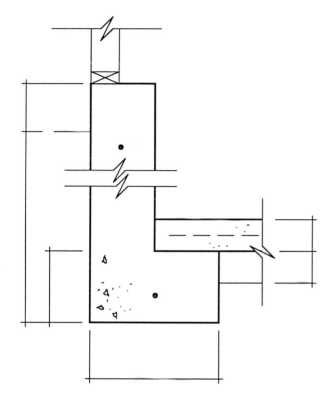

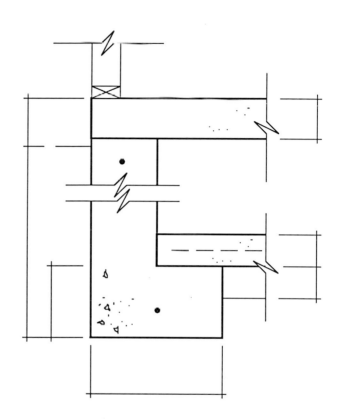

CONC. FOUNDATION WALL
Basement
1"=1'-0"   03306-1

CONC. FOUNDATION WALL
Basement/Slab 1st. Fl.
1"=1'-0"   03306-2

03306 CONCRETE FOUNDATION WALLS

FULL-SCALE GENERIC DETAILS continued

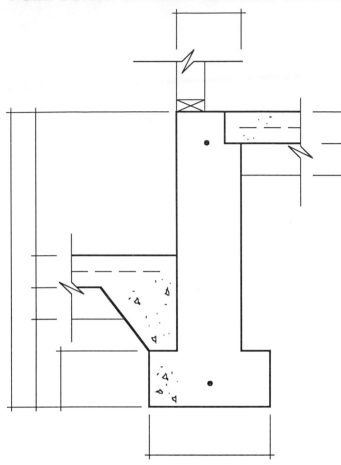

CONC. FOUNDATION WALL
Split Level
1"=1'-0"   03306-11

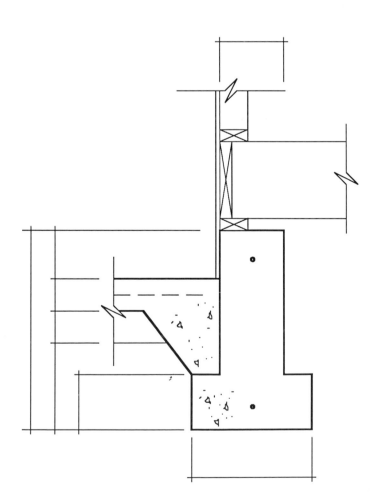

CONC. FOUNDATION WALL
Split Level
1"=1'-0"   03306-12

03306 CONCRETE FOUNDATION WALLS

FULL-SCALE GENERIC DETAILS continued

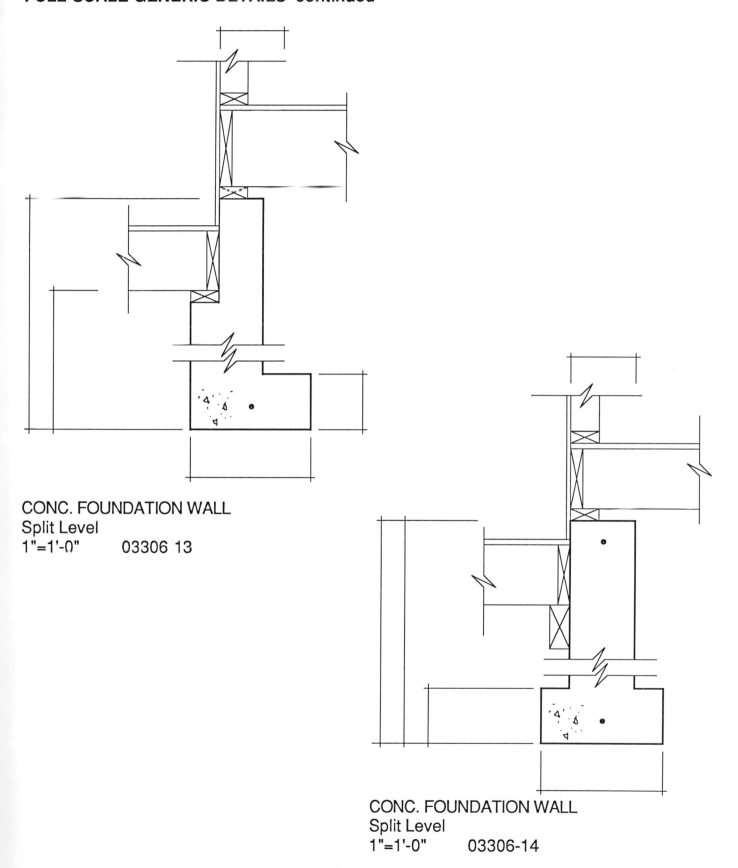

CONC. FOUNDATION WALL
Split Level
1"=1'-0"   03306 13

CONC. FOUNDATION WALL
Split Level
1"=1'-0"   03306-14

**NOTATION CHECKLIST,
 SAMPLE NOTES**

2 X   STUDS @ "O.C.
2 X   PLATE
SUBFLOOR
2 X   SOLID BLOCKING
2 X   FLOOR JOISTS @   "O.C.
MUDSILL W/ LEVELING GROUT
ANCHOR BOLTS
CONCRETE FOUNDATION WALL
NAILER
CONSTRUCTION JOINT
STEEL DOWELS
WELDED WIRE MESH REINFORCING
WATERPROOF MEMBRANE
CRUSHED ROCK OR TAMPED SAND
CONCRETE FOOTING
CONCRETE FOOTING REINFORCING BARS
FILLED & TAMPED EARTH
VAPOR BARRIER W.SAND COVER
FOOTING DRAIN TILE

2" RIGID INSUL.(@foundation wall)
DAMPROOFING (@foundation wall)
#15 FELT (over fill surrounding drain tile)
4" PERFORATED PIPE, 1/8" PER FOOT MIN. SLOPE
4" DRAIN TILE, SLOPE1/8" PER 12"
POROUS GRANULAR FILL
6" COMPACTED EARTH FILL
BACKFILL
FINISH GRADE ELEV.
FINISH FLOOR ELEV.
CONC. FTG. W/#4 REBARS @12"O.C. EA. WAY.
2 X 4 KEYWAY
BOTTOM OF FOOTING ELEV.
FOOTING, SEE PLAN FOR MARK / SEE
     SCHED. FOR SIZE & REINF.
#5 @ 10" O.C. HORIZ.
#5 @ 7" O.C. VERT. EXTEND THRU PIERS
PROVIDE CORNER BARS @ ALL EXT. & INT. CORNERS
CONCRETE FOUNDATION WALL
DBL. 2 X 6 TOP PLATE
2 X 6 SILL W/ POWER DRIVEN ANCHORS 48" O.C.
PVC WATERSTOP TYP @ CONSTRUCTION JOINT
SEE SPECS FOR WATERPROOFING

03308 CONCRETE SLABS ON GRADE

DETAIL DATA CHECKLIST

CONCRETE SLABS & FOOTINGS
__Slab on grade & reinforcing
   __Light frame buildings typically have a 4" thick slab w/ 6"x6" #10 welded wire mesh
   __Larger building slabs are 6" and thicker as required by floor loads and soil conditions
__Slab sub-base
   __Typically 4" of crushed rock over undisturbed earth
      __Tamp or otherwise compact loose soil as per engineer's recommendation
   __Add a layer of polyethelene over the rock sub-base to prevent excessive loss of water from the slab concrete mix
__Slab control joints
   __Typically tool-cut to 1/3rd slab depth every 20' both ways to direct and control cracks
   __Provide control joints around piers and columns
__Slab construction joints
   __Typically required at 20' to 30' max. both ways and at intersections with other construction
__Doweled joints
   __For movement joints, use graphite or other lubrication at one end for a bond break that facilitates free expansion
      and contraction
   __Size and space dowels as per engineer's recommendations
   __Use dowels to connect two different pours of concrete
   __Put short rods into first slab and leave exposed for second adjacent pour
__Garage slabs
   __5" or 6" thick instead of 4"
   __Slope slab to garage door and apron or to floor drain
   __Slope apron slab 1" to 3" to driveway
   __Separate apron from driveway slab with 1/2" construction joint

See other Detail Data for concrete foundations preceding 05505 (a)

SMALL-SCALE GENERIC DETAILS

CONCRETE SLAB ON GRADE
T & G Joint
03308-1

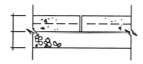

CONCRETE SLAB ON GRADE
Butt Joint
03308-2

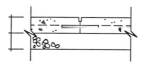

CONCRETE SLAB ON GRADE
Construction Joint
03308-3

CONCRETE SLAB ON GRADE
Control Joint
03308-4

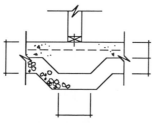

CONCRETE SLAB
& FOOTING
03308-5

CONCRETE SLAB
ON GRADE
03308-6

FULL-SCALE GENERIC DETAILS

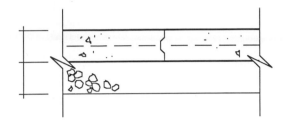

CONCRETE SLAB ON GRADE
T & G Joint
1"=1'-0"   03308-1

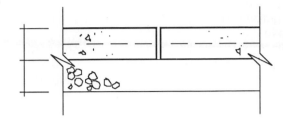

CONCRETE SLAB ON GRADE
Butt Jt.
1"=1'-0"   03308-2

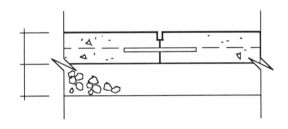

CONCRETE SLAB ON GRADE
Construction Joint
1"=1'-0"   03308-3

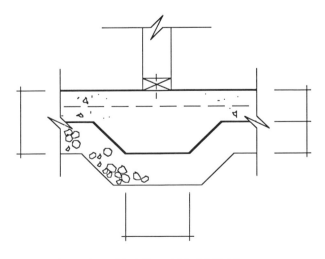

CONCRETE SLAB & FOOTING
1"=1'-0"   03308-5

CONCRETE SLAB ON GRADE
Control Joint
1"=1'-0"   03308-4

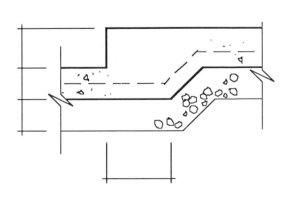

CONCRETE SLAB ON GRADE
1"=1'-0"   03308-6

03308 CONCRETE SLABS ON GRADE

NOTATION CHECKLIST,
SAMPLE NOTES

JOINT--CONTROL/CONSTRUCTION/EXPANSION
CONCRETE SLAB
WELDED WIRE MESH REINFORCING
STEEL DOWEL CONNECTORS
WATERPROOF MEMBRANE
CRUSHED ROCK OR TAMPED SAND
FILLED & TAMPED EARTH

CONC. SLAB, SEE PLAN FOR REINF.
6" COMPACTED FILL
6" MIN. GRAVEL
REINFORCING BARS
CONT. ANGLES EMBEDDED IN SLAB W/ ANCHORS
VAPOR BARRIER
NEW COMPACTED FILL
4" CONC. SLAB W/ 6X6-#10 W.W.M.
6" CONC. SLAB, SEE FOUNDATION PLAN FOR REINF.
#3 @ 12" O.C.
#4 @ 16" O.C. EACH WAY
FORMED METAL KEYED JOINT
1 X 2 SHEAR KEY
DOWELS X @   O.C.
1/8" SAWED JOINT, FILL W/ JOINT FILLER
1/4" X 1/4" SAWED EXP. CONTRACTION JOINT.
1/2" ISOLATION JOINT W/ SEALER
1/2" PREFORMED EXP. JOINT FILLER
CONTROL JOINT OR CONSTRUCTION JOINT
STOP SLAB REINF. @ JOINT.
FINISH FLOOR
SEALANT

dim. lines   break line

notation boundary

break line

cut mark

dim. line ——

dim. line ——

break line ——

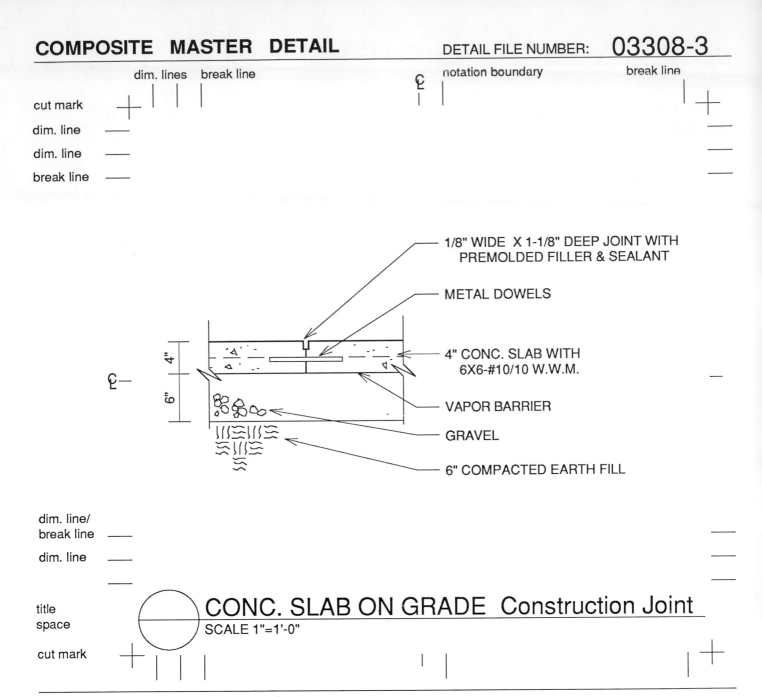

1/8" WIDE X 1-1/8" DEEP JOINT WITH
PREMOLDED FILLER & SEALANT

METAL DOWELS

4" CONC. SLAB WITH
6X6-#10/10 W.W.M.

VAPOR BARRIER

GRAVEL

6" COMPACTED EARTH FILL

dim. line/
break line ——

dim. line ——

title
space

cut mark

CONC. SLAB ON GRADE Construction Joint
SCALE 1"=1'-0"

DETAIL INFORMATION
References, jobsite feedback, job history

CHAPTER 4

Masonry
04000

DETAIL DATA CHECKLIST FOR UNIT MASONRY

CONCRETE BLOCK

__Concrete block is also often referred to as "hollow masonry units" and "concrete masonry units"
__Most data on brick or block grades, types, mortar, anchors, reinforcing, ASTM categories, etc. will be in
  specifications rather than details

__Concrete block sizes
  __Nominal thickness: 4", 6", 8", 10" & 12"
  __Nominal lengths: 16" & 18"
  __Nominal heights: 4" & 8"
    __Actual sizes are 3/8" less than nominal sizes to allow for typical mortar joint thickness

__Concrete block types
  __Solid load-bearing units
  __Hollow load-bearing units
  __Hollow non-load-bearing units

__Grades of load-bearing concrete block units are "N" and "S"
  __Grade N
    __Use for veneers and facings requiring:
      __High strength
      __High resistance to water penetration
      __High resistance to frost action
  __Grade S
    __Use for typical conditions
    __Moderate strength
    __Moderate moisture resistance

  __Grades N and S come as Types I and II
    __Type I--moisture resistant
    __Type II--non-moisture resistant

__Provide concrete block wall movement control joints at:
  __All columns or pilasters at wall
  __Each corner within distance equal to 1/2 wall height
  __Each side of openings over 5' wide
  __One side of openings less than 5' wide
  __Variations in wall height
  __Offsets and intersections
  __Intersection of load-bearing and non-load-bearing construction

__Provide concrete block wall movement control joint spacings of:
  __20' min., 8' high walls
  __25' min., 8-1/2' high walls
  __30' min., 12' and higher walls

__Concrete block at jambs
  __Reinforce and grout concrete block cells adjacent to door and window openings

__Movement control joints typically 1/2" minimum wide
  __With premolded compressible filler insert and elastic joint sealant over filler
  __Provide waterstop at solid masonry walls
  __Provide building paper as gasket at one side for complete bond break through wall expansion
    joints
  __Extend movement joints through facings rigidly attached to walls such as stucco or tile

__Wall movement is minimal below grade, so control joints aren't normally provided at block foundation walls
  __Use bond beam atop block foundation walls as boundary for control joints above

__Add slip joint material between slabs and load-bearing masonry control joints

DETAIL DATA CHECKLIST FOR UNIT MASONRY continued

BRICK

__Brick sizes
    __Standard modular brick is 4 x 2-2/3 x 8
    __Standard non-modular brick is 3-1/4 x 2-1/4 x 8
    __SCR is 6 x 2-2/3 x 12
    __There are a wide variety of special shapes and sizes, see Sweets, Time Saver Standards or other references
        __Actual size is smaller than nominal size by 3/8"to 1/2", to allow for typical mortar joint thickness

__Brick types and grades
    __Common building brick
        __SW--high moisture resistance for exposure to severe weather
        __MW--for exposure to moderate weather
        __NW--non-weather exposure
    __Face brick
    __Glazed
    __Hollow
    __Sand-lime
    __Concrete

    __Special-purpose bricks
        __Brick paving (grade SW is OK)
        __Chemical resistant
        __Industrial floor brick
        __Fire brick
        __Prefabricated brick panels

__Metal ties at brick walls
    __Double wythes of brick and block are typically linked by 3/16" diameter metal ties
        __Z or rectangular shaped
        __Spaced every 6th course maximum vertically and 36" horizontally
            __As necessary to have at least one tie for every 4.5 sq. ft. of wall area
        __Z shaped ties are NOT recommended for use with concrete block

__Brick veneer and metal ties
    __To link brick veneer to wood framing through sheathing, corrugated metal ties; 22 gauge, 7/8" wide, 6" long are typical
        __Maximum spacing at 24" o.c.
    __To fasten brick to metal studs, 9 gauge wire ties are typical

__Brick veneer air space and waterproofing
    __Add waterproof building paper on wall sheathing between grout or air space behind masonry
    __Air or grout space is typically 1" thick

__Anchors
    __To anchor unit masonry to concrete, dovetailed flexible anchors are typical
    __To tie brick or block to steel framing members, flexible anchors are typical

__Weep holes
    __Weep hole drain spacings at 24" o.c. maximum are typical
        __At bottom of wall
        __At all openings
        __In head joints right above flashing

BRICK continued

__Movement control joints typically 1/2" minimum wide
    __With premolded compressible filler insert and elastic joint sealant over filler
    __Provide waterstop at solid masonry walls
    __Provide building paper as gasket at one side for complete bond break through wall expansion
        joints
    __Extend movement joints through facings rigidly attached to walls such as stucco or tile

__Lintels and bond beams
    __Steel sizes and bond beam reinforcing are typically engineered for specific loads and spans
        and referenced to Lintel Schedules

See literature from the National Concrete Masonry Association, the Brick Institute of America, and your building code for complete engineering, specification, and construction application information.

04201 (a) BRICK & BLOCK CAVITY WALLS

See DETAIL DATA CHECKLIST for unit masonry preceding 04201(a).

DETAIL DATA CHECKLIST

BRICK AND CONCRETE BLOCK WALLS
These wall section details are to be combined with related
construction such as door frames, window frames, furred walls,
wall mounted fixtures, and wall penetrations such as for
pipe sleeves, access panels, etc.

Design limits of wall types, thickness and heights are strictly
limited by most building codes, so consult your local code for
the last word on preliminary design assumptions and final design.

Also, see literature from the National Concrete Masonry Association,
the Brick Institute of America, and the Construction Specifications
Institute for complete engineering, specification, and construction
application information.

SMALL-SCALE GENERIC DETAILS

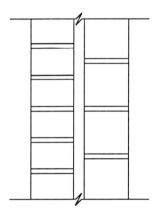

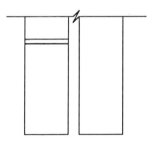

JAMB (8" CAVITY WALL)
04201-6

VERTICAL SECTION (8" CAVITY WALL)
04201-12

LINTEL (8" CAVITY WALL)
04201-14

239

04201 (a) BRICK & BLOCK CAVITY WALLS

FULL-SCALE GENERIC DETAILS

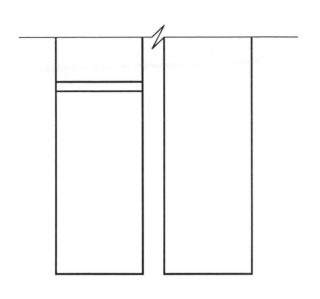

JAMB (8" CAVITY WALL)
3" = 1'-0"   04201-6

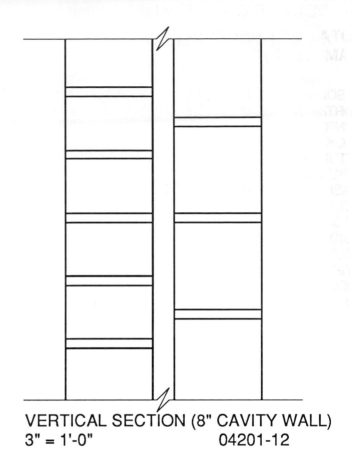

VERTICAL SECTION (8" CAVITY WALL)
3" = 1'-0"   04201-12

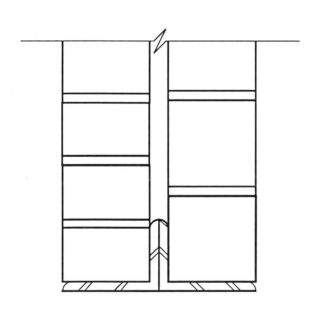

LINTEL (8" CAVITY WALL)
3" = 1'-0"   04201-14

04201 (a) BRICK & BLOCK CAVITY WALLS

**NOTATION CHECKLIST,
SAMPLE NOTES**

MASONRY UNIT TYPE & SIZE
MORTAR JOINT TYPE & SIZE
REINFORCING
HOOKS/TRACKS/WALL-MOUNTED
FIXTURES
THRU-WALL SLEEVES
FLASHING/WATERPROOFING/CAULKING
METAL TIES
AIR SPACE/GROUT
RIGID INSULATION
WEEP HOLES
INTERIOR FURRING/FINISH
DOOR/WINDOW/LOUVER FRAME
LINTEL

CONCRETE BLOCK
4" LIGHTWEIGHT CONC. BLOCK
FACE BRICK
BRICK VENEER W/ METAL TIES TO STUD WALL
CONT. SEALANT
4" STARTER COURSE
CONT. FLASHING
FABRIC FLASHING SET IN REGLET
GROUT
SHIM
5" X 3" X 1/4" CONT. SHELF ANGLE
STEEL LINTEL ELEV.
STEEL ANGLE LINTEL
WEEP HOLES @ 32" O.C.
METAL STRAP ANCHORS EVERY 6TH COURSE
BRICK ANCHORS
VERT. CONT. ANCHOR SLOTS SPACED 2'-O" O.C.
#4 @ 16" O.C., GROUT CORES
REINF. @ 16" O.C. TYP.
1" RIGID INSULATION
FOAM INSULATION

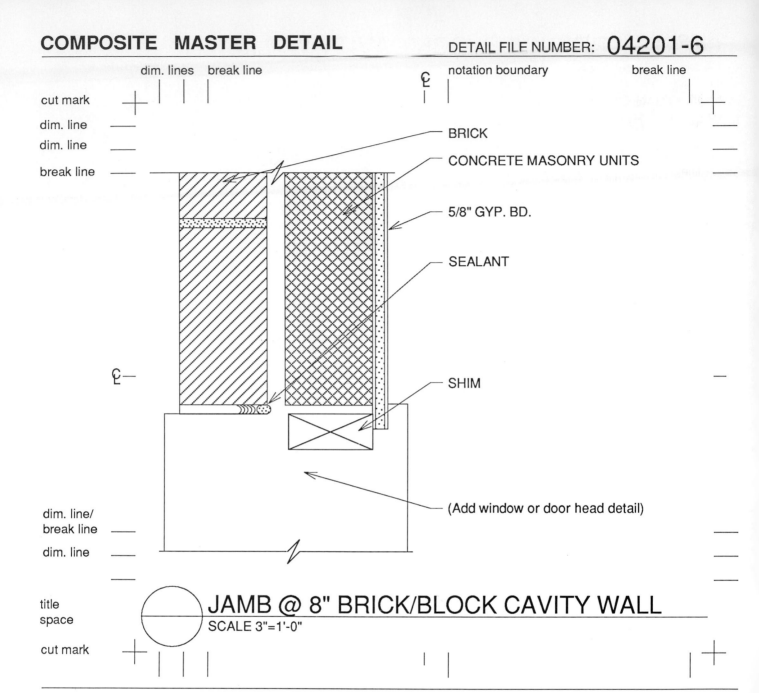

dim. lines   break line

notation boundary   break line

cut mark

dim. line

dim. line

break line

BRICK

CONCRETE MASONRY UNITS

5/8" GYP. BD.

SEALANT

SHIM

(Add window or door head detail)

dim. line/
break line

dim. line

title
space

JAMB @ 8" BRICK/BLOCK CAVITY WALL
SCALE 3"=1'-0"

cut mark

DETAIL INFORMATION
References, jobsite feedback, job history

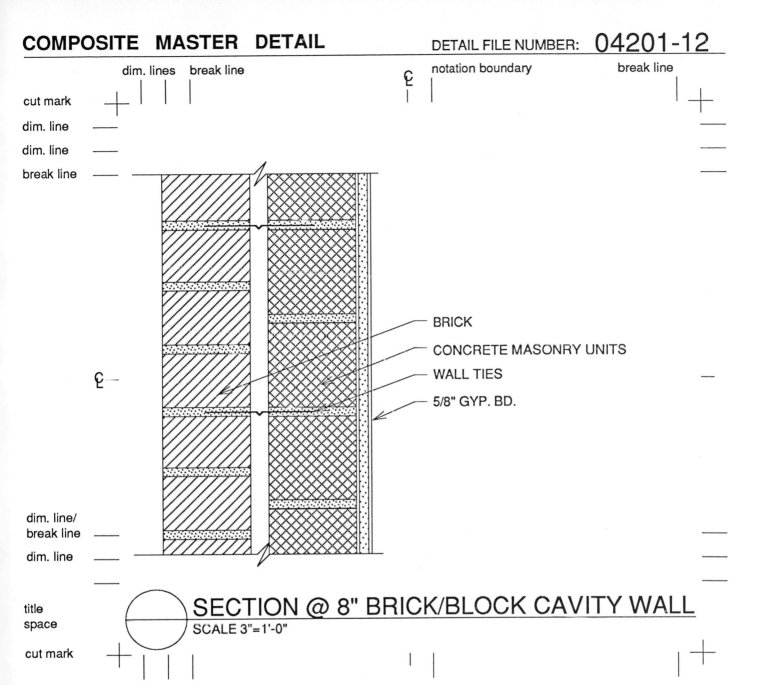

dim. lines   break line   notation boundary   break line

cut mark

dim. line

dim. line

break line

BRICK

CONCRETE MASONRY UNITS

WALL TIES

5/8" GYP. BD.

dim. line/
break line

dim. line

title
space

SECTION @ 8" BRICK/BLOCK CAVITY WALL
SCALE 3"=1'-0"

cut mark

DETAIL INFORMATION
References, jobsite feedback, job history

COMPOSITE MASTER DETAIL

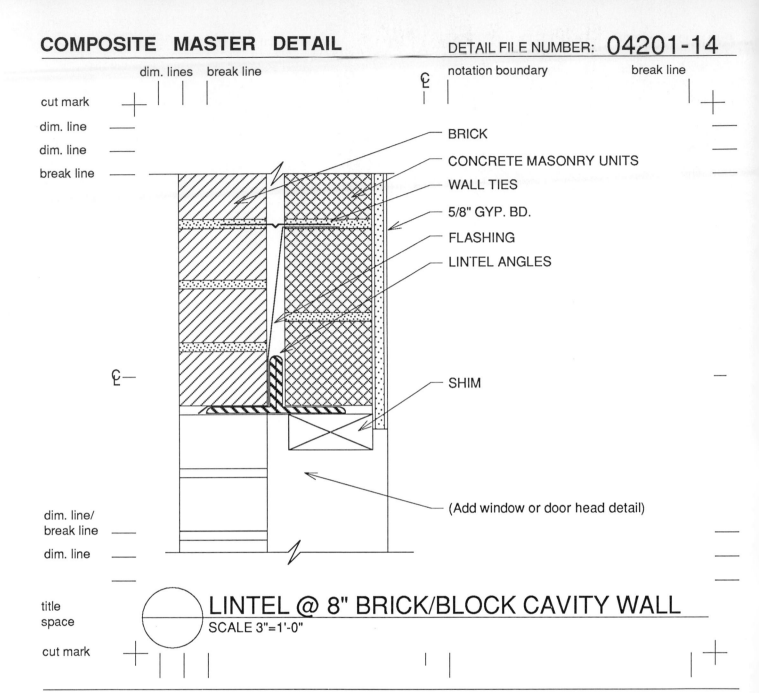

cut mark

dim. lines   break line

notation boundary   break line

dim. line

dim. line

break line

BRICK

CONCRETE MASONRY UNITS

WALL TIES

5/8" GYP. BD.

FLASHING

LINTEL ANGLES

SHIM

(Add window or door head detail)

dim. line/
break line

dim. line

title
space

LINTEL @ 8" BRICK/BLOCK CAVITY WALL
SCALE 3"=1'-0"

cut mark

DETAIL INFORMATION
References, jobsite feedback, job history

04201 (b) BRICK & BLOCK CAVITY WALLS

See DETAIL DATA CHECKLIST for unit masonry preceding 04201(a).

DETAIL DATA CHECKLIST

BRICK AND CONCRETE BLOCK WALLS
These wall section details are to be combined with related
construction such as door frames, window frames, furred walls,
wall mounted fixtures, and wall penetrations such as for
pipe sleeves, access panels, etc.

Design limits of wall types, thickness and heights are strictly
limited by most building codes, so consult your local code for
the last word on preliminary design assumptions and final design.

Also, see literature from the National Concrete Masonry Association,
the Brick Institute of America, and the Construction Specifications
Institute for complete engineering, specification, and construction
application information.

SMALL-SCALE GENERIC DETAILS

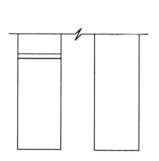

JAMB
(10" CAVITY WALL)
04201-26

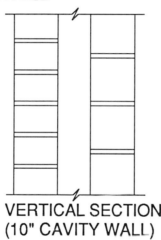

VERTICAL SECTION
(10" CAVITY WALL)
04201-32

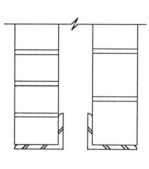

LINTEL
(10" CAVITY WALL)
04201-34

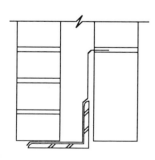

LINTEL
(10" CAVITY WALL)
04201-35

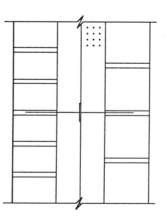

VERTICAL SECTION
(INSULATED CAV. WALL)
04201-42

04201 (b) BRICK & BLOCK CAVITY WALLS

FULL-SCALE GENERIC DETAILS

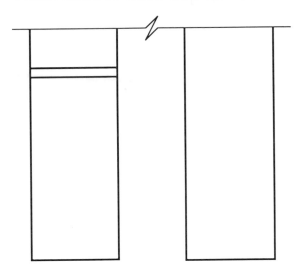

JAMB (10" CAVITY WALL)
3" = 1'-0"   04201-26

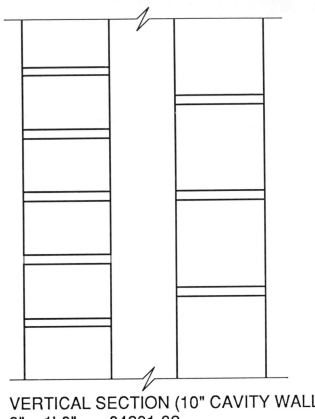

VERTICAL SECTION (10" CAVITY WALL)
3" = 1'-0"   04201-32

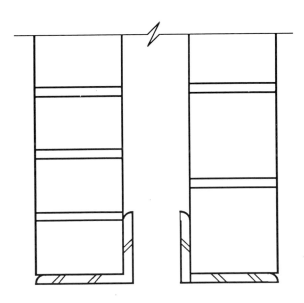

LINTEL (10" CAVITY WALL)
3" = 1'-0"   04201-34

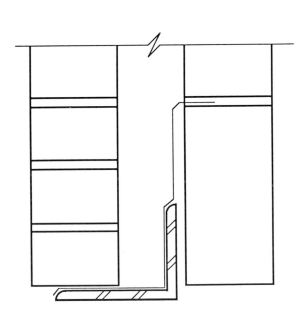

LINTEL (10" CAVITY WALL)
3" = 1'-0"   04201-35

04201 (b) BRICK & BLOCK CAVITY WALLS

FULL-SCALE GENERIC DETAILS
continued

CONCRETE BLOCK
4" LIGHTWEIGHT CONC. BLOCK
FACE BRICK
BRICK VENEER W/ METAL TIES TO STUD WALL
CONT. SEALANT
4" STARTER COURSE
CONT. FLASHING
FABRIC FLASHING SET IN REGLET
GROUT
SHIM
5" X 3" X 1/4" CONT. SHELF ANGLE
STEEL LINTEL ELEV.
STEEL ANGLE LINTEL
WEEP HOLES @ 32" O.C.
METAL STRAP ANCHORS EVERY 6TH COURSE
BRICK ANCHORS
VERT. CONT. ANCHOR SLOTS SPACED 2'-0" O.C.
#4 @ 16" O.C., GROUT CORES
REINF. @ 16" O.C. TYP.
1" RIGID INSULATION
FOAM INSULATION

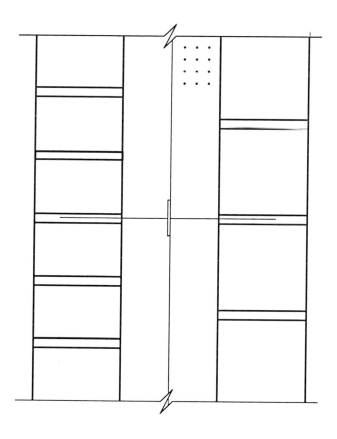

VERTICAL SECTION
(INSULATED CAV. WALL)
3" = 1'-0"   04201-42

NOTATION CHECKLIST,
SAMPLE NOTES

MASONRY UNIT TYPE & SIZE
MORTAR JOINT TYPE & SIZE
REINFORCING
HOOKS/TRACKS/WALL-MOUNTED
FIXTURES
THRU-WALL SLEEVES
FLASHING/WATERPROOFING/CAULKING
METAL TIES
AIR SPACE/GROUT
RIGID INSULATION
WEEP HOLES
INTERIOR FURRING/FINISH
DOOR/WINDOW/LOUVER FRAME
LINTEL

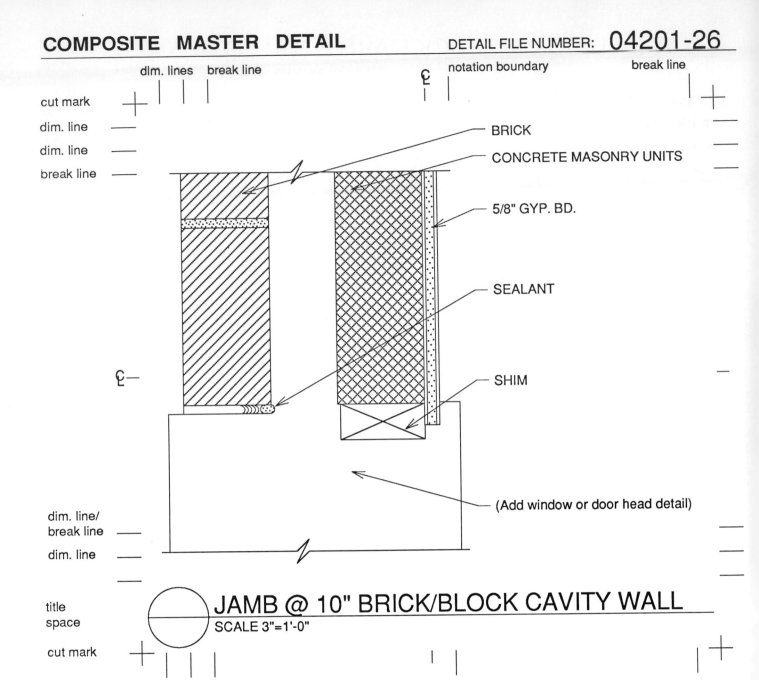

cut mark

dim. lines   break line

notation boundary   break line

dim. line

dim. line

break line

BRICK

CONCRETE MASONRY UNITS

5/8" GYP. BD.

SEALANT

SHIM

(Add window or door head detail)

dim. line/
break line

dim. line

title
space

JAMB @ 10" BRICK/BLOCK CAVITY WALL
SCALE 3"=1'-0"

cut mark

DETAIL INFORMATION
References, jobsite feedback, job history

DETAIL FILE NUMBER: 04201-35

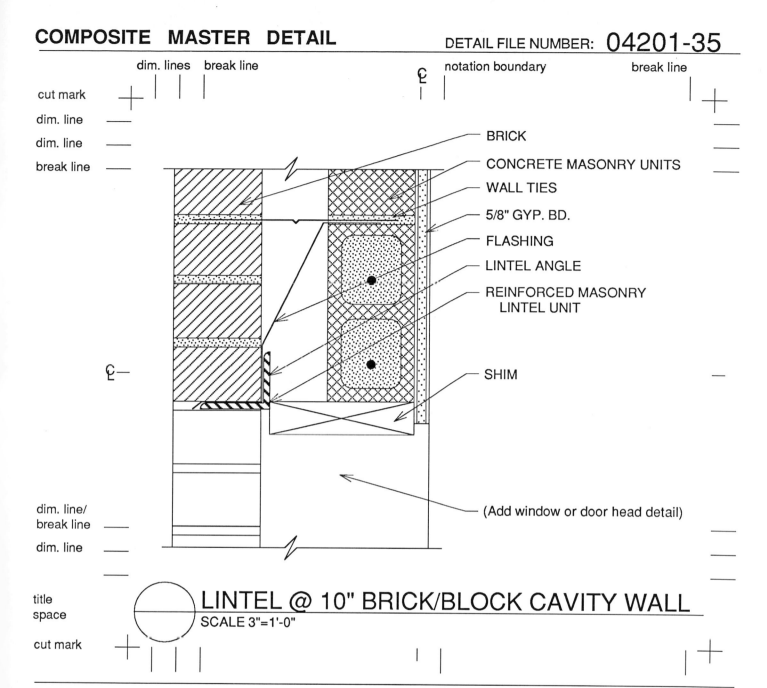

BRICK

CONCRETE MASONRY UNITS

WALL TIES

5/8" GYP. BD.

FLASHING

LINTEL ANGLE

REINFORCED MASONRY
LINTEL UNIT

SHIM

(Add window or door head detail)

dim. lines   break line

notation boundary   break line

cut mark

dim. line

dim. line

break line

dim. line/
break line

dim. line

title
space

cut mark

LINTEL @ 10" BRICK/BLOCK CAVITY WALL
SCALE 3"=1'-0"

DETAIL INFORMATION
References, jobsite feedback, job history

04210, 04214 BRICK CAVITY WALLS

See DETAIL DATA CHECKLIST for unit masonry preceding 04201(a).

DETAIL DATA CHECKLIST

BRICK AND CONCRETE BLOCK WALLS
These wall section details are to be combined with related
construction such as door frames, window frames, furred walls,
wall mounted fixtures, and wall penetrations such as for
pipe sleeves, access panels, etc.

Design limits of wall types, thickness and heights are strictly
limited by most building codes, so consult your local code for
the last word on preliminary design assumptions and final design.

Also, see literature from the National Concrete Masonry Association,
the Brick Institute of America, and the Construction Specifications
Institute for complete engineering, specification, and construction
application information.

SMALL-SCALE GENERIC DETAILS

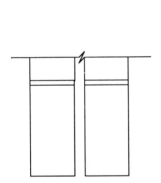

JAMB
(8" BRICK WALL)
04210-26

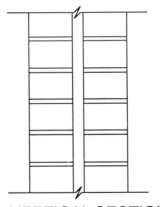

VERTICAL SECTION
(8" BRICK WALL)
04210-32

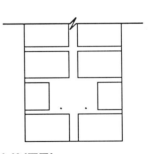

LINTEL
(8" BRICK WALL)
04210-34

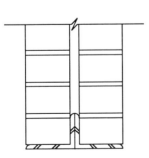

LINTEL
(8" BRICK WALL)
04210-35

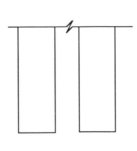

JAMB
(8" BRICK CAVITY WALL)
04214-6

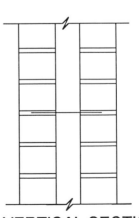

VERTICAL SECTION
(8" BRICK CAVITY WALL)
04214-12

04210, 04214 BRICK CAVITY WALLS

FULL-SCALE GENERIC DETAILS

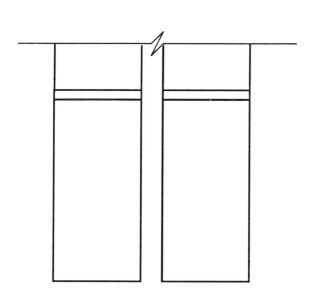

JAMB
(8" BRICK WALL)
3" = 1'-0"   04210-26

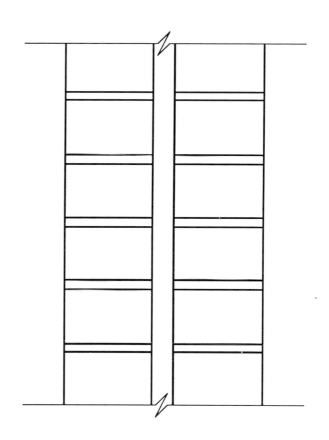
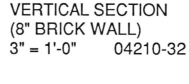

VERTICAL SECTION
(8" BRICK WALL)
3" = 1'-0"   04210-32

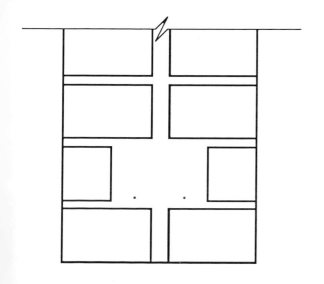

LINTEL (8" BRICK WALL)
3" = 1'-0"   04210-34

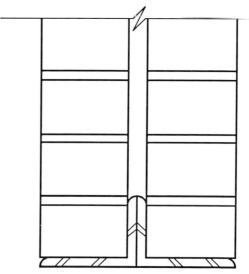

LINTEL (8" BRICK WALL)
3" = 1'-0"   04210-35

FULL-SCALE GENERIC DETAILS
continued

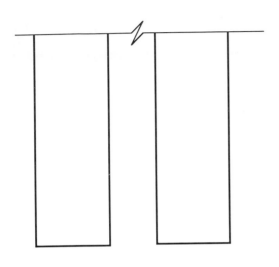

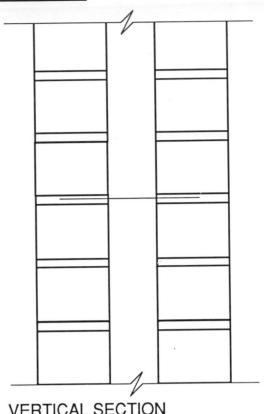

JAMB
(8" BRICK CAVITY WALL)
3" = 1'-0"   04214-6

VERTICAL SECTION
(8" BRICK CAVITY WALL)
3" = 1'-0"   04214-12

NOTATION CHECKLIST, SAMPLE NOTES

MASONRY UNIT TYPE & SIZE
MORTAR JOINT TYPE & SIZE
REINFORCING
HOOKS/TRACKS/WALL-MOUNTED
FIXTURES
THRU-WALL SLEEVES
FLASHING/WATERPROOFING/CAULKING
METAL TIES
AIR SPACE/GROUT
RIGID INSULATION
WEEP HOLES
INTERIOR FURRING/FINISH
DOOR/WINDOW/LOUVER FRAME
LINTEL

CONCRETE BLOCK
4" LIGHTWEIGHT CONC. BLOCK
FACE BRICK
BRICK VENEER W/ METAL TIES TO STUD WALL
CONT. SEALANT
4" STARTER COURSE
CONT. FLASHING
FABRIC FLASHING SET IN REGLET
GROUT
SHIM
5" X 3" X 1/4" CONT. SHELF ANGLE
STEEL LINTEL ELEV.
STEEL ANGLE LINTEL
WEEP HOLES @ 32" O.C.
METAL STRAP ANCHORS EVERY 6TH COURSE
BRICK ANCHORS
VERT. CONT. ANCHOR SLOTS SPACED 2'-0" O.C.
#4 @ 16" O.C., GROUT CORES
REINF. @ 16" O.C. TYP.
1" RIGID INSULATION
FOAM INSULATION

04214 BRICK CAVITY WALLS

See DETAIL DATA CHECKLIST for unit masonry preceding 04201(a).

DETAIL DATA CHECKLIST

BRICK AND CONCRETE BLOCK WALLS
These wall section details are to be combined with related
construction such as door frames, window frames, furred walls,
wall mounted fixtures, and wall penetrations such as for
pipe sleeves, access panels, etc.

Design limits of wall types, thickness and heights are strictly
limited by most building codes, so consult your local code for
the last word on preliminary design assumptions and final design.

Also, see literature from the National Concrete Masonry Association,
the Brick Institute of America, and the Construction Specifications
Institute for complete engineering, specification, and construction application information.

SMALL-SCALE GENERIC DETAILS

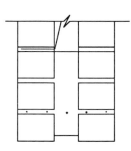
LINTEL
(8" BRICK CAVITY WALL)
04214-14

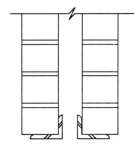
LINTEL
(8" BRICK CAVITY WALL)
04214-15

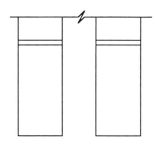
JAMB
(8" BRICK CAVITY WALL)
04214-26

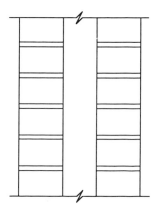
VERTICAL SECTION
(8" BRICK CAVITY WALL)
04214-32

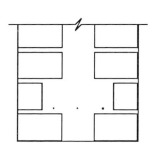
LINTEL
(10" BRICK CAVITY WALL)
04214-34

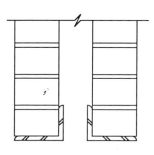
LINTEL
(10" BRICK CAVITY WALL)
04214-35

O4214 BRICK CAVITY WALLS

FULL-SCALE GENERIC DETAILS

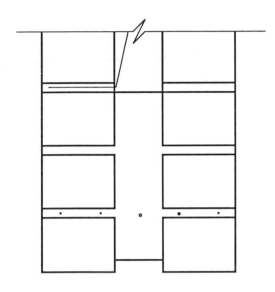

LINTEL
(8" BRICK CAVITY WALL)
3" = 1'-0"   04214-14

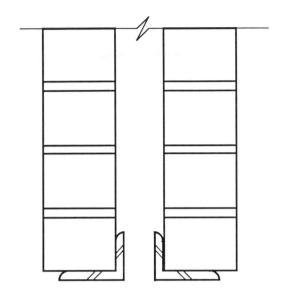

LINTEL
(8" BRICK CAVITY WALL)
3" = 1'-0"   04214-15

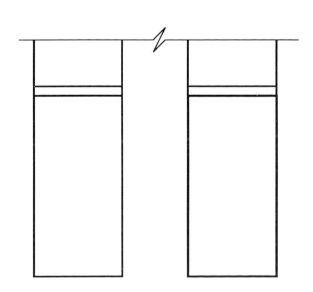

JAMB
(8" BRICK CAVITY WALL)
3" = 1'-0"   04214-26

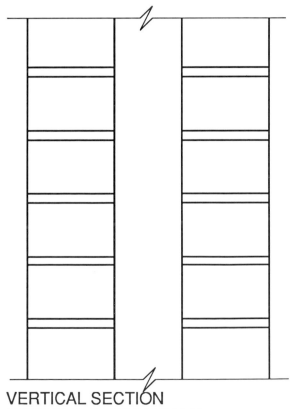

VERTICAL SECTION
(8" BRICK CAVITY WALL)
3" = 1'-0"   04214-32

O4214 BRICK CAVITY WALLS

FULL-SCALE GENERIC DETAILS continued

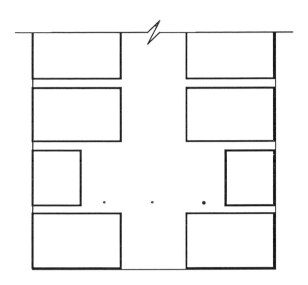

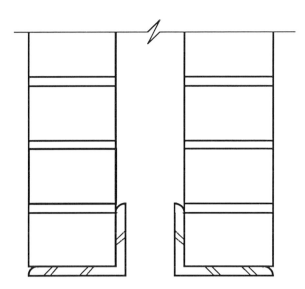

LINTEL
(10" BRICK CAVITY WALL)
3" = 1'-0"   04214-34

LINTEL
(10" BRICK CAVITY WALL)
3" = 1'-0"   04214-35

NOTATION CHECKLIST,
SAMPLE NOTES

MASONRY UNIT TYPE & SIZE
MORTAR JOINT TYPE & SIZE
REINFORCING
HOOKS/TRACKS/WALL MOUNTED
FIXTURES
THRU-WALL SLEEVES
FLASHING/WATERPROOFING/CAULKING
METAL TIES
AIR SPACE/GROUT
RIGID INSULATION
WEEP HOLES
INTERIOR FURRING/FINISH
DOOR/WINDOW/LOUVER FRAME
LINTEL

CONCRETE BLOCK
4" LIGHTWEIGHT CONC. BLOCK
FACE BRICK
BRICK VENEER W/ METAL TIES TO STUD WALL
WEEP HOLES
CONT. SEALANT
4" STARTER COURSE
CONT. FLASHING
FABRIC FLASHING SET IN REGLET
GROUT
SHIM
5" X 3" X 1/4" CONT. SHELF ANGLE
STEEL LINTEL ELEV.
STEEL ANGLE LINTEL
WEEP HOLES @ 32" O.C.
METAL STRAP ANCHORS EVERY 6TH COURSE HORIZ.
BRICK ANCHORS
VERT. CONT. ANCHOR SLOTS SPACED 2'-O" O.C.
#4 @ 16" O.C. GROUT CORES
REINF. @ 16" O.C. TYP.
1" RIGID INSULATION
FOAMED INSULATION

04215 BRICK VENEER

See DETAIL DATA CHECKLIST for unit masonry preceding 04201(a).

DETAIL DATA CHECKLIST

BRICK AND CONCRETE BLOCK WALLS
These wall section details are to be combined with related
construction such as door frames, window frames, furred walls,
wall mounted fixtures, and wall penetrations such as for
pipe sleeves, access panels, etc.

Design limits of wall types, thickness and heights are strictly
limited by most building codes, so consult your local code for
the last word on preliminary design assumptions and final design.

Also, see literature from the National Concrete Masonry Association,
the Brick Institute of America, and the Construction Specifications
Institute for complete engineering, specification, and construction
application information.

SMALL-SCALE GENERIC DETAILS

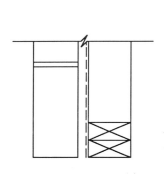

JAMB
(4" BRICK VENEER)
04215-6

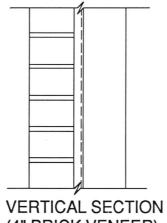

VERTICAL SECTION
(4" BRICK VENEER)
04215-12

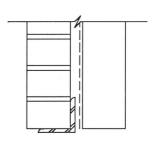

LINTEL
(4" BRICK VENEER)
04215-14

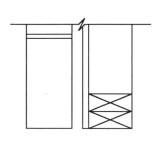

JAMB
(4" BRICK VENEER)
04215-26

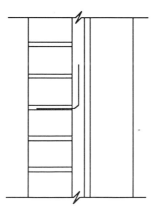

VERTICAL SECTION
(4" BRICK VENEER)
04215-32

LINTEL
(4" BRICK VENEER)
04215-34

04215 BRICK VENEER

FULL-SCALE GENERIC DETAILS

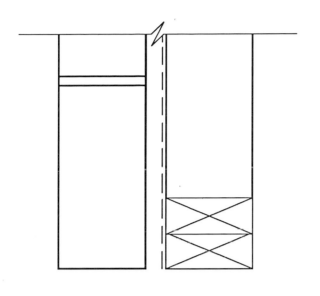

JAMB (4" BRICK VENEER)
3" = 1'-0"   04215-6

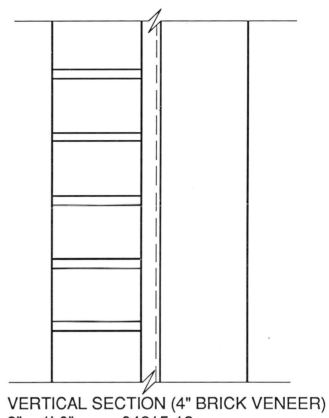

VERTICAL SECTION (4" BRICK VENEER)
3" = 1'-0"   04215-12

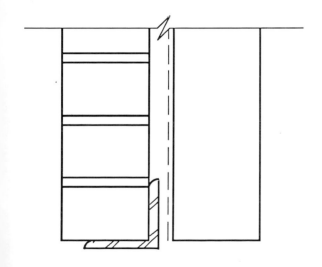

LINTEL (4" BRICK VENEER)
3" = 1'-0"   04215-14

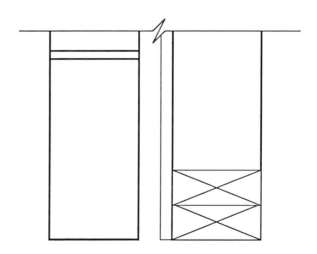

JAMB (4" BRICK VENEER)
3" = 1'-0"   04215-26

04215 BRICK VENEER

FULL-SCALE GENERIC DETAILS continued

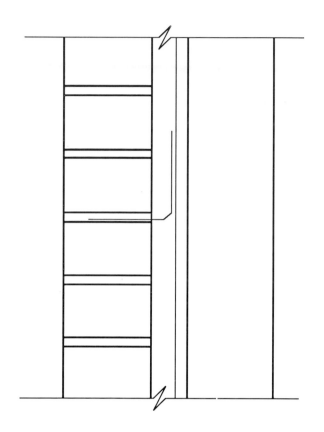

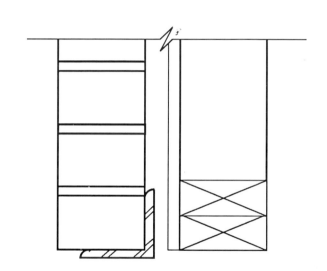

VERTICAL SECTION (4" BRICK VENEER)
3" = 1'-0"   04215-32

LINTEL (4" BRICK VENEER)
3" = 1'-0"   04215-34

258

04215 BRICK VENEER

NOTATION CHECKLIST, SAMPLE NOTES

MASONRY UNIT TYPE & SIZE
MORTAR JOINT TYPE & SIZE
REINFORCING
HOOKS/TRACKS/WALL MOUNTED
FIXTURES
THRU-WALL SLEEVES
FLASHING/WATERPROOFING/CAULKING
METAL TIES
AIR SPACE/GROUT
RIGID INSULATION
WEEP HOLES
INTERIOR FURRING/FINISH
DOOR/WINDOW/LOUVER FRAME
LINTEL

BATT INSULATION
INSULATION BOARD
WOOD SIDING
15# FELT
1/2" FOIL FACE INSULATION
AIR SPACE
1/2 X 6 BEVELED LAP SIDING
1/2" PLYWOOD SHEATH
PLYWOOD SIDING
VAPOR BARRIER
WOOD TRIM
2 X   JOISTS @   " O.C.
2 X   RAFTERS @   " O.C.
BLOCKING
FLASHING
GYP. BD. CEILING
HARDWOOD STOPS
HARDWOOD JAMB
2 X 4 CONT. WOOD BLOCKING
SOUND INSULATION
PREFINISHED PANELING
DOOR FRAME
DOOR SIZE
WOOD DRIP
1 X   WOOD STOP
SOUND ISOLATION PLATE
SOUND ISOLATION CLIPS

CONCRETE BLOCK
4" LIGHTWEIGHT CONC. BLOCK
FACE BRICK
BRICK VENEER W/ METAL TIES TO STUD WALL
WEEP HOLES
CONT. SEALANT
4" STARTER COURSE
CONT. FLASHING
FABRIC FLASHING SET IN REGLET
GROUT
SHIM
5" X 3" X 1/4" CONT. SHELF ANGLE
STEEL LINTEL ELEV.
STEEL ANGLE LINTEL
WEEP HOLES @ 32" O.C.
METAL STRAP ANCHORS EVERY 6TH COURSE HORIZ.
BRICK ANCHORS
VERT. CONT. ANCHOR SLOTS SPACED 2'-O" O.C.
#4 @ 16" O.C. GROUT CORES
REINF. @ 16" O.C. TYP.
1" RIGID INSULATION
FOAMED INSULATION

COMPOSITE MASTER DETAIL

DETAIL FILE NUMBER: **04215-12**

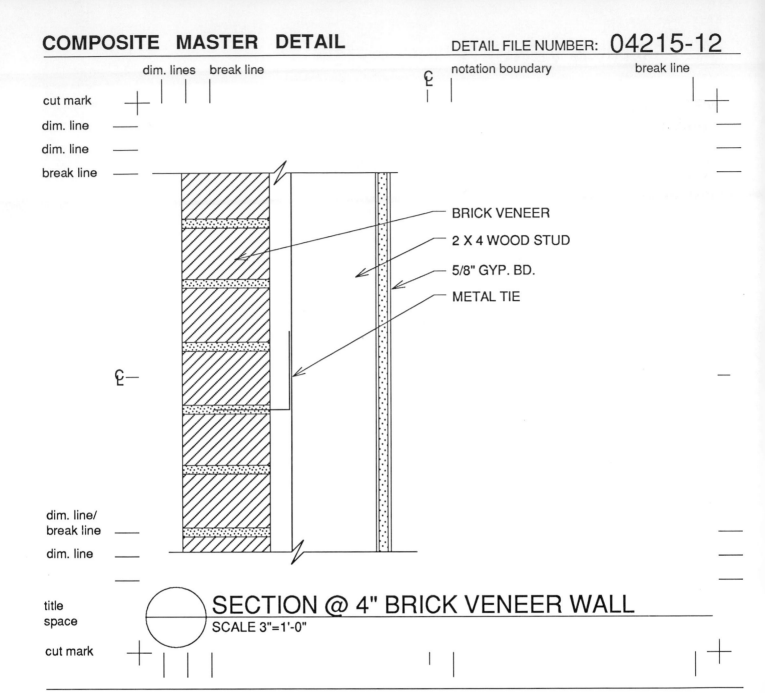

cut mark

dim. line

dim. line

break line

dim. lines   break line

notation boundary

break line

BRICK VENEER

2 X 4 WOOD STUD

5/8" GYP. BD.

METAL TIE

dim. line/
break line

dim. line

title
space

SECTION @ 4" BRICK VENEER WALL
SCALE 3"=1'-0"

cut mark

DETAIL INFORMATION
References, jobsite feedback, job history

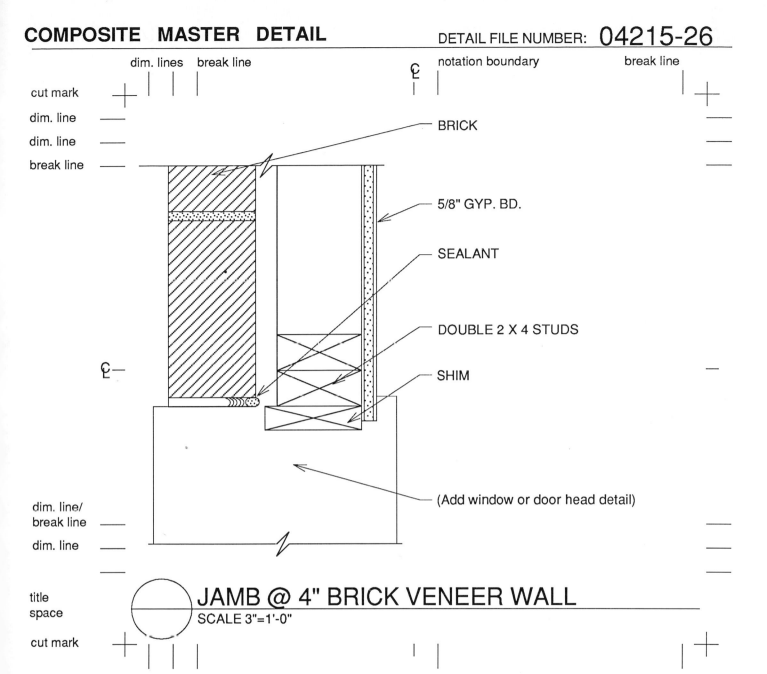

dim. lines   break line   notation boundary   break line

cut mark

dim. line

dim. line

break line

BRICK

5/8" GYP. BD.

SEALANT

DOUBLE 2 X 4 STUDS

SHIM

(Add window or door head detail)

dim. line/
break line

dim. line

title
space

JAMB @ 4" BRICK VENEER WALL
SCALE 3"=1'-0"

cut mark

DETAIL INFORMATION
References, jobsite feedback, job history

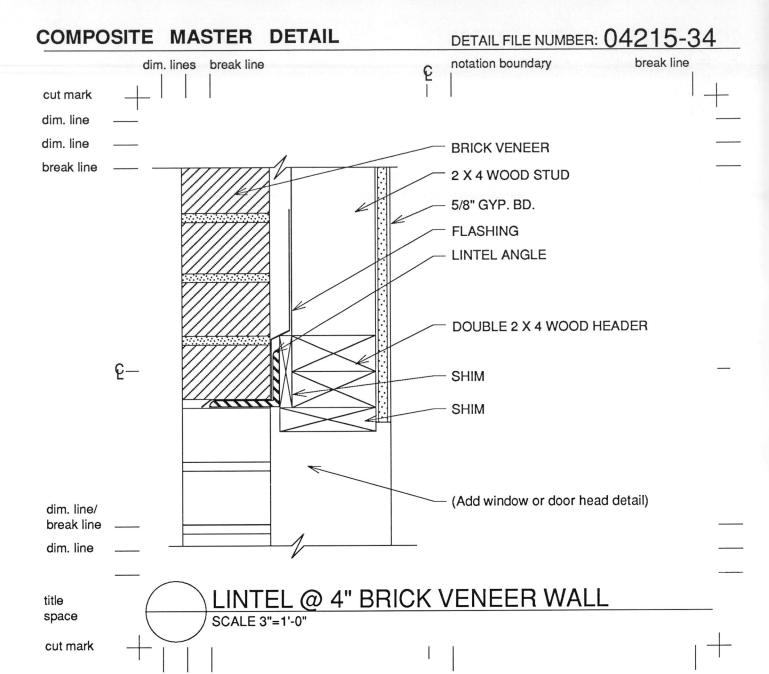

dim. lines   break line

notation boundary

break line

cut mark

dim. line

dim. line

break line

BRICK VENEER

2 X 4 WOOD STUD

5/8" GYP. BD.

FLASHING

LINTEL ANGLE

DOUBLE 2 X 4 WOOD HEADER

SHIM

SHIM

(Add window or door head detail)

dim. line/
break line

dim. line

title
space

LINTEL @ 4" BRICK VENEER WALL
SCALE 3"=1'-0"

cut mark

DETAIL INFORMATION
References, jobsite feedback, job history

04216 BRICK WALLS

See DETAIL DATA CHECKLIST for unit masonry preceding 04201(a).

DETAIL DATA CHECKLIST

BRICK AND CONCRETE BLOCK WALLS
These wall section details are to be combined with related
construction such as door frames, window frames, furred walls,
wall mounted fixtures, and wall penetrations such as for
pipe sleeves, access panels, etc.

Design limits of wall types, thickness and heights are strictly
limited by most building codes, so consult your local code for
the last word on preliminary design assumptions and final design.

Also, see literature from the National Concrete Masonry Association,
the Brick Institute of America, and the Construction Specifications
Institute for complete engineering, specification, and construction
application Information.

SMALL-SCALE GENERIC DETAILS

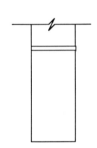

JAMB
(4" BRICK)
04216-6

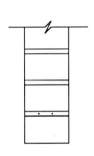

LINTEL
(4" BRICK)
04216-14

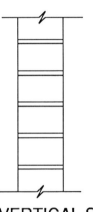

VERTICAL SECTION
(4" BRICK)
04216-12

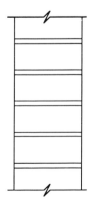

VERTICAL SECTION
(6" SCR BRICK)
04216-32

LINTEL
(6" SCR BRICK)
04216-34

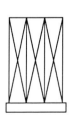

LINTEL
(6" SCR BRICK)
04216-35

LINTEL
(6" SCR BRICK)
04216-36

04216 BRICK WALLS

FULL-SCALE GENERIC DETAILS

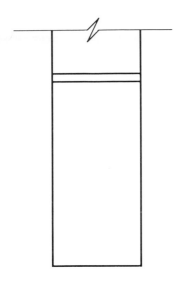

JAMB (4" BRICK)
3" = 1'-0"   04216-6

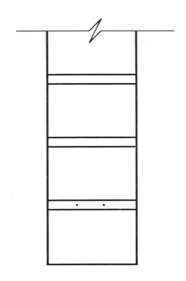

LINTEL (4" BRICK)
3" = 1'-0"   04216-14

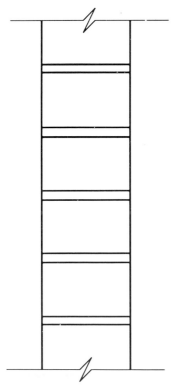

VERTICAL SECTION (4" BRICK)
3" = 1'-0"   04216-12

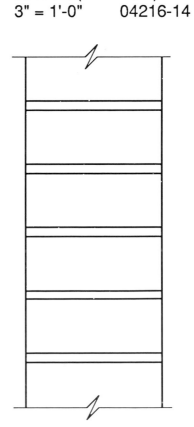

VERTICAL SECTION (6" SCR BRICK)
3" = 1'-0"   04216-32

04216 BRICK WALLS

FULL-SCALE GENERIC DETAILS continued

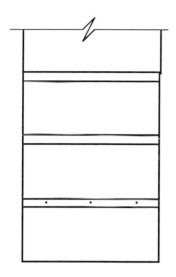

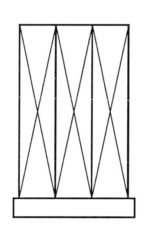

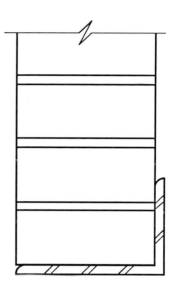

LINTEL (6" SCR BRICK)
3" = 1'-0"   04216-34

LINTEL (6" SCR BRICK)
3" = 1'-0"   04216-35

LINTEL (6" SCR BRICK)
3" = 1'-0"   04216-36

NOTATION CHECKLIST, SAMPLE NOTES

MASONRY UNIT TYPE & SIZE
MORTAR JOINT TYPE & SIZE
REINFORCING
HOOKS/TRACKS/WALL-MOUNTED FIXTURES
THRU-WALL SLEEVES
FLASHING/WATERPROOFING/CAULKING
INTERIOR FURRING/FINISH
DOOR/WINDOW/LOUVER FRAME
LINTEL

STARTER COURSE
FLASHING CONT.
FABRIC FLASHING SET IN REGLET
GROUT
CONT. SHELF ANGLE
STEEL LINTEL ELEV.
STEEL ANGLE LINTEL
BRICK ANCHORS
HORIZ. JOINT REINF.

04220 CONCRETE BLOCK CAVITY WALLS

See DETAIL DATA CHECKLIST for unit masonry preceding 04201(a).

DETAIL DATA CHECKLIST

BRICK AND CONCRETE BLOCK WALLS
These wall section details are to be combined with related
construction such as door frames, window frames, furred walls,
wall mounted fixtures, and wall penetrations such as for
pipe sleeves, access panels, etc.

Design limits of wall types, thickness and heights are strictly
limited by most building codes, so consult your local code for
the last word on preliminary design assumptions and final design.

Also, see literature from the National Concrete Masonry Association,
the Brick Institute of America, and the Construction Specifications
Institute for complete engineering, specification, and construction application information.

SMALL-SCALE GENERIC DETAILS

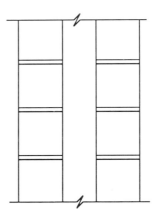

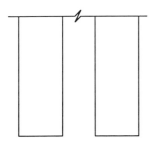

JAMB
(10" HMU CAVITY WALL)
04220-6

VERTICAL SECTION
(10" HMU CAVITY WALL)
04220-12

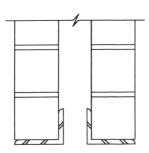

LINTEL
(10" HMU CAVITY WALL)
04220-14

266

04220 CONCRETE BLOCK CAVITY WALLS

FULL-SCALE GENERIC DETAILS

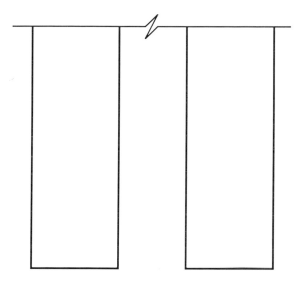

JAMB
(10" HMU CAVITY WALL)
3" = 1'-0"   04220-6

VERTICAL SECTION
(10" HMU CAVITY WALL)
3" = 1'-0"   04220-12

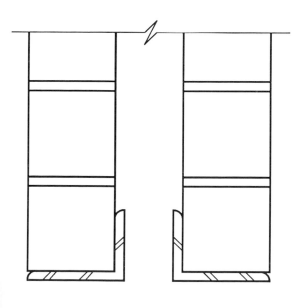

LINTEL
(10" HMU CAVITY WALL)
3" = 1'-0"   04220-14

04220 CONCRETE BLOCK CAVITY WALLS

NOTATION CHECKLIST,
SAMPLE NOTES

MASONRY UNIT TYPE & SIZE
MORTAR JOINT TYPE & SIZE
REINFORCING
HOOKS/TRACKS/WALL MOUNTED FIXTURES
THRU-WALL SLEEVES
FLASHING/WATERPROOFING/CAULKING
METAL TIES
AIR SPACE/GROUT
RIGID INSULATION
WEEP HOLES

8" CONCRETE BLOCK, GROUT CORES FULL &
   BREAK OUT WEB AS REQ'D. FOR #4 BAR VERT.
8" LINTEL BLOCK
CONC. BLOCK
FLASHING
SEALANT
CAULK
#4 @ 48" O.C. ALTERNATE - GROUT REINF. CELLS
#4 VERT. REINFORCEMENT @ 2'-0" O.C.
HORIZ. JOINT REINF. @ 16" O.C.
1/2" PREMOLDED JOINT FILLER
EXTRUDED CONTROL JOINT FILLER
FACE BRICK
1" PERIMETER INSULATION
BOND BEAM W/#5 CONT. @ 32" O.C.
#4 CONT. IN BOND BEAM
SASH BLOCK - EACH SIDE
16 GA. STEEL MESH EVERY OTHER COURSE
   (@ masonry interior partition joint)
INSULATION
DISCONTINUE MASONRY REINF. @ CONTROL
JOINT
EXPANSION SHIELD

STARTER COURSE
FLASHING CONT.
FABRIC FLASHING SET IN REGLET
GROUT
CONT. SHELF ANGLE
STEEL LINTEL ELEV.
STEEL ANGLE LINTEL
BRICK ANCHORS
HORIZ. JOINT REINF.

8" CONCRETE BLOCK
CONC. SLAB
SEE FOUNDATION PLAN FOR SLAB THICKNESS
   & FIN. FLOOR ELEV.
SEE FOUNDATION PLAN FOR TOP OF FTG. ELEV.
FLASHING
#4 @ 48" O.C. ALTERNATE - GROUT REINF. CELLS
HORIZ. JOINT REINF. @ 16" O.C.
FINISH GRADE HEIGHT VARIES
1/2" PREMOLDED JOINT FILLER
EXTRUDED CONTROL JOINT FILLER
FACE BRICK
1" PERIMETER INSULATION
BOND BEAM
STEP FTG., SEE DETAIL

04229 (a) CONCRETE BLOCK FOUNDATION WALLS

See DETAIL DATA CHECKLIST for unit masonry preceding 04201(a).

DETAIL DATA CHECKLIST

CONCRETE BLOCK FOUNDATION WALLS
Design limits of unit masonry wall types, thickness and heights are strictly
limited by most building codes, so consult your local code for the last word
on preliminary design assumptions and final design.

Unless specially engineered, concrete block foundation walls should be limited
to small, one-story residential or utility buildings.

SMALL-SCALE GENERIC DETAILS

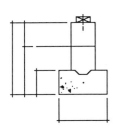

CONC. BLOCK FOUNDATION WALL
1 Story
04229-1

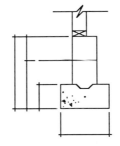

CONC. BLOCK FOUNDATION WALL
1 Story
04229-2

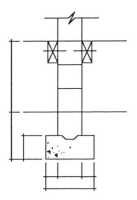

CONC. BLOCK FOUNDATION WALL
1 Story
04229-3

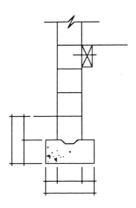

CONC. BLOCK FOUNDATION WALL
1 Story
04229-4

04229 (a) CONCRETE BLOCK FOUNDATION WALLS

FULL-SCALE GENERIC DETAILS

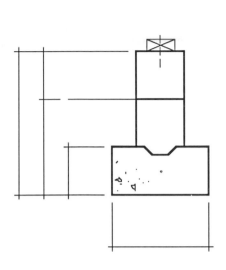

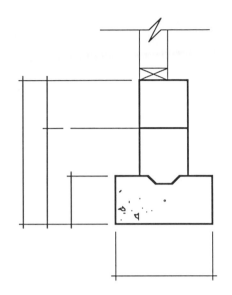

CONC. BLOCK FOUNDATION WALL
1 Story
1"=1'-0"   04229-1

CONC. BLOCK FOUNDATION WALL
1 Story
1"=1'-0"   04229-2

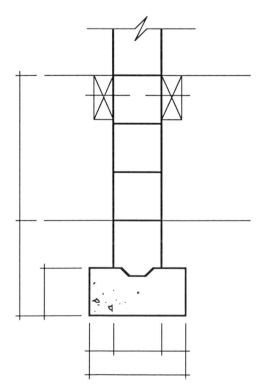

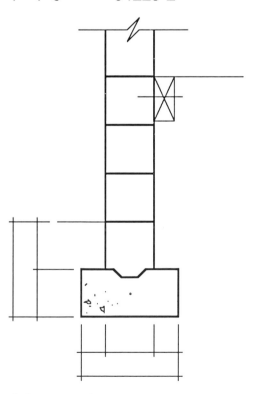

CONC. BLOCK FOUNDATION WALL
1 Story
1"=1'-0"   04229-3

CONC. BLOCK FOUNDATION WALL
1 Story
1"=1'-0"   04229-4

04229 (a) CONCRETE BLOCK FOUNDATION WALLS

NOTATION CHECKLIST,
SAMPLE NOTES

MUDSILL W/ LEVELING GROUT
ANCHOR BOLTS
LEDGER
ANCHOR FOR LEDGER
GROUTED CONCRETE BLOCK
FOUNDATION WALL REINFORCING
CONCRETE FOOTING W/GROUT KEY
CONCRETE FOOTING REINFORCING BARS
INSULATION
TERMITE SHIELD
CRAWLSPACE
RODENT BARRIER
VAPOR BARRIER W/ SAND COVER
GRADE
DRAINAGE

8" CONCRETE BLOCK
CONC. SLAB
SEE FOUNDATION PLAN FOR SLAB THICKNESS
    & FIN. FLOOR ELEV.
SEE FOUNDATION PLAN FOR TOP OF FTG. ELEV.
FLASHING
#4 @ 48" O.C. ALTERNATE - GROUT REINF. CELLS
HORIZ. JOINT REINF. @ 16" O.C.
FINISH GRADE HEIGHT VARIES
1/2" PREMOLDED JOINT FILLER
EXTRUDED CONTROL JOINT FILLER
FACE BRICK
1" PERIMETER INSULATION
BOND BEAM
STEP FTG., SEE DETAIL

04229 (b) CONCRETE BLOCK FOUNDATION WALLS

See DETAIL DATA CHECKLIST for unit masonry preceding 04201(a).

DETAIL DATA CHECKLIST

CONCRETE BLOCK FOUNDATION WALLS

Design limits of unit masonry wall types, thickness and heights are strictly limited by most building codes, so consult your local code for the last word on preliminary design assumptions and final design.

Unless specially engineered, concrete block foundation walls should be limited to small, one-story residential or utility buildings.

SMALL-SCALE GENERIC DETAILS

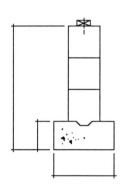

CONC. BLOCK
FOUNDATION WALL
2 Story   04229-5

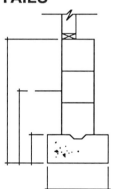

CONC. BLOCK
FOUNDATION WALL
2 Story   04229-6

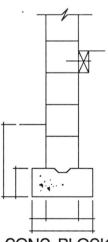

CONC. BLOCK
FOUNDATION WALL
2 Story   04229-7

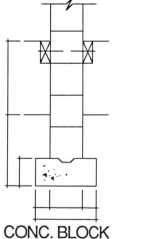

CONC. BLOCK
FOUNDATION WALL
2 Story   04229-8

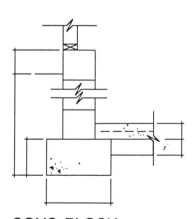

CONC. BLOCK
FOUNDATION WALL
Basement   04229-9

04229 (b) CONCRETE BLOCK FOUNDATION WALLS

FULL-SCALE GENERIC DETAILS

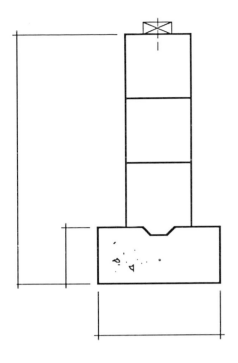

CONC. BLOCK FOUNDATION WALL
2 Story
1"=1'-0"   04229-5

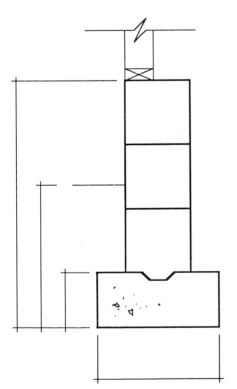

CONC. BLOCK FOUNDATION WALL
2 Story
1"=1'-0"   04229-6

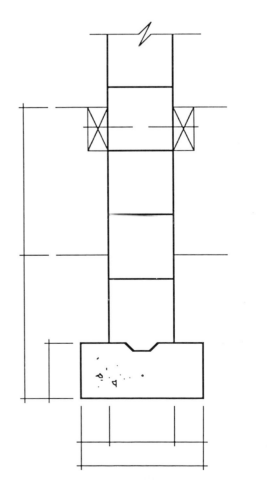

CONC. BLOCK FOUNDATION WALL
2 Story
1"=1'-0"   04229-7

FULL-SCALE GENERIC DETAILS continued

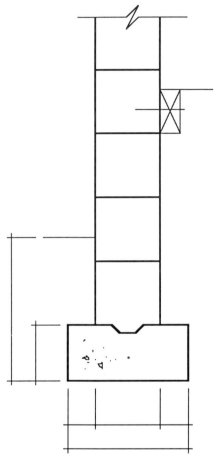

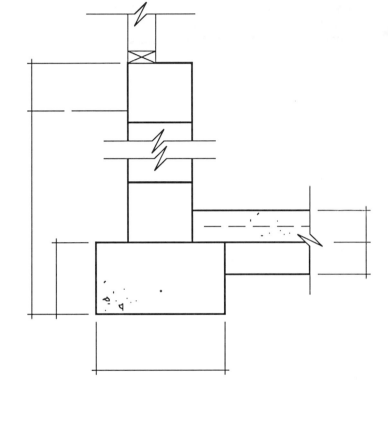

CONC. BLOCK FOUNDATION WALL
2 Story
1"=1'-0"   04229-8

CONC. BLOCK FOUNDATION WALL
Basement
1"=1'-0"   04229-9

NOTATION CHECKLIST, SAMPLE NOTES

MUDSILL W/ LEVELING GROUT
ANCHOR BOLTS
LEDGER
ANCHOR FOR LEDGER
GROUTED CONCRETE BLOCK
FOUNDATION WALL REINFORCING
CONCRETE FOOTING W/GROUT KEY
CONCRETE FOOTING REINFORCING BARS
INSULATION
TERMITE SHIELD
CRAWLSPACE
RODENT BARRIER
VAPOR BARRIER W/SAND COVER
GRADE
DRAINAGE

8" CONCRETE BLOCK
12" CONCRETE BLOCK
CONC. SLAB
SEE FOUNDATION PLAN FOR SLAB THICKNESS
    & FIN. FLOOR ELEV.
SEE FOUNDATION PLAN FOR TOP OF FTG. ELEV.
FLASHING
#4 @ 48" O.C. ALTERNATE - GROUT REINF. CELLS
HORIZ. JOINT REINF. @ 16" O.C.
FINISH GRADE HEIGHT VARIES
1/2" PREMOLDED JOINT FILLER
EXTRUDED CONTROL JOINT FILLER
FACE BRICK
1" PERIMETER INSULATION
BOND BEAM
STEP FTG., SEE DETAIL

04230 (a) CONCRETE BLOCK WALLS

See DETAIL DATA CHECKLIST for unit masonry preceding 04201(a).

DETAIL DATA CHECKLIST

BRICK AND CONCRETE BLOCK WALLS
These wall section details are to be combined with related
construction such as door frames, window frames, furred walls,
wall mounted fixtures, and wall penetrations such as for
pipe sleeves, access panels, etc.

Design limits of wall types, thickness and heights are strictly
limited by most building codes, so consult your local code for
the last word on preliminary design assumptions and final design.

Also, see literature from the National Concrete Masonry Association,
the Brick Institute of America, and the Construction Specifications
Institute for complete engineering, specification, and construction application information.

SMALL-SCALE GENERIC DETAILS

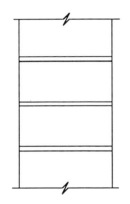

VERTICAL SECTION (8" HMU WALL)
04230-52

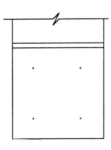

LINTEL (8" HMU WALL)
04230-54

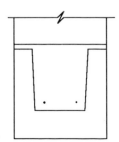

LINTEL (8" HMU WALL)
04230-55

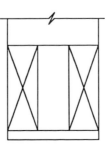

LINTEL (8" HMU WALL)
04230-56

04230 (a) CONCRETE BLOCK WALLS

FULL-SCALE GENERIC DETAILS

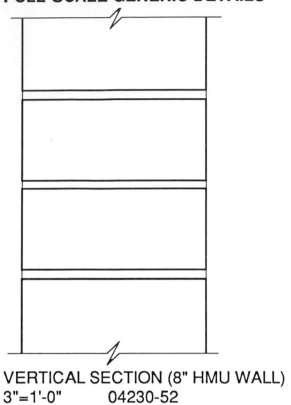

VERTICAL SECTION (8" HMU WALL)
3"=1'-0"   04230-52

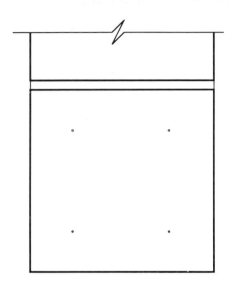

LINTEL (8" HMU WALL)
3"=1'-0"   04230-54

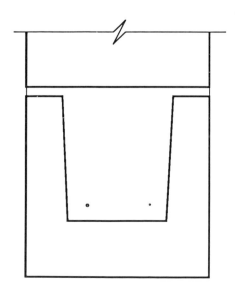

LINTEL (8" HMU WALL)
3"=1'-0"   04230-55

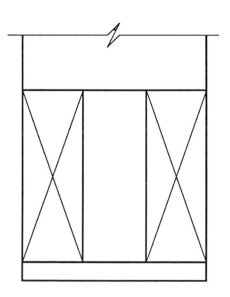

LINTEL (8" HMU WALL)
3"=1'-0"   04230-56

04230 (a) CONCRETE BLOCK WALLS

NOTATION CHECKLIST,
SAMPLE NOTES

MASONRY UNIT TYPE & SIZE
MORTAR JOINT TYPE & SIZE
REINFORCING
HOOKS/TRACKS/WALL MOUNTED FIXTURES
THRU-WALL SLEEVES
FLASHING/WATERPROOFING/CAULKING
INTERIOR FURRING/FINISH
DOOR/WINDOW/LOUVER FRAME
LINTEL

8" CONCRETE BLOCK, GROUT CORES FULL &
   BREAK OUT WEB AS REQ'D. FOR #4 BAR VERT.
8" LINTEL BLOCK
CONC. BLOCK
FLASHING
SEALANT
CAULK
#4 @ 48" O.C. ALTERNATE - GROUT REINF. CELLS
#4 VERT. REINFORCEMENT @ 2'-0" O.C.
HORIZ. JOINT REINF. @ 16" O.C.
1/2" PREMOLDED JOINT FILLER
EXTRUDED CONTROL JOINT FILLER
FACE BRICK
1" PERIMETER INSULATION
BOND BEAM W/#5 CONT. @ 32" O.C.
#4 CONT. IN BOND BEAM
SASH BLOCK - EACH SIDE
16 GA. STEEL MESH EVERY OTHER COURSE
   (@ masonry interior partition joint)
INSULATION
DISCONTINUE MASONRY REINF. @ CONTROL JOINT
EXPANSION SHIELD

04230 (b) CONCRETE BLOCK WALLS

See DETAIL DATA CHECKLIST for unit masonry preceding 04201(a).

DETAIL DATA CHECKLIST

BRICK AND CONCRETE BLOCK WALLS
These wall section details are to be combined with related
construction such as door frames, window frames, furred walls,
wall mounted fixtures, and wall penetrations such as for
pipe sleeves, access panels, etc.

Design limits of wall types, thickness and heights are strictly
limited by most building codes, so consult your local code for
the last word on preliminary design assumptions and final design.

Also, see literature from the National Concrete Masonry Association,
the Brick Institute of America, and the Construction Specifications
Institute for complete engineering, specification, and construction application information.

SMALL-SCALE GENERIC DETAILS

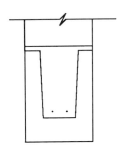

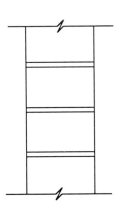

LINTEL (6" HMU WALL)
04230-32

VERTICAL SECTION (6" HMU WALL)
04230-34

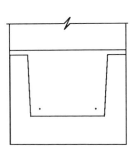

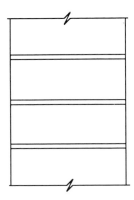

LINTEL (10" HMU WALL)
04230-72

VERTICAL SECTION (10" HMU WALL)
04230-74

04230 (b) CONCRETE BLOCK WALLS

FULL-SCALE GENERIC DETAILS

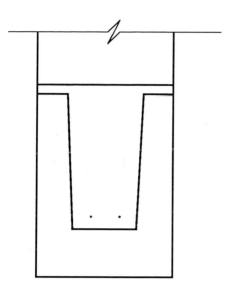

LINTEL (6" HMU WALL)
3"=1'-0"   04230-32

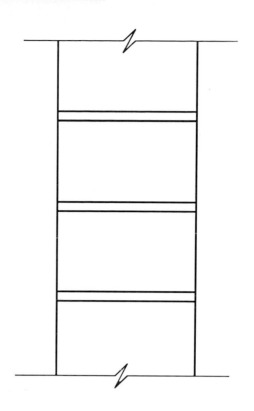

VERTICAL SECTION (6" HMU WALL)
3"=1'-0"   04230-34

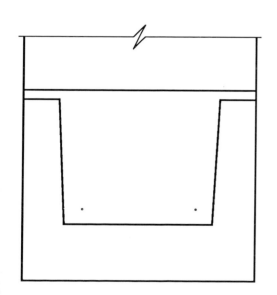

LINTEL (10" HMU WALL)
3"=1'-0"   04230-72

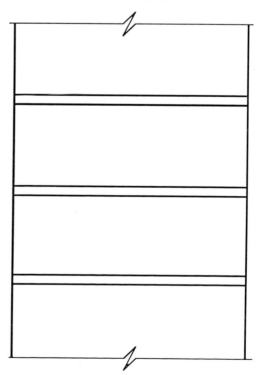

VERTICAL SECTION (10" HMU WALL)
3"=1'-0"   04230-74

04230 (b) CONCRETE BLOCK WALLS

NOTATION CHECKLIST, SAMPLE NOTES

MASONRY UNIT TYPE & SIZE
MORTAR JOINT TYPE & SIZE
REINFORCING
HOOKS/TRACKS/WALL-MOUNTED FIXTURES
THRU-WALL SLEEVES
FLASHING/WATERPROOFING/CAULKING
INTERIOR FURRING/FINISH
DOOR/WINDOW/LOUVER FRAME
LINTEL
8" CONCRETE BLOCK, GROUT CORES FULL &
   BREAK OUT WEB AS REQ'D. FOR #4 BAR VERT.
8" LINTEL BLOCK
CONC. BLOCK
FLASHING
SEALANT
CAULK
#4 @ 48" O.C. ALTERNATE - GROUT REINF. CELLS
#4 VERT. REINFORCEMENT @ 2'-0" O.C.
HORIZ. JOINT REINF. @ 16" O.C.
1/2" PREMOLDED JOINT FILLER
EXTRUDED CONTROL JOINT FILLER
FACE BRICK
1" PERIMETER INSULATION
BOND BEAM W/#5 CONT. @ 32" O.C.
#4 CONT. IN BOND BEAM
SASH BLOCK - EACH SIDE
16 GA. STEEL MESH EVERY OTHER COURSE
   (@ masonry interior partition joint)
INSULATION
DISCONTINUE MASONRY REINF. @ CONTROL JOINT
EXPANSION SHIELD

4" CMU
6" CMU
8" CMU
12" CMU
8" CMU, GROUT CORES FULL & BREAK OUT WEB
   AS REQ'D. FOR #4 BAR VERT
8" LINTEL BLOCK
CONC. BLOCK
SEE FOUNDATION PLAN FOR SLAB THICKNESS
   & FIN. FLOOR ELEV.
FLASHING
SEALANT
#4 @ 48" O.C. ALTERNATE - GROUT REINF. CELLS
HORIZ. JOINT REINF. @ 16" O.C.
1/2" PREMOLDED JOINT FILLER
FACE BRICK
1" PERIMETER INSULATION
BOND BEAM W/#5 CONT. @ 32" O.C.
#4 CONT. IN BOND BEAM
EXTRUDED CONTROL JOINT FILLER
SASH BLOCK - EACH SIDE
16 GA. STEEL MESH EVERY OTHER COURSE
   (@ masonry interior partition joint)
CAULK
SEMI-RIGID INSULATION

DISCONTINUE MASONRY REINF. @ CONTROL
JOINT
EXPANSION SHIELD
#4 VERT. @ 2'-0" O.C., GROUT CELLS WHERE
   REBAR OCCURS
#4 DOWEL @ 2'-0" O.C. W/ 4" HOOK @ BOTTOM
#4 VERT. REINFORCEMENT @ 2'-0" O.C.
METAL CLOSURE REQ'D. @ EXPOSED DECK ONLY
STUFF CAP W/ FIBERGLASS BLANKET INSUL.

04260 (a) MASONRY PARAPETS

See DETAIL DATA CHECKLIST for unit masonry preceding 04201(a).

DETAIL DATA CHECKLIST

BRICK AND CONCRETE BLOCK WALLS
Design limits of wall types, thickness and heights are strictly
limited by most building codes, so consult your local code for
the last word on preliminary design assumptions and final design.

Also, see literature from the National Concrete Masonry Association,
the Brick Institute of America, and the Construction Specifications
Institute for complete engineering, specification, and construction
application information.

SMALL-SCALE GENERIC DETAILS

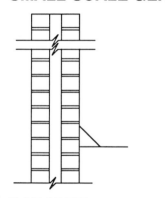

PARAPET
(8" Cav. Wall--3" Brick)
04260-1

PARAPET
(8" Wall--4" Brick)
04260-3

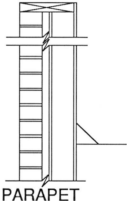

PARAPET
(4" Brick & Metal Frame)
04260-11

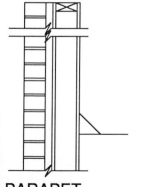

PARAPET
(4" Brick & Wood Frame)
04260-13

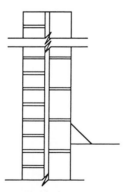

PARAPET (8" Wall--
4" Brick & 4" HMU)
04260-21

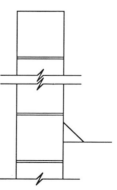

PARAPET
(8" HMU Wall)
04260-23

04260 (a) MASONRY PARAPETS

FULL-SCALE GENERIC DETAILS

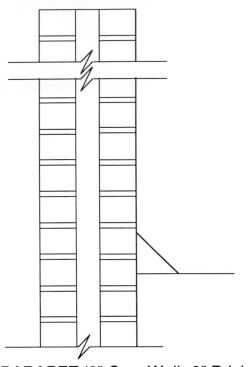

PARAPET (8" Cav. Wall--3" Brick)
1-1/2"=1'-0"   04260-1

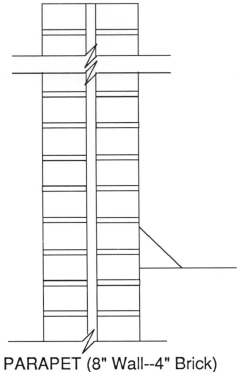

PARAPET (8" Wall--4" Brick)
1-1/2"=1'-0"   04260-3

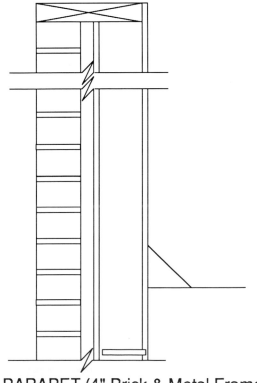

PARAPET (4" Brick & Metal Frame)
1-1/2"=1'-0"   04260-11

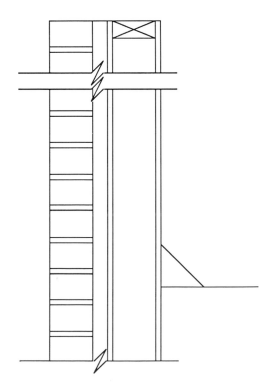

PARAPET (4" Brick & Wood Frame)
1-1/2"=1'-0"   04260-13

04260 (a) MASONRY PARAPETS

FULL-SCALE GENERIC DETAILS continued

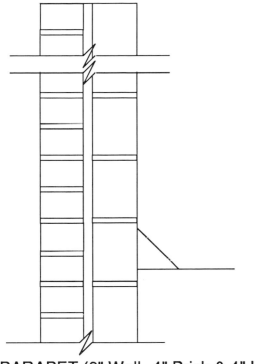

PARAPET (8" Wall--4" Brick & 4" HMU)
1-1/2"=1'-0"   04260-21

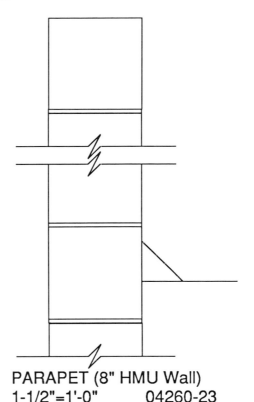

PARAPET (8" HMU Wall)
1-1/2"=1'-0"   04260-23

NOTATION CHECKLIST,
SAMPLE NOTES

COPING/CAP FLASHING
PARAPET WALL CONSTRUCTION
FLASHING/COUNTERFLASHING
WEEP
ANCHORS/TIES
SEALANT/CAULKING
CANT
ROOFING SURFACE
   (TYPE, LAYERS & COVER MATERIAL)
ROOF DECK INSULATION
ROOF CONSTRUCTION/FRAMING

FACE BRICK
METAL COPING SET W/ MASTIC SEALANT @
   SPLICE JOINTS
BASE FLASHING
TWO-PIECE METAL FLASHING
BRICK ANCHORS
CONT. 4" CANT
1" X 4" PREFORMED CANT
BLOCKING
RIGID THICK INSULATION
FOAMED-IN INSULATION
VAPOR BARRIER
1/2" PREMOLDED FILLER
5# FELT ON GYPSUM SHEATHING ON
   METAL STUDS @ 2'-0" O.C.
BRICK VENEER W/METAL TIES TO STUD WALL
WOOD BLKG. SECURED TO METAL STUD &
   BRICK W/1/4" DIA. BOLT @ 48" O.C.

04260 (b) MASONRY PARAPETS
See DETAIL DATA CHECKLIST for unit masonry preceding 04201(a).

DETAIL DATA CHECKLIST

BRICK AND CONCRETE BLOCK WALLS
Design limits of wall types, thickness and heights are strictly
limited by most building codes, so consult your local code for
the last word on preliminary design assumptions and final design.

Also, see literature from the National Concrete Masonry Association,
the Brick Institute of America, and the Construction Specifications
Institute for complete engineering, specification, and construction
application information.

SMALL-SCALE GENERIC DETAILS

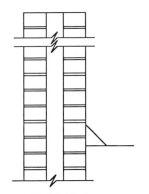

PARAPET
(10" Cav. Wall- 4" Brick)
04260-31

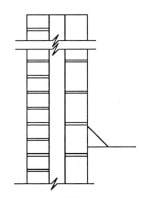

PARAPET
(10" Cav. Wall--4" Brick
& 4" HMU)   04260-32

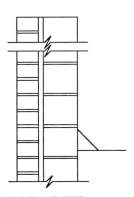

PARAPET
(10" Wall--4" HMU)
04260-33

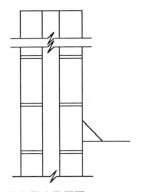

PARAPET
(10" Wall--4" Brick &
6" HMU)   04260-35

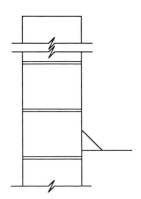

PARAPET
(10" HMU Wall)
04260-37

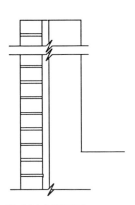

PARAPET
(10" Wall--Brick & Conc.)
04260-39

04260 (b) MASONRY PARAPETS

FULL-SCALE GENERIC DETAILS

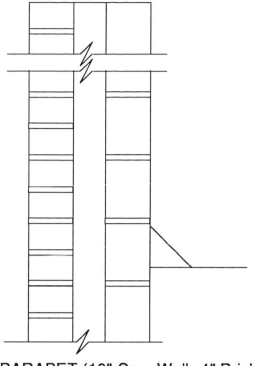

PARAPET (10" Cav. Wall--4" Brick)
1-1/2"=1'-0"   04260-31

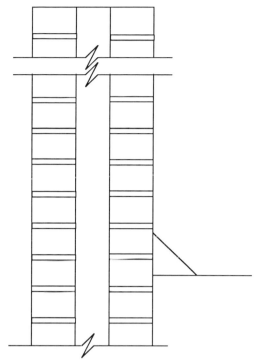

PARAPET (10" Cav. Wall--4" Brick &
4" HMU)   1-1/2"=1'-0"   04260-32

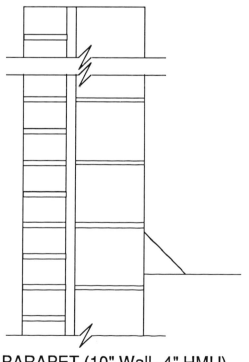

PARAPET (10" Wall--4" HMU)
1-1/2"=1'-0"   04260-33

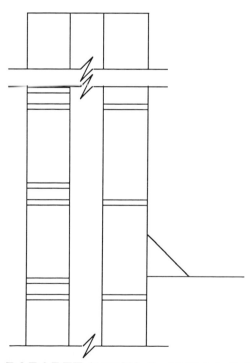

PARAPET (10" Wall--4" Brick & 6" HMU)
1-1/2"=1'-0"   04260-35

04260 (c) MASONRY PARAPETS

FULL-SCALE GENERIC DETAILS

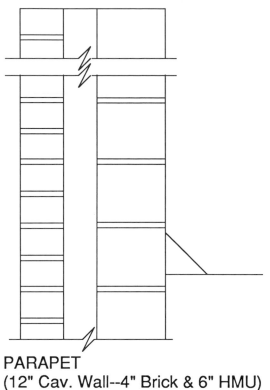

PARAPET
(12" Cav. Wall--4" Brick & 6" HMU)
1-1/2"=1'-0"   04260-41

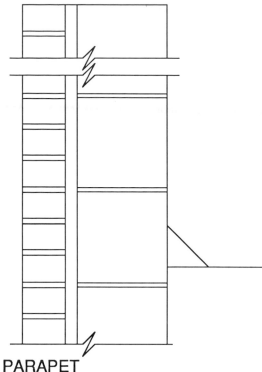

PARAPET
(12" Wall--4" Brick & 8" HMU)
1-1/2"=1'-0"   04260-42

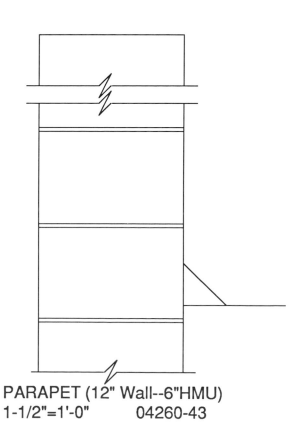

PARAPET (12" Wall--6"HMU)
1-1/2"=1'-0"   04260-43

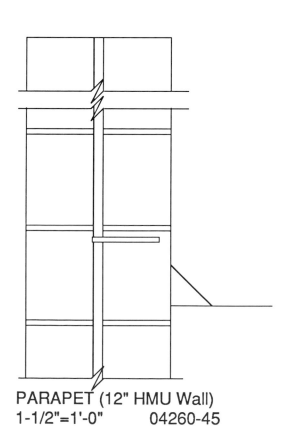

PARAPET (12" HMU Wall)
1-1/2"=1'-0"   04260-45

<u>04260 (c) MASONRY PARAPETS</u>

FULL-SCALE GENERIC DETAILS continued

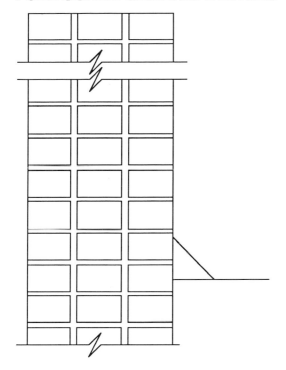

PARAPET (12" Wall--4" Brick)
1-1/2"=1'-0"   04260-47

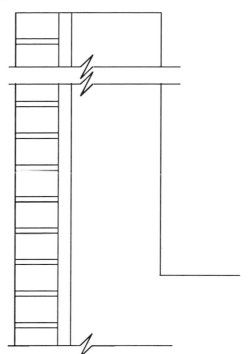

PARAPET (12" Wall--Brick & Conc.)
1-1/2"=1'-0"   04260-49

NOTATION CHECKLIST,
SAMPLE NOTES

COPING/CAP FLASHING
PARAPET WALL CONSTRUCTION
FLASHING/COUNTERFLASHING
WEEP
ANCHORS/TIES
SEALANT/CAULKING
CANT
ROOFING SURFACE
   (TYPE, LAYERS & COVER MATERIAL)
ROOF DECK INSULATION
ROOF CONSTRUCTION/FRAMING

METAL COPING SET W/ MASTIC SEALANT @
   SPLICE JOINTS ONLY
2 X 10 WOOD BLKG. SECURED TO METAL STUD &
   BRICK W/1/4" DIA. BOLT 8" LONG @ 48" O.C.
BASE FLASHING
TWO-PIECE METAL FLASHING
FACE BRICK
FOAMED-IN INSULATION
BRICK ANCHORS
CONT. 4" H. CANT
1" X 4" PREFORMED CANT
BLOCKING
2-1/4" THICK INSULATION
VAPOR BARRIER
1/2" PREMOLDED FILLER
5# FELT ON 2" GYPSUM SHEATHING ON
   4" METAL STUDS @ 2'-0" O.C.
BRICK VENEER W/METAL TIES TO STUD WALL

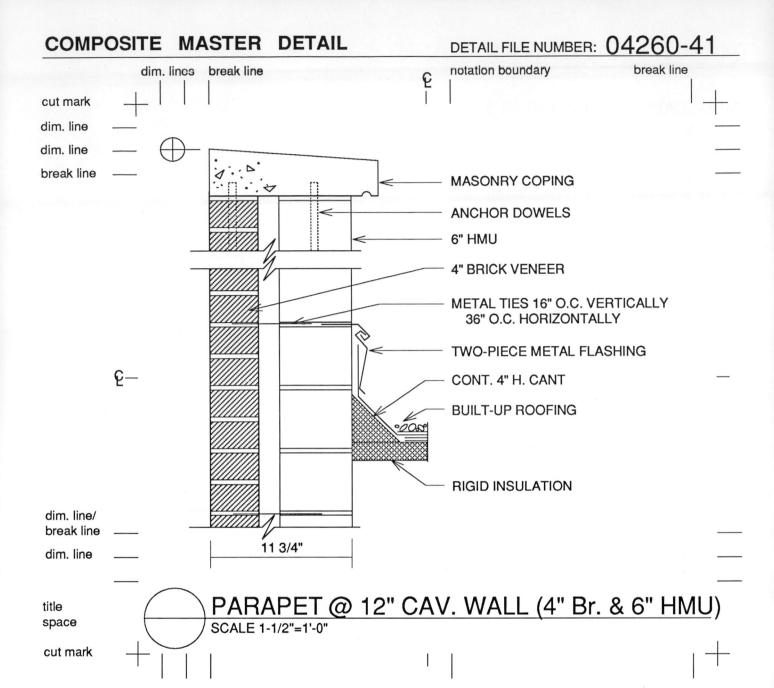

dim. lines   break line   notation boundary   break line

cut mark

dim. line

dim. line

break line

MASONRY COPING

ANCHOR DOWELS

6" HMU

4" BRICK VENEER

METAL TIES 16" O.C. VERTICALLY
36" O.C. HORIZONTALLY

TWO-PIECE METAL FLASHING

CONT. 4" H. CANT

BUILT-UP ROOFING

RIGID INSULATION

dim. line/
break line

dim. line

11 3/4"

title
space

cut mark

PARAPET @ 12" CAV. WALL (4" Br. & 6" HMU)
SCALE 1-1/2"=1'-0"

DETAIL INFORMATION
References, jobsite feedback, job history

04270 GLASS BLOCK

See DETAIL DATA CHECKLIST for unit masonry preceding 04201(a).

DETAIL DATA CHECKLIST

GLASS BLOCK
Basic use and characteristics:
__Use as panels or wall inserts as light diffusers for exterior screens and interior partitions
__Typical block sizes
    __3-7/8" thick x :
        __5-3/4" square
        __7-3/4" square
        __11-3/4" square
__Visible inside joint typically 1/4" thick, exterior joint 5/8" max.
__For non-bearing partitions or infill
    __Laid only in stackbond
__Provide movement joints and anchors as per manufacturers' instructions
__Maximum panel sizes
    __Let into wall frame: 24' long, 20 ' high without intermediate mullions (or max. area of 144 sq. ft.)
    __Anchored to wall: 10' x 10' without intermediate mullions (or max. area of 100 sq. ft.)
__Wall anchors
    __Metal strips to fasten glass block panels to adjacent walls
        __Typically 1-3/4" wide x 24" x 20 gauge galvanized steel strips
__Wall ties
    __Galvanized wire reinforcing lattice laid through horizontal mortar joints
        __Typically spaced at 24"
        __Not to extend across vertical movement joints
__Provide wall expansion strips at heads and jambs
__Details vary with manufacturer; see manufacturers' data on:
    __Special molded patterns
    __Diffusion characteristics (directed light such as exterior light directed to ceiling)
    __Modular patterning for integration with brick and concrete block
    __Anchors and wall ties
    __Expansion joints and strips
    __Mullions and stiffeners

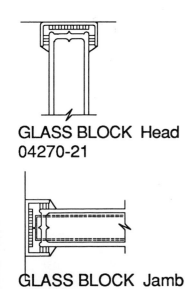

GLASS BLOCK Head
04270-21

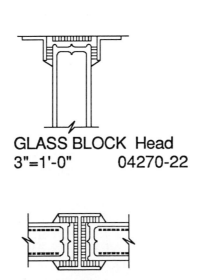

GLASS BLOCK Head
3"=1'-0"   04270-22

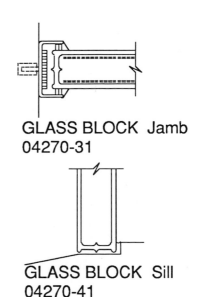

GLASS BLOCK Jamb
04270-31

GLASS BLOCK Jamb
04270-32

GLASS BLOCK Stiffener
04270-36

GLASS BLOCK Sill
04270-41

04270 GLASS BLOCK

FULL-SCALE GENERIC DETAILS

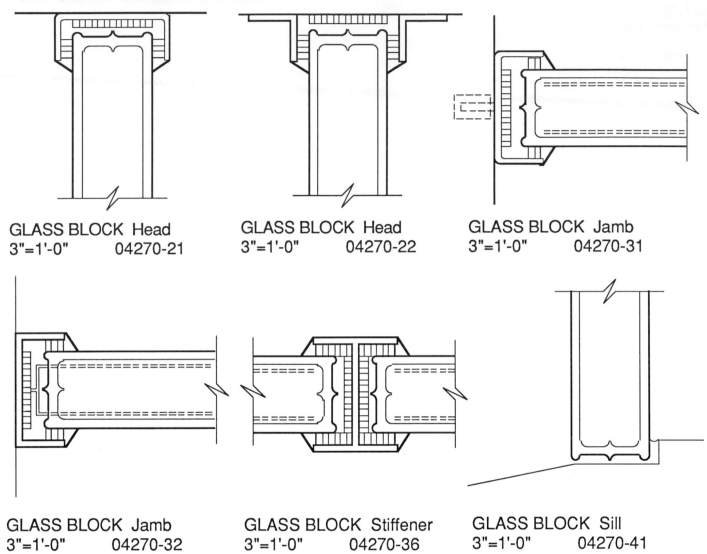

GLASS BLOCK Head
3"=1'-0"   04270-21

GLASS BLOCK Head
3"=1'-0"   04270-22

GLASS BLOCK Jamb
3"=1'-0"   04270-31

GLASS BLOCK Jamb
3"=1'-0"   04270-32

GLASS BLOCK Stiffener
3"=1'-0"   04270-36

GLASS BLOCK Sill
3"=1'-0"   04270-41

NOTATION CHECKLIST, SAMPLE NOTES

METAL
CHANNEL/ANGLE
ANCHOR
FLASHING
EXPANSION STRIP
CAULKING
JOINT REINFORCING

OAKUM
EXPANSION STRIP
ASPHALT EMULSION
PANEL REINFORCING
PANEL ANCHOR
HOOKED WIRE ANCHOR
ROOFERS FELT
GALV. DOVETAIL ANCHOR
DOVETAIL ANCHOR SLOT @ 24"
O.C.

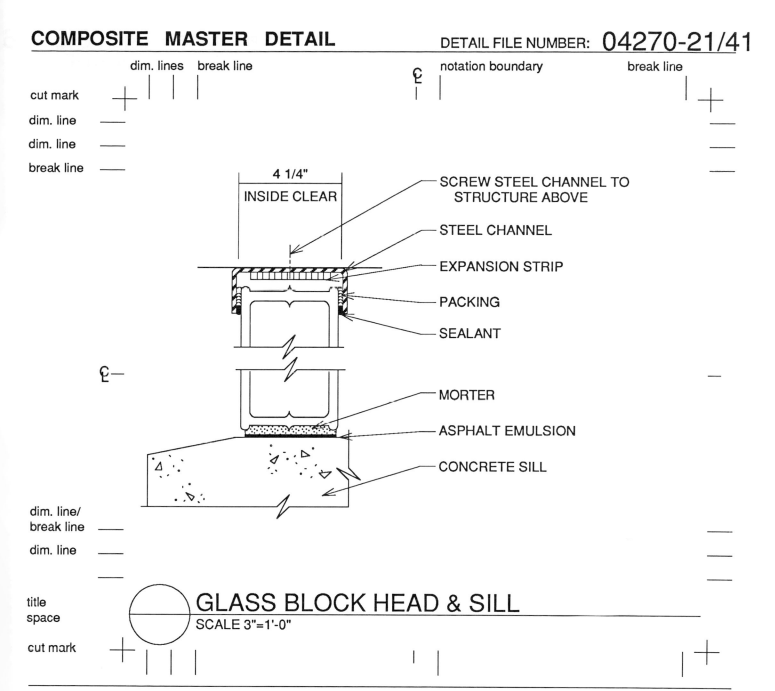

cut mark
dim. line
dim. line
break line

dim. lines   break line

notation boundary   break line

4 1/4"
INSIDE CLEAR

SCREW STEEL CHANNEL TO STRUCTURE ABOVE

STEEL CHANNEL

EXPANSION STRIP

PACKING

SEALANT

MORTER

ASPHALT EMULSION

CONCRETE SILL

dim. line/
break line

dim. line

title
space

GLASS BLOCK HEAD & SILL
SCALE 3"=1'-0"

cut mark

DETAIL INFORMATION
References, jobsite feedback, job history

04420 MASONRY COPINGS

FULL-SCALE GENERIC DETAILS

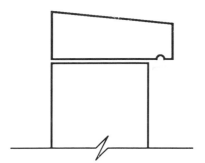

MASONRY COPING (8" Parapet)
1-1/2"=1'-0"   04420-51

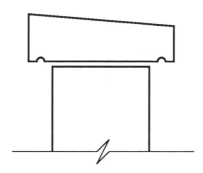

MASONRY COPING (8" Parapet)
1 1/2"=1'-0"   04420-52

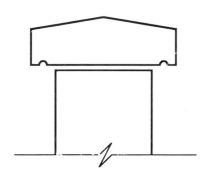

MASONRY COPING (8" Parapet)
1-1/2"=1'-0"   04420-53

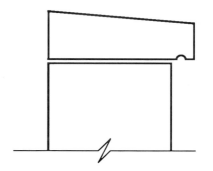

MASONRY COPING (10" Parapet)
1-1/2"=1'-0"   04420-61

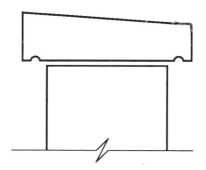

MASONRY COPING (10" Parapet)
1 1/2"=1'-0"   04420-62

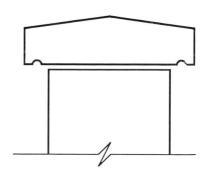

MASONRY COPING (10" Parapet)
1-1/2"=1'-0"   04420-63

04420 MASONRY COPINGS

FULL-SCALE GENERIC DETAILS continued

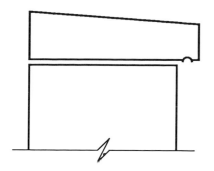

MASONRY COPING (12" Parapet)
1-1/2"=1'-0"   04420-71

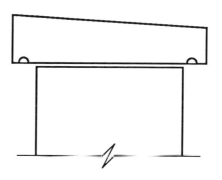

MASONRY COPING (12" Parapet)
1-1/2"=1'-0"   04420-72

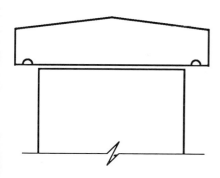

MASONRY COPING (12" Parapet)
1-1/2"=1'-0"   04420-73

NOTATION CHECKLIST,
SAMPLE NOTES

COPING (TYPE, MATERIAL & SIZE)
SETTING BED
ANCHOR/DOWELS
DRIP EDGE
NAILER
FLASHING/COUNTERFLASHING
PARAPET CONSTRUCTION

COPING STONE
JOINT COVER
TIE BACK ANCHOR
CANT
ROOFING

04450 STONE VENEER

See DETAIL DATA CHECKLIST for unit masonry preceding 04201(a).

DETAIL DATA CHECKLIST

STONE MASONRY VENEER
__Facing panels or unit stone typical sizes
    __Limestone -- 7/8", 2-1/4", 3", thick; 5' x 14' typical maximum panel
    __Marble -- 1/2" to 2" thick; 6' x 7' typical maximum panel
    __Granite -- 1-1/4" and thicker , 4' x 10' typical maximum panel
    __Slate -- 1", 1-1/2" thick; 4' x 8' typical maximum panel
__Water resistance
    __Limestone -- Low water resistance
       (middle grade absorption by weight max. % = 7.5)
    __Marble -- High water resistance
       (absorption by weight max. % = .75)
    __Granite -- Very high water resistance
       (absorption by weight max. % = .04)
    __Slate -- High water resistance
       (absorption by weight max. % = .25 exterior)
__Contact suppliers and trade associations for data and consultation
on anchoring systems

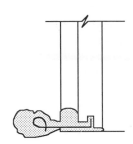

STONE VENEER @ BASE
Wire Anchor
04450-41

SMALL-SCALE GENERIC DETAILS

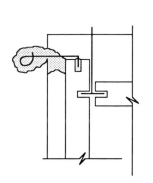

STONE VENEER @ CEILING
Wire Anchor
04450-43

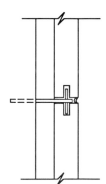

STONE VENEER @
VERT. JOINT   Wire Anchor
04450-46

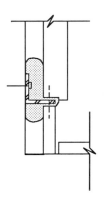

STONE VENEER @ BASE
Steel Angle
04450-51

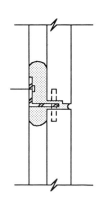

STONE VENEER @
HORIZ. JOINT   Steel Angle
04450-52

STONE VENEER
Dovetail Joint
04450-56

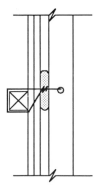

STONE VENEER
Wire tie to Wood Stud
04450-61

04450 STONE VENEER

FULL-SCALE GENERIC DETAILS

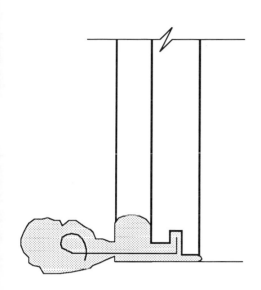

STONE VENEER @ BASE
Wire Anchor
3"=1'-0"   04450-41

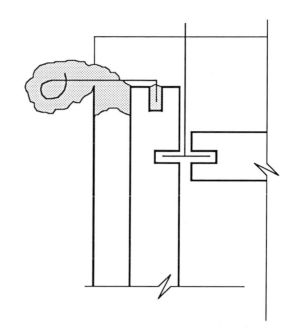

STONE VENEER @ CEILING
Wire Anchor
3"=1'-0"   04450-43

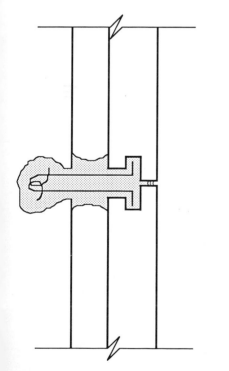

STONE VENEER @ VERT. JOINT
Wire Anchor
3"=1'-0"   04450-46

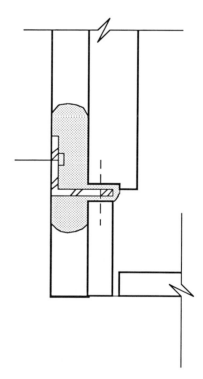

STONE VENEER @ BASE
Steel Angle
3"=1'-0"   04450-51

04450 STONE VENEER

FULL-SCALE GENERIC DETAILS continued

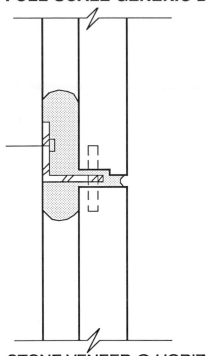

STONE VENEER @ HORIZ. JOINT
Steel Angle
3"=1'-0"   04450-52

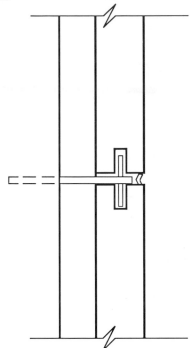

STONE VENEER
Dovetail Joint
3"=1'-0"   04450-56

NOTATION CHECKLIST,
SAMPLE NOTES

STONE (TYPE & THICKNESS)
ANCHOR/TIE (TYPE, MATERIAL & SIZE)
MORTAR BED
ADJACENT WALL MATERIAL
WALL CONSTRUCTION/FRAMING
04450 STONE VENEER

TIE WIRE, CEMENTED INTO HOLES
PIN ANCHOR
DOVETAIL INSERT
DOVETAIL ANCHOR
THREADED INSERT & EYE BOLT & STRIP LINER
LOOP TIE THRY DRILLED HOLE
STRIP LINER WITH DOWELS
STRIP HANGER
THREADED ROSETTE
RELIEF ANGLE & ANCHOR
WELD TO CLIP

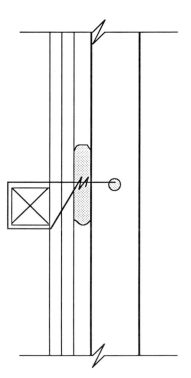

STONE VENEER
Wire tie to Wood Stud
3"=1'-0"   04450-61

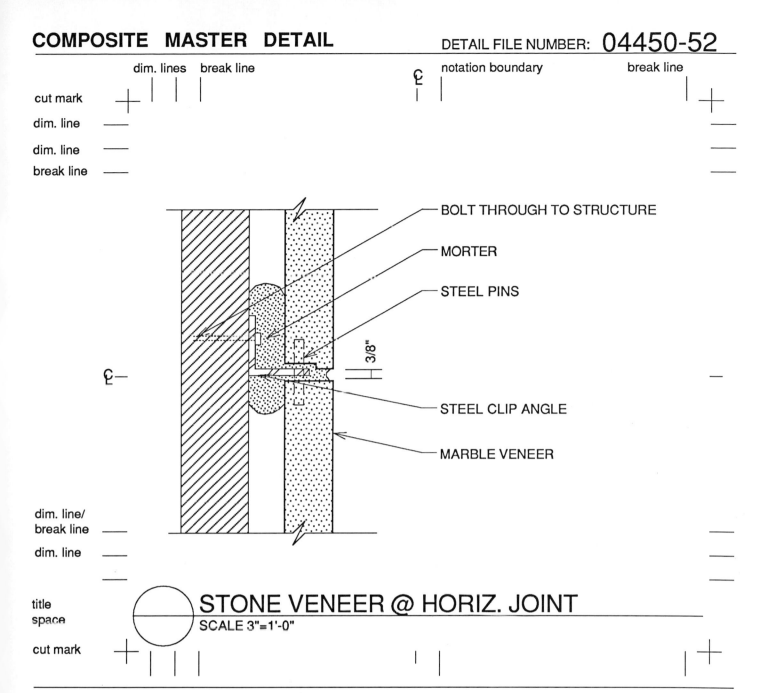

dim. lines   break line

cut mark

dim. line

dim. line

break line

notation boundary   break line

BOLT THROUGH TO STRUCTURE

MORTER

STEEL PINS

3/8"

STEEL CLIP ANGLE

MARBLE VENEER

dim. line/
break line

dim. line

title
space

STONE VENEER @ HORIZ. JOINT

SCALE 3"=1'-0"

cut mark

DETAIL INFORMATION
References, jobsite feedback, job history

CHAPTER 5

Metals
05000

05   METALS

05055 METAL FASTENINGS

DETAIL DATA CHECKLIST

METAL FASTENINGS
Wall-mounted fixtures and equipment are often packaged with the required anchors and fastenings so, in general, details only show generic dash- or dot-line indications of screw or bolt attachments.

Adequate backing, framing, blocking, or other mount supports are the most crucial aspect of detailing and constructing wall-hung fixtures, and the most common point of failure. The best rule is to over-design the attachment system as long as it isn't oversized for the item to be attached or for the support framing and backing systems.

Component sizes:
    __Lag bolts, machine bolts, and carriage bolts come in 1/4", 3/8", 1/2", 5/8", 7/8" and 1" diameters
    __Screws and bolts are commonly sized in 1/8" increments from 1/4" diameter to 1-1/4"
    __Lengths of bolts range from 1" to 12"
    __Lengths of wood screws range from 1/4" to 6"

__Toggle bolts and Molly bolts are for connections through the surfaces of hollow walls
    (a spring or tumbler activated expansion device opens when the bolt is turned to grip the fastener to the wall)
__Lag bolts and expansion shields are for insertion in masonry walls
    (a lead or fiber casing in a pre-drilled hole will expand to grip the masonry wall when a lag bolt or machine bolt is locked in)

SMALL-SCALE GENERIC DETAILS

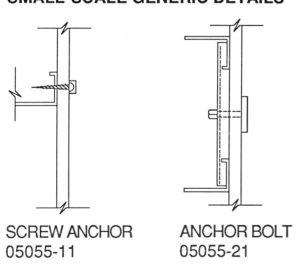

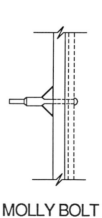

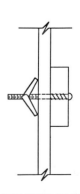

SCREW ANCHOR
05055-11

ANCHOR BOLT
05055-21

MOLLY BOLT
05055-31

TOGGLE BOLT
05055-41

05055 METAL FASTENINGS

FULL-SCALE GENERIC DETAILS

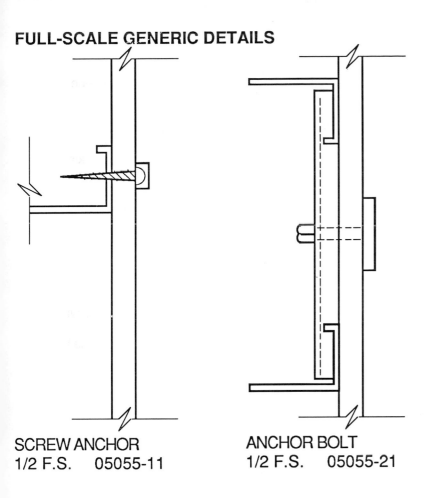

SCREW ANCHOR
1/2 F.S.   05055-11

ANCHOR BOLT
1/2 F.S.   05055-21

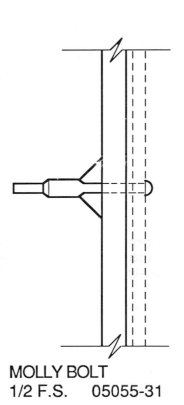

MOLLY BOLT
1/2 F.S.   05055-31

NOTATION CHECKLIST,
SAMPLE NOTES

WALL FRAMING
WALL FINISH
CONNECTOR
CONNECTOR REINFORCING
ATTACHED FIXTURE
ANCHOR TO BLOCK WALL W/EXPANSION ANCHORS
HEX NUT
WASHER
TOP PAD
MALE/FEMALE FASTENER THRU PRE-DRILLED HOLES
3/4" DIA. BOLT & LEAD PLUG
THRU BOLT

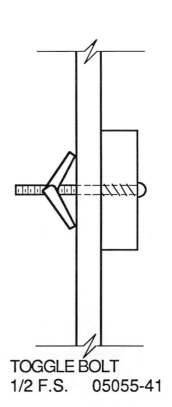

TOGGLE BOLT
1/2 F.S.   05055-41

05310 METAL DECKS

DETAIL DATA CHECKLIST

METAL DECKS FOR FLOORS AND ROOFS
__Typically used in steel framed buildings atop open web steel joists
__Painted or galvanized to prevent corrosion
__Welded wire steel mesh for temperature reinforcement if using lightweight insulating concrete

Component sizes:
    __"Centering" metal, 22, 24, 26 gauge with 2-1/2" to 4" wide corrugation, 1" deep, spans 2' to 10'
    __Narrow rib deck: 6" rib centers, 1-1/2" deep, 30" wide panels, spans 4' - 8'
    __Intermediate rib deck: 6" rib centers, 1-1/2" deep, 30" wide panels), spans 5' - 10'
    __Wide rib deck: 8" rib centers, 3" deep, 24" wide panels, spans 10' - 16'
    __Lengths to 48'

__Attach metal decking to framing every 36" minimum

SMALL-SCALE GENERIC DETAILS

METAL DECK Steel Deck
W/Insul. & Slab
05310-11

METAL DECK Steel Deck
W/Insul. & Slab
05310-13

METAL DECK Steel Deck
W/Rigid Insul.
05310-17

METAL DECK Steel Deck
W/Insul. Conc.
05310-15

METAL DECK Steel Deck
W/3" Insul.
05310-19

05310 METAL DECKS

FULL-SCALE GENERIC DETAILS

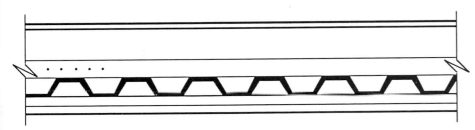

METAL DECK Steel Deck W/Insul. & Slab
1-1/2"=1'-0"   05310-11

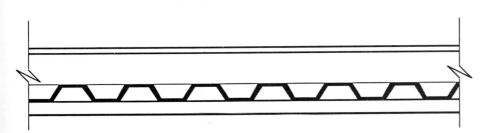

METAL DECK Steel Deck W/Insul. & Slab
1-1/2"=1'-0"   05310-13

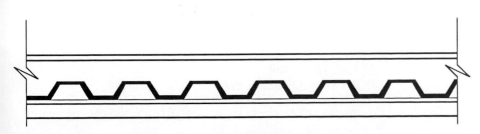

METAL DECK Steel Deck W/Insul. Conc.
1-1/2"=1'-0"   05310-15

05310 METAL DECKS

FULL-SCALE GENERIC DETAILS continued

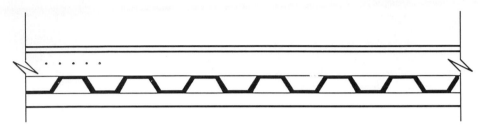

METAL DECK Steel Deck W/Rigid Insul.
1-1/2"=1'-0"　　　　　05310-17

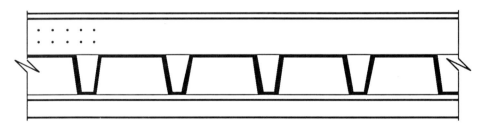

METAL DECK Steel Deck W/3" Insul.
1-1/2"=1'-0"　　　　　05310-19

NOTATION CHECKLIST,
SAMPLE NOTES

ROOFING SURFACE
　　(TYPE, LAYERS & COVER MATERIAL)
ROOF SLAB
METAL DECK
ROOF DECK INSULATION
ROOF CONSTRUCTION/FRAMING

CONCRETE
LIGHTWEIGHT CONCRETE
GALV. CORRUGATED METAL DECKING
CORR. METAL
PLATE STIFFENER
FILLER
CLOSURE STRIP
BOLT W/NEOPRENE WASHER
SHEET METAL FLASHING W/FASTENERS & EXP.
　　SHIELDS @ 12" O.C., STAGGERED, PROVIDE
　　NEOPRENE WASHERS
METAL ANGLE
EXP. BOLTS @ 24" O.C.

05420 METAL FRAME CHASE WALLS

DETAIL DATA CHECKLIST

METAL FRAME CHASE WALLS

See the Detail Data Checklist prior to detail 09110 in Chapter 09000 --Finishes for detail design data pertaining to metal stud framing, furring, and channels.

SMALL-SCALE GENERIC DETAILS

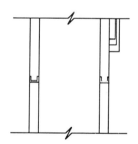

5" CHASE WALL
Plan
05420-11

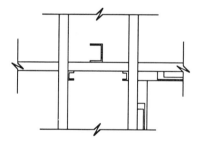

CHASE WALL
@ THRU SUSP. CLG.
05420-13

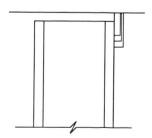

CHASE WALL
@ CLG. OR SLAB
05420-15

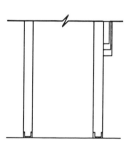

CHASE WALL
@ FLOOR
05420-17

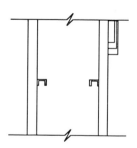

CHASE WALL
@ BRACING Sect.
05420-19

05516 SHIPS LADDER

DETAIL DATA CHECKLIST

SHIPS LADDER

Metal ships ladders are typically used in tight spaces in mechanical rooms or industrial spaces They're usually selected prefabricated from a stock catalog or fabricated to order at a specialist metal shop.

__60 degree mounting angle is typical
__Width: 18" minimum, 24" preferred
__Treads of checkered plate or open grating steel to ensure non-slip surface and prevent accumulation of slippery substances such as water and grease
__Tread-to-tread height is 12" maximum, 10" preferred
__Stringers are from stock steel channels
__Anchor the stringers to floor and wall construction with minimum 3/4" diameter expansion bolts, pre- set bolts, or through-bolts
__1" or larger diameter pipe rail at one or both sides

SMALL-SCALE GENERIC DETAILS

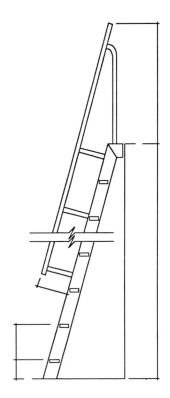

SHIPS LADDER
05516-11

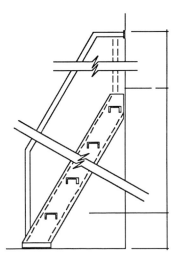

SHIPS LADDER
05516-16

05516 SHIPS LADDER

FULL-SCALE GENERIC DETAILS

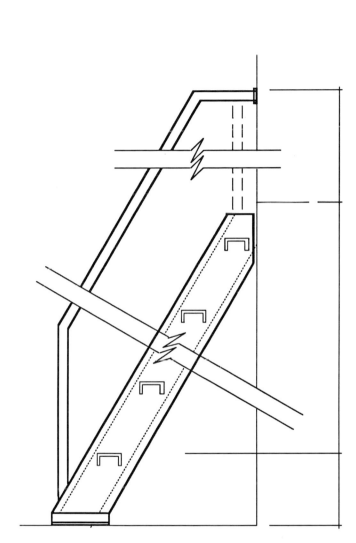

SHIPS LADDER
3/4"=1'-0"   05516-16

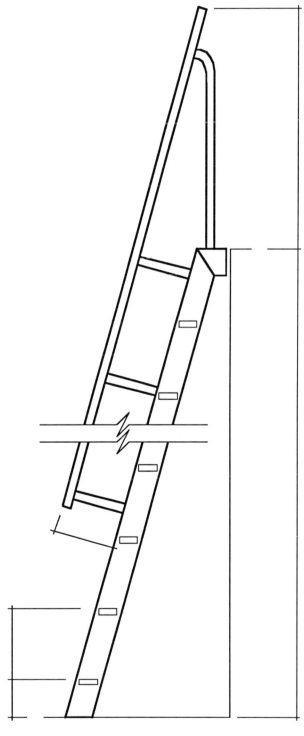

SHIPS LADDER
3/4"=1'-0"   05516-11

NOTATION CHECKLIST

PIPE RAIL
METAL TREADS
STRINGER
TREAD BRACKETS
ANGLE
WALL ANCHOR/FLOOR
ANCHOR

317

DETAIL FILE NUMBER: 05516-16

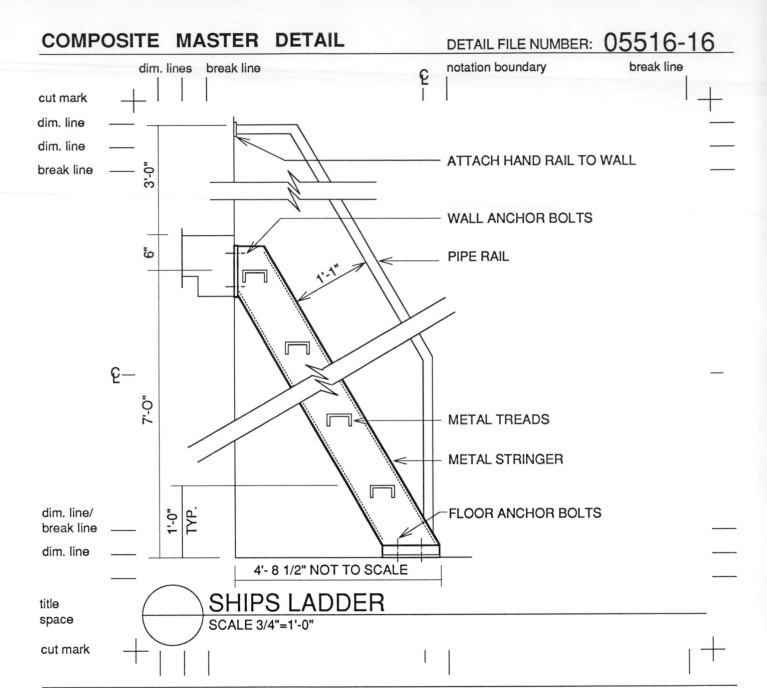

dim. lines   break line   notation boundary   break line

cut mark

dim. line

dim. line

break line

3'-0"

6"

ATTACH HAND RAIL TO WALL

WALL ANCHOR BOLTS

PIPE RAIL

1'-1"

7'-0"

METAL TREADS

METAL STRINGER

dim. line/
break line

dim. line

1'-0"
TYP.

FLOOR ANCHOR BOLTS

4'- 8 1/2" NOT TO SCALE

title
space

SHIPS LADDER
SCALE 3/4"=1'-0"

cut mark

DETAIL INFORMATION
References, jobsite feedback, job history

05517 ROOF LADDERS

DETAIL DATA CHECKLIST

VERTICAL LADDER OR ROOF LADDER
Roof ladders are usually selected prefabricated from a stock catalog or fabricated to order at a specialist metal shop.

__Treads: 1" steel pipe or 3/4" steel bars
__Width: 18" minimum, 24" preferred
    __Top handrail, or grab bars, spaced 24" apart
    __Top of handrail or grab bars 3'-6" high minimum
    Mount vertical stringer 7" from wall
__Roof ladder at parapet must include a metal grid stepping platform above the parapet supported by the handrail or
    grab bars

SMALL-SCALE GENERIC DETAILS

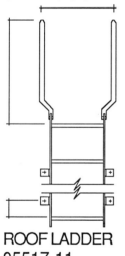
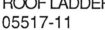

ROOF LADDER
05517-11

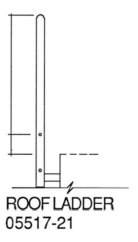

ROOF LADDER
05517-21

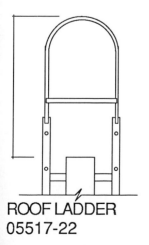

ROOF LADDER
05517-22

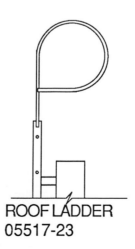

ROOF LADDER
05517-23

05517 ROOF LADDERS

FULL-SCALE GENERIC DETAILS

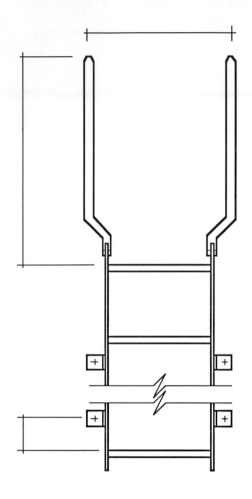

ROOF LADDER
3/4"=1'-0"   05517-11

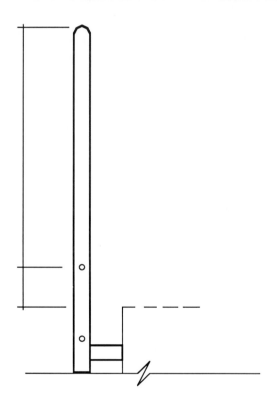

ROOF LADDER
3/4"=1'-0"   05517-21

05517 ROOF LADDERS

FULL-SCALE GENERIC DETAILS continued

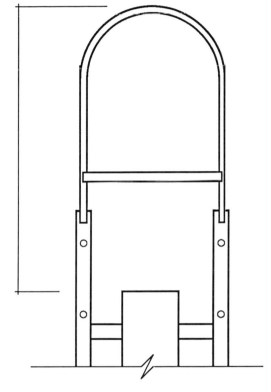

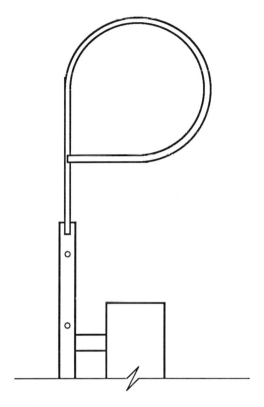

ROOF LADDER
3/4"=1'-0"   05517-22

ROOF LADDER
3/4"=1'-0"   05517-23

NOTATION CHECKLIST,
SAMPLE NOTES

TOP RAIL
PARAPET COPING/CAP
PARAPET CONSTRUCTION
LADDER RUNGS (SIZE & SPACING)
BENT BAR BRACKET
ANCHORS TO WALL

TOP OF COPING
PLUG WELD
EXP. BOLT.
BENT BAR BRACKET; WELD TO
 LADDER
1-1/4" PIPE
WELD ALL AROUND CLOSED END
3/4" DIA. RUNGS 1'-0" O.C.
2-1/2" X 3/8" FLAT BAR
2-1/2" X 3/8" BENT BAR BRACKET

COMPOSITE MASTER DETAIL

DETAIL FILE NUMBER: **05517-11**

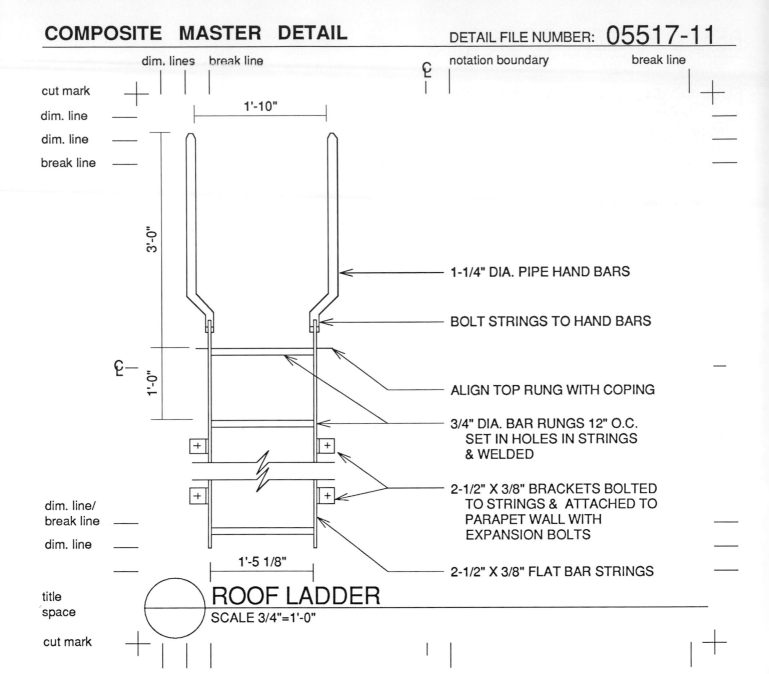

dim. lines   break line   notation boundary   break line

cut mark

dim. line

dim. line

break line

1'-10"

3'-0"

1'-0"

1-1/4" DIA. PIPE HAND BARS

BOLT STRINGS TO HAND BARS

ALIGN TOP RUNG WITH COPING

3/4" DIA. BAR RUNGS 12" O.C.
SET IN HOLES IN STRINGS
& WELDED

2-1/2" X 3/8" BRACKETS BOLTED
TO STRINGS & ATTACHED TO
PARAPET WALL WITH
EXPANSION BOLTS

dim. line/
break line

dim. line

1'-5 1/8"

2-1/2" X 3/8" FLAT BAR STRINGS

title
space

ROOF LADDER
SCALE 3/4"=1'-0"

cut mark

DETAIL INFORMATION
References, jobsite feedback, job history

05521 METAL HANDRAILS

DETAIL DATA CHECKLIST

HANDRAILS, BRACKETS, AND ANCHORS
Wall connection systems include:

__Horizontal steel stud fastened to vertical metal wall studs; anchor handrail through wall with expansion bolts

__Steel plate welded to wall studs

__Metal spacer set in plaster wall with space for expansion bolt insert

__Expansion bolts in concrete or masonry walls threaded end connection for handrail support

__Cast in place brackets, such as for newels and handrail posts supported at the edge of landings and floor slabs

__All railings must be able to sustain a load of 200 pounds applied in any way at any point

__Wall-mounted handrails must be at least 1-1/2" from the wall and not intrude on the legally required stair width

__Ends of handrails must be turned into newel posts, floors, to walls

__See manufacturers' catalogs and building code requirements for additional detailing instructions, references, and sample notation

SMALL-SCALE GENERIC DETAILS

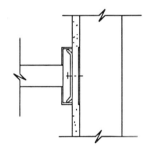

RAILING @ WOOD FRAME
WALL
05521-11

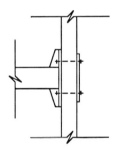

RAILING @
METAL PARTITION
05521-13

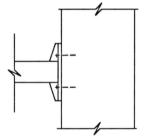

RAILING @
MASONRY OR CONC.
05521-15

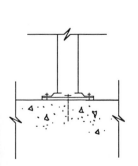

RAIL POST @ SLAB
05521-17

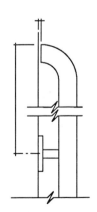

STAIR HANDRAIL
Wall Mounted
05521-21

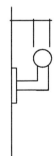

STAIR HANDRAIL
Wall Mounted
05521-22

05521 METAL HANDRAILS

FULL-SCALE GENERIC DETAILS

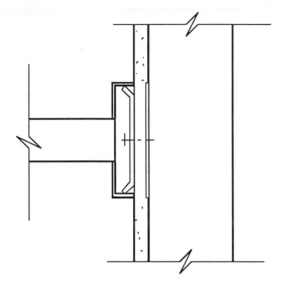

RAILING @ WOOD FRAME WALL
3"=1'-0"   05521-11

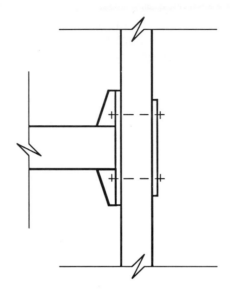

RAILING @ METAL PARTITION
3"=1'-0"   05521-13

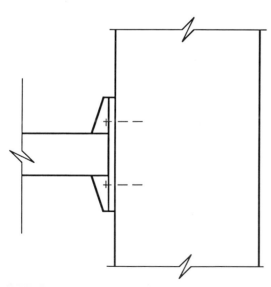

RAILING @ MASONRY OR CONC.
3"=1'-0"   05521-15

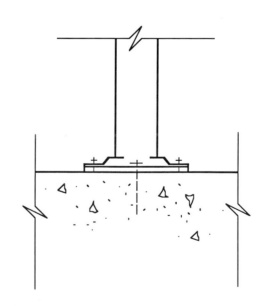

RAIL POST @ SLAB
3"=1'-0"   05521-17

05521 METAL HANDRAILS

FULL-SCALE GENERIC DETAILS continued

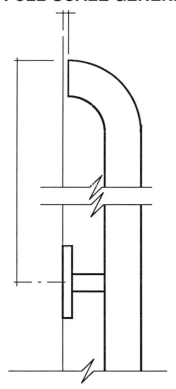

STAIR HANDRAIL Wall-Mounted
3"=1'-0"   05521-21

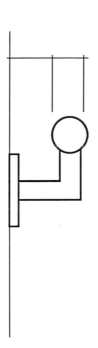

STAIR HANDRAIL Wall-Mounted
3"=1'-0"   05521-22

NOTATION CHECKLIST, SAMPLE NOTES

HANDRAIL (MATERIAL & SIZE)
HANDRAIL SUPPORT
ANCHOR TO WALL (TYPE & SIZE)
WALL CONSTRUCTION/FRAMING
PIPE RAILING, WELD & GRIND JOINTS SMOOTH,
    PAINTED
PIPE HANDRAIL, WELDED CONNECTION,
    GRIND SMOOTH, PAINTED
STD. MTL. PIPE. CONT. TOP RAIL
PIPE VERT. SUPPORTS @ 4'-0" O.C.
    MAX. SPACING
INTERMEDIATES
1-1/2" PIPE RAILING, HORIZ. & VERT., ALL
    JOINTS TO BE WELDED, GRIND SMOOTH
STEEL PIPE SLEEVE
FLOOR LINE
WELD ALL AROUND, TYP.
3" DIA. X 1/4" THICK BEVELED STEEL PLATE
STEEL PIPE SLEEVE, FILL W/MOLTEN LEAD

COUNTERSUNK HOLE FOR POURING LEAD;
    INSERT 1/4" FLAT HEAD METAL SCREW INTO LEAD-
    SEAL JOINT WITH NON-PREFORMED JOINT SEALANT
    BEFORE PAINTING
GROUT FILL BEHIND BRACKET
STAINLESS STEEL BOLT THRU STEEL PLATE
METAL BRACKETS @ 48" O.C. MAX. & WITHIN
    12" OF ENDS
SUPPORTS @ 4'-0" O.C.
    MAX. SPACING
ANCHOR BOLTS
DEFORMED BAR, WELD TO PLATE, GROUT IN PLACE
BED PLATE IN SEALANT FOR EXTERIOR USE
STEEL STUD WALL BLOCKING
CAST WALL BRACKET @ 4'-0" O.C., SECURE TO CONC.
    WALL W/ANCHOR BOLTS INTO EXT.
    SHIELDS. USE LAG SCREWS @ STL. STUD CONST.
WALL BRACKET
METAL SPACER
METAL BACKING
EXPANSION BOLTS

dim. lines   break line   notation boundary   break line

cut mark

dim. line

dim. line

break line

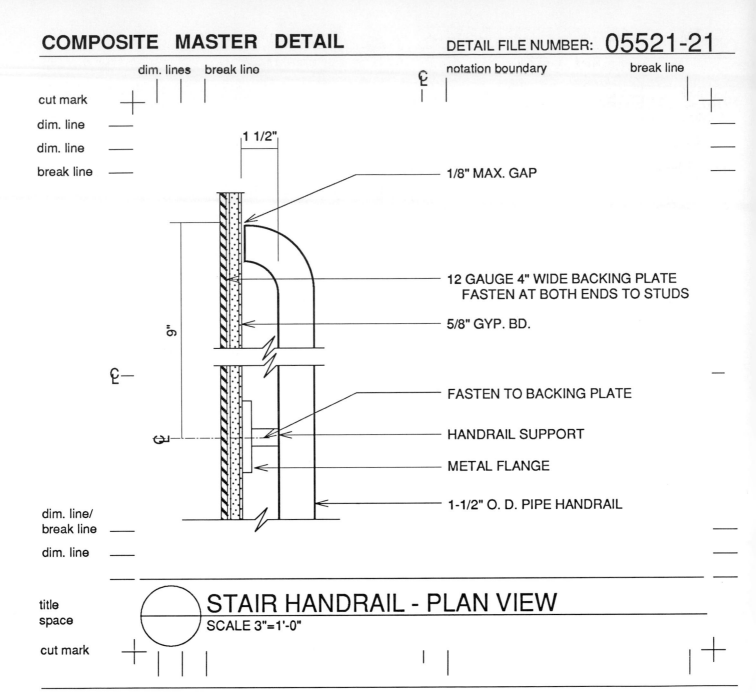

1 1/2"

1/8" MAX. GAP

12 GAUGE 4" WIDE BACKING PLATE
FASTEN AT BOTH ENDS TO STUDS

5/8" GYP. BD.

9"

FASTEN TO BACKING PLATE

HANDRAIL SUPPORT

METAL FLANGE

1-1/2" O. D. PIPE HANDRAIL

dim. line/
break line

dim. line

title
space

STAIR HANDRAIL - PLAN VIEW
SCALE 3"=1'-0"

cut mark

DETAIL INFORMATION
References, jobsite feedback, job history

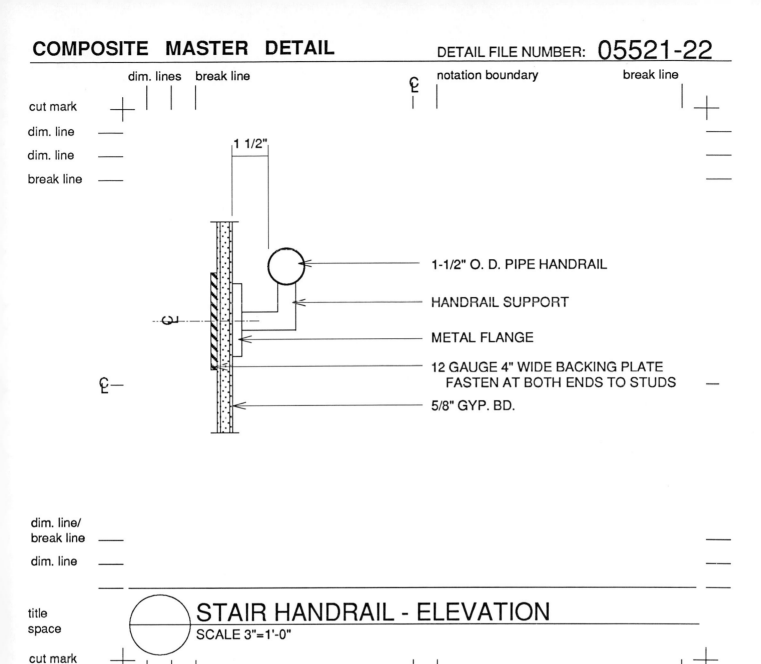

cut mark

dim. lines   break line   ₵   notation boundary   break line

dim. line

dim. line

break line

1 1/2"

1-1/2" O. D. PIPE HANDRAIL

HANDRAIL SUPPORT

METAL FLANGE

12 GAUGE 4" WIDE BACKING PLATE
FASTEN AT BOTH ENDS TO STUDS

5/8" GYP. BD.

dim. line/
break line

dim. line

title
space

STAIR HANDRAIL - ELEVATION
SCALE 3"=1'-0"

cut mark

DETAIL INFORMATION
References, jobsite feedback, job history

CHAPTER 6

Wood
06000

06102 WOOD POST @ BASE

DETAIL DATA CHECKLIST

POST AND BEAM CONSTRUCTION

BASE CONNECTORS FOR WOOD POSTS
__Wood post nominal and actual sizes
    __4 x 4 = 3-1/2" x 3-1/2"
    __6 x 6 = 5-1/2" x 5-1/2"
    __8 x 8 = 7-1/2" x 7-1/2"

__Base types:
    __Base plate with side plates
    __Precast metal shoe plate
    __U plate embedded in concrete
    __H plate embedded in concrete

__Provide approx. 3/4" leveling grout under base plate on concrete slabs or footings
__Embed 1/2" anchor bolts with hook ends into concrete slab or footing
__Use galvanized steel connectors
    __Size and number of bolts, nails, and other connectors as required by engineering calculations
__Match the fitted base support size to wood post size
    __Don't use oversized base connectors and try to compensate with wood wedges or shims

SMALL-SCALE GENERIC DETAILS

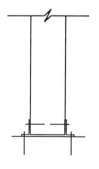

WOOD POST
@ BASE
06102-1

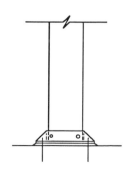

WOOD POST
@ BASE
06102-2

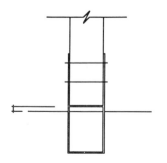

WOOD POST
@ BASE
06102-3

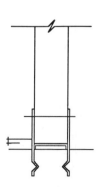

WOOD POST
@ BASE
06102-4

06102 WOOD POST @ BASE

FULL-SCALE GENERIC DETAILS

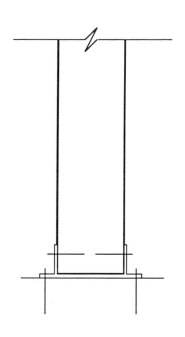

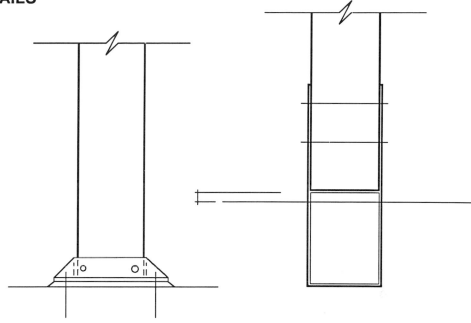

WOOD POST @ BASE
1-1/2"=1'-0"
06102-1

WOOD POST @ BASE
1-1/2"=1'-0"
06102-2

WOOD POST @ BASE
1-1/2"=1'-0"
06102-3

NOTATION CHECKLIST,
SAMPLE NOTES

    X   WOOD POST
STEEL BASE
WEEP HOLES
BOLTS TO SLAB
CONCRETE SLAB

CONCRETE FOOTING
CONCRETE PEDESTAL
SLOPE TOP OF FOOTING TO
DRAIN
STEEL PIN
MOISTURE BARRIER
TOP OF FLOOR SLAB ELEVATION
WELDED STEEL BASE PLATE
ANCHOR
BEARING PLATE
STEEL 'U'-STRAP

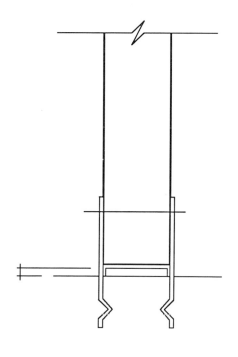

WOOD POST @ BASE
1-1/2"=1'-0"
06102-4

331

06104 (a) WOOD POST @ BEAM

DETAIL DATA CHECKLIST

POST AND BEAM CONSTRUCTION

WOOD POST AND BEAM CONNECTORS
__Connector types:
    __Nailed metal side plates
      __For light framing with minimal lateral forces
    __Bolted metal side plates
      __Sizes and spaces of bolts as per code or engineering calculations
    __U plate connector, nailed or bolted as required by engineering calculations or manufacturer's tables
    __Sheet metal connector, sized and nailed as required by engineering calculations or manufacturer's tables

SMALL-SCALE GENERIC DETAILS

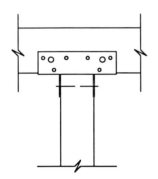

WOOD POST @ BEAM
06104-1

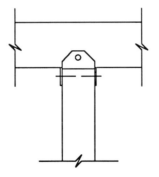

WOOD POST @ BEAM
06104-2

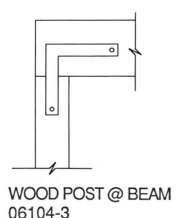

WOOD POST @ BEAM
06104-3

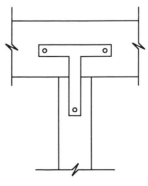

WOOD POST @ BEAM
06104-4

06104 (a) WOOD POST @ BEAM

FULL-SCALE GENERIC DETAILS

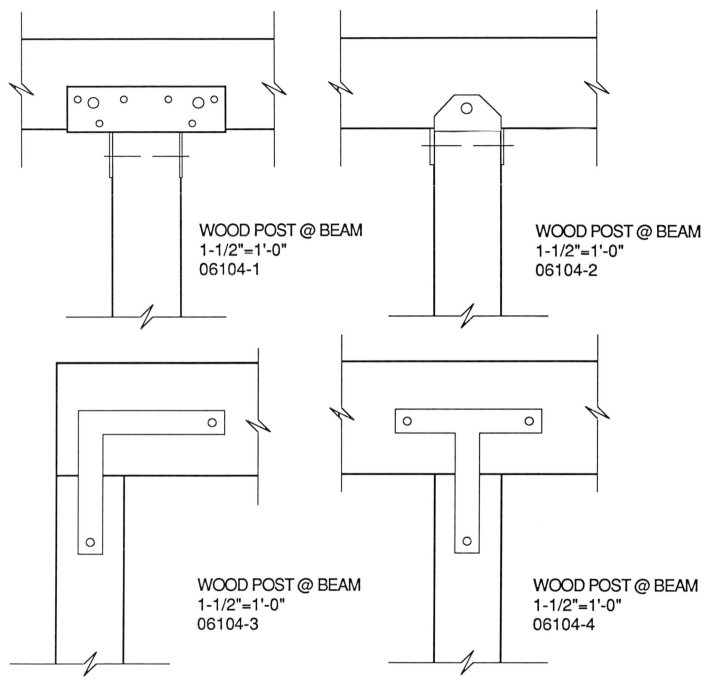

WOOD POST @ BEAM
1-1/2"=1'-0"
06104-1

WOOD POST @ BEAM
1-1/2"=1'-0"
06104-2

WOOD POST @ BEAM
1-1/2"=1'-0"
06104-3

WOOD POST @ BEAM
1-1/2"=1'-0"
06104-4

**NOTATION CHECKLIST,
SAMPLE NOTES**

X   WOOD BEAM
X   WOOD POST
STEEL POST CAP
BOLT/NAIL CONNECTORS
STEEL STRAP TIE
CROSS RAFTERS
BOLTS

HOLES FOR BOLTS
STEEL PLATE
FULL WELD BOTH CORNERS
MACHINE BOLTS W/COUNTERSUNK HEADS
   & NUTS, HOLES PLUGGED
SPLICE PLATE
BEAM HANGER

06104 (b) WOOD POST @ BEAM

FULL-SCALE GENERIC DETAILS

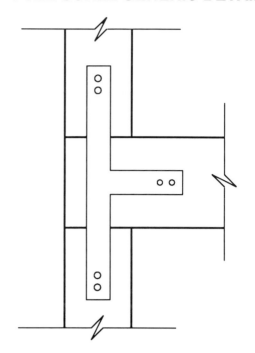

WOOD POST @ BEAM
1-1/2"=1'-0"   06104-5

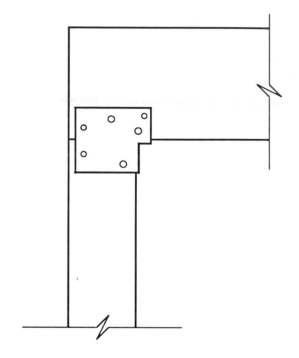

WOOD POST @ BEAM
1-1/2"=1'-0"   06104-6

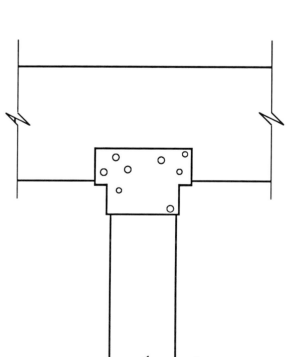

WOOD POST @ BEAM
1-1/2"=1'-0"   06104-7

06104 (b) WOOD POST @ BEAM

FULL-SCALE GENERIC DETAILS continued

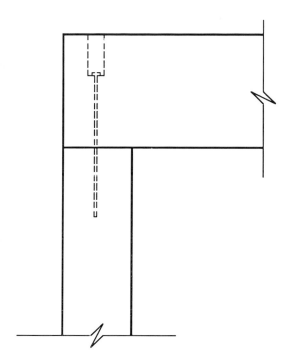

WOOD POST @ BEAM Concealed Anchor
1-1/2"=1'-0"   06104-8

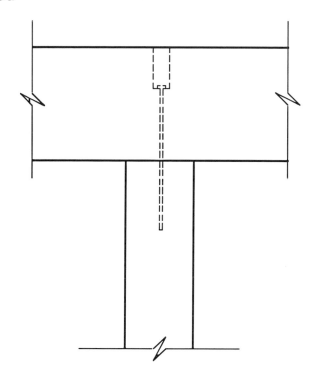

WOOD POST @ BEAM Concealed Anchor
1-1/2"=1'-0"   06104-9

NOTATION CHECKLIST,
SAMPLE NOTES

X   WOOD BEAM
X   WOOD POST
STEEL POST CAP
BOLT/NAIL CONNECTORS
STEEL STRAP TIE

CROSS RAFTERS
BOLTS
HOLES FOR BOLTS
STEEL PLATE
FULL WELD BOTH CORNERS
MACHINE BOLTS W/ COUNTERSUNK
HEADS & NUTS, HOLES PLUGGED
SPLICE PLATE
BEAM HANGER

06105, 06106 WOOD BEAM SPLICE & WOOD BEAM @ GLUE LAM BEAM

DETAIL DATA CHECKLIST

POST AND BEAM CONSTRUCTION

WOOD POST AND BEAM CONNECTORS
__Connector types:
    __Nailed metal side plates
       __For light framing with minimal lateral forces
    __Bolted metal side plates
       __Sizes and spaces of bolts as per code or engineering calculations
    __U plate connector, nailed or bolted as required by engineering calculations or manufacturer's tables
    __Sheet metal connector, sized and nailed as required by engineering calculations or manufacturer's tables

SMALL-SCALE GENERIC DETAILS

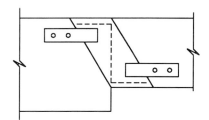

WOOD BEAM SPLICE
06105-1

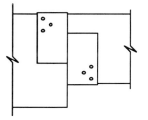

WOOD BEAM @ SPLICE
06105-2

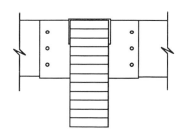

WOOD BEAM @ GLU LAM
06106-1

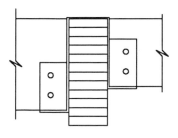

WOOD BEAM @ GLU LAM
06106-2

06105, 06106 WOOD BEAM SPLICE & WOOD BEAM @ GLUE LAM BEAM

FULL-SCALE GENERIC DETAILS

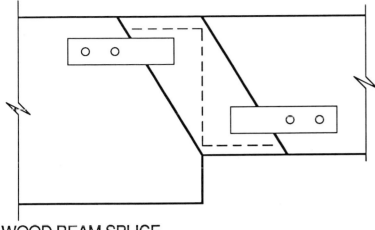

WOOD BEAM SPLICE
1-1/2"=1'-0"   06105-1

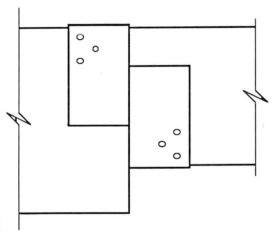

WOOD BEAM @ SPLICE
1-1/2"=1'-0"   06105-2

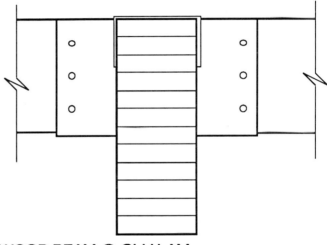

WOOD BEAM @ GLU LAM
1-1/2"=1'-0"   06106-1

NOTATION CHECKLIST, SAMPLE NOTES

X   WOOD BEAM
X   WOOD BEAM
STEEL HINGE CONNECTOR
BOLT CONNECTORS
STEEL SADDLE HANGER

FLUSH TOP SURFACE
SUPPORTED BEAM
CANTILEVERED BEAM

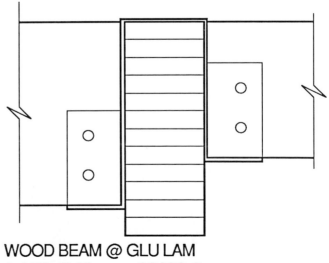

WOOD BEAM @ GLU LAM
1-1/2"=1'-0"   06106-2

DETAIL DATA CHECKLIST FOR WOOD FRAMING

WOOD FRAMING

__Nailing
Most building codes provide a nailing schedule for all wood framing, sheathing, and siding. These schedules are sometimes copied directly and included as part of working drawings.

__Joists, Joist Hangers & Rafters
Most joists are 2x framing members spaced at 16" O.C. See your local code for maximum joist spans for various joist depths.

__Double Floor Joists, Header Joists
Usually included at thru-floor openings, under parallel partitions, at bathtubs and other concentrated loads.)

__Joist Bridging or Blocking
Blocking or cross bridging is usually provided at each 8' of joist span to stiffen joist framing. 2x solid members used as bridging are usually bottom nailed only after the subfloor is completed.

__Studs
Typical stud framing is 2x4 @ 16" O.C. for single story construction. Exterior framing of 2x6 @ 24" O.C. has become more common in recent years.

__Stud Blocking
2x members at mid-point of framed walls are used as fire blocking where required by code or as nailing surface for horizontal plywood sheathing or siding.

__Double Top Plates
Joints are usually overlapped by at least 4' with no overlaps allowed at corners.

__Exterior Wall Bracing
Let-in wood diagonal bracing or metal nailer bracing strips are typically set at 45 degrees at corners and approximately at every 25 linear feet of structure. Diagonal bracing isn't normally required if the wall is sheathed with 1/2" plywood.

__Thermal Insulation
Insulation is usually identified by type--foam, rigid panel, or batt--thickness and R rating. The R rating is commonly reserved for specifications but may be in drawing notation for simpler buildings.

__Framing Members. Other members that may require notation include:

--Structural sheathing diaphragm   --Hip & Jack rafters
   w/ engineered nailing schedule   --Valley rafter
--Spaced wood sheathing   --Collar beam
--Wood decking   --Purlin
--Ledger   --Cross tie
--Trimmer   --Truss chords
--Scab
--Ribbon strip
--Girt
--Knee brace
--Kick block
--Cripple

DETAIL DATA CHECKLIST FOR WOOD FRAMING

FINISH WALL CONSTRUCTION

__Gypsum wallboard and other finish material manufacturers provide comprehensive instructions and details for their products; use the data here as a preliminary guide.

__Building codes provide extensive instructions on fireproofing requirements; those requirements have evolved from many years of fire experience and should be followed with extreme care

__Common wall finishes combined with metal frame partitions include:

      __Interior Single Layer:
          --3/8" plywood paneling
          --3/8" gypsum wallboard
          --1/2" gypsum wallboard
          --5/8" gypsum wallboard
          --3/4" 7/8" 1" metal lath and plaster

      __Interior Double Layer:
          --2 - 3/8" gypsum wallboard
          --2 - 1/2" gypsum wallboard
          --2 - 5/8" gypsum wallboard
          --1/2" gypsum wallboard plus 3/8" plywood paneling
          --3/8" gypsum lath plus 1/2" plaster (7/8")
          --3/8" gypsum lath plus 5/8" plaster (1")
          --3/8" gypsum lath plus 3/4" plaster (1-1/8")

__Gypsum Wallboard Walls & Ceilings. Special types of gypsum wallboard that might be noted in details include:
     --Type X for fire resistance
     --Water resistant
     --Waterproof
     --Sound deadening
     --Insulative foil backed

__Gypsum wallboard assembly components commonly identified in detail drawing notes include:
     --Corner beads
     --Edge trim
     --Corner guards
     --Edge trim sealant @ floor and ceiling
     --Resilient channels
     --Angle clip reinforcement @ ceilings

__Lath & Plaster Walls & Ceilings. Plaster coats sometimes identified in large scale details are:
     --Scratch coat
     --Brown coat
     --Finish coat

__Lath and plaster components commonly identified in detail notation include:
     --Expanded metal lath
     --Wire lath
     --Gypsum lath
     --Base screeds
     --Corner beads
     --Edge casing beads
     --Grounds
     --Picture mouldings
     --Window stools
     --Corner lath reinforcement
     --Control joints

DETAIL DATA CHECKLIST FOR WOOD FRAMING

FINISH WALL CONSTRUCTION   continued

Other wall and ceiling finishes that might be noted include veneer plaster, sprayed acoustical surface, fabric or carpet, vinyl, laminated plastic, etc. Such applied finishes may be named in details but are commonly referenced to the finish schedule and specifications.

OTHER DETAIL AND NOTATION DATA THAT MAY BE USED WITH THESE DETAILS

__Wall-related detail items:
   --Mirrors
   --Attached casework
   --Shelving
   --Tack and chalk boards
   --Ornamental trim, casings, and special moldings
   --Casework at end walls and jambs
   --Coves and valances
   --Signs and support backing
   --Recessed compartments
   --Pass-thru openings
   --Access panels
   --Louvers or vents

06111 FLOOR @ WALL

See DETAIL DATA CHECKLIST for wood framing preceding 06111

SMALL-SCALE GENERIC DETAILS

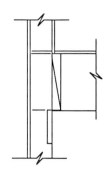

EXTERIOR WALL @
FLOOR (2X4) Balloon Frame
06111-6

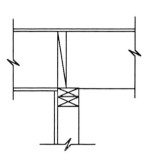

CANTILEVERED FLOOR @
EXT. WALL (2x4)
06111-21

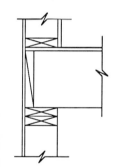

EXTERIOR WALL @
FLOOR (2x6)
06111-51

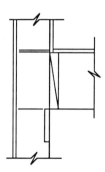

EXTERIOR WALL @
FLOOR (2x6) Balloon Frame
06111-56

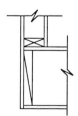

CANTILEVERED FLOOR @
WALL (2x4)
06111-57

CANTILEVERED FLOOR @
WALL (2x6)
06111-61

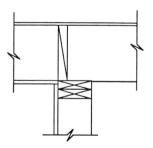

CANTILEVERED FLOOR @
EXT. WALL (2x6)
06111-71

343

06111 FLOOR @ WALL

FULL-SCALE GENERIC DETAILS

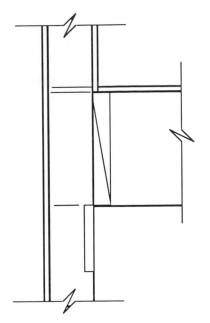

EXTERIOR WALL @ FLOOR
(2x4) Baloon Frame
1-1/2" = 1'-0"
06111-6

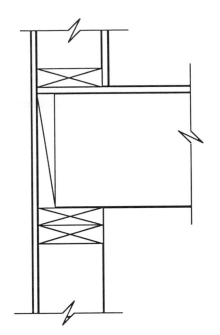

EXTERIOR WALL @ FLOOR
(2x6)
1-1/2" = 1'-0"
06111-51

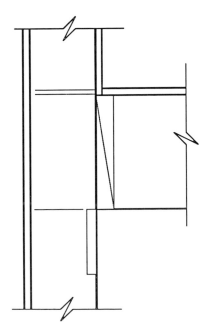

EXTERIOR WALL @ FLOOR
(2x6) Baloon Frame
1-1/2" = 1'-0"
06111-56

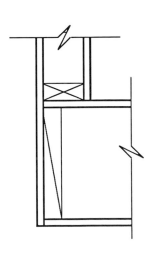

CANTILEVERED FLOOR
@ WALL (2x4)
1-1/2" = 1'-0"
06111-57

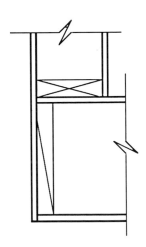

CANTILEVERED FLOOR
@ WALL (2x6)
1-1/2" = 1'-0"
06111-61

06111 FLOOR @ WALL

FULL-SCALE GENERIC DETAILS continued

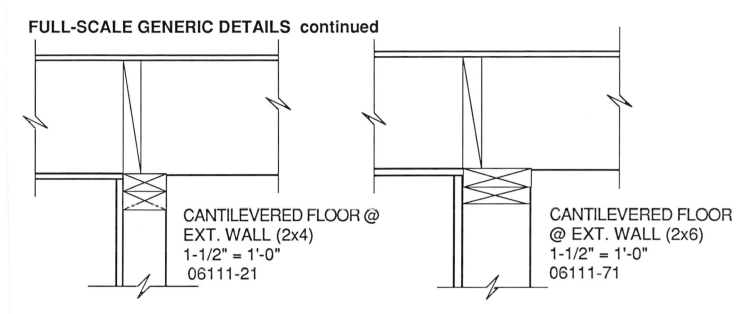

CANTILEVERED FLOOR @
EXT. WALL (2x4)
1-1/2" = 1'-0"
 06111-21

CANTILEVERED FLOOR
@ EXT. WALL (2x6)
1-1/2" = 1'-0"
06111-71

NOTATION CHECKLIST,
SAMPLE NOTES

CEILING LINE @
2 X   STUDS @   " O.C.
HEADER
TRIM FOR CASED OPENING
2 X   BOTTOM PLATE
2 X   TOP PLATE
BASE (FINISH BASE SIZE/MATERIAL)
FINISH FLOOR

INTERIOR:
GYPSUM WALLBOARD
LATH & PLASTER
WOOD PANELING
TILE
MASONRY VENEER
RAILINGS/WALL GUARDS
HOOKS/TRACKS
ANCHORS/MOUNTING BRACKETS
THRU-WALL SLEEVES
PASS-THRU
SOUND ISOLATION PLATE
SOUND ISOLATION CLIPS

EXTERIOR:
THERMAL INSULATION
GYPSUM WALLBOARD SHEATHING
WOOD SHEATHING
MOISTURE BARRIER
LATH & PLASTER/STUCCO
WOOD SIDING
MASONRY VENEER
FLASHING/WATERPROOFING
ANCHORS/MOUNTING BRACKETS
THRU-WALL SLEEVES

BATT INSULATION
INSULATION BOARD
WOOD SIDING
15# FELT
1/2" FOIL FACE INSULATION
AIR SPACE
1/2" X 6"BEVELED LAP SIDING
1/2" PLYWOOD SHEATH
PLYWOOD SIDING
VAPOR BARRIER
WOOD TRIM
2 X   JOISTS @   " O.C.
2 X   RAFTERS @   " O.C.
BLOCKING
FLASHING
GYPSUM BOARD CEILING
HARDWOOD STOPS
HARDWOOD JAMB
2 X 4 CONT. WOOD BLOCKING
SOUND INSULATION
PREFINISHED PANELING
DOOR FRAME
DOOR SIZE
WOOD DRIP
1 X   WOOD STOP

06116, 06118, 06122, 06124 (a) 2X4 WOOD FRAME WALLS

FULL-SCALE GENERIC DETAILS

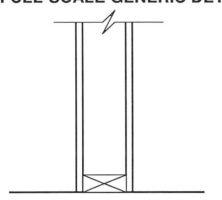

WALL @ FLOOR (2x4)
1-1/2" = 1'-0"   06116-11

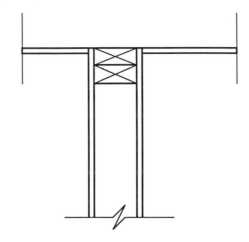

WALL @ CLG. (2x4)
1-1/2" = 1'-0"   06118-11

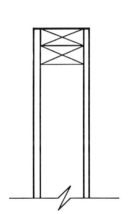

JAMB OR SILL (2x4)
1-1/2" = 1'-0"   06122-1

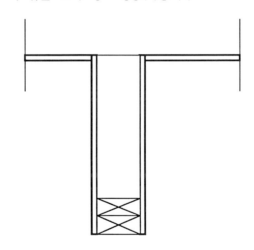

HEAD (2x4)
1-1/2" = 1'-0"   06124-11

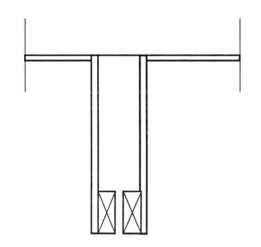

HEADER (2x4)
1-1/2" = 1'-0"   06124-13

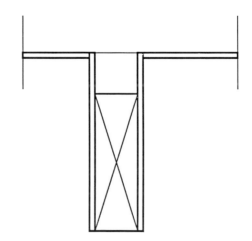

HEADER (2x4)
1-1/2" = 1'-0"   06124-15

06116, 06118, 06122, 06124 (a) 2X4 WOOD FRAME WALLS

NOTATION CHECKLIST, SAMPLE NOTES

CEILING LINE @
2 X   STUDS @   "O.C.
HEADER
TRIM FOR CASED OPENING
2 X   BOTTOM PLATE
2 X   TOP PLATE
BASE (FINISH BASE SIZE/MATERIAL)
FINISH FLOOR

INTERIOR:
GYPSUM WALLBOARD
LATH & PLASTER
WOOD PANELING
TILE
MASONRY VENEER
RAILINGS/WALL GUARDS
HOOKS/TRACKS
ANCHORS/MOUNTING BRACKETS
THRU-WALL SLEEVES
PASS-THRU
SOUND ISOLATION PLATE
SOUND ISOLATION CLIPS

EXTERIOR:
THERMAL INSULATION
GYPSUM WALLBOARD SHEATHING
WOOD SHEATHING
MOISTURE BARRIER
LATH & PLASTER/STUCCO
WOOD SIDING
MASONRY VENEER
FLASHING/WATERPROOFING
ANCHORS/MOUNTING BRACKETS
THRU-WALL SLEEVES

SAMPLE NOTES:
BATT INSULATION
INSULATION BOARD
WOOD SIDING
15# FELT
1/2" FOIL FACE INSULATION
AIR SPACE
1/2" X 6" BEVELED LAP SIDING
1/2" PLYWOOD SHEATH
PLYWOOD SIDING
VAPOR BARRIER
WOOD TRIM
2 X   JOISTS @   " O.C.
2 X   RAFTERS @   " O.C.
BLOCKING
FLASHING
GYPSUM BOARD CEILING
HARDWOOD STOPS
HARDWOOD JAMB
2 X 4 CONT. WOOD BLOCKING
SOUND INSULATION
PREFINISHED PANELING
DOOR FRAME
DOOR SIZE
WOOD DRIP
1 X   WOOD STOP

DETAIL FILE NUMBER: **06116-11**

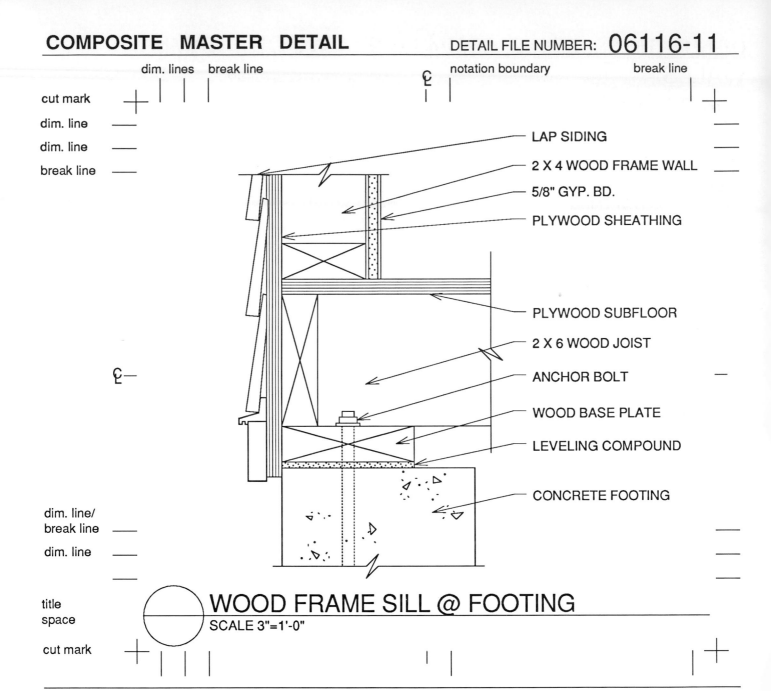

dim. lines break line   notation boundary   break line

cut mark

dim. line

dim. line

break line

LAP SIDING

2 X 4 WOOD FRAME WALL

5/8" GYP. BD.

PLYWOOD SHEATHING

PLYWOOD SUBFLOOR

2 X 6 WOOD JOIST

ANCHOR BOLT

WOOD BASE PLATE

LEVELING COMPOUND

CONCRETE FOOTING

dim. line/
break line

dim. line

title
space

WOOD FRAME SILL @ FOOTING
SCALE 3"=1'-0"

cut mark

DETAIL INFORMATION
References, jobsite feedback, job history

COMPOSITE MASTER DETAIL

DETAIL FILE NUMBER: **06122-1**

dim. lines   break line   notation boundary   break line

cut mark

dim. line

dim. line

break line

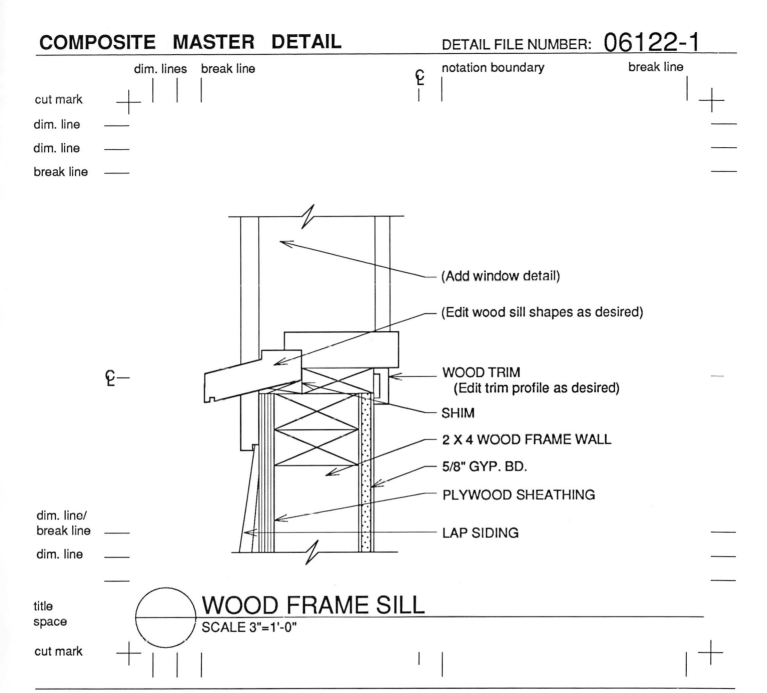

(Add window detail)

(Edit wood sill shapes as desired)

WOOD TRIM
  (Edit trim profile as desired)

SHIM

2 X 4 WOOD FRAME WALL

5/8" GYP. BD.

PLYWOOD SHEATHING

dim. line/
break line

LAP SIDING

dim. line

title
space   **WOOD FRAME SILL**
        SCALE 3"=1'-0"

cut mark

DETAIL INFORMATION
References, jobsite feedback, job history

06116, 06118, 06122, 06124 (b) 2X6 WOOD FRAME WALLS   See DETAIL DATA CHECKLIST for wood framing preceding 06111

SMALL-SCALE GENERIC DETAILS

WALL @ FLOOR (2x6)
06116-61

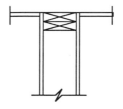

WALL @ CLG. (2x6)
06118-61

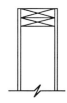

JAMB OR SILL (2x6)
06122-51

HEAD (2x6)
06124-61

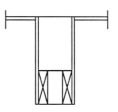

HEADER (2x6)
06124-63

COMPOSITE MASTER DETAIL

DETAIL FILE NUMBER: **01624-13**

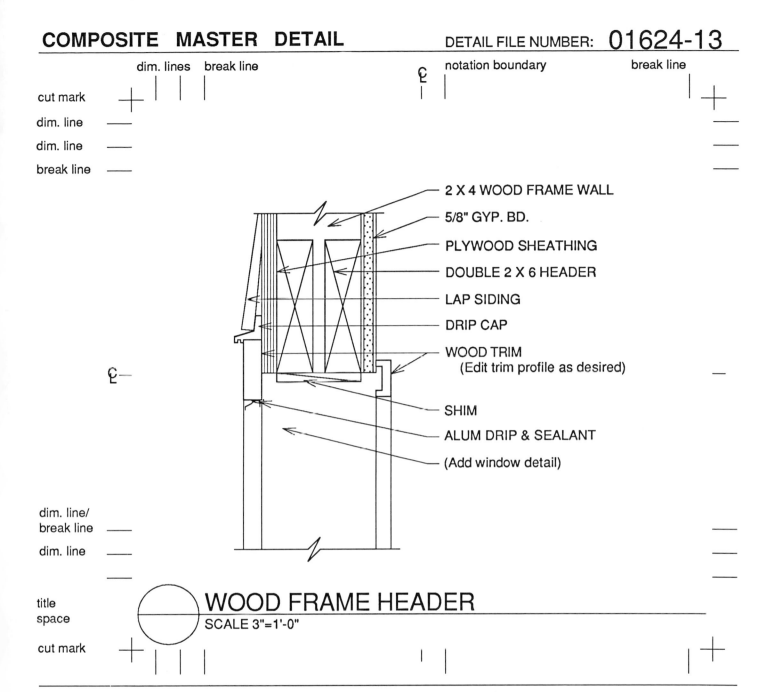

dim. lines   break line

cut mark

dim. line   ——

dim. line   ——

break line   ——

notation boundary   break line

2 X 4 WOOD FRAME WALL

5/8" GYP. BD.

PLYWOOD SHEATHING

DOUBLE 2 X 6 HEADER

LAP SIDING

DRIP CAP

WOOD TRIM
   (Edit trim profile as desired)

SHIM

ALUM DRIP & SEALANT

(Add window detail)

dim. line/
break line   ——

dim. line   ——

title
space

WOOD FRAME HEADER
SCALE 3"=1'-0"

cut mark

DETAIL INFORMATION
References, jobsite feedback, job history

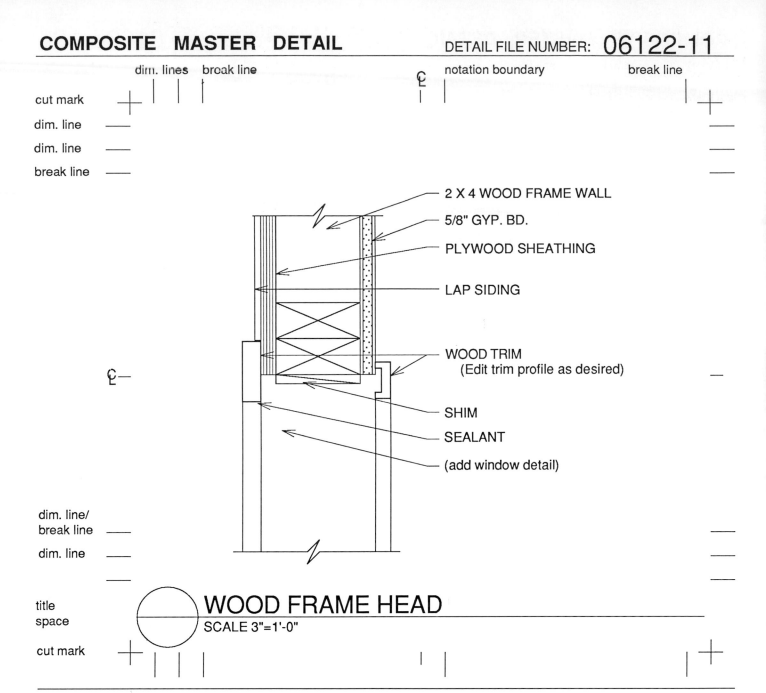

cut mark

dim. lines   break line   notation boundary   break line

dim. line

dim. line

break line

2 X 4 WOOD FRAME WALL

5/8" GYP. BD.

PLYWOOD SHEATHING

LAP SIDING

WOOD TRIM
  (Edit trim profile as desired)

SHIM

SEALANT

(add window detail)

dim. line/
break line

dim. line

title
space

cut mark

WOOD FRAME HEAD
SCALE 3"=1'-0"

DETAIL INFORMATION
References, jobsite feedback, job history

06116, 06118, 06122, 06124 (b) 2X6 WOOD FRAME WALLS

FULL-SCALE GENERIC DETAILS

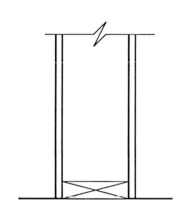

WALL @ FLOOR (2x6)
1-1/2" = 1'-0"
06116-61

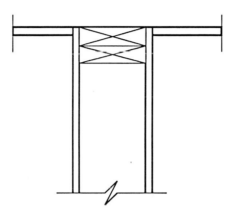

WALL @ CLG. (2x6)
1-1/2" = 1'-0"
06118-61

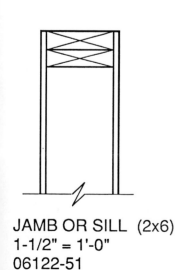

JAMB OR SILL (2x6)
1-1/2" = 1'-0"
06122-51

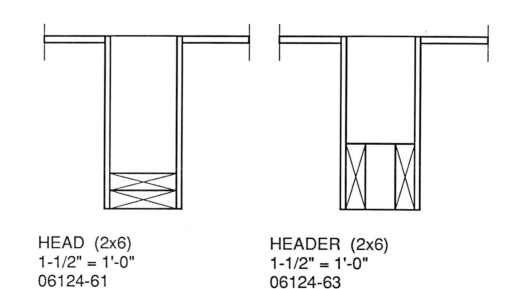

HEAD (2x6)
1-1/2" = 1'-0"
06124-61

HEADER (2x6)
1-1/2" = 1'-0"
06124-63

06116, 06118, 06122, 06124 (b) 2X6 WOOD FRAME WALLS

NOTATION CHECKLIST, SAMPLE NOTES

CEILING LINE @
2 X   STUDS @   " O.C.
HEADER
TRIM FOR CASED OPENING
2 X   BOTTOM PLATE
2 X   TOP PLATE
BASE (FINISH BASE SIZE/MATERIAL)
FINISH FLOOR

INTERIOR:
GYPSUM WALLBOARD
LATH & PLASTER
WOOD PANELING
TILE
MASONRY VENEER
RAILINGS/WALL GUARDS
HOOKS/TRACKS
ANCHORS/MOUNTING BRACKETS
THRU-WALL SLEEVES
PASS-THRU

EXTERIOR:
THERMAL INSULATION
GYPSUM WALLBOARD SHEATHING
WOOD SHEATHING
MOISTURE BARRIER
LATH & PLASTER/STUCCO
WOOD SIDING
MASONRY VENEER
FLASHING/WATERPROOFING
ANCHORS/MOUNTING BRACKETS
THRU-WALL SLEEVES

SAMPLE NOTES:
BATT INSULATION
INSULATION BOARD
WOOD SIDING
15# FELT
1/2" FOIL FACE INSULATION
AIR SPACE
1/2 X 6 BEVELED LAP SIDING
1/2" PLYWOOD SHEATH
PLYWOOD SIDING
VAPOR BARRIER
WOOD TRIM
2 X   JOISTS @   " O.C.
2 X   RAFTERS @   " O.C.
BLOCKING
FLASHING
GYPSUM BOARD CEILING
HARDWOOD STOPS
HARDWOOD JAMB
2 X 4 CONT. WOOD BLOCKING
SOUND INSULATION
PREFINISHED PANELING
DOOR FRAME
DOOR SIZE
WOOD DRIP
1 X   WOOD STOP
SOUND ISOLATION PLATE
SOUND ISOLATION CLIPS

06120 2X4 INTERIOR WALL FRAMING

See DETAIL DATA CHECKLIST for wood framing preceding 06111

SMALL-SCALE GENERIC DETAILS

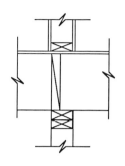 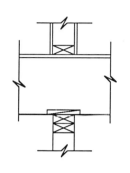 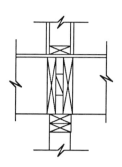 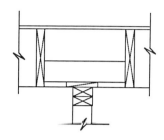

INTERIOR WALL
FRAMING (2x4)
06120-1

INTERIOR WALL
FRAMING (2x4)
06120-2

INTERIOR WALL
FRAMING (2x4)
06120-3

INTERIOR WALL
RAMING (2x4)
06120-4

FULL-SCALE GENERIC DETAILS

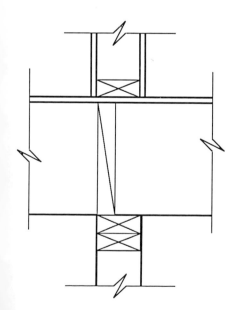 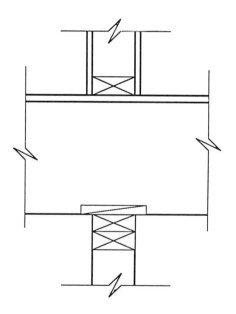

INTERIOR WALL FRAMING (2x4)
1-1/2" = 1'-0"   06120-1

INTERIOR WALL FRAMING (2x4)
1-1/2" = 1'-0"   06120-2

06120 2X4 INTERIOR WALL FRAMING

FULL-SCALE GENERIC DETAILS continued

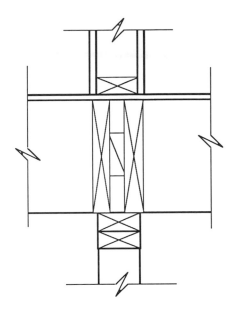

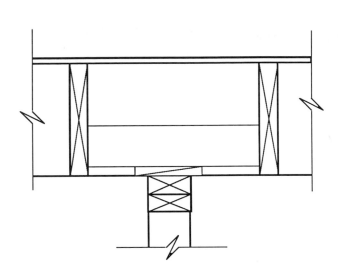

INTERIOR WALL FRAMING (2x4)
1-1/2" = 1'-0"   06120-3

INTERIOR WALL FRAMING (2x4)
1-1/2" = 1'-0"   06120-4

NOTATION CHECKLIST,
SAMPLE NOTES

2 X   STUDS @   " O.C.
2 X   BOTTOM PLATE
SUBFLOOR
2 X   FLOOR JOISTS @   " O.C.
2 X   SOLID BLOCKING
2 X   DOUBLE TOP PLATE

INTERIOR:
GYPSUM WALLBOARD
LATH & PLASTER
WOOD PANELING
TILE
SOUND INSULATION
PLYWOOD SHEATHING
SOUND ISOLATION PLATE
SOUND ISOLATION CLIPS

06121(a) 2X4 WOOD FRAMING

See DETAIL DATA CHECKLIST for wood framing preceding 06111

SMALL-SCALE GENERIC DETAILS

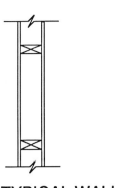

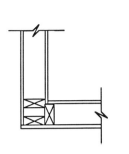

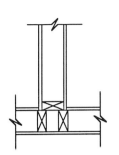

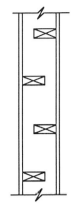

TYPICAL WALL
(2x4) Plan
06121-1

WALL @ CORNER
(2x4)
06121-3

WALL @ T
INTERSECTION (2x4)
06121-5

SOUND ISOLATION
WALL (2x4)
06121-11

FULL-SCALE GENERIC DETAILS

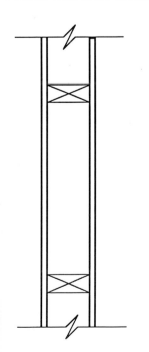

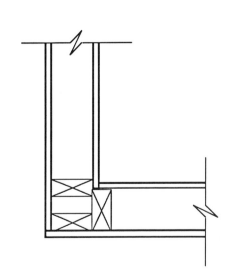

TYPICAL WALL (2x4) Plan
1-1/2" = 1'-0"   06121-1

WALL @ CORNER (2x4)
1-1/2" = 1'-0"   06121-3

06121(a) 2x4 WOOD FRAMING

FULL-SCALE GENERIC DETAILS continued

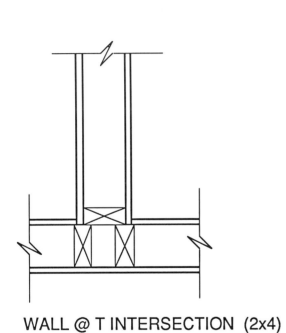

WALL @ T INTERSECTION (2x4)
1-1/2" = 1'-0"   06121-5

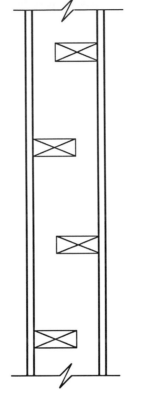

SOUND ISOLATION WALL (2x4)
1-1/2" = 1'-0"   06121-11

NOTATION CHECKLIST,
SAMPLE NOTES

CEILING LINE @
2 X   STUDS @   " O.C.
HEADER
TRIM FOR CASED OPENING
2 X   BOTTOM PLATE
2 X   TOP PLATE
BASE (FINISH BASE SIZE/MATERIAL)
FINISH FLOOR

INTERIOR:
 GYPSUM WALLBOARD
 LATH & PLASTER
 WOOD PANELING
 TILE
 MASONRY VENEER
 RAILINGS/WALL GUARDS
 HOOKS/TRACKS
 ANCHORS/MOUNTING BRACKETS
 THRU-WALL SLEEVES
 PASS-THRU
 SOUND ISOLATION PLATE
 SOUND ISOLATION CLIPS

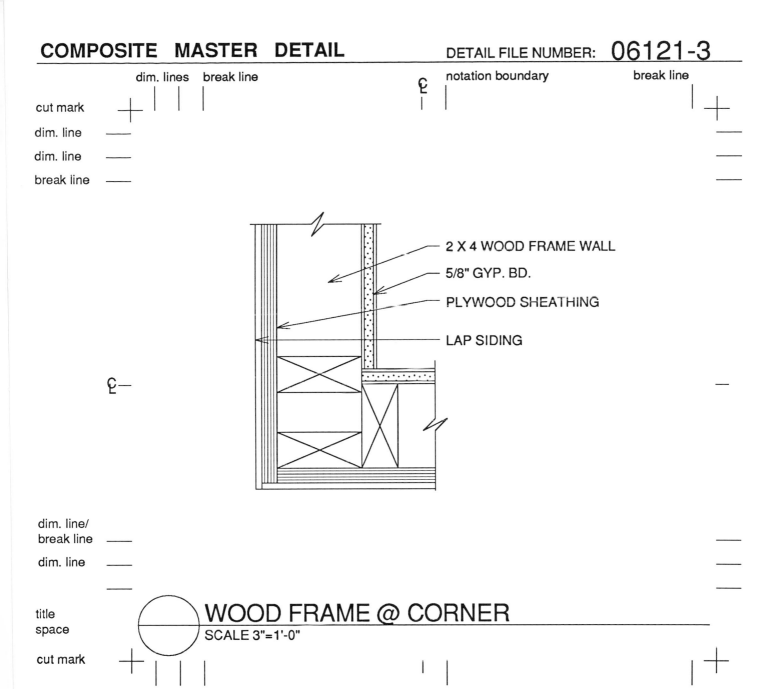

dim. lines   break line   ₵   notation boundary   break line

cut mark

dim. line

dim. line

break line

₵

- 2 X 4 WOOD FRAME WALL
- 5/8" GYP. BD.
- PLYWOOD SHEATHING
- LAP SIDING

dim. line/
break line

dim. line

title
space

WOOD FRAME @ CORNER

SCALE 3"=1'-0"

cut mark

DETAIL INFORMATION
References, jobsite feedback, job history

06160, 06161 ROOF OVERHANG

See DETAIL DATA CHECKLIST for wood framing preceding 06111

SMALL-SCALE GENERIC DETAILS

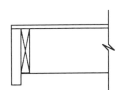

ROOF OVERHANG @ FASCIA
Flat
06160-1

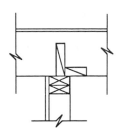

ROOF OVERHANG @ WALL
(2 X 4) Flat
06161-1

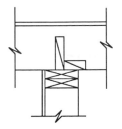

ROOF OVERHANG @ WALL
(2 X 6) Flat
06161-5

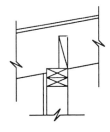

ROOF OVERHANG @ WALL
(2 X 4) 2:12 Slope
06161-11

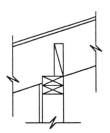

ROOF OVERHANG @ WALL
(2 X 4) 4:12 Slope
06161-12

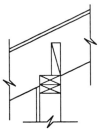

ROOF OVERHANG @ WALL
(2 X 4) 6:12 Slope
06161-13

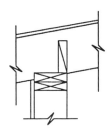

ROOF OVERHANG @ WALL
(2 X 6) 2:12 Slope
06161-51

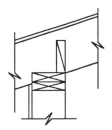

ROOF OVERHANG @ WALL
(2 X 6) 4:12 Slope
06161-52

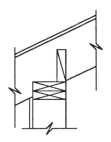

ROOF OVERHANG @ WALL
(2 X 6) 6:12 Slope
 06161-53

06160, 06161 ROOF OVERHANG

FULL-SCALE GENERIC DETAILS

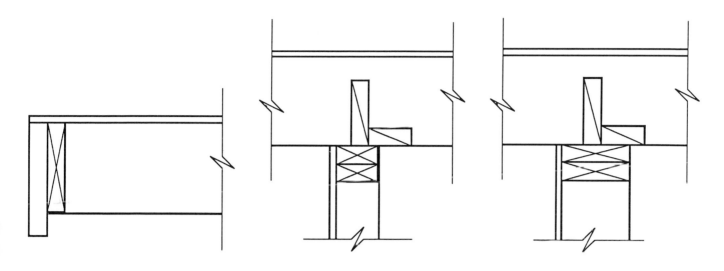

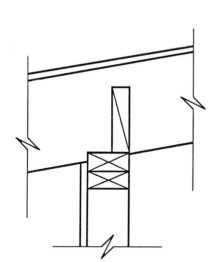

ROOF OVERHANG @ FASCIA
Flat
1-1/2" = 1'-0"
06160-1

ROOF OVERHANG @ WALL
(2 X 4) Flat
1-1/2" = 1'-0"
06161-1

ROOF OVERHANG @ WALL
(2 X 6) Flat
1-1/2" = 1'-0"
06161-5

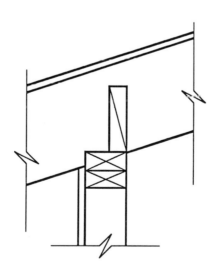

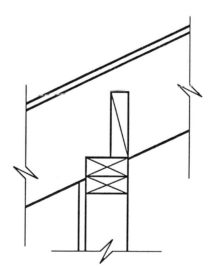

ROOF OVERHANG @ WALL
(2 X 4) 2:12 Slope
1-1/2" = 1'-0"
06161-11

ROOF OVERHANG @ WALL
(2 X 4) 4:12 Slope
1-1/2" = 1'-0"
06161-12

ROOF OVERHANG @ WALL
(2 X 4) 6:12 Slope
1-1/2" = 1'-0"
06161-13

06160, 06161 ROOF OVERHANG

FULL-SCALE GENERIC DETAILS continued

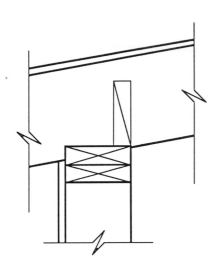 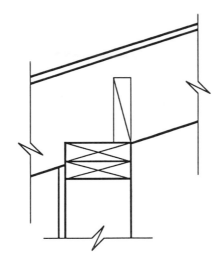 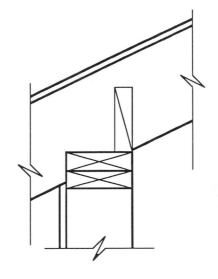

ROOF OVERHANG @ WALL
(2 X 6) 2:12 Slope
1-1/2" = 1'-0"
06161-51

ROOF OVERHANG @ WALL
(2 X 6) 4:12 Slope
1-1/2" = 1'-0"
06161-52

ROOF OVERHANG @ WALL
(2 X 6) 6:12 Slope
1-1/2" = 1'-0"
06161-53

NOTATION CHECKLIST, SAMPLE NOTES

ROOFING
ROOF SHEATHING
FLASHING/WATERPROOFING
2 X   JOISTS @   " O.C.
2 X   BLOCKING / NAILER
2 X   DOUBLE TOP PLATE
2 X   STUDS @   " O.C.

INTERIOR:
GYPSUM WALLBOARD
LATH & PLASTER
WOOD PANELING
TILE

EXTERIOR:
THERMAL INSULATION
GYPSUM WALLBOARD
SHEATHING
WOOD SHEATHING
MOISTURE BARRIER
LATH & PLASTER/STUCCO
WOOD SIDING
MASONRY VENEER
VENTILATION

EXTERIOR continued:
ROOF PITCH
BUILT-UP ROOFING
ROOFING SHINGLE
ROOF SHEATHING
ROOF PLANKS
RIDGE BOARD
METAL STRAP
METAL PLATE
ROOF BEAM
RAFTER
BEVELED RAFTER
NOTCHED RAFTER
RAFTER TIE
STRAP @ EACH RAFTER
CEILING JOISTS
ATTIC FLOOR
TOP PLATE
TYING
SCREEN VENT
INSULATION
SOFFIT
CEILING

06162 (a) ROOF FLUSH @ WALL (2 X 4 FRAMING)

See DETAIL DATA CHECKLIST for wood framing preceding 06111

SMALL-SCALE GENERIC DETAILS

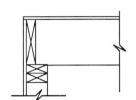

ROOF FLUSH @ WALL
(2 X 4) Flat
06162-1

ROOF FLUSH @ WALL
(2 X 4) 2:12 Slope
06162-21

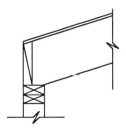

ROOF FLUSH @ WALL
(2 X 4) 4:12 Slope
06162-22

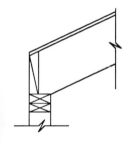

ROOF FLUSH @ WALL
(2 X 4) 6:12 Slope
06162-23

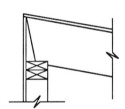

ROOF FLUSH @ WALL
(2 X 4) 2:12 Slope
06162-31

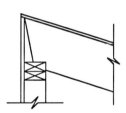

ROOF FLUSH @ WALL
(2 X 4) 4:12 Slope
06162-32

ROOF FLUSH @ WALL
(2 X 4) 6:12 Slope
06162-33

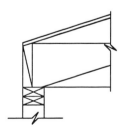

ROOF FLUSH @ WALL
(2 X 4) 4:12 Slope
06162-41

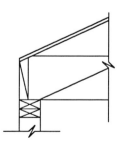

ROOF FLUSH @ WALL
(2 X 4) 6:12 Slope
06162-42

06162 (a) ROOF FLUSH @ WALL (2 X 4 FRAMING)

FULL-SCALE GENERIC DETAILS

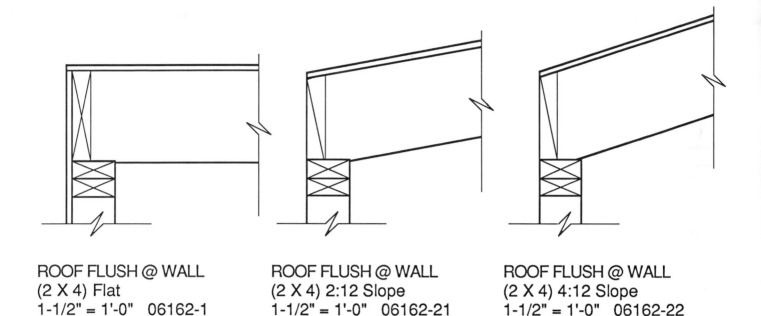

ROOF FLUSH @ WALL
(2 X 4) Flat
1-1/2" = 1'-0"   06162-1

ROOF FLUSH @ WALL
(2 X 4) 2:12 Slope
1-1/2" = 1'-0"   06162-21

ROOF FLUSH @ WALL
(2 X 4) 4:12 Slope
1-1/2" = 1'-0"   06162-22

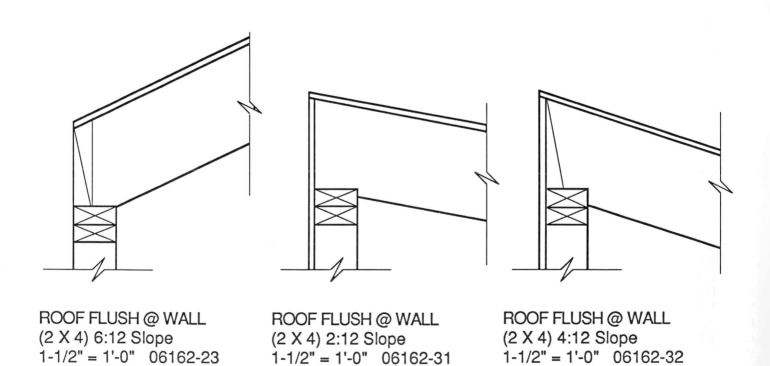

ROOF FLUSH @ WALL
(2 X 4) 6:12 Slope
1-1/2" = 1'-0"   06162-23

ROOF FLUSH @ WALL
(2 X 4) 2:12 Slope
1-1/2" = 1'-0"   06162-31

ROOF FLUSH @ WALL
(2 X 4) 4:12 Slope
1-1/2" = 1'-0"   06162-32

06162 (a) ROOF FLUSH @ WALL (2 X 4 FRAMING)

FULL-SCALE GENERIC DETAILS continued

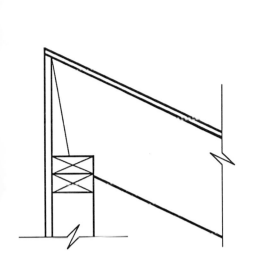

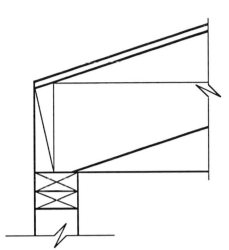

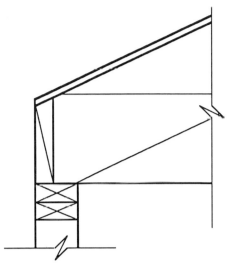

ROOF FLUSH @ WALL
(2 X 4) 6:12 Slope
1-1/2" = 1'-0"   06162-33

ROOF FLUSH @ WALL
(2 X 4) 4:12 Slope
1-1/2" = 1'-0"   06162-41

ROOF FLUSH @ WALL
(2 X 4) 6:12 Slope
1-1/2" = 1'-0"   06162-42

NOTATION CHECKLIST, SAMPLE NOTES

ROOFING
ROOF SHEATHING
FLASHING/WATERPROOFING
2 X   JOISTS @   " O.C.
2 X   BLOCKING/NAILER
2 X   DOUBLE TOP PLATE
2 X   STUDS @   " O.C.
FASCIA/TRIM

INTERIOR:
GYPSUM WALLBOARD
LATH & PLASTER
WOOD PANELING
TILE

EXTERIOR:
THERMAL INSULATION
GYPSUM WALLBOARD
SHEATHING
WOOD SHEATHING
MOISTURE BARRIER
LATH & PLASTER/STUCCO
WOOD SIDING
MASONRY VENEER

EXTERIOR continued:
ROOF PITCH
BUILT-UP ROOFING
ROOFING SHINGLE
ROOF SHEATHING
ROOF PLANKS
RIDGE BOARD
METAL STRAP
METAL PLATE
ROOF BEAM
RAFTER
BEVELED RAFTER
NOTCHED RAFTER
RAFTER TIE
STRAP @ EACH RAFTER
CEILING JOISTS
ATTIC FLOOR
TOP PLATE
TYING
SCREEN VENT
INSULATION
SOFFIT
GUTTER
CEILING

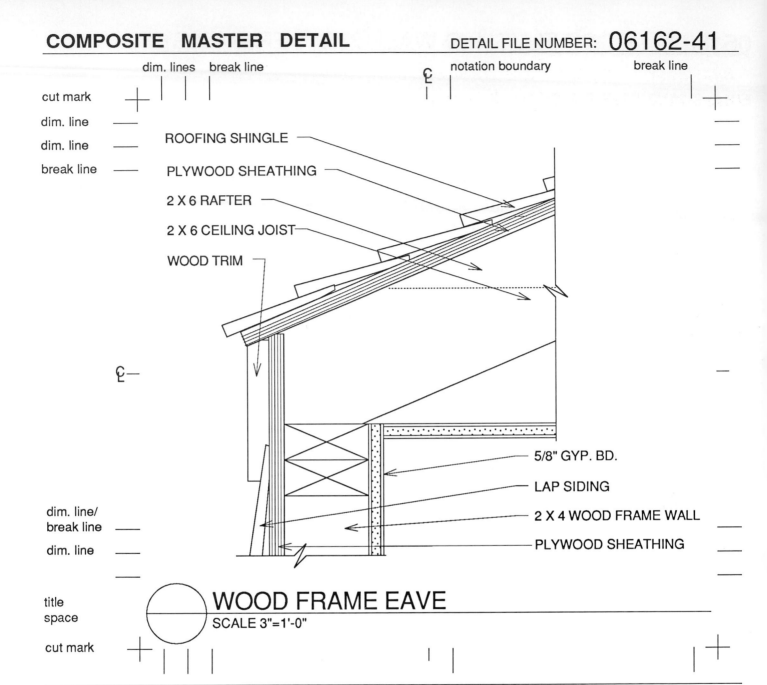

dim. lines   break line   notation boundary   break line

cut mark

dim. line

dim. line   ROOFING SHINGLE

break line   PLYWOOD SHEATHING

2 X 6 RAFTER

2 X 6 CEILING JOIST

WOOD TRIM

5/8" GYP. BD.

LAP SIDING

dim. line/
break line   2 X 4 WOOD FRAME WALL

dim. line   PLYWOOD SHEATHING

title
space   **WOOD FRAME EAVE**
             SCALE 3"=1'-0"

cut mark

DETAIL INFORMATION
References, jobsite feedback, job history

06162 (b) ROOF FLUSH @ WALL (2 X 6 FRAMING)

See DETAIL DATA CHECKLIST for wood framing preceding 06111

SMALL-SCALE GENERIC DETAILS

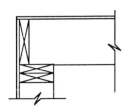

ROOF FLUSH @ WALL
(2 X 6) Flat
06162-51

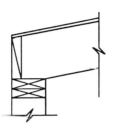

ROOF FLUSH @ WALL
(2 X 6) 2:12 Slope
06162-71

ROOF FLUSH @ WALL
(2 X 6) 4:12 Slope
06162-72

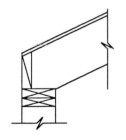

ROOF FLUSH @ WALL
(2 X 6) 6:12 Slope
06162-73

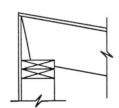

ROOF FLUSH @ WALL
(2 X 6) 2:12 Slope
06162-81

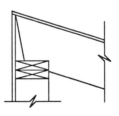

ROOF FLUSH @ WALL
(2 X 6) 4:12 Slope
06162-82

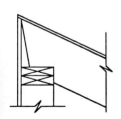

ROOF FLUSH @ WALL
(2 X 6) 6:12 Slope
06162-83

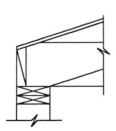

ROOF FLUSH @ WALL
(2 X 6) 4:12 Slope
06162-91

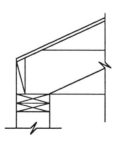

ROOF FLUSH @ WALL
(2 X 6) 6:12 Slope
06162-92

06162 (b) ROOF FLUSH @ WALL (2 X 6 FRAMING)

FULL-SCALE GENERIC DETAILS

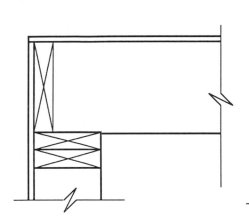

ROOF FLUSH @ WALL
(2 X 6) Flat
1-1/2" = 1'-0"
06162-51

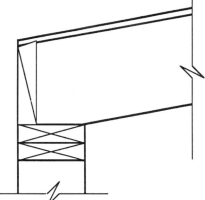

ROOF FLUSH @ WALL
(2 X 6) 2:12 Slope
1-1/2" = 1'-0"
06162-71

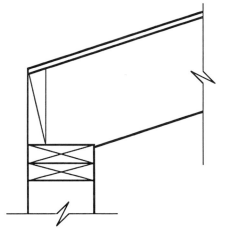

ROOF FLUSH @ WALL
(2 X 6) 4:12 Slope
1-1/2" = 1'-0"
06162-72

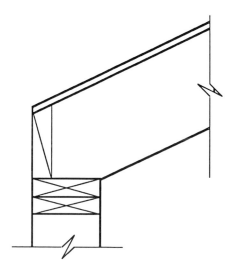

ROOF FLUSH @ WALL
(2 X 6) 6:12 Slope
1-1/2" = 1'-0"
06162-73

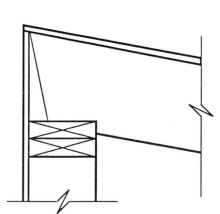

ROOF FLUSH @ WALL
(2 X 6) 2:12 Slope
1-1/2" = 1'-0"
06162-81

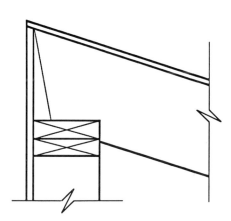

ROOF FLUSH @ WALL
(2 X 6) 4:12 Slope
1-1/2" = 1'-0"
06162-82

06162 (b) ROOF FLUSH @ WALL (2 X 6 FRAMING)

FULL-SCALE GENERIC DETAILS continued

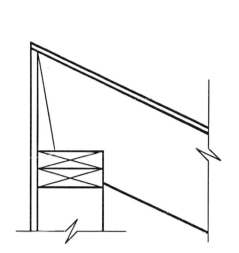 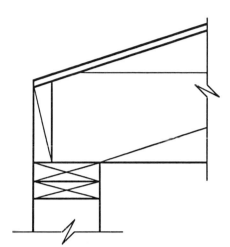 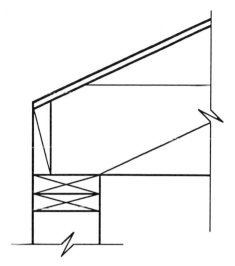

ROOF FLUSH @ WALL
(2 X 6) 6:12 Slope
1-1/2" = 1'-0"
06162-83

ROOF FLUSH @ WALL
(2 X 6) 4:12 Slope
1-1/2" = 1'-0"
06162-91

ROOF FLUSH @ WALL
(2 X 6) 6:12 Slope
1-1/2" = 1'-0"
06162-92

NOTATION CHECKLIST, SAMPLE NOTES

ROOFING
ROOF SHEATHING
FLASHING/WATERPROOFING
2 X   JOISTS @   " O.C.
2 X   BLOCKING/NAILER
2 X   DOUBLE TOP PLATE
2 X   STUDS @   " O.C.
FASCIA/TRIM

INTERIOR:
GYPSUM WALLBOARD
LATH & PLASTER
WOOD PANELING
TILE

EXTERIOR:
THERMAL INSULATION
GYPSUM WALLBOARD
SHEATHING
WOOD SHEATHING
MOISTURE BARRIER
LATH & PLASTER/STUCCO
WOOD SIDING
MASONRY VENEER

EXTERIOR continued:
ROOF PITCH
BUILT-UP ROOFING
ROOFING SHINGLE
ROOF SHEATHING
ROOF PLANKS
RIDGE BOARD
METAL STRAP
METAL PLATE
ROOF BEAM
RAFTER
BEVELED RAFTER
NOTCHED RAFTER
RAFTER TIE
STRAP @ EACH RAFTER
CEILING JOISTS
ATTIC FLOOR
TOP PLATE
TYING
SCREEN VENT
INSULATION
SOFFIT
GUTTER
CEILING

06167, 06168 SHED ROOF @ WALL/ROOF @ PARAPET

See DETAIL DATA CHECKLIST for wood framing preceding 06111

SMALL-SCALE GENERIC DETAILS

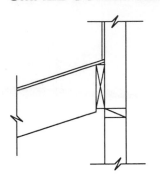

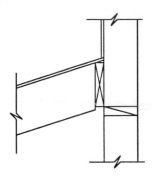

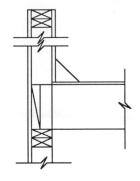

SHED ROOF @ WALL
(2 X 4) 4:12 Slope
06167-1

SHED ROOF @ WALL
(2 X 6) 4:12 Slope
06167-11

ROOF @ PARAPET WALL
(2 X 4)
06168-1

FULL-SCALE GENERIC DETAILS

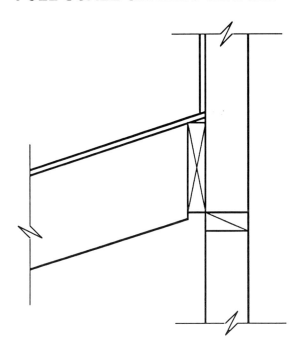

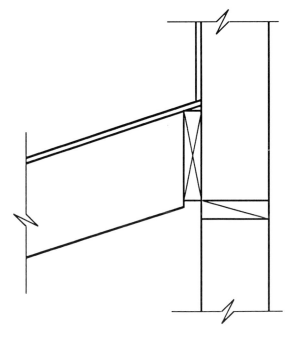

SHED ROOF @ WALL
(2 X 4) 4:12 Slope
1-1/2" = 1'-0"   06167-1

SHED ROOF @ WALL
(2 X 6) 4:12 Slope
1-1/2" = 1'-0"   06167-11

FULL-SCALE GENERIC DETAILS continued

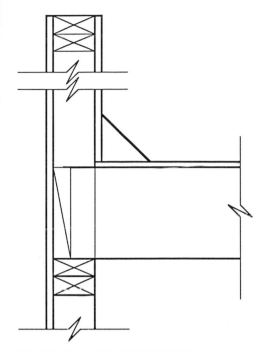

ROOF @ PARAPET WALL
(2 X 4)
1-1/2" = 1'-0"   06168-1

NOTATION CHECKLIST,
 SAMPLE NOTES

2 X   STUDS @   " O.C.
2 X   SOLID BLOCKING/NAILER
ROOFING
ROOF SHEATHING
FLASHING/WATERPROOFING
2 X   JOISTS/RAFTERS @   " O.C.
LEDGER

INTERIOR:
GYPSUM WALLBOARD
LATH & PLASTER
WOOD PANELING
TILE

EXTERIOR:
THERMAL INSULATION
GYPSUM WALLBOARD SHEATHING
WOOD SHEATHING
MOISTURE BARRIER
LATH & PLASTER/STUCCO
WOOD SIDING
MASONRY VENEER
ROOF PITCH

EXTERIOR continued:
BUILT-UP ROOFING
ROOFING SHINGLE
ROOF SHEATHING
ROOF PLANKS
RIDGE BOARD
METAL STRAP
METAL PLATE
ROOF BEAM
RAFTER
BEVELED RAFTER
NOTCHED RAFTER
RAFTER TIE
STRAP @ EACH RAFTER
CEILING JOISTS
ATTIC FLOOR
TOP PLATE
TYING
SCREEN VENT
INSULATION
SOFFIT
GUTTER
CEILING

06169 ROOF RIDGE

See DETAIL DATA CHECKLIST for wood framing preceding 06111

SMALL-SCALE GENERIC DETAILS

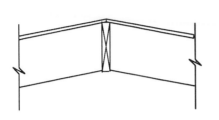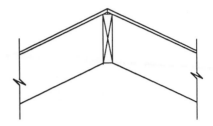

ROOF RIDGE 2:12 Slope
06169-3

ROOF RIDGE 4:12 Slope
06169-7

ROOF RIDGE 6:12 Slope
06169-11

FULL-SCALE GENERIC DETAILS

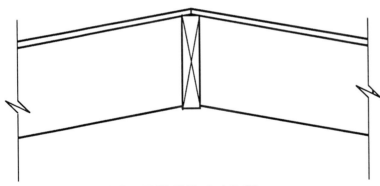

ROOF RIDGE 2:12 Slope
1-1/2" = 1'-0"   06169-3

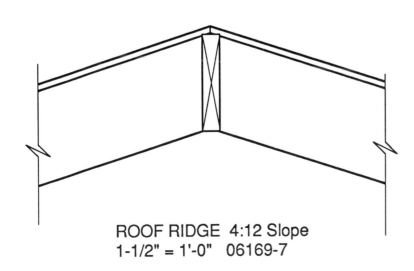

ROOF RIDGE 4:12 Slope
1-1/2" = 1'-0"   06169-7

06169 ROOF RIDGE

FULL-SCALE GENERIC DETAILS continued

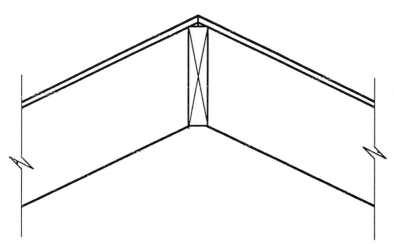

ROOF RIDGE 6:12 Slope
1-1/2" = 1'-0"   06169-11

NOTATION CHECKLIST,
SAMPLE NOTES

ROOFING
ROOF SHEATHING
FLASHING/WATERPROOFING
2 X   JOISTS/RAFTERS @   " O.C.
RIDGE BEAM
ROOF PITCH
 BUILT-UP ROOFING
 ROOFING SHINGLE
 ROOF SHEATHING
 ROOF PLANKS
 RIDGE BOARD
 METAL STRAP
 METAL PLATE
ROOF BEAM

RAFTER
BEVELED RAFTER
NOTCHED RAFTER
RAFTER TIE
STRAP @ EACH RAFTER
CEILING JOISTS
ATTIC FLOOR
TOP PLATE
TYING
SCREEN VENT
INSULATION
SOFFIT
GUTTER
CEILING

377

CABINETS

DETAIL DATA CHECKLIST

CABINETS

Most cabinets are prefabricated units which are ordered in modules to fit the required building space. See manufacturers' catalogs for specifics.

When cabinets are custom-designed, they are usually shop fabricated rather than built on site. The cabinet shop will submit shop drawings based on your design and specifications. Their construction details will be as per the standards of a trade associations such as the Architectural Woodwork Institute Manual of Millwork or the Woodwork Institute of California, unless you specify otherwise.

Detailing for on-site construction usually pertains to fastening the cabinets to the floor, walls, ceiling, or soffit.

The two main types of cabinets are "architectural mill" and "showcase." Showcase cabinets are custom designed with unusually precise detailing, and fabricated like fine furniture. "Casework" refers to specialty cabinets such as for merchandise display, or medical, laboratory, and school storage. They're usually ordered from catalogs as prefab units.

"Architectural mill" cabinet work is fabricated in three grades:
    __Economy: No backs on the cabinets, lip doors, wood edges are exposed open frame divisions between sections, undersides of counters are untreated, drawer guides are of inexpensive hardware, and base cabinet dividers rest directly on the floor.
    __Custom: Backs are included, edges are covered, panels divide the cabinet sections, drawer guides are solid hardware or of hardwood, and base cabinet dividers rest on base cabinet floor panels.
    __Premium: The features of Custom, plus mitered corners, horizontal dividers under drawers, hardwood drawers, joints solidly glued or screw fastened, tops and counters solidly attached with clips or screws, and sleeper supports are under floor panels of base cabinets spaced at 3' maximum.

Cabinet door types:
    __Lip: Thin door panels that slightly overlap the front frames. Used for economy units.
    __Flush: Fits snugly within frame opening. Used for custom or premium cabinets.
    __Flush overlay: Full-thickness doors mounted over frames; closely fit to match, align, and snugly abut the adjacent doors.
    __Limit door sizes to 24" wide maximum to minimize the chance of warpage
Shelves & supports:
    __3/4" thick minimum, with 3' maximum length between supports to avoid deflection
    __Adjustable shelf support standards with clips, or shelf support clips with pins for drilled shelf support pin holes
Sizes of wood members (thickness):
    __Nominal 1" = actual 3/4"
    __Nominal 1-1/4" = actual 1"
    __Nominal 1-1/2" = actual 1-1/4"
    __Nominal 2" = 1-1/2"
    __Nominal 3" = 2-1/2" etc. up to 11"
__Kick or toe space at base: 3-1/2" high and deep (usually matches 2x4 base support)

Drawers:
    __12" high by 16" wide is standard all-purpose size
    __6" high, minimum for utility drawers
    __Tilt strips at sides of drawers prevent drawers from tipping upwards when they're pulled outwards
Countertop finishes:
    __Ceramic tile in two grades:
        __Economy: 1/2" epoxy, mortar, or tile glue, atop Exterior Grade plywood counter platform
            __stain-resistant grout for tile joints.
        __Preferred: 15" building felt atop Exterior Grade plywood counter platform
            __A layer of metal lath and 3/4" to 1-1/2" mortar bed
            __Final thin coat (Neat Cement Coat) is added to the mortar bed to adhere the tile
Two other common counter top finishes:
    __Laminated plastic, which is reasonably heat and stain resistant.
    __"Corian" (dense, imitation marble-like material), 1/4" to 3/4" thick sheets.

06412, 06413 WOOD SHELVING

See DETAIL DATA CHECKLIST for cabinets preceding 06412

SMALL-SCALE GENERIC DETAILS

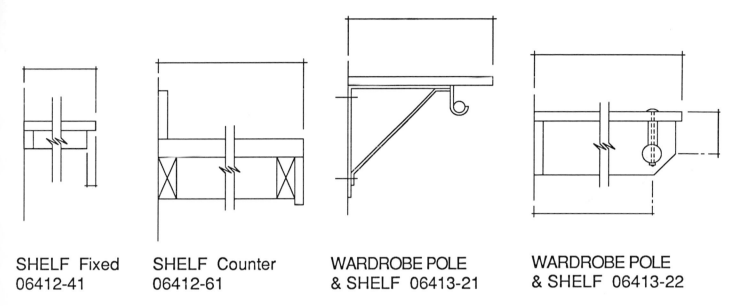

SHELF Fixed
06412-41

SHELF Counter
06412-61

WARDROBE POLE
& SHELF 06413-21

WARDROBE POLE
& SHELF 06413-22

FULL-SCALE GENERIC DETAILS

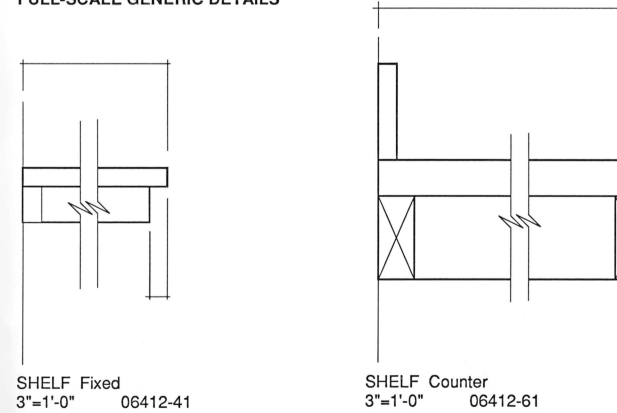

SHELF Fixed
3"=1'-0"   06412-41

SHELF Counter
3"=1'-0"   06412-61

FULL-SCALE GENERIC DETAILS continued

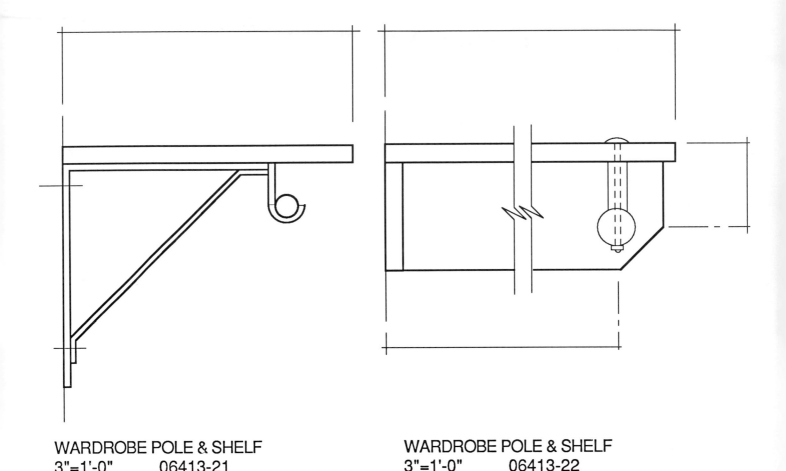

WARDROBE POLE & SHELF
3"=1'-0"   06413-21

WARDROBE POLE & SHELF
3"=1'-0"   06413-22

NOTATION CHECKLIST,
SAMPLE NOTES

FINISH SURFACE
PLYWOOD/PARTICLE BOARDS
TRIM (MATERIAL & SIZE)
BLOCKING (MATERIAL & SIZE)
ADJACENT MATERIALS
HARDWARE/ANCHOR
SHELF (MATERIAL, SIZE & FINISH)
POLE (MATERIAL & SIZE)
POLE SUPPORT/BRACKET
BLOCKING (MATERIAL & SIZE)
WALL MATERIAL

2 X 4 CONT., FRAME INTO SIDE WALLS
3/4" CORE MATERIAL, TOP & FRONT
SOLID BLOCKING BEHIND SHELF
PLASTIC LAMINATE TOP, EDGES, FRONT, SELF
EDGE
FACE OF WALL
CHROME ROD
SHELF & ROD BRACKET MAX. SPACING @ 4'-0"
5'-0" ABOVE FINISHED FLOOR

06412, 06415 WOOD SHELVING, BASE CABINET

See DETAIL DATA CHECKLIST for cabinets preceding 06412

SMALL-SCALE GENERIC DETAILS

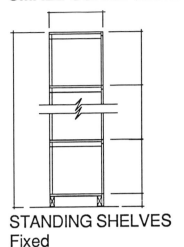

STANDING SHELVES
Fixed
06412-21

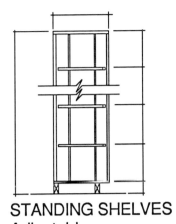

STANDING SHELVES
Adjustable
06412-31

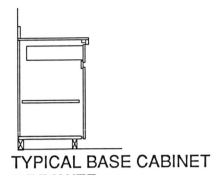

TYPICAL BASE CABINET
& DRAWER
06415-1

FULL-SCALE GENERIC DETAILS

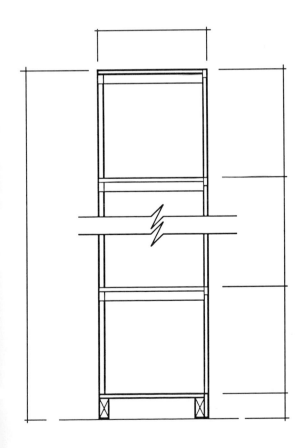

STANDING SHELVES Fixed
3/4"=1'-0"   06412-21

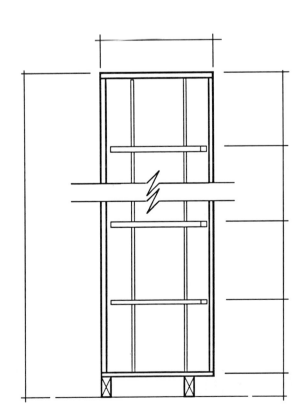

STANDING SHELVES Adjustable
3/4"=1'-0"   06412-31

FULL-SCALE GENERIC DETAILS continued

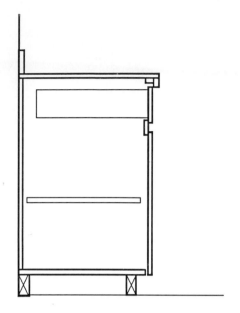

TYPICAL BASE CABINET & DRAWER
3/4"=1'-0"   06415-1

NOTATION CHECKLIST,
 ## SAMPLE NOTES

FINISH SURFACE
PLYWOOD/PARTICLE BOARDS
TRIM (MATERIAL & SIZE)
BLOCKING (MATERIAL & SIZE)
ADJACENT MATERIALS
HARDWARE/ANCHOR
DOOR/DRAWER
SHELF (MATERIAL, SIZE & FINISH)
BLOCKING (MATERIAL & SIZE)
WALL MATERIAL

2 X 4 CONT., FRAME INTO SIDE WALLS
3/4" CORE MATERIAL, TOP & FRONT
SOLID BLOCKING BEHIND SHELF
PLASTIC LAMINATE TOP, EDGES, FRONT, SELF
EDGE
FACE OF WALL
CHROME ROD
SHELF & ROD BRACKET MAX. SPACING @ 4'-0"
5'-0" ABOVE FINISHED FLOOR

06414 (a) BASE CABINETS

See DETAIL DATA CHECKLIST for cabinets preceding 06412

SMALL-SCALE GENERIC DETAILS

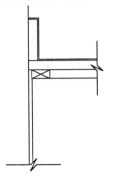

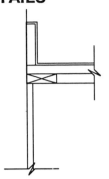

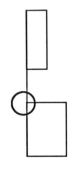

Splash
06414-51

Splash
06414-52

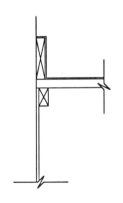

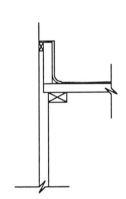

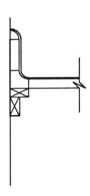

Splash
06414-53

Splash
06414-54

Splash
06414-55

06414 (a) BASE CABINETS

FULL-SCALE GENERIC DETAILS

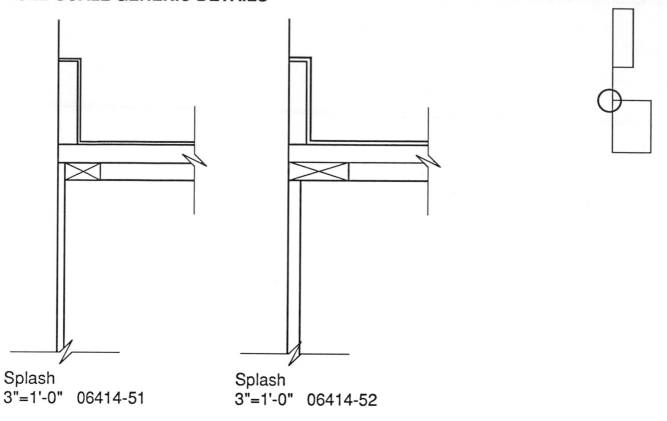

Splash
3"=1'-0"   06414-51

Splash
3"=1'-0"   06414-52

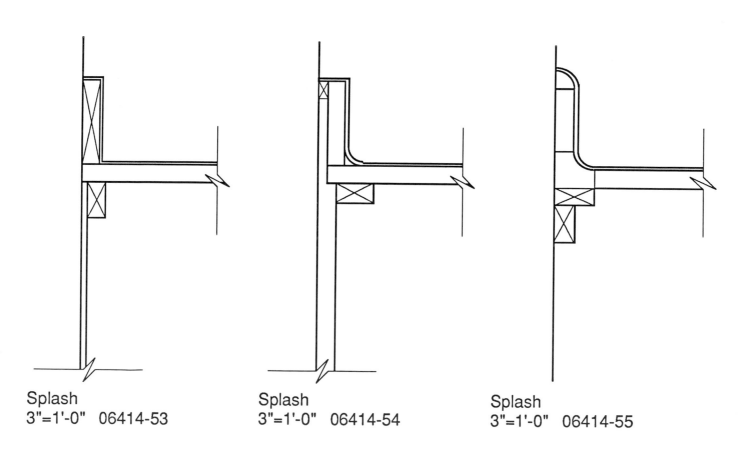

Splash
3"=1'-0"   06414-53

Splash
3"=1'-0"   06414-54

Splash
3"=1'-0"   06414-55

384

06414 (a) BASE CABINETS

NOTATION CHECKLIST, SAMPLE DETAILS

FINISH SURFACE
PLYWOOD/PARTICLE BOARD
TRIM (MATERIAL & SIZE)
BLOCKING (MATERIAL & SIZE)
ADJACENT MATERIALS
HARDWARE/ANCHOR
DOOR/DRAWER
PROVIDE BLOCKING TO RECEIVE MILLWORK ITEMS
    PLASTIC LAMINATE
3/4" PLYWOOD TOP W/ HDWD. EDGING
PLASTIC LAM. BACKING SHEET
PLASTIC LAM. TO EDGE & COVER BACKSPLASH,
    PROVIDE END SPLASH @ WALLS
3/4" PLYWOOD TOP, SIDES, DIVIDERS &
    SHELVES W/1/2" X 3/4" HDWD. NOSE
FACE OF WALL
SPLASH
PLASTIC LAM. SCRIBE STRIP
3/4" PLYWOOD DIVIDERS
1/4" PLYWOOD BACK
RECESS 1/4" HARDBOARD OR PLYWOOD BACK
2 X 4 FRAMING
3/4" PLYWOOD BOTTOM W/ WOOD EDGING
CHAMFERED TRIM PIECE
FLUSH DOORS, OAK VENEER ON PLYWOOD
3/4" X 3-1/16" HARDWOOD EDGE, EASE EDGES
2 X 4 FRAME @ FLOOR
ADJUSTABLE SHELVES
RECESSED SHELF STANDARDS
SURFACE-MOUNTED ADJ. SHELF STD'S.
    W/ BRACKETS
FIXED SHELF
3/4" PLYWOOD SHELF W/1X2 SUPPORT CLEAT &
  1 X 3 EDGE STRIP
1 X 12 SHELVES & BACKING
1 X 12 DIVIDER @ 44" O.C. MAX.
3/4" PLYWD. SHELVES W/HARDWOOD EDGING
1 X 2 WOOD SUPPORT @ WALL ANCHOR W/1/4" DIA.
    TOGGLE BOLTS @ 24" O.C.
STEEL CHANNEL, ATTACHED TO END WALL,
    W/ STUDS @ 1'-0" O.C. @ LAV. PERIMETER
DRAWER
SOLID WOOD DRAWER SIDES, HDWD. DRAWER
FRONTS
DRAWERS ON EXTENSION SLIDES
1/4" DRAWER BOTTOM
3/4" X 1-3/4" RAILS & STILES
SLIDING GLASS DOORS IN K-V TRACK,
    PROVIDE FINGER PULLS & LOCK, SAFETY GLASS

06414 (b) BASE CABINETS

See DETAIL DATA CHECKLIST for cabinets preceding 06412

SMALL-SCALE GENERIC DETAILS

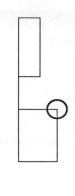

Front Edge/Lip
06414-71

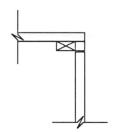

Front Edge/Lip
06414-72

Front Edge/Lip
06414-73

Front Edge/Lip
06414-74

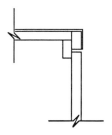

Front Edge/Lip
06414-75

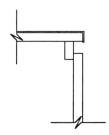

Front Edge/Lip
06414-76

Front Edge/Lip
06414-77

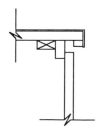

Front Edge/Lip
06414-78

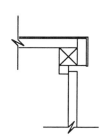

Front Edge/Lip
06414-79

Front Edge/Lip
06414-80

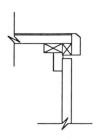

Front Edge/Lip
06414-81

06414 (b) BASE CABINETS

FULL-SCALE GENERIC DETAILS

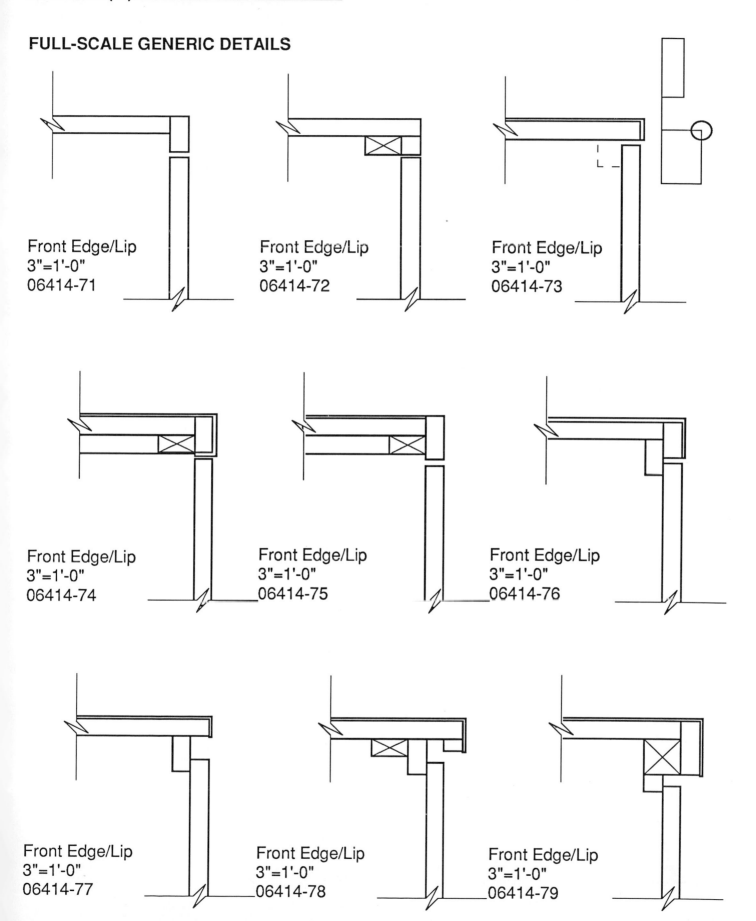

Front Edge/Lip
3"=1'-0"
06414-71

Front Edge/Lip
3"=1'-0"
06414-72

Front Edge/Lip
3"=1'-0"
06414-73

Front Edge/Lip
3"=1'-0"
06414-74

Front Edge/Lip
3"=1'-0"
06414-75

Front Edge/Lip
3"=1'-0"
06414-76

Front Edge/Lip
3"=1'-0"
06414-77

Front Edge/Lip
3"=1'-0"
06414-78

Front Edge/Lip
3"=1'-0"
06414-79

06414 (b) BASE CABINETS

FULL-SCALE GENERIC DETAILS continued

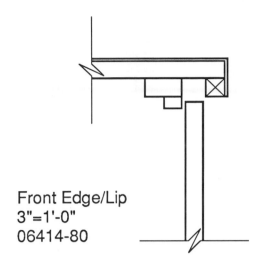

Front Edge/Lip
3"=1'-0"
06414-80

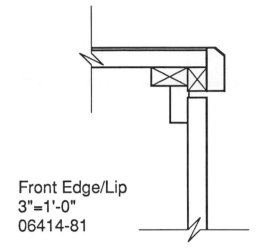

Front Edge/Lip
3"=1'-0"
06414-81

NOTATION CHECKLIST,
SAMPLE NOTES

FINISH SURFACE
PLYWOOD/PARTICLE BOARD
TRIM (MATERIAL & SIZE)
BLOCKING (MATERIAL & SIZE)
ADJACENT MATERIALS
HARDWARE/ANCHOR
DOOR/DRAWER
PROVIDE BLOCKING TO RECEIVE MILLWORK ITEMS
 PLASTIC LAMINATE
 3/4" PLYWD. TOP W/ HDWD. EDGING
 PLASTIC LAM. BACKING SHEET
 PLASTIC LAM. TO EDGE & COVER BACKSPLASH,
 PROVIDE END SPLASH @ WALLS
 3/4" PLYWD. TOP, SIDES, DIVIDERS &
     SHELVES W/ 1/2" X 3/4" HDWD. NOSE
 FACE OF WALL
 SPLASH
 PLASTIC LAM. SCRIBE STRIP
 3/4" PLYWD DIVIDERS
 1/4" PLYWD. BACK
  RECESS 1/4" HARDBOARD OR PLYWD. BACK
 2 X 4 FRAMING
 3/4" PLYWD. BOTTOM W/ WOOD EDGING
 4" TOE SPACE

CHAMFERED TRIM PIECE
FLUSH DOORS, OAK VENEER ON PLYWD.
3/4" X 3-1/16" HARDWOOD EDGE, EASE EDGES
2 X 4 FRAME @ FLOOR
ADJUSTABLE SHELVES
RECESSED SHELF STANDARDS
SURFACE MOUNTED ADJ. SHELF STD'S. W/ BRACKETS
FIXED SHELF
3/4" PLYWD. SHELF W/ 1X2 SUPPORT CLEAT &
   1 X 3 EDGE STRIP
1 X 12 SHELVES & BACKING
1 X 12 DIVIDER @ 44" O.C. MAX.
3/4" PLYWD. SHELVES W/ HDWD. EDGING
1 X 2 WD. SUPPORT @ WALL ANCHOR W/ 1/4" DIA.
   TOGGLE BOLTS @ 24" O.C.
STEEL CHANNEL, ATTACHED TO END WALL,
   W/ STUDS @ 1'-0" O.C. @ LAV. PERIMETER
DRAWER
SOLID WOOD DRAWER SIDES, HDWD. DRAWER
FRONTS
DRAWERS ON EXTENSION SLIDES
1/4" DRAWER BOTTOM
3/4" X 1-3/4" RAILS & STILES
SLIDING GLASS DOORS IN K-V TRACK,
   PROVIDE FINGER PULLS & LOCK, SAFETY GLASS

06415, 06416 BASE CABINETS

See DETAIL DATA CHECKLIST for cabinets preceding 06412

SMALL-SCALE GENERIC DETAILS

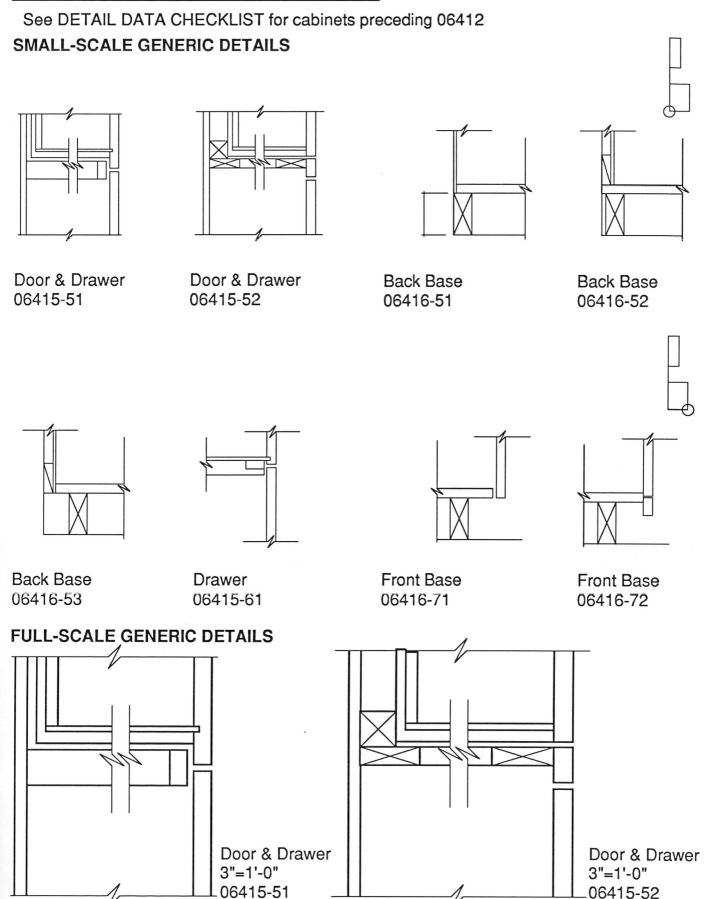

Door & Drawer
06415-51

Door & Drawer
06415-52

Back Base
06416-51

Back Base
06416-52

Back Base
06416-53

Drawer
06415-61

Front Base
06416-71

Front Base
06416-72

FULL-SCALE GENERIC DETAILS

Door & Drawer
3"=1'-0"
06415-51

Door & Drawer
3"=1'-0"
06415-52

06415, 06416 BASE CABINETS

FULL-SCALE GENERIC DETAILS

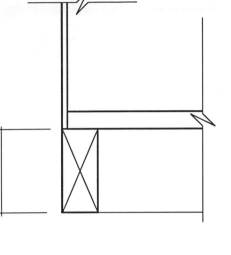

Back Base
3"=1'-0" 06416-51

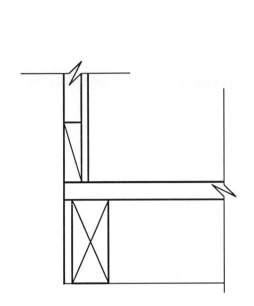

Back Base
3"=1'-0" 06416-52

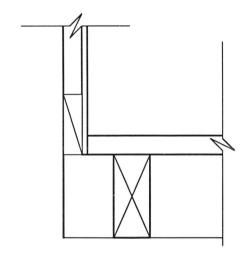

Back Base
3"=1'-0" 06416-53

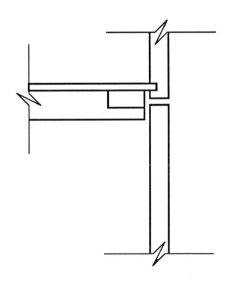

Drawer
3"=1'-0" 06415-61

06415, 06416 BASE CABINETS

FULL-SCALE GENERIC DETAILS continued

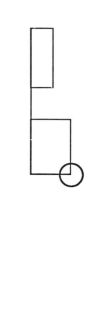

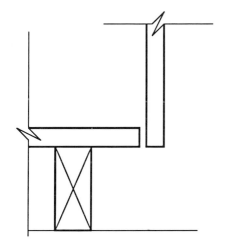

Front Base
3"=1'-0" 06416-71

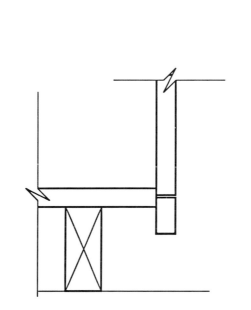

Front Base
3"=1'-0" 06416-72

NOTATION CHECKLIST,
SAMPLE NOTES

FINISH SURFACE
PLYWOOD/PARTICLE BOARD
TRIM (MATERIAL & SIZE)
BLOCKING (MATERIAL & SIZE)
ADJACENT MATERIALS
HARDWARE/ANCHOR
DOOR/DRAWER
PROVIDE BLOCKING TO RECEIVE MILLWORK
ITEMS
PLASTIC LAMINATE
3/4" PLYWD. TOP W/HARDWOOD. EDGING
PLASTIC LAM. BACKING SHEET
PLASTIC LAM. TO EDGE & COVER
BACKSPLASH,
    PROVIDE END SPLASH @ WALLS
3/4" PLYWOOD TOP, SIDES, DIVIDERS &
    SHELVES W/1/2" X 3/4" HARDWOOD NOSE
FACE OF WALL
SPLASH
PLASTIC LAM. SCRIBE STRIP
3/4" PLYWOOD DIVIDERS
1/4" PLYWOOD BACK
RECESS 1/4" HARDBOARD OR PLYWOOD BACK
2 X 4 FRAMING

3/4" PLYWWOOD BOTTOM W/WOOD EDGING
4" TOE SPACE
CHAMFERED TRIM PIECE
FLUSH DOORS, OAK VENEER ON PLYWOOD
3/4" X 3-1/16" HARDWOOD EDGE, EASE EDGES
2 X 4 FRAME @ FLOOR
ADJUSTABLE SHELVES
RECESSED SHELF STANDARDS
SURFACE MOUNTED ADJ. SHELF STD'S. W/BRACKETS
FIXED SHELF
3/4" PLYWOOD SHELF W/1X2 SUPPORT CLEAT &
    1 X 3 EDGE STRIP
1 X 12 SHELVES & BACKING
1 X 12 DIVIDER @ 44" O.C. MAX.
3/4" PLYWOOD SHELVES W/HARDWOOD EDGING
1 X 2 WD. SUPPORT @ WALL ANCHOR W/1/4" DIA.
    TOGGLE BOLTS @ 24" O.C.
STEEL CHANNEL, ATTACHED TO END WALL,
    W/ STUDS @ 1'-0" O.C. @ LAV. PERIMETER
DRAWER
SOLID WOOD DRAWER SIDES, HARDWOOD DRAWER
    FRONTS
DRAWERS ON EXTENSION SLIDES
1/4" DRAWER BOTTOM
3/4" X 1-3/4" RAILS & STILES
SLIDING GLASS DOORS IN K-V TRACK,
    PROVIDE FINGER PULLS & LOCK, SAFETY GLASS

06417 (a) OVERHEAD CABINETS

See DETAIL DATA CHECKLIST for cabinets preceding 06412

SMALL-SCALE GENERIC DETAILS

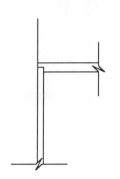

Top Back
06417-51

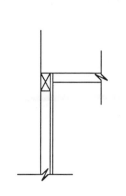

Top Back
06417-52

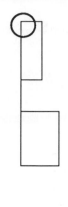

Top Back
06417-53

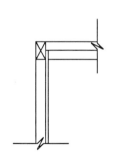

Top Back
06417-54

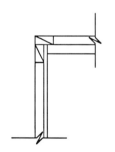

Top Back
06417-55

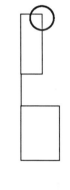

Top Front
06417-61

Top Front
06417-62

Top Front
06417-63

Top Front
06417-64

06417 (a) OVERHEAD CABINETS

FULL-SCALE GENERIC DETAILS continued

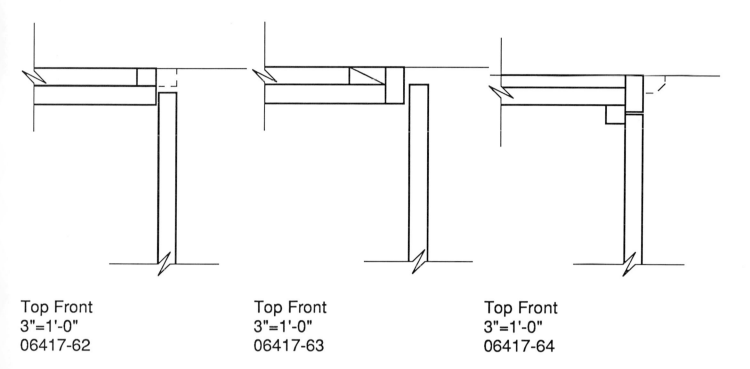

Top Front
3"=1'-0"
06417-62

Top Front
3"=1'-0"
06417-63

Top Front
3"=1'-0"
06417-64

NOTATION CHECKLIST, SAMPLE NOTES

FINISH SURFACE
PLYWOOD/PARTICLE BOARD
TRIM (MATERIAL & SIZE)
BLOCKING (MATERIAL & SIZE)
ADJACENT MATERIALS
HARDWARE/ANCHOR
DOOR/DRAWER
PROVIDE BLOCKING TO RECEIVE MILLWORK ITEMS
PLASTIC LAMINATE
3/4" PLYWOOD TOP W/HARDWOOD EDGING
PLASTIC LAM. BACKING SHEET
PLASTIC LAM. TO EDGE & COVER BACKSPLASH,
    PROVIDE END SPLASH @ WALLS
3/4" PLYWOOD TOP, SIDES, DIVIDERS &
    SHELVES W/1/2" X 3/4" HARDWOOD NOSE
FACE OF WALL
SPLASH
PLASTIC LAM. SCRIBE STRIP
3/4" PLYWOOD DIVIDERS
1/4" PLYWOOD BACK
RECESS 1/4" HARDBOARD OR PLYWOOD BACK
2 X 4 FRAMING
3/4" PLYWOOD BOTTOM W/WOOD EDGING
CHAMFERED TRIM PIECE

FLUSH DOORS, OAK VENEER ON PLYWOOD
3/4" X 3-1/16" HARDWOOD EDGE, EASE EDGES
2 X 4 FRAME @ FLOOR
ADJUSTABLE SHELVES
RECESSED SHELF STANDARDS
SURFACE MOUNTED ADJ. SHELF STD'S. W/ BRACKETS
FIXED SHELF
3/4" PLYWD. SHELF W/1X2 SUPPORT CLEAT &
    1 X 3 EDGE STRIP
1 X 12 SHELVES & BACKING
1 X 12 DIVIDER @ 44" O.C. MAX.
3/4" PLYWOOD SHELVES W/HARDWOOD EDGING
1 X 2 WD. SUPPORT @ WALL ANCHOR W/1/4"
    DIA. TOGGLE BOLTS @ 24" O.C.
STEEL CHANNEL, ATTACHED TO END WALL,
    W/ STUDS @ 1'-0" O.C. @ LAV. PERIMETER
DRAWER
SOLID WOOD DRAWER SIDES, HARDWOOD DRAWER
FRONTS
DRAWERS ON EXTENSION SLIDES
1/4" DRAWER BOTTOM
3/4" X 1-3/4" RAILS & STILES
SLIDING GLASS DOORS IN K-V TRACK,
    PROVIDE FINGER PULLS & LOCK, SAFETY GLASS

06417 (a) OVERHEAD CABINETS

FULL-SCALE GENERIC DETAILS

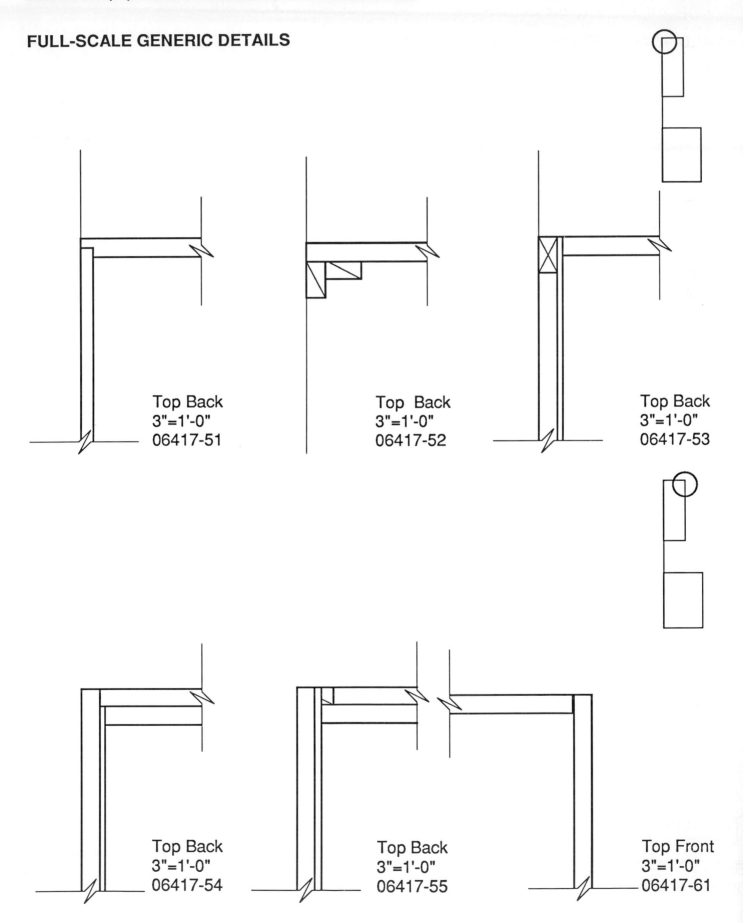

Top Back
3"=1'-0"
06417-51

Top Back
3"=1'-0"
06417-52

Top Back
3"=1'-0"
06417-53

Top Back
3"=1'-0"
06417-54

Top Back
3"=1'-0"
06417-55

Top Front
3"=1'-0"
06417-61

06417 (b) OVERHEAD CABINETS

See DETAIL DATA CHECKLIST for cabinets preceding 06412

SMALL-SCALE GENERIC DETAILS

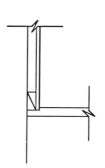

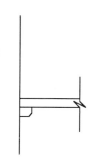

Bottom Back
06417-71

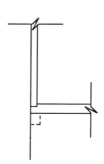

Bottom Back
06417-72

Bottom Back
06417-73

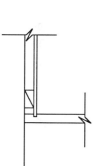

Bottom Back
06417-74

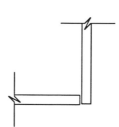

Bottom Front
06417-81

Bottom Front
06417-82

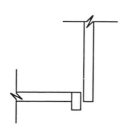

Bottom Front
06417-83

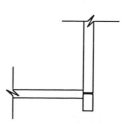

Bottom Front
06417-84

06417 (b) OVERHEAD CABINETS

FULL-SCALE GENERIC DETAILS

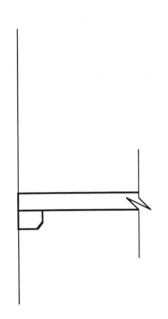

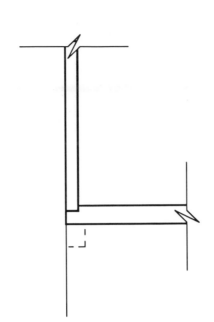

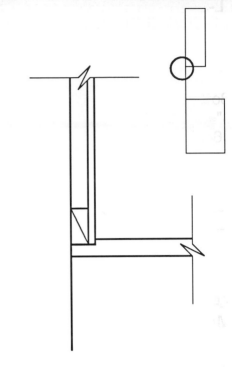

Bottom Back
3"=1'-0"
06417-71

Bottom Back
3"=1'-0"
06417-72

Bottom Back
3"=1'-0"
06417-73

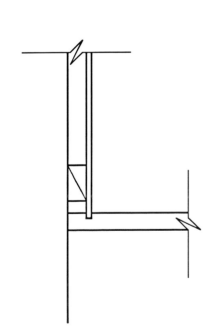

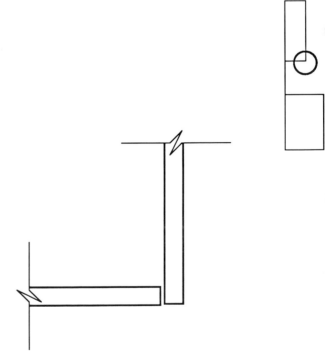

Bottom Back
3"=1'-0"
06417-74

Bottom Front
3"=1'-0"
06417-81

06417 (b) OVERHEAD CABINETS

FULL-SCALE GENERIC DETAILS continued

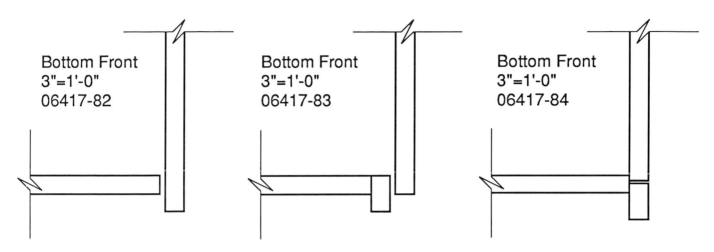

Bottom Front
3"=1'-0"
06417-82

Bottom Front
3"=1'-0"
06417-83

Bottom Front
3"=1'-0"
06417-84

NOTATION CHECKLIST, SAMPLE NOTES

FINISH SURFACE
PLYWOOD/PARTICLE BOARD
TRIM (MATERIAL & SIZE)
BLOCKING (MATERIAL & SIZE)
ADJACENT MATERIALS
HARDWARE/ANCHOR
DOOR/DRAWER
PROVIDE BLOCKING TO RECEIVE MILLWORK ITEMS
 PLASTIC LAMINATE
3/4" PLYWD. TOP W/ HDWD. EDGING
PLASTIC LAM. BACKING SHEET
PLASTIC LAM. TO EDGE & COVER BACKSPLASH,
PROVIDE END SPLASH @ WALLS
3/4" PLYWD. TOP, SIDES, DIVIDERS &
    SHELVES W/ 1/2" X 3/4" HDWD. NOSE
FACE OF WALL
SPLASH
PLASTIC LAM. SCRIBE STRIP
3/4" PLYWD DIVIDERS
1/4" PLYWD. BACK
RECESS 1/4" HARDBOARD OR PLYWD. BACK
2 X 4 FRAMING
3/4" PLYWD. BOTTOM W/ WOOD EDGING
CHAMFERED TRIM PIECE
FLUSH DOORS, OAK VENEER ON PLYWD.

3/4" X 3-1/16" HARDWOOD EDGE, EASE EDGES
2 X 4 FRAME @ FLOOR
ADJUSTABLE SHELVES
RECESSED SHELF STANDARDS
SURFACE MOUNTED ADJ. SHELF STD'S. W/ BRACKETS
FIXED SHELF
3/4" PLYWD. SHELF W/ 1X2 SUPPORT CLEAT &
    1 X 3 EDGE STRIP
1 X 12 SHELVES & BACKING
1 X 12 DIVIDER @ 44" O.C. MAX.
3/4" PLYWD. SHELVES W/ HDWD. EDGING
1 X 2 WD. SUPPORT @ WALL ANCHOR W/ 1/4" DIA.
    TOGGLE BOLTS @ 24" O.C.
STEEL CHANNEL, ATTACHED TO END WALL,
    W/ STUDS @ 1'-0" O.C. @ LAV. PERIMETER
DRAWER
SOLID WOOD DRAWER SIDES, HDWD. DRAWER
FRONTS
DRAWERS ON EXTENSION SLIDES
1/4" DRAWER BOTTOM
3/4" X 1-3/4" RAILS & STILES
SLIDING GLASS DOORS IN K-V TRACK,
    PROVIDE FINGER PULLS & LOCK, SAFETY GLASS

06418 CABINET DOORS

See DETAIL DATA CHECKLIST for cabinets preceding 06412

SMALL-SCALE GENERIC DETAILS

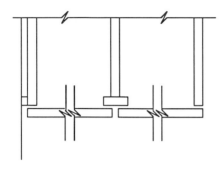

CABINET DOORS & FRAME
Horiz. Section
06418-51

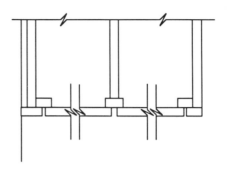

CABINET DOORS & FRAME
Horiz. Section
06418-52

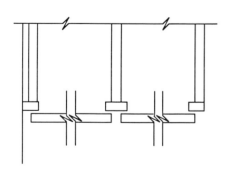

CABINET DOORS & FRAME
Horiz. Section
06418-53

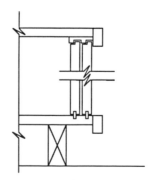

CABINET SLIDING DOORS
Vert. Section
06418-61

06418 CABINET DOORS

FULL-SCALE GENERIC DETAILS

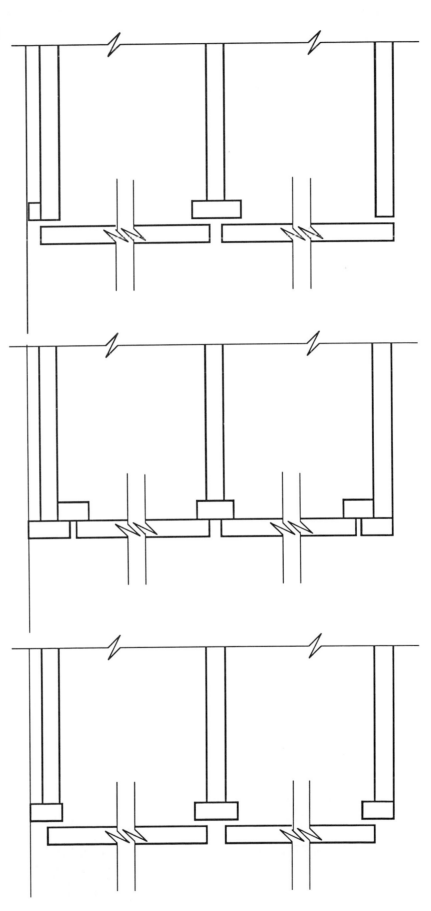

CABINET DOORS & FRAME
Horiz. Section
3"=1'-0"   06418-51

CABINET DOORS & FRAME
Horiz. Section
3"=1'-0"   06418-52

CABINET DOORS & FRAME
Horiz. Section
3"=1'-0"   06418-53

06418 CABINET DOORS

FULL-SCALE GENERIC DETAILS
continued

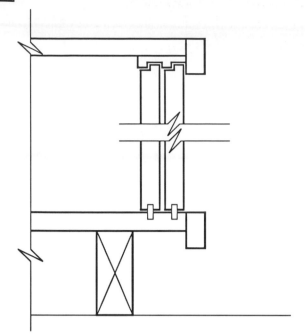

CABINET SLIDING DOORS
Vert. Section
3"=1'-0"   06418-61

NOTATION CHECKLIST,
SAMPLE NOTES

PLYWOOD/PARTICLE BOARD
DRAWER FACE FINISH SURFACE
DRAWER SIDES (MATERIAL & SIZE)
FACE FRAME (MATERIAL & SIZE)
CABINET SIDE PANELS
   (MATERIAL & THICKNESS)
TRIM (MATERIAL & SIZE)
BLOCKING (MATERIAL & SIZE)
ADJACENT MATERIALS
HARDWARE
PROVIDE BLOCKING TO RECEIVE MILLWORK ITEMS
 PLASTIC LAMINATE
3/4" PLYWD. TOP W/ HDWD. EDGING
 PLASTIC LAM. BACKING SHEET
 PLASTIC LAM. TO EDGE & COVER BACKSPLASH,
PROVIDE END SPLASH @ WALLS
3/4" PLYWD. TOP, SIDES, DIVIDERS &
   SHELVES W/ 1/2" X 3/4" HDWD. NOSE
FACE OF WALL
SPLASH
PLASTIC LAM. SCRIBE STRIP
3/4" PLYWD DIVIDERS

1/4" PLYWD. BACK
 RECESS 1/4" HARDBOARD OR PLYWD. BACK
2 X 4 FRAMING
3/4" PLYWD. BOTTOM W/ WOOD EDGING
CHAMFERED TRIM PIECE

FLUSH DOORS, OAK VENEER ON PLYWD.
3/4" X 3-1/16" HARDWOOD EDGE, EASE EDGES
2 X 4 FRAME @ FLOOR
ADJUSTABLE SHELVES
RECESSED SHELF STANDARDS
SURFACE MOUNTED ADJ. SHELF STD'S. W/ BRACKETS
FIXED SHELF
3/4" PLYWD. SHELF W/ 1X2 SUPPORT CLEAT &
   1 X 3 EDGE STRIP
1 X 12 SHELVES & BACKING
1 X 12 DIVIDER @ 44" O.C. MAX.
3/4" PLYWD. SHELVES W/ HDWD. EDGING
1 X 2 WD. SUPPORT @ WALL ANCHOR W/ 1/4" DIA.
   TOGGLE BOLTS @ 24" O.C.
STEEL CHANNEL, ATTACHED TO END WALL,
   W/ STUDS @ 1'-0" O.C. @ LAV. PERIMETER
DRAWER
SOLID WOOD DRAWER SIDES, HDWD. DRAWER
FRONTS
DRAWERS ON EXTENSION SLIDES
1/4" DRAWER BOTTOM
3/4" X 1-3/4" RAILS & STILES
SLIDING GLASS DOORS IN K-V TRACK,
   PROVIDE FINGER PULLS & LOCK, SAFETY GLASS

06419 CABINET DRAWERS

See DETAIL DATA CHECKLIST for cabinets preceding 06412

SMALL-SCALE GENERIC DETAILS

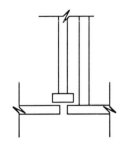

CABINET DOOR & DRAWER
Horiz. Section
06419-51

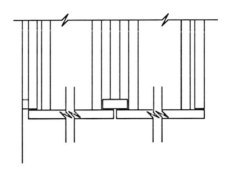

CABINET DRAWERS & FRAME
Horiz. Section
06419-61

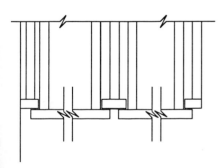

CABINET DRAWERS & FRAME
Horiz. Section
06419-62

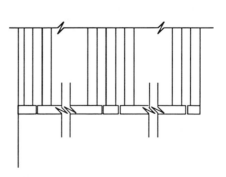

CABINET DRAWERS & FRAME
Horiz. Section
06419-63

06419 CABINET DRAWERS

FULL-SCALE GENERIC DETAILS

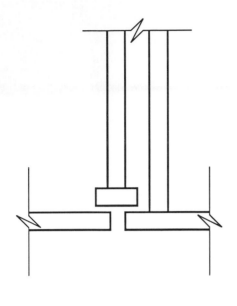

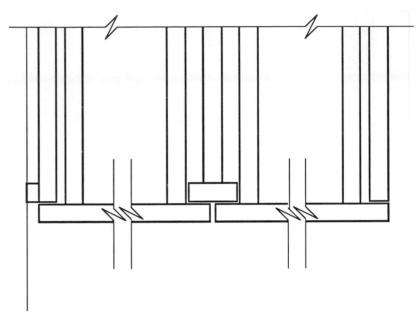

CABINET DOOR & DRAWER
Horiz. Section
3"=1'-0"   06419-51

CABINET DRAWERS & FRAME
Horiz. Section
3"=1'-0"   06419-61

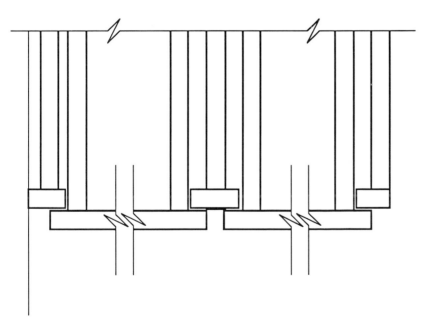

CABINET DRAWERS & FRAME
Horiz. Section
3"=1'-0"   06419-62

06419 CABINET DRAWERS

FULL-SCALE GENERIC DETAILS continued

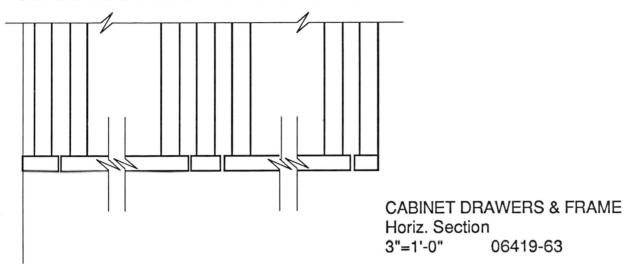

CABINET DRAWERS & FRAME
Horiz. Section
3"=1'-0"   06419-63

NOTATION CHECKLIST, SAMPLE NOTES

PLYWOOD/PARTICLE BOARD
DRAWER FACE FINISH SURFACE
DRAWER SIDES (MATERIAL & SIZE)
FACE FRAME (MATERIAL & SIZE)
CABINET SIDE PANELS
    (MATERIAL & THICKNESS)
TRIM (MATERIAL & SIZE)
BLOCKING (MATERIAL & SIZE)
ADJACENT MATERIALS
HARDWARE
PROVIDE BLOCKING TO RECEIVE MILLWORK ITEMS
 PLASTIC LAMINATE
 3/4" PLYWD. TOP W/ HDWD. EDGING
 PLASTIC LAM. BACKING SHEET
 PLASTIC LAM. TO EDGE & COVER BACKSPLASH,
 PROVIDE END SPLASH @ WALLS
 3/4" PLYWD. TOP, SIDES, DIVIDERS &
    SHELVES W/ 1/2" X 3/4" HDWD. NOSE
FACE OF WALL
SPLASH
PLASTIC LAM. SCRIBE STRIP
3/4" PLYWD DIVIDERS
1/4" PLYWD. BACK

RECESS 1/4" HARDBOARD OR PLYWD. BACK
2 X 4 FRAMING
3/4" PLYWD. BOTTOM W/ WOOD EDGING
CHAMFERED TRIM PIECE
FLUSH DOORS, OAK VENEER ON PLYWD.
3/4" X 3-1/16" HARDWOOD EDGE, EASE EDGES
2 X 4 FRAME @ FLOOR
ADJUSTABLE SHELVES
RECESSED SHELF STANDARDS
SURFACE MOUNTED ADJ. SHELF STD'S. W/ BRACKETS
FIXED SHELF
3/4" PLYWD. SHELF W/ 1X2 SUPPORT CLEAT &
  1 X 3 EDGE STRIP
1 X 12 SHELVES & BACKING
1 X 12 DIVIDER @ 44" O.C. MAX.
3/4" PLYWD. SHELVES W/ HDWD. EDGING
1 X 2 WD. SUPPORT @ WALL ANCHOR W/ 1/4" DIA.
    TOGGLE BOLTS @ 24" O.C.
STEEL CHANNEL, ATTACHED TO END WALL,
    W/ STUDS @ 1'-0" O.C. @ LAV. PERIMETER
DRAWER
SOLID WOOD DRAWER SIDES, HDWD. DRAWER
FRONTS
DRAWERS ON EXTENSION SLIDES
1/4" DRAWER BOTTOM
3/4" X 1-3/4" RAILS & STILES
SLIDING GLASS DOORS IN K-V TRACK,
    PROVIDE FINGER PULLS & LOCK, SAFETY GLASS

06421 WOOD PANELING

DETAIL DATA CHECKLIST

PANELING
Paneling can be applied to wood or metal framing with or without furring. Use furring strips or channels for thermal or acoustic isolation, or to compensate for uneven wall construction.

Use wood or metal furring when installing panels over masonry walls. 1 x 2 wood furring over masonry is typical spaced at 16" vertically and horizontally.

Grades of hardwood plywood paneling:
    __Premium and Good: Minimum flaws, for stain finish
    __Sound: For paint finish
    __Utility: Some visible defects, unmatched, for paint finish
    __Backing: Many flaws, not for visible use

__Thicknesses: 1/8" to 1", in 1/16" or 1/8" layers

__Textures and finishes come in wide variety; see the suppliers' catalogs

SMALL-SCALE GENERIC DETAILS

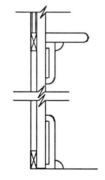

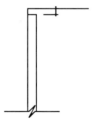

WOOD PANELING
@ BASE
06421-41

WOOD PANELING
@ BASE & WAINSCOT
06421-61

WOOD PANELING
@ CEILING
06421-81

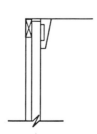

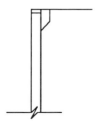

WOOD PANELING
@ CEILING
06421-82

WOOD PANELING
@ CEILING
06421-83

WOOD PANELING
@ CEILING
06421-84

06421 WOOD PANELING

FULL-SCALE GENERIC DETAILS

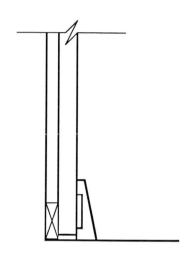

WOOD PANELING @ BASE
3"=1'-0"   06421-41

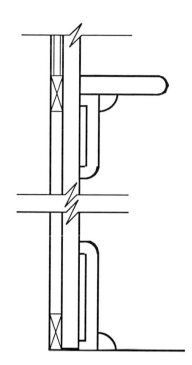

WOOD PANELING
@ BASE & WAINSCOT
3"=1'-0"   06421-61

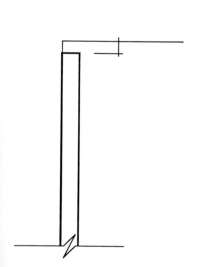

WOOD PANELING @ CEILING
3"=1'-0"   06421-81

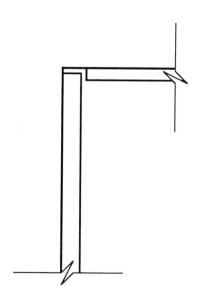

WOOD PANELING @ CEILING
3"=1'-0"   06421-82

06421 WOOD PANELING

FULL-SCALE GENERIC DETAILS continued

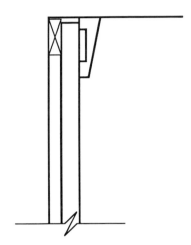

WOOD PANELING @ CEILING
3"=1'-0"   06421-83

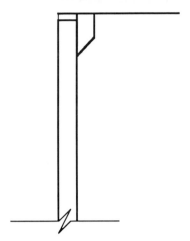

WOOD PANELING @ CEILING
3"=1'-0"   06421-84

NOTATION CHECKLIST, SAMPLE NOTES

PANEL (MATERIAL & THICKNESS)
FURRING/BLOCKING (TYPE & SIZE)
AIR SPACE
TRIM (TYPE & SIZE)
ADJACENT MATERIALS
LINE OF WALL
LINE OF CEILING
WALL CONSTRUCTION
CEILING CONSTRUCTION

BOOK MATCH VENEER
SLIP MATCH VENEER
'V' MATCH VENEER
RANDOM MATCH VENEER
FURRING STRIPS
BLOCK ALL UNSUPPORTED
EDGES
FILL SPLICES BETWEEN FURRING
RECESSED JOINT
'V' JOINT
BUTT JOINT
OUTSIDE MITERED CORNER

06432 WOOD STAIRS

DETAIL DATA CHECKLIST

WOOD STAIRS
Stairs may be shop built and installed as a unit. Use the design and construction standards of Architectural Woodwork Institute.

Rules of thumb:
__Provide landing at every 15 risers maximum
__Stair angle of 30 to 35 degrees is most comfortable
__Treads and risers must not vary in size over 1/8" or they'll cause accidents
__Optimum riser size is 7 to 7-1/2" with optimal tread of 9-1/2" to 10-1/2"
__Minimum residential stair width is 36", 44" to 48" preferred

Handrails:
__Height: 30" to 34"
__Balcony or landing guardrail: 42"
__Handrail or guardrail stiles: 9" minimum spacing.
__Turn end of handrail into newel post, to floor or to wall
__Wood tread and risers, use minimum 3/4" actual thickness

__Attach wood treads and risers with screw connections and glue to prevent movement and squeaks
__Wood stringers are usually cut from 2 x 12
__Two side stringers are mandatory and one center stringer recommended
__Provide fire blocking across stringer in closed riser with exposed soffit

SMALL-SCALE GENERIC DETAILS

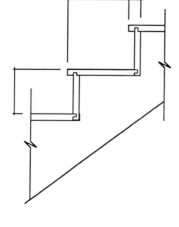

WOOD STAIR TREAD
& RISER Closed
06432-31

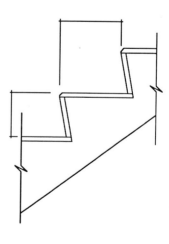

WOOD STAIR TREAD
& RISER Closed
06432-32

06432 WOOD STAIRS

SMALL-SCALE GENERIC DETAILS continued

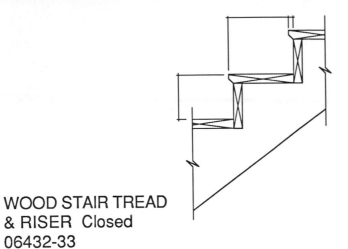

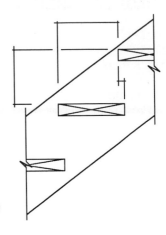

WOOD STAIR TREAD
& RISER Closed
06432-33

WOOD STAIR TREAD
& RISER Open
06432-34

FULL-SCALE GENERIC DETAILS

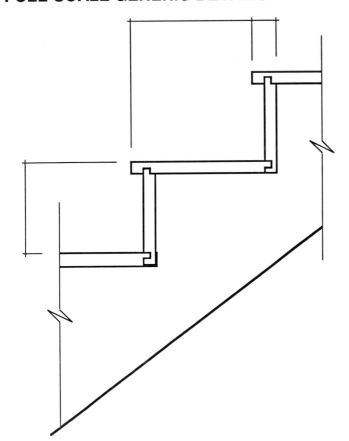

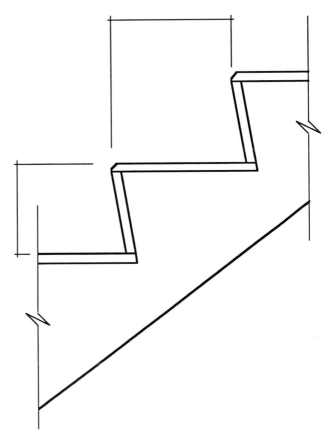

WOOD STAIR TREAD
& RISER Closed
1-1/2"=1'-0"
06432-31

WOOD STAIR TREAD
& RISER Closed
1-1/2"=1'-0"
06432-32

06432 WOOD STAIRS

FULL-SCALE GENERIC DETAILS continued

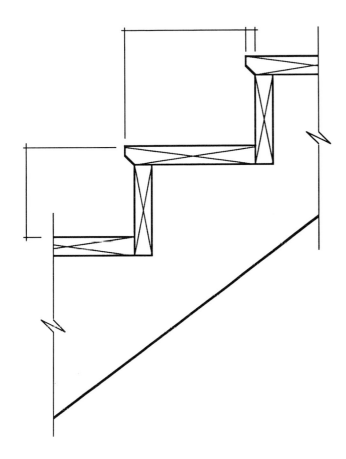

WOOD STAIR TREAD
& RISER Closed
1-1/2"=1'-0"
06432-33

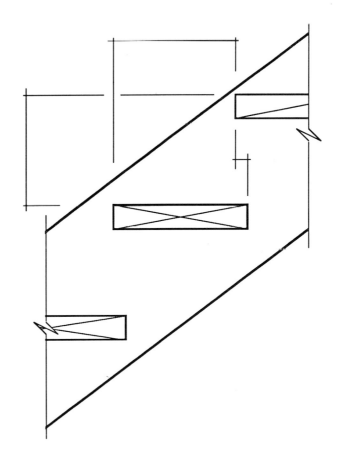

WOOD STAIR TREAD
& RISER Open
1-1/2"=1'-0"
06432-34

NOTATION CHECKLIST,
SAMPLE NOTES

TREADS & RISERS
FASTENERS
STRINGER (TYPE & SIZE)
BLOCKING
FURRING/SOFFIT
3/4" PLYWD. TREADS & RISERS
2 X 12 TREAD
1 X 8 RISER
1 X 2 NOSE
RESILIENT SQUARE SAFETY NOSE
3/4" X 3/4" QUARTER ROUND NOSING
2 X 12 STRINGERS, 1 @ CENTERLINE & 2 @ EA. SIDE
2 X 12 STRINGERS
STRINGERS FROM 2 X 12'S @ 16" O.C.
OAK BASE, OAK TREAD

06455 WOOD BASEBOARDS

DETAIL DATA CHECKLIST

BASEBOARDS
__Baseboards are manufactured in a large variety of standard sizes and profiles; see suppliers' catalogs for all the
    options available

__When choosing a baseboard design or material, consider maintenance needs
    __Provide hardness and surface finish resistance to damage from:
        __Cleaning equipment
        __Furniture legs
        __Floor cleaning chemicals.

__Some contractors will attempt to use up scrap baseboard material by piecing together short lengths of
    baseboard
    __Specify or note that all baseboards be installed full length and continuous without joints in any run

SMALL-SCALE GENERIC DETAILS

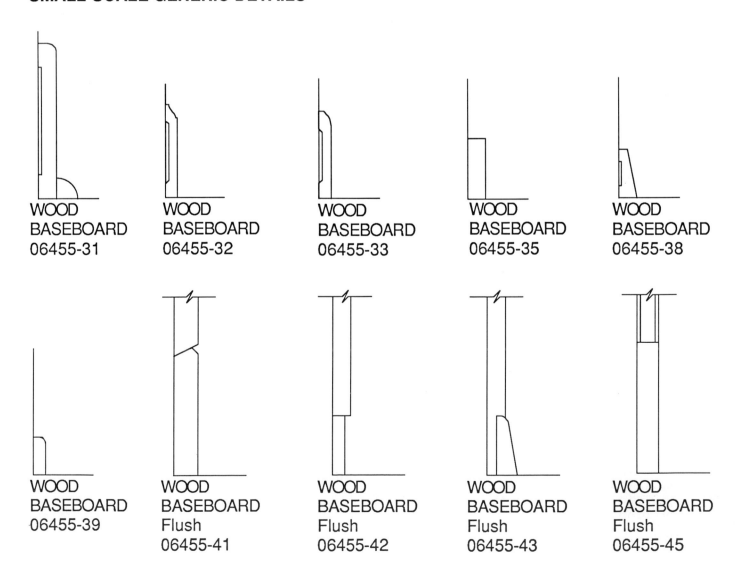

WOOD
BASEBOARD
06455-31

WOOD
BASEBOARD
06455-32

WOOD
BASEBOARD
06455-33

WOOD
BASEBOARD
06455-35

WOOD
BASEBOARD
06455-38

WOOD
BASEBOARD
06455-39

WOOD
BASEBOARD
Flush
06455-41

WOOD
BASEBOARD
Flush
06455-42

WOOD
BASEBOARD
Flush
06455-43

WOOD
BASEBOARD
Flush
06455-45

06455 WOOD BASEBOARDS

FULL-SCALE GENERIC DETAILS

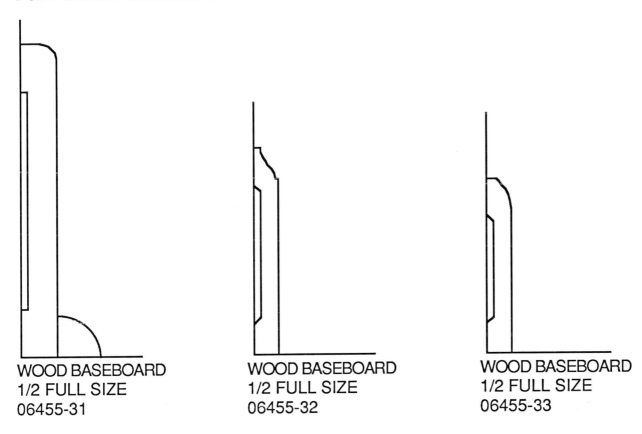

WOOD BASEBOARD
1/2 FULL SIZE
06455-31

WOOD BASEBOARD
1/2 FULL SIZE
06455-32

WOOD BASEBOARD
1/2 FULL SIZE
06455-33

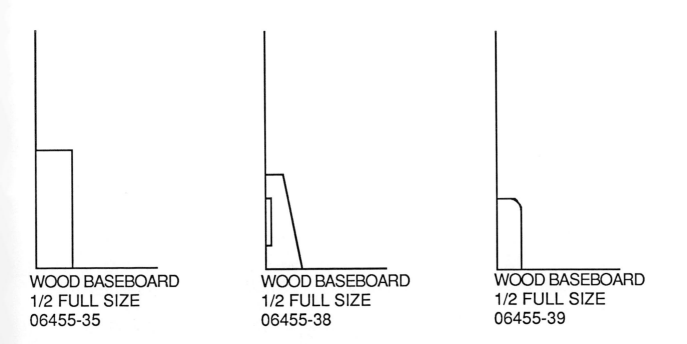

WOOD BASEBOARD
1/2 FULL SIZE
06455-35

WOOD BASEBOARD
1/2 FULL SIZE
06455-38

WOOD BASEBOARD
1/2 FULL SIZE
06455-39

06455 WOOD BASEBOARDS

FULL-SCALE GENERIC DETAILS continued

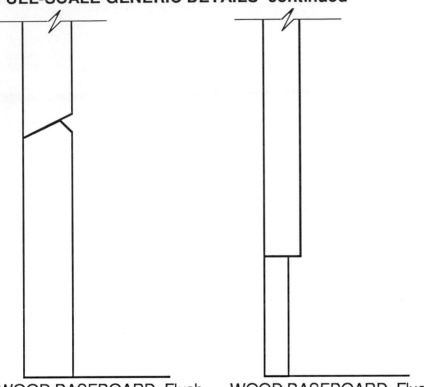

WOOD BASEBOARD Flush
1/2 FULL SIZE 06455-41

WOOD BASEBOARD Flush
1/2 FULL SIZE 06455-42

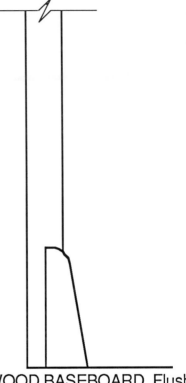

WOOD BASEBOARD Flush
1/2 FULL SIZE 06455-43

NOTATION CHECKLIST,
SAMPLE NOTES

BASE (MATERIAL & TYPE)
BASE HEIGHT & THICKNESS
ADJACENT WALL MATERIAL
WALL MEMBRANE/WATERPROOFING
ADJACENT FLOOR MATERIAL
FLOOR
MEMBRANE/WATERPROOFING
SUBFLOOR/SLAB
SEALANT/ADHESIVE
FASTENERS
TRIM/SHOE MOLD
BLOCKING STRIP
EDGE TRIM

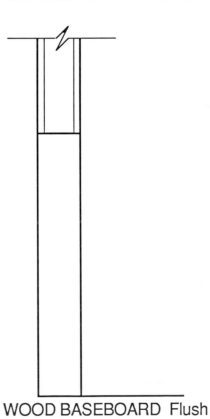

WOOD BASEBOARD Flush
1/2 FULL SIZE 06455-45

CHAPTER 7

Thermal and Roofing
07000

07321, 07322 ROOFING TILE

DETAIL DATA CHECKLIST

TILE ROOFS

__See tile suppliers' literature for tile shapes and specific recommended details and installation instructions
__Special trim pieces and fasteners are provided for ridges, end bands, eave closure, rake closure, and hips

__Heavy roof framing is required to carry roof tiles, check dead load allowances carefully
    __Spanish tile: 900 pounds sq. ft.
    __Barrel mission tile: 1250 pounds sq. ft.
    __Flat tiles: 800 pounds sq. ft.
    __French, Roman, Greek tiles: 1250 pounds sq. ft.

Tile sizes:
    __Spanish: 9-3/4" x 13-1/4" with 10-1/4" exposure
    __Barrel Mission: 8" x 18" with 15" exposure
    __Flat: 9" x 14" with 11" exposure

Minimum slopes and laps:
    __Spanish, Barrel Mission, French, Greek, Roman tile
        __Minimum slope: 4.5" per foot
        __Minimum lap 3"
    __Flat tiles
        __Minimum slope: 4.5" per foot, 6" per foot minimum recommended
        __Minimum lap as per precast attachment grooves (about 5")

Application:
    __Apply tiles over solid plywood or plank sheathing with 30# or 40# roofing felt
        __Use heavier felt in more extreme climates
        __Two ply felt recommended
        __Hot mopped building felt preferred, especially for lower slopes

    __Fasten with:
        __Copper nails
        __Other non-corrosive nails
        __12 gauge galvanized wire, 10 gauge copper wire, or .084
            stainless steel wire
        __Wires are hooked to perforated non-corrosive metal fastening strips which are nailed
            across the roof sheathing

    __Copper flashing is preferred; galvanized metal acceptable in most cases

__Main problem spots and points of failure:
    __Wind uplift at eaves and rakes
    __Insufficient cement, flashing, or building felt at ridges
    __Snow and ice build-up in roof valleys

07321, 07322 (a) ROOFING TILE

See DETAIL DATA CHECKLIST for tile roof preceding 07321

SMALL-SCALE GENERIC DETAILS

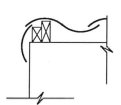

ROOFING TILE Curved S Tile @ Rake
07321-21

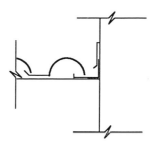

ROOFING TILE Curved S Tile @ Wall
07321-22

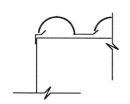

ROOFING TILE Curved Tile @ Rake
07321-26

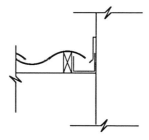

ROOFING TILE Curved Tile @ Wall
07321-27

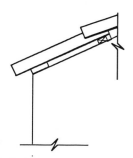

ROOFING TILE Curved Tile @ Eave
07321-31

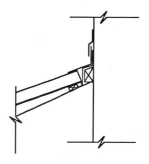

ROOFING TILE Curved Tile @ Wall
07321-32

07321, 07322 (a) ROOFING TILE

FULL-SCALE GENERIC DETAILS

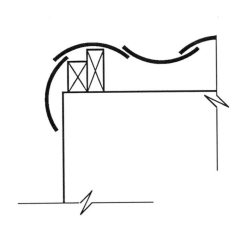

ROOFING TILE Curved S Tile @ Rake
1-1/2"=1'-0"   07321-21

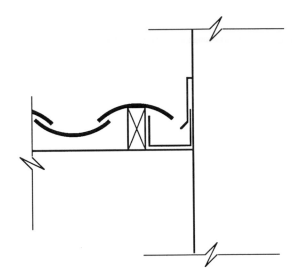

ROOFING TILE Curved S Tile @ Wall
1-1/2"=1'-0"   07321-22

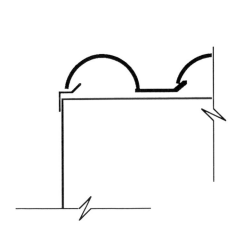

ROOFING TILE Curved Tile @ Rake
1-1/2"=1'-0"   07321-26

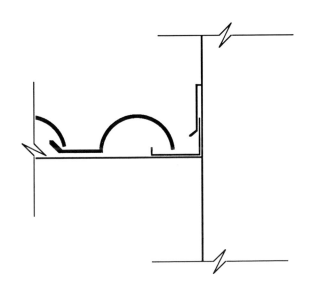

ROOFING TILE Curved Tile @ Wall
1-1/2"=1'-0"   07321-27

07321, 07322 (a) ROOFING TILE

FULL-SCALE GENERIC DETAILS continued

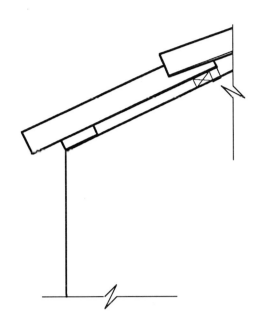

ROOFING TILE Curved Tile @ Eave
1-1/2"=1'-0"   07321-31

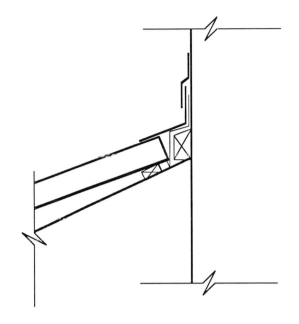

ROOFING TILE Curved Tile @ Wall
1-1/2"=1'-0"   07321-32

NOTATION CHECKLIST,
SAMPLE NOTES

RIDGE TILE
NAILER
CEMENT
FIELD TILE
GRAVEL STOP
FLASHING
NAILER
FASCIA
BUILDING FELT
ROOF DECK/INSULATION
ROOF CONSTRUCTION
SLOPE
ELASTIC CEMENT

TOP FIXTURE
EAVE CLOSURE
WOOD DECKING
CONCRETE ROOF
PLASTER LATH
RAKE
END BAND
DECK MOULD
STARTER
CLEATS
ROOF EDGE
CAP FLASHING
VALLEY FLASHING
CANT STRIP

07321, 07322 (b) ROOFING TILE

See DETAIL DATA CHECKLIST for tile roof preceding 07321

SMALL-SCALE GENERIC DETAILS

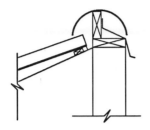

ROOFING TILE S Parapet Ridge
07321-33

ROOFING TILE S Tile @ Flat Ridge
07321-34

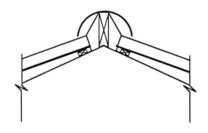

ROOFING TILE S Tile @ Ridge
07321-35

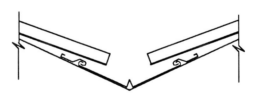

ROOFING TILE Curved Tile @ Valley
07321-38

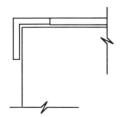

FLAT ROOFING TILE Rake
07322-21

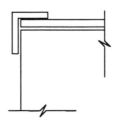

FLAT ROOFING TILE Rake
07322-22

07321, 07322 (b) ROOFING TILE

FULL-SCALE GENERIC DETAILS

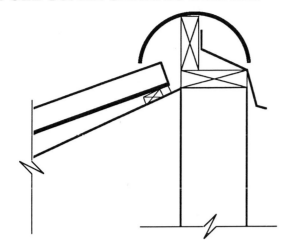

ROOFING TILE S Parapet Ridge
1-1/2"=1'-0"   07321-33

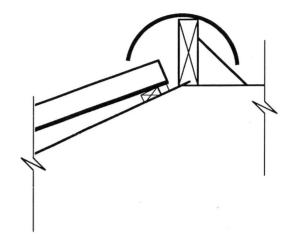

ROOFING TILE S Tile @ Flat Ridge
1-1/2"=1'-0"   07321-34

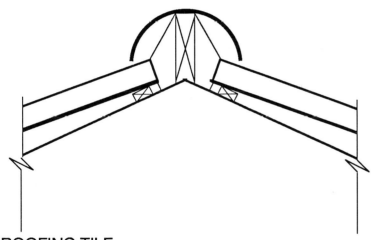

ROOFING TILE
S Tile @ Ridge
1-1/2"=1'-0"   07321-35

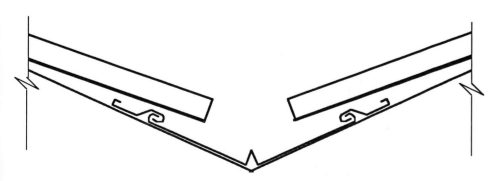

ROOFING TILE
Curved Tile @ Valley
1-1/2"=1'-0"   07321-38

FULL-SCALE GENERIC DETAILS continued

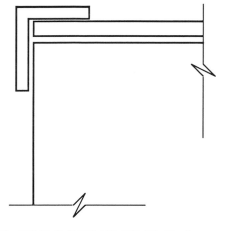

FLAT ROOFING TILE Rake
1-1/2"=1'-0"   07322-22

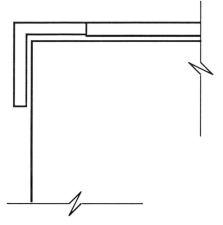

FLAT ROOFING TILE Rake
1-1/2"=1'-0"   07322-21

NOTATION CHECKLIST,
SAMPLE NOTES

RIDGE TILE
NAILER
CEMENT
FIELD TILE
GRAVEL STOP
FLASHING
NAILER
FASCIA
BUILDING FELT
ROOF DECK/INSULATION
ROOF CONSTRUCTION
SLOPE
ELASTIC CEMENT

TOP FIXTURE
EAVE CLOSURE
WOOD DECKING
CONCRETE ROOF
PLASTER LATH
RAKE
END BAND
DECK MOULD
STARTER
CLEATS
ROOF EDGE
CAP FLASHING
VALLEY FLASHING
CANT STRIP

07321, 07322 (c) ROOFING TILE

See DETAIL DATA CHECKLIST for roof tile preceding 07321

SMALL-SCALE GENERIC DETAILS

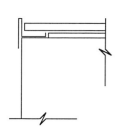

FLAT ROOFING TILE
Rake Flashing
07322-23

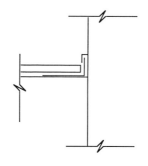

FLAT ROOFING TILE
Flashing @ Wall
07322-26

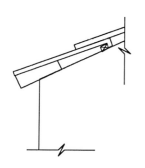

FLAT ROOFING TILE
Eave
07322-30

FLAT ROOFING TILE
Eave
07322-31

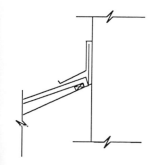

FLAT ROOFING TILE
Flashing @ Wall
07322-32

FLAT ROOFING TILE
Parapet Ridge
07322-33

07321, 07322 (c) ROOFING TILE

FULL-SCALE GENERIC DETAILS

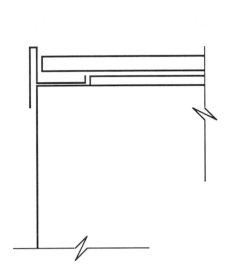

FLAT ROOFING TILE Rake Flashing
1-1/2"=1'-0"   07322-23

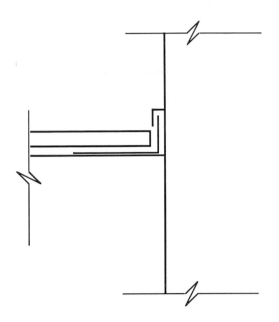

FLAT ROOFING TILE Flashing @ Wall
1-1/2"=1'-0"   07322-26

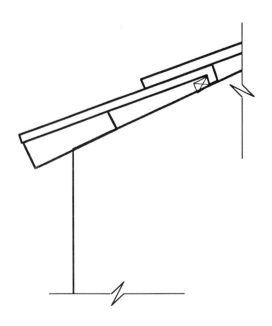

FLAT ROOFING TILE Eave
1-1/2"=1'-0"   07322-30

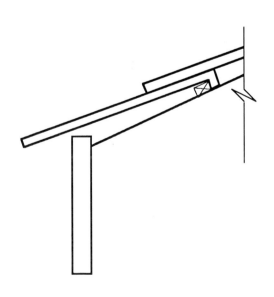

FLAT ROOFING TILE Eave
1-1/2"=1'-0"   07322-31

07321, 07322 (c) ROOFING TILE

FULL-SCALE GENERIC DETAILS continued

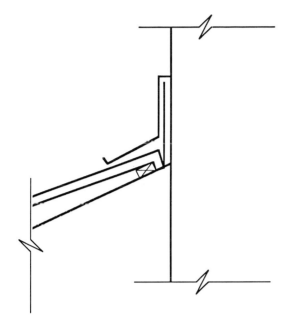

FLAT ROOFING TILE Flashing @ Wall
1-1/2"=1'-0"   07322-32

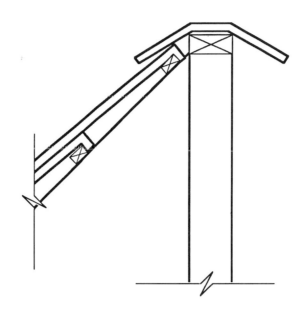

FLAT ROOFING TILE Parapet Ridge
1-1/2"=1'-0"   07322-33

NOTATION CHECKLIST,
SAMPLE NOTES

RIDGE TILE
NAILER
CEMENT
FIELD TILE
GRAVEL STOP
FLASHING
NAILER
FASCIA
BUILDING FELT
ROOF DECK/INSULATION
ROOF CONSTRUCTION
SLOPE
ELASTIC CEMENT

TOP FIXTURE
EAVE CLOSURE
WOOD DECKING
CONCRETE ROOF
PLASTER LATH
RAKE
END BAND
DECK MOULD
STARTER
CLEATS
ROOF EDGE
CAP FLASHING
VALLEY FLASHING
CANT STRIP

07321, 07322 (d) ROOFING TILE

See DETAIL DATA CHECKLIST for roof tile preceding 07321

SMALL-SCALE GENERIC DETAILS

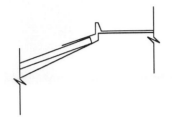

FLAT ROOFING TILE Flat Roof Ridge
07322-34

FLAT ROOFING TILE Ridge Piece
07322-35

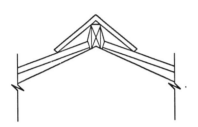

FLAT ROOFING TILE Ridge Piece
07322-36

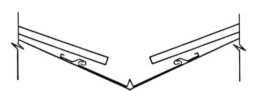

FLAT ROOFING TILE Valley
07322-38

FULL-SCALE GENERIC DETAILS

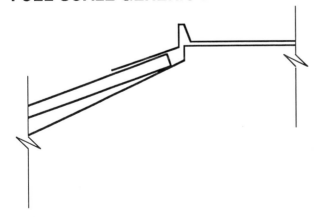

FLAT ROOFING TILE Flat Roof Ridge
1-1/2"=1'-0"   07322-34

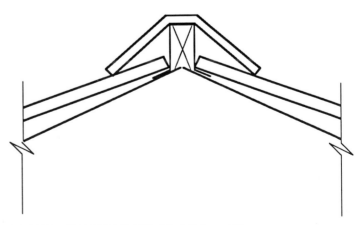

FLAT ROOFING TILE Ridge Piece
1-1/2"=1'-0"   07322-35

07321, 07322 (d) ROOFING TILE

FULL-SCALE GENERIC DETAILS continued

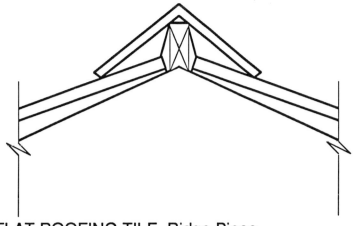

FLAT ROOFING TILE Ridge Piece
1-1/2"=1'-0"   07322-36

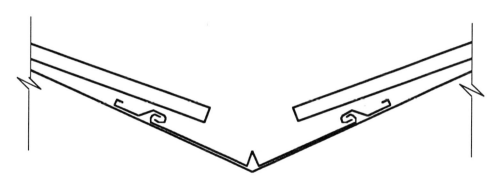

FLAT ROOFING TILE Valley
1-1/2"=1'-0"   07322-38

NOTATION CHECKLIST,
SAMPLE NOTES

RIDGE TILE
NAILER
CEMENT
FIELD TILE
GRAVEL STOP
FLASHING
NAILER
FASCIA
BUILDING FELT
ROOF DECK/INSULATION
ROOF CONSTRUCTION
SLOPE
ELASTIC CEMENT
TOP FIXTURE

EAVE CLOSURE
WOOD DECKING
CONCRETE ROOF
PLASTER LATH
RAKE
END BAND
DECK MOULD
STARTER
CLEATS
ROOF EDGE
CAP FLASHING
VALLEY FLASHING
CANT STRIP

07603 FLASHING @ PARAPETS

DETAIL DATA CHECKLIST

FLASHING AT PARAPETS

The primary cost of flashing is labor, so the best materials add little to the cost of this crucially important part of construction.

Commonly used flashing materials:
  __Copper
  __Lead
  __Zinc
  __Aluminum
  __Galvanized steel
  __Plastic
  __Copper-backed paper
  __Building paper felt and impregnated fabric

__Parapet flashing typically consists of two overlapping L sections:
  __One L section is attached to the roof
  __The other is counterflashing, an inverted L that fits into a parapet reglet and slips down over the
      top of the lower base flashing

__26 gauge flashing is commonly used because it affords good protection while still being thin enough to
      bend, form, and work with comfortably
__Base flashing is bent upwards at 45 degrees to avoid sharp corners that might splet the metal or roofing
__Minimum flashing width for most flashing situations is 8"
__Any extended lengths of flashing requires expansion joints

__Refer to the Manual of standards of the Sheet Metal and Air Conditioning Contractors National
      Association for varied detail conditions and installation standards

07603 FLASHING @ PARAPETS

See DETAIL DATA CHECKLIST for flashing preceding 07603

SMALL-SCALE GENERIC DETAILS

FLASHING
@ CONCRETE PARAPET
1-1/2"=1'-0"
07603-1

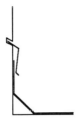

FLASHING
@ CONCRETE PARAPET
1-1/2"=1'-0"
07603-2

FLASHING
@ CONCRETE PARAPET
1-1/2"=1'-0"
07603-11

FLASHING
@ CONCRETE PARAPET
1-1/2"=1'-0"
07603-12

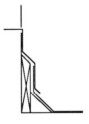

FLASHING
@ CONCRETE PARAPET
1-1/2"=1'-0"
07603-13

FLASHING
@ MASONRY PARAPET
1-1/2"=1'-0"
07603-43

FLASHING
@ PARAPET
1-1/2"=1'-0"
07603-51

07603 FLASHING @ PARAPETS

FULL-SCALE GENERIC DETAILS

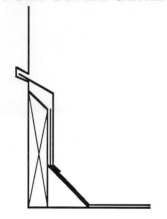

FLASHING @ CONCRETE PARAPET
1-1/2"=1'-0"   07603-1

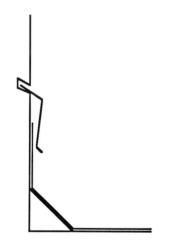

FLASHING @ CONCRETE PARAPET
1-1/2"=1'-0"   07603-2

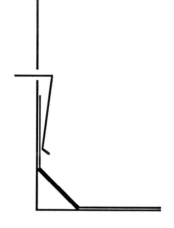

FLASHING @ MASONRY PARAPET
1-1/2"=1'-0"   07603-11

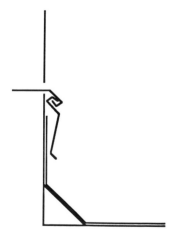

FLASHING @ MASONRY PARAPET
1-1/2"=1'-0"   07603-12

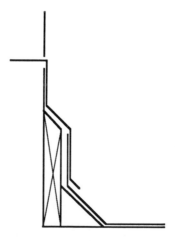

FLASHING @ MASONRY PARAPET
1-1/2"=1'-0"   07603-13

428

07603 FLASHING @ PARAPETS

FULL-SCALE GENERIC DETAILS continued

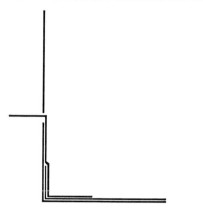

FLASHING @ MASONRY PARAPET
1-1/2"=1'-0"   07603-43

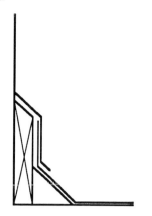

FLASHING @ PARAPET
1-1/2"=1'-0"   07603-51

NOTATION CHECKLIST, SAMPLE NOTES

PARAPET WALL CONSTRUCTION
REGLET
FLASHING/COUNTERFLASHING
CANT/NAILER
ADHESIVE/SEALANT/CAULKING
ROOFING SURFACE
    (TYPE, LAYERS & COVER MATERIAL)
ROOF DECK/INSULATION
ROOF CONSTRUCTION
COPING

SAMPLE NOTES:
24 GA. CLIP-ON FLASHING, ATTACH @
    CTR. OF EA. PIECE
2 X   TREATED PLATE, 1/2" EXP. BOLTS
    @ 24" O.C.
2 X 10 WOOD BLKG., SECURE TO MTL.
STUD & BRICK W/1/2" DIA. ANCHOR
    BOLT 8" LONG @ 48" O.C.
MANUFACTURED REGLET & FLASHING
    SYSTEM
G.I. FLASHING
ELASTOMERIC FLASHING

BASE FLASHING OVER PLATE
FLASHING APPLIED W/ ADHESIVE
LEAD OR ALUMINUM FLASHING
CONT. CLEAT
SHIM (to slope)
BASE FLASHING NAILS @ 8" O.C.
WEDGE & SEAL
FLASHING JOINT SET IN ROOFING CEMENT
METAL CAP FLASHING
S.S. FLASHING INTO PRESET REGLET
FLASH. REGLET, BEND DOWN AFTER INSTALLING
    FLUSH TIGHT AGAINST WALL
METAL FLASHING SET IN MORTAR BED
METAL CLIP @ 3'-0" O.C.
COMPOSITION FLASHING
BUILT-UP ROOFING
BASE SHEET INSULATION
FELT VAPOR BARRIER
FILL, PITCH TO DRAIN
WOOD BLOCKING
NAILABLE CANT
CONT. 4" HIGH CANT

FULL-SCALE GENERIC DETAILS

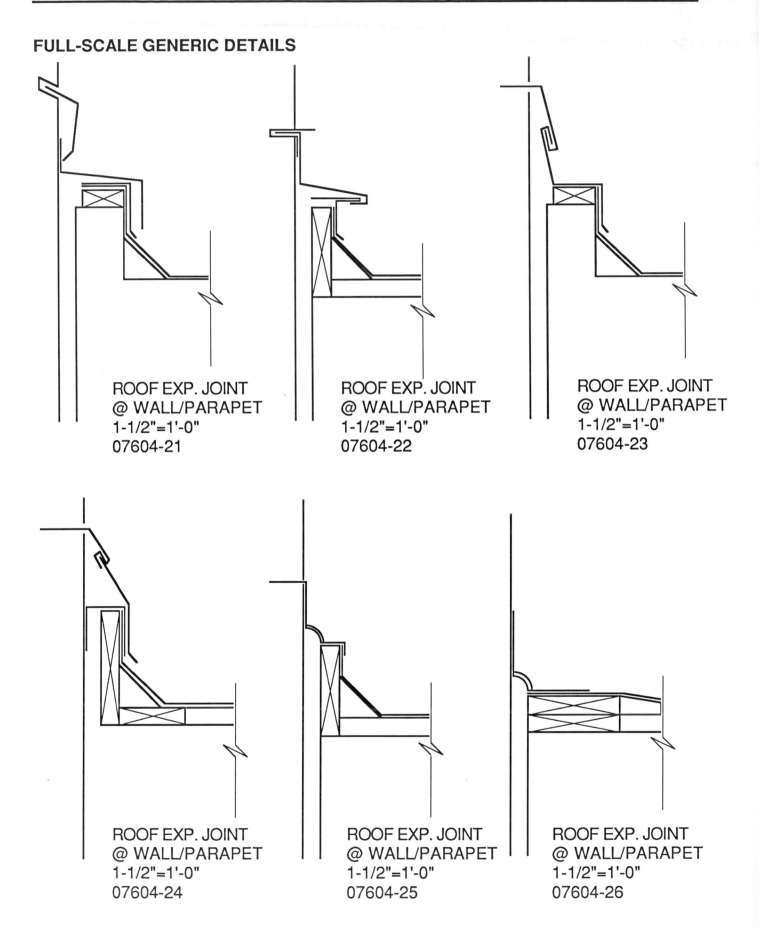

ROOF EXP. JOINT
@ WALL/PARAPET
1-1/2"=1'-0"
07604-21

ROOF EXP. JOINT
@ WALL/PARAPET
1-1/2"=1'-0"
07604-22

ROOF EXP. JOINT
@ WALL/PARAPET
1-1/2"=1'-0"
07604-23

ROOF EXP. JOINT
@ WALL/PARAPET
1-1/2"=1'-0"
07604-24

ROOF EXP. JOINT
@ WALL/PARAPET
1-1/2"=1'-0"
07604-25

ROOF EXP. JOINT
@ WALL/PARAPET
1-1/2"=1'-0"
07604-26

FULL-SCALE GENERIC DETAILS continued

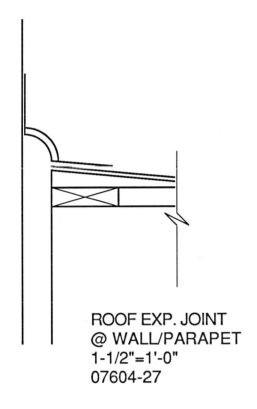

ROOF EXP. JOINT
@ WALL/PARAPET
1-1/2"=1'-0"
07604-27

NOTATION CHECKLIST,
SAMPLE NOTES

EXPANSION JOINT COVER
CANT/NAILER/BLOCKING
ADHESIVE/SEALANT/CAULKING
ROOFING SURFACE
   (TYPE, LAYERS & COVER MATERIAL)
ROOF DECK/INSULATION
ROOF CONSTRUCTION
COPING

SAMPLE NOTES:
24 GA. CLIP-ON FLASHING, ATTACH @ CTR. OF EA.
   PIECE
2 X   TREATED PLATE, 1/2" EXP. BOLTS @ 24" O.C.
2 X 10 WOOD BLKG., SECURE TO MTL.
STUD & BRICK W/1/2" DIA. ANCHOR BOLT 8" LONG
   @ 48" O.C.
MANUFACTURED REGLET & FLASHING SYSTEM
G.I. FLASHING
ELASTOMERIC FLASHING
BASE FLASHING OVER PLATE

FLASHING APPLIED W/ADHESIVE
LEAD OR ALUMINUM FLASHING
CONT. CLEAT
SHIM (to slope)
BASE FLASHING NAILS @ 8" O.C.
WEDGE & SEAL
FLASHING JOINT SET IN ROOFING CEMENT
METAL CAP FLASHING
S.S. FLASHING INTO PRESET REGLET
FLASH. REGLET, BEND DOWN AFTER INSTALLING
   FLUSH TIGHT AGAINST WALL
METAL FLASHING SET IN MORTAR BED
METAL CLIP @ 3'-0" O.C.
COMPOSITION FLASHING
BUILT-UP ROOFING
BASE SHEET INSULATION
FELT VAPOR BARRIER
FILL, PITCH TO DRAIN
WOOD BLOCKING
NAILABLE CANT
CONT. 4" HIGH CANT

07606 VENT FLASHING

See DETAIL DATA CHECKLIST for flashing preceding 07603

SMALL-SCALE GENERIC DETAILS

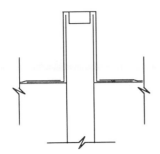

VENT FLASHING
Sleeve Type
07606-21

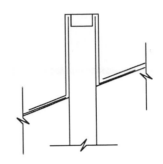

VENT FLASHING
Sleeve Type
07606-22

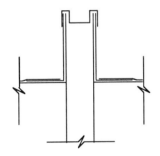

VENT FLASHING
Sleeve Type
07606-23

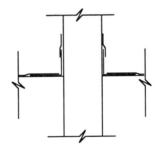

VENT FLASHING
Sleeve Type
07606-31

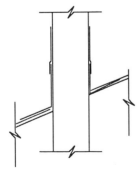

VENT FLASHING
Collar Type
07606-32

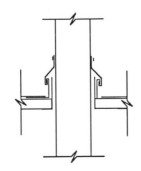

VENT FLASHING
Collar Type
07606-33

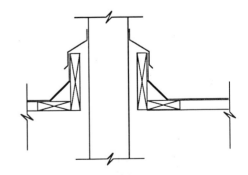

VENT FLASHING
Collar Type
07606-34

434

07606 VENT FLASHING

FULL-SCALE GENERIC DETAILS

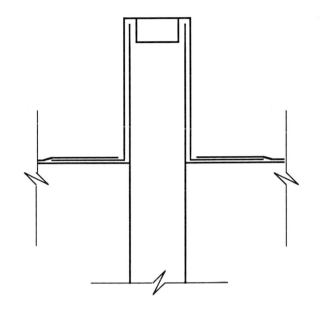

VENT FLASHING Sleeve Type
1-1/2"=1'-0"   07606-21

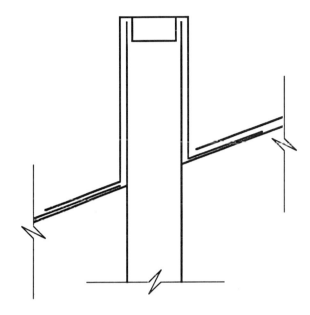

VENT FLASHING Sleeve Type
1-1/2"=1'-0"   07606-22

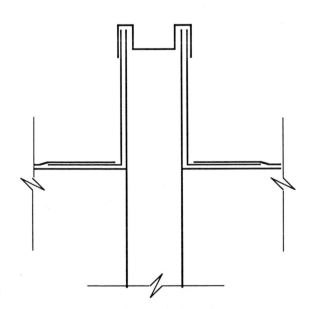

VENT FLASHING Sleeve Type
1-1/2"=1'-0"   07606-23

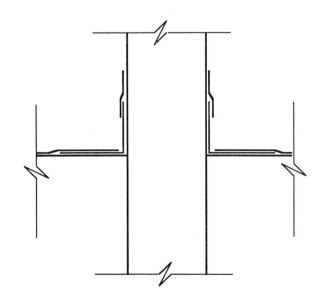

VENT FLASHING Sleeve Type
1-1/2"=1'-0"   07606-31

07606 VENT FLASHING

FULL-SCALE GENERIC DETAILS continued

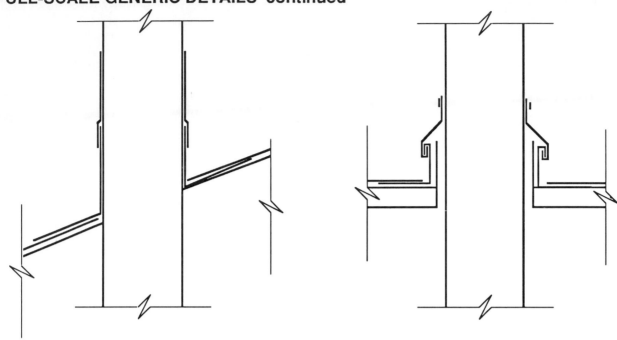

VENT FLASHING
Collar Type
1-1/2"=1'-0"   07606-32

VENT FLASHING
Collar Type
1 1/2"=1'-0"   07606-33

NOTATION CHECKLIST,
SAMPLE NOTES

VENT PIPE/STACK
   (TYPE, SIZE & MINIMUM HEIGHT)
SLEEVE FLASHING
COLLAR FLASHING
INNER FLANGE
ADHESIVE/SEALANT/CAULKING
ROOFING SURFACE
   (TYPE, LAYERS & COVER MATERIAL)
ROOF DECK/INSULATION
ROOF CONSTRUCTION
METAL VENT
PREMOLDED PIPE SEAL
SEALANT
FLASHING FELT
STAINLES STEEL CLAMPING RING
WATER CUTOFF MASTIC
CORE HOLE AS REQUIRED
OPENINGS FOR VENTS TO BE
   PREFORMED
BUILT-UP ROOF
ROOF PLIES UNDER CAP
FACTORY CURB
RIGID INSULATION
METAL DECKING
DUCT

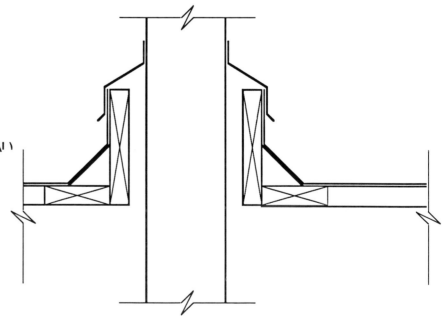

VENT FLASHING Collar Type
1-1/2"=1'-0"   07606-34

dim. lines   break line   notation boundary   break line

cut mark

dim. line

dim. line

break line

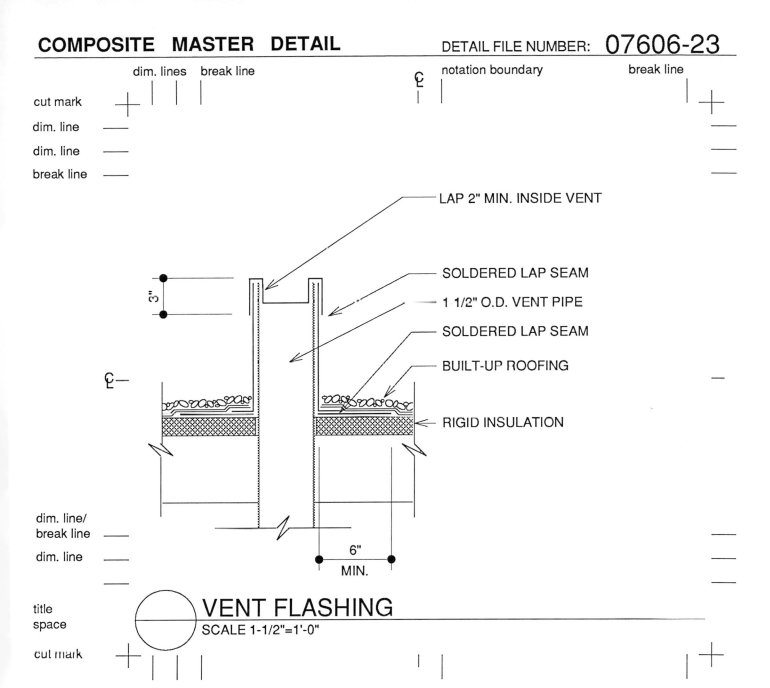

LAP 2" MIN. INSIDE VENT

SOLDERED LAP SEAM

1 1/2" O.D. VENT PIPE

SOLDERED LAP SEAM

BUILT-UP ROOFING

RIGID INSULATION

3"

dim. line/
break line

dim. line

6"
MIN.

title
space

VENT FLASHING
SCALE 1-1/2"=1'-0"

cut mark

DETAIL INFORMATION
References, jobsite feedback, job history

07610 (a) SHEET METAL ROOFING

DETAIL DATA CHECKLIST

SHEET METAL ROOFING

Sheet metal roofs are usually installed as ready-made products and will be designed and detailed as per manufacturers' instructions.

__Minimum allowable roof slope is 3" per linear foot, 4" is a preferred minimum
__Lower slopes may be used if using flat, locked, and soldered seams
__Prepare dry wood substrate with 20# building felt as backing and leak protection
__Add rosin paper atop building felt as a bond break between metal felt

__Since sheet metal expands a great deal, a primary consideration is expansion control by means of standing seams, batten seams, ribbed joints, and V crimps.

__Metal attachment cleats to hold roofing are typically nailed at 8" to 12" intervals and locked into seams

__Nail metal must match or be compatible with roofing metal
    __Nailing must not penetrate sheet metal

__Seam types:
    __Flat
    __Standing
    __Batten

__Standing seams:
    __Spacings typically range from 12" to 28"
    __Heights are 7/8" to 1-1/4"
    __26 to 24 gauge galvanized steel, 16 to 20 oz. copper are typical depending on sheet width
        __Larger sheets require the heavier metal
    __Prefabricated seams are sometimes not as watertight as job formed seams

__Batten seams:
    __Wood battens are nailed to wood sheathing or bolted to non-wood construction
    __Batten fasteners are countersunk
    __Maximum spacing is typically 20"

__Materials are chosen on the basis of job requirements for appearance and durability:
    __Aluminum, usually preformed and prefinished
    __Copper 16 to 20 oz., and lead coated copper
    __Monel metal
    __Galvanized steel, usually preformed and prefinished
    __Stainless steel
    __Terne plate
    __Zinc

__Cleats, nails, snap locks, linings, ridges, closures, valley flashing, rake pieces, and expansion joints are as provided or recommended by manufacturers
__Refer to the Manual of standards of the Sheet Metal and Air Conditioning Contractors National Association for varied detail conditions and installation standards

Trouble spots:
__Inadequate cleat and edge supports to prevent wind up lift
__Inadequate allowance for thermal expansion
__Corrosion due to contact of dissimilar metals, especially incompatible metal nails
__Inadequate slopes for rapid drainage
__Prefabricated or on-site battens and standing seams that aren't sufficiently tight
__Partial weathering, dirt streaking, and staining because of uneven water dispersal

07610 (a) SHEET METAL ROOFING

See DETAIL DATA CHECKLIST for metal roof preceding 07610 (a)

SMALL-SCALE GENERIC DETAILS

SHEET METAL ROOF EAVE
07610-1

SHEET METAL ROOF
PITCH BREAK
07610-2

SHEET METAL ROOF
FLUSH @ WALL
07610-3

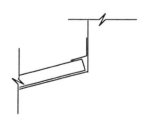

SHEET METAL ROOF
EAVE @ WALL
07610-4

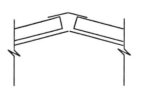

SHEET METAL ROOF
@ RIDGE
07610-5

07610 (a) SHEET METAL ROOFING

FULL-SCALE GENERIC DETAILS

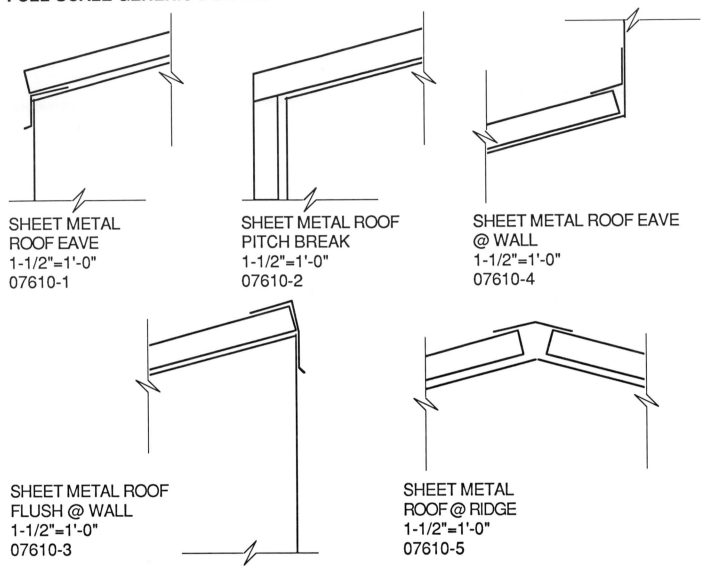

SHEET METAL
ROOF EAVE
1-1/2"=1'-0"
07610-1

SHEET METAL ROOF
PITCH BREAK
1-1/2"=1'-0"
07610-2

SHEET METAL ROOF EAVE
@ WALL
1-1/2"=1'-0"
07610-4

SHEET METAL ROOF
FLUSH @ WALL
1-1/2"=1'-0"
07610-3

SHEET METAL
ROOF @ RIDGE
1-1/2"=1'-0"
07610-5

NOTATION CHECKLIST, SAMPLE NOTES

FLAT SEAM
BATTEN
FLASHING
STANDING SEAM
SNAP CAP ANCHOR CLIP
CLEAT
METAL ROOFING
ROOFING FELT
ROOF DECK/INSULATION
ROOF CONSTRUCTION
PREFAB RIDGE PIECE

METAL ROOFING HIP COVER
PLYWOOD SHEATHING
MTL. ROOFING, 1-1/2" W. X 2" H. BATTEN @ 24" O.C.
TYPE "W" VALLEY CONT. FLASH. BY MTL.
   ROOFING MFR.
CLOSURE BY MTL. ROOFING MFR.
PEAK LAP BY MTL. ROOFING MFR.
26 GA. GALV. MTL. ROOFING, CLIP & SEAM

07610 (b) SHEET METAL ROOFING

See DETAIL DATA CHECKLIST for metal roof preceding 07610 (a)

SMALL-SCALE GENERIC DETAILS

SHEET METAL ROOF
Flat Seam @ Eave
07610-51

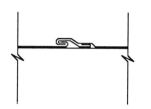

SHEET METAL ROOF
Flat Seam
07610-52

SHEET METAL ROOF
Flat Seam
07610-53

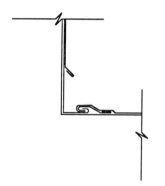

SHEET METAL ROOF
Flat Seam @ Parapet
07610-54

SHEET METAL ROOF
Flat Seam @ Ridge
07610-55

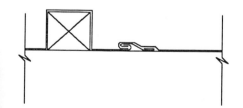

SHEET METAL ROOF
Flat Seam & Batten
07610-61

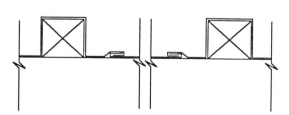

SHEET METAL ROOF
Flat Seam & Batten
07610-62

441

07610 (b) SHEET METAL ROOFING

FULL-SCALE GENERIC DETAILS

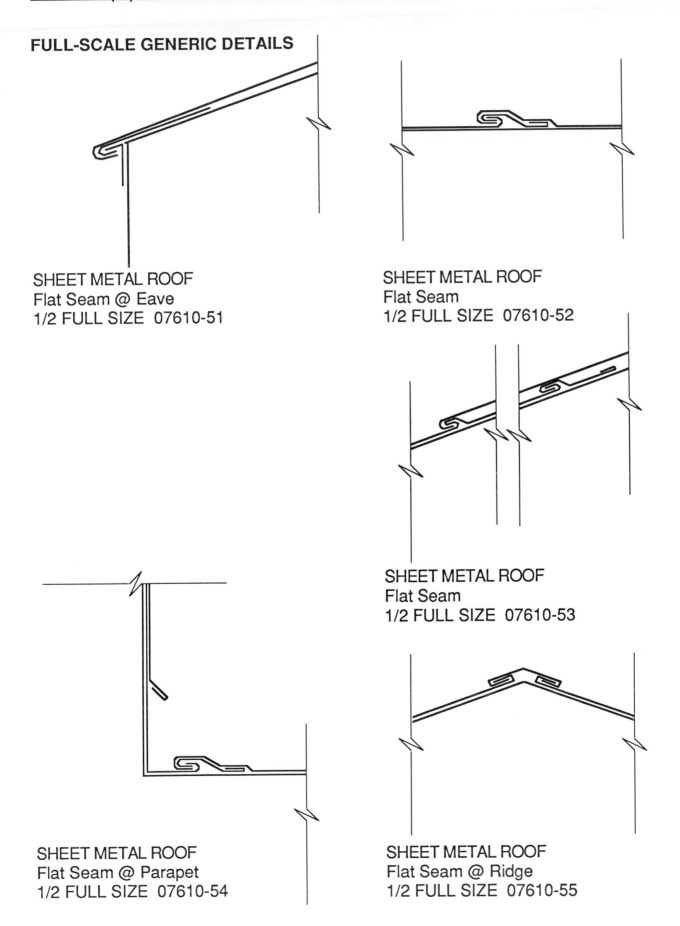

SHEET METAL ROOF
Flat Seam @ Eave
1/2 FULL SIZE 07610-51

SHEET METAL ROOF
Flat Seam
1/2 FULL SIZE 07610-52

SHEET METAL ROOF
Flat Seam
1/2 FULL SIZE 07610-53

SHEET METAL ROOF
Flat Seam @ Parapet
1/2 FULL SIZE 07610-54

SHEET METAL ROOF
Flat Seam @ Ridge
1/2 FULL SIZE 07610-55

07610 (b) SHEET METAL ROOFING

FULL-SCALE GENERIC DETAILS continued

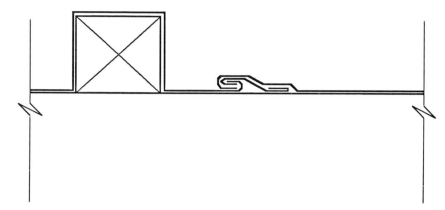

SHEET METAL ROOF Flat Seam & Batten
1/2 FULL SIZE   07610-61

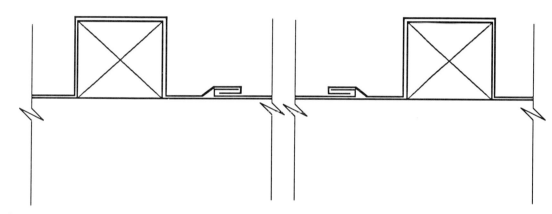

SHEET METAL ROOF Flat Seam & Batten
1/2 FULL SIZE   07610-62

NOTATION CHECKLIST,
SAMPLE NOTES

FLAT SEAM
BATTEN
FLASHING
STANDING SEAM
SNAP CAP ANCHOR CLIP
CLEAT
METAL ROOFING
ROOFING FELT
ROOF DECK/INSULATION

ROOF CONSTRUCTION
PREFAB RIDGE PIECE
METAL ROOFING HIP COVER
PLYWOOD SHEATHING
MTL. ROOFING, 1-1/2" W. X 2" H. BATTEN @ 24" O.C.
TYPE "W" VALLEY CONT. FLASH. BY MTL.
    ROOFING MFR.
CLOSURE BY MTL. ROOFING MFR.
PEAK LAP BY MTL. ROOFING MFR.
26 GA. GALV. MTL. ROOFING, CLIP & SEAM

07610 (c) SHEET METAL ROOFING

See DETAIL DATA CHECKLIST for metal roof preceding 07610 (a)

SMALL-SCALE GENERIC DETAILS

SHEET METAL ROOF
Batten @ Eave
07610-63

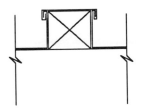

SHEET METAL ROOF
Batten Seam
07610-64

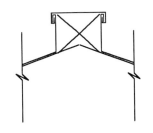

SHEET METAL ROOF
Batten Seam @ Ridge
07610-65

SHEET METAL ROOF
Batten Seam @ Ridge
07610-66

SHEET METAL ROOF
Standing Seam @ Eave
07610-76

SHEET METAL ROOF
Standing Seam @ Eave
07610-77

07610 (c) SHEET METAL ROOFING

FULL-SCALE GENERIC DETAILS

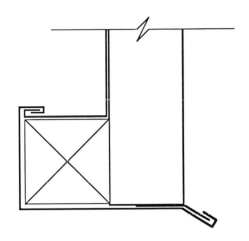

SHEET METAL ROOF
Batten @ Eave
1/2 FULL SIZE   07610-63

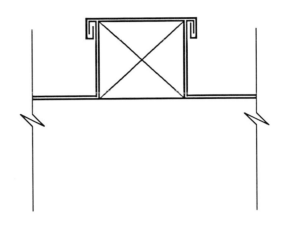

SHEET METAL ROOF
Batten Seam
1/2 FULL SIZE   07610-64

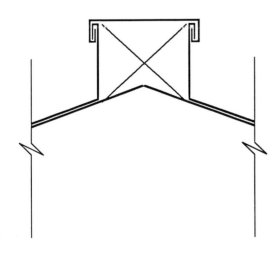

SHEET METAL ROOF
Batten Seam @ Ridge
1/2 FULL SIZE   07610-65

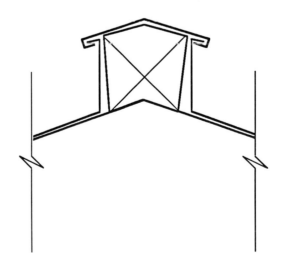

SHEET METAL ROOF
Batten Seam @ Ridge
1/2 FULL SIZE   07610-66

07610 (c) SHEET METAL ROOFING

FULL-SCALE GENERIC DETAILS continued

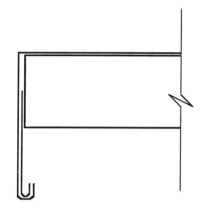

SHEET METAL ROOF
Standing Seam @ Eave
1/2 FULL SIZE   07610-76

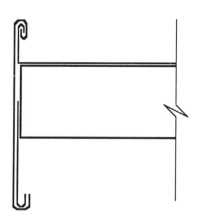

SHEET METAL ROOF
Standing Seam @ Eave
1/2 FULL SIZE   07610-77

NOTATION CHECKLIST,
SAMPLE NOTES

FLAT SEAM
BATTEN
FLASHING
STANDING SEAM
SNAP CAP ANCHOR CLIP
CLEAT
METAL ROOFING
ROOFING FELT
ROOF DECK/INSULATION

ROOF CONSTRUCTION
PREFAB RIDGE PIECE
METAL ROOFING HIP COVER
PLYWOOD SHEATHING
MTL. ROOFING, 1-1/2" W. X 2" H. BATTEN @ 24" O.C.
TYPE "W" VALLEY CONT. FLASH. BY MTL.
    ROOFING MFR.
CLOSURE BY MTL. ROOFING MFR.
PEAK LAP BY MTL. ROOFING MFR.
26 GA. GALV. MTL. ROOFING, CLIP & SEAM

07610 (d) SHEET METAL ROOFING

See DETAIL DATA CHECKLIST for metal roof preceding 07610 (a)

SMALL-SCALE GENERIC DETAILS

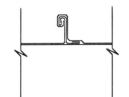

SHEET METAL ROOF
Standing Seam
07610-78

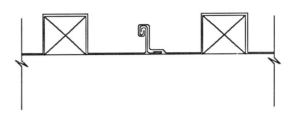

SHEET METAL ROOF
Standing Seam @ Batten
07610-79

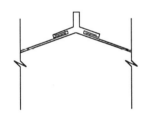

SHEET METAL ROOF
Ridge Piece
07610-85

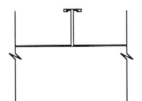

SHEET METAL ROOF
Prefab Standing Seam
07610-86

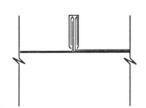

SHEET METAL ROOF
Prefab Standing Seam
07610-87

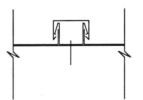

SHEET METAL ROOF
Prefab Batten
07610-88

07610 (d) SHEET METAL ROOFING

FULL-SCALE GENERIC DETAILS

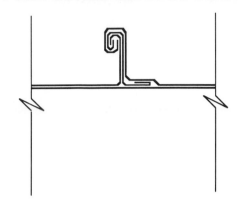

SHEET METAL ROOF Standing
Seam
1/2 FULL SIZE   07610-78

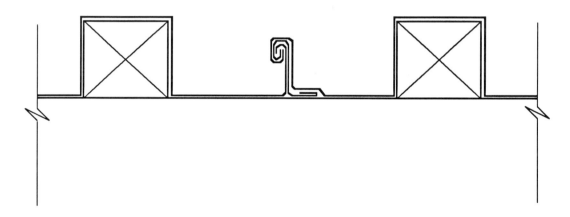

SHEET METAL ROOF Standing Seam @
Batten
1/2 FULL SIZE   07610-79

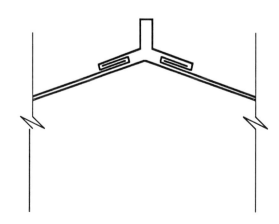

SHEET METAL ROOF Ridge Piece
1/2 FULL SIZE   07610-85

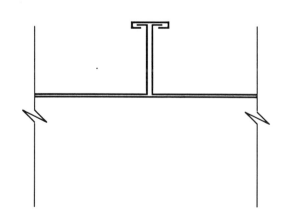

SHEET METAL ROOF Prefab Standing Seam
1/2 FULL SIZE   07610-86

07610 (d) SHEET METAL ROOFING

FULL-SCALE GENERIC DETAILS continued

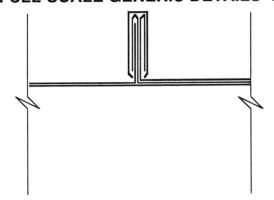

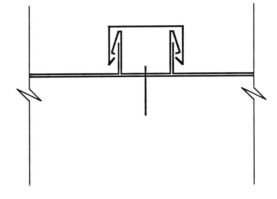

SHEET METAL ROOF
 Prefab Standing Seam
 1/2 FULL SIZE   07610-87

SHEET METAL ROOF
 Prefab Batten
 1/2 FULL SIZE   07610-88

NOTATION CHECKLIST,
 SAMPLE NOTES

FLAT SEAM
BATTEN
FLASHING
STANDING SEAM
SNAP CAP ANCHOR CLIP
CLEAT
METAL ROOFING
ROOFING FELT
ROOF DECK/INSULATION

ROOF CONSTRUCTION
PREFAB RIDGE PIECE
METAL ROOFING HIP COVER
PLYWOOD SHEATHING
MTL. ROOFING, 1-1/2" W. X 2" H. BATTEN @ 24" O.C.
TYPE "W" VALLEY CONT. FLASH. BY MTL.
    ROOFING MFR.
CLOSURE BY MTL. ROOFING MFR.
PEAK LAP BY MTL. ROOFING MFR.
26 GA. GALV. MTL. ROOFING, CLIP & SEAM

07631 GUTTERS (06225-Wood Gutters Included)

DETAIL DATA CHECKLIST

GUTTERS

DESIGN OF BUILT-UP ROOF SLOPES
When designing for roof drainage, the old standard minimum slope of 1/4" per linear foot for built-up roofs is not sufficient to allow for building settlement, structural deflection, clogged drains, etc.

Handbook values for roof drain sizes and gutter sizes are also inadequate for increasingly erratic and extreme storm conditions.

Recommend 1/2" slope per linear foot as minimum for built-up roof construction. Increase other handbook minimum slopes for shingle, tile, and other roof types by at least a half inch to help avoid roofing uplift and driven rain infiltration.

WOOD GUTTERS
__Provide 1/2" to 1" air space between gutter and wall surface to allow for overflow and allow ventilation

__Splice wood gutter joints with brass screws and lead splice plates or with brass joint connectors

ALL RAIN WATER GUTTERS
__See manufacturers' catalogs for selection of materials, sizes, hangers, closures, other fittings and special
        design and detail considerations

__Downspout Sizes:
        __3" minimum to 6" maximum for rounds, squares and rectangles
__Gutter sizes:
        __4" wide x 3" high minimum except for small porch roofs or other partial roofs
        __Maximum size typically 8" wide x 6" high

__Lap metal gutter joints 6" in direction of slope
        __Seal joints with solder or mastic
        __Provide expansion joints on gutters over 35 feet long to allow for thermal expansion (or as per
                manufacturers' instructions)

__Provide support brackets attached to wall at top and bottom of downspout, and at joints
__Gutter hangers at 3' o.c. maximum for normal rain loads
__Hangers at 1'-6" if gutters carry long-term ice and snow loads
__Electrical heat cables may be used to eliminate sustained ice and snow loads:
__Slope gutters towards rain water leaders minimum of 1/16" per linear foot, 1/8" per linear foot preferred
__Provide a snow slide clearance line between the top of the front edge of the gutter and the roof edge of
        from 1/2" for steepest roofs to to 1" for flat roofs
__Provide sufficient roof edge overhang to stop "back dripping" of water and assure water runoff directly to
        the gutters
__Provide strainers at top of downspouts

Trouble spots:
__Inadequate slopes in roof and gutters
__Deflection from full water load and inadequate gutter supports
__Clogged leaders
__Small spaces between gutter and roof that allows debris build up, clogging, and rot
__Snow and ice accumulation and backup under eaves
__Corrosion from galvanic action due to contact of dissimilar metals

07631 (a) GUTTERS (06225-Wood Gutters Included)

See DETAIL DATA CHECKLIST for gutters preceding 07631 (a)

SMALL-SCALE GENERIC DETAILS

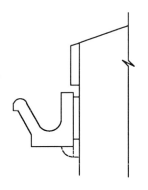

WOOD GUTTER Ogee
(06225-51)

3x4

4x4

4x5

4x6

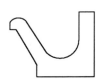

5x7

07631 (a) GUTTERS (06225-Wood Gutters Included)

FULL-SCALE GENERIC DETAILS

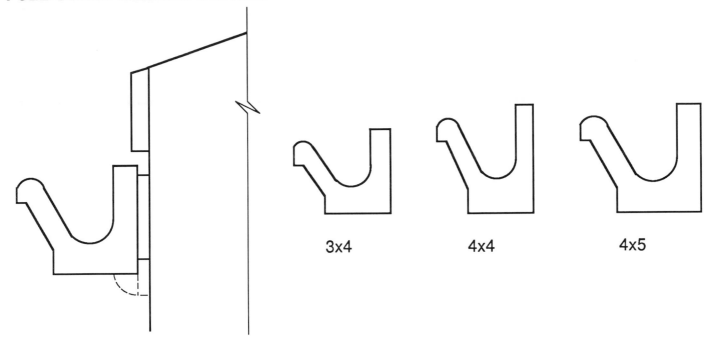

WOOD GUTTER Ogee
3"=1'-0"   (06225-51)

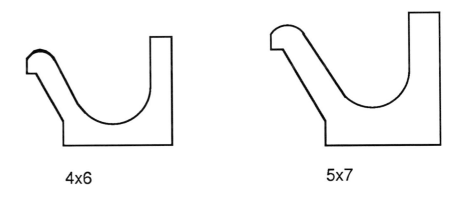

3x4   4x4   4x5

4x6   5x7

NOTATION CHECKLIST,
SAMPLE NOTES

GUTTER
HANGER
BRACKET
METAL GRAVEL STOP
CANT/NAILER
CLEAT/EDGE STRIP/FASCIA PLATE
WALL CONSTRUCTION
REGLET
FLASHING/COUNTERFLASHING
ADHESIVE/SEALANT/CAULKING
ROOFING SURFACE
    (TYPE, LAYERS & COVER MATERIAL)
ROOF DECK/INSULATION
ROOF CONSTRUCTION

07631 (b) GUTTERS

See DETAIL DATA CHECKLIST for gutters preceding 07631 (a)

SMALL-SCALE GENERIC DETAILS

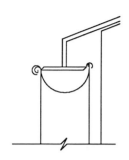

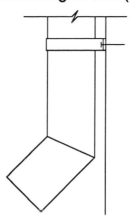

METAL GUTTER
07631-19

METAL DOWNSPOUT
07631-21

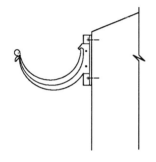

METAL GUTTER Half Round
07631-22

METAL GUTTER Half Round
07631-23

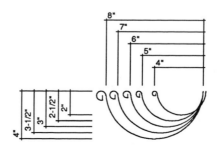

07631 (b) GUTTERS

FULL-SCALE GENERIC DETAILS

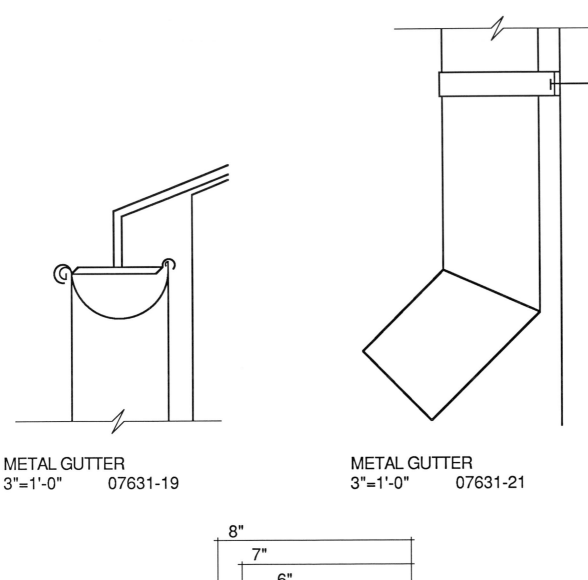

METAL GUTTER
3"=1'-0"   07631-19

METAL GUTTER
3"=1'-0"   07631-21

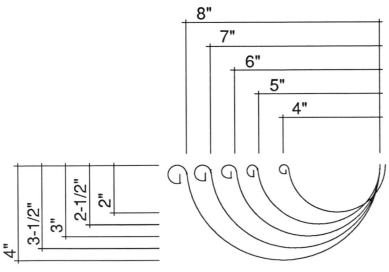

07631 (b) GUTTERS

FULL-SCALE GENERIC DETAILS continued

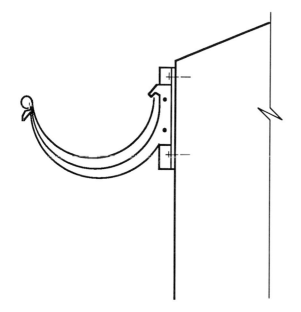

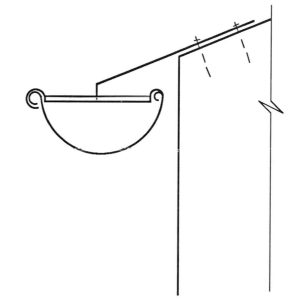

METAL GUTTER Half Round
3"=1'-0"   07631-22

METAL GUTTER Half Round
3"=1'-0"   07631-23

NOTATiON CHECKLIST, SAMPLE NOTES

GUTTER
HANGER
BRACKET
METAL GRAVEL STOP
CANT/NAILER
CLEAT/EDGE STRIP/FASCIA PLATE
PARAPET WALL CONSTRUCTION
REGLET
FLASHING/COUNTERFLASHING
ADHESIVE/SEALANT/CAULKING
ROOFING SURFACE
   (TYPE, LAYERS & COVER MATERIAL)
ROOF DECK/INSULATION
ROOF CONSTRUCTION

SAMPLE NOTES:
1/16" x 1" SHEET METAL GUTTER
   SPACER @ 6'-0" O.C.
SHEET METAL GUTTER
CONT. SHEET METAL CLEAT
BLOCKING
RIVETS
OPTIONAL GUTTER PROFILE
1/8" X 1" SHT. MTL. GUTTER
   BRACKET @ 3'-0" O.C.
DOWNSPOUT
SPLASH BLOCK

07631 (c) GUTTERS

See DETAIL DATA CHECKLIST for gutters preceding 07631 (a)

SMALL-SCALE GENERIC DETAILS

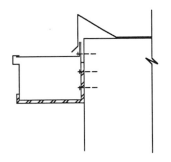

METAL GUTTER Rectangular
07631-31

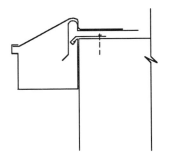

METAL GUTTER Rectangular
07631-32

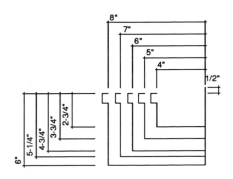

07631 (c) GUTTERS

FULL-SCALE GENERIC DETAILS

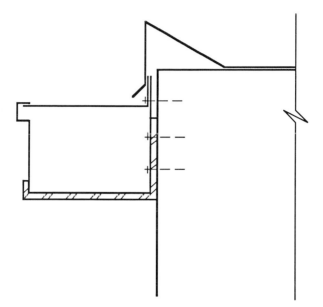

METAL GUTTER Rectangular
3"=1'-0"   07631-31

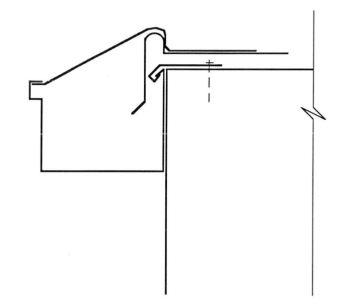

METAL GUTTER Rectangular
3"=1'-0"   07631-32

NOTATION CHECKLIST,
SAMPLE NOTES

GUTTER
HANGER
BRACKET
METAL GRAVEL STOP
CANT/NAILER
CLEAT/EDGE STRIP/FASCIA PLATE
WALL CONSTRUCTION
REGLET
FLASHING/COUNTERFLASHING
ADHESIVE/SEALANT/CAULKING
ROOFING SURFACE
    (TYPE, LAYERS & COVER MATERIAL)
ROOF DECK/INSULATION
ROOF CONSTRUCTION
1/16" x 1" SHEET METAL GUTTER
    SPACER @ 6'-0" O.C.
SHEET METAL GUTTER
CONT. SHEET METAL CLEAT
BLOCKING
RIVETS
OPTIONAL GUTTER PROFILE
1/8" X 1" SHT. MTL. GUTTER
    BRACKET @ 3'-0" O.C.
DOWNSPOUT
SPLASH BLOCK

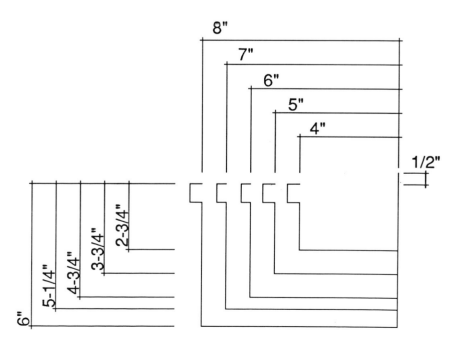

07631 (e) GUTTERS

See DETAIL DATA CHECKLIST for gutters preceding 07631 (a)

SMALL-SCALE GENERIC DETAILS

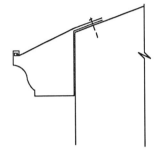

METAL GUTTER Ogee
07631-51

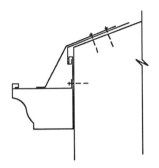

METAL GUTTER Ogee
07631-52

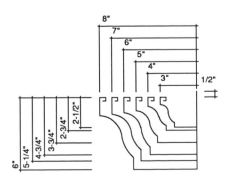

07631 (e) GUTTERS

FULL-SCALE GENERIC DETAILS

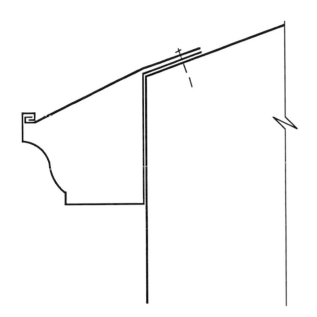

METAL GUTTER Ogee
3"=1'-0"   07631-51

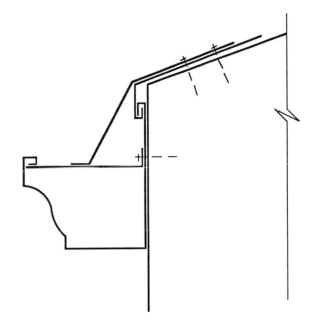

METAL GUTTER Ogee
3"=1'-0"   07631-52

NOTATION CHECKLIST, SAMPLE DETAILS

GUTTER
HANGER
BRACKET
METAL GRAVEL STOP
CANT/NAILER
CLEAT/EDGE STRIP/FASCIA PLATE
PARAPET WALL CONSTRUCTION
REGLET
FLASHING/COUNTERFLASHING
ADHESIVE/SEALANT/CAULKING
ROOFING SURFACE
    (TYPE, LAYERS & COVER MATERIAL)
ROOF DECK/INSULATION
ROOF CONSTRUCTION
1/16" x 1" SHEET METAL GUTTER
    SPACER @ 6'-0" O.C.
SHEET METAL GUTTER
CONT. SHEET METAL CLEAT
BLOCKING
RIVETS
OPTIONAL GUTTER PROFILE
1/8" X 1" SHT. MTL. GUTTER
    BRACKET @ 3'-0" O.C.
DOWNSPOUT
SPLASH BLOCK

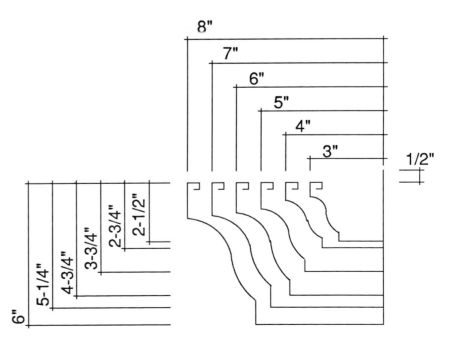

07633 SCUPPERS

FULL-SCALE GENERIC DETAILS continued

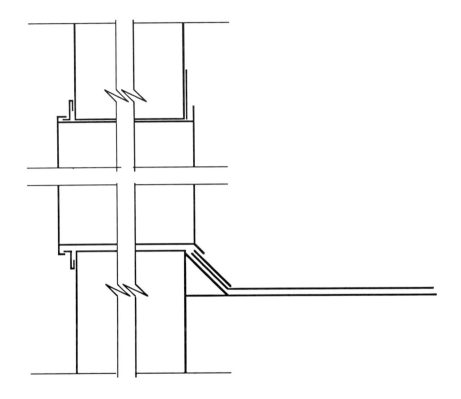

OVERFLOW SCUPPER THRU PARAPET
1-1/2"=1'-0"   07633-22

NOTATION CHECKLIST,
SAMPLE NOTES

GUTTER
HANGER
BRACKET
METAL GRAVEL STOP
CANT/NAILER
CLEAT/EDGE STRIP/FASCIA PLATE
PARAPET WALL CONSTRUCTION
REGLET
FLASHING/COUNTERFLASHING
ADHESIVE/SEALANT/CAULKING
ROOFING SURFACE
    (TYPE, LAYERS & COVER MATERIAL)
ROOF DECK/INSULATION
ROOF CONSTRUCTION

SAMPLE NOTES:
EDGE OF ROOF MEMBRANE
FASCIA COVER
STAINLESS STEEL TUBE LINER
CONDUCTOR HEAD, MIN. 2" WIDER THAN SCUPPER
PROVIDE 3" OVERLAP TO GO OVER ADJ. FIBER CANT
CAULK & MAKE WEATHER TIGHT
GALV. SHEET METAL OVERFLOW SCUPPER,
    SOLDER ALL JOINTS
GALV. SHEET METAL SCUPPER & HEADER
TREATED WOOD BLOCKING
ELEV. OF ROOF
SEALANT ALL AROUND
EMBED FLANGES COMPLETELY IN PLAS. CEMENT
FIBER GLASS CLOTH IN PLAS. CEM.
FEATHERED EDGE STRIP
TAPERED EDGE STRIP

DETAIL FILE NUMBER: **07633-21**

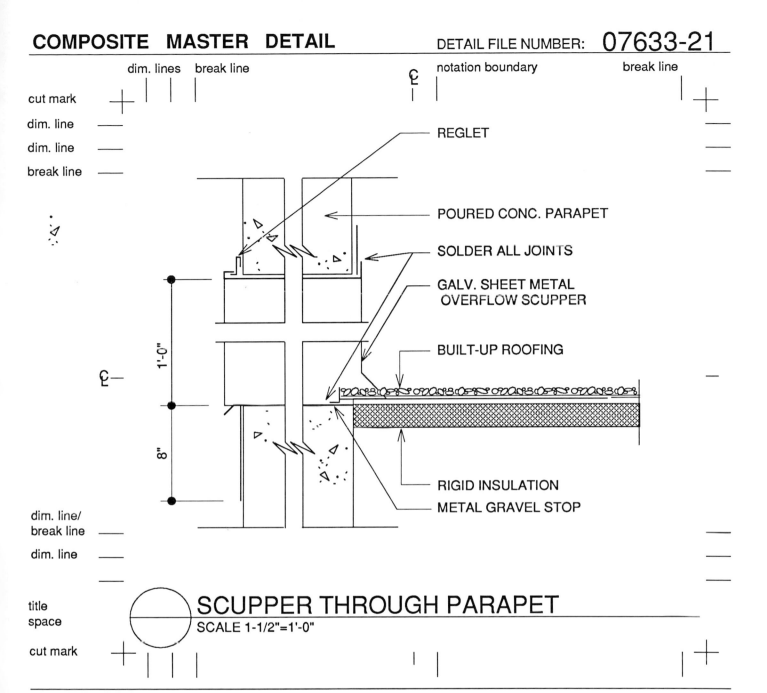

dim. lines   break line   notation boundary   break line

cut mark

dim. line

dim. line

break line

REGLET

POURED CONC. PARAPET

SOLDER ALL JOINTS

GALV. SHEET METAL
OVERFLOW SCUPPER

BUILT-UP ROOFING

1'-0"

8"

RIGID INSULATION

METAL GRAVEL STOP

dim. line/
break line

dim. line

title
space

SCUPPER THROUGH PARAPET
SCALE 1-1/2"=1'-0"

cut mark

DETAIL INFORMATION
References, jobsite feedback, job history

07660 (a) GRAVEL STOPS

DETAIL DATA CHECKLIST

GRAVEL STOPS
Materials: Sheet metal such as coated galvanized steel or copper nailed to roof substrate, wide variety of materials and finishes available. Gauges and sizes:
__4" to 8" high lip at fascia   __24 gauge for 4" to 5" lip   __22 gauge for 6" to 8" lip
    __16 oz. copper 4" to 6" lip   __20 oz. copper 7" to 8" lip.
Provide expansion joints to allow for: __1/2" thermal movement in a 40' length of galvanized steel
    __1/2" movement for 40' copper   __3/4" movement for 40' aluminum
__Set one side of overlapping joint fasteners in mastic so that one half adheres and the other half is free to allow thermal movement
__If fascia lip of gravel stop is 4" or higher, apply continuous interlocking cleat at bottom of stop at vertical edge to secure against wind uplift
__Use neoprene or similar watertight washer where cleats are nailed to wall
__Install on raised curb with 1" minimum top lip
Trouble spots:
__Gravel stops that are not above ponding line are subject to water infiltration
__Concealed gravel stops that stop at the top of a wall rather than over-hanging are subject to leaks
__Direct nailing or attachment of coping to wall surface doesn't allow for differential movement

SMALL-SCALE GENERIC DETAILS

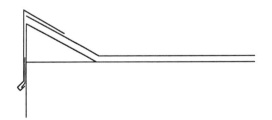

GRAVEL STOP 4x6 Cant
07660-41

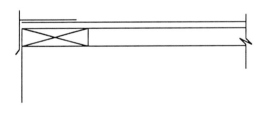

GRAVEL STOP Extruded
07660-42

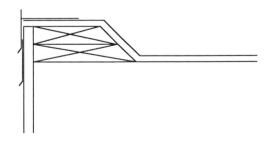

GRAVEL STOP W/Fascia Plate
07660-43

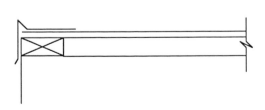

GRAVEL STOP Formed
07660-44

466

07660 (a) GRAVEL STOPS

FULL-SCALE GENERIC DETAILS

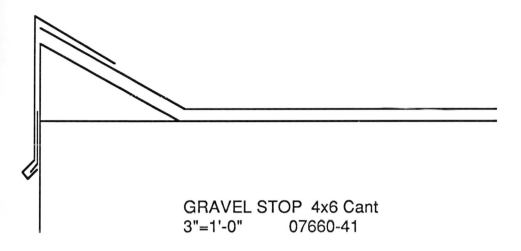

GRAVEL STOP 4x6 Cant
3"=1'-0"   07660-41

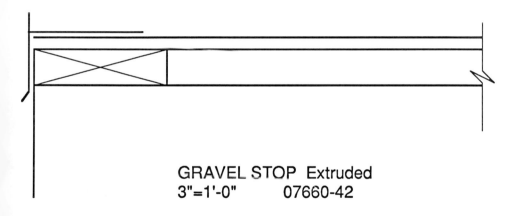

GRAVEL STOP Extruded
3"=1'-0"   07660-42

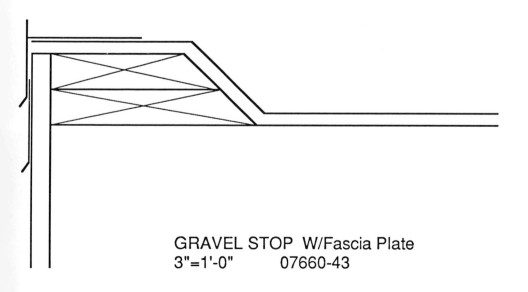

GRAVEL STOP W/Fascia Plate
3"=1'-0"   07660-43

07660 (a) GRAVEL STOPS

FULL-SCALE GENERIC DETAILS continued

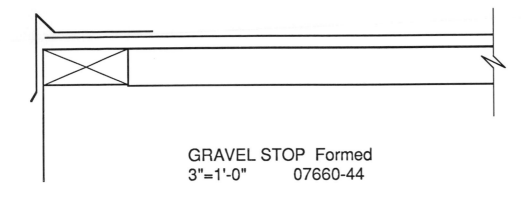

GRAVEL STOP Formed
3"=1'-0"   07660-44

NOTATION CHECKLIST,
SAMPLE NOTES

METAL GRAVEL STOP
CANT/NAILER
CLEAT/EDGE STRIP/FASCIA PLATE
ROOFING SURFACE
    (TYPE, LAYERS & COVER MATERIAL)
ROOF DECK/INSULATION
ROOF CONSTRUCTION
ROOF FASCIA
EXTRUDED ALUM. FASCIA
TREATED CANT
TREATED 2 X 6 MIN. BOLTED TO STRUCTURE
TREATED WOOD BLOCKING
ELASTOMERIC SEALANT ALONG ENTIRE LENGTH
    OF FLASH. TYPICAL
COMPRESSIBLE FILLER RD.
STEEL ANGLE, SEE STRUCTURAL

MEMBRANE BASE FLASHING CONT. TO COVER
    CANT & WOOD BLKG.
6" MIN. BASE FLASHING
SECOND PLY TO LAP OTHER PLY'S FULL LENGTH OF
    CANT
FLASHING APPLIED W/ADHESIVE
LEAD OR ALUMINUM FLASHING
CONT. CLEAT
SEALANT
SHIM (to slope)
BASE FLASHING NAILS @ 8" O.C.
SEALANT
COMPOSITION FLASHING
BUILT-UP ROOFING
BASE SHEET INSULATION
VAPOR BARRIER
FILL, PITCH TO DRAIN
NAILABLE CANT
CONT. 4" HIGH CANT

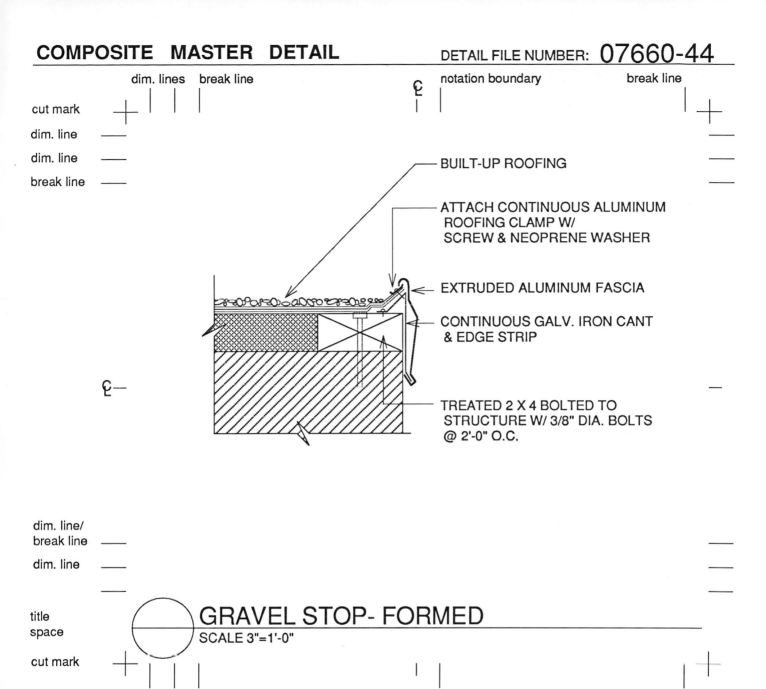

dim. lines   break line

notation boundary   break line

cut mark

dim. line

dim. line

break line

BUILT-UP ROOFING

ATTACH CONTINUOUS ALUMINUM
ROOFING CLAMP W/
SCREW & NEOPRENE WASHER

EXTRUDED ALUMINUM FASCIA

CONTINUOUS GALV. IRON CANT
& EDGE STRIP

TREATED 2 X 4 BOLTED TO
STRUCTURE W/ 3/8" DIA. BOLTS
@ 2'-0" O.C.

dim. line/
break line

dim. line

title
space

GRAVEL STOP- FORMED
SCALE 3"=1'-0"

cut mark

DETAIL INFORMATION
References, jobsite feedback, job history

07660 (b) GRAVEL STOPS

DETAIL DATA CHECKLIST

GRAVEL STOPS
Materials: Sheet metal such as coated galvanized steel or copper nailed to roof substrate, wide variety of materials and finishes available. Gauges and sizes:
__4" to 8" high lip at fascia   __24 gauge for 4" to 5" lip   __22 gauge for 6" to 8" lip
    __16 oz. copper 4" to 6" lip   __20 oz. copper 7" to 8" lip.
Provide expansion joints to allow for: __1/2" thermal movement in a 40' length of galvanized steel
    __1/2" movement for 40' copper   __3/4" movement for 40' aluminum
__Set one side of overlapping joint fasteners in mastic so that one half adheres and the other half is free to allow thermal movement
__If fascia lip of gravel stop is 4" or higher, apply continuous interlocking cleat at bottom of stop at vertical edge to secure against wind uplift
__Use neoprene or similar watertight washer where cleats are nailed to wall
__Install on raised curb with 1" minimum top lip
Trouble spots:
__Gravel stops that are not above ponding line are subject to water infiltration
__Concealed gravel stops that stop at the top of a wall rather than over-hanging are subject to leaks
__Direct nailing or attachment of coping to wall surface doesn't allow for differential movement

SMALL-SCALE GENERIC DETAILS

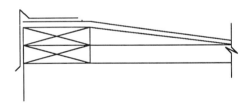

GRAVEL STOP
Formed/Tapered Edge
07660-45

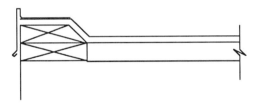

GRAVEL STOP
Formed/Raised Edge
07660-46

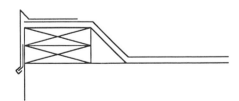

GRAVEL STOP
Formed/Raised Edge
07660-47

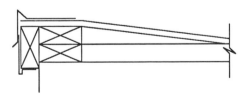

GRAVEL STOP
Formed/Tapered Edge/Soffit
07660-48

07660 (b) GRAVEL STOPS

FULL-SCALE GENERIC DETAILS

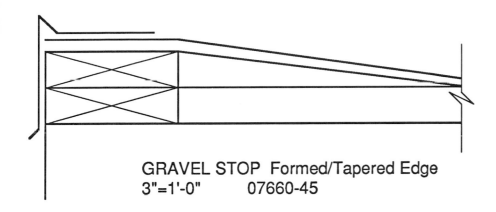

GRAVEL STOP Formed/Tapered Edge
3"=1'-0"   07660-45

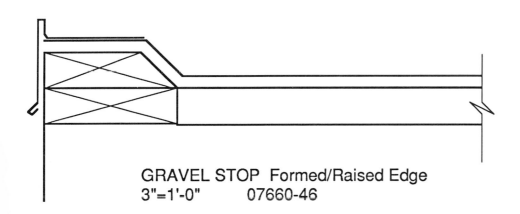

GRAVEL STOP Formed/Raised Edge
3"=1'-0"   07660-46

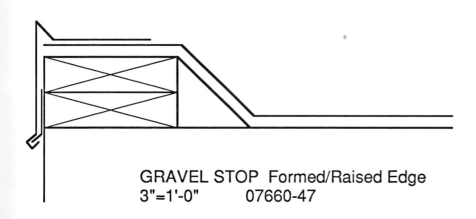

GRAVEL STOP Formed/Raised Edge
3"=1'-0"   07660-47

07660 (b) GRAVEL STOPS

FULL-SCALE GENERIC DETAILS continued

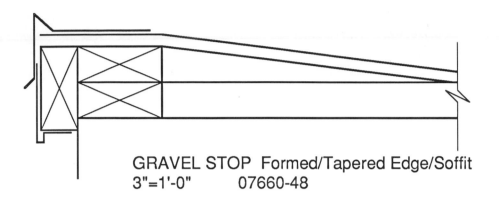

GRAVEL STOP Formed/Tapered Edge/Soffit
3"=1'-0"   07660-48

NOTATION CHECKLIST,
SAMPLE NOTES

METAL GRAVEL STOP
CANT/NAILER
CLEAT/EDGE STRIP/FASCIA PLATE
ROOFING SURFACE
    (TYPE, LAYERS & COVER MATERIAL)
ROOF DECK/INSULATION
ROOF CONSTRUCTION
ROOF FASCIA
EXTRUDED ALUM. FASCIA
TREATED CANT
TREATED 2 X 6 MIN. BOLTED TO STRUCTURE
TREATED WOOD BLOCKING
ELASTOMERIC SEALANT ALONG ENTIRE LENGTH
    OF FLASH. TYPICAL
COMPRESSIBLE FILLER RD.
STEEL ANGLE, SEE STRUCTURAL

MEMBRANE BASE FLASHING CONT. TO COVER
    CANT & WOOD BLKG.
6" MIN. BASE FLASHING
SECOND PLY TO LAP OTHER PLY'S FULL LENGTH OF
    CANT
FLASHING APPLIED W/ADHESIVE
LEAD OR ALUMINUM FLASHING
CONT. CLEAT
SEALANT
SHIM (to slope)
BASE FLASHING NAILS @ 8" O.C.
SEALANT
COMPOSITION FLASHING
BUILT-UP ROOFING
BASE SHEET INSULATION
VAPOR BARRIER
FILL, PITCH TO DRAIN
NAILABLE CANT
CONT. 4" HIGH CANT

07665 (a) METAL COPINGS

DETAIL DATA CHECKLIST

METAL COPINGS Materials, sizes and gauges:
__4" to 12" coping width: 24-ga. galvanized steel, 16-oz. copper, 26-ga. stainless steel, .232 alum.
__13" to 18" coping width: 22-ga. galvanized steel, 20-oz. copper, 24-ga. stainless steel, .040 alum.

__Provide expansion joints to allow for:
__1/2" thermal movement in a 40' length of galvanized steel
__1/2" movement for 40' copper
__3/4" movement for 40' aluminum

__Apply continuous interlocking cleats at bottom of coping at vertical edge to secure against wind uplift
__Use neoprene or similar watertight washer where cleats are nailed to wall

Trouble spots:
__Corrosion from use of dissimilar metals, especially incompatible connectors
__Direct nailing or attachment of coping to wall surface that doesn't allow for differential expansion and contraction

SMALL-SCALE GENERIC DETAILS

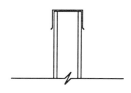

METAL COPING
Formed (4" Parapet)
07665-36

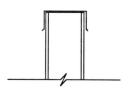

METAL COPING
Formed (6" Parapet)
07665-37

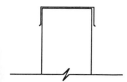

METAL COPING
Formed (8" Parapet)
07665-38

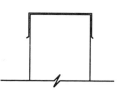

METAL COPING
Formed (10" Parapet)
07665-39

473

07665 (a) METAL COPINGS

SMALL-SCALE GENERIC DETAILS continued

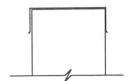

METAL COPING
Formed (12" Parapet)
07665-40

METAL COPING
Formed (4" Parapet)
07665-45

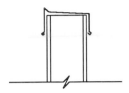

METAL COPING
Formed (6" Parapet)
07665-46

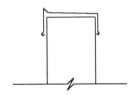

METAL COPING
Formed (8" Parapet)
07665-47

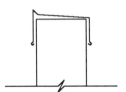

METAL COPING
Formed (10" Parapet)
07665-48

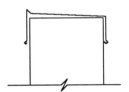

METAL COPING
Formed (12" Parapet)
07665-49

FULL-SCALE GENERIC DETAILS

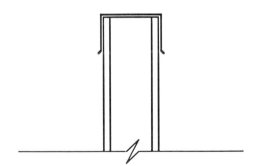

METAL COPING
Formed (4" Parapet)
1-1/2"=1'-0"
07665-36

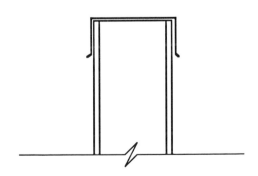

METAL COPING
Formed (6" Parapet)
1-1/2"=1'-0"
07665-37

07665 (a) METAL COPINGS

FULL-SCALE GENERIC DETAILS continued

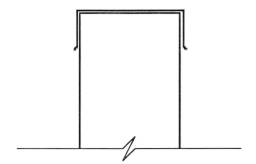

METAL COPING
Formed (8" Parapet)
1-1/2"=1'-0"
07665-38

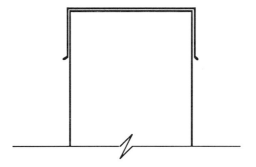

METAL COPING
Formed (10" Parapet)
1-1/2"=1'-0"
07665-39

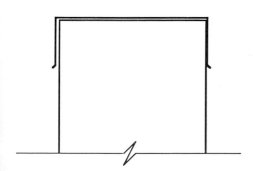

METAL COPING
Formed (12" Parapet)
1-1/2"=1'-0"
07665-40

METAL COPING
Formed (4" Parapet)
1-1/2"=1'-0"
07665-45

07665 (a) METAL COPINGS

FULL-SCALE GENERIC DETAILS continued

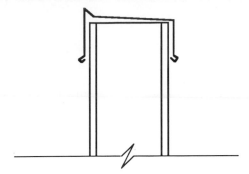

METAL COPING
Formed (6" Parapet)
1-1/2"=1'-0"
07665-46

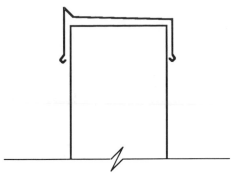

METAL COPING
Formed (8" Parapet)
1-1/2"=1'-0"
07665-47

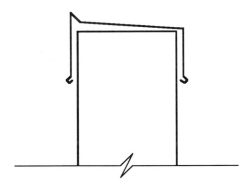

METAL COPING
Formed (10" Parapet)
1-1/2"=1'-0"
07665-48

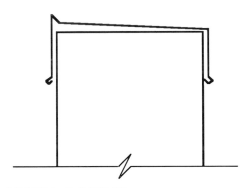

METAL COPING
Formed (12" Parapet)
1-1/2"=1'-0"
07665-49

NOTATION CHECKLIST, SAMPLE NOTES

FORMED METAL COPING
CLEAT
NAILER
SEALANT/CAULKING
EXTRUDED METAL
COPING
ANCHOR BOLT
COVER PLATE
GUTTER BAR
COPING
PREFIN. ALUM. COPING
FLASHING OVER COPING

METAL CAP
CLIP-ON FLASHING, ATTACH @ CTR. OF EA. PIECE
MTL. COPING, SET W/MASTIC SEALANT @ SPLICE
    JTS. ONLY
MANUFACTURED COPING & FLASHING SYSTEM
G.I. FLASHING
ELASTOMERIC FLASHING
BASE FLASHING OVER PLATE
FLASHING APPLIED W/ADHESIVE
LEAD OR ALUMINUM FLASHING
CONT. CLEAT
SEALANT
SHIM (to slope)

07665 (b) METAL COPINGS

DETAIL DATA CHECKLIST

METAL COPINGS Materials, sizes and gauges:
__4" to 12" coping width: 24-ga. galvanized steel, 16-oz. copper, 26-ga. stainless steel, .232 alum.
__13" to 18" coping width: 22-ga. galvanized steel, 20-oz. copper, 24-ga. stainless steel, .040 alum.

__Provide expansion joints to allow for:
__1/2" thermal movement in a 40' length of galvanized steel
__1/2" movement for 40' copper
__3/4" movement for 40' aluminum

__Apply continuous interlocking cleats at bottom of coping at vertical edge to secure against wind uplift
__Use neoprene or similar watertight washer where cleats are nailed to wall

Trouble spots:
__Corrosion from use of dissimilar metals, especially incompatible connectors
__Direct nailing or attachment of coping to wall surface that doesn't allow for differential expansion and contraction

SMALL-SCALE GENERIC DETAILS

METAL COPING
Formed
(4" Parapet)
07665-54

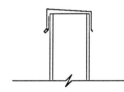

METAL COPING
Formed
(6" Parapet)
07665-55

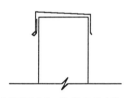

METAL COPING
Formed
(8" Parapet)
07665-56

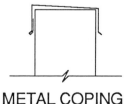

METAL COPING
Formed
(10" Parapet)
07665-57

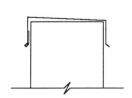

METAL COPING
Formed
(12" Parapet)
07665-58

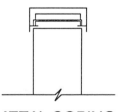

METAL COPING
Extruded
(8" Parapet)
07665-64

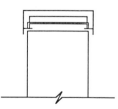

METAL COPING
Extruded
(10" Parapet)
07665-65

07665 (b) METAL COPINGS

SMALL-SCALE GENERIC DETAILS continued

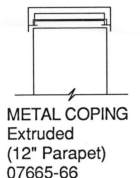

METAL COPING
Extruded
(12" Parapet)
07665-66

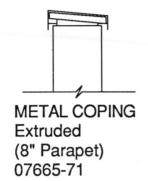

METAL COPING
Extruded
(8" Parapet)
07665-71

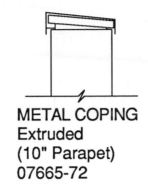

METAL COPING
Extruded
(10" Parapet)
07665-72

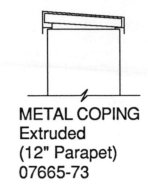

METAL COPING
Extruded
(12" Parapet)
07665-73

FULL-SCALE GENERIC DETAILS

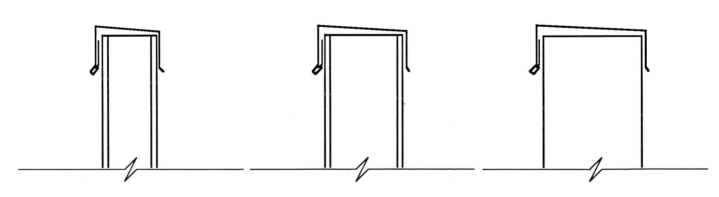

METAL COPING
Formed (4" Parapet)
1-1/2"=1'-0"
07665-54

METAL COPING
Formed (6" Parapet)
1-1/2"=1'-0"
07665-55

METAL COPING
Formed (8" Parapet)
1-1/2"=1'-0"
07665-56

07665 (b) METAL COPINGS

FULL-SCALE GENERIC DETAILS continued

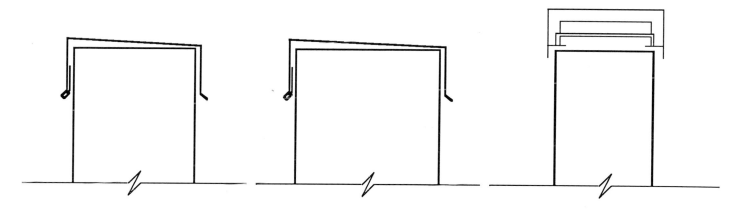

METAL COPING
Formed (10" Parapet)
1-1/2"=1'-0"
07665-57

METAL COPING
Formed (12" Parapet)
1-1/2"=1'-0"
07665-58

METAL COPING
Extruded (8" Parapet)
1-1/2"=1'-0"
07665-64

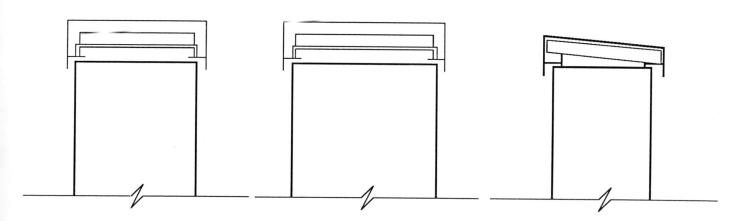

METAL COPING
Extruded (10" Parapet)
1-1/2"=1'-0"
07665-65

METAL COPING
Extruded (12" Parapet)
1-1/2"=1'-0"
07665-66

METAL COPING
Extruded (8" Parapet)
1-1/2"=1'-0"
07665-71

07665 (b) METAL COPINGS

FULL-SCALE GENERIC DETAILS continued

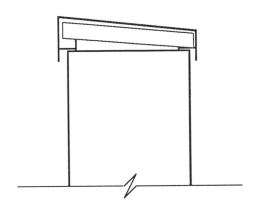

METAL COPING
Extruded (10" Parapet)
1-1/2"=1'-0"
07665-72

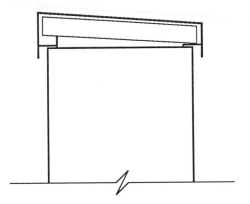

METAL COPING
Extruded (12" Parapet)
1-1/2"=1'-0"
07665-73

NOTATION CHECKLIST,
SAMPLE NOTES

FORMED METAL COPING
CLEAT
NAILER
SEALANT/CAULKING
EXTRUDED METAL
COPING
ANCHOR BOLT
COVER PLATE
GUTTER BAR
COPING
PREFIN. ALUM. COPING
FLASHING OVER COPING

METAL CAP
CLIP-ON FLASHING, ATTACH @ CTR. OF EA. PIECE
MTL. COPING, SET W/MASTIC SEALANT @ SPLICE
    JTS. ONLY
MANUFACTURED COPING & FLASHING SYSTEM
G.I. FLASHING
ELASTOMERIC FLASHING
BASE FLASHING OVER PLATE
FLASHING APPLIED W/ADHESIVE
LEAD OR ALUMINUM FLASHING
CONT. CLEAT
SEALANT
SHIM (to slope)

07810 (a) SKYLIGHTS

DETAIL DATA CHECKLIST

SKYLIGHTS

Skylights are usually installed as ready-made manufactured units so most detailing and installation will be as per manufacturers' recommendations. The catalogs provide numerous options of glazing types, fixed or operable, single or double glazing, etc. Skylight design is highly regulated, so consult all applicable building code standards.

__Materials and sizes:
   __Extruded aluminum frame with integral base and acrylic dome is typical
   __Square and rectangular units are typically sized at from 2' to 8' in each direction
__Curbs are required to block penetration of water, ice and snow at roof level
   __Curbs may be integral or designed as part of roof construction
__Provide sloping gutters between adjacent skylights to drain condensation
   __Double glazing helps mitigate condensation
__Exposed gaskets will fail due to solar and weather exposure

SMALL-SCALE GENERIC DETAILS

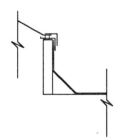

SKYLIGHT Pyramid--
Wood or Prefab Curb
07810-21

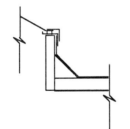

SKYLIGHT Pyramid--
Insulated Deck
07810-22

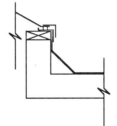

SKYLIGHT Pyramid--
Concrete Curb
07810-23

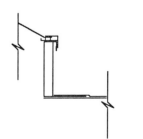

SKYLIGHT Pyramid--
Integral Curb
07810-24

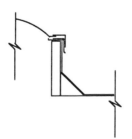

SKYLIGHT Single Dome--
Wood or Prefab Curb
07810-31

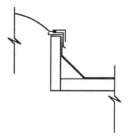

SKYLIGHT Single Dome--
Insulated Deck
07810-32

07810 (b) SKYLIGHTS

DETAIL DATA CHECKLIST

SKYLIGHTS

Skylights are usually installed as ready-made manufactured units so most detailing and installation will be as per manufacturers' recommendations. The catalogs provide numerous options of glazing types, fixed or operable, single or double glazing, etc. Skylight design is highly regulated, so consult all applicable building code standards.

__Materials and sizes:
    __Extruded aluminum frame with integral base and acrylic dome is typical
    __Square and rectangular units are typically sized at from 2' to 8' in each direction
__Curbs are required to block penetration of water, ice and snow at roof level
    __Curbs may be integral or designed as part of roof construction
__Provide sloping gutters between adjacent skylights to drain condensation
    __Double glazing helps mitigate condensation
__Exposed gaskets will fail due to solar and weather exposure

SMALL-SCALE GENERIC DETAILS

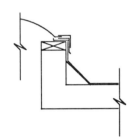

SKYLIGHT Single Dome--
Concrete Curb
07810-33

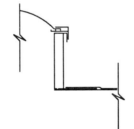

SKYLIGHT Single Dome--
Integral Curb
07810-34

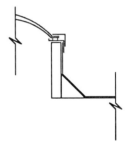

SKYLIGHT Double Dome--
Wood or Prefab Curb
07810-36

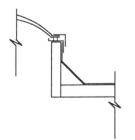

SKYLIGHT Double Dome--
Insulated Deck
07810-37

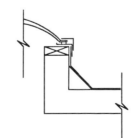

SKYLIGHT Double Dome--
Concrete Curb
07810-38

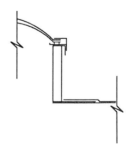

SKYLIGHT Double Dome--
Integral Curb
07810-39

07810 (b) SKYLIGHTS

FULL-SCALE GENERIC DETAILS

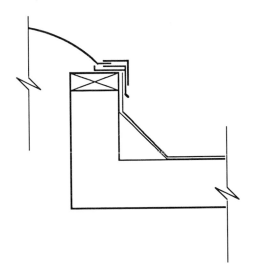

SKYLIGHT Sngl. Dome--
Concrete Curb
1-1/2"=1'-0"
07810-33

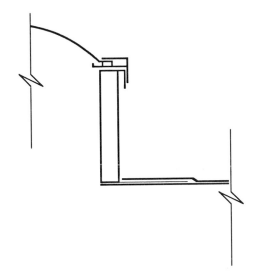

SKYLIGHT Sngl. Dome--
Integral Curb
1-1/2"=1'-0"
07810-34

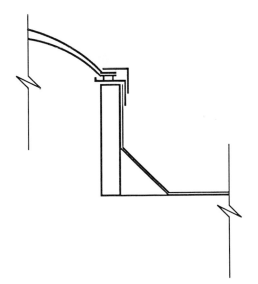

SKYLIGHT Dbl. Dome--
Wood or Prefab Curb
1-1/2"=1'-0"
07810-36

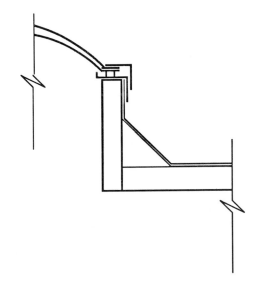

SKYLIGHT Dbl. Dome--
Insulated Deck
1-1/2"=1'-0"
07810-37

07810 (b) SKYLIGHTS

FULL-SCALE GENERIC DETAILS continued

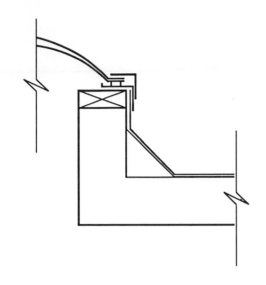

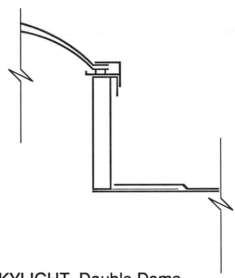

SKYLIGHT Double Dome--
Concrete Curb
1-1/2"=1'-0"
07810-38

SKYLIGHT Double Dome--
Integral Curb
1-1/2"=1'-0"
07810-39

NOTATION CHECKLIST,
SAMPLE NOTES

FRAME
FRAME CONDENSATE GUTTER/WEEP HOLES
CURB
CANT/NAILER
SEALANT/CAULKING
ROOFING SURFACE
    (TYPE, LAYERS & COVER MATERIAL)
ROOFING DECK/INSULATION
ROOF CONSTRUCTION
PLASTIC SKYLIGHT
45° SQUARE PYRAMID DOUBLE GLAZED
    SKYLIGHT SYSTEM
COVER METAL FRAME TO AVOID
    CONDENSATION
ACRYLIC PLASTIC SKYLIGHT W/EXTRUDED ALUM.
    CURB FRAME & CONDENSATE GUTTER

ALUM. FRAME BY SKYLIGHT MFR., INSTALL
    AS PER MFR'S. INSTRUCTIONS
ALUM. INNER LINER
CONT. APRON FLASHING
MEMBRANE FLASHING
TOP LINE OF CURB
MULLION
WOOD CURB
ALUM. CURB
4 X 4 CANT
WOOD BLOCKING
STEEL ANGLE
PERIMETER OPENING CHANNEL
MEMBRANE ROOFING
BUILT-UP ROOF
RIGID INSULATION
ROOF JOISTS
CEILING

COMPOSITE MASTER DETAIL

DETAIL FILE NUMBER: 07810-36

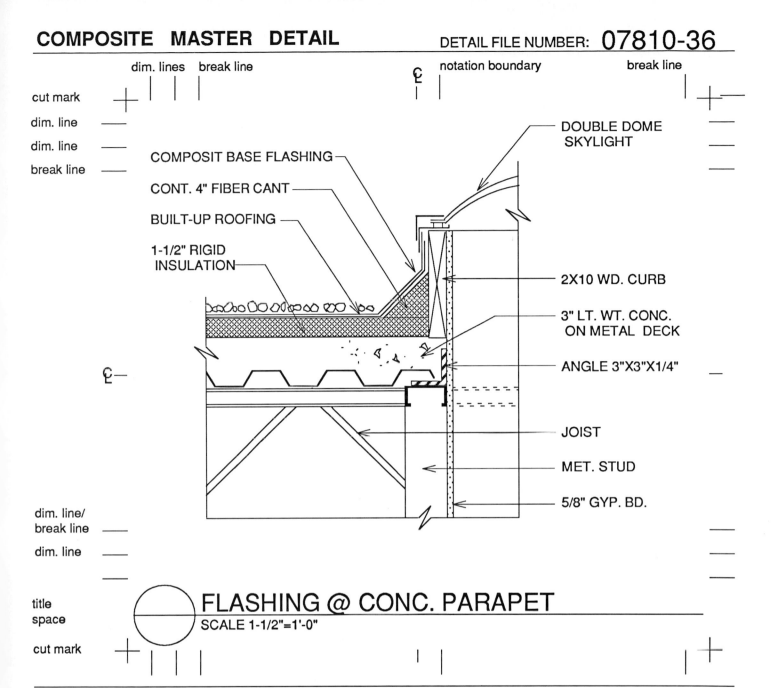

dim. lines   break line   C̸   notation boundary   break line

cut mark

dim. line

dim. line

break line

COMPOSIT BASE FLASHING

CONT. 4" FIBER CANT

BUILT-UP ROOFING

1-1/2" RIGID
INSULATION

C̸

DOUBLE DOME
SKYLIGHT

2X10 WD. CURB

3" LT. WT. CONC.
ON METAL DECK

ANGLE 3"X3"X1/4"

JOIST

MET. STUD

5/8" GYP. BD.

dim. line/
break line

dim. line

title
space

FLASHING @ CONC. PARAPET
SCALE 1-1/2"=1'-0"

cut mark

DETAIL INFORMATION
References, jobsite feedback, job history

07822 ROOF DRAINS

DETAIL DATA CHECKLIST

ROOF DRAINS

Recommend 1/2" slope per linear foot as minimum slope for built-up roof construction. Roof drains at columns, midspan of long-span roof trusses, and perimeter of roof may end up at high points due to framing deflection, wood frame shrinkage, concrete frame shrinkage or creep, or building settlement. Include more and larger roof drains to help compensate for these common circumstances.

Drains will be selected and sized by your plumbing consultant and may be installed as part of the plumbing contract or the roofing contract. In any case the work has to be coordinated with roofing and be reviewed during the roofing preconstruction meeting

Drain types:
___High strainer, narrow and wide, to block debris from entering the drains
___Flat drain for flat roof areas or roof paving where there will be foot traffic
___Bellows connection, allows differential movement

SMALL-SCALE GENERIC DETAILS

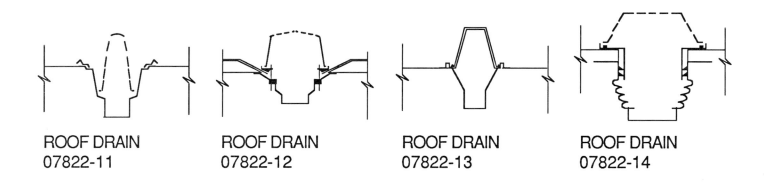

ROOF DRAIN
07822-11

ROOF DRAIN
07822-12

ROOF DRAIN
07822-13

ROOF DRAIN
07822-14

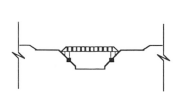

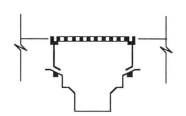

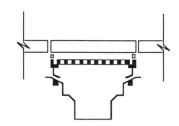

ROOF DRAIN
07822-21

ROOF DRAIN
07822-22

ROOF DRAIN
07822-23

07822 ROOF DRAINS

FULL-SCALE GENERIC DETAILS

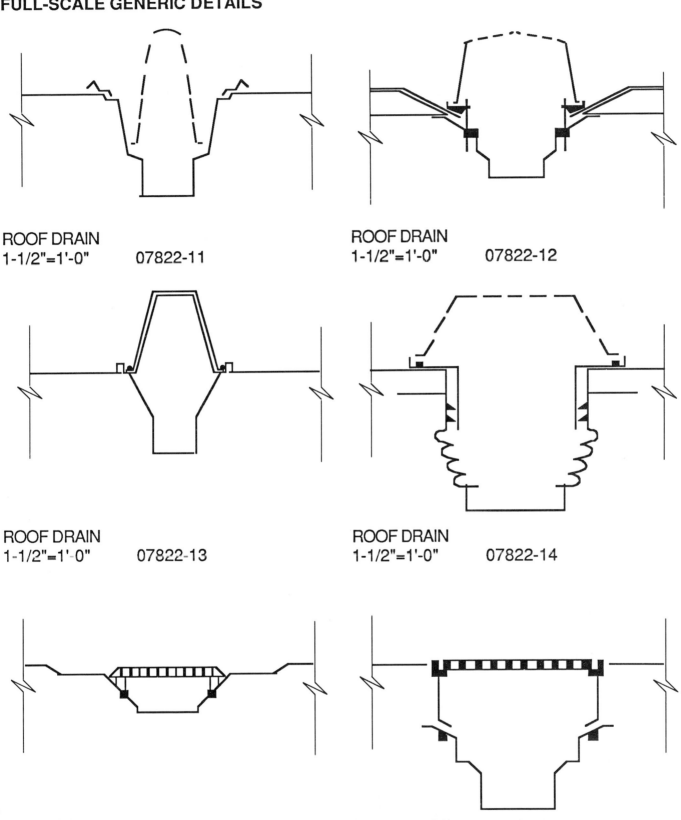

ROOF DRAIN
1-1/2"=1'-0"   07822-11

ROOF DRAIN
1-1/2"=1'-0"   07822-12

ROOF DRAIN
1-1/2"=1'-0"   07822-13

ROOF DRAIN
1-1/2"=1'-0"   07822-14

ROOF DRAIN
1-1/2"=1'-0"   07822-21

ROOF DRAIN
1-1/2"=1'-0"   07822-22

07822 ROOF DRAINS

FULL-SCALE GENERIC DETAILS continued

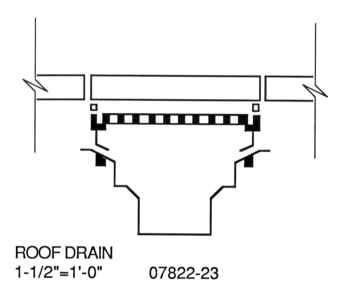

ROOF DRAIN
1-1/2"=1'-0"   07822-23

NOTATION CHECKLIST,
SAMPLE NOTES

DRAIN STRAINER
FLASHING CLAMP/GRAVEL STOP
FLASHING
ROOFING SURFACE
    (TYPE, LAYERS & COVER MATERIAL)
ROOFING DECK/INSULATION
ROOF CONSTRUCTION
ROOF DRAIN AS SPECIFIED, OPENINGS FOR
    ROOF DRAINS TO BE PREFORMED
STRAINER BASKET DRAIN GUARD
STRAINER
CLAMPING RING
WATER CUTOFF MASTIC
DECK FLANGE
NEOPRENE FLEXIBLE BELLOWS BODY
SCREW TYPE CLAMP
NO-HUB CONNECTION
MEMBRANE ROOFING
BUILT-UP ROOF
RIGID INSULATION
PRECAST CONC. SLAB ON STEEL DECKING

COMPOSITE MASTER DETAIL

DETAIL FILE NUMBER: **07822-12**

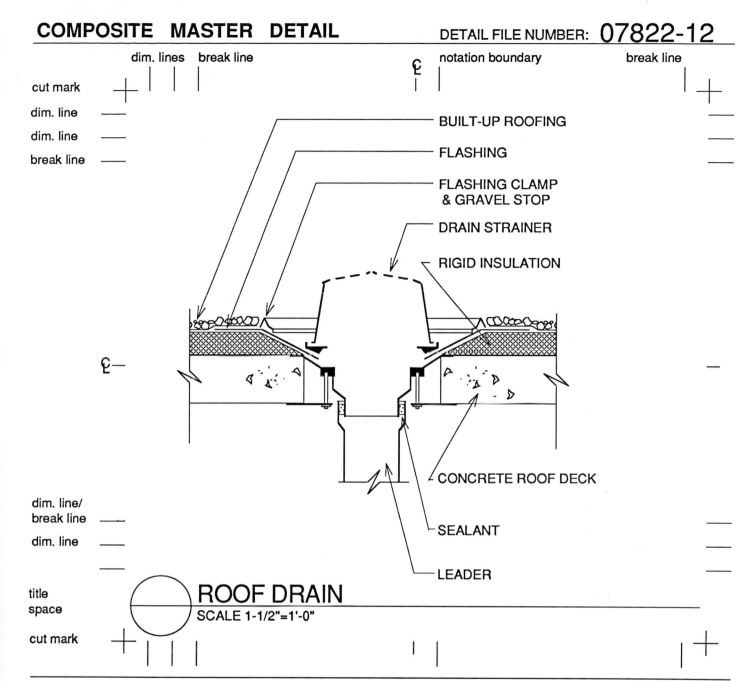

dim. lines   break line   notation boundary   break line

cut mark

dim. line

dim. line

break line

BUILT-UP ROOFING

FLASHING

FLASHING CLAMP
& GRAVEL STOP

DRAIN STRAINER

RIGID INSULATION

CONCRETE ROOF DECK

dim. line/
break line

dim. line

SEALANT

LEADER

title
space

ROOF DRAIN
SCALE 1-1/2"=1'-0"

cut mark

DETAIL INFORMATION
References, jobsite feedback, job history

07825 BREATHER VENTS

DETAIL DATA CHECKLIST

BREATHER VENT, ROOFING VENT, MEMBRANE VENT, RELIEF VENT
__Breather vents allow entrapped moisture to escape from layers of built-up roofing membranes

__They are manufactured items and should be sized and installed as per manufacturers' instructions, and roofing manufacturers' recommendations

__Some manufactured units close under exterior air pressure to prevent evaporated moisture in the air from reversing flow and entering the membrane through the vent

Sizes and installation:
  __Units are 4 to 6" diameter, 12" high
  __Install on wood blocks or nailer atop roof substrate and even with roof insulation
      __Mount on blocks or nailers with 1/2" vent holes at 2" o.c.
  __Mount 12" to top of vent with sheet metal peaked cap above
  __Provide bird screen to prevent nesting under cap

SMALL-SCALE GENERIC DETAILS

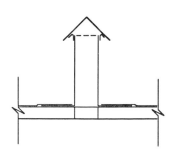

BREATHER VENT
07825-11

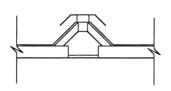

BREATHER VENT
07825-16

07825 BREATHER VENTS

FULL-SCALE GENERIC DETAILS

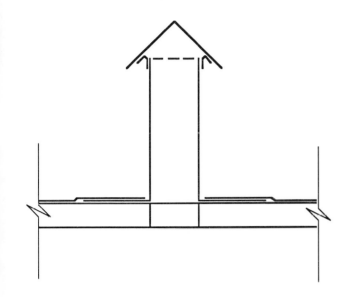

BREATHER VENT
1-1/2"=1'-0"   07825-11

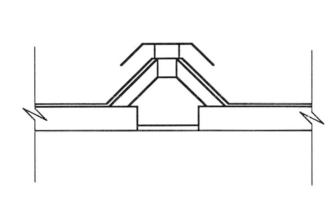

BREATHER VENT
1-1/2"=1'-0"   07825-16

NOTATION CHECKLIST, SAMPLE NOTES

METAL HOOD & FASTENERS
FLANGED METAL VENT STACK
ROOFING SURFACE
    (TYPE, LAYERS & COVER MATERIAL)
ROOFING DECK/INSULATION
ROOF CONSTRUCTION
GALV. PIPE W/TREADED END CAP
METAL PIPE
PREMOLDED PIPE SEAL
SEALANT
FLASHING FELT
STAINLES STEEL CLAMPING RING
WATER CUTOFF MASTIC
CORE HOLE AS REQUIRED
OPENINGS FOR ROOF VENTS TO BE PREFORMED
ALLOW 1-1/2" MIN. CLEAR AIR PASSAGE TO VENT
BUILT-UP ROOF
RIGID INSULATION
METAL DECKING

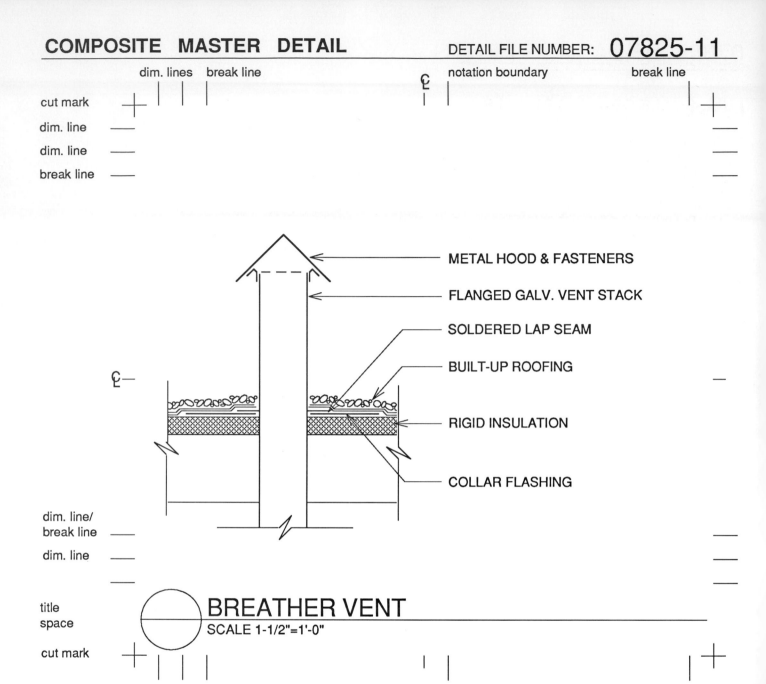

cut mark

dim. lines   break line

notation boundary   break line

dim. line

dim. line

break line

METAL HOOD & FASTENERS

FLANGED GALV. VENT STACK

SOLDERED LAP SEAM

BUILT-UP ROOFING

RIGID INSULATION

COLLAR FLASHING

dim. line/
break line

dim. line

title
space

BREATHER VENT

SCALE 1-1/2"=1'-0"

cut mark

DETAIL INFORMATION
References, jobsite feedback, job history

07830 ROOF HATCHES

DETAIL DATA CHECKLIST

ROOF HATCHES AND SCUTTLES
__See manufacturers' catalogs for choices of sizes, fittings, and special detail conditions
__Check building code fire and smoke control restrictions regarding hatches
__Check whether curb roof supports are built-in to the manufactured units or whether curbs have to be
    detailed and installed separately
__A framed opening should be provided to receive roof hatch unit, coordinate with the structural drawings
__Check whether the manufactured unit includes all required flashing, counter flashing, and blocking for
    flashing

Common trouble spots:
__Insufficient height above roof to block water entry, particularly from ice-dam water ponding in freezing
    weather
__Location in low or ponding area of roof
__Insufficient flashing and counter flashing

SMALL-SCALE GENERIC DETAILS

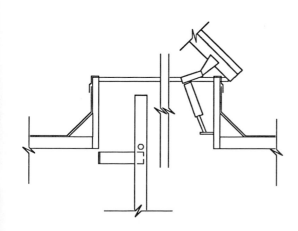

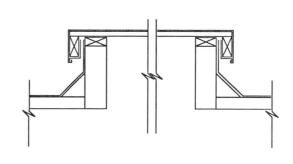

ROOF HATCH & SCUTTLE
07830-11

ROOF HATCH
07830-16

07830 ROOF HATCHES

FULL-SCALE GENERIC DETAILS

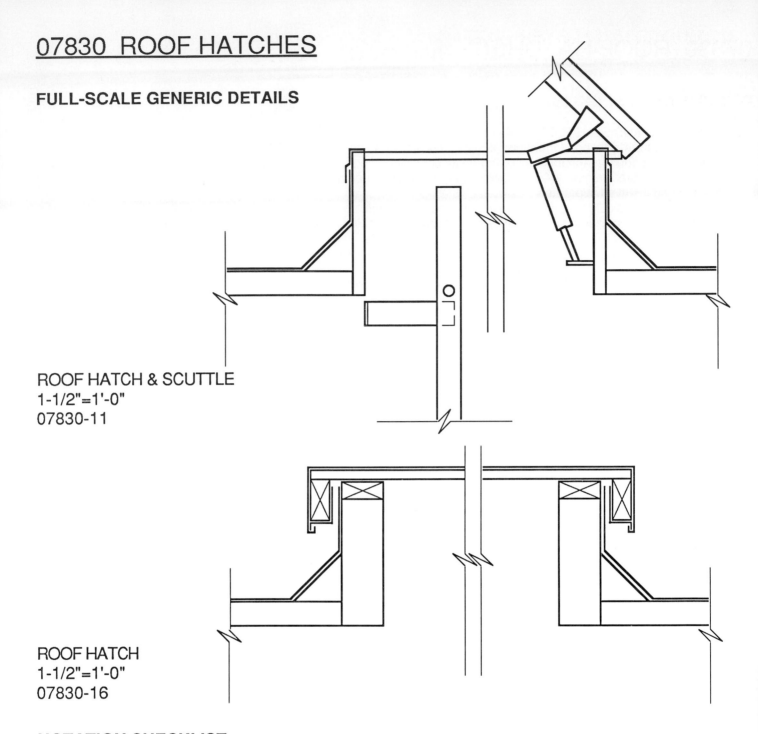

ROOF HATCH & SCUTTLE
1-1/2"=1'-0"
07830-11

ROOF HATCH
1-1/2"=1'-0"
07830-16

NOTATION CHECKLIST,
SAMPLE NOTES

ROOF HATCH & HARDWARE
SCUTTLE SIZE
FLASHING
CANT/NAILER
METAL LADDER
ROOFING SURFACE
   (TYPE, LAYERS & COVER MATERIAL)
ROOFING DECK/INSULATION
ROOF CONSTRUCTION
CEILING CONSTRUCTION

ROOF SCUTTLE
INSULATED HATCH DOOR
ROOF HATCH 2'-6" X 4'-6"
MANUFACTURED ROOF HATCH
4" CANT
BUILT-UP ROOF
SINGLE PLY MEMBRANE
STEEL ANGLE
DECK CLOSURE
LADDER
RIGID INSULATION
RIGID INSULATION BASE FLASHING
FOLD-DOWN STAIR
CEILING JOISTS

COMPOSITE MASTER DETAIL

DETAIL FILE NUMBER: **07830-11**

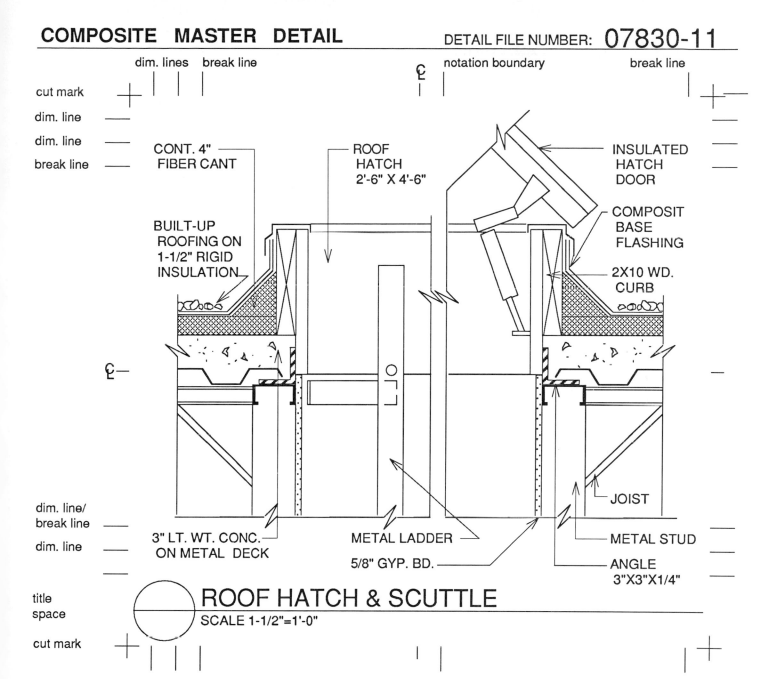

dim. lines   break line   notation boundary   break line

cut mark

dim. line

dim. line

break line

CONT. 4"
FIBER CANT

ROOF
HATCH
2'-6" X 4'-6"

INSULATED
HATCH
DOOR

COMPOSIT
BASE
FLASHING

BUILT-UP
ROOFING ON
1-1/2" RIGID
INSULATION

2X10 WD.
CURB

JOIST

dim. line/
break line

dim. line

3" LT. WT. CONC.
ON METAL DECK

METAL LADDER

5/8" GYP. BD.

METAL STUD

ANGLE
3"X3"X1/4"

title
space

cut mark

ROOF HATCH & SCUTTLE
SCALE 1-1/2"=1'-0"

DETAIL INFORMATION
References, jobsite feedback, job history

07850-07852 ROOF CURBS

DETAIL DATA CHECKLIST

ROOF CURBS
__Curbs are to prevent water entry to roof expansion joints, skylights, roof hatches, etc.
__Curb materials:
    __Wood sleepers nailed or bolted to roof substrate
    __Concrete sections
    __Prefabricated metal
__Installation:
    __Curbs are placed prior to finish roofing
    __Finish roofing is installed up and usually over the top of the curb
    __Curb top is covered with a metal cap, coping, or similar flashing

Work must be coordinated with roofing, may be part of the roofing contract and, if possible, included in the roofing warranty. It must be reviewed as part of the roofing preconstruction meeting.

SMALL-SCALE GENERIC DETAILS

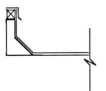

PREFAB ROOF CURB
07850-11

PREFAB ROOF CURB
W/ Insulation
07850-12

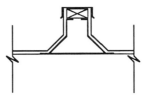

PREFAB ROOF CURB
07850-13

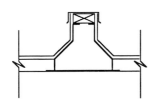

PREFAB ROOF CURB
W/ Insulation
07850-14

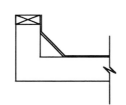

CONCRETE ROOF CURB
07851-11

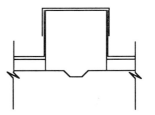

CONCRETE ROOF CURB
07851-12

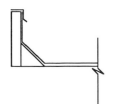

WOOD OR PREFAB
ROOF CURB
07852-11

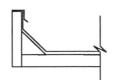

WOOD OR PREFAB
ROOF CURB
W/ Insul.
07852-12

WOOD SLEEPER
ROOF CURB
07852-16

07850-07852 ROOF CURBS

FULL-SCALE GENERIC DETAILS

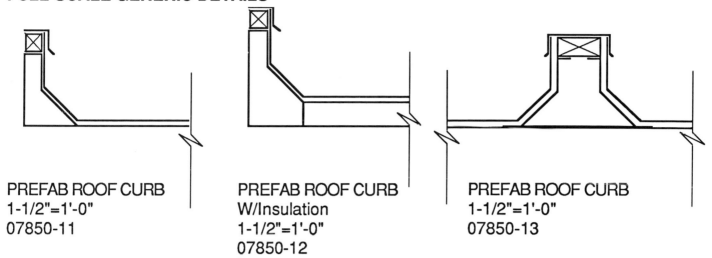

PREFAB ROOF CURB
1-1/2"=1'-0"
07850-11

PREFAB ROOF CURB
W/Insulation
1-1/2"=1'-0"
07850-12

PREFAB ROOF CURB
1-1/2"=1'-0"
07850-13

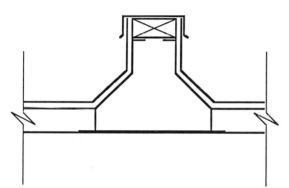

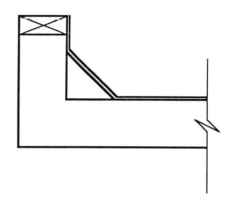

PREFAB ROOF CURB
W/Insulation
1-1/2"=1'-0"
07850-14

CONCRETE ROOF CURB
1-1/2"=1'-0"
07851-11

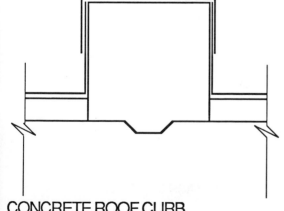

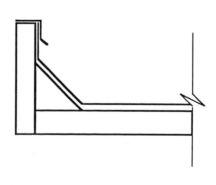

CONCRETE ROOF CURB
1-1/2"=1'-0"
07851-12

WOOD OR PREFAB ROOF CURB
W/Insulation
1-1/2"=1'-0" 07852-12

07850-07852 ROOF CURBS

FULL-SCALE GENERIC DETAILS continued

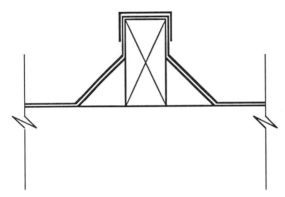

WOOD SLEEPER ROOF CURB
1-1/2"=1'-0"
07852-16

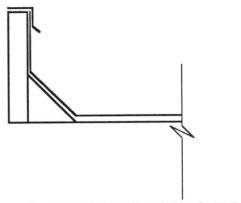

WOOD OR PREFAB ROOF CURB
1-1/2"=1'-0"
07852-11

NOTATION CHECKLIST, SAMPLE NOTES

CURB (TYPE, MATERIAL & SIZE)
METAL CAP/FLASHING
CANT/NAILER
ROOFING SURFACE
   (TYPE, LAYERS & COVER MATERIAL)
ROOFING DECK/INSULATION
ROOF CONSTRUCTION
2 X WOOD FRAME
ROOF CURB
PREFABRICATED ROOF CURB W/2 X 2 WOOD
   NAILER & INSUL. TREATED WOOD NAILER

2 X NAILERS
THRU-BOLT TO ANGLE
STEEL ANGLE
SEALANT
EXTEND ROOFING FELTS TO TOP OF CURB
26 GA. FLASHING
ELASTOMERIC FLASHING
CAP FLASHING
ROOFING MEMBRANE & FLASHING
CANT

07860, 07861 ROOF EXPANSION JOINTS

DETAIL DATA CHECKLIST

ROOF EXPANSION JOINT COVERS
    __Expansion joints consist of:
    __An opening or separation across a building to allow for movement, typically 1/2" to 1" wide
    __A waterstop between the separated structures
    __A premolded expansion joint filler
    __A block or curb to keep the joint above the roof surface and block water from entering the joint
    __An expansion joint cover

__Expansion joint cover types:
    __Type A: aluminum, stainless steel, or copper
        __Type A are best quality covers for most roofing conditions
    __Type B: elastomeric such as neoprene, with metal flanges
        __For intersection of roof slab and parapets or walls
    __Type C: plastic low profile cover
        __Not recommended except for minimal joints such as
            intermediate expansion joints for membrane

SMALL-SCALE GENERIC DETAILS

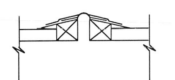

ROOF EXPANSION JOINT
Flexible Cover 07860-11

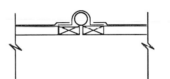

ROOF EXPANSION JOINT
Flexible Cover 07860-12

ROOF EXPANSION JOINT
Flexible Cover 07860-13

ROOF EXPANSION JOINT
Flexible Cover 07860-14

ROOF EXPANSION JOINT
Metal Cover 07861-11

FULL-SCALE GENERIC DETAILS

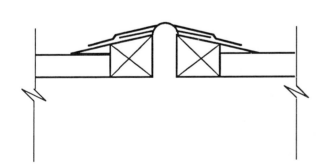

ROOF EXPANSION JOINT Flexible Cover
1-1/2"=1'-0"   07860-11

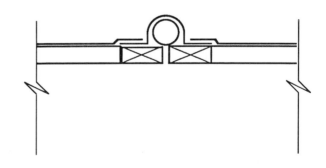

ROOF EXPANSION JOINT Flexible Cover
1-1/2"=1'-0"   07860-12

07860, 07861 ROOF EXPANSION JOINTS

FULL-SCALE GENERIC DETAILS

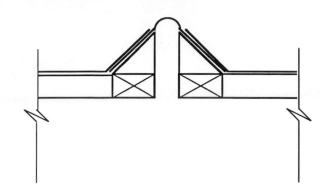

ROOF EXPANSION JOINT Flexible Cover
1-1/2"=1'-0"   07860-13

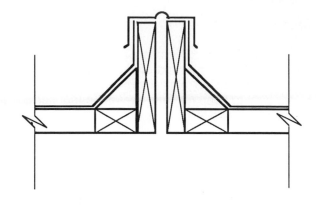

ROOF EXPANSION JOINT Flexible Cover
1-1/2"=1'-0"   07860-14

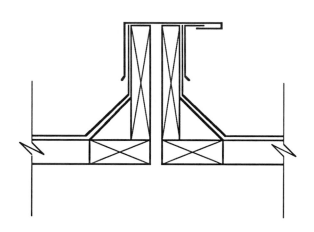

ROOF EXPANSION JOINT Metal Cover
1-1/2"=1'-0"   07861-11

NOTATION CHECKLIST, SAMPLE NOTES

EXPANSION JOINT COVER
FLASHING/FLEXIBLE FLASHING
CANT/NAILER/BLOCKING
ADHESIVE/SEALANT/CAULKING
ROOFING SURFACE
     (TYPE, LAYERS & COVER MATERIAL)
ROOFING DECK/INSULATION
ROOF CONSTRUCTION
WIDTH OF JOINT
BASE FLASHING, EXTEND. OVER TOP OF
     NAILER
EXP. JT. COVER, SET FLANGES IN PLASTIC
     CEMENT
FLEXIBLE JT. COVER.
24 GA. STAINLESS STEEL COPING
ALUM. COPING
ALUM. COUNTERFLASHING
COMPRESSIBLE INSULATION
BATT INSULATION
FIBER GLASS INSULATION
FIBER GLASS EXPANSION
TREATED NAILERS

CONT. FIRE RETARD. WOOD BLOCKING
2 PIECES TREATED WOOD BLOCKING CONT. W/3/8"
     BOLTS @ 24" O.C. , FILL VOID W/LOOSE
     INSULATION
BASE FLASH IN FULL BED OF PLASTIC CEMENT
FIBER GLASS CLOTH EMBEDDED IN & COVERED
     W/PLASTIC CEMENT
FIBER CANT
4" CANT STRIP CONTINUOUS
FLASHING FELTS
STEEL ANGLE

COMPOSITE MASTER DETAIL

DETAIL FILE NUMBER: **07860-11**

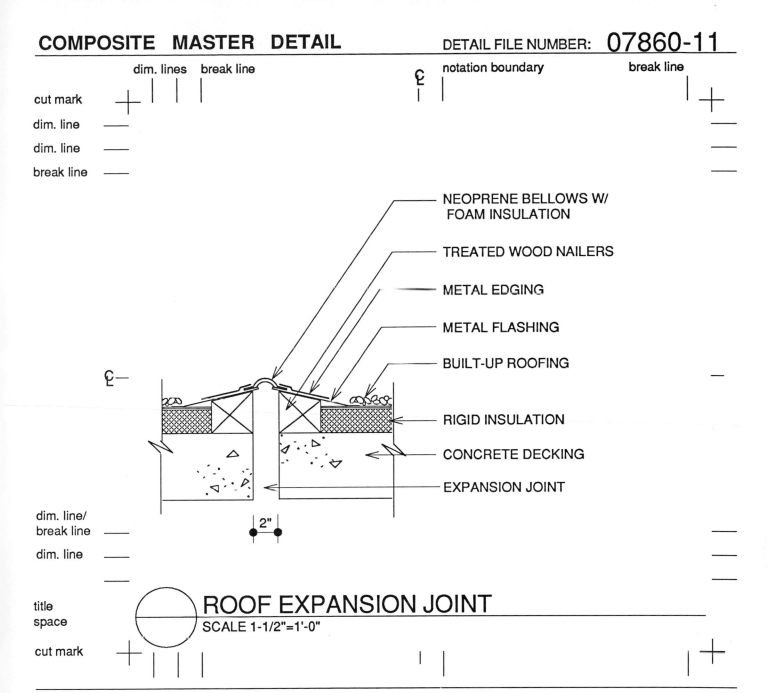

cut mark

dim. lines   break line

dim. line —

dim. line —

break line —

notation boundary   break line

NEOPRENE BELLOWS W/
FOAM INSULATION

TREATED WOOD NAILERS

METAL EDGING

METAL FLASHING

BUILT-UP ROOFING

RIGID INSULATION

CONCRETE DECKING

EXPANSION JOINT

2"

dim. line/
break line —

dim. line —

title
space

ROOF EXPANSION JOINT
SCALE 1-1/2"=1'-0"

cut mark

DETAIL INFORMATION
References, jobsite feedback, job history

07870 PITCH POCKETS

DETAIL DATA CHECKLIST

PITCH POCKETS

Pitch pockets are enclosed caulk-filled holes or pans around a pipe, conduit, or structural support that penetrates a roof.

Ideally, pipes, conduit, or structural supports should not penetrate a roof surface. Such penetrations require extra maintenance and are likely to be a source of leaks. In general, the best rule is to avoid roof-mounted equipment as much as possible.

If such work has to be done, the connections should be in the form of well-caulked and sealed pockets. Hot-or cold-applied bitumin with fiber filler is poured or packed around the penetration, sometimes in a galvanized steel pitch pan. Then it's covered with flashing and a cap or counterflashing and integrated with the roofing seal. Coordinate the detailing for such work with the structural engineers and make sure it's reviewed during the roofing preconstruction meeting.

This work should be part of the roofing contract and included in the roofing warranty.

SMALL-SCALE GENERIC DETAILS

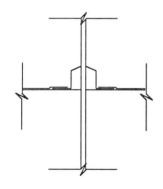

PITCH POCKET Conduit
07870-11

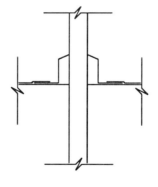

PITCH POCKET Pipe
07870-12

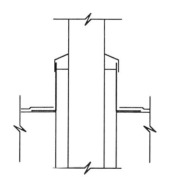

PITCH POCKET Pipe or Structural
07870-16

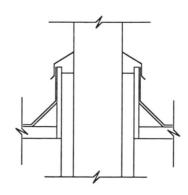

PITCH POCKET Pipe or Structural
07870-17

07870 PITCH POCKETS

FULL-SCALE GENERIC DETAILS

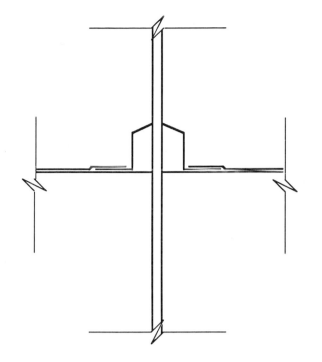

PITCH POCKET Conduit
1 1/2"=1'-0"   07870-11

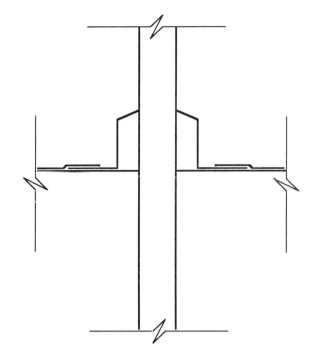

PITCH POCKET Pipe
1 1/2"=1'-0"   07870-12

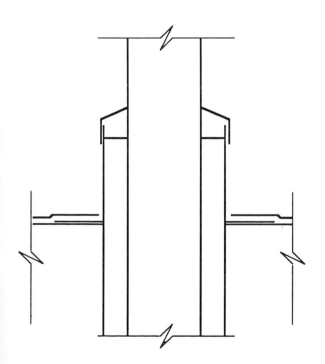

PITCH POCKET Pipe or Structural
1 1/2"=1'-0"   07870-16

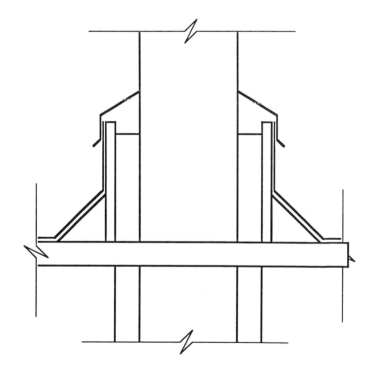

PITCH POCKET Pipe or Structural
1 1/2"=1'-0"   07870-17

505

07870 PITCH POCKETS

**NOTATION CHECKLIST,
SAMPLE NOTES**

PIPE/STRUCTURAL SUPPORT
   (MATERIAL & SIZE)
CAP FLASHING
PITCH PAN/PITCH WELL
PITCH/FLASHING COMPOUND
CANT/NAILER
ROOFING SURFACE
   (TYPE, LAYERS & COVER MATERIAL)
ROOFING DECK/INSULATION
ROOF CONSTRUCTION
PITCH POCKET FILLED BY ROOFER
SEALANT
GALV. METAL UMBRELLA, ROUND,
   W/DRAW BAND
GALV. METAL PITCH POCKET FILLED
   W/FLASHING CEMENT
GALV. PITCH PAN, STRIPPED IN, FILL W/PITCH
24 GA. GALV. STEEL CAP FLASHING,
   WELD OR SEAM ALL SEAMS & JOINTS
24 GA. GALV. STEEL PITCH PAN,
   EXTEND FLANGE 4" ONTO ROOF
NAILERS
BASE FLASHING
INSULATION CANT
RIGID INSULATION

COMPOSITE MASTER DETAIL

DETAIL FILE NUMBER: **07870-16**

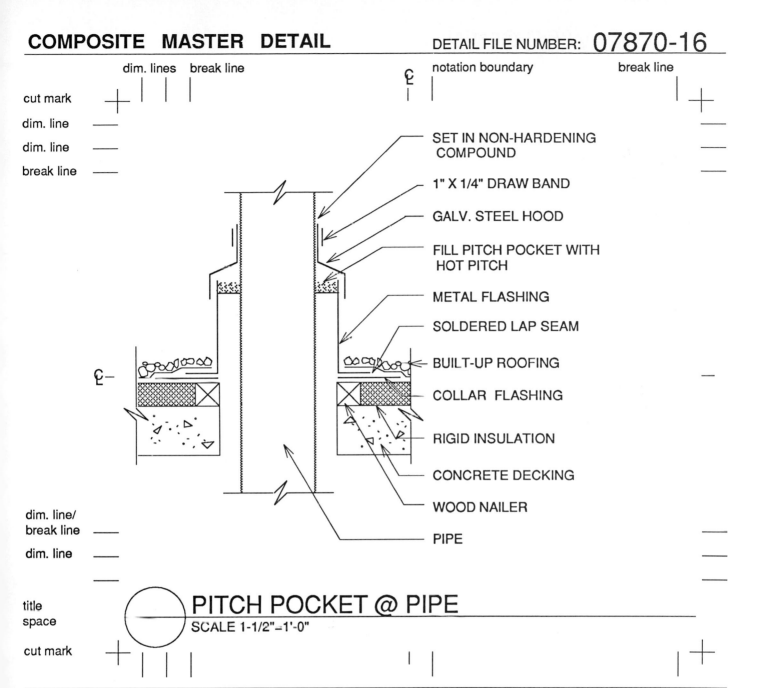

cut mark — dim. lines — break line

dim. line

dim. line

break line

notation boundary — break line

SET IN NON-HARDENING COMPOUND

1" X 1/4" DRAW BAND

GALV. STEEL HOOD

FILL PITCH POCKET WITH HOT PITCH

METAL FLASHING

SOLDERED LAP SEAM

BUILT-UP ROOFING

COLLAR FLASHING

RIGID INSULATION

CONCRETE DECKING

WOOD NAILER

PIPE

dim. line/ break line

dim. line

title space

PITCH POCKET @ PIPE
SCALE 1-1/2"=1'-0"

cut mark

DETAIL INFORMATION
References, jobsite feedback, job history

07871 GUY WIRE CONNECTION

DETAIL DATA CHECKLIST

GUY WIRE

Guy wire connections are usually an afterthought; a way of securing add-on equipment on a rooftop after it's built. It's not good construction practice to penetrate the roof with connectors of any sort and especially connectors that will be subject to stress and possible movement.

If they must be included, they're handled as pitch pockets: enclosed, caulk-filled holes around the penetrating guy-wire eyebolt. Hot- or cold-applied caulk such as bitumin with fiber filler is poured and/or packed around the penetration.

Coordinate the detailing for such work closely with the structural engineers and make sure the operation is covered in the roofing preconstruction meeting. This work should be part of the roofing contract and included in the roofing warranty.

SMALL-SCALE GENERIC DETAIL

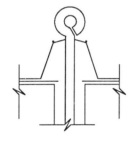

GUY WIRE CONNECTION
07871-11

FULL-SCALE GENERIC DETAIL

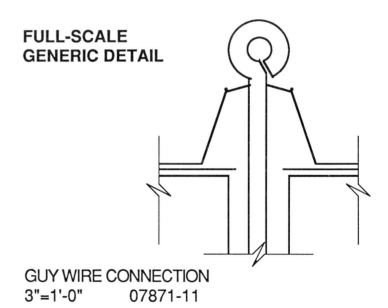

GUY WIRE CONNECTION
3"=1'-0"   07871-11

NOTATION CHECKLIST, SAMPLE NOTES

EYE BOLT (MATERIAL & SIZE)
MOLDED FLASHING/METAL DAM
SEALER/PITCH
ROOFING SURFACE
   (TYPE, LAYERS & COVER MATERIAL)
ROOFING DECK/INSULATION
ROOF CONSTRUCTION

3/4" STAINLESS STEEL EYEBOLT
   W/1" DIA. EYE
POURABLE SEALER
MOLDED FLASHING
GALV. METAL DAM
MEMBRANE IN CONTACT W/POURABLE SEALER
ROOFING MEMBRANE
TREATED WOOD BLOCKING
METAL DECK
FILLER

CHAPTER 8

Doors and Windows
08000

08000 WINDOWS & GLAZING

DETAIL DATA CHECKLIST

Windows are usually bought as manufactured products in stock sizes. Window types, materials and sizes are shown in the Window Schedule, details of manufacture, finishes and workmanship are described in specifications.

Glazing
__Single, double, insulated, removable
__Glass types: obscure, wire, reflective, safety or tempered
__Thickness may be noted but is commonly sized in specifications

Glazing Clearances
__Commonly required clearances are 1/4" between glass to frame,1/8" between glass and rabbet, and 5/8" depth of rabbit

Rough Opening
__The difference between finish window frame and rough opening is often dimensioned or noted as a guide for the framing carpenters
__1/2" all way around is a common rough opening tolerance

Shim Space
__A commonly accepted rough opening framing tolerance is 1/4" on a side so that's often the space allowed for shim

Vents, Weep Holes, Wind Guards, Hardware, Sill Tracks, & Screens
__All vary according to window type and specific manufacture
__Consult catalogs of preferred manufacturers for notation

Background Frame Lines; Lines of Construction, & Finishes
__Lines of sills, Jambs, portions of frame and adjacent or background wall construction are commonly outline drawing and noted

Anchors & Screws
__Connection of window frames to walls is determined by wall type and manufacturers' specifications
__Attachment devices are commonly drawn in simple single line symbols and noted by generic material and type

Extension Jamb & Extension Sill
__See manufacturer's data sheets for variations in frame extenders

Sill, Sub-sill & Stool
__These are usually unique to a project, and sized and noted accordingly

Wood Trim & Casing
__Commonly drawn at net size to scale, and referenced to a Trim Schedule
__Wood type and quality is often noted on the drawing as well as referenced to specifications

Flashing & Caulking
__Typically named generically by material and function and referenced to specifications
__Drawings for small, simple projects often include flashing material and thickness

Sliding Glass Doors
__Notation and detail data is similar to window construction
__Add notes, drawing, and specifications for visual safety barriers, safety guardrails, added lock devices, interlocks, etc

08111 METAL DOOR FRAMES

METAL DOOR FRAMES
 Rabbet, Single or Double
__1-9/16" for 1-3/8" doors, 1-15/16" for 1-3/4" doors
__A glazing stop may be added if the frame is used as a side light
__Rubber grommets may be provided to silence door slamming
__Include weather-stripping for exterior doors

Metal Gauges
__Typical standard: #14, #16, #18, usually in specifications

Frame Sizes
__Typical sizes are shown on the tracer sheets
__Other dimensions are 5/8" for the depth of rabbet, 2" for standard frames, 1" for narrow line
__Backbends are usually 1/2" each so the back opening or throat is a total of 1" narrower than the overall frame

Frame Anchors to Wall
__Anchors vary to fit either wood, masonry, or metal stud walls
__These are usually mounted 3 per jamb and dotted in outline in the detail drawing

Grout in Frame
__Full grouting in frames is used to resist damage in heavy traffic areas and/or for fire resistance

SMALL-SCALE GENERIC DETAILS

| 4-3/4" | 5-3/4" | 6-3/4" | 7-3/4" | 8-3/4" |

| 4-3/4" | 5-3/4" | 6-3/4" | 7-3/4" | 8-3/4" |

| 4-3/4" | 5-3/4" | 6-3/4" | 7-3/4" | 8-3/4" |

STEEL DOOR FRAME
4-3/4" Frame/
6" Wall
3"=1'-0"

STEEL DOOR FRAME
4-3/4" Frame/
8" Wall
3"=1'-0"

STEEL DOOR FRAME
5-3/4" Frame/
8" Wall
3"=1'-0"

STEEL DOOR FRAME
5-3/4" Frame/
10" Wall
3"=1'-0"

08111 METAL DOOR FRAMES

SCALE 3"=1'-0"

FULL-SCALE GENERIC DETAILS

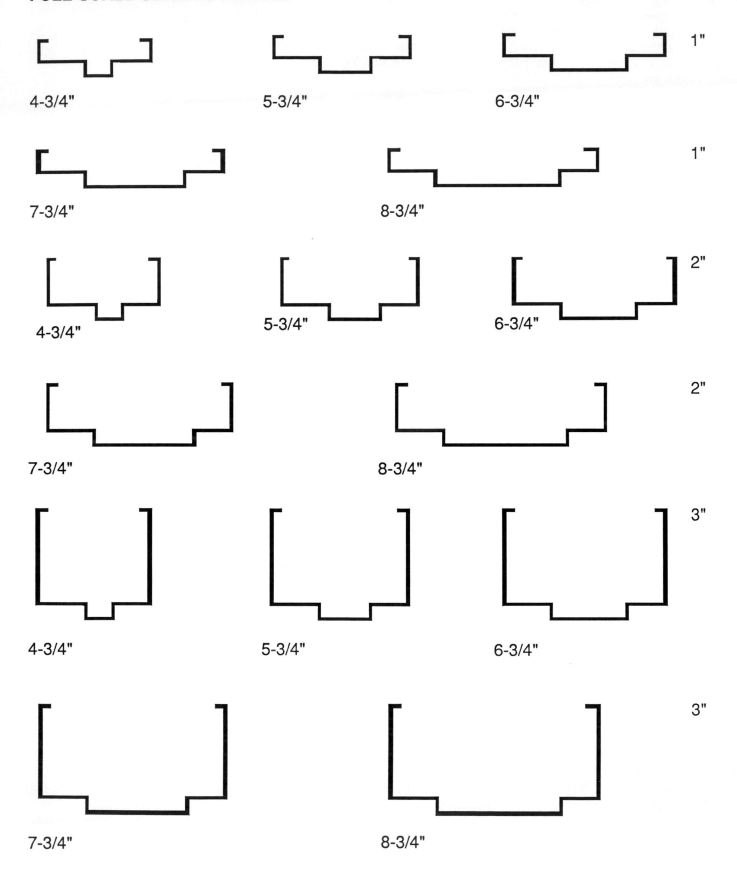

4-3/4"

5-3/4"

6-3/4"

1"

7-3/4"

8-3/4"

1"

4-3/4"

5-3/4"

6-3/4"

2"

7-3/4"

8-3/4"

2"

4-3/4"

5-3/4"

6-3/4"

3"

7-3/4"

8-3/4"

3"

08111 METAL DOOR FRAMES

FULL-SCALE GENERIC DETAILS continued

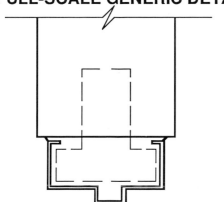

STEEL DOOR FRAME
4-3/4" Frame/6" Wall
3"=1'-0"

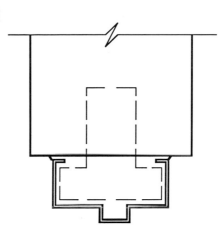

STEEL DOOR FRAME
4-3/4" Frame/8" Wall
3"=1'-0"

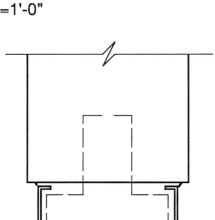

STEEL DOOR FRAME
5-3/4" Frame/8" Wall
3"=1'-0"

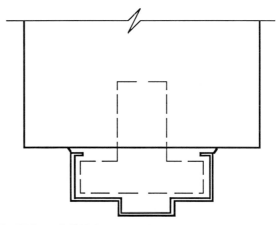

STEEL DOOR FRAME
5-3/4" Frame/10" Wall
3"=1'-0"

NOTATION CHECKLIST, SAMPLE NOTES

METAL FRAME
GROUT
CAULKING
SHIM SPACE
ADJACENT FINISHES
CASING/TRIM
JAMB OR HEAD CONSTRUCTION
ANCHOR TO WALL
DOOR, SEE SCHEDULE
SEE DOOR SCHEDULE FOR
   OPENING SIZE
HOLLOW METAL FRAME
HOLLOW METAL FRAME,
   GROUT FULL

METAL STOP
18 GA. METAL FRAME
PRESSED METAL FRAME
   W/MASONRY ANCHORS
DOOR STOP
RATED FRAME
FRAME ANCHOR
DOOR OPENING
CORNER BEAD
CONT. CAULK EACH SIDE
SHIM AS REQUIRED
PROVIDE 3 ADJUSTABLE
   ANCHORS
PER JAMB, GROUT JAMB FULL

GLASS STOP
F.H. SCREWS
WELDED ZEE REINFORCEMENT
EXPANSION SHIELD
METAL PLATE DOOR
METAL CHANNEL RUNNER
WOOD BLOCKING
STUDS @ 16" O.C.
DOUBLE STUDS @ EACH JAMB
NESTED STUDS
PAINT ALL EXPOSED METAL
CORNER BEAD
JAMB ANCHOR CLIP
FACE OF FINISH WALL

08201--08206 WOOD DOORS AND DOOR FRAMES

DETAIL DATA CHECKLIST

Door Types & Sizes
__Hollow core wood doors are commonly 1-3/8" thick, solid core1-3/4"
__Thickness, finish, width and door type are usually referenced to the door schedule
__Metal door frames are usually referenced to a separate frame schedule.

Louvers, View Panel, Undercut for Ventilation
__Such items may be noted on the plans or details for smaller buildings but otherwise
   are commonly shown in the door schedule

Door Frames With Stop
__Stops may be integral rabbeted or applied, if applied, note fastening
__Net actual size of door frame may be dimensioned, referred to schedule, or noted

Fire Rating, Acoustical Treatment, Lead Lining
__These are all normally specified and/or shown in the door schedule

Wood Trim & Casing
__Commonly drawn at net size to scale, and referenced to a Trim Schedule
__Wood type and quality is sometimes noted on the drawing but more often referenced to specifications

Rough Opening
__The difference between finish door frame and rough opening is sometimes dimensioned or noted
   as a guide for the framing carpenters.
__1/2" to 1" all way around is a common rough-opening size
__Provide shims in the rough opening shim space to plumb and straighten the door frame

Flashing & Caulking
__Flash and/or caulk where door frames are exposed to weather
__Flashing is usually named generically by material and function and referenced to specifications
__Drawings for small, simple projects often include flashing material and thickness
__Include weather-stripping at exterior doors

08201--08206 WOOD DOORS AND DOOR FRAMES

Also see DETAIL DATA CHECKLIST for wood doors and frames preceding 08201

DETAIL DATA CHECKLIST

Pocket and Sliding Doors
__Usually made of standard hollow or solid core doors with top-mounted hanging slider hardware
__3/16" to 1/4" clearance is normally provided between the face of the door and the pocket recess framing and trim
__Floor tracks and door pull hardware are referenced in specifications, general notes, or door hardware schedule
__Trim at the header is usually designed to hide the hanging hardware so rough opening to header may be higher
    than for a regular interior door.

Bifold Door
__Sometimes includes bottom pivot and special hardware
__Trim may be required as in preceding note
__Magnetic or other surface-mounted catch may be used and so noted

Accordion door
__These are bought as manufactured units, either in standard sizes or custom sizes
__Usually a vinyl covered metal frame door surface-mounted In a cased opening
__Magnetic or other surface-mounted catch may be used and so noted

SMALL-SCALE GENERIC DETAILS

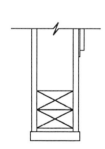

CASED OPENING
08201-1

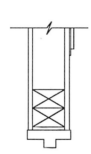

JAMB
08202-1

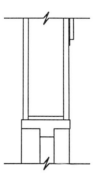

HEAD
08202-4

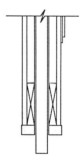

POCKET DOOR
08203-1

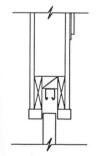

POCKET
DOOR HEAD
08203-4

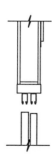

DOUBLE SLIDING
DOOR HEAD
08204-4

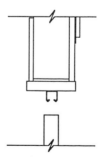

BI-FOLD
DOOR HEAD
08205-4

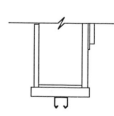

ACCORDION
DOOR HEAD
08206-4

FULL-SCALE GENERIC DETAILS

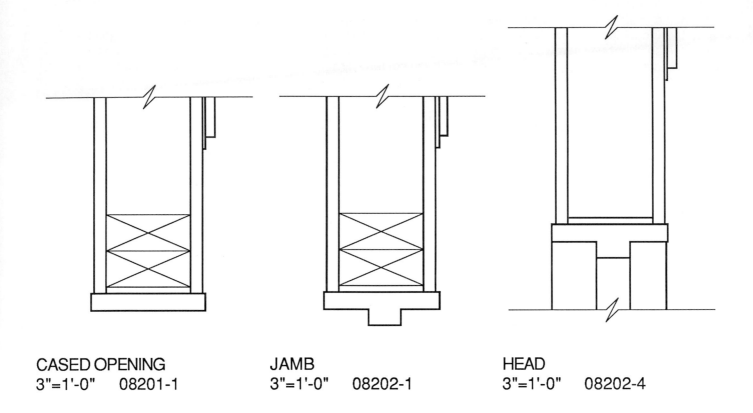

CASED OPENING
3"=1'-0"   08201-1

JAMB
3"=1'-0"   08202-1

HEAD
3"=1'-0"   08202-4

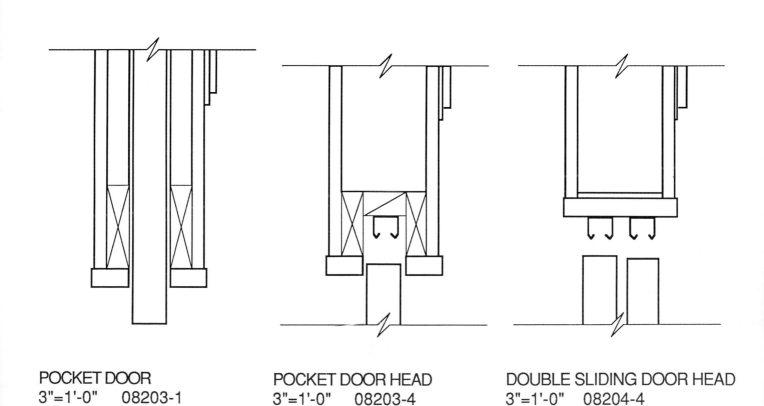

POCKET DOOR
3"=1'-0"   08203-1

POCKET DOOR HEAD
3"=1'-0"   08203-4

DOUBLE SLIDING DOOR HEAD
3"=1'-0"   08204-4

08201--08206 WOOD DOORS AND DOOR FRAMES

FULL-SCALE GENERIC DETAILS continued

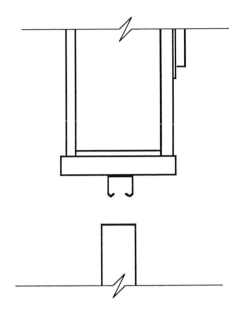

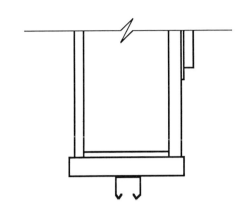

BI-FOLD DOOR HEAD
3"=1'-0"   08205-4

ACCORDION DOOR HEAD
3"=1'-0"   08206-4

NOTATION CHECKLIST,
SAMPLE NOTES

WALL CONSTRUCTION
SHIM SPACE
FINISH HEAD/JAMB
ADJACENT FINISHES
CASING/TRIM
DOOR TYPE, MATERIAL & FINISH
FIXTURES/ATTACHMENTS/HARDWARE
ROUGH OPENING/FINISH OPENING

DBL. 2 X 4 HEADER
BLOCKING
    X   WOOD CASING
WOOD TRIM
MOULDING
STEEL ANGLE
PREHUNG DOOR UNIT
THRESHOLD
1/2" X 1-1/2" WOOD STOP
GYPSUM WALLBOARD
VENEER

08330 ROLLING DOORS

DETAIL DATA CHECKLIST

ROLLING DOORS
__These are manufactured products provided in standard widths and heights.
__Detail drawings are included mainly to show special anchoring conditions--thru-bolts, anchor bolts,
  expansion bolts, etc. in wood frame, masonry, or concrete wall construction.
__See manufacturers' and suppliers' catalogs for design data, details, and specifications
__See manufacturer's recommendations for wall and header anchors.

SMALL-SCALE GENERIC DETAILS

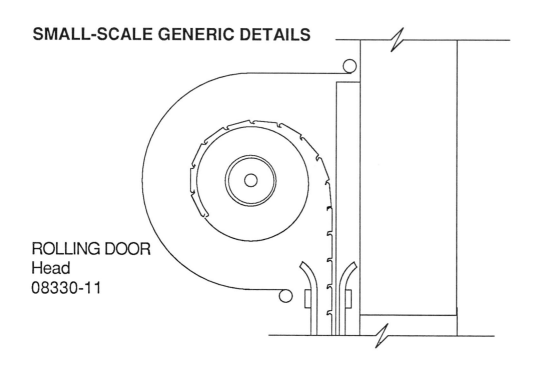

ROLLING DOOR
Head
08330-11

FACE-MOUNTED
JAMB GUIDE
Wood or Masonry
08330-31

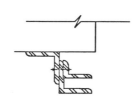

FACE-MOUNTED
JAMB GUIDE
Concrete
08330-32

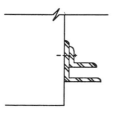

JAMB-MOUNTED
GUIDE
08330-35

BOTTOM BAR
W/WEATHERSTRIPPING
08330-37

08330 ROLLING DOORS

FULL-SCALE GENERIC DETAILS

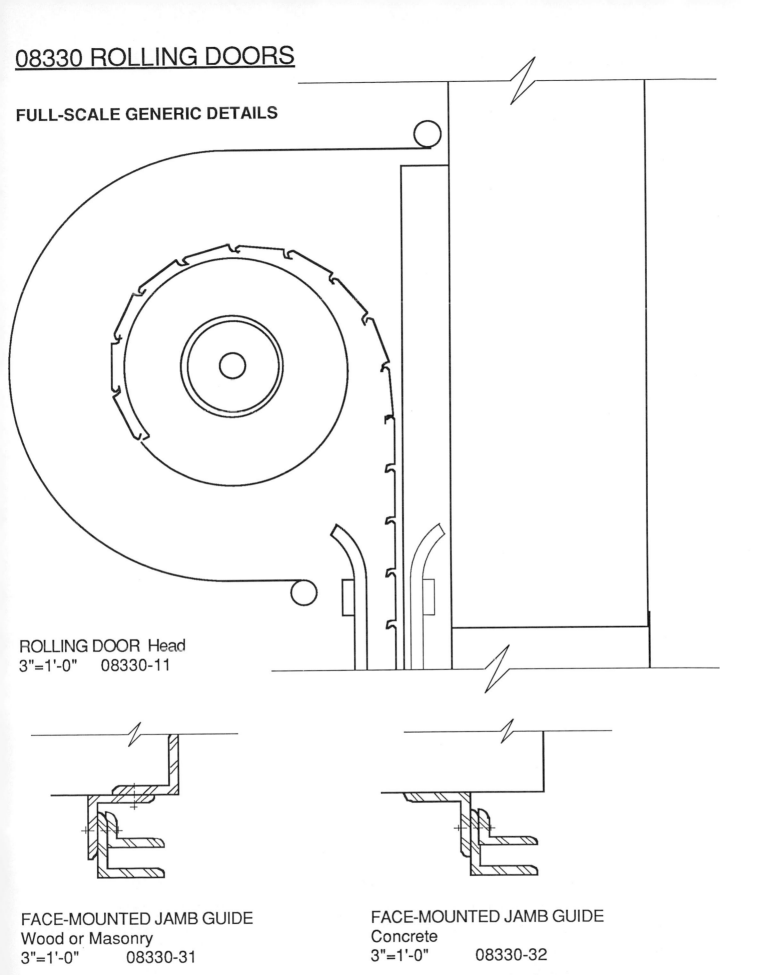

ROLLING DOOR Head
3"=1'-0"   08330-11

FACE-MOUNTED JAMB GUIDE
Wood or Masonry
3"=1'-0"   08330-31

FACE-MOUNTED JAMB GUIDE
Concrete
3"=1'-0"   08330-32

08330 ROLLING DOORS

FULL-SCALE GENERIC DETAILS continued

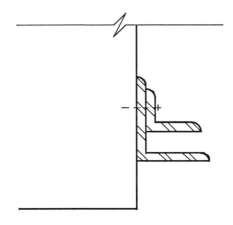

JAMB-MOUNTED GUIDE
3"=1'-0"   08330-35

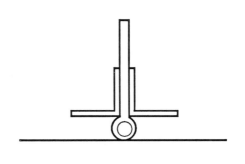

BOTTOM BAR W/WEATHERSTRIPPING
3"=1'-0"   08330-37

NOTATION CHECKLIST,
SAMPLE NOTES

MOTOR MOUNT/OPERATING CHAIN
HOOD/HOOD BAFFLE
DOOR SLATS/GRILLE
CHANNEL/ANCHOR
METAL ANGLE SLAT GUIDE
LOCKBAR
BOTTOM BAR/ASTRAGAL

BRACING TO STRUCTURE ABOVE
SECURE TO STRUCTURE
STRUCTURAL LINTELS
SECURE HOOD AS PER MFR'S. RECOMMENDATIONS
FUSIBLE LINK
CHAIN- 0R MOTOR-OPERATED ROLLING DOOR
ROLL-UP DOOR HOOD
ROLLING COUNTER DOOR
ROLL-UP GRILLE
DOOR GUIDE
OPENING HEIGHT

08372 ALUMINUM SLIDING GLASS DOORS

DETAIL DATA CHECKLIST

ALUMINUM SLIDING GLASS DOORS
__These are manufactured products provided in standard widths and heights.
__Detail drawings are included mainly to show special anchoring conditions: Screws, anchor bolts,
    expansion bolts, etc., in wood frame, masonry, or concrete wall construction.
__See manufacturers' and suppliers' catalogs for design data, details, and specifications.
__See manufacturer's recommendations for wall and header anchors.

SMALL-SCALE GENERIC DETAILS
Aluminum Sliding Glass Door -- Single Glazed

HEAD   08372-1

JAMB   08372-2

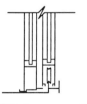

SILL   08372-3

Aluminum Sliding Glass Door -- Double Glazed

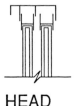

HEAD   08372-21

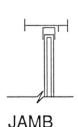

JAMB   08372-22

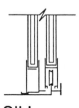

SILL   08372-23

08373 WOOD SLIDING GLASS DOORS AND WINDOWS

FULL-SCALE GENERIC DETAILS

Wood Sliding. Glass Door -- Single Glazed

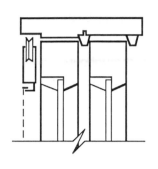

HEAD   3"=1'-0"
08373-1

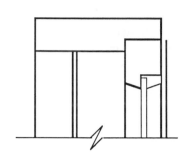

JAMB   3"=1'-0"
08373-2

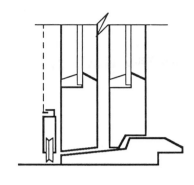

SILL   3"=1'-0"
08373-3

Wood Sliding. Glass Door -- Double Glazed

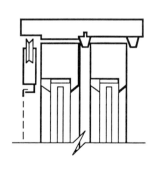

HEAD   3"=1'-0"
08373-21

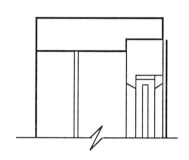

JAMB   3"=1'-0"
08373-22

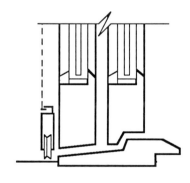

SILL   3"=1'-0"
08373-23

NOTATION CHECKLIST
SAMPLE NOTES

WALL CONSTRUCTION
SHIM SPACE
DRIP CAP/WEATHERSTRIPPING/FLASHING
CAULKING/GROUT
FINISH HEAD/SILL/JAMB
WINDOW TYPE, MATERIAL & FINISH
HARDWARE/OPERATOR
VENT/WEEP HOLE/WIND GUARD
GLAZING: SINGLE/DOUBLE/REMOVABLE
SCREEN/SCREEN FRAME
CASING/TRIM/ADJACENT FINISH
ROUGH OPENING/FINISH OPENING

08411 STOREFRONT WINDOWS

DETAIL DATA CHECKLIST

STORE FRONTS & ENTRANCES

__Since these are manufactured products, components need only be drawn in profile and noted in one or two words: Glazing Bar, Vertical Mullion, Transom, etc.
__Materials are typically aluminum, stainless steel or bronze
__Allow for expansion and contraction of large storefront units
__See manufacturer's instructions for allowances for movement

Connectors, hardware, vents, etc.
__These items are determined by manufacturers' specifications

Adjacent Construction
__Soffits or ceiling heights are often drawn, noted, and dimensioned
__Show enough of adjacent wall construction to indicate and note fastening of frame to structure and what finishes occur adjacent to frames
__Show caulking of contact of window frames to surrounding material or structure

Glazing
__Single, double, insulated, removable
__Glass types: obscure, wire, reflective, safety or tempered
__Thickness may be noted but is commonly sized in specifications

Glazing Clearances
__Commonly required clearances are 1/4" between glass to frame, 1/8" between glass and rabbet, and 5/8" depth of rabbit

Vents, Weep Holes, Wind Guards, Hardware, Sill Tracks, & Screens
__All vary according to window type and specific manufacture
__Consult catalogs of preferred manufacturers for notation

Anchors & Screws
__Connection of window frames to walls is determined by wall type and manufacturers' specifications
__Attachment devices are commonly drawn in simple single line symbols and noted by generic material and type

Flashing & Caulking
__Typically named generically by material and function and referenced to specifications
__Drawings for small, simple projects often include flashing material and thickness

08411 STOREFRONT WINDOWS

See DETAIL DATA CHECKLIST for storefronts preceding 08411

SMALL-SCALE GENERIC DETAILS

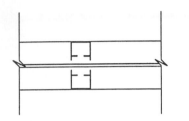

VERTICAL GLAZING BAR
Single Glazed
08411-1

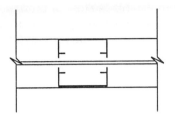

MULLION
Single Glazed
08411-3

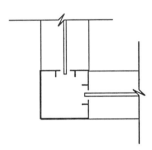

CORNER MULLION
Single Glazed
08411-5

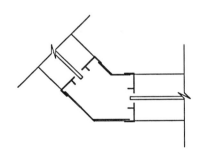

ANGLE CORNER MULLION
Single Glazed
08411-7

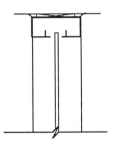

MULLION @ WALL
08411-9
MULLION HEAD
Single Glazed   08411-17

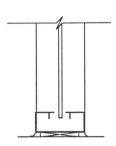

MULLION BASE
Single Glazed
08411-11

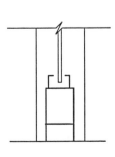

BASE @ SIDE LIGHT
Single Glazed
08411-13

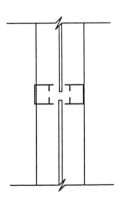

HORIZONTAL GLAZING BAR
Single Glazed
08411-15

08411 STOREFRONT WINDOWS

FULL-SCALE GENERIC DETAILS

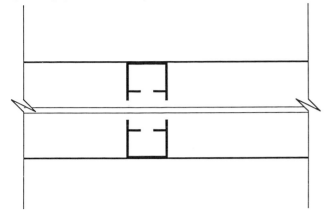

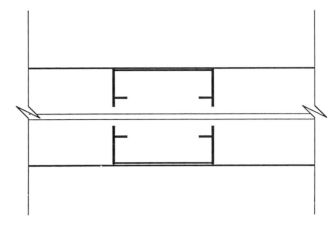

VERTICAL GLAZING BAR Single Glazed
3"=1'-0"   08411-1

MULLION Single Glazed
3"=1'-0"   08411-3

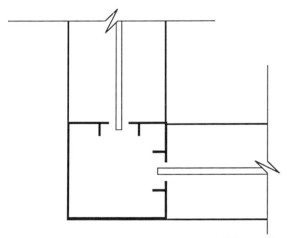

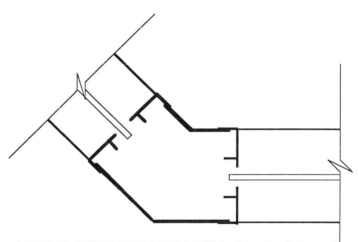

CORNER MULLION Single Glazed
3"=1'-0"   08411-5

ANGLE CORNER MULLION Single Glazed
3"=1'-0"   08411-7

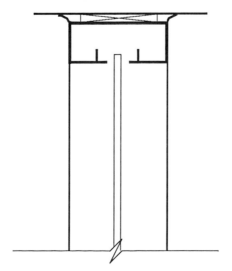

MULLION @ WALL 08411-9
MULLION HEAD   08411-17
Single Glazed 3"=1'-0"

08412 STOREFRONT WINDOWS

FULL-SCALE GENERIC DETAILS

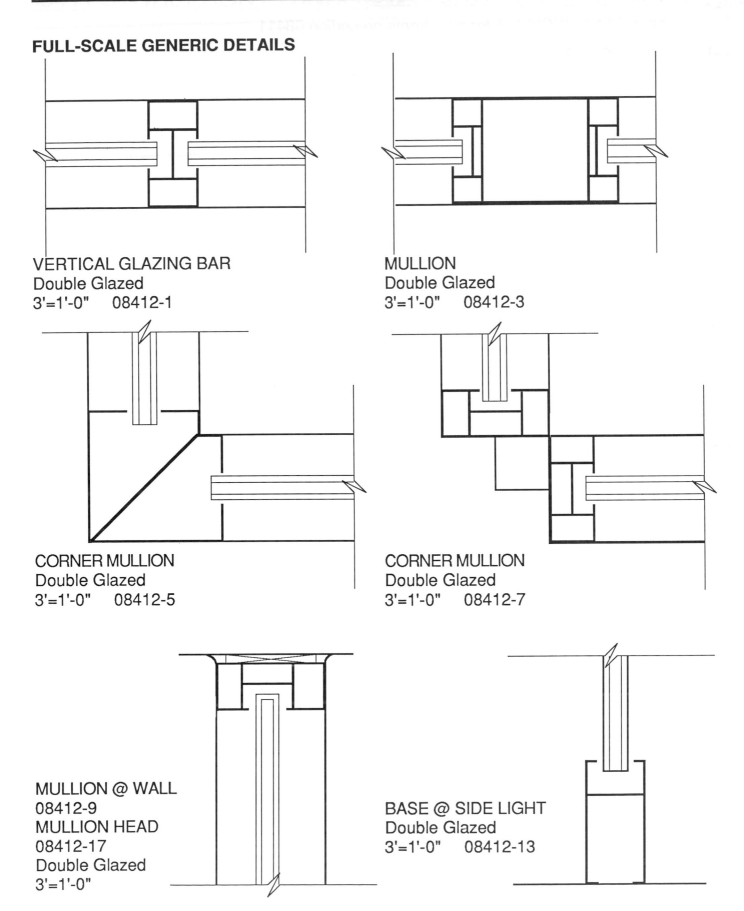

VERTICAL GLAZING BAR
Double Glazed
3'=1'-0"   08412-1

MULLION
Double Glazed
3'=1'-0"   08412-3

CORNER MULLION
Double Glazed
3'=1'-0"   08412-5

CORNER MULLION
Double Glazed
3'=1'-0"   08412-7

MULLION @ WALL
08412-9
MULLION HEAD
08412-17
Double Glazed
3'=1'-0"

BASE @ SIDE LIGHT
Double Glazed
3'=1'-0"   08412-13

08412 STOREFRONT WINDOWS

FULL-SCALE GENERIC DETAILS continued

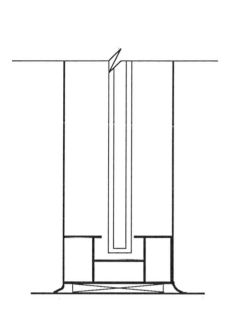

MULLION BASE
Double Glazed
3" = 1'-0"   08412-11

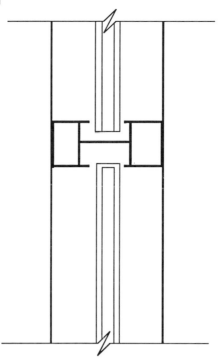

HORIZONTAL GLAZING BAR
Double Glazed
3" = 1'-0"   08412-15

NOTATION CHECKLIST,
SAMPLE NOTES

FRAME TYPE, MATERIAL & SIZE
GLAZING: SINGLE/DOUBLE
GASKET
BEAD
SHIM SPACE
CAULKING
WALL CONSTRUCTION
ANCHORS
ADJACENT FINISHES

FLOOR MATERIAL
HOLLOW METAL FRAME
BASE ANCHOR
STOPS
SINGLE GLAZING
THERMOPANE INSULATING
GLASS
FRAMING
HEADER

08413 STOREFRONT WINDOWS

See DETAIL DATA CHECKLIST for storefronts preceding 08411

SMALL-SCALE GENERIC DETAILS

MULLION @ WALL
08413-3
MULLION HEAD
08413-9
Single Glazed

MULLION BASE
Single Glazed
08413-5

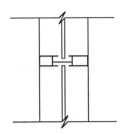

HORIZONTAL
GLAZING BAR
Single Glazed
08413-7

FULL-SCALE GENERIC DETAILS

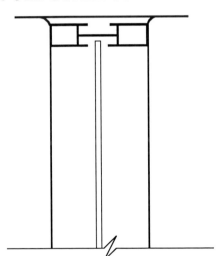

MULLION @ WALL 08413-3
MULLION HEAD 08413-9
Single Glazed   3'=1'-0"

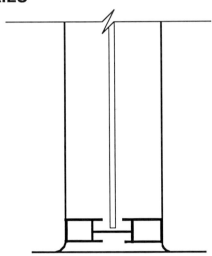

MULLION BASE
Single Glazed
3'=1'-0"   08413-5

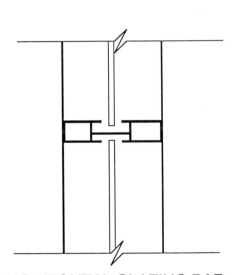

HORIZONTAL GLAZING BAR
Single Glazed
3'=1'-0"   08413-7

NOTATION CHECKLIST, SAMPLE NOTES

FRAME TYPE, MATERIAL & SIZE
GLAZING: SINGLE/DOUBLE
GASKET
BEAD
SHIM SPACE
CAULKING
WALL CONSTRUCTION
ANCHORS
ADJACENT FINISHES

FLOOR MATERIAL
HOLLOW METAL FRAME
BASE ANCHOR
STOPS
SINGLE GLAZING
THERMOPANE INSULATING
GLASS
FRAMING
HEADER

08421 STOREFRONT DOORS

See DETAIL DATA CHECKLIST for storefronts preceding 08411

SMALL-SCALE GENERIC DETAILS

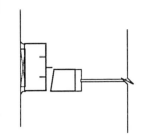

JAMB @ WALL
Single Acting
08421-1

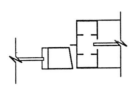

JAMB @ SIDE LIGHT
Single Acting
08421-3

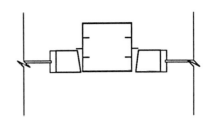

MULLION JAMB
Single Acting
08421-5

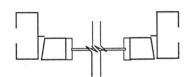

MULLION JAMBS
Single Acting
08421-7

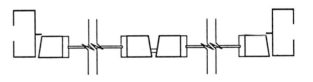

MULLION JAMBS
Paired Single Acting
08421-9

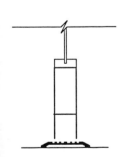

SILL
Single Acting
08421-11

HEAD
Single Acting
08421-13

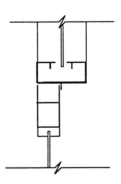

HEAD @ TRANSOM
Single Acting
08421-15

08421 STOREFRONT DOORS

FULL-SCALE GENERIC DETAILS

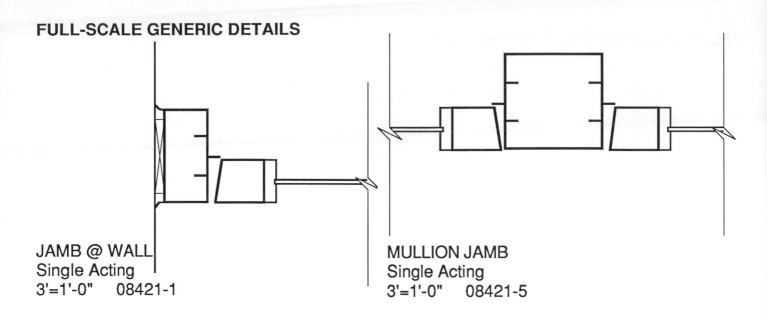

JAMB @ WALL
Single Acting
3'=1'-0"   08421-1

MULLION JAMB
Single Acting
3'=1'-0"   08421-5

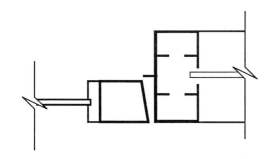

JAMB @ SIDE LIGHT
Single Acting
3'=1'-0"   08421-3

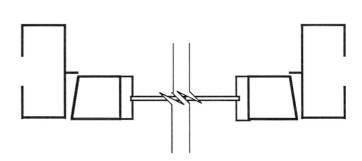

MULLION JAMBS
Single Acting
3'=1'-0"   08421-7

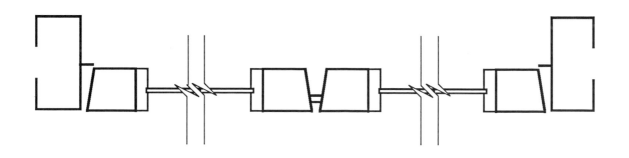

MULLION JAMBS
Paired Single Acting
3'=1'-0"   08421-9

08421 STOREFRONT DOORS

FULL-SCALE GENERIC DETAILS continued

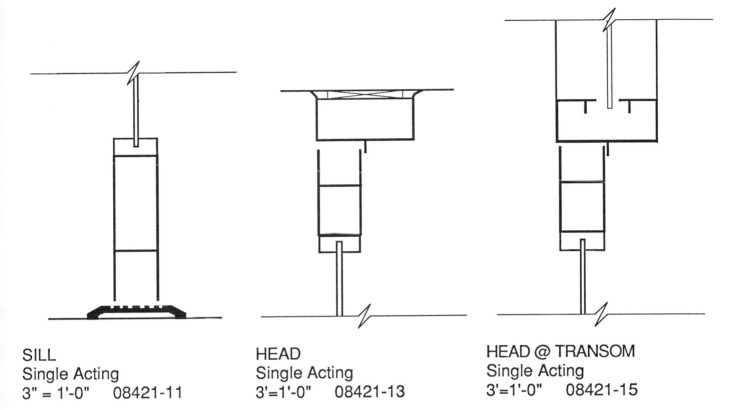

SILL
Single Acting
3" = 1'-0"   08421-11

HEAD
Single Acting
3'=1'-0"   08421-13

HEAD @ TRANSOM
Single Acting
3'=1'-0"   08421-15

NOTATION CHECKLIST,
SAMPLE NOTES

SINGLE GLAZED DOOR
THRESHOLD SET IN FULL BED BED OF
CAULKING
DOOR SWEEP
WEATHERSTRIPPING @ HEAD & JAMB
JAMB STIFFENERS, FULL HT. OF JAMB
FLOOR MATERIAL
HOLLOW METAL FRAME
BASE ANCHOR
STOPS
SINGLE GLAZING
THERMOPANE INSULATING GLASS
FRAMING
HEADER

WALL CONSTRUCTION
ANCHORS
ADJACENT FINISHES
SHIM SPACE
CAULKING
FRAME TYPE, MATERIAL & SIZE
DOOR FRAME
BEAD
GLAZING: SINGLE/DOUBLE
GASKET
BRACING

08422 STOREFRONT DOORS

See DETAIL DATA CHECKLIST for storefronts preceding 08411

SMALL-SCALE GENERIC DETAILS

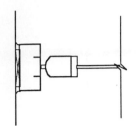

JAMB @ WALL
Double Acting
08422-1

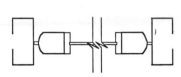

JAMB @ SIDE LIGHT
Double Acting
08422-3

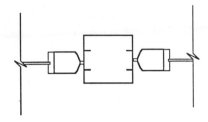

MULLION JAMB
Double Acting
08422-5

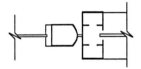

MULLION JAMBS
Double Acting
08422-7

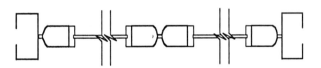

MULLION JAMBS
Paired Double Acting
08422-9

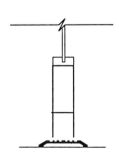

SILL
Double Acting
08422-11

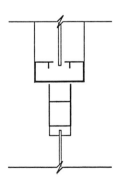

HEAD @ TRANSOM
Double Acting
08422-13

HEAD
Double Acting
08422-13

08422 STOREFRONT DOORS

FULL-SCALE GENERIC DETAILS

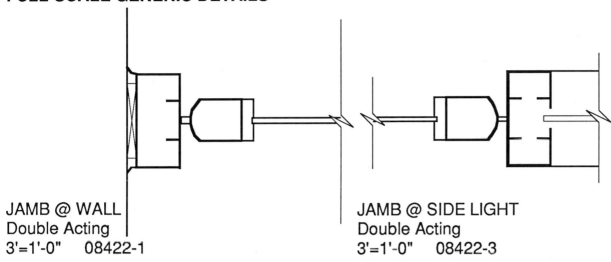

JAMB @ WALL
Double Acting
3'=1'-0"   08422-1

JAMB @ SIDE LIGHT
Double Acting
3'=1'-0"   08422-3

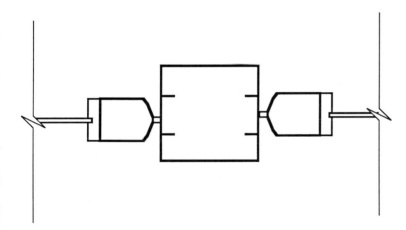

MULLION JAMB
Double Acting
3'=1'-0"   08422-5

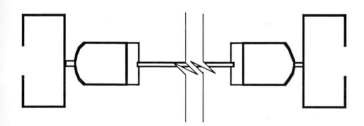

MULLION JAMBS
Double Acting
3'=1'-0"   08422-7

08422 STOREFRONT DOORS

FULL-SCALE GENERIC DETAILS continued

MULLION JAMBS
Paired Double Acting
3'=1'-0"   08422-9

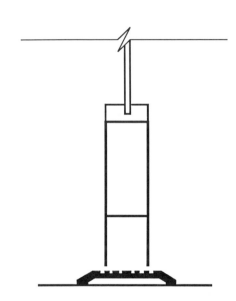

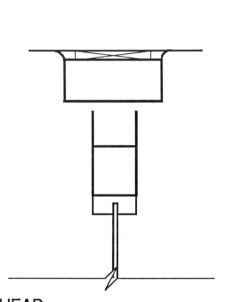

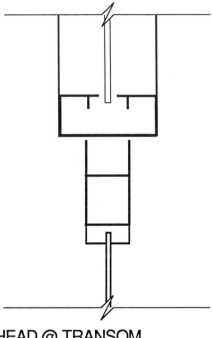

SILL
Double Acting
3'=1'-0"   08422-11

HEAD
Double Acting
3'=1'-0"   08422-13

HEAD @ TRANSOM
Double Acting
3'=1'-0"   08422-15

NOTATION CHECKLIST,
SAMPLE NOTES

WALL CONSTRUCTION
ANCHORS
ADJACENT FINISHES
SHIM SPACE
CAULKING
FRAME TYPE, MATERIAL & SIZE
DOOR FRAME
BEAD
GLAZING: SINGLE/DOUBLE
GASKET
BRACING

SINGLE GLAZED DOOR
THRESHOLD SET IN FULL BED OF CAULKING
DOOR SWEEP
WEATHERSTRIPPING @ HEAD & JAMB
JAMB STIFFENERS, FULL HT. OF JAMB
FLOOR MATERIAL
HOLLOW METAL FRAME
BASE ANCHOR
STOPS
SINGLE GLAZING
THERMOPANE INSULATING GLASS
FRAMING
HEADER

08423 STOREFRONT DOORS

See DETAIL DATA CHECKLIST for storefronts preceding 08411

SMALL-SCALE GENERIC DETAILS

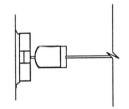

JAMB @ WALL
(Narrow) Double Acting
08423-1

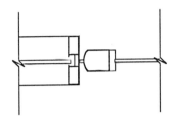

JAMB @ WALL
(Narrow) Double Acting
08423-3

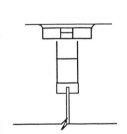

HEAD
(Narrow) Double Acting
08423-5

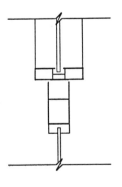

HEAD @ TRANSOM
(Narrow) Double Acting
08423-7

08423 STOREFRONT DOORS

FULL-SCALE GENERIC DETAILS

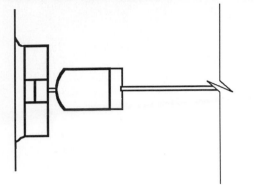

JAMB @ WALL
(Narrow) Double Acting
3'=1'-0"   08423-1

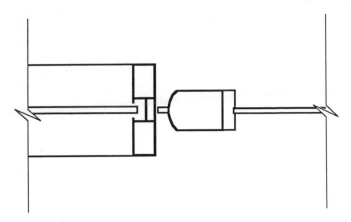

JAMB @ WALL
(Narrow) Double Acting
3'=1'-0"   08423-3

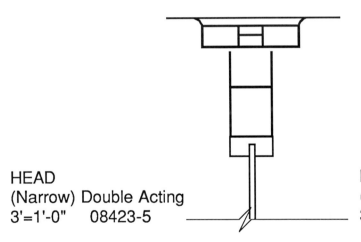

HEAD
(Narrow) Double Acting
3'=1'-0"   08423-5

HEAD @ TRANSOM
(Narrow) Double Acting
3'=1'-0"   08423-7

NOTATION CHECKLIST, SAMPLE NOTES

WALL CONSTRUCTION
ANCHORS
ADJACENT FINISHES
SHIM SPACE
CAULKING
FRAME TYPE, MATERIAL & SIZE
DOOR FRAME
BEAD
GLAZING: SINGLE/DOUBLE
GASKET
BRACING

SINGLE GLAZED DOOR
THRESHOLD SET IN FULL BED OF CAULKING
DOOR SWEEP
WEATHERSTRIPPING @ HEAD & JAMB
JAMB STIFFENERS, FULL HT. OF JAMB
FLOOR MATERIAL
HOLLOW METAL FRAME
BASE ANCHOR
STOPS
SINGLE GLAZING
THERMOPANE INSULATING GLASS
FRAMING
HEADER

08425 STOREFRONT AUTOMATIC DOORS

DETAIL DATA CHECKLIST

AUTOMATIC DOORS

__See manufacturer's catalogs for standard sizes, finishes, and materials.
__Detail drawings are included mainly to show special anchoring conditions--screws, anchor bolts,
    etc., in wood frame, metal frame, masonry, or concrete construction.
__See manufacturers' and suppliers' catalogs for detail design data and specifications.
__See manufacturer's recommendations for special anchor requirements for different kinds of construction.

SMALL-SCALE GENERIC DETAILS

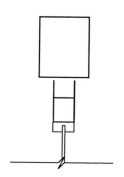

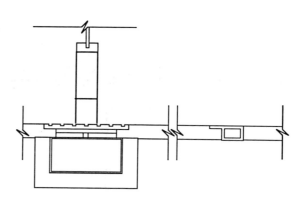

HEAD @ AUTOMATIC DOOR CLOSER
08425-3

SILL Double Acting
08422-11

08425 STOREFRONT AUTOMATIC DOORS

FULL-SCALE GENERIC DETAILS

NOTATION CHECKLIST

DOOR GLAZING
DOOR FRAME
THRESHOLD
RECESSED MAT
AUTOMATIC DOOR OPERATOR
CONCRETE SLAB RECESS

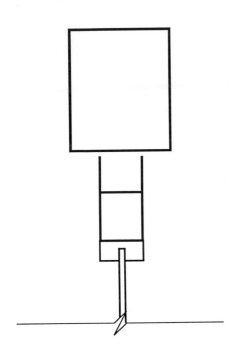

HEAD @ AUTOMATIC DOOR CLOSER
3'=1'-0"   08425-3

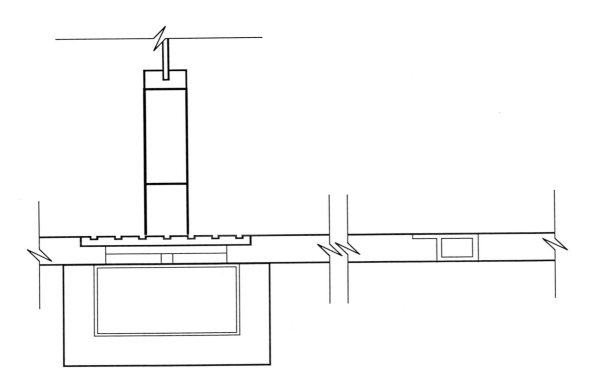

SILL Double Acting
3'=1'-0"   08422-11

COMPOSITE MASTER DETAIL

DETAIL FILE NUMBER: 08511-1-4

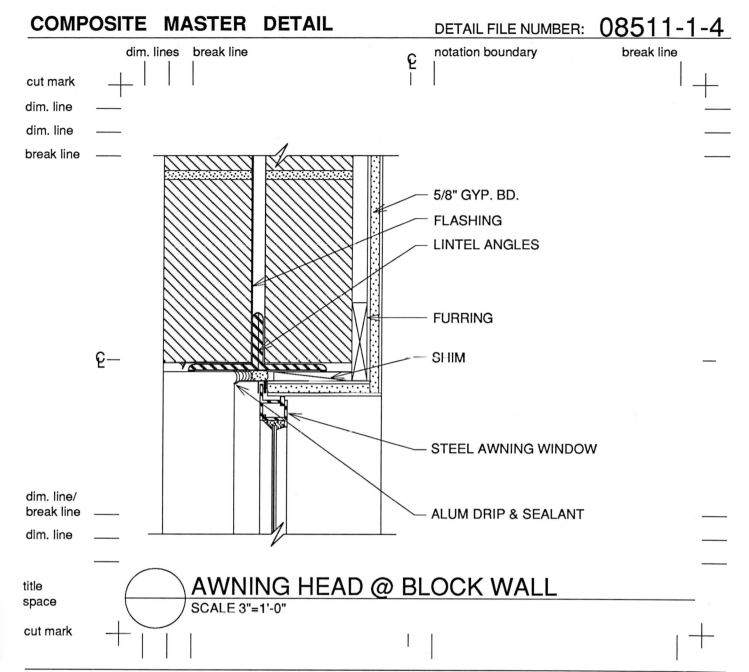

dim. lines   break line   notation boundary   break line

cut mark

dim. line

dim. line

break line

— 5/8" GYP. BD.

— FLASHING

— LINTEL ANGLES

— FURRING

— SHIM

— STEEL AWNING WINDOW

dim. line/
break line

dim. line

— ALUM DRIP & SEALANT

title
space

AWNING HEAD @ BLOCK WALL
SCALE 3"=1'-0"

cut mark

DETAIL INFORMATION
References, jobsite feedback, job history

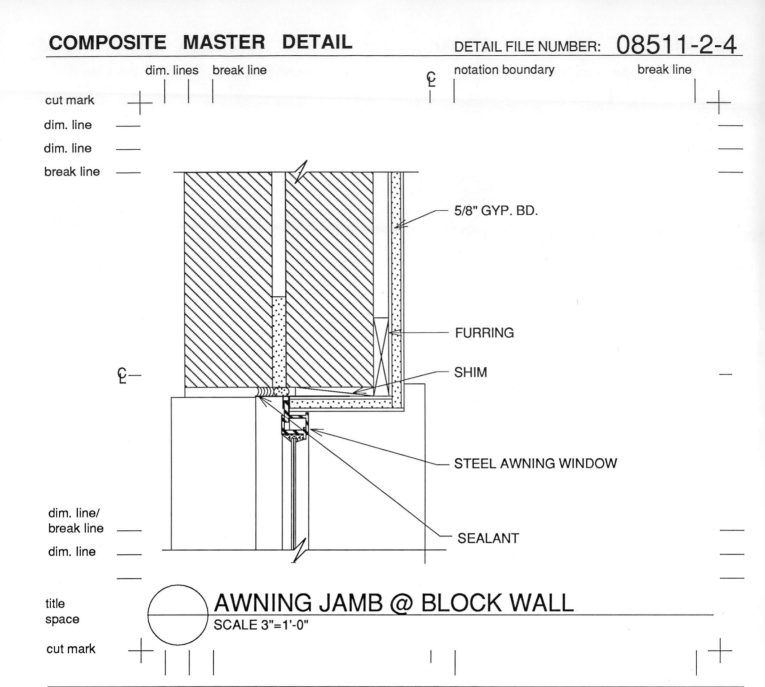

cut mark

dim. line

dim. line

break line

5/8" GYP. BD.

FURRING

SHIM

STEEL AWNING WINDOW

dim. line/
break line

dim. line

SEALANT

title
space

AWNING JAMB @ BLOCK WALL
SCALE 3"=1'-0"

cut mark

DETAIL INFORMATION
References, jobsite feedback, job history

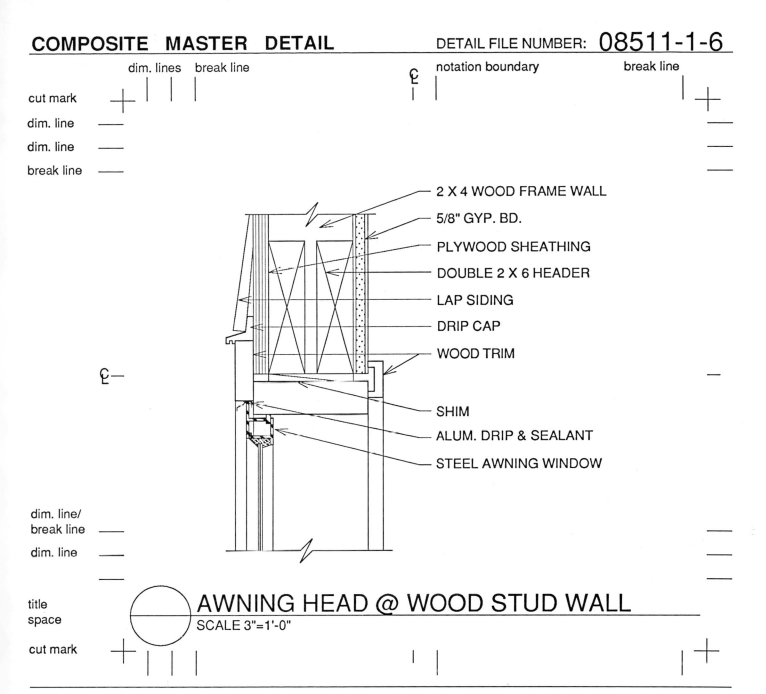

cut mark

dim. lines | break line

notation boundary | break line

cut mark
dim. line
dim. line
break line

2 X 4 WOOD FRAME WALL
5/8" GYP. BD.
PLYWOOD SHEATHING
DOUBLE 2 X 6 HEADER
LAP SIDING
DRIP CAP
WOOD TRIM
SHIM
ALUM. DRIP & SEALANT
STEEL AWNING WINDOW

dim. line/
break line
dim. line

title
space

AWNING HEAD @ WOOD STUD WALL
SCALE 3"=1'-0"

cut mark

DETAIL INFORMATION
References, jobsite feedback, job history

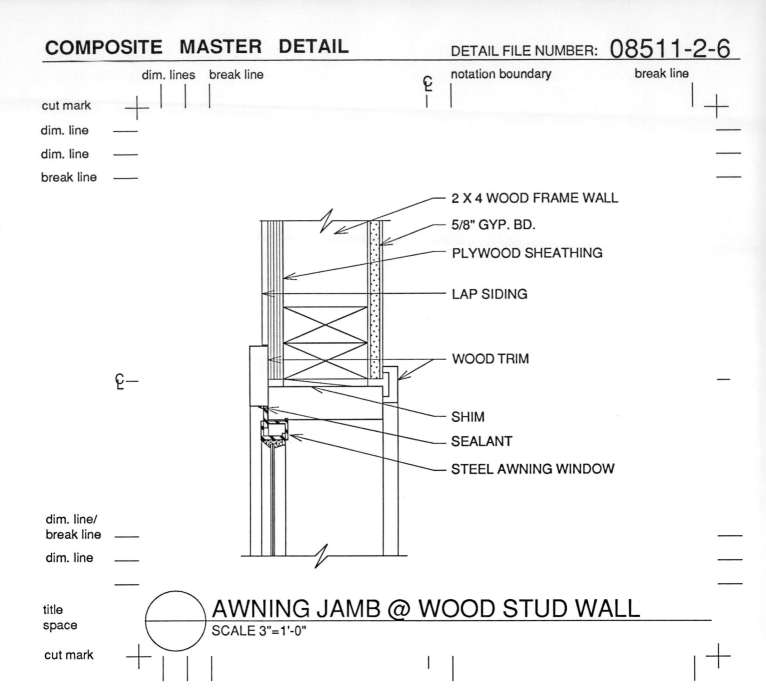

dim. lines   break line

notation boundary

break line

cut mark

dim. line

dim. line

break line

2 X 4 WOOD FRAME WALL

5/8" GYP. BD.

PLYWOOD SHEATHING

LAP SIDING

WOOD TRIM

SHIM

SEALANT

STEEL AWNING WINDOW

dim. line/
break line

dim. line

title
space

AWNING JAMB @ WOOD STUD WALL
SCALE 3"=1'-0"

cut mark

DETAIL INFORMATION
References, jobsite feedback, job history

COMPOSITE MASTER DETAIL

DETAIL FILE NUMBER: **08511-3-6**

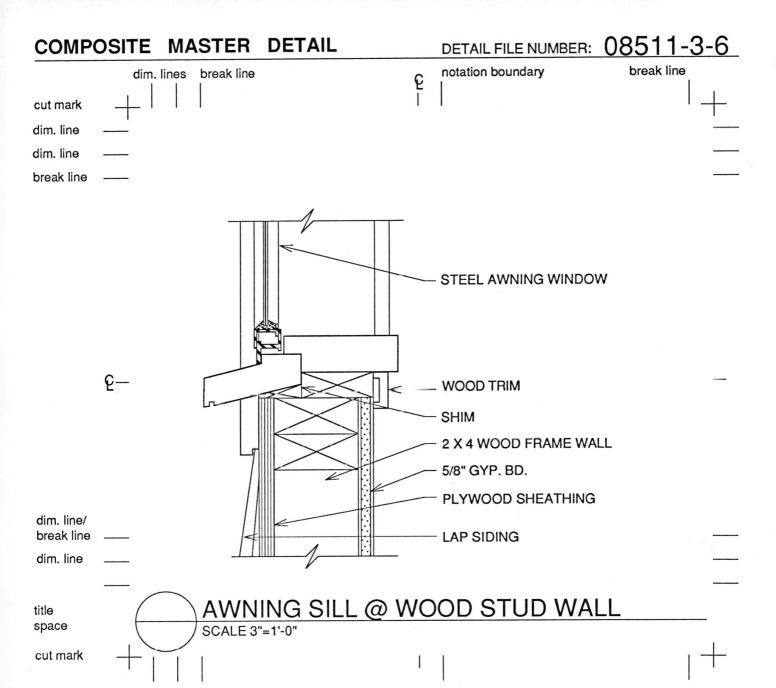

cut mark
dim. line
dim. line
break line

dim. lines break line

notation boundary break line

STEEL AWNING WINDOW

WOOD TRIM

SHIM

2 X 4 WOOD FRAME WALL

5/8" GYP. BD.

PLYWOOD SHEATHING

LAP SIDING

dim. line/
break line

dim. line

title
space

cut mark

AWNING SILL @ WOOD STUD WALL
SCALE 3"=1'-0"

DETAIL INFORMATION
References, jobsite feedback, job history

08512 STEEL CASEMENT WINDOWS

DETAIL DATA CHECKLIST

STEEL CASEMENT WINDOWS

Note: You can combine these generic window details with varied exterior wall construction details in this book to create many hundreds of possible special combinations.

__See manufacturers' and suppliers' catalogs for standard sizes, detail design data, materials, and finishes.
__Detail drawings are required mainly to show the relationship of windows to wall construction such as connections to wood frame, masonry, or concrete wall construction.
__Details or window schedules should show rough-opening sizes and shim tolerance allowances (1/2" all around is a common allowance for shim space).
__Details should show flashing and caulking at heads, jambs, and sills.
__See manufacturers' recommendations for connections to varied wall construction.
__See the Detail Data Checklist for Windows and Glazing at the beginning of this chapter for more information.

SMALL-SCALE GENERIC DETAILS

Steel Casement -- Single Glazed

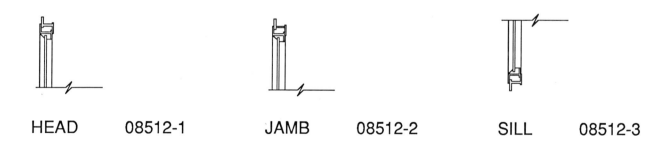

HEAD   08512-1   JAMB   08512-2   SILL   08512-3

Steel Casement -- Double Glazed

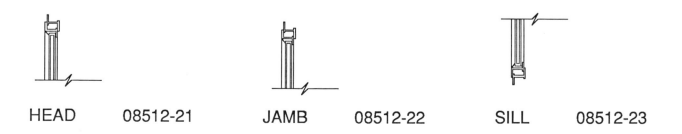

HEAD   08512-21   JAMB   08512-22   SILL   08512-23

08512 STEEL CASEMENT WINDOWS

FULL-SCALE GENERIC DETAILS
Steel Casement -- Single Glazed

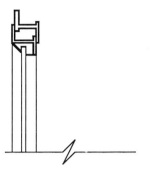

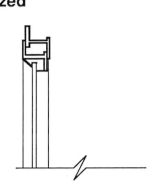

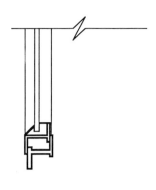

HEAD   3"=1'-0"
08512-1

JAMB   3"=1'-0"
08512-2

SILL   3"=1'-0"
08512-3

Steel Casement -- Double Glazed

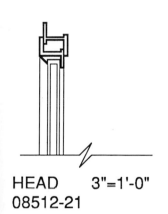

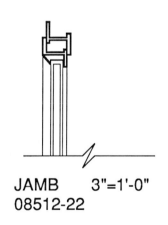

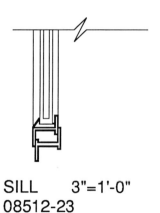

HEAD   3"=1'-0"
08512-21

JAMB   3"=1'-0"
08512-22

SILL   3"=1'-0"
08512-23

NOTATION CHECKLIST, SAMPLE NOTES

WALL CONSTRUCTION
SHIM SPACE
DRIP CAP/WEATHERSTRIPPING/FLASHING
CAULKING/GROUT
FINISH HEAD/SILL/JAMB
WINDOW TYPE, MATERIAL & FINISH
HARDWARE/OPERATOR
VENT/WEEP HOLE/WIND GUARD
GLAZING: SINGLE/DOUBLE/REMOVABLE
SCREEN/SCREEN FRAME
CASING/TRIM/ADJACENT FINISH
ROUGH OPENING/FINISH OPENING

STEEL WINDOW SYSTEM
METAL SILL BELOW
THERMOPANE INSULATING GLASS
SINGLE PANE GLASS
HEAD, SEALANT BOTH SIDES
SILL W/SEALANT EACH SIDE
WOOD NAILER
TREATED BLOCKING
1 X   WOOD TRIM
METAL EDGE BEAD
STUD
FLASHING
SEALANT

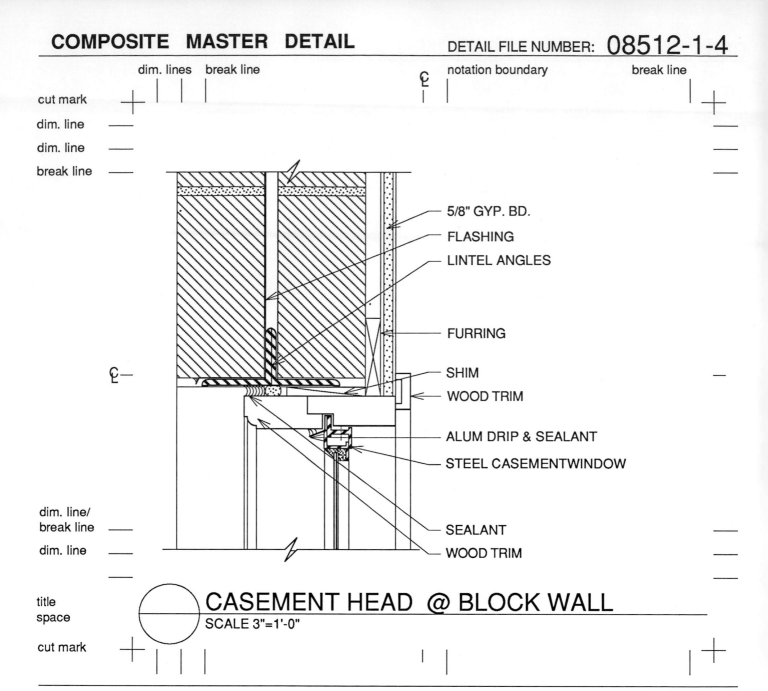

cut mark

dim. lines   break line   notation boundary   break line

dim. line

dim. line

break line

5/8" GYP. BD.

FLASHING

LINTEL ANGLES

FURRING

SHIM

WOOD TRIM

ALUM DRIP & SEALANT

STEEL CASEMENTWINDOW

dim. line/
break line

dim. line

SEALANT

WOOD TRIM

title
space

CASEMENT HEAD @ BLOCK WALL
SCALE 3"=1'-0"

cut mark

DETAIL INFORMATION
References, jobsite feedback, job history

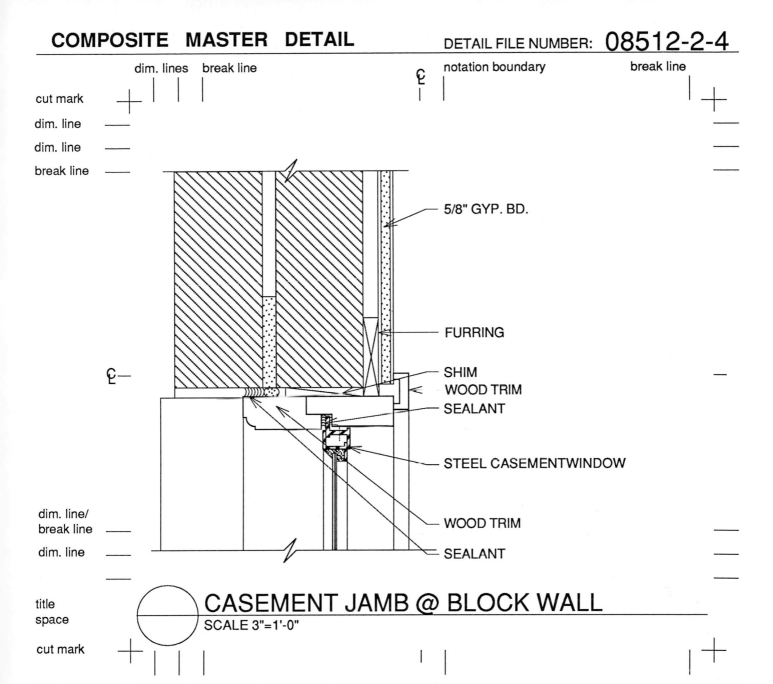

dim. lines   break line

notation boundary   break line

cut mark

dim. line

dim. line

break line

5/8" GYP. BD.

FURRING

SHIM
WOOD TRIM
SEALANT

STEEL CASEMENTWINDOW

WOOD TRIM

SEALANT

dim. line/
break line

dim. line

title
space

CASEMENT JAMB @ BLOCK WALL
SCALE 3"=1'-0"

cut mark

DETAIL INFORMATION
References, jobsite feedback, job history

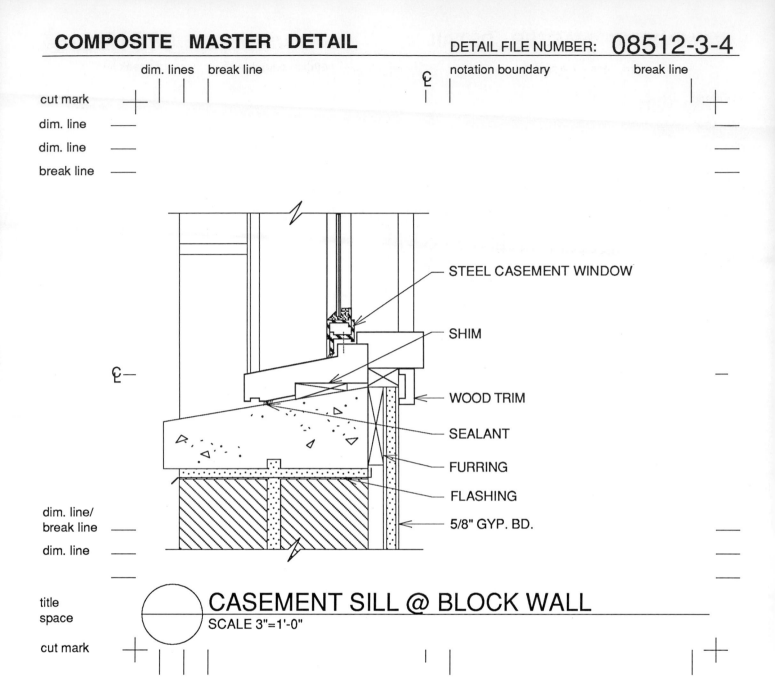

dim. lines   break line

notation boundary   break line

cut mark

dim. line

dim. line

break line

STEEL CASEMENT WINDOW

SHIM

WOOD TRIM

SEALANT

FURRING

FLASHING

5/8" GYP. BD.

dim. line/
break line

dim. line

title
space

CASEMENT SILL @ BLOCK WALL
SCALE 3"=1'-0"

cut mark

DETAIL INFORMATION
References, jobsite feedback, job history

COMPOSITE MASTER DETAIL

DETAIL FILE NUMBER: 08512-1-6

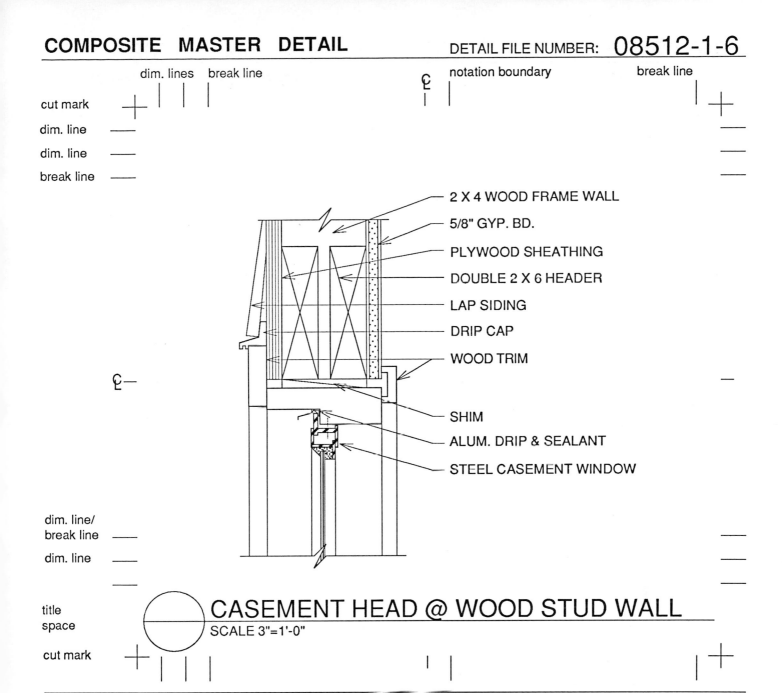

cut mark

dim. lines   break line

dim. line

dim. line

break line

notation boundary

break line

2 X 4 WOOD FRAME WALL

5/8" GYP. BD.

PLYWOOD SHEATHING

DOUBLE 2 X 6 HEADER

LAP SIDING

DRIP CAP

WOOD TRIM

SHIM

ALUM. DRIP & SEALANT

STEEL CASEMENT WINDOW

dim. line/
break line

dim. line

title
space

CASEMENT HEAD @ WOOD STUD WALL
SCALE 3"=1'-0"

cut mark

DETAIL INFORMATION
References, jobsite feedback, job history

dim. lines   break line

notation boundary   break line

cut mark

dim. line

dim. line

break line

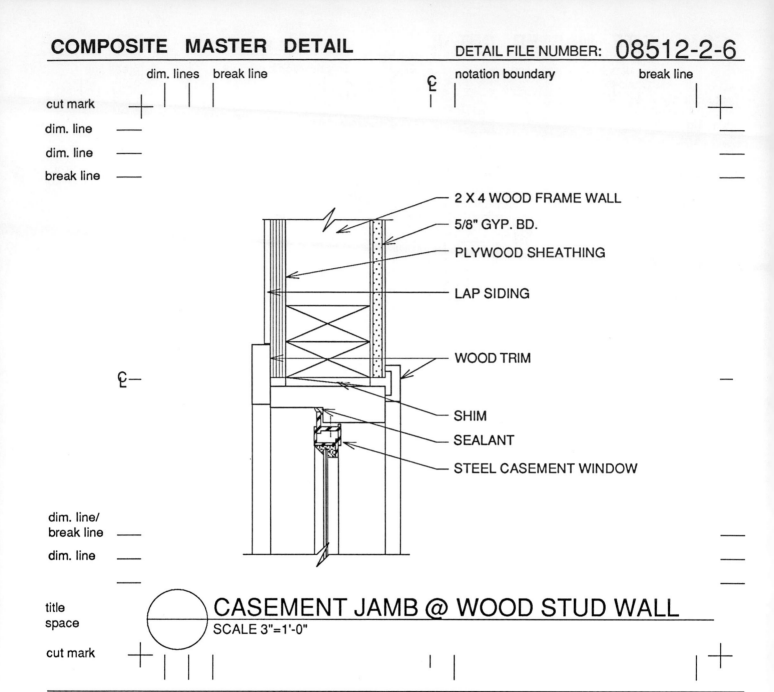

2 X 4 WOOD FRAME WALL

5/8" GYP. BD.

PLYWOOD SHEATHING

LAP SIDING

WOOD TRIM

SHIM

SEALANT

STEEL CASEMENT WINDOW

dim. line/
break line

dim. line

title
space

CASEMENT JAMB @ WOOD STUD WALL

SCALE 3"=1'-0"

cut mark

DETAIL INFORMATION
References, jobsite feedback, job history

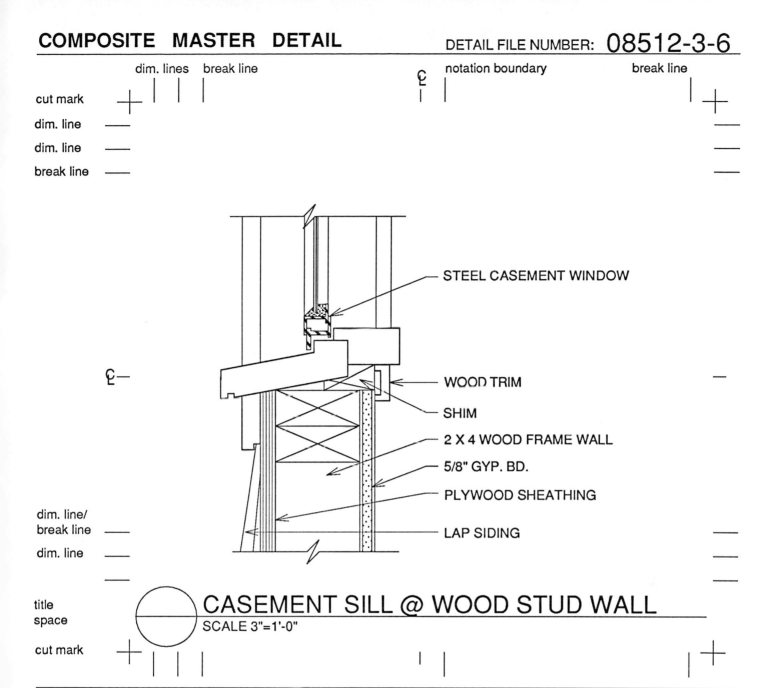

dim. lines   break line

notation boundary   break line

cut mark

dim. line

dim. line

break line

STEEL CASEMENT WINDOW

WOOD TRIM

SHIM

2 X 4 WOOD FRAME WALL

5/8" GYP. BD.

PLYWOOD SHEATHING

dim. line/
break line

LAP SIDING

dim. line

title
space

CASEMENT SILL @ WOOD STUD WALL

SCALE 3"=1'-0"

cut mark

DETAIL INFORMATION
References, jobsite feedback, job history

08515 STEEL PIVOTED WINDOWS

DETAIL DATA CHECKLIST

STEEL PIVOTED WINDOWS

Note: You can combine these generic window details with varied exterior wall construction details in this book
to create many hundreds of possible special combinations.

__See manufacturers' and suppliers' catalogs for standard sizes, detail design data, materials, and finishes.
__Detail drawings are required mainly to show the relationship of windows to wall construction such as
connections to wood frame, masonry, or concrete wall construction.
__Details or window schedules should show rough-opening sizes and shim tolerance allowances
(1/2" all around is a common allowance for shim space).
__Details should show flashing and caulking at heads, jambs, and sills.
__See manufacturers' recommendations for connections to varied wall construction.
__See the Detail Data Checklist for Windows and Glazing at the beginning of this chapter for more information.

SMALL-SCALE GENERIC DETAILS

Steel Pivoted -- Single Glazed

HEAD   08515-1   JAMB   08515-2   SILL   08515-3

Steel Pivoted -- Double Glazed

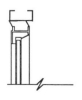

HEAD   08515-21   JAMB   08515-22   SILL   08515-23

08515 STEEL PIVOTED WINDOWS

FULL-SCALE GENERIC DETAILS

Steel Pivoted -- Single Glazed

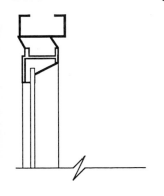

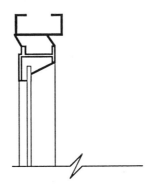

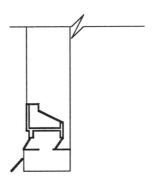

HEAD   3"=1'-0"
08515-1

JAMB   3"=1'-0"
08515-2

SILL   3"=1'-0"
08515-3

Steel Pivoted -- Double Glazed

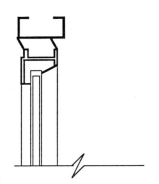

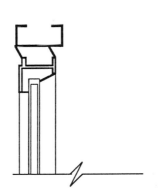

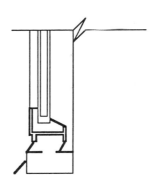

HEAD   3"=1'-0"
08515-21

JAMB   3"=1'-0"
08515-22

SILL   3"=1'-0"
08515-23

NOTATION CHECKLIST, SAMPLE NOTES

WALL CONSTRUCTION
SHIM SPACE
DRIP CAP/WEATHERSTRIPPING/FLASHING
CAULKING/GROUT
FINISH HEAD/SILL/JAMB
WINDOW TYPE, MATERIAL & FINISH
HARDWARE/OPERATOR
VENT/WEEP HOLE/WIND GUARD
GLAZING: SINGLE/DOUBLE/REMOVABLE
SCREEN/SCREEN FRAME
CASING/TRIM/ADJACENT FINISH
ROUGH OPENING/FINISH OPENING

STEEL WINDOW SYSTEM
METAL SILL BELOW
THERMOPANE INSULATING GLASS
SINGLE PANE GLASS
HEAD, SEALANT BOTH SIDES
SILL W/SEALANT EACH SIDE
WOOD NAILER
TREATED BLOCKING
1 X   WOOD TRIM
METAL EDGE BEAD
STUD
FLASHING
SEALANT

08521, 08522 ALUMINUM AWNING & CASEMENT WINDOWS

DETAIL DATA CHECKLIST

ALUMINUM AWNING & CASEMENT WINDOWS

Note: You can combine these generic window details with varied exterior wall construction details in this book to create many hundreds of possible special combinations.

__See manufacturers' and suppliers' catalogs for standard sizes, detail design data, materials, and finishes.
__Detail drawings are required mainly to show the relationship of windows to wall construction such as connections to wood frame, masonry, or concrete wall construction.
__Details or window schedules should show rough-opening sizes and shim tolerance allowances (1/2" all around is a common allowance for shim space).
__Details should show flashing and caulking at heads, jambs, and sills.
__See manufacturers' recommendations for connections to varied wall construction.
__See the Detail Data Checklist for Windows and Glazing at the beginning of this chapter for more information.

SMALL-SCALE GENERIC DETAILS

Aluminum Awning Window -- Single Glazed

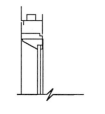   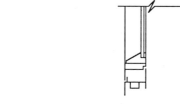

HEAD   08521-1   JAMB   08521-2   SILL   08521-3

Aluminum Awning Window -- Double Glazed

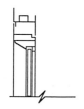   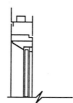

HEAD   08521-21   JAMB   08521-22   SILL   08521-23

Aluminum Casement -- Single Glazed

HEAD   08522-1   JAMB   08522-2   SILL   08522-3

08521, 08522 ALUMINUM AWNING & CASEMENT WINDOWS

SMALL-SCALE GENERIC DETAILS continued
Aluminum Casement -- Double Glazed

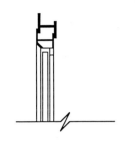

HEAD   3"=1'-0"
08522-21

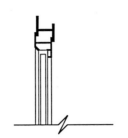

JAMB   3"=1'-0"
08522-22

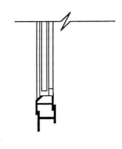

SILL
08522-23

FULL-SCALE GENERIC DETAILS
Aluminum Awning Window -- Single Glazed

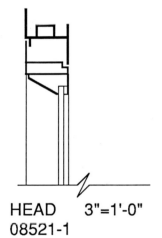

HEAD   3"=1'-0"
08521-1

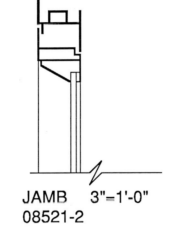

JAMB   3"=1'-0"
08521-2

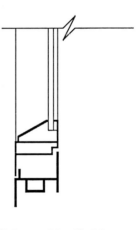

SILL   3"=1'-0"
08521-3

Aluminum Awning Window -- Double Glazed

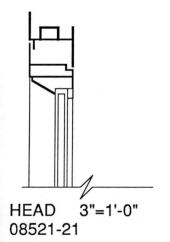

HEAD   3"=1'-0"
08521-21

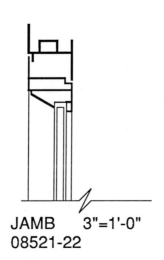

JAMB   3"=1'-0"
08521-22

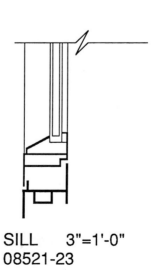

SILL   3"=1'-0"
08521-23

08521, 08522 ALUMINUM AWNING & CASEMENT WINDOWS

FULL-SCALE GENERIC DETAILS continued
Aluminum Casement -- Single Glazed

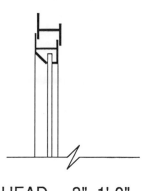

HEAD   3"=1'-0"
08522-1

JAMB   3"=1'-0"
08522-2

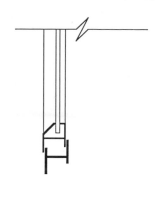

SILL
08522-3

Aluminum Casement -- Double Glazed

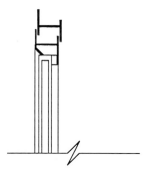

HEAD   3"=1'-0"
08522-21

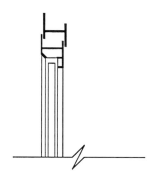

JAMB   3"=1'-0"
08522-22

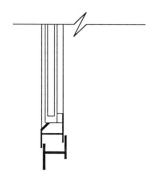

SILL
08522-23

NOTATION CHECKLIST, SAMPLE NOTES

WALL CONSTRUCTION
SHIM SPACE
DRIP CAP/WEATHERSTRIPPING/FLASHING
CAULKING/GROUT
FINISH HEAD/SILL/JAMB
WINDOW TYPE, MATERIAL & FINISH
HARDWARE/OPERATOR
VENT/WEEP HOLE/WIND GUARD
GLAZING: SINGLE/DOUBLE/REMOVABLE
SCREEN/SCREEN FRAME
CASING/TRIM/ADJACENT FINISH
ROUGH OPENING/FINISH OPENING

ANODIZED ALUM. TRIM
1/4" TEMP. GLASS
EXTRUDED ALUM. SILL TO MATCH WINDOW
METAL SILL BELOW
THERMOPANE INSULATING GLASS
SINGLE PANE GLASS
ALUM. HEAD, SEALANT BOTH SIDES
ALUM. SILL W/SEALANT EACH SIDE
WOOD NAILER
TREATED BLOCKING
1 X   WOOD TRIM
METAL EDGE BEAD
STUD
GYPSUM WALLBOARD
FLASHING
SEALANT

08523 ALUMINUM DOUBLE HUNG WINDOWS

DETAIL DATA CHECKLIST

ALUMINUM DOUBLE HUNG WINDOWS

Note: You can combine these generic window details with varied exterior wall construction details in this book to create many hundreds of possible special combinations.

__See manufacturers' and suppliers' catalogs for standard sizes, detail design data, materials, and finishes.
__Detail drawings are required mainly to show the relationship of windows to wall construction such as connections to wood frame, masonry, or concrete wall construction.
__Details or window schedules should show rough-opening sizes and shim tolerance allowances (1/2" all around is a common allowance for shim space).
__Details should show flashing and caulking at heads, jambs, and sills.
__See manufacturers' recommendations for connections to varied wall construction.
__See the Detail Data Checklist for Windows and Glazing at the beginning of this chapter for more information.

SMALL-SCALE GENERIC DETAILS
Aluminum Double Hung -- Single Glazed

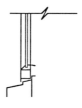

HEAD   08523-1   JAMB   08523-2   SILL   08523-3

Aluminum Double Hung -- Double Glazed

HEAD   08523-21   JAMB   08523-22   SILL   08523-23

08523 ALUMINUM DOUBLE HUNG WINDOWS

FULL-SCALE GENERIC DETAILS
Aluminum Double Hung -- Single Glazed

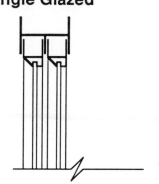

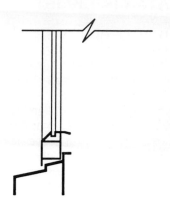

HEAD   3"=1'-0"
08523-1

JAMB   3"=1'-0"
08523-2

SILL   3"=1'-0"
08523-3

Aluminum Double Hung -- Double Glazed

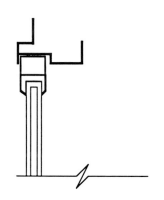

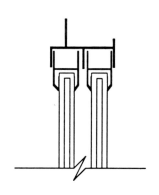

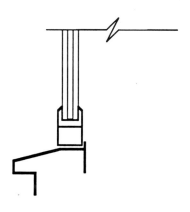

HEAD   3"=1'-0"
08523-21

JAMB   3"=1'-0"
08523-22

SILL   3"=1'-0"
08523-23

08523 ALUMINUM DOUBLE HUNG WINDOWS

NOTATION CHECKLIST, SAMPLE NOTES

WALL CONSTRUCTION
SHIM SPACE
DRIP CAP/WEATHERSTRIPPING/FLASHING
CAULKING/GROUT
FINISH HEAD/SILL/JAMB
WINDOW TYPE, MATERIAL & FINISH
HARDWARE/OPERATOR
VENT/WEEP HOLE/WIND GUARD
GLAZING: SINGLE/DOUBLE
REMOVABLE SCREEN/SCREEN FRAME
CASING/TRIM/ADJACENT FINISH
ROUGH OPENING/FINISH OPENING
ANODIZED ALUM. TRIM
1/4" TEMP. GLASS
EXTRUDED ALUM. SILL TO MATCH WINDOW
METAL SILL BELOW
THERMOPANE INSULATING GLASS
SINGLE PANE GLASS
ALUM. HEAD, SEALANT BOTH SIDES
ALUM. SILL W/SEALANT EACH SIDE
WOOD NAILER
TREATED BLOCKING
1 X   WOOD TRIM
METAL EDGE BEAD
STUD
GYPSUM WALLBOARD
FLASHING
SEALANT

08527 ALUMINUM SLIDING WINDOWS

DETAIL DATA CHECKLIST

ALUMINUM SLIDING WINDOWS

Note: You can combine these generic window details with varied exterior wall construction details in this book to create many hundreds of possible special combinations.

__See manufacturers' and suppliers' catalogs for standard sizes, detail design data, materials, and finishes.
__Detail drawings are required mainly to show the relationship of windows to wall construction such as connections to wood frame, masonry, or concrete wall construction.
__Details or window schedules should show rough-opening sizes and shim tolerance allowances (1/2" all around is a common allowance for shim space).
__Details should show flashing and caulking at heads, jambs, and sills.
__See manufacturers' recommendations for connections to varied wall construction.
__See the Detail Data Checklist for Windows and Glazing at the beginning of this chapter for more information.

SMALL-SCALE GENERIC DETAILS

Aluminum Sliding -- Single Glazed

HEAD   08527-1   JAMB   08527-2   SILL   08527-3

Aluminum Sliding -- Double Glazed

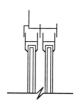

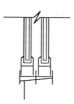

HEAD   08527-21   JAMB   08527-22   SILL   08527-23

08527 ALUMINUM SLIDING WINDOWS

FULL-SCALE GENERIC DETAILS

Aluminum Sliding -- Single Glazed

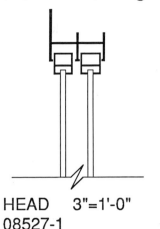

HEAD   3"=1'-0"
08527-1

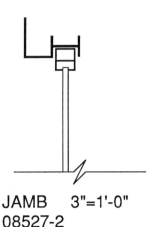

JAMB   3"=1'-0"
08527-2

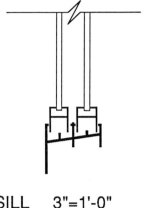

SILL   3"=1'-0"
08527-3

Aluminum Sliding -- Double Glazed

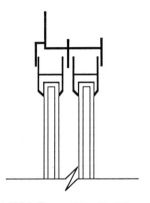
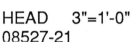

HEAD   3"=1'-0"
08527-21

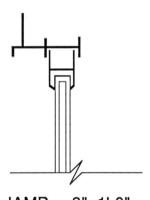

JAMB   3"=1'-0"
08527-22

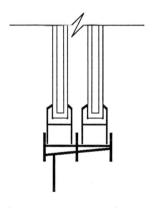

SILL   3"=1'-0"
08527-23

NOTATION CHECKLIST, SAMPLE NOTES

WALL CONSTRUCTION
SHIM SPACE
DRIP CAP/WEATHERSTRIPPING/FLASHING
CAULKING/GROUT
FINISH HEAD/SILL/JAMB
WINDOW TYPE, MATERIAL & FINISH
HARDWARE/OPERATOR
VENT/WEEP HOLE/WIND GUARD
GLAZING: SINGLE/DOUBLE/REMOVABLE
SCREEN/SCREEN FRAME
CASING/TRIM/ADJACENT FINISH
ROUGH OPENING/FINISH OPENING

ANODIZED ALUM. TRIM
1/4" TEMP. GLASS
EXTRUDED ALUM. SILL TO MATCH WINDOW
METAL SILL BELOW
THERMOPANE INSULATING GLASS
SINGLE PANE GLASS
ALUM. HEAD, SEALANT BOTH SIDES
ALUM. SILL W/SEALANT EACH SIDE
WOOD NAILER
TREATED BLOCKING
1 X   WOOD TRIM
METAL EDGE BEAD
STUD
GYPSUM WALLBOARD
FLASHING
SEALANT

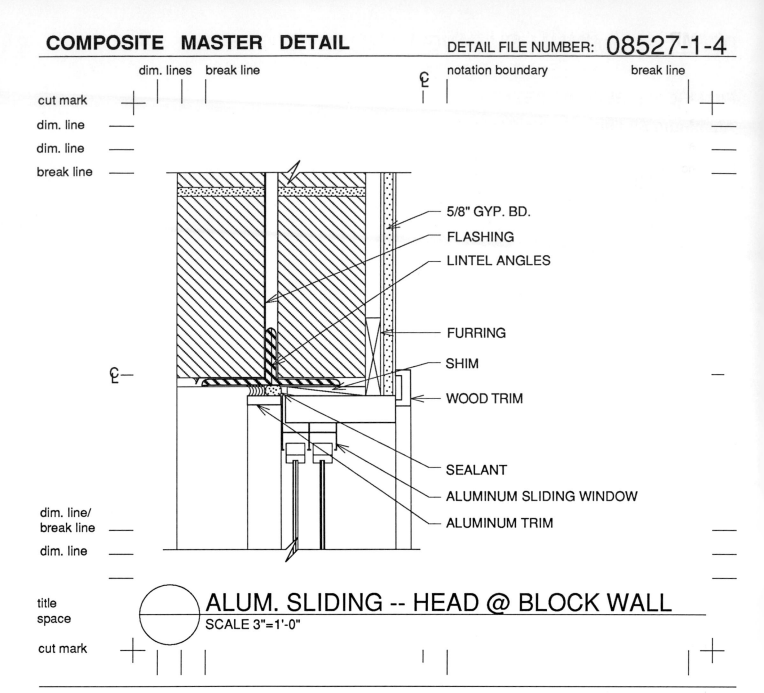

dim. lines   break line

notation boundary

break line

cut mark

dim. line

dim. line

break line

5/8" GYP. BD.

FLASHING

LINTEL ANGLES

FURRING

SHIM

WOOD TRIM

SEALANT

ALUMINUM SLIDING WINDOW

ALUMINUM TRIM

dim. line/
break line

dim. line

title
space

cut mark

ALUM. SLIDING -- HEAD @ BLOCK WALL

SCALE 3"=1'-0"

DETAIL INFORMATION
References, jobsite feedback, job history

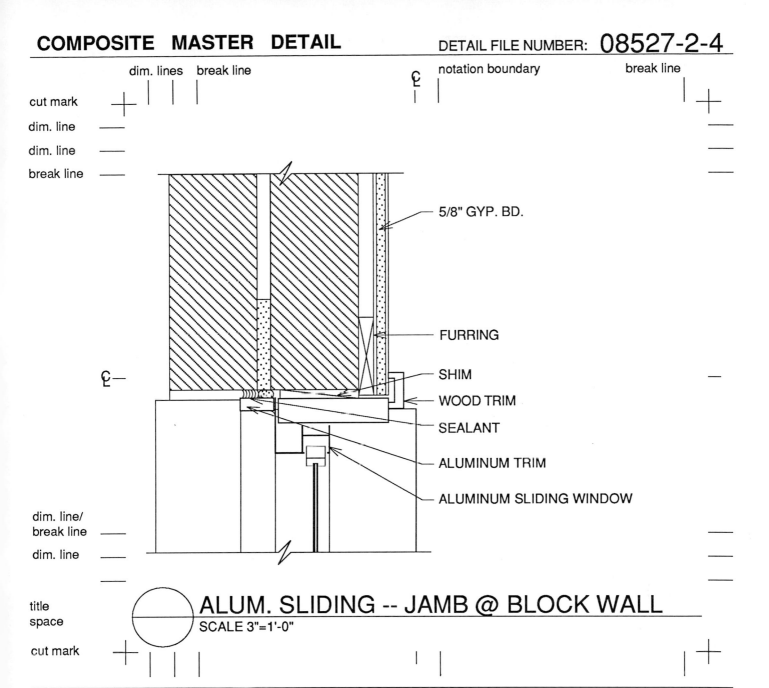

cut mark

dim. lines   break line

notation boundary   break line

dim. line

dim. line

break line

5/8" GYP. BD.

FURRING

SHIM

WOOD TRIM

SEALANT

ALUMINUM TRIM

ALUMINUM SLIDING WINDOW

dim. line/
break line

dim. line

title
space

ALUM. SLIDING -- JAMB @ BLOCK WALL
SCALE 3"=1'-0"

cut mark

DETAIL INFORMATION
References, jobsite feedback, job history

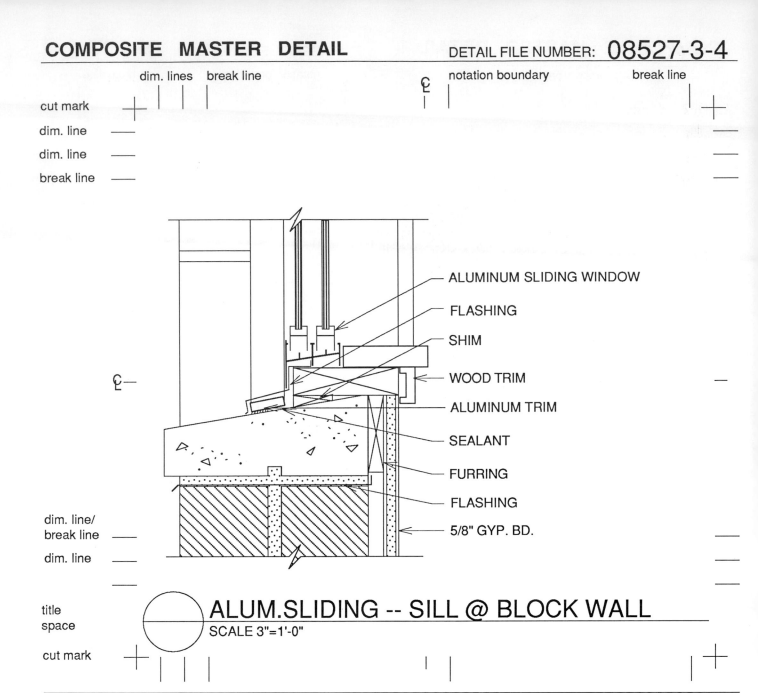

cut mark

dim. lines   break line

notation boundary   break line

dim. line

dim. line

break line

ALUMINUM SLIDING WINDOW

FLASHING

SHIM

WOOD TRIM

ALUMINUM TRIM

SEALANT

FURRING

FLASHING

5/8" GYP. BD.

dim. line/
break line

dim. line

ALUM. SLIDING -- SILL @ BLOCK WALL
SCALE 3"=1'-0"

title
space

cut mark

DETAIL INFORMATION
References, jobsite feedback, job history

COMPOSITE MASTER DETAIL

DETAIL FILE NUMBER: **08527-1-6**

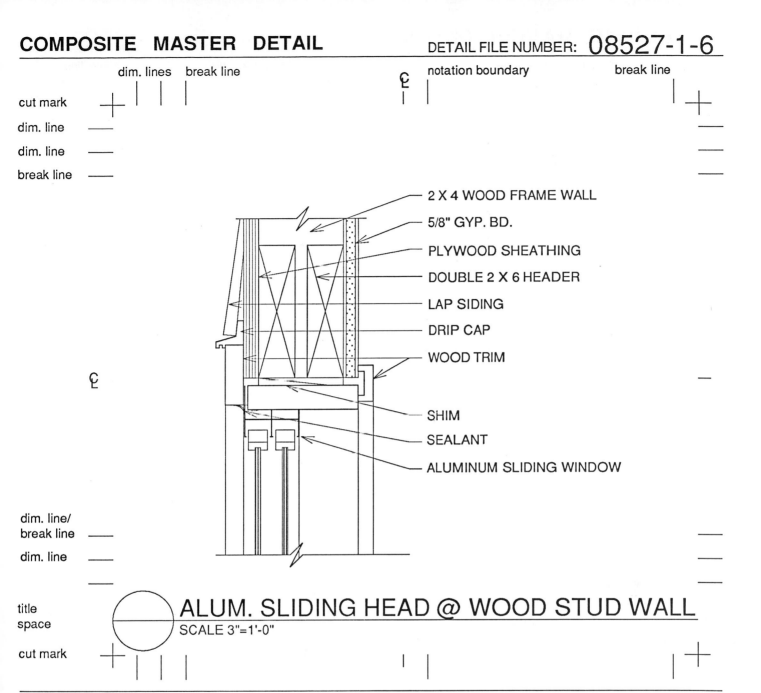

dim. lines   break line

notation boundary   break line

cut mark

dim. line

dim. line

break line

- 2 X 4 WOOD FRAME WALL
- 5/8" GYP. BD.
- PLYWOOD SHEATHING
- DOUBLE 2 X 6 HEADER
- LAP SIDING
- DRIP CAP
- WOOD TRIM
- SHIM
- SEALANT
- ALUMINUM SLIDING WINDOW

dim. line/
break line

dim. line

title
space

ALUM. SLIDING HEAD @ WOOD STUD WALL
SCALE 3"=1'-0"

cut mark

DETAIL INFORMATION
References, jobsite feedback, job history

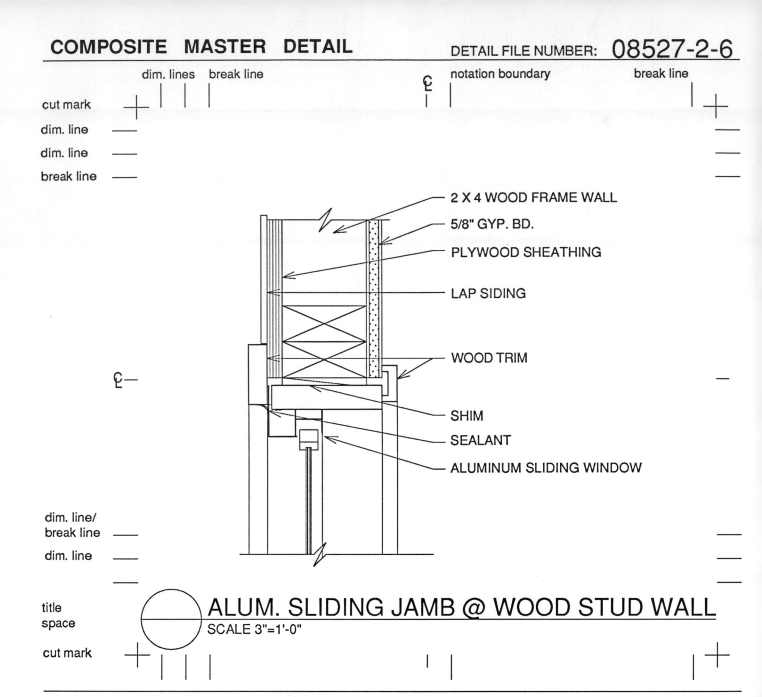

dim. lines break line

notation boundary

break line

cut mark

dim. line ——

dim. line ——

break line ——

2 X 4 WOOD FRAME WALL

5/8" GYP. BD.

PLYWOOD SHEATHING

LAP SIDING

WOOD TRIM

SHIM

SEALANT

ALUMINUM SLIDING WINDOW

dim. line/
break line ——

dim. line ——

title
space

ALUM. SLIDING JAMB @ WOOD STUD WALL
SCALE 3"=1'-0"

cut mark

DETAIL INFORMATION
References, jobsite feedback, job history

COMPOSITE MASTER DETAIL

DETAIL FILE NUMBER: **08527-3-6**

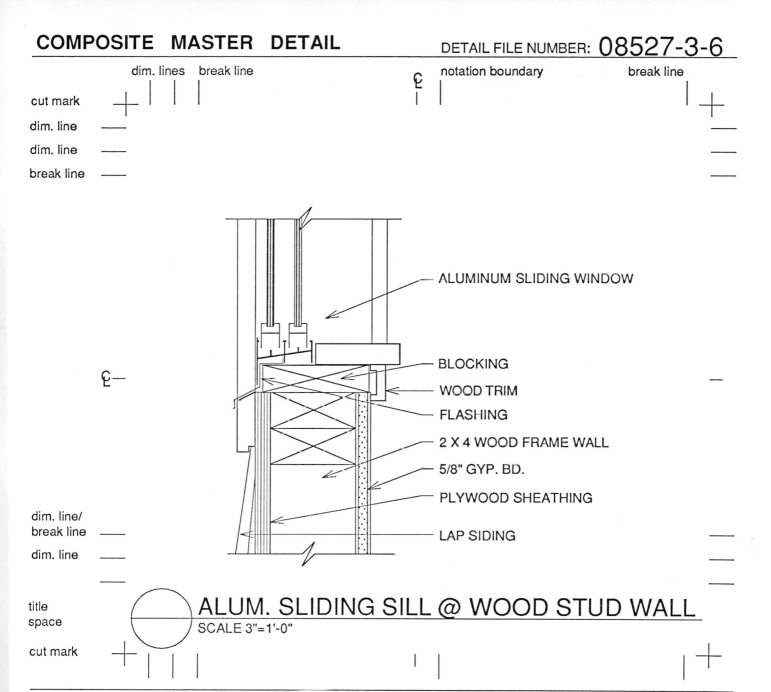

cut mark — dim. lines — break line — notation boundary — break line

cut mark
dim. line
dim. line
break line

ALUMINUM SLIDING WINDOW

BLOCKING

WOOD TRIM

FLASHING

2 X 4 WOOD FRAME WALL

5/8" GYP. BD.

PLYWOOD SHEATHING

LAP SIDING

dim. line/
break line
dim. line

title
space

ALUM. SLIDING SILL @ WOOD STUD WALL

SCALE 3"=1'-0"

cut mark

DETAIL INFORMATION
References, jobsite feedback, job history

08611 (a) WOOD AWNING WINDOWS

DETAIL DATA CHECKLIST

WOOD AWNING WINDOWS

Note: You can combine these generic window details with varied exterior wall construction details in this book
to create many hundreds of possible special combinations.

__Wood windows are especially subject to moisture damage and warping; they require extra care throughout
design, detailing, and specification, and extra protection during construction.
__See manufacturers' and suppliers' catalogs for standard sizes, detail design data, materials, and finishes.
__Detail drawings are required mainly to show the relationship of windows to wall construction such as
connections to wood frame, masonry, or concrete wall construction.
__Details or window schedules should show rough-opening sizes and shim tolerance allowances
(1/2" all around is a common allowance for shim space).
__Details should show flashing and caulking at heads, jambs, and sills.
__See manufacturers' recommendations for connections to varied wall construction.
__See the Detail Data Checklist for Windows and Glazing at the beginning of this chapter for more information.

SMALL-SCALE GENERIC DETAILS

Wood Awning Window -- Single Glazed

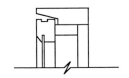
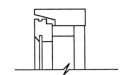
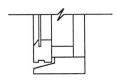

HEAD   08611-1   JAMB   08611-2   SILL   08611-4

Wood Awning Window W/Operator -- Single Glazed

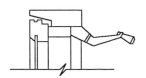
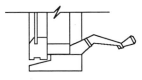

JAMB   08611-3   SILL   08611-5

08611 (a) WOOD AWNING WINDOWS

FULL-SCALE GENERIC DETAILS
Wood Awning Window -- Single Glazed

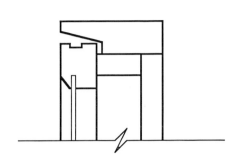

HEAD   3"=1'-0"
08611-1

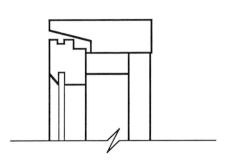

JAMB   3"=1'-0"
08611-2

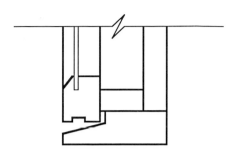

SILL   3"=1'-0"
08611-4

Wood Awning Window W/Operator -- Single Glazed

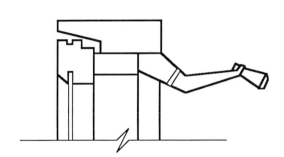

JAMB   3"=1'-0"
08611-3

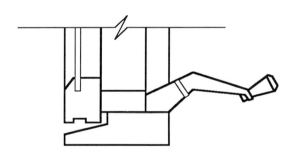

SILL   3"=1'-0"
08611-5

NOTATION CHECKLIST,
SAMPLE NOTES

WALL CONSTRUCTION
SHIM SPACE
DRIP CAP/WEATHERSTRIPPING/FLASHING
CAULKING/GROUT
FINISH HEAD/SILL/JAMB
WINDOW TYPE, MATERIAL & FINISH
HARDWARE/OPERATOR
VENT/WEEP HOLE/WIND GUARD
GLAZING: SINGLE/DOUBLE/REMOVABLE
SCREEN/SCREEN FRAME
CASING/TRIM/ADJACENT FINISH
ROUGH OPENING/FINISH OPENING
WOOD AWNING WINDOW
WOOD WINDOW
WOOD STOP, 1/2" X 1"

2 X   WOOD NAILER
1/4" GLASS
3/4" JAMB
CAULK OR SEALANT
WOOD CASING
2" WOOD DRIP
WOOD STOOL
    X   HEADER
3/4" WOOD FASCIA
1/3" WOOD TRIM
1 X   INTERIOR CASING
1 X 8 WOOD SIDING
1/2" INSUL. BOARD
5/8" GYPSUM BOARD
BRICK VENEER
EYE HOOK W/EYE SCREW
SCREEN MOLDING

08611 (b) WOOD AWNING WINDOWS

DETAIL DATA CHECKLIST

WOOD AWNING WINDOWS

Note: You can combine these generic window details with varied exterior wall construction details in this book to create many hundreds of possible special combinations.

__Wood windows are especially subject to moisture damage and warping; they require extra care throughout design, detailing, and specification, and extra protection during construction.
__See manufacturers' and suppliers' catalogs for standard sizes, detail design data, materials, and finishes.
__Detail drawings are required mainly to show the relationship of windows to wall construction such as connections to wood frame, masonry, or concrete wall construction.
__Details or window schedules should show rough-opening sizes and shim tolerance allowances (1/2" all around is a common allowance for shim space).
__Details should show flashing and caulking at heads, jambs, and sills.
__See manufacturers' recommendations for connections to varied wall construction.
__See the Detail Data Checklist for Windows and Glazing at the beginning of this chapter for more information.

SMALL-SCALE GENERIC DETAILS

Wood Awning Window -- Double Glazed

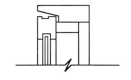 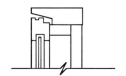 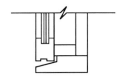

HEAD   08611-21   JAMB   08611-22   SILL   08611-24

Wood Awning Window W/Operator -- Double Glazed

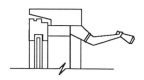 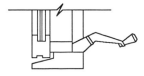

JAMB   08611-23   SILL   08611-25

08611 (b) WOOD AWNING WINDOWS

FULL-SCALE GENERIC DETAILS

Wood Awning Window -- Double Glazed

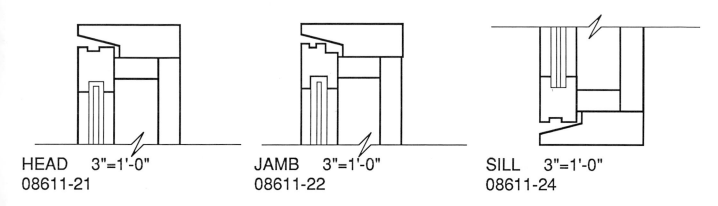

HEAD   3"=1'-0"
08611-21

JAMB   3"=1'-0"
08611-22

SILL   3"=1'-0"
08611-24

Wood Awning Window W/Operator -- Double Glazed

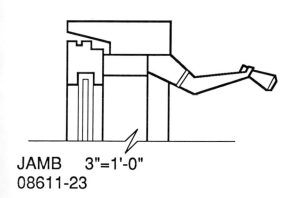

JAMB   3"=1'-0"
08611-23

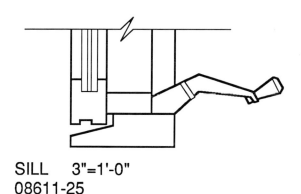

SILL   3"=1'-0"
08611-25

NOTATION CHECKLIST, SAMPLE NOTES

WALL CONSTRUCTION
SHIM SPACE
DRIP CAP/WEATHERSTRIPPING/FLASHING
CAULKING/GROUT
FINISH HEAD/SILL/JAMB
WINDOW TYPE, MATERIAL & FINISH
HARDWARE/OPERATOR
VENT/WEEP HOLE/WIND GUARD
GLAZING: SINGLE/DOUBLE/REMOVABLE
SCREEN/SCREEN FRAME
CASING/TRIM/ADJACENT FINISH
ROUGH OPENING/FINISH OPENING
WOOD AWNING WINDOW
WOOD WINDOW
WOOD STOP, 1/2" X 1"

2 X   WOOD NAILER
1/4" GLASS
3/4" JAMB
CAULK OR SEALANT
WOOD CASING
2" WOOD DRIP
WOOD STOOL
    X   HEADER
3/4" WOOD FASCIA
1/3" WOOD TRIM
1 X   INTERIOR CASING
1 X 8 WOOD SIDING
1/2" INSUL. BOARD
5/8" GYPSUM BOARD
BRICK VENEER
EYE HOOK W/EYE SCREW
SCREEN MOLDING

08612 WOOD CASEMENT WINDOWS

DETAIL DATA CHECKLIST

WOOD CASEMENT WINDOWS

Note: You can combine these generic window details with varied exterior wall construction details in this book to create many hundreds of possible special combinations.

__Wood windows are especially subject to moisture damage and warping; they require extra care throughout design, detailing, and specification, and extra protection during construction.
__See manufacturers' and suppliers' catalogs for standard sizes, detail design data, materials, and finishes.
__Detail drawings are required mainly to show the relationship of windows to wall construction such as connections to wood frame, masonry, or concrete wall construction.
__Details or window schedules should show rough-opening sizes and shim tolerance allowances (1/2" all around is a common allowance for shim space).
__Details should show flashing and caulking at heads, jambs, and sills.
__See manufacturers' recommendations for connections to varied wall construction.
__See the Detail Data Checklist for Windows and Glazing at the beginning of this chapter for more information.

SMALL-SCALE GENERIC DETAILS

Wood Casement -- Single Glazed

HEAD   08612-1

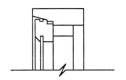

JAMB   08612-2

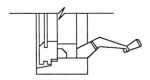

SILL   08612-3

Wood Casement -- Double Glazed

HEAD   08612-21

JAMB   08612-22

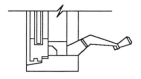

SILL   08612-23

08612 WOOD CASEMENT WINDOWS

FULL-SCALE GENERIC DETAILS
Wood Casement -- Single Glazed

HEAD   3"=1'-0"
08612-1

JAMB   3"=1'-0"
08612-2

SILL   3"=1'-0"
08612-3

Wood Casement -- Double Glazed

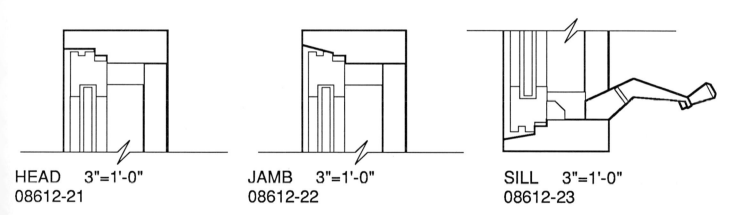

HEAD   3"=1'-0"
08612-21

JAMB   3"=1'-0"
08612-22

SILL   3"=1'-0"
08612-23

NOTATION CHECKLIST, SAMPLE NOTES

WALL CONSTRUCTION
SHIM SPACE
DRIP CAP/WEATHERSTRIPPING/FLASHING
CAULKING/GROUT
FINISH HEAD/SILL/JAMB
WINDOW TYPE, MATERIAL & FINISH
HARDWARE/OPERATOR
VENT/WEEP HOLE/WIND GUARD
GLAZING: SINGLE/DOUBLE/REMOVABLE
SCREEN/SCREEN FRAME
CASING/TRIM/ADJACENT FINISH
ROUGH OPENING/FINISH OPENING
CASEMENT WOOD WINDOW
WOOD WINDOW
WOOD STOP, 1/2" X 1"

2 X   WOOD NAILER
1/4" GLASS
3/4" JAMB
CAULK OR SEALANT
WOOD CASING
2" WOOD DRIP
WOOD STOOL
  X   HEADER
3/4" WOOD FASCIA
1/3" WOOD TRIM
1 X INTERIOR CASING
1 X 8 WOOD SIDING
1/2" INSUL. BOARD
5/8" GYP.BD.
BRICK VENEER
EYE HOOK W/ EYE SCREW
SCREEN MOLDING

08613 WOOD DOUBLE HUNG WINDOWS

DETAIL DATA CHECKLIST

DOUBLE HUNG WINDOWS

Note: You can combine these generic window details with varied exterior wall construction details in this book to create many hundreds of possible special combinations.

__Wood windows are especially subject to moisture damage and warping; they require extra care throughout design, detailing, and specification, and extra protection during construction.
__See manufacturers' and suppliers' catalogs for standard sizes, detail design data, materials, and finishes.
__Detail drawings are required mainly to show the relationship of windows to wall construction such as connections to wood frame, masonry, or concrete wall construction.
__Details or window schedules should show rough-opening sizes and shim tolerance allowances (1/2" all around is a common allowance for shim space).
__Details should show flashing and caulking at heads, jambs, and sills.
__See manufacturers' recommendations for connections to varied wall construction.
__See the Detail Data Checklist for Windows and Glazing at the beginning of this chapter for more information.

SMALL-SCALE GENERIC DETAILS

Wood Double Hung -- Single Glazed

HEAD   08613-1

JAMB   08613-2

SILL   08613-3

Wood Double Hung -- Double Glazed

HEAD   08613-21

JAMB   08613-22

SILL   08613-23

08613 WOOD DOUBLE HUNG WINDOWS

FULL-SCALE GENERIC DETAILS

Wood Double Hung -- Single Glazed

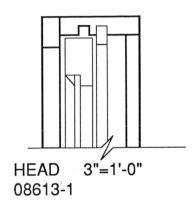

HEAD   3"=1'-0"
08613-1

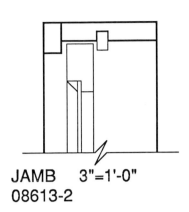

JAMB   3"=1'-0"
08613-2

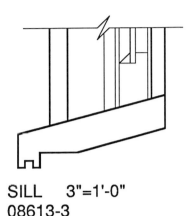

SILL   3"=1'-0"
08613-3

Wood Double Hung -- Double Glazed

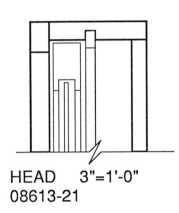

HEAD   3"=1'-0"
08613-21

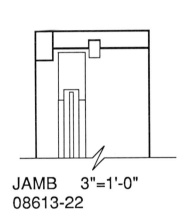

JAMB   3"=1'-0"
08613-22

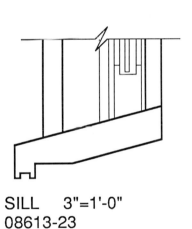

SILL   3"=1'-0"
08613-23

NOTATION CHECKLIST, SAMPLE NOTES

WALL CONSTRUCTION
SHIM SPACE
DRIP CAP/WEATHERSTRIPPING/FLASHING
CAULKING/GROUT
FINISH HEAD/SILL/JAMB
WINDOW TYPE, MATERIAL & FINISH
HARDWARE/OPERATOR
VENT/WEEP HOLE/WIND GUARD
GLAZING: SINGLE/DOUBLE/REMOVABLE
SCREEN/SCREEN FRAME
CASING/TRIM/ADJACENT FINISH
ROUGH OPENING/FINISH OPENING
DOUBLE HUNG WOOD WINDOW
WOOD STOP, 1/2" X 1"
2 X   WOOD NAILER

1/4" GLASS
3/4" JAMB
CAULK OR SEALANT
WOOD CASING
2" WOOD DRIP
WOOD STOOL
    X   HEADER
3/4" WOOD FASCIA
1/3" WOOD TRIM
1 X   INTERIOR CASING
1 X 8 WOOD SIDING
1/2" INSUL. BOARD
5/8" GYP.BD.
BRICK VENEER
EYE HOOK W/EYE SCREW
SCREEN MOLDING

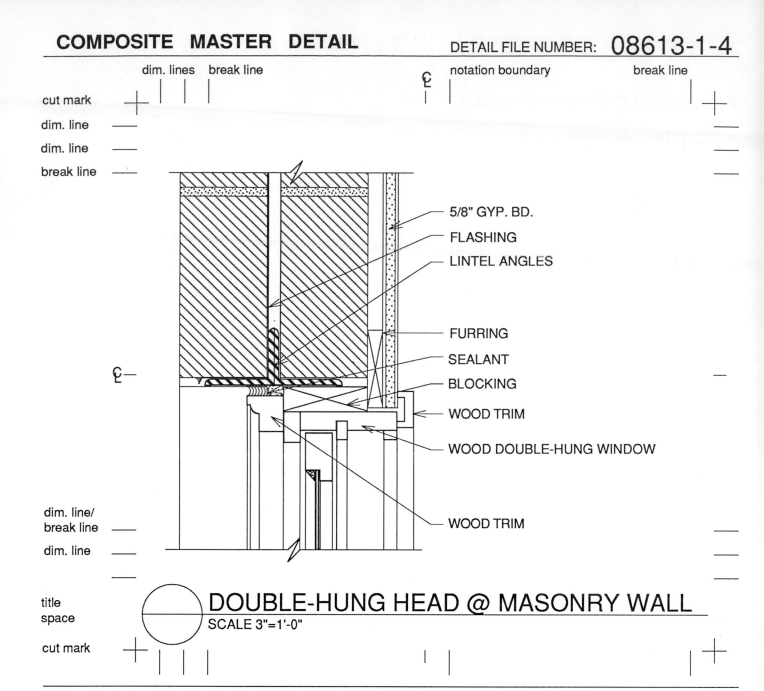

dim. lines   break line

notation boundary   break line

cut mark

dim. line

dim. line

break line

5/8" GYP. BD.

FLASHING

LINTEL ANGLES

FURRING

SEALANT

BLOCKING

WOOD TRIM

WOOD DOUBLE-HUNG WINDOW

WOOD TRIM

dim. line/
break line

dim. line

title
space

DOUBLE-HUNG HEAD @ MASONRY WALL
SCALE 3"=1'-0"

cut mark

DETAIL INFORMATION
References, jobsite feedback, job history

COMPOSITE MASTER DETAIL

DETAIL FILE NUMBER: **08613-2-4**

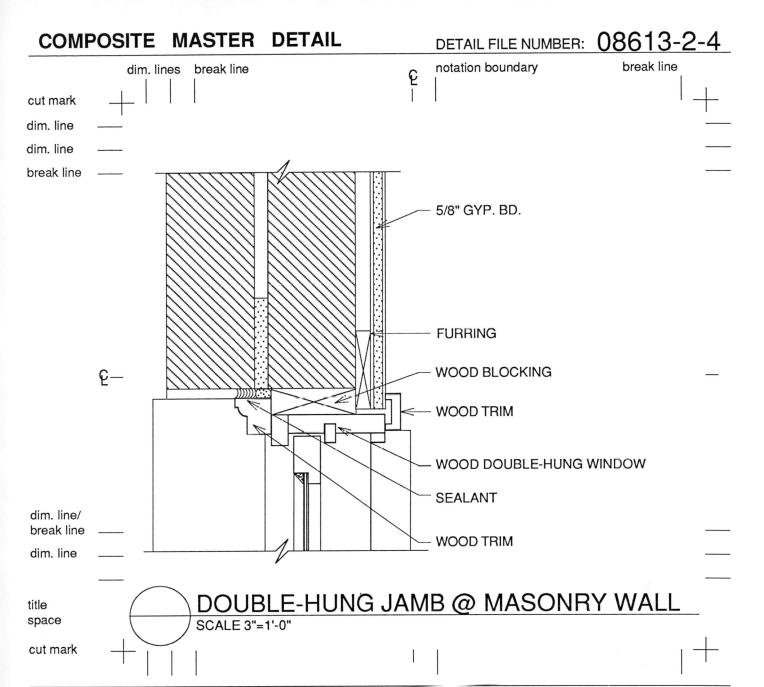

dim. lines   break line   notation boundary   break line

cut mark

dim. line

dim. line

break line

— 5/8" GYP. BD.

— FURRING

— WOOD BLOCKING

— WOOD TRIM

— WOOD DOUBLE-HUNG WINDOW

— SEALANT

dim. line/
break line

dim. line

— WOOD TRIM

title
space

DOUBLE-HUNG JAMB @ MASONRY WALL
SCALE 3"=1'-0"

cut mark

DETAIL INFORMATION
References, jobsite feedback, job history

COMPOSITE MASTER DETAIL

DETAIL FILE NUMBER: **08613-3-4**

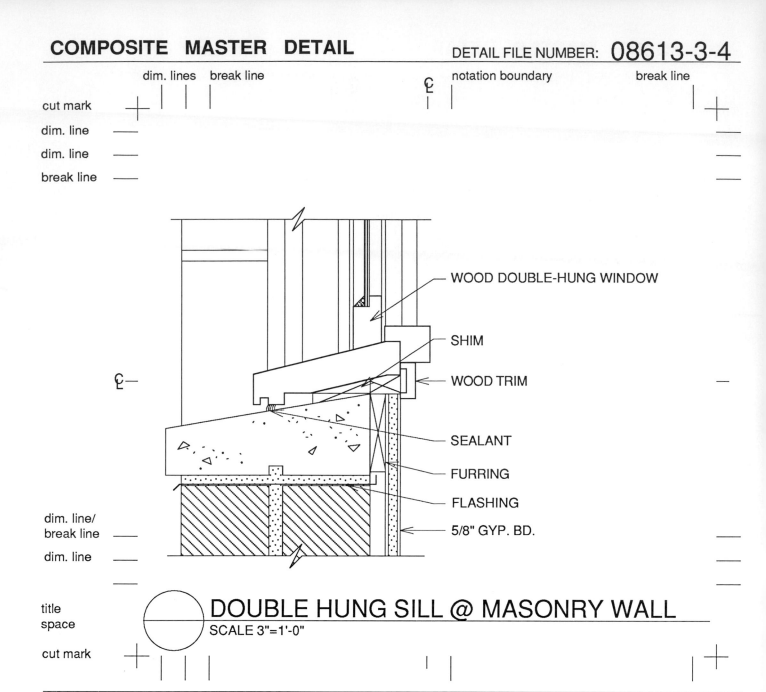

dim. lines   break line   ℄   notation boundary   break line

cut mark

dim. line —

dim. line —

break line —

WOOD DOUBLE-HUNG WINDOW

SHIM

WOOD TRIM

SEALANT

FURRING

FLASHING

5/8" GYP. BD.

dim. line/
break line —

dim. line —

title
space

DOUBLE HUNG SILL @ MASONRY WALL
SCALE 3"=1'-0"

cut mark

DETAIL INFORMATION
References, jobsite feedback, job history

COMPOSITE MASTER DETAIL

DETAIL FILE NUMBER: **08613-1-6**

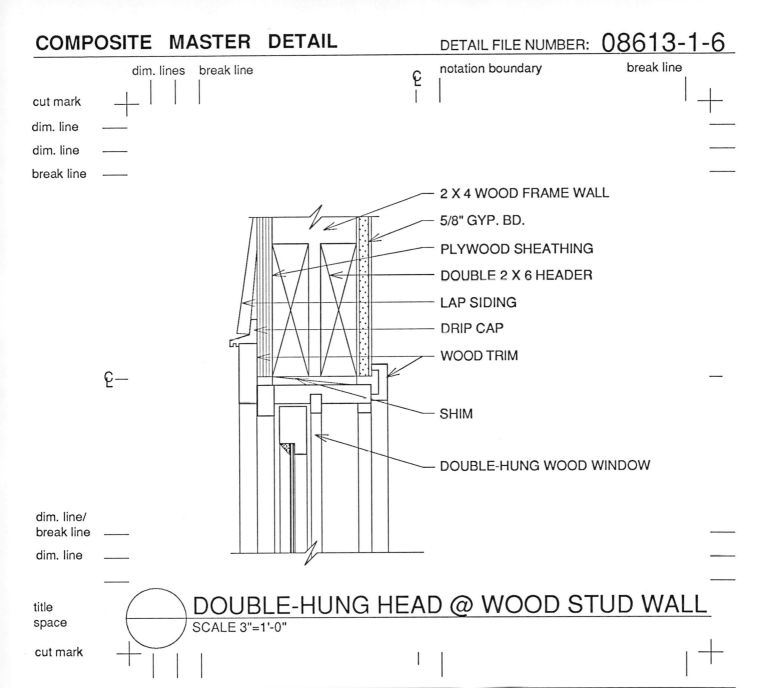

dim. lines   break line   ₵   notation boundary   break line

cut mark

dim. line

dim. line

break line

2 X 4 WOOD FRAME WALL

5/8" GYP. BD.

PLYWOOD SHEATHING

DOUBLE 2 X 6 HEADER

LAP SIDING

DRIP CAP

WOOD TRIM

SHIM

DOUBLE-HUNG WOOD WINDOW

₵—

dim. line/
break line

dim. line

title space

DOUBLE-HUNG HEAD @ WOOD STUD WALL
SCALE 3"=1'-0"

cut mark

DETAIL INFORMATION
References, jobsite feedback, job history

DETAIL FILE NUMBER: **08613-2-6**

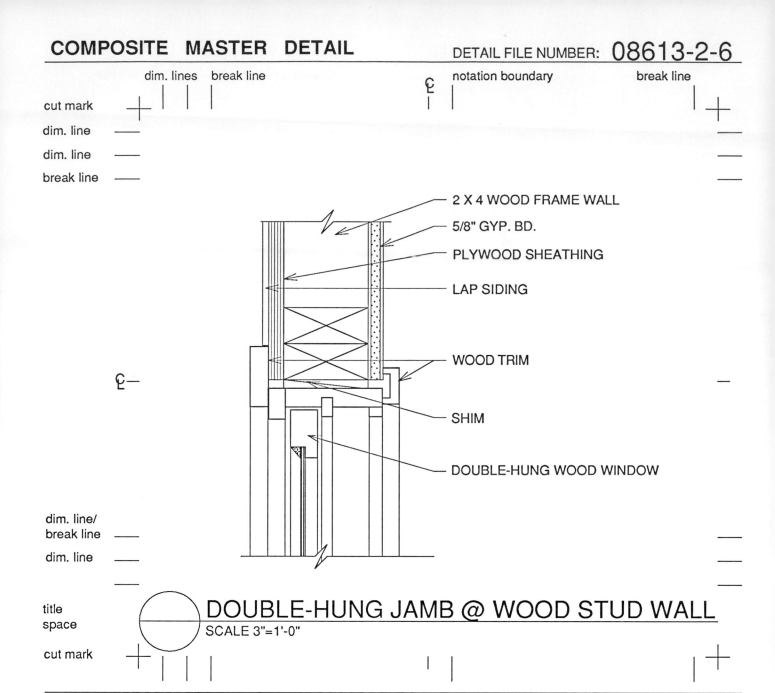

dim. lines   break line

cut mark

dim. line

dim. line

break line

notation boundary   break line

— 2 X 4 WOOD FRAME WALL

— 5/8" GYP. BD.

— PLYWOOD SHEATHING

— LAP SIDING

— WOOD TRIM

— SHIM

— DOUBLE-HUNG WOOD WINDOW

dim. line/
break line

dim. line

title
space

DOUBLE-HUNG JAMB @ WOOD STUD WALL

SCALE 3"=1'-0"

cut mark

DETAIL INFORMATION
References, jobsite feedback, job history

COMPOSITE MASTER DETAIL

DETAIL FILE NUMBER: **08613-3-6**

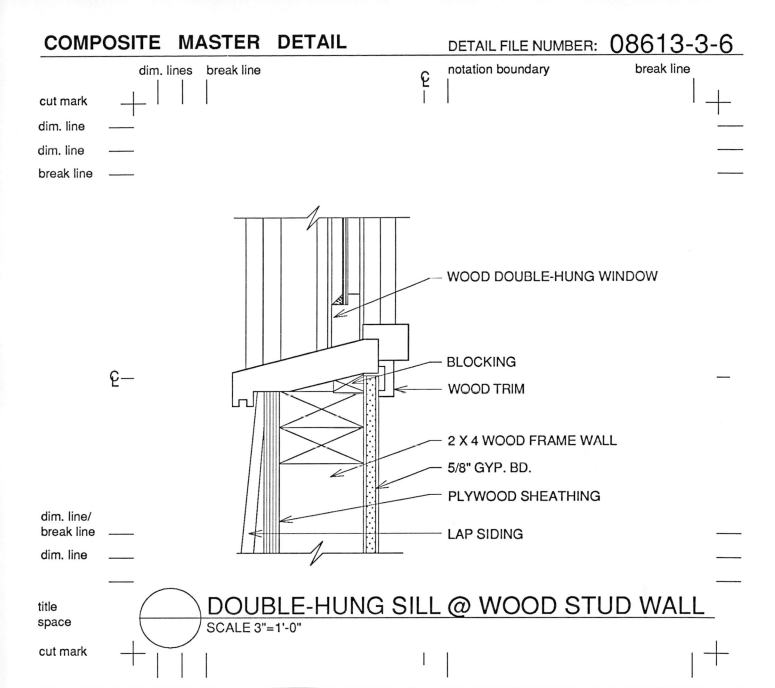

cut mark

dim. lines   break line

notation boundary   break line

dim. line

dim. line

break line

WOOD DOUBLE-HUNG WINDOW

BLOCKING

WOOD TRIM

2 X 4 WOOD FRAME WALL

5/8" GYP. BD.

PLYWOOD SHEATHING

dim. line/
break line

dim. line

LAP SIDING

title
space

cut mark

DOUBLE-HUNG SILL @ WOOD STUD WALL
SCALE 3"=1'-0"

DETAIL INFORMATION
References, jobsite feedback, job history

08617 WOOD SLIDING WINDOWS

DETAIL DATA CHECKLIST

WOOD SLIDING WINDOWS

Note: You can combine these generic window details with varied exterior wall construction details in this book
to create many hundreds of possible special combinations.

__Wood windows are especially subject to moisture damage and warping; they require extra care throughout
design, detailing, and specification, and extra protection during construction.
__See manufacturers' and suppliers' catalogs for standard sizes, detail design data, materials, and finishes.
__Detail drawings are required mainly to show the relationship of windows to wall construction such as
connections to wood frame, masonry, or concrete wall construction.
__Details or window schedules should show rough-opening sizes and shim tolerance allowances
(1/2" all around is a common allowance for shim space).
__Details should show flashing and caulking at heads, jambs, and sills.
__See manufacturers' recommendations for connections to varied wall construction.
__See the Detail Data Checklist for Windows and Glazing at the beginning of this chapter for more information.

SMALL-SCALE GENERIC DETAILS

Wood Sliding -- Single Glaze

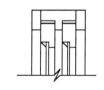

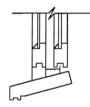

HEAD   08617-1   JAMB   08617-2   SILL   08617-3

Wood Sliding -- Double Glazed

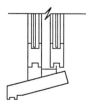

HEAD   08617-21   JAMB   08617-22   SILL   08617-23

08617 WOOD SLIDING WINDOWS

FULL-SCALE GENERIC DETAILS

Wood Sliding -- Single Glazed

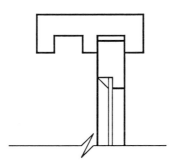

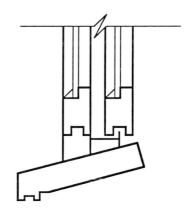

HEAD   3"=1'-0"
08617-1

JAMB   3"=1'-0"
08617-2

SILL   3"=1'-0"
08617-3

Wood Sliding -- Double Glazed

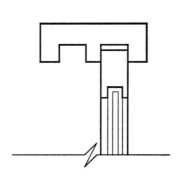

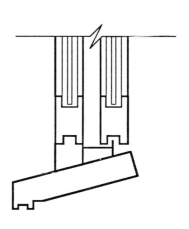

HEAD   3"=1'-0"
08617-21

JAMB   3"=1'-0"
08617-22

SILL   3"=1'-0"
08617-23

NOTATION CHECKLIST, SAMPLE NOTES

WALL CONSTRUCTION
SHIM SPACE
DRIP CAP/WEATHERSTRIPPING/FLASHING
CAULKING/GROUT
FINISH HEAD/SILL/JAMB
WINDOW TYPE, MATERIAL & FINISH
HARDWARE/OPERATOR
VENT/WEEP HOLE/WIND GUARD
GLAZING: SINGLE/DOUBLE/REMOVABLE
SCREEN/SCREEN FRAME
CASING/TRIM/ADJACENT FINISH
ROUGH OPENING/FINISH OPENING
SLIDING WOOD WINDOW
WOOD WINDOW
WOOD STOP, 1/2" X 1"

2 X   WOOD NAILER
1/4" GLASS
3/4" JAMB
FLASHING, UP 8" MIN.
WOOD CASING
2" WOOD DRIP
WOOD STOOL
WOOD HEADER
WOOD FASCIA
WOOD TRIM
INTERIOR CASING
WOOD SIDING
INSUL. BOARD
GYPSUM WALLBOARD
EYE HOOK W/EYE SCREW
SCREEN MOLDING

08730 METAL THRESHOLDS

DETAIL DATA CHECKLIST

THRESHOLDS

Note: You can combine these threshold details with varied flooring details in this book to create many special combinations.

__Thresholds are primarily to hide the joint-line at changes in flooring and block weather, air infiltration and sound
__See manufacturers' and suppliers' catalogs for standard sizes, detail design data, materials, and finishes.
__Detail drawings are mainly to show:
    __The profile of thresholds
    __Floor construction
    __Change in floor materials at joint lines
    __Connection to the floor
    __Exterior caulking, flashing, weatherstripping
    __Required special sound or light insulation

__See manufacturers' recommendations for connections to varied floor construction.

SMALL-SCALE GENERIC DETAILS

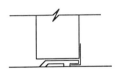

EXTERIOR THRESHOLD
Interlocking
08730-31

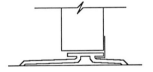

EXTERIOR THRESHOLD
Interlocking
08730-32

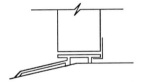

EXTERIOR THRESHOLD
Interlocking
08730-33

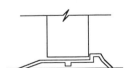

EXTERIOR THRESHOLD
Flat Saddle
08730-41

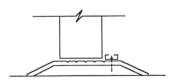

EXTERIOR THRESHOLD
Flat W/Latch Track
08730-42

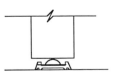

EXTERIOR THRESHOLD
Vinyl Insert
08730-46

08730 METAL THRESHOLDS

FULL-SCALE GENERIC DETAILS

EXTERIOR THRESHOLD Interlocking
1/2 FULL SIZE   08730-31

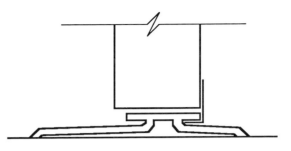

EXTERIOR THRESHOLD Interlocking
1/2 FULL SIZE   08730-32

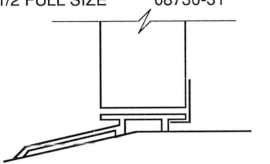

EXTERIOR THRESHOLD Interlocking
1/2 FULL SIZE   08730-33

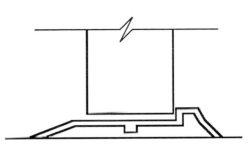

EXTERIOR THRESHOLD Flat Saddle
1/2 FULL SIZE   08730-41

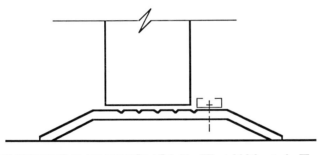

EXTERIOR THRESHOLD Flat W/Latch Track
1/2 FULL SIZE   08730-42

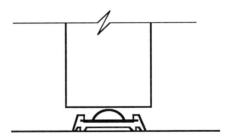

EXTERIOR THRESHOLD Vinyl Insert
1/2 FULL SIZE   08730-46

NOTATION CHECKLIST,
SAMPLE NOTES

DOOR TYPE
HOOK STRIP
BUMPER STRIP
CAULKING OR PAN W/WEEP

DOOR, SEE DOOR SCHEDULE
THRESHOLD
METAL THRESHOLD SET IN CAULK
SADDLE & PLATE SIZE VARY W/HINGE SIZE
ANCHORS
GROUT
SEALANT
SET IN MASTIC
FRAME STOP
BUMPER STRIP
FLOORING, SEE FINISH SCHEDULE
FINISH FLOOR
SETTING BED

dim. lines   break line   ℄   notation boundary   break line

cut mark

dim. line

dim. line

break line

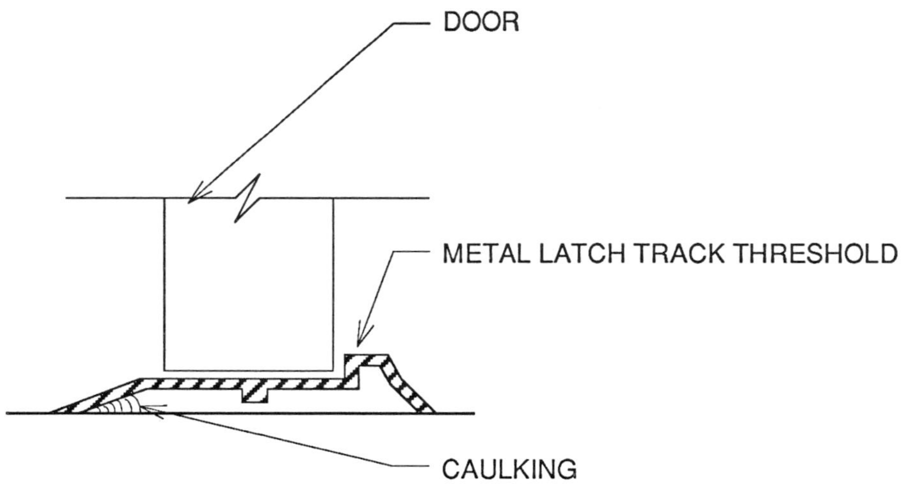

℄

— DOOR

— METAL LATCH TRACK THRESHOLD

dim. line/
break line

dim. line

— CAULKING

title
space

DOOR THRESHOLD
SCALE 6"=1'-0"

cut mark

DETAIL INFORMATION
References, jobsite feedback, job history

CHAPTER 9

Finishes
09000

09110   METAL FRAME PARTITIONS

DETAIL DATA CHECKLIST

METAL STUD WALLS

__Studs shown in this series are steel members in the sizes indicated in the detail titles
__Metal wall manufacturers' instructions and details for these products are very comprehensive; use the data here
    as a preliminary design guide

__Partition notation mainly consists of naming the various components such as:
    __Metal studs:
        __Channel,
        __"C"
        __Open web
        __Nailable
    __Floor and ceiling tracks
    __Tracks connecting to other wall construction
    __Jamb anchor clips
    __Bolt or toggle bolt connection to ceiling
    __Movement sleeve at ceiling
    __Sealant at top and bottom tracks
    __Horizontal 3/4" channel stiffeners:
        __ At door jambs
        __Above door heads
        __Usually within 12" of other wall openings

FINISH WALL CONSTRUCTION

__Gypsum wallboard and other finish material manufacturers provide comprehensive instructions and details for their
    products; use the data here as a preliminary guide.
__Building codes provide extensive instructions on fireproofing requirements; those requirements have evolved
    from many years of fire experience and should be followed with extreme care

__Common wall finishes combined with metal frame partitions include:

    __Interior Single Layer:
        --3/8" plywood paneling
        --3/8" gypsum wallboard
        --1/2" gypsum wallboard
        --5/8" gypsum wallboard
        --3/4" 7/8" 1" metal lath and plaster

    __Interior Double Layer:
        --2 - 3/8" gypsum wallboard
        --2 - 1/2" gypsum wallboard
        --2 - 5/8" gypsum wallboard
        --1/2" gypsum wallboard plus 3/8" plywood paneling
        --3/8" gypsum lath plus 1/2" plaster (7/8")
        --3/8" gypsum lath plus 5/8" plaster (1")
        --3/8" gypsum lath plus 3/4" plaster (1-1/8")

__Gypsum Wallboard Walls & Ceilings. Special types of gypsum wallboard that might be noted in details include:
    --Type X for fire resistance
    --Water resistant
    --Waterproof
    --Sound deadening
    --Insulative foil backed

09110   METAL FRAME PARTITIONS

DETAIL DATA CHECKLIST   continued

FINISH WALL CONSTRUCTION continued

__Gypsum wallboard assembly components commonly identified in detail drawing notes include:
- --Corner beads
- --Edge trim
- --Corner guards
- --Edge trim sealant @ floor and ceiling
- --Resilient channels
- --Angle clip reinforcement @ ceilings

__Lath & Plaster Walls & Ceilings. Plaster coats sometimes identified in large.scale details are:
- --Scratch coat
- --Brown coat
- --Finish coat

__Lath and plaster components commonly identified in detail notation include:
- --Expanded metal lath
- --Wire lath
- --Gypsum lath
- --Base screeds
- --Corner beads
- --Edge casing beads
- --Grounds
- --Picture mouldings
- --Window stools
- --Corner lath reinforcement
- --Control joints

Other wall and ceiling finishes that might be noted include veneer plaster, sprayed acoustical surface, fabric or carpet, vinyl, laminated plastic, etc. Such applied finishes may be named in details but are commonly referenced to the finish schedule and specifications.

OTHER DETAIL AND NOTATION DATA THAT MAY BE USED WITH THESE DETAILS

__Wall-related detail items:
- --Mirrors
- --Attached casework
- --Shelving
- --Tack and chalk boards
- --Ornamental trim, casings, and special moldings
- --Casework at end walls and jambs
- --Coves and valances
- --Signs and support backing
- --Recessed compartments
- --Pass-thru openings
- --Access panels
- --Louvers or vents

09110 (a) 2-1/2" METAL FRAME PARTITION

See DETAIL DATA CHECKLIST for metal partitions preceding 09110 (a)

SMALL-SCALE GENERIC DETAILS

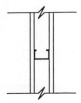

TYPICAL
PARTITION
(2-1/2" STUD)
1-1/2"=1'-0"

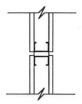

PARTITION @
CONTROL JOINT
(2-1/2" STUD)
1-1/2"=1'-0"

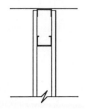

PARTITION @
BEARING WALL
(2-1/2" STUD)
1-1/2"=1'-0"

PARTITION
@ CORNER
(2-1/2" STUD)
1-1/2"=1'-0"

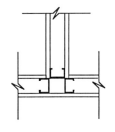

PARTITION @
T INTERSECTION
(2-1/2" STUD)
1-1/2"=1'-0"

PARTITION THRU
SUSP. CLG.
(2-1/2" STUD)
1-1/2"=1'-0"

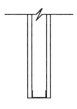

HEAD
(2-1/2" STUD)
1-1/2"=1'-0"

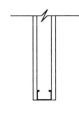

JAMB
(2-1/2" STUD)
1-1/2"=1'-0"

FULL-SCALE GENERIC DETAILS

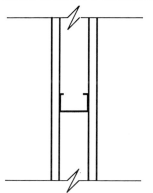

TYPICAL PARTITION
(2-1/2" STUD)
1-1/2"=1'-0"

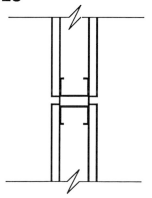

PARTITION @ CONTROL
JOINT (2-1/2" STUD)
1-1/2"=1'-0"

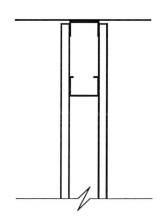

PARTITION @ BEARING
WALL (2-1/2" STUD)
1-1/2"=1'-0"

09110 (a) 2-1/2" METAL FRAME PARTITION

FULL-SCALE GENERIC DETAILS continued

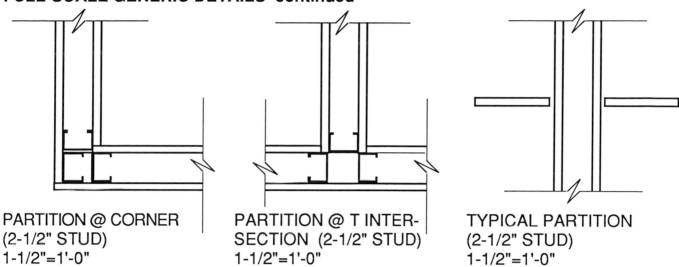

PARTITION @ CORNER
(2-1/2" STUD)
1-1/2"=1'-0"

PARTITION @ T INTER-
SECTION (2-1/2" STUD)
1-1/2"=1'-0"

TYPICAL PARTITION
(2-1/2" STUD)
1-1/2"=1'-0"

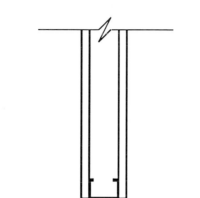

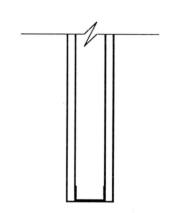

JAMB
(2-1/2" STUD)
1-1/2"=1'-0"

HEAD
(2-1/2" STUD)
1-1/2"=1'-0"

NOTATION CHECKLIST, SAMPLE NOTES

METAL STUDS (SIZE & SPACING)
METAL RUNNER/ANCHORS
METAL TRACK/HEADER
ADJACENT CEILING OR SLAB
GYPSUM WALLBOARD
LATH & PLASTER
SPECIAL FINISHES/
   WATERPROOFING
HOOKS/TRACKS
WALL MOUNTED FIXTURES
WALL ANCHORS/
   MOUNTING BRACKETS
RAILINGS/WALL GUARDS
THRU-WALL SLEEVE
SEALANT/SOUND BARRIER/
   LEAD LINING
JOINTS (CONTROL OR EXPANSION)
ADJACENT FINISHES
GYPSUM WALL BOARD
WATER-RESISTANT GYP.BD.
CORNER BEAD
CONTROL JOINT
SOUND ATTENUATION BLANKET
RIGID INSULATION

PLYWOOD
METAL WALL ANGLE @ CLG.
FURRING CHANNEL
METAL RUNNER
SUSP. METAL FURRING CHANNEL
METAL STUDS @ 24" O.C.
METAL STUDS @ 16" O.C.
STAGGER STUDS
BRACING TO STRUCTURE
STUD TO CLG. @ 48" O.C.
CHASE WALL
FLOOR TRACK
SEALANT EACH SIDE
RESILIENT BASE, 4"
CONT. SPONGE RUBBER GASKET, 1/2" X 3" (@ clg.)
SUSPENDED CEILING
FASTEN METAL STUDS TO CLG. 'T'

09110 (b) 4" METAL FRAME PARTITIONS

See DETAIL DATA CHECKLIST for metal partitions preceding 09110 (a)

SMALL-SCALE GENERIC DETAILS

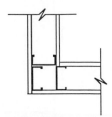

TYPICAL
PARTITION
(4" STUD)
1-1/2"=1'-0"

PARTITION
@ CONTROL JOINT
(4" STUD)
1-1/2"=1'-0"

PARTITION
@ BEARING WALL
(4" STUD)
1-1/2"=1'-0"

PARTITION
@ CORNER
(4" STUD)
1-1/2"=1'-0"

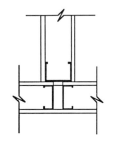

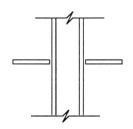

PARTITION @ T
INTERSECTION
(4" STUD)
1-1/2"=1'-0"

PARTITION THRU
SUSP.CEILING
(4" STUD)
1-1/2"=1'-0"

JAMB
(4" STUD)
1-1/2"=1'-0"

HEAD
(4" STUD)
1-1/2"=1'-0"

FULL-SCALE GENERIC DETAILS

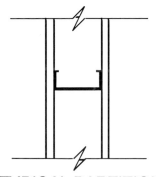

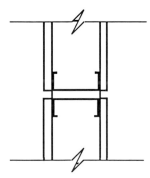

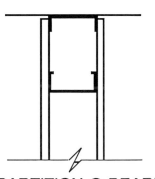

TYPICAL PARTITION
(4" STUD)
1-1/2"=1'-0"

PARTITION @ CONTROL
JOINT (4" STUD)
1-1/2"=1'-0"

PARTITION @ BEARING
WALL (4" STUD)
1-1/2"=1'-0"

FULL-SCALE GENERIC DETAILS continued

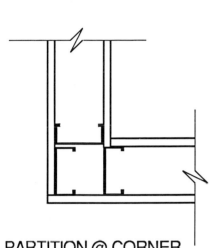

PARTITION @ CORNER (4" STUD)
1-1/2"=1'-0"

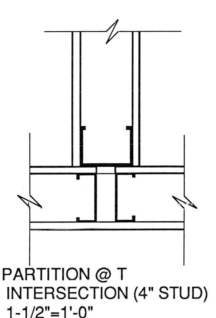

PARTITION @ T INTERSECTION (4" STUD)
1-1/2"=1'-0"

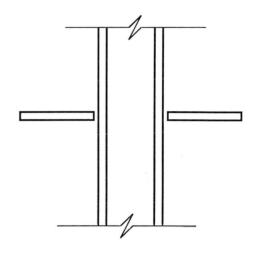

PARTITION THRU SUSP. CEILING (4" STUD)
1-1/2"=1'-0"

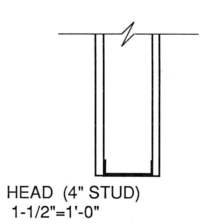

HEAD (4" STUD)
1-1/2"=1'-0"

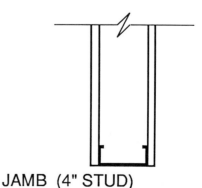

JAMB (4" STUD)
1-1/2"=1'-0"

NOTATION CHECKLIST, SAMPLE NOTES

METAL STUDS (SIZE & SPACING)
METAL RUNNER/ANCHORS
METAL TRACK/HEADER
ADJACENT CEILING OR SLAB
GYPSUM WALLBOARD
LATH & PLASTER
SPECIAL FINISHES/
    WATERPROOFING
HOOKS/TRACKS
WALL MOUNTED FIXTURES
WALL ANCHORS/MOUNTING
    BRACKETS
RAILINGS/WALL GUARDS
THRU-WALL SLEEVE
SEALANT/SOUND BARRIER/
    LEAD LINING
JOINTS (CONTROL OR
    EXPANSION)
ADJACENT FINISHES
GYPSUM WALL BOARD
WATER-RESISTANT GYP.BD.
CORNER BEAD
CONTROL JOINT

SOUND ATTENUATION BLANKET
RIGID INSULATION
PLYWOOD
METAL WALL ANGLE @ CLG.
FURRING CHANNEL
METAL RUNNER
SUSP. METAL FURRING
    CHANNEL
METAL STUDS @ 24" O.C.
METAL STUDS @ 16" O.C.
STAGGER STUDS
BRACING TO STRUCTURE
STUD TO CLG. @ 48" O.C.
CHASE WALL
FLOOR TRACK
SEALANT EACH SIDE
RESILIENT BASE, 4"
CONT. SPONGE RUBBER
    GASKET, 1/2" X 3" (@ clg.)
SUSPENDED CEILING
FASTEN METAL STUDS
    TO CLG. 'T'

09110 (c) 5-1/2" METAL FRAME PARTITION

See DETAIL DATA CHECKLIST for metal partitions preceding 09110 (a)

SMALL-SCALE GENERIC DETAILS

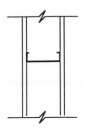

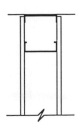

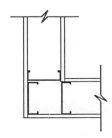

TYPICAL PARTITION
(5-1/2" STUD)
1-1/2"=1'-0"

PARTITION @ CONTROL
JOINT (5-1/2" STUD)
1-1/2"=1'-0"

PARTITION @ BEARING
WALL (5-1/2" STUD)
1-1/2"=1'-0"

PARTITION @ CORNER
(5-1/2" STUD)
1-1/2"=1'-0"

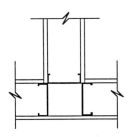

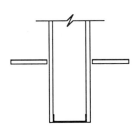

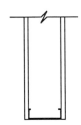

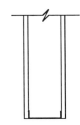

PARTITION @
T INTERSECTION
(5-1/2" STUD)
1-1/2"=1'-0"

PARTITION THRU
SUSP. CLG.
(5-1/2" STUD)
1-1/2"=1'-0"

JAMB
(5-1/2" STUD)
1-1/2"=1'-0"

HEAD
(5-1/2" STUD)
1-1/2"=1'-0"

FULL-SCALE GENERIC DETAILS

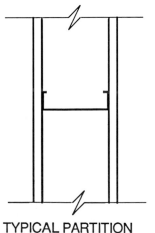

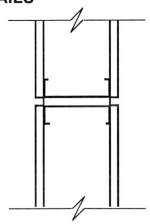

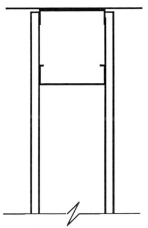

TYPICAL PARTITION
(5-1/2" STUD)
1-1/2"=1'-0"

PARTITION @ CONTROL
JOINT (5-1/2" STUD)
1-1/2"=1'-0"

PARTITION @ BEARING
WALL (5-1/2" STUD)
1-1/2"=1'-0"

09110 (c) 5-1/2" METAL FRAME PARTITION

FULL-SCALE GENERIC DETAILS continued

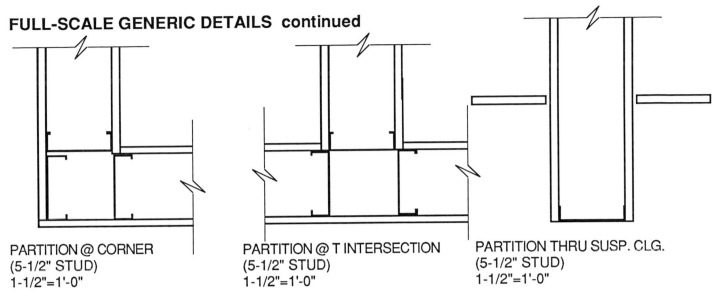

PARTITION @ CORNER
(5-1/2" STUD)
1-1/2"=1'-0"

PARTITION @ T INTERSECTION
(5-1/2" STUD)
1-1/2"=1'-0"

PARTITION THRU SUSP. CLG.
(5-1/2" STUD)
1-1/2"=1'-0"

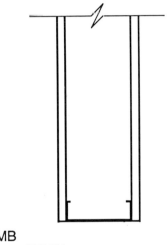

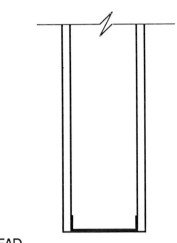

NOTATION CHECKLIST,
SAMPLE NOTES

METAL STUDS (SIZE & SPACING)
METAL RUNNER/ANCHORS
METAL TRACK/HEADER
ADJACENT CEILING OR SLAB
GYPSUM WALLBOARD
LATH & PLASTER
SPECIAL FINISHES/
   WATERPROOFING
HOOKS/TRACKS
WALL MOUNTED FIXTURES
WALL ANCHORS/MOUNTING
   BRACKETS
RAILINGS/WALL GUARDS
THRU-WALL SLEEVE
SEALANT/SOUND BARRIER/
   LEAD LINING
JOINTS (CONTROL OR EXPANSION)
ADJACENT FINISHES
GYPSUM WALL BOARD
WATER-RESISTANT GYP.BD.
CORNER BEAD
CONTROL JOINT
SOUND ATTENUATION BLANKET
RIGID INSULATION

JAMB
(5-1/2" STUD)
1-1/2"=1'-0"

HEAD
(5-1/2" STUD)
1-1/2"=1'-0"

PLYWOOD
METAL WALL ANGLE @ CLG.
FURRING CHANNEL
METAL RUNNER
SUSP. METAL FURRING CHANNEL
METAL STUDS @ 24" O.C.
METAL STUDS @ 16" O.C.
STAGGER STUDS
BRACING TO STRUCTURE
STUD TO CLG. @ 48" O.C.
CHASE WALL
FLOOR TRACK
SEALANT EACH SIDE
RESILIENT BASE, 4"
CONT. SPONGE RUBBER GASKET, 1/2" X 3" (@ clg.)
SUSPENDED CEILING
FASTEN MTL. STUDS TO CLG. 'T'

09115 METAL FURRING -- WALLS & CEILINGS

DETAIL DATA CHECKLIST

METAL FURRING
__Typically consists of metal furring strips added to rough wall or ceiling construction for attachment of lath or gypsum wall board
__A typical gypsum board support system:
    __Hanger wires are typically spaced 48" o.c. and within 6" of the end of carrying channel
    __Hanger wires support 1-1/2" carrying channels set at 48" o.c. and within 6" of walls
    __7/8" metal furring channels are supported at right angles to the carrying channels
__Furred spaces may be used for chases and soffits and are constructed of combinations of wood or metal studs and furring strips
__See manufacturers' recommendations regarding attachment of hanger wire and furring strips to various types of substructure

__Common wall finishes combined with metal framed partitions and furring include:
--3/8" plywood paneling
--3/8" gypsum wallboard
--1/2" gypsum wallboard
--5/8" gypsum wallboard
--3/4" 7/8" 1" metal lath and plaster
--2 - 3/8" gypsum wallboard
--2 - 1/2" gypsum wallboard
--2 - 5/8" gypsum wallboard
--1/2" gypsum wallboard plus 3/8" plywood paneling
--3/8" gypsum lath plus 1/2" plaster (7/8")
--3/8" gypsum lath plus 5/8" plaster (1")
--3/8" gypsum lath plus 3/4" plaster (1 1/8")

Gypsum Wallboard Walls & Ceilings -- special types of gypsum wallboard that might be required:
--Type X for fire resistance
--Water resistant
--Waterproof
--Sound deadening
--Insulative foil backed

Gypsum wallboard assembly components commonly identified in detail drawing notes include:
--Corner beads
--Edge trim
--Corner guards
--Edge trim sealant @ floor and ceiling
--Resilient channels
--Angle clip reinforcement @ ceilings

Lath and plaster components commonly identified in detail notation include:
--Expanded metal lath
--Wire lath
--Gypsum lath
--Base screeds
--Corner beads
--Edge casing beads
--Grounds
--Picture mouldings
--Window stools
--Corner lath reinforcement
--Control joints

09115 METAL FURRING -- WALLS & CEILINGS

SMALL-SCALE GENERIC DETAILS

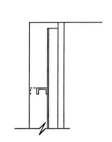

FURRED WALL
@ CEILING

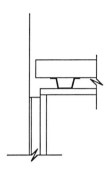

FURRED WALL
@ FURRED CEILING

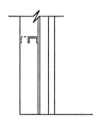

FURRED WALL
@ FLOOR

FURRED WALL
@ FLOOR

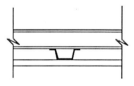

FURRED CEILING

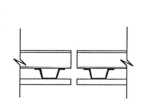

FURRED CEILING
@ EXPANSION JOINT

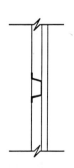

FURRED WALL
Plan

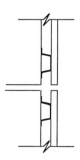

FURRED WALL
@ EXPANSION JOINT

09115 METAL FURRING -- WALLS & CEILINGS

FULL-SCALE GENERIC DETAILS

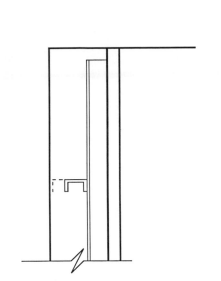

FURRED WALL
@ CEILING
3"=1'-0"   09115-3

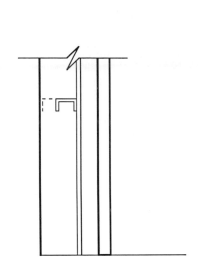

FURRED WALL
@ FLOOR
3"=1'-0"   09115-5

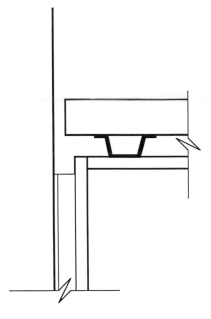

FURRED WALL
@ FURRED CEILING
3"=1'-0"   09115-9

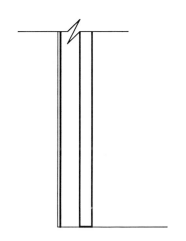

FURRED WALL
@ FLOOR
3"=1'-0"   09115-11

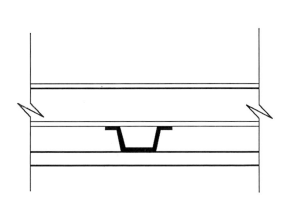

FURRED CEILING
3"=1'-0"   09115-21

09115 METAL FURRING -- WALLS & CEILINGS

FULL-SCALE GENERIC DETAILS continued

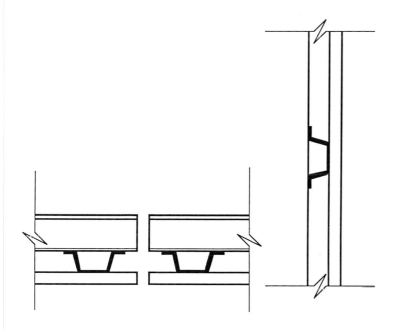

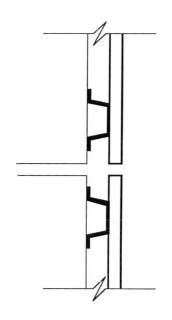

FURRED CEILING
@ EXPANSION JOINT
3"=1'-0"   09115-23

FURRED WALL
Plan
3"=1'-0"   09115-27

FURRED WALL
@ EXPANSION JOINT
3"=1'-0"   09115-29

NOTATION CHECKLIST,
SAMPLE NOTES

HANGER WIRE
1-1/2" CARRYING CHANNEL
3/4" FURRING CHANNEL
ADJACENT WALL CONSTRUCTION
CHANNEL STUDS
FURRING STUDS/BRACKET/TIE
GYPSUM WALLBOARD
LATI I & PLASTER
SPECIAL FINISHES/WATERPROOFING
HOOKS/TRACKS/WALL-MOUNTED FIXTURES
WALL ANCHORS/MOUNTING BRACKETS
BASE (FINISH BASE SIZE/MATERIAL)
CHANNEL FLOOR RUNNER/ANCHORS
FINISH FLOOR/SUBFLOOR/SLAB

GYPSUM WALLBOARD
WATER-RESISTANT GYP.BD.
GYPSUM BOARD, TYPE 'X'
CORNER BEAD
CONTROL JOINT
SOUND ATTENUATION BLANKET
RIGID INSULATION
PLYWOOD
METAL WALL ANGLE @ CLG.
FURRING CHANNEL
METAL RUNNER
SUSP. MTL. FURRING CHANNEL
METAL STUDS @ 24" O.C.
METAL STUDS @ 16" O.C.
STAGGER STUDS
BRACING TO STRUCTURE
STUD TO CLG. @ 48" O.C.
CHASE WALL
FLOOR TRACK
SEALANT EACH SIDE
RESILIENT BASE, 4"
CONT. SPONGE RUBBER GASKET, 1/2" X 3" (@ clg.)
SUSPENDED CEILING
FASTEN METAL STUDS TO CLG. ' T '

09120 SUSPENDED CEILINGS

FULL-SCALE GENERIC DETAILS continued

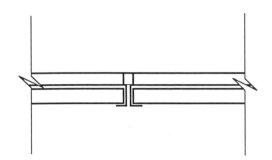

EXPOSED GRID FOR
CEILING TILE
3"=1'-0"   09120-5

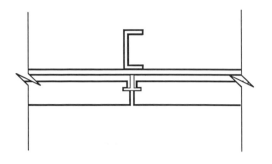

CONCEALED GRID FOR
CEILING TILE
3"=1'-0"   09120-6

NOTATION CHECKLIST,
SAMPLE NOTES

HANGER WIRE
1-1/2" CARRYING CHANNEL
MAIN RUNNER
CROSS TEE
CEILING TILE
3/4" FURRING CHANNEL
GYPSUM WALLBOARD
LATH & PLASTER
SPECIAL FINISHES
CORNER BEAD
TRACKS/ANCHORS/FIXTURES

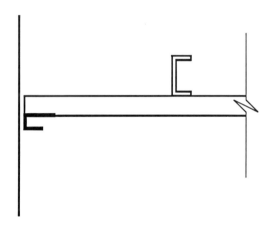

SUSPENDED PLASTER CEILING
@ WALL
3"=1'-0"   09120-7

HANGER WIRES, 3 TURNS AROUND ITSELF
MAIN BEAM, SUPPORT W/HANGER WIRE
ACOUSTICAL TILE CLG.
CAULK GYPSUM BOARD AROUND CLG.
    PENETRATIONS
'S' SCREW
METAL WALL ANGLE
SECURE META; WALL TRIM TO CLG.
    SUSPENSION SYSTEM (not wall)
LINE @ WALL
BATT INSULATION
PROVIDE FIRE DAMPERS WHERE DUCTS
    PENETRATE ENVELOPE
LIGHT FIXTURES

COMPOSITE MASTER DETAIL

DETAIL FILE NUMBER: **09120-1**

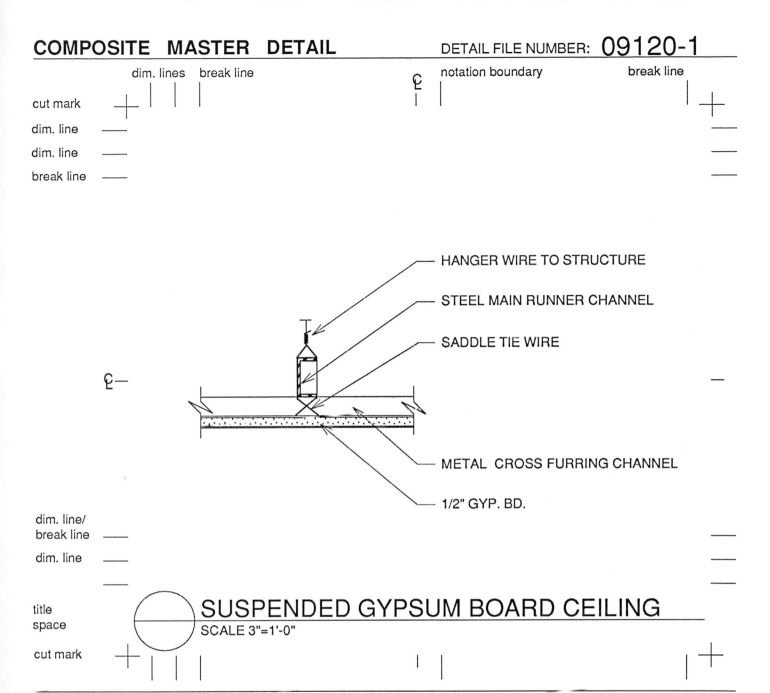

dim. lines   break line

cut mark

dim. line

dim. line

break line

notation boundary   break line

HANGER WIRE TO STRUCTURE

STEEL MAIN RUNNER CHANNEL

SADDLE TIE WIRE

METAL CROSS FURRING CHANNEL

1/2" GYP. BD.

dim. line/
break line

dim. line

title
space

SUSPENDED GYPSUM BOARD CEILING
SCALE 3"=1'-0"

cut mark

DETAIL INFORMATION
References, jobsite feedback, Job history

09125 SUSPENDED CEILINGS

DETAIL DATA CHECKLIST

SUSPENDED CEILINGS
__There are many varied suspended ceiling systems and products; see manufacturers' catalogs for recommendations for specifications, detailing, and application.

__A typical gypsum board support system:
    __Hanger wires are typically spaced 48" o.c. and within 6" of the end of carrying channel
    __Hanger wires support 1-1/2" carrying channels set at 48" o.c. and within 6" of walls
    __7/8" metal furring channels are supported at right angles to the carrying channels

__Integrated lighting and acoustical tile systems come complete with all hardware and accessories.
__Use manufacturers' shop drawings as guides for any special customized detailing of a selected product.
__See manufacturers' recommendations regarding attachment of hanger wire to various types of overhead construction.

SMALL-SCALE GENERIC DETAILS

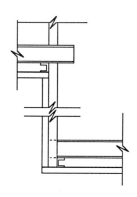

SUSPENDED CEILING @ SOFFIT
09125-1

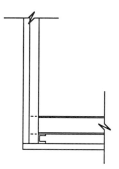

SUSPENDED CEILING @ SOFFIT
09125-2

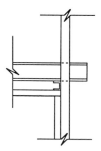

SUSPENDED CEILING @ FURRED WALL
09125-3

09125 SUSPENDED CEILINGS

FULL-SCALE GENERIC DETAILS

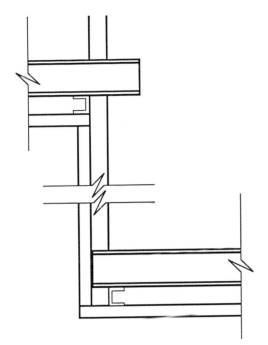

SUSPENDED CEILING @ SOFFIT
3"=1'-0"   09125-1

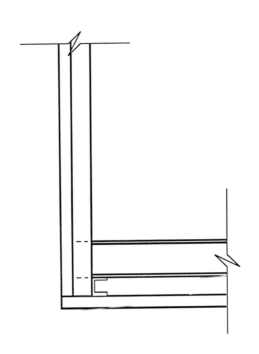

SUSPENDED CEILING @ SOFFIT
3"=1'-0"   09125-2

NOTATION CHECKLIST, SAMPLE NOTES

HANGER WIRE
1-1/2" CARRYING CHANNEL
MAIN RUNNER
CROSS TEE
CEILING TILE
3/4" FURRING CHANNEL
GYPSUM WALLBOARD
LATH & PLASTER
SPECIAL FINISHES
CORNER BEAD
TRACKS/ANCHORS/FIXTURES
HANGER WIRES, 3 TURNS AROUND ITSELF
MAIN BEAM, SUPPORT W/HANGER WIRE
ACOUSTICAL TILE CLG.
CAULK GYPSUM BOARD AROUND CLG.
    PENETRATIONS
'S' SCREW
METAL WALL ANGLE
SECURE METAL WALL TRIM TO CLG.
    SUSPENSION SYSTEM (not wall)
LINE @ WALL
BATT INSULATION
PROVIDE FIRE DAMPERS WHERE
    DUCTS PENETRATE ENVELOPE
LIGHT FIXTURES

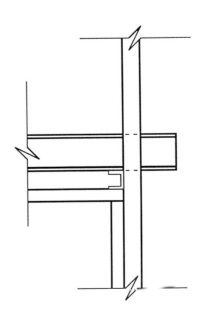

SUSPENDED CEILING @ FURRED WALL
3"=1'-0"   09125-3

611

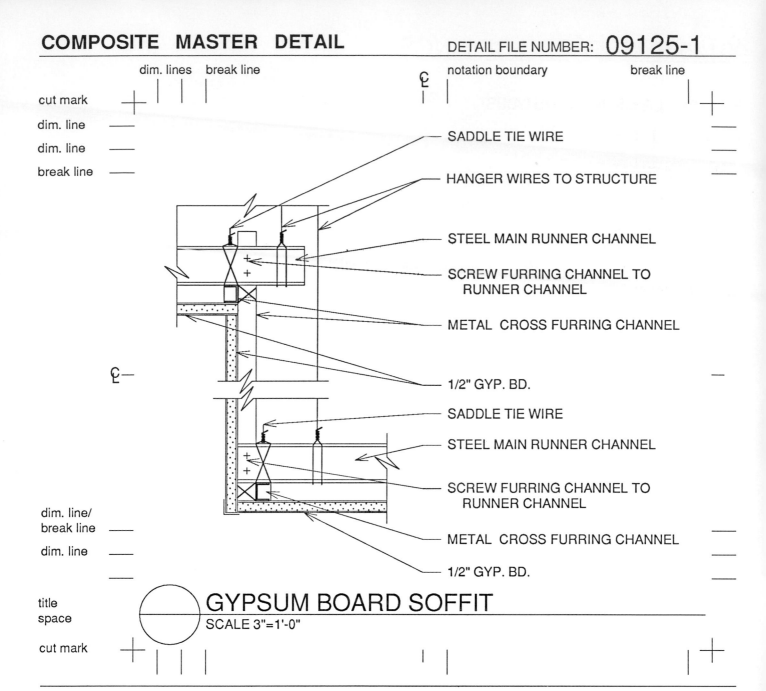

SADDLE TIE WIRE

HANGER WIRES TO STRUCTURE

STEEL MAIN RUNNER CHANNEL

SCREW FURRING CHANNEL TO RUNNER CHANNEL

METAL CROSS FURRING CHANNEL

1/2" GYP. BD.

SADDLE TIE WIRE

STEEL MAIN RUNNER CHANNEL

SCREW FURRING CHANNEL TO RUNNER CHANNEL

METAL CROSS FURRING CHANNEL

1/2" GYP. BD.

cut mark
dim. lines   break line
notation boundary   break line
dim. line
dim. line
break line

GYPSUM BOARD SOFFIT
SCALE 3"=1'-0"

title space
cut mark

dim. line/ break line
dim. line

DETAIL INFORMATION
References, jobsite feedback, job history

09311 CERAMIC TILE

DETAIL DATA CHECKLIST

CERAMIC TILE

__Mosaic tiles are 1" x 1", 1" x 2", 2" x 2" and 1/4" thick
__Glazed wall tiles are 4-1/4" x 4-1/4", 4-1/4" x 6", and 6" x 6"; typically 5/16" thick
__Quarry tiles and floor pavers are 2-3/4" x 6", 4" x 4", 4" x 6", 6" x 6", 6" x 9", 9" x 9"; 1/2" to 3/4" thick

__Wall tile on wood frame walls:
    __Apply with waterproof glue over water resistant backing such as gypsum wallboard
    __Sometimes applied on cement mortar on metal or gypsum lath over wood frame
    __When using gypsum wallboard tile backing in wet rooms, use water proof or water resistant grade
__Tile on concrete or masonry walls:
    __Walls must be stable, not subject to extremes of expansion/contraction, soil movement, etc.

__Primary variations of tile setting are:
    __Mortar method on wood or metal frame: 3/4" to 1-1/2" mortar bed over scratch coat, lath and felt
    __Mortar method on masonry: 3/4" to 1-1/2" mortar bed over scratch coat
    __Thin-set over masonry or concrete: tile over 1/8" to 1/4" thick dry set mortar
    __Adhesive method: Tile over 1/16" adhesive over primed solid backing

__Cement mortar scratch coat is typically 3/4", with a leveling coat of 1/4" to 1/2"
__Reinforce floor mortar to prevent cracking
__Tile flooring substrate may have to be recessed to allow for different adjacent finish-floor thicknesses
__Floor reinforced mortar bed is typically 1-1/4" thick
__Quarry tile and pavers are typically 1/2" to 1-1/2" thick
__Promenade tile are 1" x 6" x 9" in size

__See tile manufacturers' and suppliers' catalogs for recommended detailing, specifications, and application
    of tile to different types of wall and floor surfaces

09311 CERAMIC TILE FLOOR

See DETAIL DATA CHECKLIST for ceramic tile preceding 09311

SMALL-SCALE GENERIC DETAILS

CERAMIC TILE FLOOR Thin-Set
09311-21

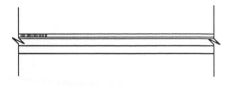

CERAMIC TILE FLOOR
Thin-Set On Wood
09311-22

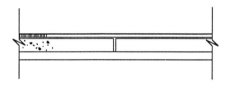

CERAMIC TILE FLOOR
Glass Mesh/Mortar
09311-23

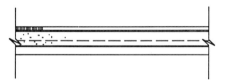

CERAMIC TILE FLOOR
Cement Mortar On Wood
09311-26

CERAMIC TILE FLOOR
Cement Mortar
09311-27

09311 CERAMIC TILE FLOOR

FULL-SCALE GENERIC DETAILS

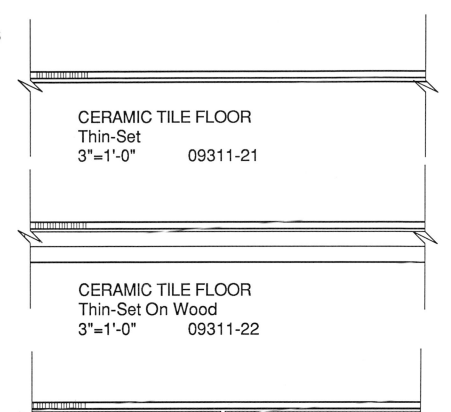

CERAMIC TILE FLOOR
Thin-Set
3"=1'-0"   09311-21

CERAMIC TILE FLOOR
Thin-Set On Wood
3"=1'-0"   09311-22

CERAMIC TILE FLOOR
Glass Mesh/Mortar
3"=1'-0"   09311-23

**NOTATION CHECKLIST,
SAMPLE NOTES**

FINISH FLOOR
   (MATERIAL & THICKNESS)
SETTING BED
   (MATERIAL & THICKNESS)
JOINT SIZE
FLOOR MEMBRANE/
   WATERPROOFING
SUBFLOOR/SLAB
REINFORCING
CERAMIC TILE
BOND COAT/MORTAR BED
SCRATCH COAT
MEMBRANE
WALL CONSTRUCTION

THINSET QUARRY TILE
QUARRY TILE
ROUND TOP COVE BASE
WATERPROOF GYP. BD.
ADHESIVE
SETTING BED
MORTAR BED W/REINFORCING
ANGLE EDGER
THRESHOLD
HARDWOOD DIVIDER STRIP
REDUCER STRIP
DOOR
SILICONE SEALER
SLOPE FROM CURB TO DRAIN

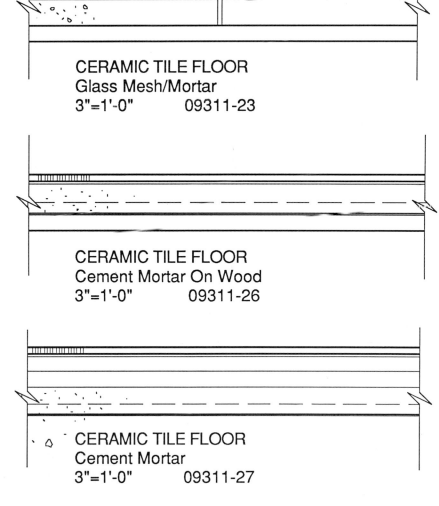

CERAMIC TILE FLOOR
Cement Mortar On Wood
3"=1'-0"   09311-26

CERAMIC TILE FLOOR
Cement Mortar
3"=1'-0"   09311-27

09312, 09313 CERAMIC TILE BASE & WAINSCOT

See DETAIL DATA CHECKLIST for ceramic tile preceding 09311

SMALL-SCALE GENERIC DETAILS

CERAMIC
TILE BASE
Thin-Set
09312-21

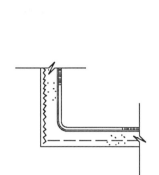

CERAMIC
TILE BASE
Cement Mortar
09312-22

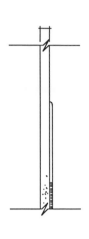

CERAMIC TILE
WAINSCOT
Thin-Set
09313-21

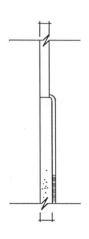

CERAMIC TILE
WAINSCOT
Cement Mortar
09313-22

FULL-SCALE GENERIC DETAILS

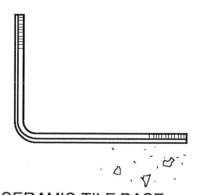

CERAMIC TILE BASE
Thin-Set
3"=1'-0"   09312-21

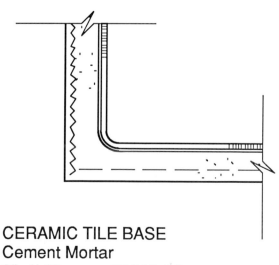

CERAMIC TILE BASE
Cement Mortar
3"=1'-0"   09312-22

09312, 09313 CERAMIC TILE BASE & WAINSCOT

FULL-SCALE GENERIC DETAILS continued

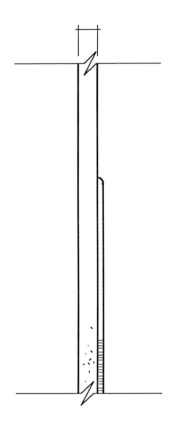

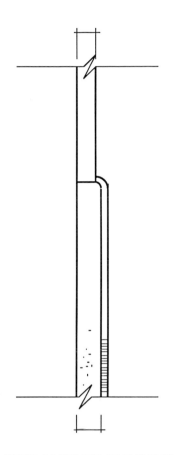

CERAMIC TILE
WAINSCOT   Thin-Set
3"=1'-0"   09313-21

CERAMIC TILE WAINSCOT
Cement Mortar
3"=1'-0"   09313-22

NOTATION CHECKLIST,
SAMPLE NOTES

FINISH FLOOR (MATERIAL & THICKNESS)
SETTING BED (MATERIAL & THICKNESS)
JOINT SIZE
FLOOR MEMBRANE/WATERPROOFING
SUBFLOOR/SLAB
REINFORCING
CERAMIC TILE
BOND COAT/MORTAR BED
SCRATCH COAT
MEMBRANE
WALL CONSTRUCTION

THINSET QUARRY TILE
QUARRY TILE
ROUND TOP COVE BASE
WATERPROOF GYPSUM BOARD
ADHESIVE
SETTING BED
MORTAR BED W/REINFORCING
ANGLE EDGER
THRESHOLD
HARDWOOD DIVIDER STRIP
REDUCER STRIP
DOOR
SILICONE SEALER
SLOPE FROM CURB TO DRAIN

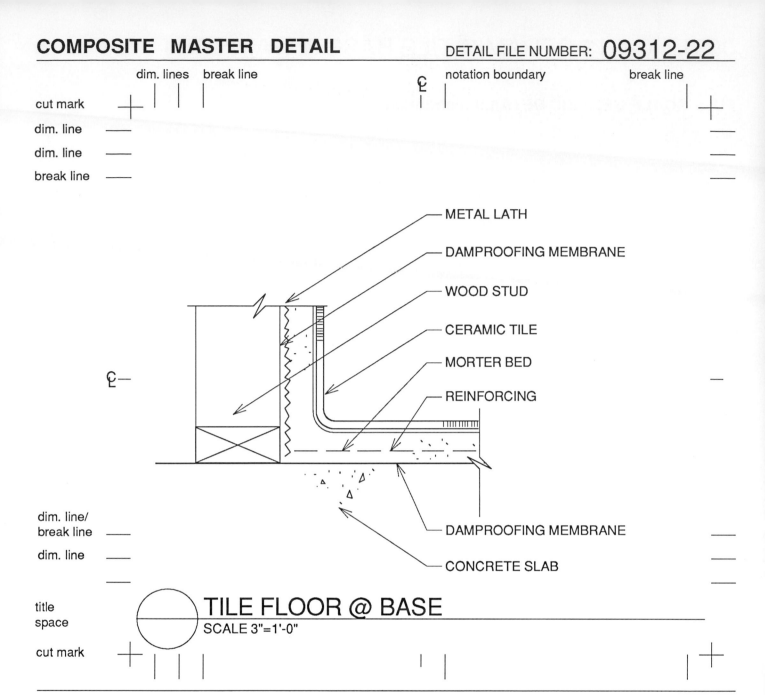

cut mark

dim. lines   break line

notation boundary   break line

dim. line

dim. line

break line

METAL LATH

DAMPROOFING MEMBRANE

WOOD STUD

CERAMIC TILE

MORTER BED

REINFORCING

dim. line/
break line

dim. line

DAMPROOFING MEMBRANE

CONCRETE SLAB

title
space

TILE FLOOR @ BASE
SCALE 3"=1'-0"

cut mark

DETAIL INFORMATION
References, jobsite feedback, job history

09314 CERAMIC TILE WALLS

See DETAIL DATA CHECKLIST for ceramic tile preceding 09311

SMALL-SCALE GENERIC DETAILS

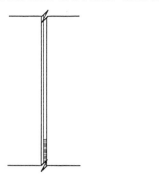

CERAMIC TILE WALL
Thin-Set
09314-21

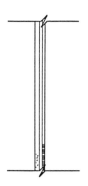

CERAMIC TILE WALL
Leveling/Bond Coat
09314-22

CERAMIC TILE WALL
Cement Mortar
09314-23

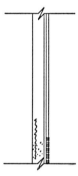

CERAMIC TILE WALL
Lath/Plaster/Mortar
09314-24

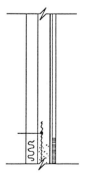

CERAMIC TILE WALL
@ STEAM ROOM
09314-25

CERAMIC TILE WALL
Thin-Set on Gypsum Board
09314-26

09314 CERAMIC TILE WALLS

FULL-SCALE GENERIC DETAILS

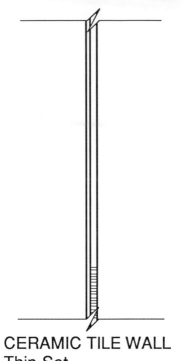

CERAMIC TILE WALL
Thin-Set
3"=1'-0"   09314-21

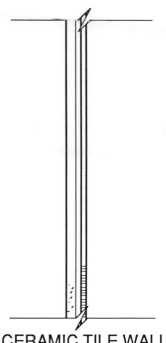

CERAMIC TILE WALL
Leveling/Bond Coat
3"=1'-0"   09314-22

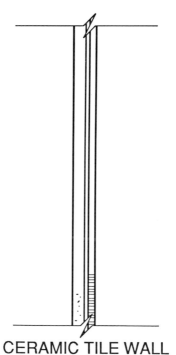

CERAMIC TILE WALL
Cement Mortar
3"=1'-0"   09314-23

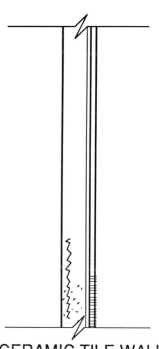

CERAMIC TILE WALL
Lath/Plaster/Mortar
3"=1'-0"   09314-24

09314 CERAMIC TILE WALLS

FULL-SCALE GENERIC DETAILS continued

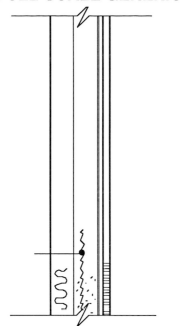

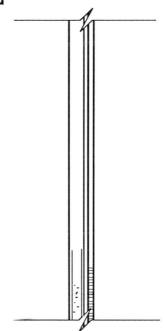

CERAMIC TILE WALL
@ STEAM ROOM
3"=1'-0"   09314-25

CERAMIC TILE WALL
Thin-Set on Gypsum Board
3"=1'-0"   09314-26

NOTATION CHECKLIST,
SAMPLE NOTES

CERAMIC TILE
ADHESIVE/DRY-SET
BOND COAT/MORTAR BED
SCRATCH COAT
MEMBRANE
WALL CONSTRUCTION

THINSET QUARRY TILE
QUARRY TILE
ROUND TOP COVE BASE
WATERPROOF GYPSUM BOARD
ADHESIVE
SETTING BED
MORTAR BED W/REINFORCING
ANGLE EDGER
THRESHOLD
HARDWOOD DIVIDER STRIP
REDUCER STRIP
DOOR
SILICONE SEALER

09314--09317 CERAMIC TILE TUBS & RECEPTORS

See DETAIL DATA CHECKLIST for ceramic tile preceding 09311

SMALL-SCALE GENERIC DETAILS

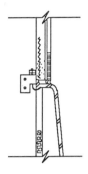

CERAMIC TILE WALL
@ TUB Plaster Wall
09314-31

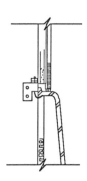

CERAMIC TILE WALL
@ TUB Gypsum Board Wall
09314-36

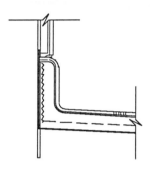

CERAMIC TILE BASE
SHOWER RECEPTOR
09315-21

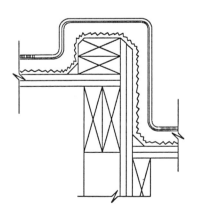

CERAMIC
TILE TUB
09316-21

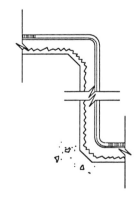

CERAMIC
TILE TUB
09316-22

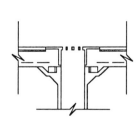

CERAMIC TILE BASE
FLOOR @ DRAIN
09317-11

09314--09317 CERAMIC TILE TUBS & RECEPTORS

FULL-SCALE GENERIC DETAILS

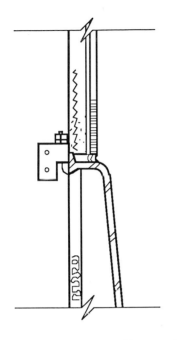

CERAMIC TILE WALL @ TUB
Plaster Wall
3"=1'-0"   09314-31

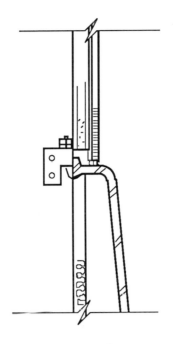

CERAMIC TILE WALL @ TUB
Gypsum Board Wall
3"=1'-0"   09314-36

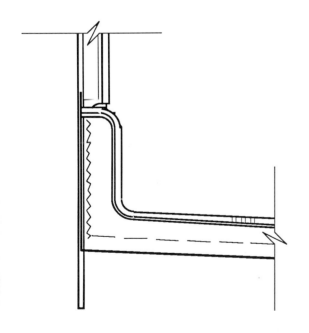

CERAMIC TILE BASE SHOWER RECEPTOR
3"=1'-0"   09315-21

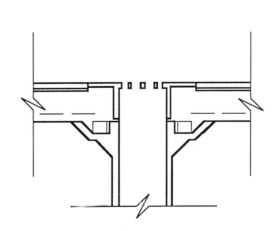

CERAMIC TILE BASE FLOOR @ DRAIN
3"=1'-0"   09317-11

FULL-SCALE GENERIC DETAILS continued

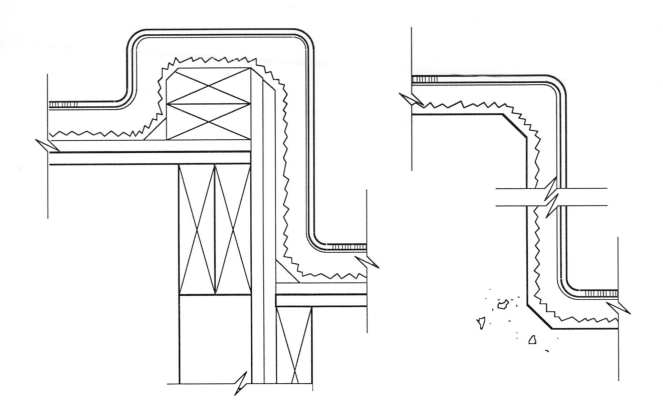

CERAMIC TILE TUB
3"=1'-0"   09316-21

CERAMIC TILE TUB
3"=1'-0"   09316-22

NOTATION CHECKLIST, SAMPLE NOTES

CERAMIC TILE
WALL CONSTRUCTION
WALL FRAMING
TUB HANGER
TUB
SETTING BED
LATH/REINFORCING
WATERPROOF MEMBRANE
DRAIN

THINSET QUARRY TILE
QUARRY TILE
ROUND TOP COVE BASE
CERAMIC CAP
BULLNOSE CAP
WATERPROOF GYPSUM BOARD
ADHESIVE
SETTING BED
MORTAR BED W/REINFORCING
ANGLE EDGER
THRESHOLD
HARDWOOD DIVIDER STRIP
REDUCER STRIP
DOOR
SILICONE SEALER
SLOPE FROM CURB TO DRAIN

09318 TILE COUNTERTOPS

See DETAIL DATA CHECKLIST for ceramic tile preceding 09311

SMALL-SCALE GENERIC DETAILS

TILE COUNTERTOP
Splash/Thin Set
09318-21

TILE COUNTERTOP
Lip/Thin Set
09318-22

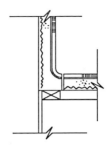

TILE COUNTERTOP
Splash/Mortar Bed
09318-31

TILE COUNTERTOP
Lip/Mortar Bed
09318-32

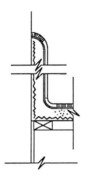

TILE COUNTERTOP
Splash/Mortar Bed
09318-41

FULL-SCALE GENERIC DETAILS

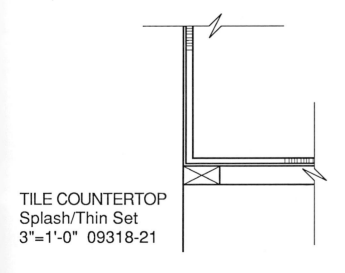

TILE COUNTERTOP
Splash/Thin Set
3"=1'-0" 09318-21

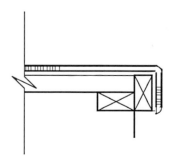

TILE COUNTERTOP
Lip/Thin Set
3"=1'-0" 09318-22

09318 TILE COUNTERTOPS

FULL-SCALE GENERIC DETAILS continued

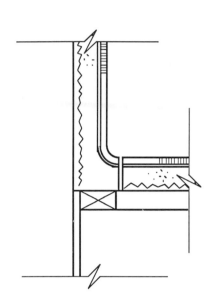

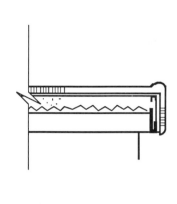

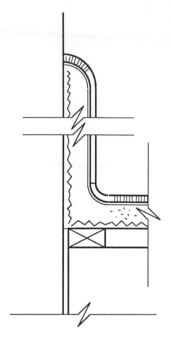

TILE COUNTERTOP
Splash/Mortar Bed
3"=1'-0" 09318-31

TILE COUNTERTOP
Lip/Mortar Bed
3"=1'-0" 09318-32

TILE COUNTERTOP
Splash/Mortar Bed
3"=1'-0" 09318-41

NOTATION CHECKLIST, SAMPLE NOTES

TILE SURFACE
ADHESIVE
BOND COAT
MORTAR BED
METAL LATH
MEMBRANE
PLYWOOD/PARTICLE BOARD
TRIM (MATERIAL & SIZE)
BLOCKING (MATERIAL & SIZE)
ADJACENT MATERIALS
THINSET QUARRY TILE
QUARRY TILE
ROUND TOP COVE BASE
CERAMIC CAP

BULLNOSE CAP
WATERPROOF GYPSUM BOARD
ADHESIVE
SETTING BED
MORTAR BED W/REINFORCING
ANGLE EDGER
THRESHOLD
HARDWOOD DIVIDER STRIP
REDUCER STRIP
DOOR
SILICONE SEALER

DETAIL FILE NUMBER:**09318-21/31**

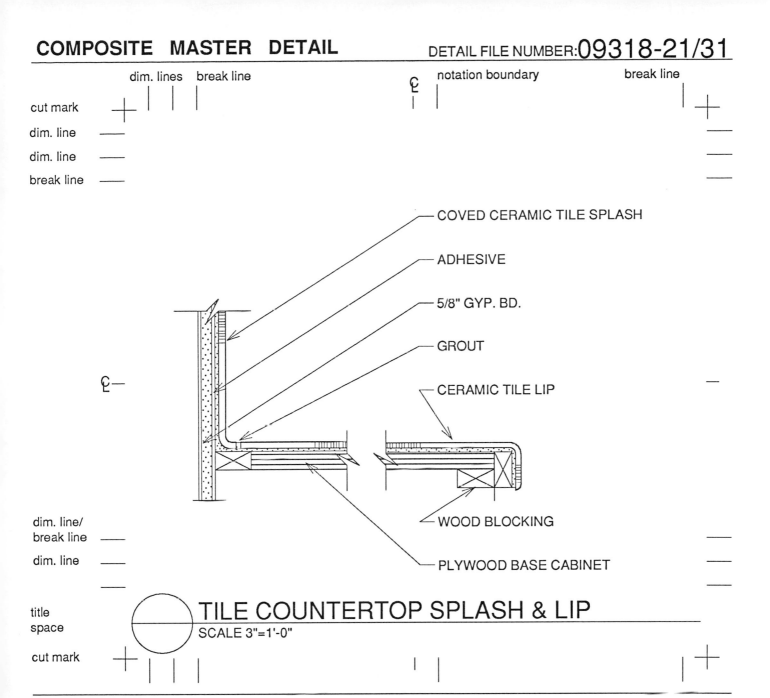

cut mark

dim. lines   break line

dim. line

dim. line

break line

notation boundary   break line

COVED CERAMIC TILE SPLASH

ADHESIVE

5/8" GYP. BD.

GROUT

CERAMIC TILE LIP

WOOD BLOCKING

PLYWOOD BASE CABINET

dim. line/
break line

dim. line

title
space

TILE COUNTERTOP SPLASH & LIP

SCALE 3"=1'-0"

cut mark

DETAIL INFORMATION
References, jobsite feedback, job history

09332 SLATE TILE FLOORS

DETAIL DATA CHECKLIST

SLATE FLOORING
__Typical slate flagstone thickness is 7/8"
__Slate flagstone comes in three types:
    __Square, four edges sawn
    __Irregular, two edges sawn
    __Irregular, no edges sawn
__Slate floor tile thicknesses are typically 1/2" to 1-1/4"
__Thicker floors are for the heavier traffic areas
__Follow supplier's recommendations for thickness in different floor traffic conditions
__Typical slate floor tile sizes are 6", 10" and 12", widths are 6" to 9", thicker panels are up to 24" square
__Slate is brittle and subject to damage from impact or bending stress
__Provide a stable substrate; movement of substrate will cause cracks in stone at mortar joints
__Provide complete, compact bedding beneath stone tile slabs to avoid bending stresses and cracking

SMALL-SCALE GENERIC DETAILS

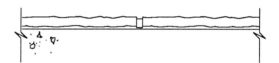

SLATE TILE FLOOR
Thin-Set on Concrete   09332-21

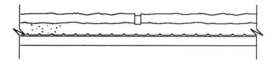

SLATE TILE FLOOR
Mortar Bed on Wood   09332-23

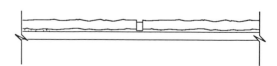

SLATE TILE FLOOR
Thin-Set on Wood 09332-26

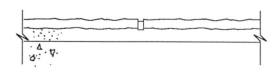

SLATE TILE FLOOR
Mortar Bed on Concrete   09332-31

09332 SLATE TILE FLOORS

FULL-SCALE GENERIC DETAILS

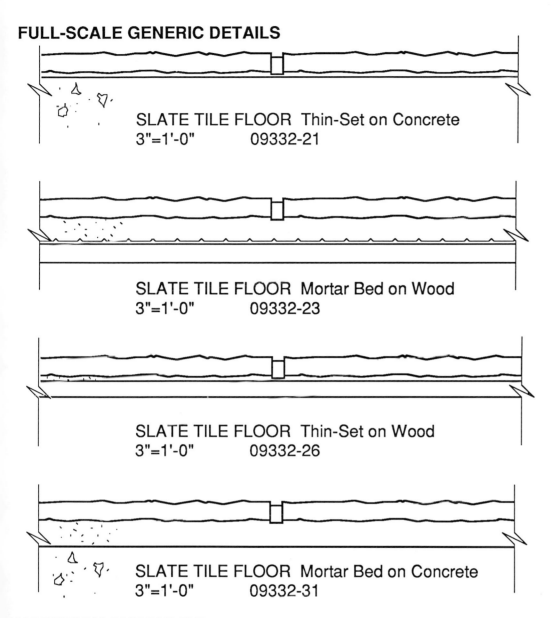

SLATE TILE FLOOR Thin-Set on Concrete
3"=1'-0"   09332-21

SLATE TILE FLOOR Mortar Bed on Wood
3"=1'-0"   09332-23

SLATE TILE FLOOR Thin-Set on Wood
3"=1'-0"   09332-26

SLATE TILE FLOOR Mortar Bed on Concrete
3"=1'-0"   09332-31

NOTATION CHECKLIST, SAMPLE NOTES

FINISH FLOOR (MATERIAL & SIZE)
SETTING BED (MATERIAL & SIZE)
JOINT SIZE
FLOOR
MEMBRANE/WATERPROOFING
SUBFLOOR/SLAB
REINFORCING

SLATE TILE
FINISH CONC.
BUILD UP CONC. FLOOR W/FLOORSTONE AS REQ'D.
PLYWOOD UNDERLAYMENT
PLYWOOD SUBFLOOR
PARTICLE BOARD UNDERLAYMENT
MASTIC
BOND COAT
ADHESIVE
SETTING BED
MORTAR BED W/REINFORCING
ANGLE EDGER
THRESHOLD
DIVIDER STRIP
REDUCER STRIP

09340 MARBLE TILE FLOORS

DETAIL DATA CHECKLIST

MARBLE FLOORING
__Typical thicknesses are 7/8" and 1-1/4"
__Joints are typically 1/16" thick
__Typical marble tile size ranges are 8" x 16", 12" x 12", and 10" x 20"
__Marble comes in hundreds of varieties, in five classes and four grades:
    __Classes are Travertine, Dolomite, Calcite, Onyx, and Serpentine, see supplier's catalogs for flooring
        characteristics and recommendations
    __Grading is according to uniformity of appearance: A, B, C, and D; A being best
__Provide a stable substrate; movement of substrate will cause cracks
__Provide complete, compact bedding beneath marble tile slabs to avoid bending stresses and cracking
__Don't use marble floors in restrooms or other areas where it would be exposed to acids or alkaline substances
__Don't use polished marble near exterior doors, restrooms or other areas where floors may be wet and slippery
__Marble can be dangerously slippery and shouldn't be used on stairs or ramps

SMALL-SCALE GENERIC DETAILS

THIN MARBLE FLOOR Thin-Set
09340-21

MARBLE TILE FLOOR Mortar Bed
09340-23

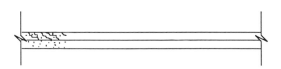

THIN MARBLE FLOOR   Mortar Bed
09340-26

MARBLE TILE FLOOR Thin-Set
09340-31

09340 MARBLE TILE FLOORS

FULL-SCALE GENERIC DETAILS

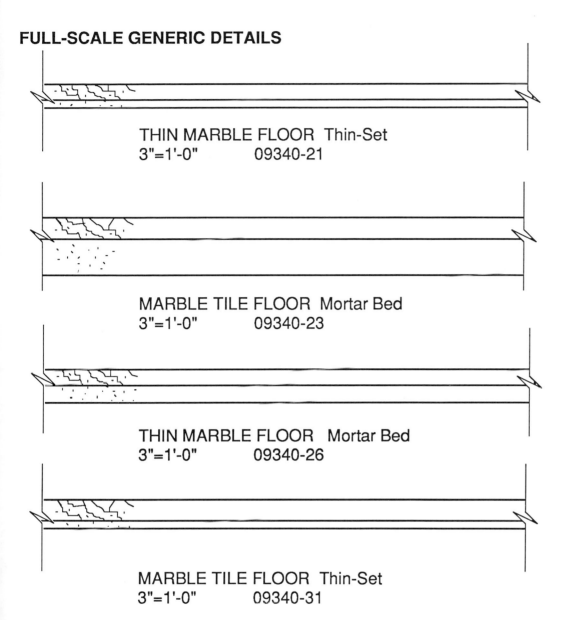

THIN MARBLE FLOOR Thin-Set
3"=1'-0"   09340-21

MARBLE TILE FLOOR Mortar Bed
3"=1'-0"   09340-23

THIN MARBLE FLOOR   Mortar Bed
3"=1'-0"   09340-26

MARBLE TILE FLOOR Thin-Set
3"=1'-0"   09340-31

NOTATION CHECKLIST,
SAMPLE NOTES

FINISH FLOOR (MATERIAL & SIZE)
SETTING BED (MATERIAL & SIZE)
JOINT SIZE
FLOOR
MEMBRANE/WATERPROOFING
SUBFLOOR/SLAB
REINFORCING

MARBLE TILE
FINISH CONC.
PLYWOOD UNDERLAYMENT
PLYWOOD SUBFLOOR
PARTICLE BOARD UNDERLAYMENT
MASTIC
BOND COAT
ADHESIVE
SETTING BED
MORTAR BED W/REINFORCING
ANGLE EDGER
THRESHOLD
DIVIDER STRIP
REDUCER STRIP

09401 TERRAZZO FLOORS

DETAIL DATA CHECKLIST

TERRAZZO
__Follow suppliers' instructions with extreme care in detailing, specifications, and construction
__Cracking is extremely common in terrazzo, strictly follow all manufacturer's instructions regarding divider and expansion strips
__Substrate for terrazzo has to be completely stable; solid concrete slabs preferred
__Terrazzo is extremely slippery and dangerous when wet; never use it where it might exposed to moisture and foot traffic at the same time
__Thin-set terrazzo topping thickness is 1/4"
__Typical terrazzo thickness is 1/2" over 2" underbed over concrete slab
__Sand cushion terrazzo is 1/2" topping over 2" underbed over 1/4" sand cushion over slab

SMALL-SCALE GENERIC DETAILS

Thin Top
Divider Strip
09401-1

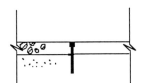

Heavy Top
Divider Strip
09401-2

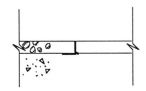

"L" Divider
Strip
09401-3

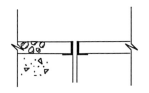

Double Angle
Divider Strip
09401-6

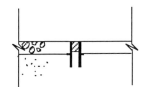

Expansion
Strip
09401-7

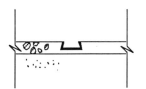

Abrasive
Channel Strip
09401-11

"L" Divider
Strip
09401-12

09401 TERRAZZO FLOORS

FULL-SCALE GENERIC DETAILS

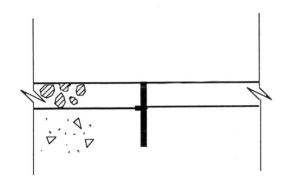

Thin Top Divider Strip
1/2 Size   09401-1

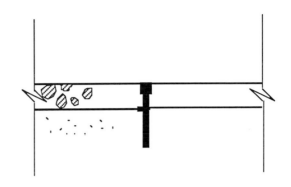

Heavy Top Divider Strip
1/2 Size   09401-2

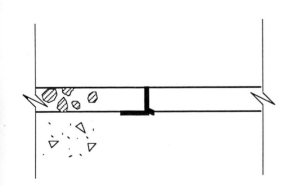

"L" Divider Strip
1/2 Size   09401-3

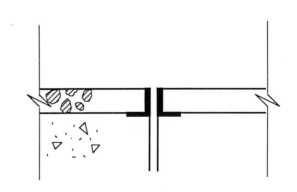

Double Angle Divider Strip
1/2 Size   09401-6

09401 TERRAZZO FLOORS

FULL-SCALE GENERIC DETAILS continued

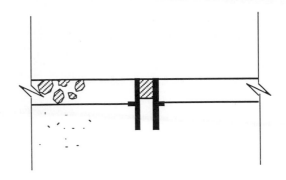

Expansion Strip
1/2 Size   09401-7

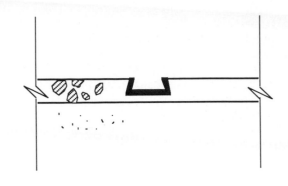

Abrasive Channel Strip
1/2 Size   09401-11

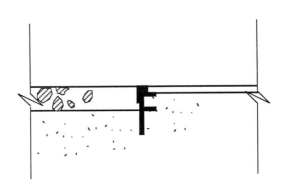

"L" Divider Strip
1/2 Size   09401-12

NOTATION CHECKLIST, SAMPLE NOTES

FINISH FLOOR (MATERIAL & SIZE)
SETTING BED (MATERIAL & SIZE)
JOINT SIZE/TYPE
FLOOR
MEMBRANE/WATERPROOFING
SUBFLOOR/SLAB
REINFORCING
BASE (MATERIAL & SIZE)
BASE HEIGHT & THICKNESS
ADJACENT WALL MATERIAL
WALL MEMBRANE/WATERPROOFING
TERRAZZO BED
FINISH CONC.

PLYWOOD UNDERLAYMENT
PLYWOOD SUBFLOOR
PARTICLE BOARD UNDERLAYMENT
MASTIC
BOND COAT
ADHESIVE
SETTING BED
MORTAR BED W/REINFORCING
ANGLE EDGER
THRESHOLD
DIVIDER STRIP
REDUCER STRIP

09402, 09410, 09411 TERRAZZO BASES & FLOORS

DETAIL DATA CHECKLIST

TERRAZZO
__Follow manufacturers' instructions with extreme care in detailing, specifications, and construction
__Cracking is extremely common in terrazzo, strictly follow all manufacturers instructions regarding divider and
    expansion strips
__Substrate for terrazzo has to be completely stable; solid concrete slabs preferred
__Terrazzo is extremely slippery and dangerous when wet; never use it where it might exposed to moisture
    and foot traffic at the same time
__Thin-set terrazzo topping thickness is 1/4"
__Typical terrazzo thickness is 1/2" over 2" underbed over concrete slab
__Sand cushion terrazzo is 1/2" topping over 2" underbed over 1/4" sand cushion over slab

SMALL-SCALE GENERIC DETAILS

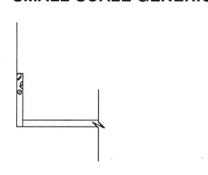

TERRAZZO BASE
Straight
09402-1

TERRAZZO BASE
Splayed
09402-2

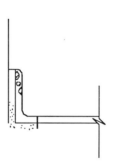

TERRAZZO BASE
Coved
09402-3

TERRAZZO FLOOR
Setting Bed On Wood
09410-31

TERRAZZO FLOOR
Sand Cushion
09410-36

TERRAZZO FLOOR
On Concrete
09411-31

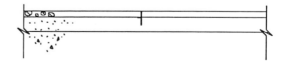

TERRAZZO FLOOR
Setting Bed On Concrete
09411-36

09402, 09410, 09411 TERRAZZO BASES & FLOORS

FULL-SCALE GENERIC DETAILS

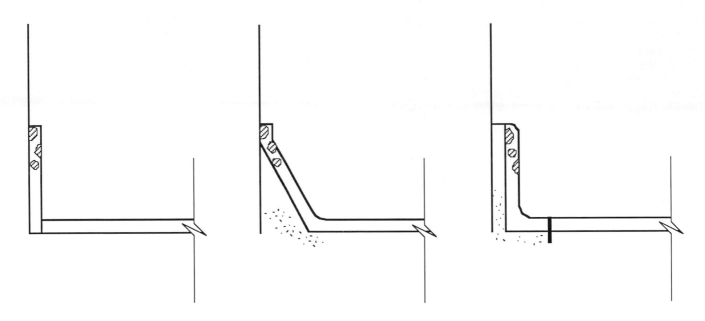

TERRAZZO BASE Straight
3"=1'-0"   09402-1

TERRAZZO BASE Splayed
3"=1'-0"   09402-2

TERRAZZO BASE Coved
3"=1'-0"   09402-3

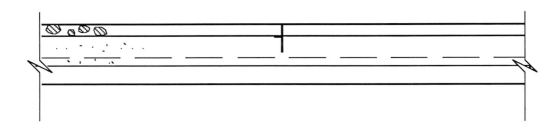

TERRAZZO FLOOR Setting Bed On Wood
3"=1'-0"   09410-31

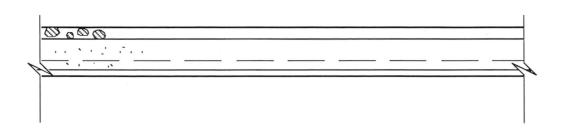

TERRAZZO FLOOR Sand Cushion
3"=1'-0"   09410-36

FULL-SCALE GENERIC DETAILS continued

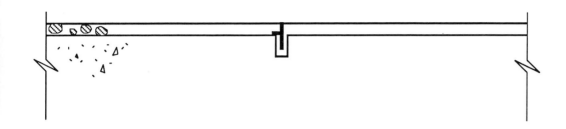

TERRAZZO FLOOR On Concrete
3"=1'-0"   09411-31

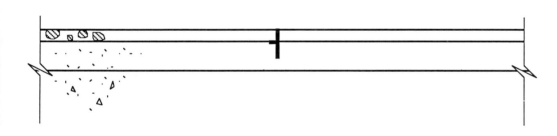

TERRAZZO FLOOR Setting Bed On Concrete
3"=1'-0"   09411-36

NOTATION CHECKLIST,
SAMPLE NOTES

FINISH FLOOR (MATERIAL & SIZE)
SETTING BED (MATERIAL & SIZE)
JOINT SIZE/TYPE
FLOOR
MEMBRANE/WATERPROOFING
SUBFLOOR/SLAB
REINFORCING
BASE (MATERIAL & SIZE)
BASE HEIGHT & THICKNESS
ADJACENT WALL MATERIAL
WALL MEMBRANE/WATERPROOFING

TERRAZZO BED
FINISH CONC.
MASTIC
BOND COAT
ADHESIVE
SETTING BED
MORTAR BED W/REINFORCING
ANGLE EDGER
THRESHOLD
DIVIDER STRIP
REDUCER STRIP

09560, 09570, 09590, 09595 WOOD FLOORS

DETAIL DATA CHECKLIST

WOOD FLOORING
__Hardwood thickness typically 3/8" to 3/4"
__Industrial wood block or strip is typically 2-1/2" to 4" thick
__Plank or strip flooring on concrete may be laid on:
    __Wood sleepers or nailers
    __Rubber-base adhesive
    __Asphalt mastic
__Wood sleepers or nailers are preferred when installing wood floors over concrete slabs to permit
    ventilation and prevent moisture swelling and/or decay
__Wood sleepers can be attached to concrete with power fasteners or mounted in an adhesive bed
__Wood flooring over concrete slab on grade requires a vapor barrier under the slab and between slab
    and the flooring
__See manufacturers' catalogs for varied sizes, species, colors, finishes, and applications of wood flooring

SMALL-SCALE GENERIC DETAILS

WOOD STRIP FLOOR
Wood Underlayment   09560-21

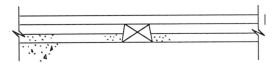

WOOD STRIP FLOOR
On Cement Topping   09560-22

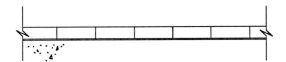

WOOD STRIP BLOCK FLOOR
 On Concrete Slab   09560-26

WOOD PARQUET FLOOR
09570-21

RESILIENT WOOD FLOOR
09590-21

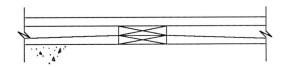

RESILIENT WOOD FLOOR
On Slab On Grade   09590-26

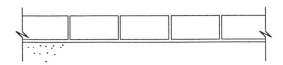

WOOD STRIP INDUSTRIAL FLOOR
09595-21

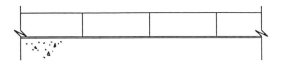

WOOD BLOCK INDUSTRIAL FLOOR
09595-26

09560, 09570, 09590, 09595 WOOD FLOORS

FULL-SCALE GENERIC DETAILS

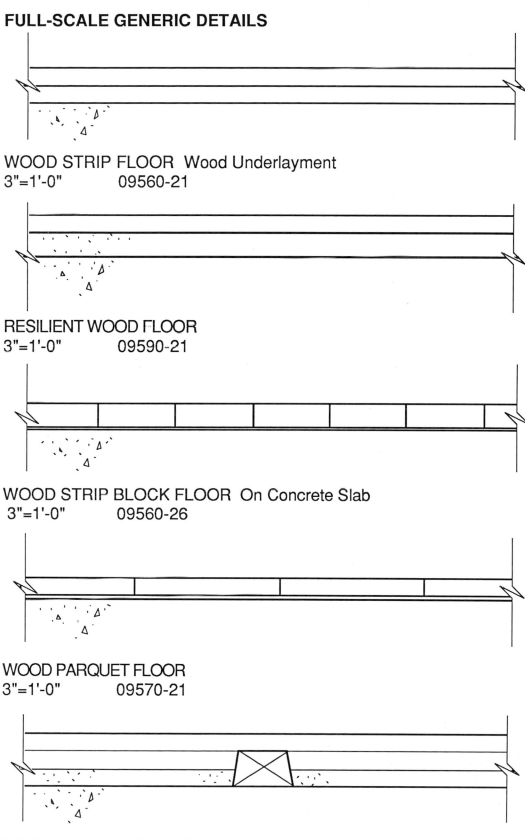

WOOD STRIP FLOOR Wood Underlayment
3"=1'-0"   09560-21

RESILIENT WOOD FLOOR
3"=1'-0"   09590-21

WOOD STRIP BLOCK FLOOR On Concrete Slab
3"=1'-0"   09560-26

WOOD PARQUET FLOOR
3"=1'-0"   09570-21

WOOD STRIP FLOOR On Cement Topping
3"=1'-0"   09560-22

09560, 09570, 09590, 09595 WOOD FLOORS

FULL-SCALE GENERIC DETAILS continued

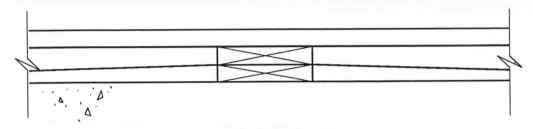

RESILIENT WOOD FLOOR On Slab On Grade
3"=1'-0"   09590-26

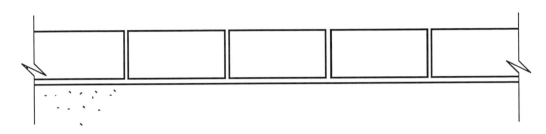

WOOD STRIP INDUSTRIAL FLOOR
3"=1'-0"   09595-21

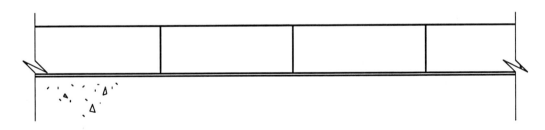

WOOD BLOCK INDUSTRIAL FLOOR
3"=1'-0"   09595-26

NOTATION CHECKLIST,
SAMPLE NOTES

FINISH FLOOR (MATERIAL & SIZE)
SLEEPER
MORTAR BED
ADHESIVE SETTING BED
UNDERLAYMENT/MEMBRANE
SUBFLOOR/SLAB

HARDWOOD FLOORING
HARDWOOD PARQUET FLOORING
CONCRETE
PLYWOOD UNDERLAYMENT
PARTICLE BOARD UNDERLAYMENT
PLYWOOD SUBFLOOR
MASTIC
ADHESIVE
SAND & POLISH

DETAIL FILE NUMBER: **09590-21**

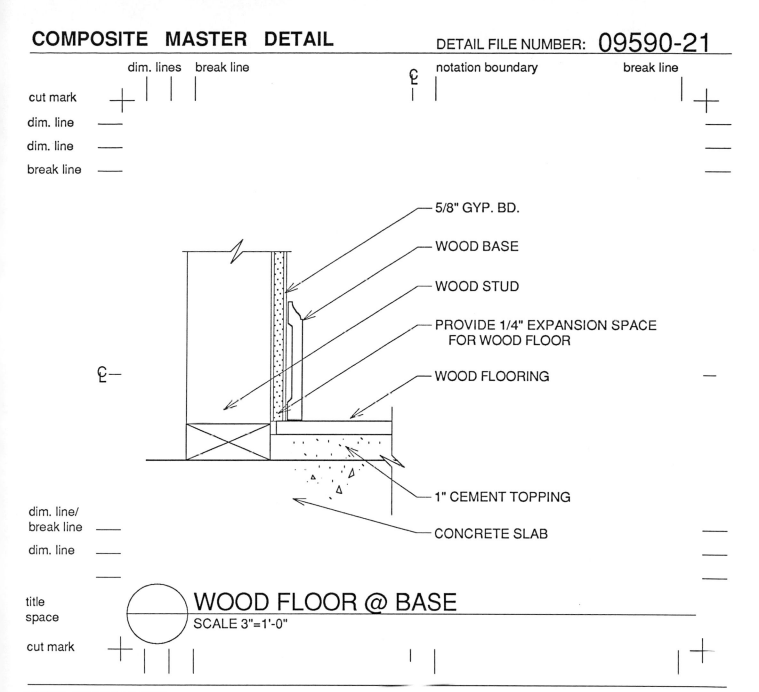

dim. lines   break line

notation boundary   break line

cut mark

dim. line

dim. line

break line

5/8" GYP. BD.

WOOD BASE

WOOD STUD

PROVIDE 1/4" EXPANSION SPACE FOR WOOD FLOOR

WOOD FLOORING

1" CEMENT TOPPING

CONCRETE SLAB

dim. line/
break line

dim. line

title
space

WOOD FLOOR @ BASE

SCALE 3"=1'-0"

cut mark

DETAIL INFORMATION
References, jobsite feedback, job history

09610 STONE FLOORS

DETAIL DATA CHECKLIST

STONE FLOORS
__Thick stone flooring is mainly used for exterior paving and finished roof decks
__Granite paver thicknesses are typically 2" to 3", typical sizes are 4" x 4", 4" x 8", 5" x 8", 8" x 8", and 12" x 12"
__See stone suppliers' catalogs for variations in thicknesses and stone sizes, bedding support, and application
__Follow suppliers' details, specifications, and application instructions carefully
__Open-joint paving is used to allow drainage of rain water to the slab or roofing beneath the finish stone surface

SMALL-SCALE GENERIC DETAILS

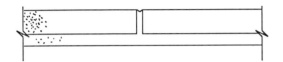

STONE FLOOR
Thin-Set
09610-31

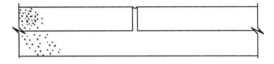

STONE FLOOR
Mortar Bed
09610-36

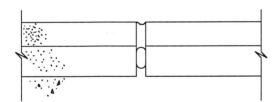

STONE FLOOR CONTROL JOINT
Mortar Bed
09610-37

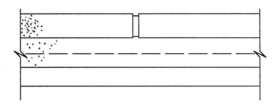

STONE FLOOR
Mortar Bed On Wood
09610-46

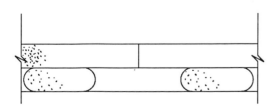

STONE FLOOR W/OPEN JOINTS
Mortar Pads
09610-51

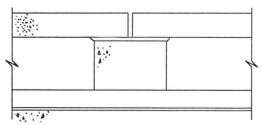

STONE FLOOR W/OPEN JOINTS
Pedestal
09610-56

09610 STONE FLOORS

FULL-SCALE GENERIC DETAILS

STONE FLOOR Thin-Set
3"=1'-0"   09610-31

STONE FLOOR Mortar Bed
3"=1'-0"   09610-36

STONE FLOOR CONTROL JOINT Mortar Bed
3"=1'-0"   09610-37

STONE FLOOR Mortar Bed On Wood
3"=1'-0"   09610-46

09610 STONE FLOORS

FULL-SCALE GENERIC DETAILS continued

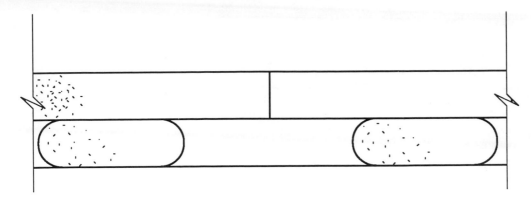

STONE FLOOR W/OPEN JOINTS Mortar Pads
3"=1'-0"   09610-51

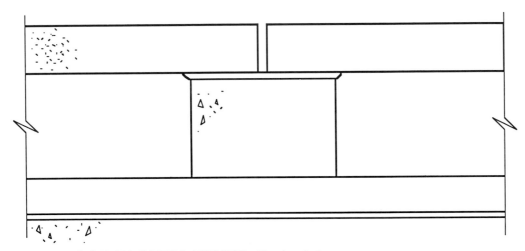

STONE FLOOR W/OPEN JOINTS Pedestal
3"=1'-0"   09610-56

NOTATION CHECKLIST,
SAMPLE NOTES

FINISH FLOOR (MATERIAL & SIZE)
JOINT SIZE
BOND COAT/MORTAR BED
FLOOR
MEMBRANE/WATERPROOFING
SUBFLOOR/SLAB
REINFORCING
SEALANT/FILLER STRIP
STONE
MARBLE TILE
GRANITE FLOORING
FINISH CONC.
BUILD UP CONC. FLOOR
W/FLOORSTONE AS REQ'D.

PLYWOOD UNDERLAYMENT
PLYWOOD SUBFLOOR
PARTICLE BOARD UNDERLAYMENT
MASTIC
BOND COAT
ADHESIVE
SETTING BED
MORTER BED W/REINFORCING
ANGLE EDGER
THRESHOLD
DIVIDER STRIP
REDUCER STRIP

09680 CARPET FLOORING

DETAIL DATA CHECKLIST

CARPET
__Typical thickness 1/2" to 1"
__Detailing is required only to show special flooring, base, or joint conditions
__Be sure carpet notation in drawings corresponds to specifications
__Carpet application is sometimes incomplete, with very serious consequences; strictly enforce
    compliance with drawings, specifications, and manufacturers' instructions
__Carpet may have to be ordered before construction begins to assure delivery in time for
    occupancy, so carpet selection and specification may precede the rest of the documents

SMALL-SCALE GENERIC DETAILS

CARPET W/PAD &
TACK STRIP
09680-11

CARPET @ VINYL
REDUCER
09680-21

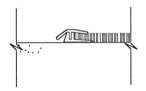

SNAP-ON CARPET
EDGE
09680-22

UNDERSLUNG HALF
SADDLE
09680-23

CARPET @ VINYL
REDUCER
09680-24

CARPET @ VINYL
REDUCER
09680-25

09680 CARPET FLOORING

SMALL-SCALE GENERIC DETAILS continued

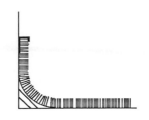

CARPET BASE
09680-31

UNDERSLUNG SADDLE
09680-41

THRESHOLD
09680-42

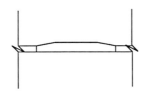

**THRESHOLD/FEATURE
STRIP   09680-43**

STAIR NOSING
09680-51

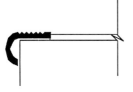

STAIR NOSING
09680-52

FULL-SCALE GENERIC DETAILS

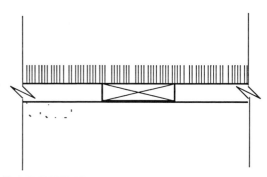

CARPET W/PAD & TACK STRIP
1/2 Size   09680-11

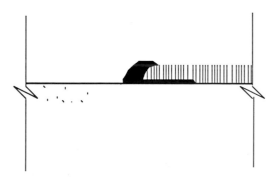

CARPET @ VINYL REDUCER
1/2 Size   09680-21

09680 CARPET FLOORING

FULL-SCALE GENERIC DETAILS continued

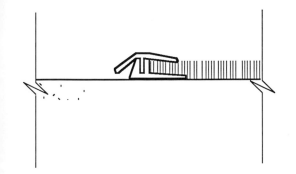

SNAP-ON CARPET EDGE
1/2 Size   09680-22

UNDERSLUNG HALF SADDLE
1/2 Size   09680-23

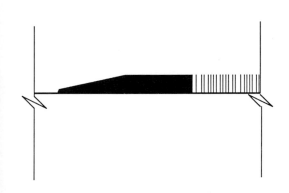

CARPET @ VINYL REDUCER
1/2 Size   09680-24

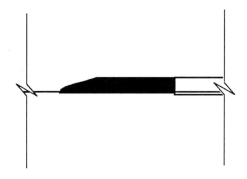

CARPET @ VINYL REDUCER
1/2 Size   09680-25

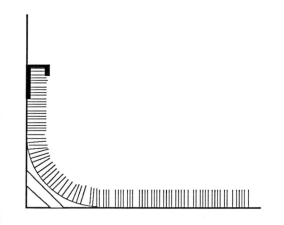

CARPET BASE
1/2 Size   09680-31

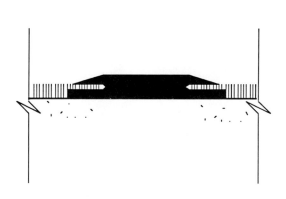

UNDERSLUNG SADDLE
1/2 Size   09680-41

09680 CARPET FLOORING

FULL-SCALE GENERIC DETAILS continued

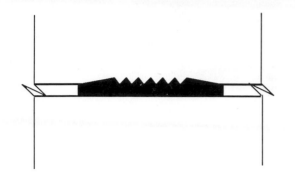

THRESHOLD
1/2 Size   09680-42

THRESHOLD/FEATURE STRIP
1/2 Size   09680-43

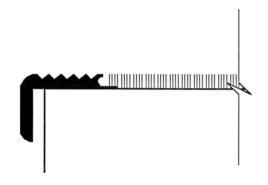

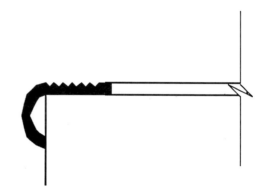

STAIR NOSING
1/2 Size   09680-51

STAIR NOSING
1/2 Size   09680-52

NOTATION CHECKLIST, SAMPLE NOTES

CARPET
PAD
TACK STRIP
REDUCER
SUBFLOOR/SLAB

GLUE DOWN CARPET
CARPET & PAD W/TACK STRIPS
FINISH CONC.
BUILD UP CONC. FLOOR W/FLOORSTONE AS
    REQ'D.
PLYWOOD SUBFLOOR
PLYWOOD UNDERLAYMENT
PARTICLE BOARD UNDERLAYMENT
MASTIC
ADHESIVE
THRESHOLD
REDUCER STRIP
CARPET TILE JOINER
CARPET EDGE STRIP

CHAPTER 10

Specialties
10000

10110, 10120 CHALKBOARDS & TACKBOARDS

DETAIL DATA CHECKLIST

CHALKBOARDS & TACKBOARDS

__See manufacturers' catalogs for standard sizes, finishes, and materials.
__Detail drawings are included mainly to show special anchoring conditions--screws, anchor bolts, etc., in
   wood frame, metal frame, masonry, or concrete wall construction.
__See manufacturers' and suppliers' catalogs for detail design data and specifications.
__See manufacturer's recommendations for special anchor requirements for different kinds of construction.

SMALL-SCALE GENERIC DETAILS

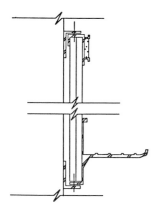

CHALKBOARD
10110-21

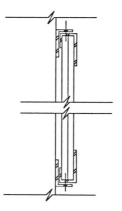

TACKBOARD
10120-21

10110, 10120 CHALKBOARDS & TACKBOARDS

FULL-SCALE GENERIC DETAILS

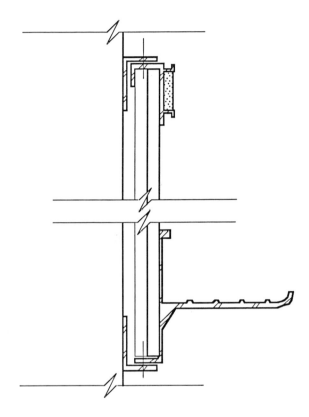

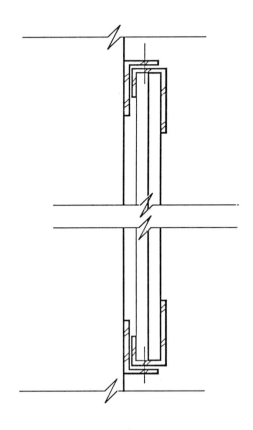

CHALKBOARD
10110-21

TACKBOARD
10120-21

NOTATION CHECKLIST, SAMPLE NOTES

CORK TACKBOARD
CHALKBOARD
HARDBOARD BACK PANEL
CHALK TRAY
ANGLE BRACKETS/FASTENERS
WALL CONSTRUCTION/FRAMING

TACK SURFACE
WOOD GROUND
STEEL SURFACE, ON BACKER BOARD
WOOD BLOCKING @ STUD WALL
METAL FRAME
PERIMETER TRIM
SCREW ON TRIM OVER WOOD GROUNDS
CHALK TROUGH

COMPOSITE MASTER DETAIL

DETAIL FILE NUMBER: **10110-21**

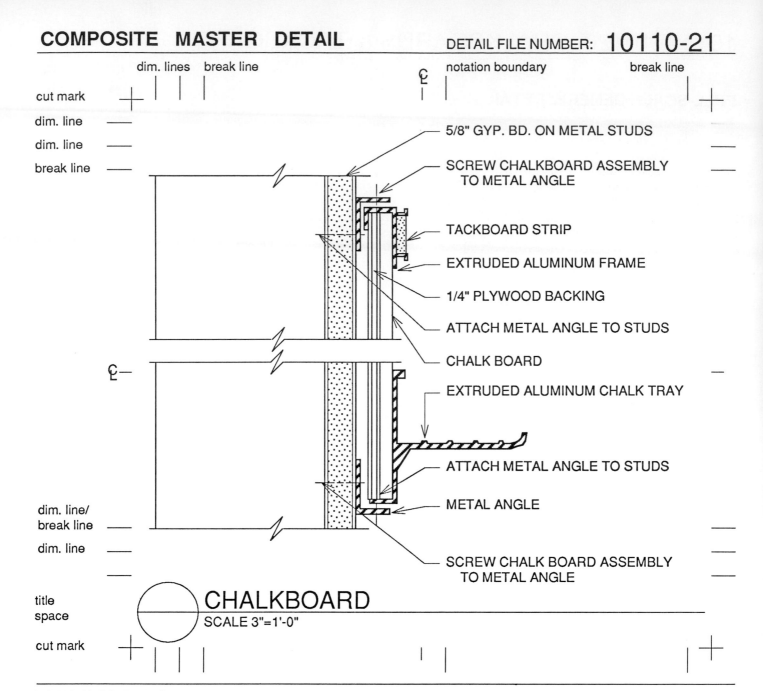

dim. lines   break line   notation boundary   break line

cut mark

dim. line

dim. line

break line

5/8" GYP. BD. ON METAL STUDS

SCREW CHALKBOARD ASSEMBLY
TO METAL ANGLE

TACKBOARD STRIP

EXTRUDED ALUMINUM FRAME

1/4" PLYWOOD BACKING

ATTACH METAL ANGLE TO STUDS

CHALK BOARD

EXTRUDED ALUMINUM CHALK TRAY

ATTACH METAL ANGLE TO STUDS

METAL ANGLE

SCREW CHALK BOARD ASSEMBLY
TO METAL ANGLE

dim. line/
break line

dim. line

title
space

CHALKBOARD
SCALE 3"=1'-0"

cut mark

DETAIL INFORMATION
References, jobsite feedback, job history

10162 METAL TOILET PARTITIONS

DETAIL DATA CHECKLIST

METAL TOILET PARTITIONS

__See manufacturers' catalogs for standard sizes, finishes, and materials.
__Detail drawings are included mainly to show special anchoring conditions--screws, anchor bolts, etc., in
    wood frame, metal frame, masonry, or concrete wall construction.
__See manufacturers' and suppliers' catalogs for detail design data and specifications.
__See manufacturer's recommendations for special anchor requirements for different kinds of construction.

SMALL-SCALE GENERIC DETAILS

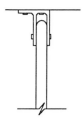

METAL TOILET PARTITION
@ Wall   10162-21

METAL TOILET PARTITION
@ Wall   10162-22

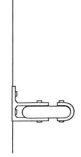

METAL TOILET PARTITION
@ Wall   10162-23

METAL TOILET PARTITION
@ Pilaster   10162-24

10162 METAL TOILET PARTITIONS

SMALL-SCALE GENERIC DETAILS continued

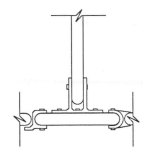

METAL TOILET PARTITION
@ Door   10162-25

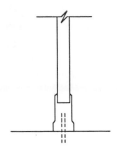

METAL TOILET PARTITION
@ Floor   10162-31

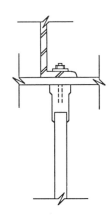

METAL TOILET PARTITION
@ Ceiling   10162-36

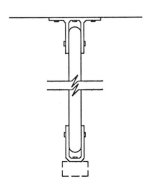

METAL TOILET PARTITION
@ Wall & Post   10162-41

FULL-SCALE GENERIC DETAILS

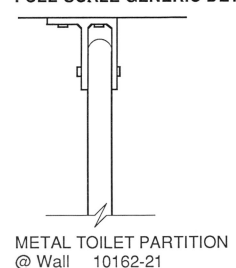

METAL TOILET PARTITION
@ Wall   10162-21

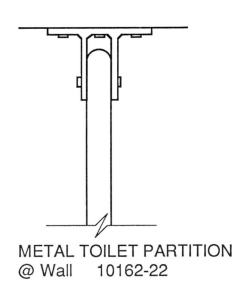

METAL TOILET PARTITION
@ Wall   10162-22

10162 METAL TOILET PARTITIONS

FULL-SCALE GENERIC DETAILS continued

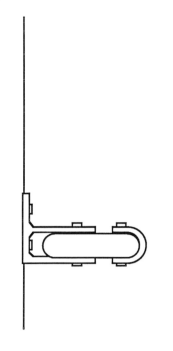

METAL TOILET PARTITION
@ Wall   10162-23

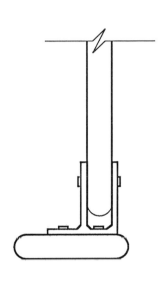

METAL TOILET PARTITION
@ Pilaster   10162-24

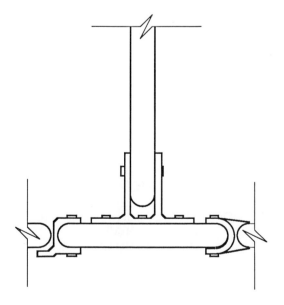

METAL TOILET PARTITION
@ Door   0162-25

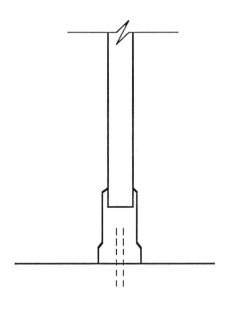

METAL TOILET PARTITION
@ Floor   10162-31

10162 METAL TOILET PARTITIONS

FULL-SCALE GENERIC DETAILS continued

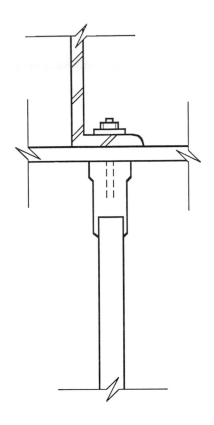

METAL TOILET PARTITION
@ Ceiling   0162-36

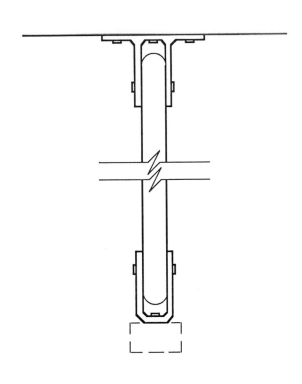

METAL TOILET PARTITION
@ Wall & Post   10162-41

NOTATION CHECKLIST,
 SAMPLE NOTES

BRACKET
FASTENERS
STALL PARTITION
PILASTER
TRIM
ANCHOR
DOOR HINGE/LATCH
FLOOR CONSTRUCTION
CEILING CONSTRUCTION

STEEL CHANNEL CONT. @ PARTITIONS, DRILL
   BOTTOM FOR SUPPORT BOLTS BY PARTITION MFR.
CEILING LINE
PROVIDE DRILLED HOLE, SLEEVE & INSERT @ CLG.
   TO SUPPORT BOLT PENETRATION AS REQ'D.
TOILET PARTITION & CLG.-MOUNTED ASSEMBLY
   BY PARTITION MFR.
TOILET PARTITION BOLT ASSEMBLY
BRACE TO STRUCTURE ABOVE
CEILING-HUNG UNITS

10210 METAL LOUVERS

DETAIL DATA CHECKLIST

METAL LOUVERS

__See manufacturers' catalogs for standard sizes, finishes, and materials.
__Detail drawings are included mainly to show special anchoring conditions--screws, anchor bolts, etc., in
    wood frame, metal frame, masonry, or concrete wall construction.
__See manufacturers' and suppliers' catalogs for detail design data and specifications.
__See manufacturer's recommendations for special anchor requirements for different kinds of construction.

SMALL-SCALE GENERIC DETAILS
Metal Louvers -- 2" Wide 10210

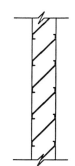

Z Louver
10210-11

Inverted V
10210-13

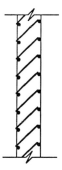

Bar Grille
10210-15

Sight Proof
10210-17

Metal Louvers -- 4" Wide 10210

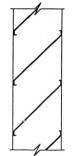

Z Louver
10210-21

Inverted V
10210-23

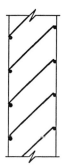

Bar Grille
10210-25

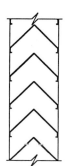

Sight Proof
10210-27

10210 METAL LOUVERS

FULL-SCALE GENERIC DETAILS
Metal Louvers -- 2" Wide 10210

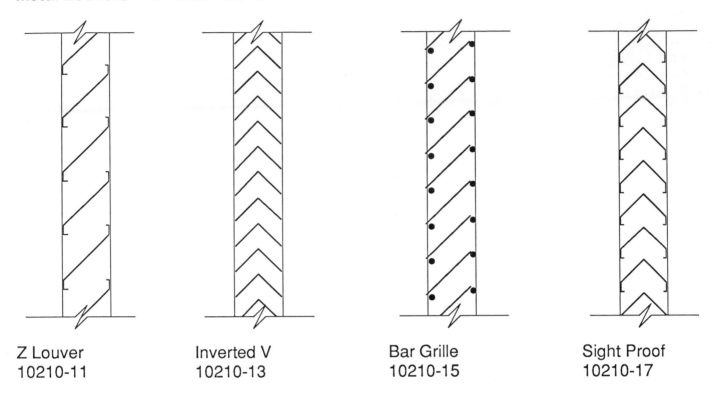

Z Louver
10210-11

Inverted V
10210-13

Bar Grille
10210-15

Sight Proof
10210-17

Metal Louvers -- 4" Wide 10210

**NOTATION
CHECKLIST**

SEALANT
CHANNEL FRAME
ANCHOR
INSECT SCREEN/BIRD
SCREEN
WEEP HOLES

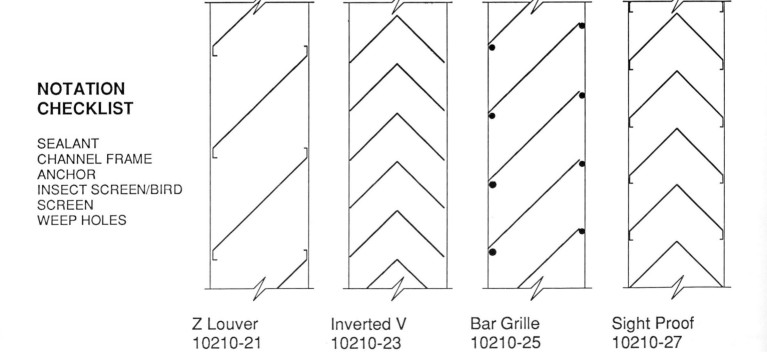

Z Louver
10210-21

Inverted V
10210-23

Bar Grille
10210-25

Sight Proof
10210-27

10221-10223 ACCESS PANELS

DETAIL DATA CHECKLIST

ACCESS PANELS

__See manufacturers' catalogs for standard sizes, finishes, and materials.
__Detail drawings are included mainly to show special anchoring conditions--screws, anchor bolts, etc., in
    wood frame, metal frame, masonry, or concrete construction.
__See manufacturers' and suppliers' catalogs for detail design data and specifications.
__See manufacturer's recommendations for special anchor requirements for different kinds of construction.

SMALL-SCALE GENERIC DETAILS

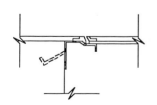

ACCESS PANEL Floor
10221-21

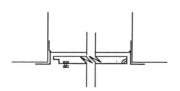

ACCESS PANEL Wall
10222-21

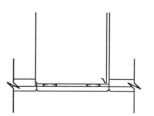

ACCESS PANEL Ceiling
10223-21

10221-10223 ACCESS PANELS

FULL-SCALE GENERIC DETAILS

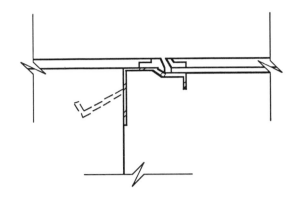

ACCESS PANEL Floor
10221-21

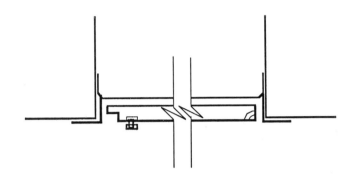

ACCESS PANEL Wall
10222-21

NOTATION CHECKLIST

FINISH FLOOR
SUBFLOOR/SLAB
WALL CONSTRUCTION/FRAMING
CEILING CONSTRUCTION
CHANNEL/SUPPORT WIRES
METAL FRAME/ANCHOR
ACCESS PANEL
HARDWARE

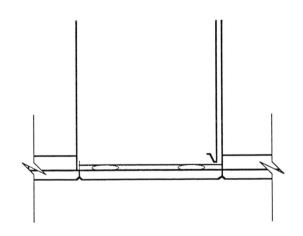

ACCESS PANEL Ceiling
10223-21

10260, 10265 CORNER GUARDS

DETAIL DATA CHECKLIST

CORNER GUARDS

__See manufacturers' catalogs for standard sizes, finishes, and materials.
__Detail drawings are included mainly to show special anchoring conditions--screws, anchor bolts, etc., in
    wood frame, metal frame, masonry, or concrete wall construction.
__See manufacturers' and suppliers' catalogs for detail design data and specifications.
__See manufacturer's recommendations for special anchor requirements for different kinds of construction.

SMALL-SCALE GENERIC DETAILS

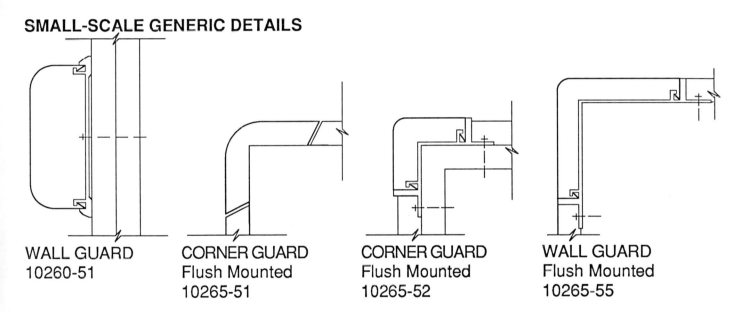

WALL GUARD
10260-51

CORNER GUARD
Flush Mounted
10265-51

CORNER GUARD
Flush Mounted
10265-52

WALL GUARD
Flush Mounted
10265-55

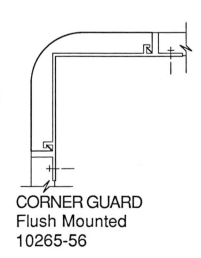

CORNER GUARD
Flush Mounted
10265-56

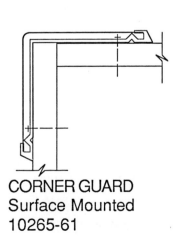

CORNER GUARD
Surface Mounted
10265-61

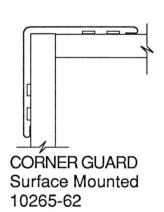

CORNER GUARD
Surface Mounted
10265-62

10260, 10265 CORNER GUARDS

FULL-SCALE GENERIC DETAILS

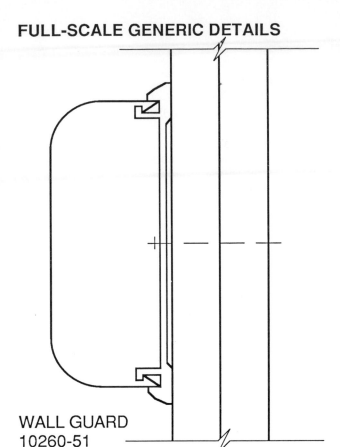

WALL GUARD
10260-51

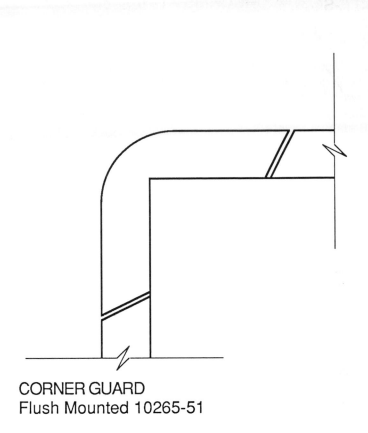

CORNER GUARD
Flush Mounted 10265-51

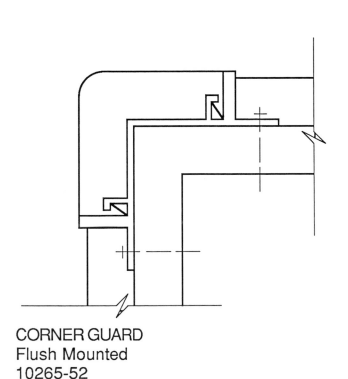

CORNER GUARD
Flush Mounted
10265-52

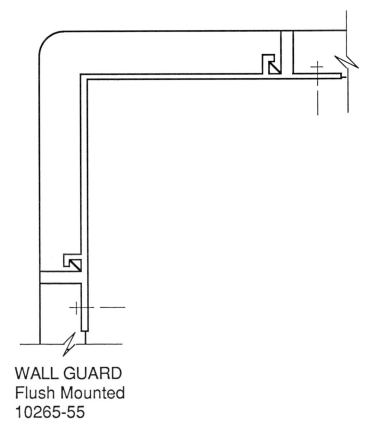

WALL GUARD
Flush Mounted
10265-55

10260, 10265 CORNER GUARDS

FULL-SCALE GENERIC DETAILS continued

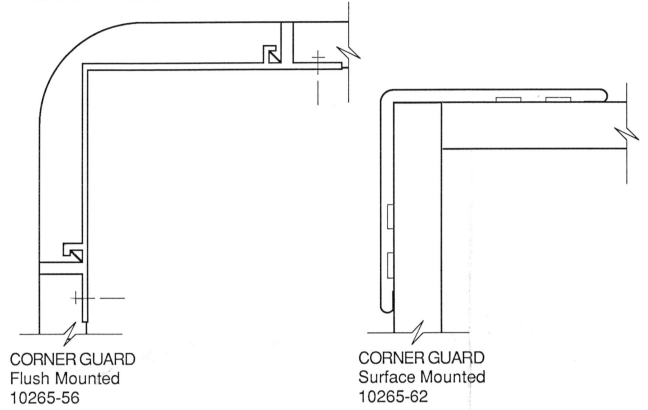

CORNER GUARD
Flush Mounted
10265-56

CORNER GUARD
Surface Mounted
10265-62

NOTATION CHECKLIST

CORNER GUARD (TYPE & MATERIAL)
ADHESIVE/FASTENERS
WALL CONSTRUCTION

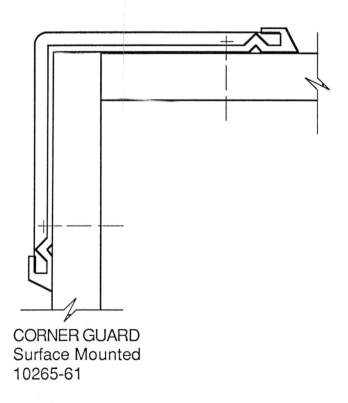

CORNER GUARD
Surface Mounted
10265-61

COMPOSITE MASTER DETAIL

DETAIL FILE NUMBER: **10265-61**

cut mark

dim. lines   break line

notation boundary   break line

dim. line

dim. line

break line

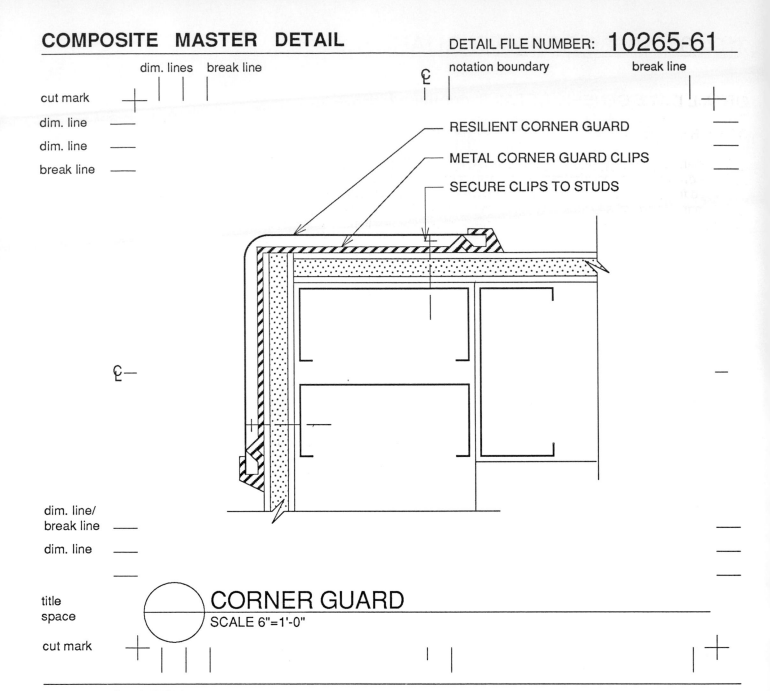

RESILIENT CORNER GUARD

METAL CORNER GUARD CLIPS

SECURE CLIPS TO STUDS

dim. line/
break line

dim. line

title
space

CORNER GUARD
SCALE 6"=1'-0"

cut mark

DETAIL INFORMATION
References, jobsite feedback, job history

10266 CORNER GUARDS

DETAIL DATA CHECKLIST

CORNER GUARDS

__See manufacturers' catalogs for standard sizes, finishes, and materials.
__Detail drawings are included mainly to show special anchoring conditions--screws, anchor bolts, etc., in
    wood frame, metal frame, masonry, or concrete wall construction.
__See manufacturers' and suppliers' catalogs for detail design data and specifications.
__See manufacturer's recommendations for special anchor requirements for different kinds of construction.

SMALL-SCALE GENERIC DETAILS

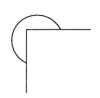

WOOD CORNER GUARD
10266-21

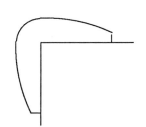

WOOD CORNER GUARD
10266-21

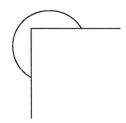

WOOD CORNER GUARD
10266-21

WOOD CORNER GUARD
10266-21

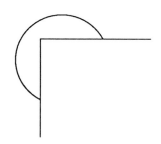

WOOD CORNER GUARD
10266-21

WOOD CORNER GUARD
10266-25

10266 CORNER GUARDS

FULL-SCALE GENERIC DETAILS

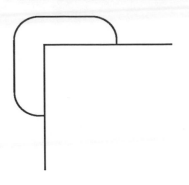

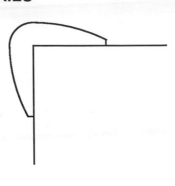

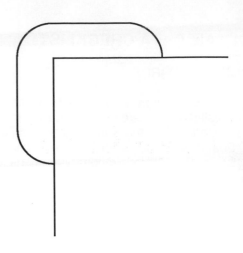

WOOD CORNER GUARD
FULL SIZE   10266-21

WOOD CORNER GUARD
FULL SIZE   10266-21

WOOD CORNER GUARD
FULL SIZE   10266-21

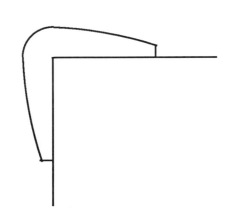

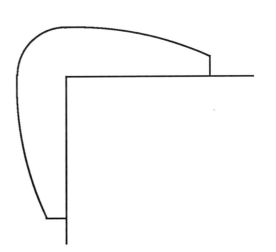

WOOD CORNER GUARD
FULL SIZE   10266-21

WOOD CORNER GUARD
FULL SIZE   10266-21

NOTATION CHECKLIST

CORNER GUARD (TYPE & MATERIAL)
ADHESIVE/FASTENERS
WALL CONSTRUCTION

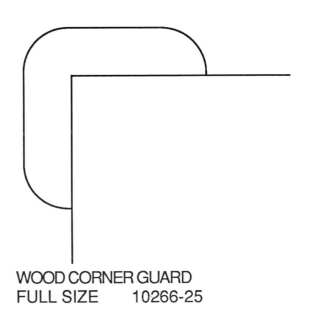

WOOD CORNER GUARD
FULL SIZE   10266-25